Modern Republican

Modern Republican

ARTHUR LARSON AND THE EISENHOWER YEARS

David L. Stebenne

INDIANA UNIVERSITY PRESS
Bloomington and Indianapolis

This book is a publication of

Indiana University Press
601 North Morton Street
Bloomington, IN 47404-3797 USA

http://iupress.indiana.edu

Telephone orders 800-842-6796
Fax orders 812-855-7931
Orders by e-mail iuporder@indiana.edu

The paper used in this publication meets the minimum requirements of American National Standard for Information Sciences—Permanence of Paper for Printed Library Materials, ANSI Z39.48-1984.

Manufactured in the United States of America

Library of Congress Cataloging-in-Publication Data

Stebenne, David.
Modern Republican : Arthur Larson and the Eisenhower years / David L. Stebenne.
p. cm.
Includes bibliographical references and index.
ISBN-13: 978-0-253-34807-4 (cloth : alk. paper)
ISBN-10: 0-253-34807-2 (cloth : alk. paper) 1. Larson, Arthur. 2. Lawyers—United States—Biography. 3. Political consultants—United States—Biography. 4. United States. Dept. of Labor—Officials and employees—Biography. 5. United States. Information Agency—Officials and employees—Biography. I. Larson, Arthur. II. Title.
KF373.L36S74 2006
973.921092—dc22
[B]

2006015063

1 2 3 4 5 11 10 09 08 07 06

To the memory of my maternal grandfather,
George C. Perkins (1897–1997)

CONTENTS

PREFACE

AMERICANS HAVE HEARD a lot about "compassionate conservatism" recently, but what that label really means in terms of basic philosophy and specific public policies is still pretty unclear. What we know for sure is that it differs significantly from Reagan-era conservatism, which sought to shrink the size and cost of government (especially by cutting domestic programs) and reduce its role in society. "Government is the problem, not the solution" was the libertarian-like mantra of 1980s-style conservatism. Since 2001, however, the opposite pattern has developed in response to changing conditions, both foreign and domestic. The size and cost of government have grown a great deal since then, and not just with respect to military spending. The administration of George W. Bush is responsible for the biggest single expansion of the welfare state (the prescription-drug-benefit program) since the mid-1960s. The "compassionate conservatives" have also pushed successfully for the highest levels of federal spending ever for AIDS research and treatment. At the same time, government intrusion into everyday life has grown, most notably with the passage of the Patriot Act. When one stops to consider that all of these initiatives emerged from a Congress controlled by Republicans, the difference between the current political situation and the Reagan era becomes even clearer.

Although the specific policies associated with "compassionate conservatism" have begun to become more concrete, what they add up to remains vague. Today's version of "compassionate conservatism" is very much a work in progress, in terms of both defining basic principles and explaining how they apply to contemporary conditions. One of the most important purposes of this book is to help with that process of defining and explaining by providing some useful historical perspective. Like so many other political philosophies, "compassionate conservatism" is not something entirely new but rather represents an effort to update something older. This book explores in depth the basic philosophy and specific public policy positions of that earlier version of "compassionate conservatism": Eisenhower-era Republicanism.

The book's focus is on a person and a point of view that were much better known half a century ago than they are today. Arthur Larson's most popular book, *A Republican Looks at His Party* (1956), made him something of a political celebrity. The *New York Times* labeled Larson the "chief theoretician" of Eisenhower-era Republicanism. However, with the passing of time and the rise of a newer, more extreme form of conservatism—the "New Right"—in the 1960s, 1970s, and 1980s, Larson's name faded from public memory. Even the label Modern Republican that Larson and Eisenhower used to describe their moderately conservative views now sounds unfamiliar to many close observers of the American political scene.

This gap in the nation's memory has yet to be filled by academic historians. A paradoxical situation has developed instead, in which moderate conservatism has become the least studied yet most influential political force in modern American history. There are, to be sure, some good recent books about more extreme kinds of American conservatism. The New Right in particular and its leading champions, Barry Goldwater and Ronald Reagan, have been the subject of several studies, but they tend to begin, chronologically speaking, toward the end of the Eisenhower era and give little attention to its distinctly different political orientation. And while there are a lot of books about Eisenhower and his administration, none of them closely addresses its point of view as such. Most academic bibliographies instead list *A Republican Looks at His Party* as the most useful source on that subject. This biography of Larson is intended to help fill in that blank spot in the political history of twentieth-century America.

Eisenhower and Larson enjoyed a close relationship during the Modern Republican heyday that grew out of similarities in background, outlook, and temperament. Like Eisenhower, Larson hailed from the middle of the country, where moderation was broadly popular. That midwestern upbringing helped give Larson, like Ike, a personality decidedly lacking in sharp edges. There was also a common quality of innocence to both men, in the sense that they both entered partisan politics from other worlds. In Larson's case that other realm was academia, where he distinguished himself as an expert on the law of the welfare state before rising to high office in Eisenhower's administration.

Larson's philosophical turn of mind makes him a very good vehicle to explore moderate conservatism as it was during the middle third of the twentieth century. Unlike Eisenhower and most of his other top aides, Larson was a theorist who excelled at providing what George Bush, Sr., once called "the vision thing." Larson held three major posts in the Eisenhower administration: under secretary of labor (1954–1956), director of the United States Information Agency (1956–1957), and chief presidential speechwriter (1957–1958). In each of these roles, Larson's most important achievement was to explain more clearly and cogently than his predecessor what the administration stood for (and not just what it stood against).

Even Larson's limitations and disappointments help explain Eisenhower-era conservatism. They illuminate the extent to which there were gaps between what the Modern Republicans believed, what they said, and what they were able to accomplish and why those were not always the same. Larson's ultimately unsuccessful efforts to prevent the rise of the New Right are especially enlightening, for they help clarify why the party of Dwight Eisenhower in the 1950s gradually became the party of the more conservative Ronald Reagan by the 1980s.

Finally, and most important to today's reader, this study of Larson's life and work is useful because they illustrate so well what "compassionate conservatism" really means and how far the GOP has to go in order truly to reclaim that political position as its own.

ACKNOWLEDGMENTS

A great many people have helped me in one way or another with this project, and I can only try to thank them all. My first real assistance came from Dwight Strandberg, Mack Teasley, and the other members of the staff at the Dwight D. Eisenhower Presidential Library, who accelerated the processing of the Arthur Larson Papers on deposit there at my request and aided me in many other ways. Also helping early on was the Eisenhower World Affairs Institute, whose research grant partly underwrote the cost of working with the Larson Papers. Special thanks go, too, to Lex, Kathy, Ken, and Anna Larson for their early interest, enthusiasm, hospitality, and willingness to share their records and memories of the life and work of Arthur Larson and Florence Newcomb Larson.

Then there are the many people who helped along the research trail: the late James Kittelson for some very helpful early suggestions; Dave Mason for help in finding and copying publications by and about Larson; the Perzans: Jeff, Karen, Cary, and Mireille for their hospitality and help in researching Larson's time in Milwaukee; Arthur Huseboe (of the Center for Western Studies at Augustana College) and Jim Bartholomew for their thoughts about Arthur Larson's hometown and the way it shaped him; the archivists at the University of Tennessee, Cornell University, the University of Pittsburgh, and Duke University for helping locate useful material from Larson's time on the faculty at those places; the research staff of the National Archives II and the Pacific Southwest Region of the National Archives and archivists at the Lyndon Baines Johnson Presidential Library and the Richard Nixon Library for their help in tracking down relevant material; David Rezelman for his much-appreciated help with using the Declassified Documents Reference System; Abbott Washburn for his memories of working with Larson; Lou Galambos and Daun van Ee for their help in finding some of the now-published Eisenhower papers; Ron Grele for his assistance in using materials in the Columbia University Oral History Collection; Russ Coil and Mike Hissam for insights drawn from their research on Eisenhower-era Republicanism; Yanek Mieczkowski for his impressions of Larson; Craig Swarts for his thoughts about the John Birch Society; Les Benedict, Jim Brudney, Debby Merritt, and others at the Ohio State University Law School for their thoughts about Larson's contributions to legal scholarship; Lon Hamby, Joan Hoff, and their colleagues at Ohio University's Contemporary History Institute for their comments on a presentation about this project; and Ev Dennis for his thoughts about the Republican Party of the 1950s and 1960s.

I am especially grateful to those colleagues and friends who took precious time away from their own work to read earlier drafts of this manuscript: Jim Bartholomew, Manse Blackford, Alan Brinkley, Mike Flamm, Eric Foner, Susan Hartmann, and Joe Mitchell. All made very useful suggestions, which I have done my best to incorporate. Also helping greatly with the writing was a year of paid sabbatical leave from my teaching and other duties at Ohio State University and Joe Pirone's tireless assistance with the vagaries of word processing.

Indispensable contributions in making the manuscript into a book also came from Bob Sloan, Jane Quinet, Miki Bird, Kate Babbitt, Greg Domber, and their colleagues at Indiana University Press.

Last but hardly least, heartfelt thanks go to family members for their assistance, interest, patience, and support, especially my parents, and Charles and Carol Simonian, and, above all, Karen. She helped make this book better in countless ways while humoring its author.

Modern Republican

CHAPTER ONE

Native Son of the Upper Midwest

THIS VERY AMERICAN STORY begins, quite appropriately, in the heart of the country on the Fourth of July, 1910. On that day in the town of Sioux Falls, South Dakota, Anna Huseboe Larson, the child of Norwegian immigrants, as was her husband Lewis, gave birth to a son they named Lewis Arthur Larson. Arthur, as they always called him, was the third of five children. They and their parents were a closely knit midwestern family that was both typical and special.[1]

The first generation of Larsons in America, Arthur's grandparents, immigrated in search of greater economic opportunity and became successful farmers. Arthur's mother's parents came for much the same reason and experienced similar success, although in real estate rather than agriculture. Their focus on earning money through owning property reflected the specific conditions in their native Norway. In the middle of the nineteenth century, Norway remained what it had long been, one of the poorest countries in Europe because it possessed so little land suitable for farming. That poverty had also made industrialization unusually slow because of the resulting shortage of investment capital. As Norway's population grew steadily during the first half of the nineteenth century, life for many of its inhabitants became more difficult. The system of primogeniture in landholding meant that the eldest son usually inherited the entire farm, which left younger brothers with diminishing options as the century wore on. Some managed to accumulate savings but could find no way to buy good farmland, given its scarcity. Others, more numerous, had little or no savings or land, and their prospects by the 1860s were much grimmer.

Religious intolerance (toward those who did not adhere to the tenets of the state-run Lutheran churches), military conscription, and a very limited franchise added to the discontent that flowed primarily from economic hardship. These conditions spurred a massive movement of Norwegians to the United States during the last four decades of the nineteenth century.[2]

Arthur only knew one of his grandparents well, his father's father, Peter Larson Sorlie (U.S. immigration officials at Ellis Island dropped the last name). By the time Arthur got to know his Grandpa Peter, he was an old man with "a magnificent white beard, twinkling eyes and a terrific sense of humor."[3] Basically retired by the time Arthur had come along, Peter liked nothing better than to tell stories about his life in the old country and early days in America. As a result, the story of his origins, much more than those of the other grandparents, has come down through the generations. Peter Larson was one of the younger sons of a small farmer who lived in Jevnaker Parish, Norway, about twenty-five miles northwest of Oslo. Ambitious and outgoing, he found a job delivering pharmaceutical supplies on foot for a druggist. In this way he managed to save enough money to pay for passage to the United States, to which he emigrated in 1866, the year he turned twenty-three. He followed the typical Norwegian route, bypassing the big American cities of the East in favor of the frontiers of the upper Midwest, where farmland could still be obtained under the provisions of the Homestead Act. Evidently wanting to make some money first that would help him get started in farming, he joined a construction gang that was building the Dakota Southern Railroad, the first in the Dakota Territory. It connected Sioux City, Iowa, the nearest urban center to the east, with the territorial capital at Yankton, in the southeast corner of the territory.[4]

The income from that job, which ended when the railroad was finished in February 1873, and a few others helped Peter Larson realize the Norwegian immigrant's dream of becoming a prosperous farmer. He acquired a quarter-section of land in Yankton County and built it, through hard work and prudent judgment, into the most successful enterprise in the area. Although ultimately satisfying, this kind of life was far from easy. Peter Larson started out by building a sod hut and contending with winter blizzards, summer droughts, prairie fires in the fall and spring, dust storms, hordes of grasshoppers, sometimes hostile Indians, and the pervasive loneliness, so common to all frontier farmers, that the treeless and seemingly lifeless prairie country made even more intense. Larson, his wife, Martha Goodman Larson, and their children lived out their own version of the Norwegian immigrant experience on the Great Plains that the Norwegian-American writer O. E. Rölvaag later captured so vividly in *Giants in the Earth*.[5]

Although Peter Larson wanted his eldest son Lewis to continue on the land, the serious, educated, and articulate young man who turned twenty-two in 1900 chose a different course. He met a young woman from Sioux Falls named Anna

Huseboe and began a courtship that drew him instead toward life in town. Like him, Anna Huseboe was a smart, serious person with Norwegian immigrant parents. Her father, Knudt, whom Arthur later described as "a tall, gaunt Scandinavian," had become moderately wealthy by acquiring houses in Sioux Falls that he rented out.[6] Eventually he came to own twenty-two of them and achieved his own version of the Norwegian immigrant's dream. Fearful, however, that word of his wealth might get around to outlaws, Knudt Huseboe "always dressed like a tramp," Arthur recalled. In later years, Knudt was viewed as something of an outsider due to his remarriage after the untimely death of Anna's mother, which led to a rift between father and daughter.[7]

At the time Lewis and Anna met, she was working ten-hour days at a local dressmaking shop and spending her free time in activities organized by Trinity Lutheran Church, where she sang in the choir. Although the story is lost to history, it seems likely that these two first met at church, as did so many other couples of Norwegian ancestry. Lewis took his faith very seriously, thanks mostly to his mother, who was as pious and strict as Peter was a free spirit. Martha's severity left a vivid impression on her grandson Arthur, whose only boyhood memory of her was as "a looming black-dressed unsmiling menace, that materialized from time to time for disciplinary purposes."[8] Martha Goodman Larson evidently made certain that her children were good Lutherans who lived their faith. For the second generation, as for the first, the Lutheran church was an anchor that tethered them to their past, their values, and one another. Lewis and Anna married at Trinity Lutheran on September 9, 1903.[9]

The couple's wedding photo revealed their relatively elite status within the Norwegian-American community of greater Sioux Falls. Most Norwegian immigrants who had settled in the area were, according to a local historian, "the poorest of the poor" and stayed that way into the second generation.[10] The Larson and Huseboe clans, so like the local Norwegian Americans in other respects, stood out from their group in terms of social class. Anna and Lewis Larson embodied the essence of middle-class respectability, as the studio photograph taken on their wedding day makes clear. In it, Lewis appeared as a handsome, light-haired young man with a dark mustache whose every hair stood neatly in place. He wore the customary dark wedding suit, but unlike those worn by so many other sons of the frontier, Lewis Larson's conservatively tailored clothes fit him perfectly. Anna was a similarly attractive and well-groomed brunette who wore both a gentle smile and an elaborate white dress while holding a bouquet of flowers neatly centered in front of her. This family portrait, and every subsequent one for which they sat, conveyed an impression of people who, while modest, had a sense of their exceptional status.[11]

Wanting to stay in Sioux Falls, Lewis and Anna moved in with her parents until the young couple could establish themselves independently. The community they called home ever afterward was in those days a regional center of about 10,000 people that was just beginning a period of steady growth. Sioux Falls stood on a flat piece of land close to the western fringe of the northern plains and thus near the western edge of the Upper Midwest itself. Approximately fifty miles northeast of Yankton, Sioux Falls had replaced it by the turn of the century as the major population center in southeastern South Dakota. Unlike much of the rest of the state, Minnehaha County, where the town was located, usually received sufficient rainfall to support diversified agriculture. Most of the farmers who lived in the outlying area grew some combination of spring wheat, corn, and oats.[12]

The site of the town that formed the county's economic hub was chosen in response to an early misconception: Sioux Falls's first settlers had envisioned it as a manufacturing area, thanks to the falls of the Big Sioux River that flowed nearby. In keeping with that plan, the transplanted Yankees from the East who laid out the town in the 1870s tried building a flour mill, meatpacking plant, and various other manufacturing enterprises. All had failed. The sorest disappointment of these had been the flour mill, which investors had hoped could tap the energy generated by the falls that stood in the town's northeast corner. Only after the very large Queen Bee mill was built in 1881 did its backers discover that the flow of water was too slow and intermittent to provide sufficient power for milling or manufacturing.[13]

The area around the falls did, however, contribute to the development of the town's economy in another way. Located nearby were large outcroppings of pink- and gray-colored quartzite rock, commonly called granite or jasper. Exceedingly durable and susceptible to a high polish, this natural resource led to the establishment of five different quarries in Sioux Falls by 1890. They served as a major source of employment for both common and skilled laborers and added to the local shipping business. Carloads of paving blocks left Sioux Falls for cities as far away as Omaha, Chicago, and St. Louis. The local stone industry also contributed to the town's growth by furnishing building material that was at once inexpensive, attractive, and imposing. Most of the major public buildings in town were built with it, including the county courthouse, completed in 1890, which was reputed to be the biggest between Minneapolis and Denver.[14]

And so Sioux Falls emerged during the 1880s and 1890s as a trade and distribution rather than a manufacturing center. Farm products and local stone were loaded onto railroad cars there and shipped to cities south and east. But the nearby farms and quarries did not produce enough to make the town a true metropolis, as the early settlers had hoped. Unlike the better-known bonanza farms of the Red River Valley to the north, where Norwegian immigrants with money to spend on large tracts and farm equipment had built big and very profitable enterprises, those around Sioux Falls had mostly been started by impoverished Norwegian immigrants who operated small, largely unmechanized, and not very lucrative operations. During the worst years of the 1890s, when grain prices reached record lows, many such farmers operated in the red or gave up farming entirely. The quarries, too, ran into trouble as the economics of building construction changed and the use of stone became less common, which diminished the demand for Sioux Falls's principal natural resource.[15]

The only new "industry" that sprang up in Sioux Falls during the late nineteenth century to supplement farming, quarrying, and trade was the highly controversial market in easy divorce. Sioux Falls had become a "divorce mill" around the turn of the century; at that time, all of the nearby states required a full year's residence before one could dissolve a marriage, whereas South Dakota required only six months. This situation produced a steady stream of well-known visitors seeking a speedy divorce in a location relatively free of publicity, a booming trade for hoteliers and merchants who catered to such guests, and a flock of divorce lawyers who handled their cases. Although this turn of events made Sioux Falls bigger and more prosperous than it would have otherwise been, many longtime residents viewed with distaste the activity that gave their town the atmosphere of a vice capital. This situation so dismayed community leaders, most notably those in the local churches such as Trinity Lutheran, that they entered into a lengthy struggle to rid their town of these unwelcome visitors and those who serviced them. Although religious leaders succeeded in pressuring the state legislature to enact a new divorce law in 1905 that extended the residency requirement to a full year, Sioux Falls's lawyers and hotel operators mounted numerous challenges to it. Only when a statewide referendum passed in 1908 was the battle truly won.[16]

Wanting to establish himself in this awkwardly growing but clearly vibrant community, Lewis Larson first tried opening a small grocery store but soon went broke after he extended credit too generously to his friends and could not bring himself to press them for repayment. The experience taught him, as his son Arthur later recalled, that he was "too soft-hearted" to succeed in business.[17] Next, he found work in local government as Sioux Falls's city clerk, a post to which he was appointed in 1906 and held, with one brief interruption, until 1911. Lewis Larson's work in this job appears to have awakened an interest in studying law, an idea that provoked more than a little tension within the Larson family. Lawyers had used their expert knowledge to win local land title disputes at the expense of honest but less knowledgeable farmers. To Peter Larson, lawyers were basically crooks, and he strongly objected to his son's plans to become one. The divorce specialists who filled Sioux Falls's courts made the profession look even worse to morally traditional Norwegian Americans like his mother. Lewis, who was determined to pursue this course, had to find a way finance his legal education himself, which he did in 1911 by taking a job with South Dakota senator Coe Crawford in Washington, D.C.[18]

This wrenching move was all the more difficult because Lewis Larson by that point was in his early thirties and had a wife and three children (including the newly arrived Arthur) to support. Anna's backing helped make Lewis's plan work. She and the children made the 1,300-mile train trip to Washington, where they settled in with him at a house located about three miles north of the Capitol and across the street from the Old Soldiers Home park. Evidently concerned about the effect of Washington's notoriously poor climate on her higher than the White House . . . so it won't be as damp as the lower places."[19] While Lewis spent most of the next three years working as an administrative assistant on Capitol Hill during the day and studying at National Law School in the evening, Anna focused on raising their young family.[20]

All in all, this new life made for an interesting change from the one they had known in Sioux Falls. The various beautification projects begun in Washington during the decade before the Larson family arrived had finally made the city an attractive place to live. Anna wrote Helen Rothie on January 18, 1912, marveling at how densely settled downtown Washington was and how convenient when compared with life back home. She pondered how motherhood had changed her life:

> Doesn't it seem funny . . . to think of me with three children already. Really sometimes I can't believe it myself for I feel as much like a kid as they do sometimes. This morning I certainly did. I left the breakfast table and all my work [and] just got all their wraps and mine on and we went out sliding over in the vacant lot just west of our place and we slid from 9:30 till 11:45 and I had so much fun I just got the head ache from laughing.[21]

Anna's strong commitment to childrearing came through in another letter to Helen, where she expressed strong disapproval of a mother who had allowed her child to go outside without enough warm clothes. "Anything like that just makes my blood boil," Anna confessed to her friend.[22] Anna's focus of concern at that time was her youngest, Arthur, a blond, blue-eyed baby who, she reported to Helen, "has been having whooping cough just awful bad."[23]

While Anna experienced the new world of childraising, Lewis Larson entered what for him was the equally foreign realm of national politics. His employer, Coe Crawford, had started out as a fairly conservative Republican railroad lawyer, but by 1903 he had caught the spirit of Progressive reform and became known as the father of the Progressive movement in South Dakota. During his tenure as governor there from 1907 to 1909, the state legislature passed laws that installed the primary election system; created a state food and drug commission; curbed corporate influence, most notably that of the railroads; and required the disclosure of campaign contributions as well as other regulations on lobbyists. Morally traditional, Crawford also supported laws that prohibited theatrical performances and baseball games on Sundays and forbade the sale of cigarettes to minors as well as the statewide referendum to lengthen the residency requirement for divorce and another one, which failed, to allow the state's counties to enact local Prohibition measures.[24]

Crawford's blend of economic populism and moral traditionalism evidently appealed to Lewis Larson, especially Crawford's willingness to support the residence requirement referendum in 1908. The following year, Crawford moved on to the U.S. Senate by ousting a conservative Republican incumbent and political rival named Alfred Kittredge, the so-called boss of the South Dakota GOP. Although the evidence on this point is sketchy, it seems likely that Crawford was impressed by Larson's work as Sioux Falls city clerk and asked him to come along as his administrative assistant. Crawford's willingness to hire a second-generation Norwegian American for such an important post reflected his greater openness to new kinds of people than more orthodox Republicans such as Kittredge.[25]

Larson's success in getting the job reflected, too, the growing importance of the Norwegian community in South Dakota politics. Although preoccupied at first with establishing farms, churches, and schools, Norwegians there became politically active during the heyday of populism in the later 1880s and early 1890s. Most of the settlers of Norwegian ancestry in the state responded enthusiastically to the Populists' call to regulate the railroads to protect the interests of small farmers. When Progressives such as Crawford later took up that cause, Norwegian-American farmers gave them strong support, as they did to the Progressive Republican president, Theodore Roosevelt. So popular was Roosevelt in the Dakotas, where he had lived briefly during the 1880s, that he actually carried South Dakota in November 1912 when he attempted to return to the White House by running on the Bull Moose ticket.[26]

Progressive strength in South Dakota also stemmed from the active role the federal government played in developing the state's economy. The Dakotas had needed and benefited from such government intervention, which encouraged residents to view the activist state in a positive way. That outlook meshed well with the views of Norwegian settlers such as the Larsons and Huseboes, who tended to be much more communitarian than individualistic. Although they were as egalitarian as most midwesterners, Norwegian immigrants, like Scandinavian settlers more generally, differed from Yankees in their tendency to see the group rather than the individual as the source of social progress. The strong Lutheran faith of Norwegian Americans also tended to make them staunch moral traditionalists who generally favored the use of state power to protect their values. All of these factors encouraged such people to embrace a broader role for the government at a time when that was a hotly contested idea. This distinctive mix of political traditions constituted the milieu in which Arthur Larson grew up.[27]

He might have spent more of his childhood in the rather different environment of Washington itself, but the Larson family had to leave while Arthur was only three years old when Coe Crawford lost his bid for reelection. Crawford's service in the Senate had proved to be a disillusioning experience for him and, one suspects, for his administrative assistant. A gifted public speaker, Crawford quickly learned to his chagrin that no one in the Senate took oratory very seriously. Although he had greatly admired Senator Robert La Follette of Wisconsin, a Progressive champion, Crawford soon discovered upon arriving in Washington that his hero was an unlikable man who demanded unswerving loyalty. A supporter of reducing trade barriers to encourage farm exports, Crawford found himself maneuvered into voting for the thoroughly inadequate Payne-Aldrich Tariff on the grounds that it was the best that could be obtained. In so doing, he alienated La Follette and many of his own constituents. An early friendship with President William Howard Taft broke down when Taft's administration negotiated a trade agreement with Canada that adversely affected South Dakota farmers. The presidential candidates Crawford supported in 1912 to replace Taft—first La Follette and then Roosevelt—both lost, and the rift within the Republican Party that year led to the election of Democrat Woodrow Wilson. That same split back home in South Dakota eventually led to a similarly frustrating outcome. In the 1914 Republican senatorial primary, Crawford lost to a more conservative challenger who in turn was beaten by Tom Johnson, the first Democrat to represent South Dakota in the U.S. Senate. That result ended Crawford's political career and appears to have also extinguished whatever interest Lewis Larson had developed in the Washington scene. By the time Crawford lost his seat, Larson had spent enough time studying law to pass the bar exam back home, so he, Anna, and their children returned to Sioux Falls in 1914. Arthur Larson would spend the next eighteen years there, maturing from boy to young man.[28]

The Larsons' hometown was in the midst of a genuine boom that year, fueled mostly by the steady rise in grain prices since 1900. The outbreak of war in Europe during the summer the Larsons returned soon pushed farmers' income even higher and encouraged a steady stream of newcomers to settle in Sioux Falls, whose population topped 25,000 by 1920. By that point Sioux Falls had begun to feel truly urban, with crowded streets shared by electric streetcars, automobiles, and pedestrians and a steady stream of trains arriving and departing from the station downtown. The community's growth slowed during the 1920s, as farming began to slump again after World War I, but still increased by about 8,000 in that decade. The 1910s and 1920s were a heyday of sorts for Sioux Falls, as they were for many similar midwestern communities. Still growing fast enough to provide jobs for most of the next generation, Sioux Falls possessed the air of a thriving, comfortable place. There were still a lot of poor farmers, mostly of Norwegian ancestry, in the surrounding countryside, but even their incomes improved until the early 1920s. Although lacking much in the way of heavy industry, in most other respects Sioux Falls then was fairly typical of the small midwestern city that sociologists Robert Lynd and Helen Merrell Lynd immortalized in their classic work *Middletown*.[29]

The Larson family soon took their place in the middling tier of the Sioux Falls's social structure that lay just below the business elite of Yankee ancestry who ran the town and considerably above the laborers and poor farm families, mostly Norwegian Americans with some Irish and German Americans, who made up a majority of the overall population. Rather than stay in the private practice of law, which would have enmeshed him in the business world that had earlier disappointed him, Lewis Larson soon ran successfully for juvenile court judge in Minnehaha County. This new job suited him so well that he stayed in it for the remainder of his working life. One of the first Norwegian Americans to sit on the county bench, he served throughout his long tenure there as a kind of informal ombudsman between the poor Norwegian farm families living in the county and the local establishment in Sioux Falls.[30]

The steady income of a county judge helped provide a stable, secure environment for the Larson children, whose ranks had expanded to five with the arrival of Arthur's younger brothers Don in 1914 and Richard one year later. All the indications are that the Larson children enjoyed a happy, healthy family life, thanks to their conscientious and highly competent parents and the safe, family-friendly community in which they grew up. Anna Huseboe Larson in particular so excelled at parenting that she was once voted South Dakota's mother of the year. She did develop something of a melancholy streak after her brother Leonard came back from World War I so troubled that he eventually committed suicide. The premature death of her mother may also have contributed to that inner sadness, but it seems not to have left any marks on her children. Theirs was a happy childhood, filled with games, music, and summers on the Larson family farm, which Lewis's younger brother Gilbert managed.[31]

Of the various family entertainments, by far the most important was music. Anna, herself a cultured and thoroughly musical person, made certain that all of her children learned to play an instrument and sing. The first thing Arthur Larson ever bought, in fact, was a used violin, which he played publicly, though unsuccessfully, for the first time at age seven. In his words,

> Someone conceived the misguided notion that I was ready to play a solo at a Sunday evening meeting of a young people's League. The selection was "Angel's Serenade," and my sister Marguerite, already an accomplished pianist at age 13, would accompany me. Needless to say, we had rehearsed many times. But when the crucial moment arrived, I was so terrified that I forgot that Marguerite had a four-bar introduction to play, and as soon as she hit her first note I hit mine too. Marguerite quickly jumped ahead and caught up with me, but the damage was done. The dreadful moment haunted me for months.[32]

Despite this unfortunate early episode, he persisted in practicing the violin and other instruments, as well as learning how to sing. Music became in time his favorite form of evening recreation, as it did for his siblings, who often practiced and performed together. The Larson "family orchestra," as Arthur later called it, featured Marguerite on piano, Palmer on coronet, himself on violin, Don on trombone, and Dick on French horn. When they switched from classical pieces to jazz, Palmer would play the banjo, Arthur the guitar, Don the accordion, and Dick the drums. The point of all of this activity was not so much to excel but simply to have fun. As Arthur put this thought later, "We all learned a little about a lot of kinds of music and instruments, but never became really outstanding at any of them."[33]

Their parents' strong encouragement helped bring that about, but as important, one suspects, was the time and place in which the Larson family lived. Radio did not arrive in Sioux Falls until Arthur was in his teens, and television would not do so until three decades after that. Nationally known figures such as the comedian Will Rogers and the composer and pianist George Gershwin did perform at the Sioux Falls Coliseum, but that kind of outing would only have been an occasional treat. Arthur Larson's generation was perhaps the last in which a middle-class family creating its own entertainment could be considered not only a virtue but also a necessity, especially in smaller cities and towns such as Sioux Falls.[34]

In that warm, supportive, and tightly knit world Arthur also began learning his first life lessons. Of these, the most important, Larson later wrote, was what his parents taught him early about making a lot of money, something to which they did not attach great value, especially when doing so conflicted with other values such as honesty, friendship, and fairness. The event that crystallized his parents' views on this subject for him was the response that greeted his first business transaction, in which, at age four, he swapped a whistle for an iron dumbbell worth several times as much. The other participant in this deal was a neighbor boy named Kenny, also four years old. When Lewis Larson came home, Arthur told him about the trade and immediately received a stern fatherly command to return the dumbbell to Kenny at once. Much later, Arthur Larson wrote of his parents' teaching in this regard:

> I have often wondered if, in some households where making money and getting ahead in business rated higher in the scale of virtues than they did in ours, the same transaction would not have been applauded as evincing promise of commercial triumphs to come. This was only the first in a number of incidents, most of them subtle and unspoken, that taught me that in this family making money was at the bottom of the scale of priorities, and that unselfish service was at the top. . . . Of the five children . . . not one ever went into business or set out to make money; all spent their lives in academia, the church or public service.[35]

Although the Larson parents did not emphasize the importance of accumulating wealth, acquiring knowledge was another matter entirely. Lewis and Anna communicated their expectations for academic success subtly but clearly and achieved the desired result. All five of their children excelled, as Anna had, in the Sioux Falls public schools. Her favorite motivational technique was to leave out her report cards for her children to find, which contained an unbroken series of "Excellents" in every subject. The great importance Lewis and Anna placed on education appears to have dictated the location of their new home, to which they moved soon after returning to Sioux Falls in 1914 and where they lived for the rest of their lives. Located at 831 South Prairie Avenue in the established southwest neighborhood where most of the middle- and upper-class families of Sioux Falls lived, their house was a substantial but not very big three-bedroom structure made of wood with two stories, an attic, and a small front porch. It stood diagonally across an intersection from the Lowell (Elementary) School and only a short walk away from Washington High School and Augustana College, the local Lutheran institution of higher learning. Arthur Larson attended all three in succession while living at home, beginning kindergarten in the fall of 1915 and graduating from college in the spring of 1931.[36]

He was from the start, like his siblings, a confident student who enjoyed and excelled at school. The Lowell School building itself was an impressive stone structure built in 1891 whose interior had been completely redone after a fire gutted it in 1906. Arthur's memories of it included the large and sunny kindergarten room with its little bentwood chairs painted in primary colors and usually arranged in a circle. Besides the occasional struggle to put on wet or shrunken overshoes in inclement weather, his only memory of that first year was being punished for accidentally sitting on a classmate's art project. He was required to stay after school, and the memory lingered because of the sense of injustice that accompanied it. The other student had put his creation on Arthur's chair, unbeknown to him, and so Arthur had concluded, with logic worthy of a judge's son, that he deserved no blame in the matter.[37]

That same pattern of successful performance marred only by an occasional bump in the educational road continued over the rest of his time at the Lowell School. He spent one year less than was normal there because Anna had prepared him so well that Arthur's teachers decided to let him skip the first grade entirely. Of the following two years, Arthur retained few memories, save for learning how to brush his teeth properly in hygiene class and how much he disliked the overly rich milk he was obliged to drink during the mid-morning break. In fourth grade, however, the single most memorable incident of his years at Lowell School took place. By that point Arthur had come to expect, thanks to his mother's outstanding report cards, his older siblings' similar performance, and his own easy success, to get every assignment exactly right. Unprepared for how to react should he fail to meet such a high standard, this eight-year-old-boy eventually made a mistake in judgment that he never forgot. When Arthur finally misspelled a word on a self-graded test, he impulsively corrected his mistake and gave himself the usual 100, an act that led to the following trauma:

> This occurred just before I went home for lunch break. In the half hour that ensued, I experienced all the torments of Hell that I ever need to know. Of course my mother knew something was terribly wrong, of course I told her my crime, and of course she gently told me what to do. Ignoring my lunch, I rushed back to the fourth-grade room and waited for the teacher to return. I blubbered out my confession, and must have cut such a heart-rending figure that she gave me my 100 anyway.
>
> And so, as in Kindergarten I had first known injustice, so in fourth grade I had first known sin. And forgiveness.[38]

The religious terminology Arthur Larson used in recounting this story reflected how central church life was to his childhood generally and to his moral instruction in particular, as it was for every member of his family. He later characterized church as "an extremely important part of our lives" and recalled that during his boyhood "I spent a large part of my time in church, one way or another."[39]

The Larson family belonged to Trinity Lutheran, as everyone there called it, the church Anna had grown up in and that Lewis had joined after they married. Founded in 1890 as the Evangelical Lutheran Trinity Congregation, its official name distinguished this church from the other Lutheran one in Sioux Falls, the St. Olaf Congregation, which had been organized thirteen years earlier. By the time Lewis Larson appeared on the scene, these two congregations had erected church buildings only a few blocks from each other in a town of only a few square miles. The older of these two churches was attached to the Norwegian Synod, which viewed as its mission the carrying forward in America of the kind of religious life known in the state churches of Norway. Trinity Lutheran, in contrast, was affiliated with the newly formed synod of the United Norwegian Lutheran Church. It tried to steer a moderate middle course between the practices of the Norwegian state church and the more extreme form of low-church pietism practiced by the Haugean Synod that flourished in nearby Minnesota and Wisconsin.[40]

The United Norwegian Lutheran churches gave greater emphasis to evangelism and more commitment to religious revivalism than the Norwegian state church. United Lutheran churches also favored more of a role for laymen than was allowed in Norway's state church, which tended to be clerically controlled. Laymen participated more actively in church governance and life in the United Norwegian Church synod and its various congregations enjoyed more autonomy from the parent body than did those affiliated with the Norwegian Synod, which emulated the organizational structure of Norway's state church. During the 1860s, 1870s, and 1880s, these differences in church doctrine and organization sparked intense and bitter debates between churches affiliated with these two synods and the Haugean synod. By the early 1900s, however, divisions had begun to heal and the differences in doctrine and organization had narrowed. Over the next decade and a half, the three synods that made up the bulk of Norwegian Lutherans in the United States moved gradually toward a merger, which eventually took place in 1917.[41]

The emergence of the new parent body, the Norwegian Lutheran Church of America, had a direct impact on the two Sioux Falls congregations, which responded by organizing a Union Committee to begin local merger negotiations. In keeping with his prominent status within the church and the Norwegian community more generally, which his work for Senator Crawford in Washington and legal training had enhanced, Lewis Larson was named the lead member of the Trinity Lutheran group on this committee. Negotiations soon broke down, however, over the thorny question of which language to use during church services. The St. Olaf congregation used Norwegian and Trinity Lutheran used English. Lewis Larson and the other leaders of Trinity Lutheran's representatives took a firm stand in favor of English only, rejecting a compromise proposal from the St. Olaf delegates to alternate languages every other Sunday. When the merger talks stalled as a result, Larson and his colleagues withdrew from them and led a reorganization of Trinity Lutheran alone to place it in compliance with the requirements of the new synod.[42]

This seemingly arcane dispute about language reflected much more basic cleavages within the Norwegian-American community in Sioux Falls. Continuing to allow the use of Norwegian half of the time in a merged church would have tended to give the clergy, fully versed in the mother tongue, more influence over worship. Such a move would also have diminished the appeal of church membership to the young, who increasingly spoke little or no Norwegian. Finally, hovering over all of this was the issue of assimilation within American society, a concern heightened in the spring of 1917 when the United States entered World War I. The resulting upsurge in nationalist sentiments and growing hostility toward "foreign elements" apparently helped Trinity Lutheran prevail on the language question. In the summer of 1920, a second Union Committee achieved a consensus in favor of using English exclusively at all services. On September 21, 1920, the two congregations formally merged and Trinity's new pastor, H. J. Glenn, whom Lewis Larson had taken the lead in recruiting, was unanimously elected the first pastor at the new church, named First Lutheran. In a letter written to Lewis Larson just prior to accepting the call there, Reverend Glenn expressed his vision of what the new church should be like with respect to matters of language and culture: "I feel strongly that the church must be planted on American soil in the language of the day and country and in harmony with the spirit and ideals of America, rightly understood. I have talked this a long time."[43] Thus, the congregation in which Arthur Larson grew up was moderate in doctrine and organization and assimilationist in outlook and sensibility.

Arthur's family was as deeply involved in the new church as any in the congregation. Lewis Larson was, his son Arthur remembered, "a true pillar of the church" who handled matters both great and small. They ranged from helping raise money to construct a new church building, a mammoth undertaking that took ten years, to performing routine maintenance on the older building that had housed Trinity Lutheran and became the interim home of the newly merged congregation. "I distinctly remember when I was quite small that he would go over and do janitor work when there wasn't anybody else to do it," Arthur later recalled.[44] Anna played a similarly important part in the various activities headed by women. So central and time-consuming were these various obligations, and the faith that sustained them, that Arthur Larson later described religion's role in his youth as "an omnipresent force in every aspect of life—personal, family and community."[45]

Unlike most churchgoers today, the Larson family's time at church far exceeded the one hour per week devoted to the main Sunday service. Arthur later described his boyhood schedule of church-related commitments as follows:

> Every Sunday there was Sunday School at 10:00, morning service at 11:00, Young People's Luther League at 7:00, and evening service at 8:00. Then there was choir practice on Thursday and Luther League on Friday, plus innumerable special events and duties, such as confirmation classes and summer Bible school. At home there were prayers before meals, at which each of the children took his turn, prayers at bedtime, and regular Bible reading.[46]

All of this religious instruction, which continued for years, did more than give Arthur Larson a clear sense of right and wrong; it also contributed to his growth as a scholar. He filled the margins of his confirmation Bible with textual exegesis until the book literally began to fall apart. He later explained the way this activity helped develop his powers of reasoning:

> For example, I had always been troubled by the doctrine, which has hurried so many missionaries into the field, that if babies were not baptized they would be condemned to eternal hellfire, on the basis of Mark 16:16: "He that believeth, and is baptized, shall be saved; but he that believeth not, shall be damned." My marginal note solves the problem with lawyerlike precision: "Doesn't say—or is not baptized."[47]

He also learned a lot of valuable lessons about life in general and public speaking in particular from Reverend Glenn, whom he described as "my idol." So deeply did Glenn impress Larson that for most of his childhood he thought that he would one day become a preacher, a notion his father strongly encouraged. This was partly because Arthur's parents considered him to be "a good boy" and thus meant for the ministry, in contrast to his older brother Palmer, who had a rebellious streak that suggested to his father that he should study law instead.[48]

Arthur gradually diverged from that path during high school and college. He became deeply involved in debate, which involved him much more in contemporary social and political controversies than theological ones. He also became seriously involved with girls, and their influence also led him eventually in other directions. He matured during high school into a tall, handsome, clean-cut young man with light brown hair, a lively wit, obvious intelligence, and a baritone voice that sounded a lot like that of the actor Jimmy Stewart. Although Arthur Larson, like his brothers, lacked the prestige that came from lettering in varsity athletics, lots of time spent playing tennis at the local YMCA had made him both strong and agile. Always interested most in brainy girls, he tended to date the smartest one in his class. The example of his own highly intelligent, educated mother appears to have been the key factor here. He always remembered the way that she, without any legal training, could analyze the cases his father talked about over dinner and invariably reach the right verdict.[49]

His official girlfriend throughout most of high school had a similarly formidable mind. She was an Irish Catholic named Shirley Kilpatrick, whom he later described as "attractive, vivacious and very bright."[50] They got to know each other well through working together on the same activities, most notably debate, orchestra, chorus, and the yearbook, of which she was editor-in-chief. Helping to encourage the romance was the simple fact of proximity. Shirley lived only two blocks away, and Arthur would always walk her home after an evening spent at school working on extracurricular activities. For a Lutheran boy to date a Catholic girl in those days would have been fairly unusual, and it certainly suggested a diminished interest in the ministry as a vocation.[51]

His next romance, the great passion of his life, proved far more distracting. Her name was Florence Newcomb and she lived in the town of Madison, South Dakota, about fifty miles northwest of Sioux Falls. The seventh of eight children, Florence was a seventeen-year-old senior at Madison High School during the 1926–1927 academic year. She and Arthur Larson first met on February 28, 1927, when the Washington High School debate team visited Madison to debate its high school team about whether the United States should grant independence to the Philippines. Larson's team was an extraordinarily talented one, whose members during his three years on it included, in addition to him and Shirley, Walt Simmons, who later became the Sunday editor of the *Chicago Tribune*; Keith Funston, a future president of Trinity College and the New York Stock Exchange; and Sig Mickelson, who rose in the journalism world to become president of CBS News. This powerhouse had always won their contests and, as Arthur explained, "I got in the habit of thinking we could never lose."[52]

After typically effective performances by the three members of their team chosen to speak that day, including Larson, who went last for them, he sat back to listen to the other side's final speaker while confidently expecting another victory. And then, to his great surprise, brainy beautiful brunette Florence Newcomb stood up and, in his words, "tore our case to pieces."[53] He and his teammates lost their first debate, and they lost again when Florence's team beat them during the district tournament on March 2nd, thereby knocking Larson's team out of contention for the state championship. Within the space of three days, he and his cohorts suffered their only two defeats in his three years on the Washington High debate team.[54]

Although no doubt annoyed and disappointed by this turn of events, Larson found himself impressed by Florence's obvious intelligence, charm, and, not the least, movie-star features that resembled those of the young Shirley MacLaine. No romance developed right away, but she had made a lasting, positive presence in his subconscious. In his words, "Although . . . I never had more than one girl at a time, I found that it made me feel good to refer to Florence as 'my girl in Madison.'"[55] They spent a few hours together when he made a trip to Madison to attend a music contest and again when she visited a friend who lived in Sioux Falls. During the second of these occasions, he recalled "showing off my ability to toss her up to the ceiling and catch her. I also took her to church."[56]

The relationship finally flowered during the summer of 1928, after his first year of college. The key fortuitous development was the location of his summer job as athletic director, lifeguard, accountant, and guitar player at a YMCA boys' camp on Lake Madison, just five miles from where Florence lived. Arriving early that summer to set things up for the first group of campers, Larson found himself with some extra time on his hands and decided to write Florence a little note, inviting her to visit. Borrowing a card from a friend and fellow camp counselor named "Doc" Borst, Larson playfully wrote the following message:

> I remember your smile,
> I remember your laugh,
> But I just can't remember
> Your autograph.
> Please write. How about coming out to see me?[57]

She drove up the next morning in a Model A Ford, ready for what became one of the most memorable days in both of their lives. Taking along swimsuits, the two got into a canoe, paddled expertly out to the changing area, and then went for a swim. In his memoir, Larson described his falling in love:

> My head reeled at the sight of the most gorgeous female figure I had ever seen—or dreamed of, for that matter—in a simple one-piece yellow bathing suit. . . .
>
> We swam for a while, and finally ventured out into the lake to the far side of a diving raft. There, hidden by the raft, we kissed. But this was nothing like any kiss I had known. It was soft and deep and lingering, even if very

> wet. I was gone-gone-gone. I knew then, more surely than I have ever known anything before or since, that this was my girl forever, and that all of the powers of heaven and hell could not change that eternal result.[58]

As if this were not enough, when he gave Florence a tour of the camp after their swim, she sat down at an upright piano in the mess hall and played "Papillon" with a grace that bowled him over. As he wrote later, "I distinctly remember that, at that moment, I turned my eyes heavenward and said in my heart, 'Oh God, all this, and she plays the piano too.'" Then she proceeded to play a series of popular tunes while he sang along. By the time she drove away later that day, Larson had acquired the overwhelming certainty of a seventeen-year-old who has fallen head over heels in love.[59]

After Florence's car disappeared down the camp road, he turned to Doc Borst and said, "Doc, I'm going to marry that girl," to which his friend chuckled in reply and asked "What about Shirley?" So profoundly affected was he by the experience of that day that his friend's question seemed to be "quite irrelevant."[60] He had never felt this way about Shirley, which put their relationship in an entirely different light. And the two of them had begun to drift apart after high school, especially after she left for a teachers' college in Cedar Falls, Iowa, some 200 miles east of Sioux Falls. Although they had written letters to each other during the previous academic year and he had made one brief visit to her campus, the sense of connection had clearly begun to wane, on his part at least. Feeling himself free to pursue this new romance, the rest of that summer was, he later wrote, "a lover's idyll," filled with evening rendezvous, moonlit canoe rides, singing, and warm embraces. All of this served only to confirm what he had already felt, that in Florence he had found what he called "True Love."[61]

More than a little disoriented by Florence, Arthur Larson began behaving, for the first time in his life, as something other than the "good boy" destined for the ministry. He began neglecting his duties at camp, with which he had been involved for years and where he had always served as a model of responsibility. Eventually worn out by his late nights with Florence, he began sleeping in a hideaway during the afternoons instead of supervising campers' games. And then came an act of irresponsibility that got him fired: he lost one of the children under his supervision during a day hike, thanks to the distraction of having Florence come along with him. Although the youngster was found unharmed, this incident placed Larson in what for him was the very unusual position of having to account for something truly inexcusable. To make matters worse, the man who called him on the carpet was the very intimidating general secretary of the Sioux Falls YMCA, who made a special trip to the camp just to deal with him. And as if that were not bad enough, this man, whom Larson described as a "terrifying Prussian type," knew his father, who was actively involved in the YMCA and served as one of its international vice presidents.[62] Ordinarily Larson would have made an abject apology, but so overwhelmed was he by his feelings for Florence that he just sat silently during the interview with an exasperating smile on his face, which eventually enraged his interrogator so much that he finally said "You're fired." By that point the summer had only one week left to run, and he spent it as a visitor in the Newcomb household before returning home to Sioux Falls for his second year in college.[63]

Once back in Sioux Falls to begin his second year at Augustana College, he went to see Shirley to explain what had happened to him that summer. Standing on the sidewalk in front of her house, he tried to tell her how his feelings had changed. Evidently hoping to get him to reconsider, Shirley suggested that they have a more private discussion that evening. Wanting to let her down as gently as he could, Larson agreed and managed to borrow his father's 1922 Packard for the occasion. He and Shirley drove out to a deserted cemetery, parked, and moved into the back seat for their talk. Much later, he described the ensuing conversation as follows:

> We talked for a while, but when it was becoming evident that my mind was not going to change, she tried one final desperate throw of the dice. She said, "If you want to, you can put your hand *there*," taking my hand and placing it on her leg, about a half-inch above her knee. Although this was a quantum leap beyond any of our prior intimacies, I could hardly tell her, after what I had experienced that summer, that it was too little and too late. Indeed, she did not need to be told; she knew. And that was that.[64]

Although partly the result simply of chance, this breakup also stemmed from deeper differences in background and beliefs, which the social structure of that time and place tended to reinforce. Shirley, the straitlaced young Catholic woman, could not compete with Florence, the less morally traditional Methodist, in the realm of physical intimacy. Nor, for that matter, would Shirley have felt at home attending First Lutheran with him, or he at her church. It seems likely as well that their parents did not mind the end of their high school romance, for that reason if for no other. This was how things worked in the world in which Arthur Larson grew up.[65]

While the breakup with Shirley may well have pleased his parents, Arthur's new romance with Florence certainly did not, at least at first. That was because it inaugurated a period of adolescent rebellion in Arthur Larson's life, during which their heretofore highly responsible son became markedly less so. With the incident at the summer camp still fresh in his mind and theirs, Arthur soon got into trouble again, thanks to his interest in Florence. During his sophomore year at Augustana, he took up hitchhiking to Madison on the weekends to visit her. What complicated things was his contract with the Sioux Falls Presbyterian Church to sing bass every Sunday in its quartet, which formed the heart of the choir. In theory he could manage both because there was a bus that traveled between Madison and Sioux Falls early Sunday morning, the fare for which was much less than his $5 weekly singing fee. However, he frequently missed the bus and thus his Sunday obligation. The unconvincing excuses he and Florence offered satisfied no one and only increased his parents' unhappiness with him and disapproval of her.[66]

Florence's parents also disapproved of the speed with which the romance appeared to be progressing and the late hours she began keeping as a result. Her father, Robert K. Newcomb, owned six chicken farms in South Dakota that by the late 1920s had become profitable enough to provide his large family with a comfortable existence and the freedom to travel for extended periods. Evidently wanting Florence to take a break from her new romance, he and his wife Ollie decided that the entire Newcomb family should spend the next summer visiting his relatives in Lorain, Ohio. Despite anguished protests from Florence and Arthur, off she went to Ohio for three months in 1929, leaving him thoroughly in the dumps. Although he made amends for his bad behavior at camp the previous year by working extra hard at his counseling duties that summer, Larson clearly missed his new girlfriend very badly. And once she came back, Florence's father continued to try to discourage her from becoming too involved with her young suitor. Feeling obliged to accede to her father's wishes, Florence wrote Larson to explain her change in behavior: "Oh gee Art I've just got to tell you this—and I hate to—and yet I must. You probably noticed my indifference last Monday—and I'll tell you why. Papa—isn't very enthusiastic about our going together so much and writing so much."[67]

And there were other obstacles besides parental objections. Florence's falling in love took place more gradually, and with less certainty, than did his. Although their romance survived the three-month separation, she rebuffed his early talk of marriage, telling him that she wanted to wait until he was established in a profession. The simple fact of physical distance also kept their bond from solidifying quickly. While he studied at Augustana in Sioux Falls, she worked toward a degree at Eastern State Normal School, the local teachers' college in Madison, and then took a teaching job at the public high school in Freeman, South Dakota, which was thirty miles southwest of Sioux Falls. An imbalance in the relationship soon developed because he greatly enjoyed his studies and campus life more generally, while she disliked hers. He pursued a liberal arts course of study and had become something of a big man on campus when he was elected president of the first-year class. Florence, however, found her creative, artistic temperament stifled by the normal school's prescribed curriculum and emphasis on learning through rote memorization. The heavy amount of coursework and student teaching also seem to have worn her down. Not surprisingly, she missed him much more during this period than he appears to have missed her. Her letters during this time mention over and over how lonely she was without him and gently complained about his failure to visit more often.[68]

They did, of course, still share their common passion for debate, but even this activity interfered in a way with the progress of their romance. As in high school, each of them played starring roles on their respective college teams and met occasionally at various contests. In keeping with the pattern established during high school, he lost only one regular-season debate during his four years at Augustana, to her team. That did not bother him, but her debate coach's efforts to discourage their romance certainly did. The meddlesome figure here was Karl Mundt, who would later go on to a long and distinguished career in Congress as a leader of the Republican Right. In the late 1920s and early 1930s, however, he was working as a speech teacher and debate coach at Eastern State. For reasons that are not entirely clear but seem to have been an outgrowth of his intensely competitive approach to his coaching duties, Mundt took a strong dislike to Arthur Larson's interest in Florence, placing her in the middle of a thoroughly awkward situation.[69]

As frustrating as this no doubt was for both of them at times, things surely could have been worse. The single biggest obstacle for most young lovers in those days, the onset of the Great Depression, seems not to have seriously interfered with their plans. Not until December 1930 did Florence's letters to him even mention the economic contraction, which hit South Dakota hard. And even the way in which the Depression touched her life then showed the degree of insulation her family enjoyed from its worst effects. The specific incident, the failure of the bank in Freeman, where she had taken a teaching job, and the one in Madison left her and her parents temporarily without cash but not impoverished. As she explained in a letter to Larson dated December 20, 1930,

> I'm all in a muddle tonight. I lost $185.00 today in the Freeman Bank. . . .
> The folks lost all of their money in the Madison bank the same time I lost mine. This is a rather unhappy household—and yet we have had several good laughs over it all. . . .
> Of course we have all of our resources in the Hatcheries. We are not quite poor—but we have nothing to use for money.[70]

Larson's family also enjoyed considerable insulation from the worst effects of the Great Depression because his father's $3,100 salary was fixed in the state constitution, which could not easily be amended. This safeguard, intended to guarantee judicial independence, had the happy consequence during the 1930s of protecting Lewis Larson's salary from the legislative cuts that affected so many other public employees. His real income actually improved substantially then, thanks to the sharp drop in prices that accompanied hard times. Although not unaware of the growing joblessness and poverty in their own communities and the nation as a whole, the relatively privileged position of their respective families allowed Florence and Arthur to remain as preoccupied with their own lives and romance as people their age are inclined to be.[71]

As is so often the case, the course of their love proved less than straight and smooth. When he tried to strengthen their connection by giving her a diamond ring in March 1930, she accepted it but still refused to become formally engaged to him and then had second thoughts about whether she should have accepted the ring at all. The seriousness of Florence's doubts can be seen in her decision early in 1931 to return his books and other things, most notably his letters to her, and her request that he return her letters to him. He seems to have thrown away the letters she sent back to him while she kept hers, thereby leaving a very one-sided record of their early relationship. All that remains, save for one short letter to her written while he was working at the summer camp, is the following description of his love letters that Florence wrote before her father insisted that she cool things off: "I can't help but notice how many different kinds of letters you write. Some brief, some long—some philosophize, some describe—some are practical and others are fanciful. I like it so much. I never know what to expect in your letters, except that you love me."[72]

Florence's decision to pull back, as she explained in her letters to him, stemmed mostly from her concerns about the potentially limiting consequences of an early marriage for both of them, as well as uncertainty over the depth of her own feelings for him. She also appears to have doubted that he really understood the sacrifices that marriage and adult life more generally would demand of him, given the rather charmed life he had thus far led. As she explained in the only seriously critical comments she ever wrote to him during their courtship,

> You see—everything has come your way—contests, everything. Your mother waits upon you. You have nothing to worry about now. . . .
>
> You have never been imposed upon—have you? You have never really given anything. You haven't had to so far.
>
> But some day you are going to be imposed upon. Someone is going to have to depend on you for a lively hood [*sic*]. And you're going to have to sacrifice and give and give and give. You're going to have to forget personal glory. You're going to have to fight with men. . . . All kinds of men—good, bad, fine, intelligent.[73]

The uncertainty in Florence's mind and heart could be seen in how she dealt with him. She tried to place their relationship on the plane of friendship and usually closed her letters to him with the words "your buddy." The phrase was a reference to "their" song, a popular one of that day called "My Buddy," but it also seems to have reflected Florence's doubts about how far their relationship could progress. Trying to be honest with him, she wrote early in 1931 that "I'm afraid I don't love you as much as I should—gee I'm terribly sorry but I can't explain anymore than I can tell you why God made the sky so blue. You're wonderful—I like you but I don't love you."[74] The clearest sign of the change in her feelings came that spring when she dated someone else briefly. At the same time, however, she kept Larson's picture and the ring he had given to her. Although understandably unhappy and frustrated by these mixed signals, he persevered, and in the process demonstrated the depth and seriousness of his feelings for her. She reciprocated by continuing to answer his letters and trying to explain the ever-changing state of her emotions. By the spring of 1932, she had finally discarded all such doubts, to her own joy and his great relief.[75]

While his relationship with Florence moved through its ups and downs, Arthur devoted the bulk of his considerable energy to excelling at college in both coursework and debate. Augustana College had, by the time he enrolled there in the fall of 1927, finally begun to blossom as a solid place in which to obtain a liberal arts education. The school had an unusual history. It had been founded in Chicago in 1860 by a Swedish Lutheran minister named Lars P. Esbjorn. He and his followers settled on the name Augustana, which was Latin for Augsburg, the place in Germany where Martin Luther had laid out Lutheranism's main doctrines in his famous "Confession." Over the following six decades, Augustana moved five times to stay close to the Norwegian Lutheran communities that supported it. This odyssey, which earned the school the nickname of "the college on wheels," finally came to an end in 1918, when, as a result of the merger of the three leading Norwegian Lutheran synods, it was formally established in Sioux Falls. Two years later, a new administration building, built with local stone in a handsome Gothic style, opened and a new, more stable chapter in the school's history began.[76]

Although at first mostly a place to study religion, music, or the basic subjects needed to become a schoolteacher, during the 1920s Augustana's faculty, student body, curriculum, and number of buildings all grew steadily. The school's "college department," which served students pursuing a general liberal arts education, expanded from just sixteen majors in 1920 to 284 during Arthur Larson's first year there, out of a total college enrollment of 486. The students were heavily of Norwegian Lutheran background and mostly from South Dakota, and women outnumbered men by a ratio of 3 to 2.[77]

The most important influences on Larson at Augustana were a professor of modern languages named Helmer Blegen and the debate coach, Hugo Carlson. Of these two, Blegen was the more significant. He arrived in the fall of 1927, just as Larson did, and made a major impact on the school's intellectual life. Blegen had studied in Europe and was widely read in philosophy, literature, and science. He could also speak and write a dozen languages and had studied with the great Ole Rölvaag, whose novel *Giants in the Earth* had appeared in English that year and become a bestseller. Sophisticated, cosmopolitan, and formally dressed in conservative suits, Blegen was just the sort of mentor to whom a bright, impressionable, middle-class young undergraduate such as Arthur Larson would be drawn. During his years at Augustana, the more intellectual students met regularly at a downtown restaurant called The Chocolate Shop, and they invited Blegen to join them. He often did, smoking his trademark cigars and holding forth on a wide variety of subjects as his audience eagerly listened.[78]

Hugo Carlson, who arrived at Augustana in 1925, also figured prominently in Arthur Larson's college years because he coached Larson in his principal extracurricular activities: forensics and debate. By the early 1920s, Augustana's forensics and debate teams had become excellent, and under Carlson's skillful direction, they stayed that way throughout Larson's time there. During his first three years on Augustana's team, it reached the semifinals of the Pi Kappa Delta (a national honorary forensic society) tournament each time. Although he and his teammates never won a national title, they set school records for winning the most debates in various national competitions, some involving teams and others individuals. The high point for Larson came in the spring of 1930, during his junior year, when he and his teammate Melvin Nelson won eight consecutive debates during the national tournament competition at Wichita, Kansas. That year, Larson won third place and a prize of $750 in the finals of the oratorical division, an individual event that was held in Los Angeles on June 9th.[79]

Confident, quick-witted, and polished, Larson excelled in particular at extemporaneous public speaking, for which he later gave the primary credit to his pastor, H. J. Glenn. He remained a familiar presence in Larson's life during his college years, partly because Glenn served as Augustana's acting president during Larson's sophomore year. Larson later explained how Glenn helped him become a champion debater:

> He volunteered to coach me in public speaking, and I owe more to him in this area than to anyone. He began by imposing the strictest discipline on posture and movements. Hand gestures were used sparingly, and were as carefully choreographed as a ballet dancer's. Then, in time, as these habits became ingrained, there was room for spontaneity, but it could never deteriorate into the pointless arm-waving and air clutching that characterizes ninety percent of public speaking today.[80]

Glenn's willingness to invest such time and energy in teaching Larson how to speak stemmed at least in part from Glenn's deeply cherished hope that Arthur would eventually enter the ministry. This had been the family assumption throughout his childhood, but soon after graduating from Augustana in June 1931 he changed his mind. Debate and his studies in college had made Larson more interested in the secular world, as did, in a different way, his relationships with Shirley and Florence. Crucial here, too, was the example of Larson's father, who had made a distinguished career in law, and his older brother Palmer, then a law student at the University of South Dakota. For all of these reasons, which even he did not fully understand at first, Arthur Larson decided during the summer after finishing college that he would become a lawyer instead. He promptly joined Palmer at the University of South Dakota Law School, which, like so many others during the Depression, simply admitted applicants on the spot if they appeared qualified and could afford the tuition.[81]

The news of Arthur's decision deeply disappointed his pastor. After moving forty miles south of Sioux Falls to Vermillion, where the law school was located, Arthur Larson wrote Glenn and tried to explain the reasons behind his change of heart. Glenn replied later that fall in a heartfelt letter which reveals how painful this news was to him and thus how difficult it must have been for Larson to dash the hopes of the man he later called "my idol." In his letter Glenn wrote: "I'm praying for you Art. And you will forgive me for being disappointed that you did not come into this work with me. I have honestly tried to respect your judgment but I have never been reconciled. And honestly, I fear I never can become reconciled to it except on the basis of your proving unworthy, which would be the great sorrow of my life."[82]

By the end of his college years Larson had diverged in another way from the example his pastor had set for him. Although Arthur Larson described Glenn as "almost excessively modest," the same could not be said of his twenty-one-year-old admirer.[83] Arthur Larson by then had acquired an exalted view of himself that he did not always take pains to conceal. The clearest indication of this appears in his college yearbook, where he chose Emerson's maxim "To be great is to be misunderstood" to appear immediately beneath his name. Success in endeavors both educational and extracurricular combined with his parents' and pastor's repeated messages that he was someone special appear to have been the key factors behind this visibly big ego, so at odds with the example set for him at home and in church. Although such immodesty was unattractive, the abundant self-confidence it reflected helped him achieve extraordinary things.[84]

The most noteworthy of his early accomplishments came during his first semester in law school, when he applied for and won a Rhodes Scholarship. Larson decided to try for the Rhodes for reasons he later explained this way:

> It grew out of a conviction going back to childhood that I was going to do something special. What better way to break out of my unpromising surroundings? The Depression had just begun to hit its lowest point, with 25 percent unemployment. As if that weren't enough, South Dakota was in the grip of the Dust Bowl days. . . . The difference between this kind of prospect and three years in the lush green countryside of Oxfordshire with a comfortable income and an exciting future was incalculable.[85]

The selection criteria for a Rhodes were academic excellence, athletic interests, other extracurricular activities of all kinds, and evidence of leadership ability. Larson's outstanding record in college debate was doubtless a major factor in getting him to the interview with the regional committee, which met that year in Des Moines, Iowa. His big break came when one of its guest members, lexicographer and co-editor of the *Oxford English Dictionary* C. T. Onions, asked Larson if he liked Ibsen. Purely by chance, Larson had spent the previous summer reading the playwright's complete works, and he mentioned that in his affirmative reply. Thus began a long discussion in which Onions, an Ibsen scholar, quizzed Larson about some of Ibsen's least-known writings, an exchange in which Larson evidently held his end up very effectively. His clear commitment to public service also impressed his examiners. Even so, the competitors that Larson met during the two-day interview process seemed so stellar that he did not hold out much hope of winning. The fact that his college alma mater had not yet been fully accredited also seemed to place him at a distinct disadvantage. When he heard his name announced as one of the four regional winners, Larson momentarily collapsed onto a table, overcome by the thought, as he later wrote, that "my world would never be the same."[86]

Larson opted to study law at Oxford and decided that the three years he would spend there (starting the following fall) would be sufficient legal training for him. Accordingly, he dropped out of South Dakota law school after his first semester. Thanks in part to Palmer's coaching, he had done well there—all A's in fact—but did not find the courses very stimulating. He also strongly disliked the dull, fattening meat-and-potatoes diet provided by the boarding house where he was staying. With no good reason to remain in Vermillion, Larson chose instead to go home and take some elective courses at Augustana in Latin and French during the winter and spring of 1932. He also sang in some musical comedies, continued to court Florence, and, in his words, "generally had a glorious time."[87] Receiving the Rhodes Scholarship also opened doors for him in Sioux Falls, giving him social contact for the first time with the Yankee elite who ran the town. In his memoir, Larson described that change as follows:

> A whole new world opened to me, whose existence I had hardly noticed, although I used to think I knew almost everybody. I was discovered by the world of Sioux Falls high society, and they swept me off my feet. They were in fact interesting company, because they made a practice of patronizing talented and witty people, like Professor Blegen, and the famous architect Harold Spitznagel. Since my social world had tended to center in the First Lutheran Church and the Y.M.C.A., this was, to say the least, a pleasant change.[88]

Winning the Rhodes Scholarship did have one serious drawback: it created new obstacles to the progress of his relationship with Florence. Under the terms of the scholarship program, recipients could not marry. Those who did would promptly forfeit their scholarship, and Florence firmly refused to allow him to make such a sacrifice. By that point her feelings for him had become sure enough to make a commitment, but not at such a cost for his future. Even so, for him to accept the scholarship would have meant his absence from the country—

and her—for three years, a prospect both of them found intolerable. Their solution was for Florence to move to England as well, where she would apply to study acting in London at the Royal Academy of Dramatic Art. This way, they could continue to see each other regularly while remaining unmarried and under separate roofs.[89]

The crucial factors in this decision were their mutual desire to be together and, less important but still significant, Florence's dislike for the daily grind of school-teaching and administration. Had she genuinely enjoyed that profession and her hard-to-get job as principal of Freeman High School, things might have turned out differently. Moving to England, however, would not only allow her to remain near the man she loved, it would also make possible a change in vocation that she strongly desired. And, of course, implicit in all of this was the understanding that they would marry once the Rhodes Scholarship ended.[90]

Helping make this unusual plan work was the support of both her parents and his, something Arthur Larson described with wonder in his memoirs: "It all seemed perfectly normal to me [then], but in retrospect (this was in 1932), I marvel at the tolerance and understanding of our families and friends as we stood, side by side, on the back of the platform of the train to Montreal, going off together unmarried, while my father—juvenile judge and Sunday School superintendent—and several hundred others waved from the platform."[91]

Sustaining him on that journey were the love, support, and wisdom his family and community had given him and the happiness and security that came from success in his one great romance. Twenty-two years old when he and Florence set sail for England in the late summer of 1932, he, like her, had matured into a typical and also exceptional young midwesterner. Flush with the seemingly boundless optimism so characteristic of that region, Larson set forth to make his mark on the world beyond it.

CHAPTER TWO

Oxford's Imprint

Although Larson would move several times throughout his life, this first experience of uprooting proved in many ways to be the hardest. The most immediate discomfort stemmed from chronic indigestion. It affected him so severely that he went to see a doctor, who prescribed what Larson later remembered as "a repellent-looking purple medicine."[1] In time, this substance succeeded in making British food edible, but nothing, insofar as he was concerned, could make it palatable. His first letter to his mentor at Augustana, Helmer Blegen, pronounced the college dining hall's fare "swinish."[2] In subsequent letters home over the next three years, Larson complained repeatedly about the poor quality and preparation of the food served there and throughout the country.[3]

Another shock to his system came when he received his first term's bill, which was much higher than he had expected. In part this stemmed from his choice of college. Oxford's system of assigning students to residential colleges, each of which had its own dormitories and dining facilities, had the effect of making the educational experience there more personal but also more variable and quirky. His college, Pembroke, was one of the smallest, but—he discovered to his chagrin that fall—also one of the most expensive. Even though his parents surprised him by sending a large check at Christmas to help out with his expenses, the high prices for room, board, and other related fees upset him deeply. In a letter to his parents written shortly after the fall term bill arrived, he called the itemized fees "outrageous" and "scandalous."[4] He followed up his uncharacteristically intemperate language with five pages that explained the fees in detail and his plans for cutting costs in the future.[5]

Larson might have found the high fees Pembroke charged more bearable had the instruction there met his expectations. Unfortunately, the faculty member assigned to supervise his academic work while at Oxford quickly proved to be a colossal disappointment. Pembroke's law tutor in those days was a man named C. M. Davidge, who owed his faculty appointment to his moneyed background, fame as a rowing star during his Oxford undergraduate days, and, crucially, his engagement to the college master's niece, which Davidge broke once his faculty appointment became secure. Lazy and often half-drunk, Davidge personified the most serious drawback to Oxford's upper-class–oriented educational system, which had been originally conceived to meet the needs of gentlemen amateurs, not genuine scholars. His weekly essay assignments consisted of asking students to restate in their own words the material discussed in the assigned readings. When Larson, impatient with such elementary requirements, tried writing a more advanced analytical piece, Davidge commented during the weekly tutorial session that "this is all very interesting, but really . . . it's not exactly what is wanted."[6] Although the university as a whole had become a more serious place by the time Larson arrived there, reminders such as Davidge of the older Oxford still remained.[7]

Larson, not wanting to upset his parents with too much bad news, confided his unhappiness with Davidge in letters to Blegen and Palmer. On January 21, 1933, Arthur Larson wrote his brother sourly that "my tutor has usually got himself into a mild and happy cognac daze by the time I get to him, and so I might as well be in . . . South Dakota with my books."[8] Making matters even worse was the fact that Larson had been granted undergraduate standing, which meant that he had to share his tutor with six other undergraduates rather than receive the individual attention he had expected. All of these other students, Larson reported to his parents, were "at least four years younger than I."[9] As for the university-wide lectures, which formed the other major mode of instruction at Oxford, Larson found them so inefficient a way of learning and so uninteresting that he informed Palmer at the start of the winter term that "I have ceased going to lectures altogether."[10]

Larson finally broke the news of his unhappiness with this state of affairs to his father in a letter written the following March, in which he characterized his program of study as "this silly Oxford law course."[11] The focus of his complaints by then had to do with the impractical course of reading that Oxford students working toward a bachelor's degree in jurisprudence were required to complete. Heavy on legal history and philosophy, the reading list struck Larson, the vocationally minded American, as largely irrelevant to someone seeking to become a practicing lawyer.[12]

Rather than simply accept this situation, Larson decided to modify his course of study to deal with Oxford's limitations. Determined to avoid having to enroll again at an American law school after he finished his Rhodes Scholarship, Larson decided to compile his own reading list on the needed subjects and study them in addition to his regular Oxford work. He also explored ways to shorten his program to two years instead of three, before giving up in frustration when the impossibility of properly completing such a heavy workload became clear. Most important, Larson eventually managed to acquire a second law tutor, who helped fill in the gaps created by Davidge's lackadaisical approach.[13]

Larson's gloomy mood that winter also stemmed from Oxford's inadequate indoor heating and overcast skies. Like so many other American visitors to Britain, Larson found remarkable that a country blessed with such a mild climate could possess such cold, damp, and drafty dwellings. Even worse from his perspective was the lack of sunshine, which created an overall impression of the university as gray and depressing. In his March 9th letter to his father, Larson described the atmosphere produced by these conditions: "Torpor hangs over this place like a fog. You have to keep shaking yourself and sticking pins in yourself or you lapse into a dazed coma. The air is dense and humid and heavy in these lowlands, the sky is an unvarying lead . . . colour, the food is heavy and stultifying."[14]

Also contributing to Larson's jaundiced view of Oxford was loneliness, something he, raised in a large family and a friendly midwestern community, had never before experienced. With Florence off studying in London, he looked to his fellow Oxonians for companionship on weekdays but found little. In part this stemmed from a disappointing experience with his assigned roommate, another Rhodes scholar named Willmoore Kendall. A prodigy from Oklahoma still possessed of an unshakable belief in his own intellectual superiority, Kendall quickly proved a major annoyance. As Larson later recalled, Kendall, like so many highly intellectual Oxford students of that era, was "an ardent leftist."[15] Although in later years he would shift his stance to the other extreme and become an editor of the *National Review*, when Larson knew him Kendall fervently advocated the left's view on the major social questions of the day. "We were," Larson later wrote, "instantly embroiled in a succession of violent arguments ranging from contemporary politics to the Civil War."[16] They quarreled, too, over the best way to tend their soft-coal fireplace, with Kendall characteristically favoring lots of intervention and Larson just as characteristically preferring a more restrained approach. These differences in outlook and temperament drove Larson and Kendall to dislike each other strongly, so much so that Larson moved in mid-October to a room of his own.[17]

That solved one problem but made his isolation from the other students even worse. Accustomed to outgoing, informal South Dakotans who would routinely strike up conversations with perfect strangers, Larson found himself ignored by the British students, whose reserve precluded such exchanges. He later recalled his seeming invisibility to the other students during his first few months at Oxford in this way: "As for the English students, not one ever spoke to me or acknowledged my existence, although most of us lived and dined together in the college. I knew this was not hostility. It was merely the well-known British standoffishness, for which I thought I was prepared. But for a Midwesterner the reality was hard to believe."[18]

One central feature of the Oxford social scene that clearly put Larson off was heavy drinking. This reaction stemmed in part from where and when he had grown up. In the year Arthur had turned nine, the U.S. Congress had passed the Volstead Act, which instituted Prohibition, and that law had remained in force until shortly after he left for Britain. The morally traditional family and collegiate environment in which he came of age would have had nothing to do with alcohol, and all the indications are that neither did he. Prohibition had also put the saloons in downtown Sioux Falls out of business, so, except for his brief time as a law student at the University of South Dakota, he would have had no exposure to drunkenness prior to arriving in England.[19]

Larson did go into English pubs, and the drunkenness he saw there and elsewhere on the Oxford campus produced a strongly negative reaction. He wrote his father in May 1933 that

> the pubs here are a most disgusting blot on this country. . . . If there is still anyone left in the U.S. who says that legalized drinking would curtail drunkenness, and that there is more drinking in American colleges than there would otherwise be, you can tell them for me that they that they are talking pure bilge. I've seen drunkenness at the U.S.D. [University of South Dakota], but I've never before seen students staggering around in broad daylight, day after day,—or what is even worse in a way, an enormous fraction of the college in a totally inefficient daze most of the time from drinking beer with lunch, beer with tea, and usually ending up quite drunk by having a quantity of beer in Hall [with dinner].[20]

The typical male Oxford undergraduate's affected manner of speaking, fondness for childish games, and penchant for wasting time in idle conversation also contributed to Larson's feelings of social alienation. To an American raised in his country's heartland such as Larson, such students seemed effete and immature. Near the end of his first year there, he proclaimed in a letter to Helmer Blegen that "I'm fed up with the touchy, gossipy, epigramming, inhibited, filter-tip cigaretted, 'just cahn't beah' product of these 500 year-old walls."[21] Florence's Sunday visits and his occasional trips to London helped ease Larson's sense of isolation but could not remedy it.[22]

This situation seems to be what drove him during his first term to join the Pembroke college rowing team, where he forged most of his lasting Oxford friendships. The one real friend Larson had made thus far, another American student named Ackerman from California who lived in the room below him, had decided to row for Pembroke and encouraged him to do so as well. To increase the coach's interest in having Larson join the team, Ackerman started a rumor that Larson had been an All-American fullback, which produced recruitment inquiries from the college rugby, soccer, hockey, squash, and crew teams. The rowing coach, confident that he had a real find in Larson, soon made him the lead rower, or "stroke," who set the pace for the three others in his boat.[23]

Happily for Larson and his teammates, all of the hours he had spent at the Sioux Falls YMCA swimming and playing tennis prepared him well for his new sport. Although his boat lost its first race on November 11th, further training and practice under the skilled direction of a Pembroke alumnus and former rowing star named White and a new boat led to a noteworthy triumph the following February. This time, Larson rowed as part of an eight-man team in a racing shell that was sixty-three feet long and less than two feet wide. So thin was its outer wall, he reported to Palmer, "If you step on the bottom of it getting in, your foot will go straight on through."[24] This new craft, which Pembroke bought for what was then considered the extraordinary sum of 200 British pounds (about $700), promised to deliver very high speeds if properly handled. In its maiden contest, both boat and rowers met the college's high expectations. During the week-long Togger Races held in February, Larson's boat caught up with, or "bumped," its opponent in five of the six races, the first time a Pembroke team had done that well in eight years. The honors after the final race included wild applause from the assembled onlookers, including Florence, an elaborate banquet dinner in the college dining hall, and the award of an oar to each of the eight rowers. Thus did Larson "win his oar" during his first year at Oxford, an achievement sufficiently noteworthy as to break down some of the social barriers that separated him from the British students in Pembroke.[25]

This success did not, however, persuade Larson to stick with rowing. He had begun to regret the time lost to other more intellectual pursuits even before the Togger Races. The toll taken on his body by such strenuous exertion also began to concern him. Even more unhealthy was the poor climate in which the practices and races were typically conducted. The Togger Races took place during "bitter, freezing, drizzle," he later wrote.[26] After the drudgery of that contest, he remembered, "I was a physical wreck."[27] His ailments included serious respiratory problems, a persistent cough, and many blisters on his hands and bottom. The worst of these took six months to disappear completely. Larson decided to drop crew the following term and instead focus his extracurricular energies on the Oxford Political Union, the most prestigious debating society on campus. Knowing that his teammates would try to dissuade him from making such a change, he sat down and wrote out a list of all of the reasons he could think of why he should stop rowing. "When I got to 26," he later wrote, "I figured I was safe."[28]

Given Larson's extensive experience as a debater, the Oxford Political Union was the most logical extracurricular activity for him from the start. Founded in 1823, it had been something of a training ground for aspiring British politicos during its first century. After a low point in the late 1920s, when clever argumentation rather than thoughtful discussion was in vogue, the Union began to become a more serious place again. The social and political crisis sparked by the arrival of the Great Depression in Europe made itself felt in Oxford Union debates. Larson's slowness to become heavily involved there had to do with his negative first impression of the place as dominated by cliques whose members seemed much more skilled at infighting than public speaking.[29]

Larson did attend the most notable debate held there during his first year at Oxford, which took place on the evening of February 9, 1933. At that meeting, the members discussed and then approved, by a margin of 275 to 153, a motion "that this House will in no circumstances fight for its King and Country." This quickly became the most widely publicized debate in the Oxford Union's history because of the social context in which it took place and the angry response it provoked from Union alumni and many British newspapers. The critics thought the Union majority dangerously naive about the best way to maintain peace in the world, but not Larson. His comments in his letters home about the debate endorsed the pacifist position. He wrote his father that "I think this, together with similar votes at the Manchester and other [university] Unions, is the most hopeful sign in the way of peace for some time."[30] Larson's thinking appears to reflect both the influence of his religious instruction and the pacifist milieu of the post–World War I era during which he had first begun to form his views about politics.[31]

His status as a Rhodes scholar helped bring him into occasional contact with the world of high politics during his first year at Oxford, though strictly as an interested observer rather than a participant. Among the more noteworthy of these experiences was a meeting arranged by a friend of his father with a prominent British parliamentary lawyer and a tea he attended at the American embassy, where he met the new American ambassador to the United Kingdom, Robert Bingham. Larson's interest in this world can clearly be seen in his letters to his parents, where he wrote of his repeated though unsuccessful efforts to get into sessions of the World Economic Conference, which met in London during the summer of 1933. That curiosity also comes through in his written comment to his mother about a conversation he witnessed at Wimbledon between the queen and her guest, the exiled King Alfonso XIII of Spain.[32]

Larson's various trips to London that year and travel on the Continent during his vacations exposed him to the social and political world of the radical and the dispossessed. In the winter of 1932–1933, the total number of unemployed in Britain reached its official Depression-era peak of approximately 3 million. Signs of the hardship and political discontent that unprecedented joblessness produced could easily be seen on the streets of London and in the inexpensive cafes Larson frequented during his visits there. From time to time he also encountered that world by stopping to listen to the soapbox speakers in the city parks and talking about social problems with the working-class customers at a local eatery.[33]

Like so many middle-class Americans during the 1930s, Larson sympathized with the plight of the unemployed but not with the more extreme solutions to their problems advocated by socialists and communists. His lack of interest in their schemes for social transformation can be seen clearly in the way he described one such speaker he heard in Regent's Park in the spring of 1933: "Next was a screaming reformer who looked like Lionel Barrymore in his worst moments. He flailed the air with stubby arms and shrieked and shouted—I caught only a few words '. . . social order . . . based on universal brotherhood . . .' etc. A red, I guess."[34]

The depth of his concern for those in need is harder to gauge from his letters to relatives back home. The overall impression one gets from his descriptions of trips with Florence to the Continent during 1932–1933 is of a light-hearted young man who only occasionally fell into a somber mood when confronted with a reminder of European social strife. After trying to describe the sights he and Florence had seen in Belgium, Luxembourg, Switzerland, and northern Italy during the summer of 1933, Larson wrote to his mother: "The trouble is, Mom, that I can't really tell you about all the little things that have made this trip the biggest thrill of my life. I think the greatest thing is that we seem to be laughing at something or other all day long—we just guffaw our way through Europe."[35] The only sad note he struck in that letter came in describing World War I cemeteries and battlefields in eastern France: "There were poppy-covered graveyards of thousands of white roses; there were remains of trenches and shell-holes; there were even abandoned cannon and other pieces. I cannot tell you the feeling inspired by these sights."[36]

Larson's letters about that trip and the others he made during his Rhodes Scholarship contained few such downbeat passages, although that may have reflected his decision to spare his family and friends a lot of alarming images of Europe's down and out and political extremists. More certain is that when the poor people he encountered became so demanding as to seem a menace, as they did during a visit to Naples in the late summer of 1933, Larson quickly turned hostile. He described his arrival there in a letter to his mother as follows:

> No sooner was I out of the compartment than three "facchini" or porters sprang at my valises, clawed away at my hands, wrestled and tugged until I thought I was verily being robbed. Of course it was only the Neapolitan idea of snappy service. Sometime later, sweaty, mussed and breathing threats on all sides, I emerged triumphant, still gripping the precious bags. The contemptible little blighters make a habit of thus snatching baggage, trotting it into a taxi a few . . . [feet] away and then screaming for four lire. I made for the "uscita" (exit) with these bounders yapping at my heels and making sporadic attacks for the valises from either flank or the rear.[37]

This experience and a few others like it led Larson to write his mother that the outstretched open palm was "the most characteristic gesture of Southern Italy" and to pronounce Naples "the foulest hole in Europe."[38] Although Larson was certainly not a hard-hearted reactionary, his actions here and the way he described them reveal the limits of his sympathy for the poor at this stage of his life.[39]

In part that stemmed from Larson's view of his own status as ordinary rather than privileged. Only occasionally did events in the outside world remind him otherwise. One of the more memorable took place the following September, when he and Florence looked around London to find a cheaper room for her. While responding to an advertisement in a local newspaper, they managed to offend the landlady in question by asking whether the rent she quoted included the customary breakfast. Angry that they had not asked about this before she had climbed five flights of stairs to show them the room, the woman roughly replied that she had no time to cook breakfast for a tenant. When Arthur and Florence suggested that her unpleasant manner was no way to attract one, the woman had flown off the handle. Larson described what happened next in a letter to his father: "She [the landlady] went completely mad, screaming as she drove us out 'Well I don't want the likes of you!! I want people as works, and hunderstands!!' "[40] Larson related to his father the insight this episode produced: "In the midst of all this toil [his studies] I was rather roughly reminded . . . that I am little better than a member of the leisure class."[41]

The elite social circles in which he and Florence mostly moved during their time in England tended, however, to make such illuminating encounters the exception rather than the rule. The friendships and connections he forged at Oxford and she at the Royal Academy of Dramatic Art appear to have been largely with upper-class Britons, who typically lived far apart from the poor and their problems during the 1930s. He and Florence mostly filled their spare time with concerts and plays in London; teas, lunches, dinners, and parties at fashionable London townhouses; and occasional visits to country homes that to middle-class Americans could only be thought of as estates. The novelty of this world, so different from the one he and she had known in South Dakota, appears to have been one of its main attractions for both of them. The following passage from one of Larson's letters to his parents in December 1932 provides a typical description of his social life outside Oxford:

> Almost every evening I've been here [in London] I've been in full dress, or at least a tuxedo. . . .
>
> Well, I cut down my London engagements to a minimum. I did go to a tea at Lady Neish's, a luncheon at Lady Wingfield-Bonsor's and a big party at Lady Trotter's, but that's about all—oh no, I had dinner with Lady Stephenson. You have no idea of the absolute classiness of these upper-class English families. I never saw such food, such service, such homes or such entertainment in my life. Servants bowing at every corner. Magnificent old homes, with art treasures and ancient carved furniture everywhere.[42]

Larson's success in gaining entrée into this world was no accident. His conscious decision a few months after he arrived in England to buy a wardrobe suitable for these kinds of occasions, including spats and a cane, made that access possible. Florence, too, helped a great deal. He usually had a date for these engagements, and a glamorous one at that. Another factor had to do with the way he spoke. Larson made a careful study of the speech he heard from the mouths of upper-class British students during his first few months at Oxford, learning the vocabulary and pronunciation so well by the end of his first term that even native Londoners sometimes mistook him for one of their own. He also proved to be a popular guest in these rather rarefied social circles thanks to the good manners his parents had taught him and his maturity, which contrasted sharply with the demeanor of so many of the other Oxford students. Larson's moderate views on politics also appear to have won approval from his upper-class British hosts, who were more used to hearing Oxonians utter the kind of extreme opinions considered fashionable there during the 1930s. Florence commented on both how England had changed her fiancé and why he was proving so popular there in a March 1933 letter to his younger brother Don:

> I saw Art this weekend. I think he is changing a lot. He seems different even to me. But it's a very satisfactory change.
>
> Everyone I introduce to Art says how much they like him. I took him to a party Friday night. I was so proud to be with him and believe me he looks wonderful in tails. At that party an elderly man who has joint interest in one of the largest airplane concerns in England, came up to me and said "Well, at last I've found a young man who can talk and at the same time be intelligent—That boy," he said, pointing to Arthur, "is most remarkable—etc.—etc."[43]

Although Larson's new environment did change him, it does not appear to have done so in any fundamental way. After rattling off his list of social engagements with the high and mighty to his parents, Larson went on to inform them that "I didn't enjoy all this half as much as the concerts I've been hearing."[44] His letters home from his time at Oxford contained far more discussion and enthusiasm for the music he had heard and plays he had seen than the upper-class social events he had attended. He also wrote his mother in March 1933 that "I am now quite satisfied that my speech is indistinguishable from that of an Englishman, but I still laugh at myself every time I talk."[45] He wrote Helmer Blegen in a similar vein that one of his accomplishments by the end of his first year at Oxford was that "I can now both look at and listen to a serious Oxfordian without guffawing in his face."[46] He also derided to his mother the stuffiness of upper-class Britons:

> You ought to hear my Oxford friends gasp when I tell them what I've been doing [while vacationing in London]—going to Hampstead Heath—canoeing in the Serpentine in Regent's Park—eating at George's all-nite lunch counter—sitting in a rented chair in Hyde Park.
>
> Preedy summed it all up—"Why my deah Lahson!"—he Gasped—"that soht of thing—well—aftah all—it just isn't done in London, y'know."

> The line between what is done and what isn't done is very clear here. Anything that's fun isn't done. How the upper classes amuse themselves is a mystery. I think they don't.[47]

What did prove to be fun during his second and third years in England, besides foreign travel, plays, concerts, and seeing the sights in London, was the Oxford Union. Larson became actively involved there during the fall of 1933 and soon attracted favorable attention from its members. He made his maiden speech on the evening of October 19th, shortly before the meeting ended. The subject of Larson's remarks has been lost to history, but not the response. As he proudly wrote his mother the next day, "The officers liked my speech so well that they invited me to supper afterward."[48] Larson so impressed the Union's president, Michael Foot, that he nominated Larson for a seat on the Library Committee, which was, as Larson excitedly wrote his brother Don, "the first step toward offices in the Union."[49] Foot and the other officers also gave Larson the honor of serving as Teller for the Noes during a debate on November 1st, a position that gave him the opportunity to speak early in the debate. The motion before the Union that night was "That this House deplores the discovery of America," and Larson made a hit with the kind of witty speech so prized by Union members. Attired in the customary formal dress suit with white tie and tails, he told the members present that tobacco, America's gift, was a substitute for thought, and an essential one, given that most people, if they thought for an hour, would all become socialists—or so the socialists said. *Isis*, the Oxford magazine that reported on Union debates, called it "a popular speech," and it led Michael Foot to urge Larson to seek elective office there.[50] An elated Larson wrote his mother three days later that "I've at last got off to a good start in the Oxford Union."[51]

Over the following eighteen months, he plunged into its activities and made a real mark for himself. Larson quickly became a very popular speaker thanks to his skill at telling jokes and the large supply of American ones at his disposal that were new to his mostly British listeners. These jokes, many of them culled by family members from the pages of the *Reader's Digest*, also went over well because Larson had developed an acute sense of timing during his years on the Augustana debate team. He explained the secret of his success to his mother as follows:

> The technique is simply to get these chaps hysterical and then keep tickling them with little jokes before they sober up each time. In this way you can have the House helpless for half an hour if you like. This is something all the aspiring Union humorists have failed to learn—they work all day and night trying to think of witty remarks for their next speech, and for lack of a little timing they fall flat.
>
> A second point one must learn in the Union is that the audience must be given a generous amount of time to get the joke. . . . immediately after a

> joke there is a slight titter, from the quick-witted, then if you pause and take a drink of water, a moment later the titter becomes a booming roar, much like the sizzling of a fuse before an explosion.[52]

Larson's remarks also met with broad approval when they dealt with more serious matters. Given his moderate Republican outlook, Larson found himself drawn to the Union's political center, then led by Michael Foot. Although Foot would evolve over the next few years into a Labour Party leftist, when Larson met him Foot was a Liberal whose eloquent speeches against the extremes of fascism and socialism had carried him to the union presidency in the spring of 1933. He encouraged Larson to follow a similar path to high Union office. Larson's November 1st speech proved so popular that it won him a seat on the Library Committee, giving him the chance to speak regularly at the Union's weekly meetings. In his speeches, Larson used the strategy of criticizing the left, often humorously, without coming across as some kind of reactionary. This offered something of interest to the socialist camp (which dominated the Union during the 1930s), the smaller, deeply divided centrist group, and the hawkish right, with its staunch defense of imperialism and calls for increasing British armaments. Larson explained his approach this way in a December 1933 letter to his mother: "The Union and the magazines are largely socialist-minded, and . . . I go out of my way at every opportunity to poke fun at the socialists."[53]

In that letter, Larson provided an assessment of the various factions within the Union then, and revealed a good deal about his own still-evolving ideas about politics. This discussion was prompted by Larson's having learned from various Union members that he needed a party's backing in order to win elective office there. Although told that the easiest route to the presidency was to join the socialists who supported the British Labour Party, he rejected that route because of a disagreement with their extremism and a far-sighted concern with the problems such an affiliation could cause him should he one day wish to run for public office in the United States. "It would be no good," he wrote his mother, "trying to convince Americans that Socialism [at Oxford] is an intellectual fad."[54] He dismissed joining the Conservatives, too, reporting that "these I wouldn't care to align myself with, because they're hopelessly narrow-minded and spend the larger part of their energies screaming for large armaments." Of the final option, the Liberals, Larson wrote: "Here is the only place I could find refuge, because the Liberals, like the Republicans and Democrats, are not bound to any political principles, but just sensible government. The only trouble with the Liberals is that they are so split up, and hence have dwindled so in actual power that they are not at all the force they used to be."[55]

Larson's observations about his own country's major political parties reflected the time in which he had come of age politically. During the late 1920s and early 1930s, the stands of the Republican and Democratic Parties on most issues were not all that different. That situation was only just beginning to change in 1933 with the advent of Franklin Roosevelt's New Deal, but the growing divisions between the Democrats and the GOP had not yet become clear to interested observers in the United States, let alone those living abroad.[56]

Although Larson considered the Republicans and Democrats of that time to be very much alike, he did identify with the GOP, thanks mostly to having grown up in a Republican household. An indication of this outlook could be seen in his sympathetic view of Herbert Hoover, whose one unhappy term as president had recently come to an end. Larson compared him with British prime minister Ramsay MacDonald in a letter to his father, observing that "I think MacDonald, like Hoover, is extremely competent, but he doesn't put up much of a show for the electorate."[57] Another clue to Larson's political leanings could be seen in his fondness for reading *Time* magazine, then entering its heyday as a vehicle for the expression of moderate Republican views.[58]

Unlike more extreme conservatives, whose ranks Hoover soon joined after leaving the White House in March 1933, Larson did not oppose the new administration of Franklin Roosevelt. In part this had to do, one suspects, with the new president's connections to his cousin, predecessor, and political role model, Theodore Roosevelt. In the early 1930s, Roosevelt was still considered a Republican political name, and a progressive one at that, which met with approval from families such as the Larsons. More important in explaining his reaction to Franklin Roosevelt's administration was the matter of timing. Larson's period of active involvement in the Oxford Union coincided with the first phase of the New Deal, the most important policies of which were federal government insurance for bank deposits, a temporary federal relief program to assist the unemployed, a system of farm production limits and price supports, and presidential efforts to enlist business community support for price and wage floors through Roosevelt's National Recovery Administration. All of these were among the most popular actions of Roosevelt's presidency, and they contributed to Larson's decision to describe himself in Oxford Union debates as a Republican who supported the New Deal.[59]

Larson also used that term in connection with the cause for which he became best known in the Oxford Union: the admission of women to its new dining room. The controversy arose in the fall term of 1934, by which point Larson had been elected treasurer of the Oxford Union in recognition of his many funny and successful speeches. This office was one of the three highest in the Union, the other two being librarian and president. Among the treasurer's various responsibilities was that of managing the Union's ongoing efforts to raise funds to build a dining facility. Larson came up with the idea of converting an existing room, no longer much used, into a place to serve meals. If the Union members agreed with this approach, he reasoned, they need not wait several more years while more money was raised for a new structure. Operating the facility was, of course, another matter, and Larson gave some careful thought to the economics of that proposition. He soon concluded that the Union, given its existing funds, could afford to operate its own dining facility only if it was heavily used and that allowing women to eat there as guests would assure such a result.[60]

At the most basic level, Larson's openness to this change in the Union's males-only policy appears to have reflected his considerable exposure to intelligent, educated women, whose company he clearly enjoyed. His previous schooling in America, all of which had been coeducational, also appears to have been an important factor. At work as well, one suspects, was the high opinion he had formed of the public speaking skills of some of the women he had debated in the States, most notably his fiancée, which contrasted sharply with the forensic ineptitude he often witnessed in the Union.[61]

Larson's challenge was to persuade the Union to back his plan, which the members considered at a meeting held on November 16, 1934. Mindful of the failure of a similar motion two terms earlier, Larson chose to make what he described to his mother as "a tactful speech."[62] Rather than try to make his case on the grand principle of equality of the sexes, which seemed certain to lose, he argued instead that his dining-room plan would make the Union the social center of Oxford and give its existing and quite modest refreshment services "a New Deal." When challenged by opponents of his proposal to allow women as guests, Larson defended his idea as both necessary and limited. To underscore the latter point and refute the alarmist predictions of those on the other side, Larson told Union members that

> Women will not overrun the premises . . . they will be strictly limited to the morning coffee hour and the afternoon tea hour and they will be strictly limited to that one room.
>
> Those members who wish to take their tea out of sight of the women guests can do so as before.
>
> For the benefit of those members who are still a little doubtful, I may add that a separate entrance will probably be provided so that women will not be all over the place.[63]

He appealed to the undecided members to give his experiment a try with the understanding that the Union could reconsider its decision at a future meeting should the result prove undesirable. That cautious approach, and the support of the librarian, Labour Party supporter J. P. Hickerton, caused the potentially broad opposition to collapse. Hickerton, a witty, popular socialist from Wales, helped solidify support for Larson's plan by telling members that he agreed that admitting women was necessary to make the dining hall a successful financial proposition. After hearing those arguments, Union members voted down a proposed amendment to eliminate that feature of Larson's plan by a margin of 400 to 46.[64]

Although this step toward equality in the Oxford Union may appear in hindsight to be a rather small one, it was nonetheless historic, for it marked the first time that women students at Oxford had been admitted to the Union's premises. This foot in the door portended other, more far-reaching changes in the future, something that knowledgeable observers grasped immediately. This can be seen in the extraordinary amount of attention Larson's achievement received in the press. Stories of his successful campaign to give the Oxford Union "a New Deal" appeared in newspapers throughout the English-speaking world.[65]

His willingness to be identified publicly in this way with Roosevelt's policies during their first phase stemmed in part from Larson's discovery while at Oxford of British economist John Maynard Keynes's new ideas about economics. Although Keynes taught at Cambridge, not Oxford, and would not publish his major work, the *General Theory of Employment, Interest, and Money*, until February 1936, his articles and commentaries appeared frequently in British publications during the years of Larson's Rhodes Scholarship and attracted a great deal of interest from the British Liberals with whom Larson allied himself in the Oxford Union. Keynesian economic ideas, which embraced a greater role for government in managing the economy and greater government spending to stimulate a lasting return to prosperity, helped persuade Larson to support the kinds of early New Deal policies that Hoover had staunchly opposed.[66]

Larson made his views known during an Oxford Union debate held on February 13, 1935. The motion before the crowded Union Hall that night was "That this House prefers the New Deal to Socialism." Speaking in favor were a trio composed of Ian Harvey, an Oxford student; Larson; and a guest speaker, British MP Megan Lloyd George, the daughter of former Liberal prime minister David Lloyd George. The trio on the other side featured two students and a leading light of British politics, Labour Party MP Sir Stafford Cripps. Larson, who spoke second for his team, characteristically began his remarks with excerpts from letters he had supposedly received from home that were as funny as they were imaginary. After bringing down the house six times with this news from middle America about the New Deal, Larson turned serious. He devoted the rest of his speech to an argument that the New Deal had put into practice Keynes's ideas, which Larson strongly endorsed. His detailed discussion of Keynesian economic theory appears, however, to have left some of his hearers confused. The correspondent for *Isis* who reported on the debate evaluated Larson's performance in this way: "Our mirth-making Librarian [the office he held that term] is to be congratulated on the success of his cracks. As an economist, however, he was not so successful. He traced the idea of a New Deal to Mr. Keynes' economic theories, the superiority of which the Librarian spent a sticky ten minutes explaining. Like Byron, I wish he would explain his explanation."[67]

Happily for Larson's cause that night, his team's final speaker, Megan Lloyd George, provided a more practical and easily understood defense of Roosevelt's policies. Lloyd George's argument in particular that the New Deal approach of paying the unemployed to work was better than the current British practice of supporting them in idleness appears to have won favor with her elite audience. After this spirited debate between speakers from the political center and the left, Union members narrowly endorsed the motion by a vote of 266 to 261.[68]

Larson's arguments during this debate, like his earlier decision to ally himself with the Liberals in the Oxford Union, are interesting for what they reveal about his relationship with conservatives at this time in his life. By the time Larson arrived in Britain, a like-minded group within the Conservative Party had begun to emerge under the leadership of MP Harold Macmillan. Macmillan had published his first solely authored book in 1933, *A Plea for a National Policy*, which called for the kind of greater government planning to bring about an end to the Depression that Keynes had suggested. The book received a good deal of attention, and Macmillan continued to promote its ideas in speeches before the House of Commons over the next few years. Just one month after the Oxford Union debate on the New Deal, Macmillan and fourteen other Conservative MPs joined in publishing a booklet called *Planning for Employment* that set out what Macmillan proposed as a New Deal for Britain. This kind of thinking was in the air by early 1935 and appears to be what inspired the Oxford Union's president, Labour Party supporter David Lewis, to sponsor the debate about the New Deal versus socialism. There is no sign, however, in Larson's correspondence from this time, or, indeed, from his entire three-year stay at Oxford, that he had heard of Macmillan or his writings.[69]

The reason for Larson's distance from Conservative Party circles and the Macmillanites had to do with the balance of power within the Tories at that time. Moderate conservatives such as Macmillan were a tiny and very isolated group within a more extreme right-wing party. He and his fourteen co-authors in the House of Commons together made up less than 4 percent of the Conservatives' 473-seat majority there. Macmillan himself was so discouraged by the dominance of the extreme right within his own party by the mid-1930s that he briefly considered trying to form a new center party in concert with the Liberal faction headed by David Lloyd George. The Conservatives in the Oxford Union, while somewhat more moderate than most Tory MPs, were sufficiently extreme, on military spending especially, to push Larson away from them and toward the Liberal camp instead.[70]

That distance from orthodox Conservatives, while principled, proved costly to Larson in one sense; it placed him in a weak position when he sought the Union presidency in the winter of 1935. His main rival was J. P. Hickerton, a formidable candidate on his own merits who received a boost when the Conservatives fielded a strong one of their own, a distinguished elegant young Englishman named Richard Kay-Shuttleworth. This split between moderate and more extreme conservatives put Larson into what he knew to be a hopeless position and made Hickerton the winner. It also vividly illustrated the difficulties Larson and like-minded conservatives faced in the polarized political world of the mid-1930s.

Liberal Party leaders consoled Larson by suggesting that he become a British citizen and run as one of their candidates for Parliament, but that unlikely prospect held no appeal for him.[71]

One of the more noteworthy aspects of Larson's political position while living abroad was the steadiness he showed in a turbulent time. Unlike some of the other Liberal Party supporters at Oxford then such as Michael Foot, Larson never moved away from his moderately conservative political stance toward a more radical leftist one. Larson had no "Marxist moment" at Oxford, something evident in his reaction to the news (in November 1934) of his election to Oxford's Carlton Club, a British conservative bastion. He proudly wrote his mother about this achievement, noting that the Carlton was "Oxford's most exclusive and most Tory club."[72]

Larson's continued adherence to moderately conservative views can be gleaned, too, from his travel destinations during this period and the observations he made in his letters about the various European political systems. Although he received lots of encouragement from friends at Oxford to visit Spain, he put off that trip until August 1934, by which time a conservative government had replaced a leftist one there. He seems never to have considered a visit to the Soviet Union, although the distance and cost might have struck him as too great even to contemplate. In the winter of 1932–1933, he and Florence made their first trip to the Continent by visiting Paris. Although he greatly enjoyed the food and the liveliness of the city's streets, calling his visit "the best time I have ever had in my life," Larson's midwestern provincialism showed in his response to the city's inhabitants and their cosmopolitan ways.[73] He observed in a letter to his father in March 1933 that "Germany seems to be the most significant country on the continent now, except possibly Russia. France is an old story—it's decadent, dirty and contemptible."[74]

Despite his interest in seeing Germany and visiting friends there, Larson never went, seemingly because of Hitler's rise to power early in 1933. Larson characterized the new German leader as "a rattle-headed demagogue who delights his people by all the time 'doing something,'" in a letter to his father written later that year.[75] Although Larson clearly disapproved of the Nazis, like so many other midwestern conservatives at that time, he tended to dismiss the potential danger posed by their demands for German rearmament. Larson poohpoohed the alarm over them in the British newspapers: "Nobody has invaded anyone's territory, no one has insulted anyone's national honor—but just because the international scene is a bit confused they [the British press] can see no way out but a war. Of course it's pure bilge. The only immediate strain arises from Germany's desire for arms equality—but how can that lead to a war when Germany is unarmed to begin with?"[76]

Larson felt that the best way to assure peace was to promote disarmament and discourage military alliances. In March 1934, he wrote his brother Don, then a student at Augustana, that "people bellow that 'we must first end the fundamental economic . . . causes of war'—that's pure bilge—it can't be done."[77] In a letter to his mother one month later he asked "Why on earth must the U.S. launch a stupendous ship and plane building program just now? The effect here is very bad."[78]

Although Larson did not embrace the isolationist cause then, he clearly felt its attraction. This came across in a January 1935 letter to his brother Don that endorsed American entry into the League of Nations only as a concession to reality rather than as a move that deserved support on its own merits: "The case for isolation is very strong,—the more I see of Europe, the less I want to have to do with it,—but if the U.S. is going to abandon that policy in fact (as it certainly has done in Europe) it may as well abandon it in form, and join the League for the prestige it would give the League."[79]

Even more revealing about Larson's basic political orientation are his comments about the only European political system that seems to have impressed him: Mussolini's Italy. He and Florence went there purely for leisure in the summer of 1933. They enjoyed Italy's many beautiful and historic sights and the favorable exchange rate. While there, however, and especially while in northern Italy, Larson was struck by the changes Mussolini's government had brought during its decade in power. He wrote to his father that "you never saw a man so respected, so loyally adhered to by an adoring country. . . . Even slums are being cleaned up . . . because Mussolini doesn't like his people to live in squalor and filth. The people discover that Mussolini would like them to ride motorcycles for economy—immediately thousands of motorcycles flood the country."[80]

Larson, like so many other conservatives then and even some liberals, was also greatly impressed by the way Mussolini's government had improved Italy's accessibility to foreign visitors. He explained to his father that Mussolini's "big idea" was that Italy must make a good impression on foreign visitors, which had led to trains running on time, modernized hotels, magnificent roads, easy travel, and a host of cultural activities aimed at tourists.[81]

Larson was impressed, too, by what he saw as the Italian fascist system's realism in recognizing formally the power that the various industries and professions exercised in Italian politics and society. He discussed this in a letter to Don, telling him to consider whether the United States ought to do something similar: "Ask yourself whether we might not just as well give official representation to big business interests as such, since it seems an ineluctable law that they will achieve political control anyway—by bribery, lobbying or other means. This goes for Federal and State, as well as municipal governments."[82] Larson advised his brother to read the autobiography of Progressive Era journalist Lincoln Steffens, which reached a similar conclusion:

> See if it does not make you think it is inevitable that money and business interests *must* govern, no matter what your structure or system of government is—and that the best thing we can do is to make the constitution of

> government correspond to the facts of government by giving official representation to businesses, as is done in Italy. Now we call such business influence in government corruption; it is really not so, for it is the working out of an inescapable principle.[83]

Here was a key clue to Arthur Larson's emerging public philosophy. If one definition of a conservative is someone who accepts an existing system as it is and tries to make it work most effectively, these remarks certainly place Larson in that camp. On the other hand, Larson's letters nowhere indicated support for the repression that lay behind Italian fascism's achievements or for Italian fascism as such. One should keep in mind, too, that Larson's visit to Italy and written observations about it came before Mussolini chose to invade Ethiopia and forge an alliance with Nazi Germany. At the time Arthur and Florence visited Italy, its fascist system of government was still widely admired in the United States, even by some New Dealers.[84]

Instead of enthusiasm for repression, fascism, or militarism, Larson's letters indicate his interest in what historians and political scientists today call corporatism, a political system based on bargaining between organized interest groups supervised by the state. In this kind of system, individual citizens express their political wishes through such interest groups rather than by trying to influence the political system more directly. The community in which Larson grew up, where families and churches tended to play a similar mediating role between individuals and the state, appears to have contributed to his receptivity to this kind of system that was so different from the older American conception that stressed the importance of direct citizen participation in government.[85]

Also important in understanding Larson's views was his sense of the likely alternative. The radicalism he saw at Oxford and elsewhere in Britain persuaded him that socialism posed a serious challenge to the established order. Larson expressed that concern at length in the same letter to Don:

> In all your thinking, Don, do not slight the imminence of Socialism. I know that at home it seems thousands of miles away, but I tell you that for two pins England would go Socialist. The London County Council, which governs Greater London, went Socialist t[he] other day. Just let the present government make one bad slip and England would return a Labor [*sic*] government in a fortnight. You have Socialists right at the elbow of Pres. Roosevelt —chaps like [Rexford] Tugwell and others—and their influence is apparent in many of Roosevelt's policies.[86]

Unlike more extreme American conservatives of that day, however, Larson was not alarmed about the future survival of the nation's existing form of government. He wrote Don that "the big argument here in England is whether the U.S. is going Fascist or Socialist. Everyone takes it for granted that it must be one or the other. My personal opinion is that it is a little of each, but that representative government is not imperilled [*sic*]."[87]

Larson explained the reason for his confidence in a highly successful speech to the Glasgow University Union, where he appeared as a guest speaker on February 15, 1935. The motion before the house that night was "That in View of Modern Conditions the Desirable Ideal of Democracy is No Longer Practicable." Larson spoke in opposition, arguing that "Democracy has not failed in any country where it has had its normal birth and growth."[88] To those who believed that the growth in executive power threatened the survival of democracy, Larson said that development was simply a temporary response to a situation of crisis. He elaborated on that last point in another letter to Don:

> In time of crisis the executive always must and does take the bulk of the power, for the simple reason that it can and does act quickly and directly, and crises demand quick and direct action. . . . That is why I am loath to believe that dictatorships are permanent—I believe they represent only the expression of that need for quick action. That is why, also, I believe that if business and trade improves, Fascism and Socialism have missed their chance in England and America, and will eventually disappear elsewhere, except perhaps in countries temperamentally unsuited to any other treatment.[89]

Larson's last point signaled his embrace of the kind of cultural chauvinism popular then with so many conservatives at Oxford and elsewhere in the English-speaking world.[90] The intellectual confusion such prejudice could cause can be seen in the way he handled this issue during an earlier debate in the Oxford Union. Making a broader argument that democracy itself could succeed only in "the hands of Anglo-Saxons and related races," Larson struggled to explain its existence in ancient Greece. He "resolved" this dilemma by finding "evidence that the Greeks were a race closely related to the Celts."[91] This sort of muddled and even silly thinking is all the more striking because it was so atypical of the lucid, mature, and highly rational way Larson generally thought and wrote then and afterward.

His Anglophilia did not stem from, or signal, any rejection of his own Norwegian ancestry. On the contrary, Larson's letters from England to his parents and Helmer Blegen indicate his continuing pride in that heritage. He had become friends with a Norwegian musician named Johan Egilsvud, joined with a group of people of Norwegian ancestry to celebrate the country's national day, continued learning the language, and persuaded his parents to join him in visiting their ancestral homeland during the summer of 1934. Oxford and England had clearly made him an Anglophile but had not led him to reject his own heritage in the process.[92]

The source of Larson's problem was his tendency to embrace stereotypes when thinking about the peoples and practices of foreign countries. He displayed that habit of thought from time to time in his letters home, generalizing and exaggerating about other nationalities, especially if he got into some kind of trouble during one of his visits on the Continent. After his trip to Paris in December 1933, for example, where he had a run-in with taxi driver that landed them both at a local police station, Larson wrote his brother Palmer that "the French are very hard to like—that is, those you meet on the street—shopkeepers, police, cabmen, and even students. They are hare-brained, dirty, unscrupulous, selfish, and incapable of reasoning coolly or acting sanely."[93] Still remembering his trouble in Paris and newly upset by his encounter with the porters and beggars of Naples, Larson described Switzerland, which he greatly enjoyed and where he had no problems, as "an oasis of cleanliness and sweetness between the sweaty filth of Italy and the hysteria of France."[94] Angry that he had been robbed repeatedly in Spain in the late summer of 1934, Larson wrote his mother that "the Spanish are lazy, excitable, fast-talking, inefficient and thievish—outside of that they are all right."[95]

Unlike those with truly deep prejudices, Larson usually found some way of acknowledging in his letters that there was something wrong with this kind of thinking. He immediately followed his comment about the Spanish, for example, by writing that "on the other hand, people like my landlady and my two Spanish friends, Eduardo and Manuelo, are fine in every way."[96] Not once did he write anything during these years that could be construed as anti-Semitic or racially prejudiced. Indeed, the overall impression conveyed by his many letters from these years is of someone who was unusually free of the prejudices and insensitivities common among Americans with his background and outlook at that time.[97]

Another sign of Larson's rejection of reactionary views can be seen in his openness to social democratic policies of the sort advanced by the more moderate voices in the British Labour Party. He wrote Don in January 1935 that "when I left America, Socialists there were still considered as in a class with the wild-eyed shaggy-maned anarchists; now you'll hear Socialism in every side—true, it's rather the English Socialism than the Marxian, but it's having a tremendous influence, and its best ideas have got to be fitted in somewhere."[98] Later in that letter, he elaborated on that last point, noting to Don "the pitiful inadequacy of social legislation in [the] U.S.—e.g. old age + unemployment + medical insurance; provisions for the poor, etc."[99]

A sign of his essentially moderate outlook emerged from his queries to Don about the future of American politics. The catalyst for Larson's inquiry was the Republican Party's disastrous showing in the elections after Roosevelt's first two years in office, the worst in the history of the GOP. The thrust of his questions to Don provide a sense of what he thought the future would bring: "What is going to happen to the party arrangement in America? Isn't the Tory Republican party to be relegated to the position of a third party, while some other party—presumably radical, or possibly a sort of Progressive Republican party, becomes the official Opposition of the government?"[100]

Yet another indication of Larson's moderate conservative outlook surfaced in his response to Don's request for suggestions about what to read regarding the rapidly changing American political scene. By then a member of Augustana's debate team, Don had written to ask for material that could help him prepare for future competitions. Arthur Larson pointed his brother toward the person who was emerging as one of the most thoughtful moderate conservative commentators in American journalism, syndicated columnist and author Walter Lippmann:

> If you want to read the soundest ideas which have emerged from the horrific mass of economic and political opinion writings in the last five years, you read anything you can get your hands on by Walter Lippman[n]. He writes a column in one of the New York papers—read that too if you like. Only a few months ago he published a little book whose title I've forgotten also, which will give you ideas aplenty for a dozen orations.[101]

Lippmann's "little book," *The Method of Freedom,* was a collection of the Godkin Lectures he had delivered at Harvard in the spring of 1934. Heavily influenced by Keynes, whom Lippmann had met and talked with extensively one year earlier, the book argued that changing social conditions required greater government intervention in the workings of the national economy. Lippmann endorsed such intervention, within certain limits, as the only way to preserve free societies in the face of increasing challenges from authoritarian systems on both the right and the left.[102]

Lippmann's qualified support for Keynesian ideas struck a chord with Arthur Larson. He explained to Don how he approached proposed solutions to the world's economic problems. His essentially cautious frame of mind, with its preference for incremental adjustments rather than drastic change, comes through strongly in the following passage:

> Every monetary or economic panacea-plan I ever studied reminds me of the way I plan a game of chess—every move seems perfect, the King will be checked completely—but in reality there's some little piece or move that I hadn't reckoned on, and the net result is either nullity or disaster. I should rather trust a government that proceeds more in the way I play checkers making each jump as it comes and hoping to come out ahead in the end—than one that trusts everything to an elaborate plan with a weakness that is probably fatal.[103]

This intellectual tendency did not rule out support for major changes in public policy. When the appearance of new social conditions and the constructive example of other comparable political systems indicated that such a change was desirable and practical, Larson could be persuaded to support it. He argued to Don that the United States should emulate Britain's decision in 1873 to create a more uniform system of national law for England, Scotland, and Wales. He wrote that while the American constitutional system of allowing the state legislatures to make the bulk of the laws affecting everyday life had made sense during earlier times, given the wide disparities then in social conditions among the various regions of the country, the increasing uniformity of social conditions across the United States made its balkanized legal system increasingly outmoded. Larson's proposed alternative, which would have horrified deeply conservative Americans, was to abolish all the various state courts and codes and replace them with "a hierarchy of [national] courts from the [U.S.] Supreme Court down administering a universal code of laws."[104] Given the much greater workload such a system would imply for Congress, which would be responsible for enacting this universal code, Larson also proposed the creation of a permanent law reform commission, like the one in Britain, to study and make needed revisions in existing laws, subject only to congressional approval.[105]

In view of the importance of federalism in his later writings and work, Larson's defense for this quite radical proposal deserves some attention here. He wrote Don that it would put an end both to the confusion that resulted from varying rules of law in different states and the poor-quality judges that sometimes managed to get appointed to state courts. Larson also argued that such a change would lead to better law enforcement, citing as evidence the FBI's success in bringing gangsters to justice after state and local police, prosecutors, and courts failed to do so. To the critics of this idea who insisted that the United States of the mid-1930s was still too much larger and more diverse than Britain for such a change to be advisable, Larson argued that the English and Welsh were more diverse than the American people, despite the much smaller size of the United Kingdom.[106]

All in all, Larson's handling of this subject speaks volumes about his willingness to break at times with traditional political ideas and about the part of the United States in which he had mostly lived and traveled. Larson was most familiar with the predominantly Republican heartland that stretched between Ohio and California. He had never lived in the vastly different South, which showed in his naively confident statements to Don about how differences among the various sections of the United States had narrowed by 1935. Greater familiarity with life outside his native Midwest and more reflection about the legitimate interests still served by the federal system would in time persuade Larson to retreat somewhat from the views he expressed to Don. More significant, though, was his continuing enthusiasm for establishing uniform national laws when necessary and his rejection of the states' rights philosophy so popular with extreme conservatives in the United States.[107]

That full maturation of Larson's views on federalism, like his public philosophy more generally, would not be complete until some years after he had left Oxford. What is clear, however, from his letters written during his Rhodes Scholarship, is that it was then and there that many of his most basic political commitments first became firmly established. Despite the drawbacks of Oxford's formal system of instruction, the experience of studying there had clearly provided him with a first-rate introduction to contemporary political thought.

Larson, however, did not spend all or even most of his time while at Oxford engaged in that kind of reflection. He devoted the bulk of his time there, especially during his second and third years, to his law books. As he became more familiar with the jurisprudence program at Oxford and its educational system more generally, his early negative assessment began to change. At the start of his second year, Larson explained in a letter to his father why Oxford's law program had begun to appear worthwhile, noting that it had proved to be much more efficient as a way of learning law than the case method prevalent in American law schools. His newfound uncertainty about which system was best came through in this letter:

> I have never yet been able to make up my mind whether the Oxford system is the world's most inspired form of education or its most nonsensical. I incline to think the latter when I contemplate how all the lectures are read to the students (as if they could not read for themselves) and how the courses are arranged with a fanatical preoccupation with origins and foundations. But then when I realize that something—something I cannot define—is constantly making me study harder and learn more than ever before . . . I have to shrug my shoulders and admit that Oxford has a little something some others haven't got.[108]

His concern that Oxford's law curriculum left out too many important subjects and information about American rules of law also faded as he became more familiar with the various required reading lists. Larson wrote how he had come to understand that the deficiencies of those lists were more apparent than real because their titles did not capture fully the breadth of the subjects addressed by the books and articles appearing on them.[109]

In what must have been the biggest surprise of all, Larson also discovered that working with Davidge yielded a benefit as valuable as it had been unexpected, which was to greatly improve Larson's writing. Looking back on the experience of working with his primary Oxford tutor much later, Larson wrote:

> He did wonders for my prose style. The detailed corrections, week after week, year after year, gradually left their mark. Not just on matters of correct syntax and punctuation, but on matters of rhythm, balance—one might almost say music. It may well be said that there is something about the English educational process ensuring that, whether you learn anything else, you learn how to handle the language.[110]

As the strengths of the Oxford law program became more evident, Larson's enthusiasm for his law studies increased and his general philosophical approach to legal questions became clearer. Both can be seen in his enthusiastic response to the writings of Benjamin Cardozo, the distinguished New York State judge

Herbert Hoover had appointed to the U.S. Supreme Court in 1932. Larson wrote his mother near the end of his first Oxford academic year that "I have been reading Cardozo's books, not because I have to, but because I am a great admirer of his decisions and ideas, and because it is a pardonable thrill when I discover again and again that he says the same things that I have been writing in essays this winter."[111]

Like Oliver Wendell Holmes, the man Cardozo replaced on the Supreme Court and always referred to as "the Master," Cardozo's writings attacked the older view of judges as simply "finding" preexisting law rather than actually making it. And like Holmes, Cardozo argued that judges should therefore restrain themselves from interfering with legislative efforts to address social problems created by an increasingly urban and industrial society. Cardozo's more than 500 opinions as a judge on the highest court in New York State from 1914 to 1932 demonstrated his commitment to adapting the law to new economic and social conditions in principled ways. His opinions in the areas of torts, contracts, and liability enjoyed national influence for their clarity, consistency, and practicality. All of this gave Cardozo a well-deserved reputation as an enlightened conservative and explains why Arthur Larson found his legal philosophy so congenial.[112]

Larson received his first real grades in the fall of 1933 for the exams he had written the previous June, and they were so good that he received congratulations not only from his tutor but also from the chief administrator of the Rhodes Program at Oxford, C. K. Allen, a professor of jurisprudence at one of the other Oxford colleges (University). Larson's best grade, an A+ in constitutional law, was an especially significant achievement. His tutor informed him that "an A+ was a very, very rare thing at Oxford."[113] So promising an omen was this, Allen told Larson, that if he worked hard he would have a realistic chance of earning a First on his final exams, which was roughly equivalent to graduating summa cum laude. Spurred on by that prospect, Larson applied himself even more diligently during his third year, especially in his final term, by which point he no longer held office in the Oxford Union and had more time to study.[114]

He was able to focus his mind on work during that final year in part due to the absence of his fiancée, who left for New York after completing her training at the Royal Academy. Florence had done extraordinarily well there, playing Ophelia in its production of *Hamlet* and the female leads in *A Doll's House* and *Children in Uniform*, all difficult roles for which she received very positive reviews. For her part as Manuela in the last of these, she received a prize from the head of the school. Her acting skills were so strong that the school awarded her two terms of advanced standing, which meant that she earned her diploma at the end of the fall term of 1933, a full six months ahead of schedule.[115]

Given this success, the natural next step would have been to act on the London stage, but Florence found that route blocked by her inability to obtain a work permit. The ultimate source of the problem here was the high unemployment rate, which made jobs in theater scarce for everyone and virtually impossible for foreign nationals to obtain. She stalled her departure for a while in the hope of catching a break, but no real job opportunity arose. Her photo did make the cover of one of England's leading magazines, *Britannia and Eve,* in April 1934, but even that kind of favorable publicity could not overcome the work-permit barrier. Stymied, Florence decided to look for acting jobs in New York until Larson finished at Oxford. A disheartened but still supportive Arthur Larson waved goodbye as her ship sailed off that same month, leaving him without much else to do for the next fourteen months except study.[116]

Florence's departure does not appear to have signaled any problems in her romance with Larson. On the contrary, all the indications from her letters home during their twenty months together in England, and his, are of a happily engaged couple enjoying each other's company and making plans to spend the rest of their lives together. Larson made certain that Florence received a weekly red rosebud from him while they were apart. And when an opportunity arose in the fall of 1934 to buy an inexpensive boat ticket to New York, he grabbed the chance and spent his winter holiday there with her, where they saw the sights, dressed up like European aristocrats for fun, and generally enjoyed each other's company.[117]

Larson also managed to get a little work done while in New York by making the rounds of the big law firms there to place applications for employment. Now it was his turn to feel the sting of Depression-era unemployment: he found the firms crowded with applicants and jobs very scarce. Larson's lack of an American law degree placed him at even more of a disadvantage. Only the Cravath firm expressed interest, and its partners insisted that he first spend a year at an American law school before starting work there. Even more discouraging, in some respects, was what he saw of what working at such a place would be like. The wan, shaky appearance of one Oxford acquaintance, another Rhodes scholar and top rower there named Pirie, who had visibly deteriorated under the strain of working at a similar firm, left a vivid and lasting negative impression. Larson described him in a letter as "the saddest-looking fellow I ever saw. A big, tough oarsman when I last saw him, now he is white and trembles like a leaf."[118]

In contrast, Larson's rather sedentary lifestyle during his final year at Oxford had helped him reach his greatest weight thus far, which he noted in a letter to his mother that fall had reached 176 pounds. Oxford had filled him out physically as well as intellectually, giving him the look that he would possess for the rest of his life. The most notable features included a six-foot-tall broad frame, bright blue eyes, and an attractive, sensitive-looking face that was usually creased in a smile. Even more distinctive was his wardrobe, which by then consisted mostly of fairly formal and conservatively tailored English clothes that made him look like a diplomat. A renewed acquaintance with America would wear away some of this Oxford influence over time, but its essence remained permanently.

Larson's three years there had given his outward appearance, like his thinking about politics, a much more fixed and durable form.[119]

By the time Larson returned to Oxford in early January, he had begun to rethink his plans for the future. Learning that there were one-year fellowships at leading American law schools, he decided to apply for one. His first choice among these was Yale Law School, the most intellectually exciting one in that group. He also seems to have considered Yale an attractive prospect because of its location in New Haven, Connecticut, then a major try-out town for theatrical productions aspiring to play on Broadway and thus a place where Florence could also progress professionally. To his great disappointment, all but three of his fellowship applications were rejected that spring, including the one to Yale. The only law schools that accepted his applications were Chicago, Northwestern, and the University of Pennsylvania, and of these, the second was by far the most financially attractive. Happily for him, Larson found the prospect of studying at Northwestern for a year quite appealing, given its location in Chicago, where there would be acting opportunities for Florence and a not-too-distant journey back home when they wanted to visit their relatives.[120]

The one other possibility was a law firm in Milwaukee that liked to hire Rhodes scholars. The following passage from a letter to his father written in January 1935 shows the drift of Larson's thinking by then: "I'm still not sure I want to practice on Wall Street. I seem to feel that I'd perhaps be a lot happier, say, in Milwaukee, where I'd feel more at home, and could perhaps have a chance in political affairs."[121] The connection at the Milwaukee firm was a partner named Leroy Burlingame, a Rhodes alumnus who had served on the Rhodes Scholarship examining committee that selected Larson. When Larson wrote him expressing interest in working at his firm, Burlingame responded with the news that there was such an opening and encouraged him to interview for it.[122]

This prospect of getting started right away in a real job appears to have counted for a lot in Larson's thinking then. He would turn twenty-five that summer, an impending milestone that probably increased his impatience. Larson conveyed that sense to his father in a letter in late May 1935: "I cannot conceal the fact that I am highly excited over this Wisconsin prospect. No doubt in Milwaukee I could even settle down and buy a house. And, above all, there won't be any one year's delay."[123] He mulled over what he should do next and decided to put off a decision until the summer, when he would return to the United States and could stop in Milwaukee for a job interview on his way home. In the meantime, he resolved to apply himself intensely to his studies and preparations for the final round of university examinations.[124]

His Rhodes Scholarship had a similarly formative influence on his professional development, for it was at Oxford that Larson became heavily engaged in the area of law in which he would eventually do his most important work: torts. This was the area of law concerned with civil as opposed to criminal wrongs. Torts deal with wrongdoing between private parties rather than between citizens and the state. Larson quickly found himself attracted to the issues raised by tort law, especially ones having to do with causation, liability, and the difficulties that arose when new kinds of wrongs arise in response to new social conditions. The Oxford approach to legal study, in particular the university's emphasis on learning the fundamental principles that lay behind specific rules of law, helped give Larson an unusually coherent grasp of the relationships among the various tort law rules.[125]

He became so interested in those relationships that he produced his own tort law "treatise," complete with graphs and charts that he thought of as comparable to Mendeleev's periodic table of the elements. He assigned each specific tort, such as assault, libel, or trespass, its own box that indicated why that tort should possess certain specific characteristics. Although this never-published work has not survived, Larson said in his memoirs that it explained how tort law as a whole could best be understood. He found the key organizing principle in a Roman law maxim, *Sic utere tuo ut alienum non laedas* (So use yours that you do not harm others).[126] In taking this approach to the study of tort law, Larson sided with the newer school of legal thought that argued that there was a general principle of law that unjustified harm of any kind exposed the person responsible for it to legal liability. This view contrasted sharply with an older, more cautious one that held that only those injuries that fell within the centuries-old tort law categories could be considered actionable.[127]

All of this thinking about tort law paid off handsomely when Larson took the last of his essay examinations in June 1935. To his delight, he discovered that one of the essay questions asked simply "Is there a Law of Tort or a Law of Torts? Comment." Delighted to address this query, which essentially asked him to choose between the newer view and the older one, Larson wrote for three hours, explaining why he thought the first of these approaches was the right one. His examiners awarded this essay a Double First, a grade so high that it earned him a B.A. in jurisprudence with highest honors.[128]

This happy ending to Larson's Oxford experience merged quickly with an even more joyous beginning. Eager to get home, he departed immediately after a final perfunctory oral exam and arrived in New York on the morning of July 24, 1935. After a quick call on the Cravath law firm to bring the partners there up to date on his situation, Larson met Florence in Chicago, made another brief stop in Milwaukee, and then went home to Sioux Falls for an event he had long and eagerly awaited. On July 31st, his odyssey of the past three years finally came to an end at First Lutheran, where he and Florence were married before a crowd so big that the church overflowed. The three long years of waiting were finally over.[129]

CHAPTER THREE

A Few False Starts

At first, life for the two newlyweds was appropriately carefree. They spent the month following their wedding at Lake Bemidji in Minnesota's North Woods enjoying a long honeymoon. Next came a move to Milwaukee, where Larson began working at the firm that had expressed interest in hiring him. His interview with the partners, which had taken place shortly before his wedding day, had gone well and led to an offer, which Arthur and Florence decided he should accept. The key factors in this decision appear to have been his desire to get started in a paying job right away, the Depression-era scarcity of good job offers that made this one seem all the more valuable, Milwaukee's proximity to their relatives, its attractive setting on the western shore of Lake Michigan, and its familiar midwestern flavor.[1]

Their choice was not unusual for highly educated South Dakotans of that day. By the 1930s, the economy of their home state and the rest of the upper Midwest had ceased creating enough jobs for aspiring professionals, who began moving eastward in search of work to such cities as Milwaukee and Chicago. The region's steadily improving network of roads and highways also contributed to this migration by making occasional visits back home much easier.[2]

One other consideration that deserves mention was Larson's interest in politics and a career in public service. Wisconsin's population, like that of South Dakota's, included a large number of Scandinavian Americans who would presumably have been receptive to a Larson candidacy for public office. Wisconsin also offered a very appealing political milieu to someone like him, with its strong Progressive Republican tradition that even Herbert Hoover's ineptitude and Franklin Roosevelt's popularity had not extinguished.[3]

All of these various pushes and pulls led Larson to Milwaukee and the law offices of Quarles, Spence and Quarles in September 1935. The heavily urban and industrial city he and Florence had chosen embodied the newer type of midwestern community that contrasted with the older one like Sioux Falls, which tended to be much smaller and more oriented toward the needs of surrounding farmers. When he and Florence arrived in Milwaukee during the late summer of 1935, the city was the twelfth largest in the country with over half a million inhabitants but had a distinctly suburban flavor. Milwaukee had a well-deserved reputation as a safe, clean family town that even the Depression did not radically change. The economic crisis of the 1930s hit the city hard, however, thanks to the central role in its economic life basic manufacturing played. Approximately 40 percent of Milwaukee's workforce during the 1930s held jobs of that kind, producing iron, steel, and durable goods, the demand for which fluctuated sharply in response to the health of the nation's economy. When it hit bottom early in 1933, one-fifth of all Milwaukee residents were receiving local relief. And when the economy began to revive, labor unrest exploded there. In 1934, Milwaukee had experienced more strikes, some 107 in all, than any other American city. They inaugurated a wave of labor organizing that over the next five years would give Milwaukee one of the most heavily unionized workforces in the nation.[4]

The makeup of the city's population also differed significantly from that of Sioux Falls. Milwaukee had many more residents of German ancestry than did Larson's hometown and much greater ethnic diversity overall. The city had a very large Polish-American community and substantial numbers of residents living in ethnic enclaves who traced their ancestry to Austria, Russia, Holland, Bohemia, Serbia, Croatia, Slovenia, Greece, Hungary, Italy, Ireland, Scotland, and Scandinavia. This patchwork of nationalities contrasted sharply with Sioux Falls in all but one respect: Milwaukee, like Sioux Falls, was overwhelmingly white. The city's black community in the mid-1930s mostly lived within a single square mile on the northwest outskirts of the business district and made up less than 2 percent of Milwaukee's population.[5]

Also familiar to Arthur and Florence were the city's affordability, family-centered social life, and moral traditionalism. In those respects, Milwaukee resembled a great big small town, blessed with cheap rents, crime rates among the lowest of the major American cities, a swift and highly effective criminal justice system, and a thrifty, fiscally responsible public sector. Among the most important community institutions were the city's many churches, by far the most numerous of which were Catholic and Lutheran.[6]

Looking back on his time there many years later, Larson remembered fondly Milwaukee's low prices and spirit of togetherness, which combined to make life pleasant even for young newcomers like him and Florence. They soon found a small apartment in the Annason, an Art Deco–style building in the Shorewood section of the city, north of downtown and near Lake Michigan. In return for parquet floors, stepped-back ceilings, and a pull-down bed, they paid $37.50 a month. The newlyweds gradually made friends with other couples in their twenties, mostly actors and artists Florence met in the course of investigating career opportunities for herself. None of them had much money, but at that stage of their lives it did not seem to matter a great deal. As Larson later explained,

> We were very happy—everybody, curiously enough, seemed to be in good spirits, even those that were the hardest up. . . . There was a spirit that we're all in this together and somehow we're going to get through, we're going to make it. And we helped each other out. There were several couples of us that were very close to each other: the Cyruses and the Clemenses, artists, they were, if anything, worse off than I was. More than once they would have no place to go. The Clemenses at the end of the month actually slept in our bed [with us] . . . to get through the month.[7]

While Florence searched for acting jobs with the local theater companies, Larson settled into the private practice of law with Quarles, Spence and Quarles at a starting salary of $100 a month. Founded in 1882, it had become one of Milwaukee's establishment law firms, with thirteen active attorneys, including its newest associate. Shortly before Larson arrived, the firm had moved to a new office building downtown, from which it serviced the various legal needs of major corporate clients. The city's big mills, factories, breweries, tanneries, and meat-packing plants gave rise to many workers' compensation cases, and one of the firm's partners, another Rhodes scholar named Arthur Doe, specialized in defending employers' interests in such matters. Doe's death in 1934 created a gap that Larson was intended to fill. The firm's partners gave him work to do in that area, which consisted of writing briefs in cases where a workers' compensation claim was being contested at the appellate level. He also worked on general corporate law matters and antitrust and patent cases and spent the first year studying part-time for the Wisconsin bar exam. The senior partner most influential in hiring him, Leroy Burlingame, played the role of primary supervisor and mentor.[8]

All of this was a real challenge to Larson, given the kinds of subjects he had mostly studied at Oxford and the fact that he had never worked even part-time in a law office before, as many law students did prior to graduation. He knew nothing about the area of law in which the firm expected him to specialize. As he explained in his memoirs, "Before Milwaukee, I had never even seen the two words 'workmen's' and 'compensation' juxtaposed." As for his other assignments, Larson recalled that "anti-trust, patents, bankruptcy, even corporations were never mentioned at Oxford."[9] The reason was simple. Most of these areas of law had been created over the past half-century and were too new to merit inclusion in Oxford's very traditional law curriculum, with its focus on origins and general principles. Burlingame, himself a Rhodes scholar, no doubt understood the limitations of the Oxford law program but expected that someone with Larson's ability and training would in time master the areas of law he had been assigned.[10]

At first, Larson performed as expected. His first big assignment dealt with a corporate client's challenge to the constitutionality of the Agricultural Adjustment Act of 1933, a New Deal measure that created a system that limited farm production in return for federal subsidies as a way to stabilize prices for agricultural commodities. Next came an assignment to help General Electric challenge a new Wisconsin tax on dividends that the legislature had passed to generate more revenue for social services. Another early assignment asked him to find out whether an injured person could recover damages for pain and suffering when the shock of the injury produced immediate unconsciousness. Another involved defending Standard Oil against a suit brought by someone who had made his living by faking workplace injuries but had finally suffered a real one, thereby raising the question of whether someone who had consistently abused his rights in this area of the law could now use it to recover damages. The quality of Larson's work on these matters so pleased the partners that they decided in November 1935 to raise his salary to $175 a month.[11]

The increasing volume of work at the firm, a consequence of the improving economy, made that boost in pay possible and fueled the firm's growth more generally. Larson and the other lawyers were so busy by the winter of 1935–1936 that the partners decided to hire another associate the following summer, another Rhodes scholar named Henry Reuss. He and Larson got to know each other well while studying together for the Wisconsin bar exam that summer. They both passed on their first try, to their great relief. Reuss, Larson, and slightly older associate Jefferson Burrus, Rhodes scholars all, became friends and socialized together after hours. And so, it seemed, Larson was nicely launched in his new profession.[12]

The first sign of serious doubts about his career choice surfaced during the summer Larson took the bar exam. When he and Florence made a short visit home and attended a service at First Lutheran, it proved to be the catalyst, as Larson later explained in his memoirs:

> All the familiar sights, sounds and associations began to bring up emotions I thought I had forgotten. Rev. Glenn preached a superb sermon, and by the time the service was over, I was belatedly experiencing something approaching the "call" that one is supposed to feel before entering the ministry. The next day, instead of heading back to Milwaukee, I pointed my new red Pontiac toward St. Paul and the Luther Theological Seminary.[13]

With Florence at his side, Larson pleaded his case for admission to the seminary's president, T. H. Gullixson, a family friend. Gullixson listened for a while and then burst Larson's balloon by saying abruptly, "I wouldn't have you." With a kindly smile he explained, "You wouldn't last six months in the Norwegian

Lutheran Church."[14] And that was that, at least insofar as a career in the ministry was concerned.

The source of Larson's doubt appears to have been the nature of the work the firm required him to do, the long hours it entailed, and, above all, the pressure from the partners to find clients of his own. With respect to the first of these, the issue of timing was crucial. Larson had arrived at Quarles, Spence and Quarles shortly after Roosevelt's New Deal entered its second phase, when Congress enacted the Social Security Act; the National Labor Relations Act, which provided broad protection for union organizing and collective bargaining; and a new tax law that promised eventually to hit the upper middle class and truly rich the hardest. These three measures, which Roosevelt signed into law during the summer of 1935, had provoked a deeply antagonistic response from large sections of the American business community. Determined to block the implementation of the new laws, businesses began filing lawsuits to invalidate them. Firms like Larson's that mostly represented big corporations thus found themselves regularly engaged from the fall of 1935 onward in fashioning legal arguments attacking the constitutionality of these laws as well as some of the earlier New Deal measures such as the Agricultural Adjustment Act and the "little" National Recovery Act for the coal industry, which had come to seem similarly objectionable to many businessmen, and state laws of the same basic sort. Although this kind of work helped pay Larson's salary, writing anti–New Deal briefs could not have appealed to him, given his more sympathetic view of what Congress and the president had done. His intellectual frame of mind may well have led him to rebel at working intensely on arcane areas of tax and corporate law.[15]

The long hours the partners expected everyone to work likewise put him off. A man with a happy home life and strong outside interests in theater and music, Larson appears to have found the adjustment to the office work regime difficult. He suggested as much in letters to his mother: "I get practically no extra time off at Christmas, it seems. I have very meager vacations. . . . I wish I could be back home for Thanksgiving, but I have only the one day off. Time seems to go so terrifically fast when you work all day."[16] The following March he reported to her that "we are still busy in the office. I haven't had an idle moment for months."[17]

As unappealing to him as some of the work and the long hours must have been, the pressure to bring in business of his own was even greater. Like so many private law firms, Quarles, Spence and Quarles's long-term financial health depended on its lawyers' ability to increase its roster of clients. Larson understood what the partners expected of him in this regard but could not bring himself to do it. Like his father, Arthur Larson found the business world alien and off-putting. He later explained his actions in this vital area: "We [Florence and I] spent a lot of our time in the artist and theater community. I suppose if I had been a little more practical, I would have spent more of my time trying to go out and hobnob with wealthy Milwaukeeans and drum up legal business, but I'm afraid that just wasn't my way. I much preferred to hang around with the sculptors, painters [and] actors."[18] Larson's decision in the winter of 1937–1938 to join the Town Club, an athletic facility favored by the local gentry, appears to have been inspired partly by a desire to make such connections, but even there he showed much more interest in actually playing racket sports than in finding clients. What few attempts he did make failed to yield much income, which eventually bred dissatisfaction among the firm's partners.[19]

Larson's failure to attract any major clients of his own finally began to produce serious consequences when the economic recovery of the mid-1930s collapsed in the fall of 1937. For the next two years, the so-called Roosevelt Recession severely depressed Milwaukee's volatile economy. Quarles, Spence and Quarles saw its income dwindle in response. Without much work for Larson or the other young associates to do, their salaries became an increasing drag on the firm's diminished income. Although the partners held back for a while, apparently hoping that the downturn would prove short-lived, by the summer of 1939, things reached a breaking point. J. V. Quarles summoned the young associates one by one, including Larson and his two friends Henry Reuss and Jeff Burrus, and informed them that "we just can't carry you young fellows any longer."[20] As it had with so many others, the Great Depression's effects had finally touched them suddenly and severely.

In Larson's case, the timing of this blow could hardly have been worse. The previous April, he and Florence had bought a small house in Shorewood, assuming the obligation of monthly mortgage payments that were higher than their rent had been. She had found a paying job directing a theater funded by the Federal Theater Project, which helped make this purchase possible, but then became pregnant early in 1939. Although both of them appear to have welcomed this turn of events, it greatly increased the weight on their shoulders. A further complication soon arose, which Larson traced back to an incident at his office two years earlier, when he had leaned back one day in his chair and felt something in his back snap. Although never entirely sure what caused this injury, he surmised that it must have been a long-term reaction to the strain he had placed on his back while rowing at Oxford. Two of his fellow Pembroke rowers had strained their backs during his time on the crew team, which suggested that rowing was the most likely culprit. Whatever the ultimate cause, Larson's doctor diagnosed him as having a herniated intervertebral disk, which caused what Larson later described as "severe pain in my legs" during the summer of 1939.[21] When all of these developments coincided with the loss of his job, Larson reached what he later called "the lowest point in my whole life."[22]

So much success had come to him easily that Larson seems never to have imagined that such a bad break could befall him. That kind of naive optimism now placed him in a very serious bind that the particular circumstances of the late 1930s made positively frightening. Larson much later wrote about this, the great personal crisis of his life: "It is difficult now for people who did not live through that period to imagine the feeling of bottomless insecurity experienced by millions of people like us. There was no safety net. Social Security and Unemployment Insurance had not yet taken hold. Unemployment, in this second trough of the Depression, once more stood at 25 percent."[23]

He and Florence plunged immediately into the task of finding a new job for him. Other Milwaukee law firms offered no real hope, given the surplus of lawyers on the market at that time. Something in state or local government might have seemed a logical choice, but Larson seems never to have seriously considered that possibility. He had done nothing since arriving in Milwaukee to follow up on his earlier interest in politics, for a variety of reasons. Years of debating politics and public policy questions on the elevated plane of the Oxford Union appear to have diminished whatever interest he might have had in the nuts-and-bolts questions that usually confronted state and local lawmakers. Larson confessed as much in a letter to his father toward the end of his time in England, writing that "the Union has almost spoiled my taste for politics."[24] His father's unpleasant experiences while seeking reelection to the bench also soured Larson on the whole notion of running for public office:

> My father's judgeship was an elective office with a term of only two years. Although only once or twice did someone presume to run against him, the cheap attacks of his opponents and my father's suffering made a deep impression on me. When in later years I tried to analyze what it was about politics that repelled me, it came down to this: in a political contest, what counts is not finding and establishing truth, but rather creating the illusion of truth just long enough to get a majority of the electorate to vote for you. I realized that in a democracy this was probably unavoidable, but that did not mean I had to be part of it.[25]

Even if Larson had not lost interest for those reasons, the local and state political milieus at that time would likely have dissuaded him. Milwaukee had been led by a Socialist-Populist mayor named Daniel Webster Hoan for twenty-three years who was held firmly in check by a nonpartisan city council. The two major political parties thus had no direct role in municipal government, which meant that a Republican such as Larson had no obvious way into the system. In the late 1930s, the state's political situation posed similar obstacles; its Republican Party had split into two warring factions. This mine-filled political landscape strongly deterred people with Larson's outlook from entering, even if they found the idea of running for office appealing.[26]

His distaste for elective politics did not, of course, imply a lack of interest in public policy. On the contrary, Larson's favorite play at that time was Shakespeare's *Henry IV, Part II*, in which the future King Henry V learned the art of good government. Given that kind of interest, seeking a civil service appointment in city government would have been a logical next step, but Larson seems not to have pursued that possibility. The key factor appears to have been the lack of real roots in the community of the sort that helped Henry Reuss obtain the post of assistant Milwaukee County corporation counsel, which put him onto a path that eventually led to the U.S. House of Representatives. Larson's decision to leave his native South Dakota had made that kind of career move far more difficult.[27]

For all of these reasons, the most attractive and promising course of action appeared to be a teaching job. Larson had already been working on some scholarly articles during the slack times before the firm had laid him off, apparently with this thought in mind. When disaster struck, he decided to apply immediately for a position as a law professor. Florence and her theater friend Edie Mahler typed letters of application to all of the 108 law schools then accredited in the United States, but this wave of applications met with a deeply discouraging response. Law schools simply were not hiring because of the economic downturn, which had depressed enrollments and deterred many older faculty members from retiring. The dean of Cornell Law School, Robert S. Stevens, wrote back offering Larson a one-year residential fellowship. With no other prospects in sight, he and Florence prepared to move there and try again for a real job next year. And then a letter arrived from the University of Tennessee announcing that an assistant professor of law position had opened and inviting him to interview for it. Larson hurried down to Knoxville and got the job, to his great relief. Although his brush with unemployment proved mercifully brief, like so many others with similar experiences during the Great Depression, he never forgot it. Some of his naive optimism had been knocked out of him for good.[28]

Moving the 650 miles from Milwaukee to Knoxville brought more than just a change of scene for Arthur and Florence. It made them residents of the South, a place where neither of them had ever lived and which Larson later described as "a whole new world to us—particularly as it was in 1939."[29] The distinctively southern aspects of their new hometown included a large black population, which the 1940 census takers counted as 16,106, or 14.4 percent, of Knoxville's 111,580 residents. Most of the city's African-American population lived in the aging city center, near but still apart from white residents, in keeping with the formal system of racial segregation still very much in place at that time. The severe economic and social problems associated with the Great Depression, combined with the poverty of the surrounding Appalachian region, had given Knoxville much higher rates of violent crime than any place Arthur and Florence had ever called home. In the year before they arrived, the list of ten leading causes of death in the city included homicide for the first time. These conditions gave Knoxville, like so much of the pre–World War II South, the aura of what today we would call a Third World country, an environment that was strikingly different from the northern cities he and Florence had earlier lived in.[30]

On the other hand, Knoxville could hardly be considered a typical southern place. For one thing it was urban, which most of the South was not. Another major difference grew out of the city's location in eastern Tennessee, an area predominantly occupied by small farmers whose forebears had strongly opposed the planter-led secession movement that culminated in the Civil War. So staunchly did the majority of Knoxvillians support the Union cause during the war that afterward they elected Republicans to represent them in Congress, something that was still the case when Larson arrived there.[31]

Another important difference between Knoxville and most of the rest of the South at that time was the city's highly diversified economic base, which from the earliest days of settlement had been industrial as well as commercial. The clay in the local soil helped make it a brick-making center, and the abundance of local soft coal encouraged the construction of factories and mills. Knoxville's location astride the Tennessee River helped make possible that kind of economic development and the city's emergence as a major trading center that served eastern Tennessee, western North Carolina and Virginia, Kentucky, South Carolina, Georgia, and Alabama. By the 1920s, Knoxville had become the wholesale center of the South, from which armies of salesmen moved into surrounding states, drumming up demand for the many goods stored in the city's warehouses. The city also was the home for the state's university and a separate institution of higher learning for blacks, known then as Knoxville College for Negroes, which attracted many highly educated whites and blacks, respectively. The creation of the Tennessee Valley Authority (TVA) in May 1933 had broadened the city's economic base even more. Although most of TVA's dam-building and related electric power construction projects took place in outlying areas, the authority established its headquarters in Knoxville, where TVA engineers, technicians, and clerical staff soon filled much local office space. These characteristics made Knoxville into a pioneer "New South" city of the sort *Atlanta Constitution* editor Henry Grady had so famously called for. In 1939, such places were still highly unusual in a region whose economy remained predominantly agricultural.[32]

Knoxville's economy also made the city's social structure atypical of the South. During the prosperous years of the mid- and late 1920s, Knoxville had a fairly large middle class. The overall impression the city tended to make on visitors then was as a place without extremes of wealth or poverty. Although the onset of the Great Depression soon changed that situation, there were some lasting consequences, such as home ownership and literacy rates that were unusually high for the South of that day. In some ways very southern and in others more northern, Knoxville in 1939 constituted something of a halfway house between those two very different parts of the country.[33]

Not surprisingly, Knoxville's southern qualities were the ones that made the most lasting impression on a transplanted northerner such as Larson. He vividly remembered his first encounter with the black caretaker who maintained the large and dilapidated old house Larson and Florence rented during their first year there. As he sat on the spacious columned porch one day, an elderly black man approached and headed toward the rear of the house. In response to Larson's quizzical look, the man announced "I'm Fred. I goes with the house."[34] Larson soon discovered that Fred's duties were to stoke the furnace, tend the yard, and make small repairs, all no doubt much appreciated given Larson's serious back problems. In the course of one such repair job on the window next to the front door, this man provided Larson with another lasting memory of the distortions in human behavior southern segregation often produced. Fixing the window entailed working both inside and outside the house. Whenever he needed to work inside, Fred, to Larson's uncomprehending annoyance, walked around to the back of the house, a distance of 108 feet, then up a long flight of steps to the back door and through the house to the window in question. After watching him do this a few times, Larson finally exclaimed, "For heaven's sake, Fred. Why don't you just go through the [front] door? Why do you take that long trip around the back?" To this Fred had replied, "Oh, suh, I just can't bring myself to go through that front door."[35]

These kinds of interactions made up Larson's first sustained exposure to African Americans. Sioux Falls, Oxford, and Milwaukee had all been overwhelmingly white during his years there. Apart from one black boy in the summer camp where Larson worked as a counselor, he seems to have had no contact with African Americans prior to moving to Knoxville. And even there, he and Florence moved in social circles at the university, which had no black faculty or students. This did not, of course, imply any antagonism toward blacks on his or her part. On the contrary, all the evidence suggests that they, like so many "Party of Lincoln" Republicans of their generation, believed strongly in the right of blacks to equal treatment in law and life but had little or no knowledge of them as individuals.[36]

Larson's good intentions in this regard can most readily be seen in the way he responded when his black maid, a bright young woman named Alice, got into serious trouble with the law. He and Florence had hired her and her 11-year-old daughter Glenzarine to help out around the house in return for $5 a week. On the third day of their employ, Alice and Glenzarine failed to appear and then Alice telephoned to say, in a very agitated voice, "Mr. Larson, could you come right down to the jail? I'm in trouble." He agreed to come and, upon arriving, explained to the officer on duty that he was Alice's employer. With the sounds of Alice's and Glenzarine's crying plainly audible, Larson asked to see Alice. "I'm not so sure," the officer had replied. "Why, what's she in for?" Larson had asked. "Murder." After pausing to digest this surprising news, Larson explained that he was a lawyer and might be of some help. That produced the desired result, and soon Larson found himself in the cell listening to Alice's story about what had happened.[37]

As Larson later related in his memoirs, Alice claimed that the death in question had been an accident. He recalled her version of what had happened:

> Alice had been carrying on an affair, which took the form of a visit by her boyfriend to her bedroom every morning on his way to work. On the fatal morning, there had been a quarrel, the revolver in the nightstand had been extracted, and while the two were grappling with it Glenzarine ran in from her room to join in the tussle. Somehow in the midst of all this the gun had gone off and shot the boyfriend, who ran into the street, *carrying the smoking gun,* and collapsed about a block away.[38]

Although the police seemed to have a good case at first glance, Larson concluded that they lacked any real evidence to convict Alice of murder. The deputy sheriff who had arrested her claimed to have a key witness, the hospital nurse who had attended to the boyfriend before he died, but failed for weeks to produce her in court. This turn of events made Larson suspicious, so he decided to represent Alice. Even though Larson was not admitted to the Tennessee bar, the judge, an obliging sort who had graduated from the law school whose faculty Larson had just joined, told him to "go right ahead."[39] Larson questioned the nurse, who told him that she had never heard of the deputy sheriff. When Larson took this information to the judge, he set an early hearing date to look into the whole matter.

The entire episode took an even stranger turn when the deputy sheriff sidled up to Larson outside the judge's chambers and offered to drop the case in return for $8.43, which, the deputy said, was the cost of the time he had spent on it thus far. Without stopping to consider the danger in which he was putting his maid, Larson spurned this sleazy offer and made his case in court. Luckily for Alice, the deputy sheriff's case against her rested only on the general testimony of several character witnesses that "Alice was no good," which had no real legal weight, and the nurse's account of the boyfriend's remarks to her at the hospital where he had been treated. Before dying there, the nurse related, he had told her that "Alice done shot me."[40]

The key legal issue raised by this evidence was whether it could be admitted at trial. Under a long-standing rule of law, such a statement could not be admitted into evidence against the accused unless the person making it believed his own death was imminent. In that case, such a statement, ordinarily inadmissible as hearsay, would be allowed as a dying declaration, on the theory that someone about to die would be strongly inclined to tell the truth. Alice's fate turned on whether the state could show that the boyfriend had believed he was dying when he made his declaration against her. The most the deputy sheriff could elicit from the nurse, however, was her recollection that the boyfriend had simply said that he was "feeling mighty low" at the time.[41] Larson argued that such a remark did not go far enough, and the judge agreed and dismissed the case. This entire episode took one final strange turn the next morning, when Alice and her daughter failed to report for work. Larson never heard from them again, and it seems likely that they simply cleared out rather than risk more trouble with the local police.

He had no time to ponder at length over all of this. The very next day, September 17, 1939, Florence gave birth to their first child, a son they named Lex Kingsbury Larson. This name was intended to honor both Lex King Souter, a collegiate debate champion and friend of Larson's from his Augustana days, and Florence's family tree, which included the surname Kingsbury. Choosing the name Lex, which was Latin for "law," reflected Arthur Larson's deep faith in it—which so many conservatives shared—as a way to address social problems. Happy but overworked, he and Florence soon found another housekeeper, a good-natured African-American woman named Hattie, who stayed with them for the next four years. Hattie handled all of the housework, cooked, helped with the baby, and did the wash for $6 a week, including carfare, a high sum by Knoxville's standards but a bargain by those of Sioux Falls and Milwaukee. Arthur and Florence greatly benefited from Hattie's assistance given their lack of nearby relatives and his back problems, which ruled out all forms of heavy lifting and prolonged stooping. The arrival of a second child fourteen months later, a daughter they named Anna Barbara in honor of his mother, helped keep all of them busy. So, too, did another move, this time to a little white house with a white picket fence in a suburb south of the city's center.[42]

Apart from these domestic concerns, Larson's time in Knoxville was mostly consumed by his work at the law school, where he firmly intended to make a name for himself in the world of legal scholarship. The setting in which Larson began that quest did not offer much encouragement, however, because the Tennessee Law School in those days did not enjoy a very distinguished reputation. Although the American Bar Association committee that surveyed the school in 1937–1938 concluded that it ranked "well among the better law schools of the South," the school, like the University of Tennessee more generally, suffered from heavy teaching loads and mediocre library facilities that deterred most professors from doing research.[43] The Tennessee Law School's small enrollment, approximately 100 students when Larson arrived, compounded this problem by keeping tuition income low and the faculty's size tiny. Although the five other law professors on staff had earned their degrees from such notable places as Chicago, Harvard, Iowa, Wisconsin, and Yale, most published nothing. Instead, they devoted their time and energies to teaching three courses each in the fall and spring semesters and, if necessary, three more during the school's summer session.[44]

This unpromising state of affairs failed to deter Larson from beginning a career as a legal scholar. Over the next two years, he somehow managed to teach the full course load and publish three articles and six book reviews in various law journals. This achievement appears all the more impressive because Larson during these same years also developed teaching materials for seven different courses: Administrative Law, Agency, Bankruptcy, Corporations, Labor Problems, Office Practice, and Partnership. When one considers that he accomplished all of this while suffering from serious back problems that required two operations and dealing with the demands of a growing family, the truly remarkable nature of his ambition and industriousness becomes clear.[45]

Although Larson always kept quiet about his back injury, what few references he and Florence made to it in their letters from this period signal just how serious the problem was. During the worst periods, a simple sneeze on his part could mean considerable pain. Shortly after arriving in Knoxville, he underwent surgery there. The surgeon gave him a large steel and leather belt to wear, which he did for the next year. This contraption led Larson to refrain from strenuous exertion and his pain subsided, which seemed briefly to indicate that the surgery had helped. When Larson tried playing Ping-Pong, however, the pain returned. It got so bad that he consulted several other doctors, none of whom could help. This turn of events left him "very discouraged," as Florence eventually confided in a letter to his father.[46] Refusing to give up, Larson went to see a specialist at Johns Hopkins Hospital in Baltimore, who took X-rays and informed him that there was a large protrusion in his spinal column that was pressing against a nerve. The doctor said that the Knoxville surgeon had operated one notch too low on Larson's spinal column and accomplished nothing. So Larson underwent another operation in the fall of 1940 at Johns Hopkins, which seemed at first to bring some improvement but did not really end his discomfort.[47]

What appears to have kept Larson moving forward then and afterward was the love and companionship he received from Florence, Lex, and Anna and the pleasure he derived from his new job. In those days, simply having one at all made many Americans feel good. In Larson's case, his affinity for the work greatly enhanced that kind of satisfaction. His highly developed public speaking skills had equipped him perfectly for teaching, and his intellectual curiosity and strong writing skills had prepared him for scholarship. Larson's letters home reveal just how much he enjoyed his new duties. He informed his mother that writing his first law review article, a substantial piece of about 20,000 words, had been "a lot of fun."[48] Two weeks later, he confessed in his next letter to her that "I'm really excited about this writing business."[49]

That it (and teaching) paid well enough to live comfortably could only have added to Larson's contentment. Although the legislature and board of trustees had cut faculty salaries by almost 20 percent during the Depression, prices had declined too, and that offset some of the effect of that reduction. Law professors also made more than the typical faculty member, so even a first-year assistant professor of law such as Larson earned an adequate income of $4,250 per year. On that he could support his family properly, given Knoxville's low cost of living.

Making this situation all the more sweet was the fact that Larson's new job paid twice what he had been making at Quarles, Spence and Quarles. Despite the various obstacles he confronted when the partners there had laid him off, Larson had managed to land on his feet.[50]

The publications he produced during these two years provide some interesting insights into Larson's still-developing public philosophy. By far the most revealing of these works was the first, a law review article about the legal controversy that arose when Franklin Roosevelt fired TVA chairman Arthur E. Morgan in March of 1938. Morgan sued for damages and reinstatement, claiming that Roosevelt had no power to remove him. In so doing, Morgan sought to bring his claim within the reach of the U.S. Supreme Court's earlier ruling in *Humphrey's Executor v. United States,* 295 U.S. 602 (1935). In that case, the Court found that Roosevelt's publicly expressed reason for firing a member of the Federal Trade Commission was not one Congress had listed in the law creating the commission as an appropriate reason for removal. The Court also found that the Federal Trade Commission was not an executive branch agency because in the course of its work it at times exercised legislative and judicial authority. The Court had therefore held that the president had exceeded his authority and ordered the government to pay damages to the estate of the former commissioner, who had died.[51]

Like *Humphrey's,* Morgan's case raised far-reaching questions about the scope of the president's power at a time when it had grown to an extraordinary degree, something that clearly interested Larson very much. After working on the research and writing day and night for several weeks, he gave the resulting article to the school's law journal, the *Tennessee Law Review,* which published it in the April 1940 issue. Larson argued that the president had no inherent power to remove Morgan because the chairman of the TVA was not an executive branch appointee. The Tennessee Valley Authority, Larson argued, was another hybrid creation, like the Federal Trade Commission, that did more than execute the nation's laws.[52]

Although the courts eventually rejected this line of reasoning, Larson's article is interesting because of the concern it showed over the effect an enlarged presidency was having on the allocation of power to the three branches of the federal government. Larson went into considerable detail on the TVA's legal status to rebut erroneous ideas that had emerged during Roosevelt's administration:

> This [discussion] is the more necessary, because of the prevalence of a popular notion that not only such agencies as the TVA, but the whole administrative system in general, was invented and created by the President, is run by him, and in general belongs to him. A similar misconception is the identification of the administrative system with the New Deal. Of course anyone with the slightest familiarity with the subject knows that that system antedates the New Deal by many years, and that many of the agencies popularly supposed to be New Deal creations were in existence long before.[53]

This passage indicates Larson's distance from both the most conservative critics and ardent admirers of Roosevelt. Unlike the most extreme right-wingers, who had formed the American Liberty League in the mid-1930s to fight Roosevelt's policies, Larson did not suggest anywhere in his article that New Deal agencies were unconstitutional encroachments on the free enterprise system. His more moderate critique focused instead on the likelihood that allowing Roosevelt and his advisors alone to control these and the older federal regulatory agencies would weaken the courts and Congress vis-à-vis the president. In pointing out the danger of allowing unrestrained presidential control over the federal regulatory agencies, Larson sounded a theme similar to the one Walter Lippmann developed more broadly in his anti–New Deal treatise *The Good Society*, which appeared in the fall of 1937. Lippmann argued that Roosevelt had gone too far in concentrating power in the presidency to meet the economic crisis and in so doing had created an even more fundamental menace to Americans' individual freedoms. Although not opposed, in principle, to most of Roosevelt's Depression-fighting policies, Larson, like Lippmann, had begun to disagree strongly and publicly with how New Dealers had chosen to implement them.[54]

These doubts about expanded presidential power showed in Larson's February 1941 review of Harold Laski's book *The American Presidency*. Laski, a well-known British political theorist, argued that the United States, whatever its earlier history, had come to have the same basic problems as the major European nations and thus needed a strong central government, with power concentrated in the executive branch, to meet the new and serious challenges that faced the nation by 1940. Larson praised the book's very clear and complete description of the president's responsibilities but criticized its failure to provide persuasive evidence to support its main arguments. Larson reserved his harshest remarks for his discussion of Laski's proposed reforms to strengthen the presidency, which included suggestions that Congress voluntarily abandon its right to initiate appropriations in favor of the executive branch and that senators likewise give up their right to be consulted by the president when making executive appointments. These notions Larson dismissed as utterly unrealistic. Here, as elsewhere in Larson's writings, his characteristically practical approach shone through.[55]

That approach tended to steer him away from more rigidly conservative views, as another of the law review articles he published in the early 1940s made clear. This piece is interesting because in it Larson discussed a federal workers' compensation statute that, like others enacted by the various states, eliminated older common law rules requiring wrongdoing on part of the employer and blamelessness on the part of the injured worker in order for him or her to receive compensation. Implicit in this legislative shift was a view that in a modern industrial economy, society bore collective responsibility for making certain that those who suffered from workplace injuries receive compensation for them, regardless of considerations of individual fault. Many American judges, however, guided by older and harsher notions of personal responsibility embedded in common law, had found workers' compensation laws hard to accept when state legislatures and Congress had begun enacting them during the first two decades of the twentieth century. When employers challenged injured employees' claims in the courts, such judges had often issued rulings that reintroduced older notions of fault, thereby creating a confused set of workers' compensation precedents.[56]

Larson, in marked contrast with that kind of conservative legal mind, showed no such prejudice against the thinking that lay behind this cornerstone of the American welfare state. Rather than resist the changing view of moral responsibility for workplace injuries that lay behind it, Larson approvingly described the way workers' compensation statutes imposed reciprocal benefits and burdens on employers, workers, and society as a whole:

> Under such a system, the employer and employee both gain certain things and undergo corresponding burdens. The employer gives up some of his defenses and gains immunity from unpredictable personal injury verdicts. The employee foregoes his right to seek large common-law damage verdicts and gains certainty of recovery. Society gains freedom from the helpless victim of industry thrown upon its charity, and for this pays a little higher price for the products of industry.[57]

The same openness to change emerged in Larson's other scholarly writings from this period. The most important of these were reviews of Thurman Arnold's *Bottlenecks of Business*, which dealt with antitrust policy, and a collection of essays entitled *A Century of Social Thought*. Of these, Arnold's book was the more significant, for its author, a onetime law professor at Yale whom Roosevelt appointed head of the Antitrust Division of the U.S. Justice Department in 1937, had vigorously used the power at his disposal during the late 1930s to increase competition in private industry. Unlike some antimonopoly enthusiasts, Arnold did not oppose bigness for its own sake. At the same time, he did not suggest, as some of his earlier writings had, that the Sherman Antitrust Act ought to be repealed or ignored. Arnold's new approach, which he explained in this book, defended antitrust investigations and prosecutions of only those business combinations engaged in anticompetitive behavior that inflated consumer prices.[58] *Bottlenecks of Business* thus staked out a kind of middle position on antitrust law, with which Arthur Larson tended to agree. He wrote enthusiastically in his review of the book that "every lawyer, and every businessman and consumer for that matter, ought to read this book."[59]

Larson's moderately conservative outlook showed through in another way in his review of *A Century of Social Thought*. The book contained a collection of lectures given at Duke University as part of its centennial celebration in 1938. The book's various contributors each discussed at length intellectual progress over the previous century in a major field of inquiry such as economics, education, law, and religion. Larson chose to focus his review on the essays on education and law. He praised the first of these for making clear that formal education until the past century had been "primarily an aristocratic thing" that needed considerable changes in light of the much broader social purpose it now served.[60] Unlike some enthusiasts for educational reform, Larson warned against the danger of going too far, noting that professionals in general and lawyers in particular needed the broad grounding in the classics the older educational approach emphasized.[61]

Larson observed that the essay on law, which was written by noted legal philosopher Roscoe Pound, dealt with the highly important question of whether rules of law derived their authority from their basis in reason and justice or simply from the force in the hands of those who had made them. This timeless debate had taken on a renewed interest in the past century, Larson wrote, as nations struggled to establish a system of international law without a supranational means of enforcement. This raised the crucial question of whether conduct could be truly characterized as illegal if no policing force existed to punish it. Larson noted that some scholars in this field had concluded that this could never be done and implicitly called for the creation of some kind of supranational enforcing authority. Although he did not endorse that conclusion, which would have horrified conservative Republicans such as former president Herbert Hoover and Ohio senator Robert Taft, Larson did not reject it either. Instead, he simply noted the disagreement within the field of international law over this key question and endorsed Pound's essay as a useful place to begin sorting out an answer. This review, like his other writings, reinforced an overall impression of a mind instinctively cautious but still open to new ideas about the role of government, which set him apart from both starry-eyed liberals such as Laski and more rigid conservatives such as Hoover and Taft.[62]

Although the quality and quantity of Larson's publications indicated that he possessed the right kind of mind and work habits for a successful career in legal scholarship, he nonetheless chose to leave the University of Tennessee as soon as an appealing alternative developed. One materialized in the summer of 1941, when Henry Reuss, who had recently become assistant general counsel of the Office of Price Administration (OPA) in Washington, called Larson to ask if he would join him on its legal staff. The changing political environment of the early 1940s no doubt made such a move more attractive to Larson than it would have been earlier. During 1940–1941, Roosevelt's New Deal entered its third and final phase, marked by massive federal spending on the military, a less confrontational posture vis-à-vis the business community, and the entry of large numbers of business executives, many of them Republicans, into management positions at the various war mobilization agencies. Even though the United States remained formally at peace in the summer of 1941, Larson, like other perceptive observers, could plainly see that the fighting in Europe and Asia was gradually drawing the nation into World War II.[63]

As strong as these pulls were, the various pushes to leave Knoxville appear to have been the truly decisive factors that persuaded him and Florence to make this change. Their sense of themselves as outsiders in Knoxville, the lack of career opportunities there for her, and the city's unattractive and even unhealthy environment gave them strong incentives to depart. The last of these likely mattered more than one might think. Although blessed with a pretty natural setting in the foothills west of the Great Smoky Mountains, Knoxville's heavily industrial and commercial economy gave the city a strikingly unpleasant appearance. Journalist John Gunther, who visited Knoxville in the mid-1940s while traveling around the country doing research for his famous bestseller *Inside USA*, found Knoxville so unattractive that he unkindly described it as "the ugliest city I ever saw in America, with the possible exception of some mill towns in New England."[64]

Related to this concern and even more serious was Knoxville's heavily reliance on local soft coal for heating, which perpetually covered the city in a cloud of coal dust. It often filled the skies so thickly that it limited visibility on West Cumberland, one of the main streets near the University of Tennessee campus, to only 200 feet. Keeping anything clean for long simply could not be done, including the air that he, Florence, and their two babies breathed every day. When the opportunity to move to Washington, D.C., arose, they immediately accepted.[65]

Leaving Florence behind to supervise the packing and move their children, Larson made his way to the capital in early September 1941 and immediately plunged into his new duties at the OPA. This agency, which Roosevelt had formally created by executive order one month earlier, had inherited its price control mission from predecessor organizations, the first of which had come into being in May 1940 under statutory authority remaining from World War I. The catalysts for this extraordinary government intervention into the nation's economic life were the inflationary pressures and shortages that accompanied the nation's increasing involvement in World War II. The OPA's objective was to maintain price stability by controlling prices for raw materials, goods, and services for which demand was rising rapidly. The OPA's director, Leon Henderson, and his chief deputy, John Kenneth Galbraith, decided at first to meet that goal by developing price ceilings for commodities experiencing that kind of inflationary demand and developing such ceilings for other commodities if and as the need arose. In taking this incremental approach, Henderson and Galbraith rejected World War I economic "czar" Bernard Baruch's advice to simply freeze all existing prices and focus on making needed adjustments. In time, the unworkability of the Henderson-Galbraith approach would become clear, given the vast number of commodities affected by inflationary demand once the nation formally entered the war in December 1941. When Larson first arrived, however, Henderson and Galbraith's initial scheme was still the order of the day, which meant that the agency's economists and lawyers were working around the clock to draft commodity price schedules.[66]

Under a dual system of administrative authority established by Henderson and Galbraith, the OPA consisted of various divisions based on the industry groupings listed in the 1940 census, each of which was headed by two people. One was either an economist or a knowledgeable civil servant from one of the peacetime agencies, who bore the title price executive. The other was a lawyer formally called an associate general counsel. These two individuals needed to agree on price schedules before they could be issued. When Larson arrived, the OPA's general counsel, David Ginsburg, made him associate general counsel for the industrial manufacturing division, which included materials used to construct buildings. By far the most important of these was lumber, prices for which had begun to rise sharply in the summer of 1941. In tandem with the division's price executive, Larson and his staff of four lawyers spent the next six months drafting price schedules for such commodities as western pine and southern hardwood lumber.[67]

The nature of his work changed suddenly and dramatically the following spring, when the OPA's inability to issue price schedules fast enough to keep up with spreading inflationary pressures led to a major change in policy. In April 1942, Henderson and Galbraith abandoned their incremental approach in favor of Baruch's method, issuing an overall price freeze order known as the General Maximum Price Regulation. "General Max," as OPA administrators informally called it, limited the price for all commodities to the highest charged by the seller to purchasers during the previous March. Understanding that unavoidable fluctuations in supply and demand would in time require some price increases, Henderson, Galbraith, and Ginsburg directed their subordinates to focus on investigating business executives' requests for such changes and approving them when necessary. This kind of adjustment was especially needed for products such as industrial materials that had earlier been subject to generally worded price regulations. When the need to spell out specific prices industry by industry, product by product reemerged in cases where the highest price during March 1943 was unclear, OPA economists and lawyers such as Larson prepared and issued them.[68]

Although he knew nothing about the lumber business prior to coming to the OPA, Larson carried out these kinds of duties very effectively and in time became a highly influential person in his particular regulatory domain. He did his work so well, in fact, that when the person serving as price executive in his division took leave from the agency, Larson's superiors gave him that responsibility as well. Even after that person returned and the OPA's new head, believing that the system of dual authority was creating more problems than it solved, did away with the lawyers' veto over pricing decisions, Larson's extensive experience tended to give him more authority than attorneys of equal rank who had arrived more recently. As a practical matter, the lawyers' continuing control over the drafting of all regulations concentrated a great deal of the real power in their hands. Larson exaggerated only slightly when he later described himself as a kind of "czar of the lumber industry" during World War II.[69]

Doing that job required Larson to make extended tours for weeks at a time to places in the South and West where the bulk of the nation's wood and wood products were produced. He would inspect lumber operations, meet with mill owners, and attempt to address their various concerns about price controls. This kind of work required strong public speaking and negotiating skills as well as patience, all of which Larson appears to have possessed. His lack of left-wing ardor seems also to have helped him establish a good rapport with industry leaders, who tended to assume OPA administrators were all ardent New Dealers like Henderson and Galbraith.[70]

Larson's OPA experience, which lasted about three years, was an intensive tutorial in applied political economy. The agency employed over a quarter of a million people during World War II either as paid staff or volunteers, and their price control activities touched every industry and community in the country. The OPA's huge size and broad reach made it an ideal place to learn practical lessons about the relationship between government and business. The unworkability of the initial incremental approach to price control exposed Larson directly to the limits of government's regulatory power, what political scientists call "state capacity." The failure of that approach also revealed the kind of conflict that sometimes arose between what was economically desirable and politically possible. While Baruch's plan for price regulation made more economic sense than the initial scheme Henderson and Galbraith developed, prior to the United States' formal entry into World War II, the support in Congress and across the country needed to implement such a drastic move did not exist. The incremental approach, while ultimately inadequate, had the virtues of exerting some control over rising prices in the period before the attack on Pearl Harbor and teaching reluctant business executives, members of Congress, and the public that a more comprehensive approach was required. Larson's day-to-day OPA work also revealed to him, as it did to so many others who worked there, the essential nature of that support, from businessmen especially, in order to make strict price controls operate effectively in an economic and political system like that of the United States.[71]

The experience of working with businessmen did not diminish Larson's sense of the business world as an alien and even off-putting place. Instead, what he saw only reinforced that outlook. In letters home to Florence, Larson complained about what he called lumbermen's "greediness" in constantly demanding price increases and the phony way lumber industry executives tried to win him over with expensive meals.[72] Toward the end of his time at the OPA, he elaborated on those themes, writing to her that "day after day I listen to the blandishments of earnest lumbermen, most of whom have no more honesty or principle than their profit margin makes expedient."[73]

Like so many other businessmen during the early 1940s, lumber industry executives had struggled to keep their enterprises afloat during the Depression and then, just as prosperity returned, found themselves faced with much higher taxes; bigger, stronger unions; and strict price controls that combined to squeeze their profit margins. This series of unwelcome developments, which stretched over fifteen years, greatly increased the pressures on lumbermen and tended to have a degrading effect on business morals and practices that led to just the sort of behavior Larson witnessed while working at the OPA. The unattractive results bred by years of intense insecurity, overwork, and cutthroat competition tended to alienate even moderate conservatives such as Larson, who explicitly rejected the anticapitalist ideologies emanating from the extreme left.[74]

Even the businessmen who came to work for the OPA as industry specialists deeply disappointed him. Inclined at first to rely on them for advice, given their firsthand knowledge of their respective industries, Larson soon discovered that the industry specialists' parochial perspective usually led them to the wrong conclusion. He explained his unhappiness with them at length in a letter to his parents:

> These transplanted business-men, on whom such high hopes are built by their fellow-business-men, are the greatest disappointments of the whole Roosevelt regime—worse even than the Brain Trust and the college professors. In my section there is a "business specialist" for each commodity and even sub-commodity—a man who has spent his life on that one product. To a man, they are hopelessly unable to administer the industries in which they have been small cogs for so long.[75]

Larson developed a similarly jaundiced view of the farm lobby in Congress, whose single-minded defense of agricultural interests struck him as wholly out of place during a time of great national crisis. The demands, in particular, from farm-state senators for increasing agricultural commodity prices above the good-times norm known as "parity" deeply disturbed him.[76]

Larson's sympathies tended to run much more toward those of the OPA's senior administrators such as Henderson and Galbraith, whose unbending support for strict price controls and impolitic manner provoked strong criticism from business circles and right-wing members of Congress. Larson formed a high opinion of Henderson in particular, who more than any other single person brought the nation's wartime price control system into being. In a January 1942 letter to his parents, he described him as "the smartest and soundest man in the whole defense set-up."[77] When growing opposition in Congress forced first Henderson and then Galbraith out, Larson lamented the discouraging signal that sent about the need for strict price controls to contain inflation. He wrote Florence in early June 1943 that Galbraith "was our symbol, so to speak, of firm price control since Henderson left. Now they're both gone. No one knows what to expect next."[78]

Although Larson appears to have genuinely respected the most senior OPA administrators, some of the lower-level ones with whom he dealt eventually alienated him. One subordinate annoyed him by needlessly offending already grouchy lumber executives with his high-handed behavior. Other members of Larson's own division sometimes frustrated him when they ignored his carefully considered advice and came to accept it only after precious time had been lost. Larson also found himself betrayed at one point by a duplicitous colleague who contrived to put the blame for unpopular price decisions on Larson alone in order to build goodwill with lumbermen who might have a job to offer once the war came to an end.[79]

These kinds of experiences helped persuade Larson that the life of a Washington bureaucrat was not for him. So, too, did the long absences from Florence, Lex, and Anna. His inability to obtain a raise from his starting OPA salary of $5,600 per year, despite having at times done the work of two senior officials, also persuaded him that he should begin looking for another job. In the summer of 1943 he began to put out feelers to law firms in Los Angeles and New York, cities he and Florence liked because of the career opportunities there for her as well as him. After more than a year of looking quietly, however, no offers materialized. In the meantime, he decided to leave OPA for another administrative agency, the Foreign Economic Administration (FEA), which would at least provide a change from the price control duties and OPA office politics.[80]

Larson found the job at the FEA by promptly responding to a tip that its general counsel, Oscar Cox, was looking for a personal legal assistant. When Larson went to see him, Cox explained that Congress had recently established the agency through the merger of the Office of Lend-Lease Administration and the Board of Economic Warfare. This reorganization seemed logical because the Lend-Lease agency had provided needed supplies to America's wartime allies while the Board of Economic Warfare purchased war matériel from foreign nations. Roosevelt had chosen Cox, one of the main authors of Lend-Lease legislation and a close confidant, as the new agency's top lawyer, and Larson, after listening to Cox explain the job's duties, decided that working for him promised to be an exciting change from the OPA. Cox, for his part, liked what he saw in Larson and offered him the job, which Larson immediately accepted.[81]

No sooner had the two men decided this when fate intervened and sent Larson in a somewhat different direction. In his memoirs, he described what happened then in this way:

> Oscar was just beginning to explain my new duties to me when Schaffner, Head of the European Section, and also the middle name in [the clothing

> firm of] Hart, Schaffner and Marx, burst into the room, exclaiming, "My God, what are we going to do? The Chief of the Scandinavian Section has just resigned." Oscar looked at me with a twinkle in his eye and said, "Your name's Larson. You take it."[82]

Like a good soldier in wartime, Larson agreed and proceeded to his new place of work in Temporary Building T, a flimsy wartime structure located on the mall. He found his new desk piled high with files in need of urgent processing and set to work. Once again, he found himself starting out in a government job that dealt with a subject about which he knew nothing: Scandinavian economic affairs. Of his early days at the FEA, he later wrote, "I processed them [the files he found] all right, but it was some months before I really understood what I was doing."[83]

He stayed for about a year, enjoying the change of scene from the OPA and the excitement that came from working, however indirectly, with the Norwegian and Danish underground. Larson's involvement grew out of his responsibility for deciding what supplies the underground needed to carry on its resistance efforts effectively and estimating postwar needs for economic assistance. Making such determinations required information about the Norwegian and Danish economies that their respective underground agents worked courageously to provide. Although he mostly stayed in Washington, Larson's FEA assignment did take him to London for a month in the spring of 1945, where he conferred with members of the Norwegian and Danish governments-in-exile about plans for postwar economic reconstruction. He also enjoyed the chance to visit some of his old haunts there, the London theaters especially, and to see friends. As at the OPA, he handled his FEA duties very effectively, so much so in this case that his London supervisors offered him a job dealing with all of the liberated areas. Wanting very much, however, to get home to Florence and their children, Larson declined, which meant that his time at the FEA would be limited. Shortly after the Japanese government surrendered on August 14, 1945, Larson cleaned out his desk in "Tempo T," thereby ending his wartime government service.[84]

Like his first wartime job at the OPA, this second one taught Larson some important lessons in political economy, although this time they were of a comparative nature. The reason his new job provided this kind of education had to do with the reading on Scandinavian economics it required. The similar and interconnected countries of that region were among the most strongly social democratic in the world, with powerful labor movements, generous welfare states, and deeply entrenched commitments to economic planning. Sweden in particular had enjoyed a vogue among American liberals during the 1930s, many of whom read journalist Marquis Child's best-selling book, which appeared in 1936, about the Swedish model of political economy. Childs called his account *Sweden: The Middle Way*, and in so doing contributed a new phrase to the national political debate. While Larson's FEA duties did not involve him much with Sweden, given its official policy of neutrality during World War II, his background reading inevitably included discussions of that subject because much of the relevant literature dealt with Scandinavia as a single entity.[85]

Larson became so familiar with the economic systems of the northern European countries while working at the FEA that he contributed a chapter on that topic to a book-length survey of the economic challenges facing the postwar world. *Towards World Prosperity: Through Industrial and Agricultural Development and Expansion,* edited by New Deal economist and economic growth advocate Mordecai Ezekiel, eventually appeared in 1947. In his chapter, Larson first discussed the economic problems and prospects of the region as a whole and then dealt with the special circumstances facing each of the four nations located there: Denmark, Finland, Norway, and Sweden. He noted their heavy dependence on foreign trade and stressed their value, economic and otherwise, to Americans:

> The stake of the United States in the Northern Countries is particularly strong. . . . They are in the vanguard of orderly democratic development, and incalculable damage would be done to the cause of democracy throughout the world if this democratic development were damaged or defeated because the United States omitted to do its part in ensuring the prosperity which is the necessary foundation for continued successful democratic governance anywhere.[86]

This passage signaled the extent to which the war had converted Larson, like so many other Americans, into a committed internationalist. In place of the cautious and grudging acceptance of America's role in the wider world that had appeared in his letters home from Oxford during the mid-1930s was a new enthusiasm for American involvement abroad as both necessary and beneficial to all concerned.[87]

World War II seems to have changed his mind, too, about the military's proper role in modern society. In place of the reflexively antimilitary attitudes he expressed in his Oxford letters appeared a new appreciation for the nation's armed forces, which had played an indispensable role in ridding the world of fascism. The clearest sign of this shift came on June 18, 1945, when the city of Washington held a parade to welcome home the commander of allied forces in Europe, Dwight D. Eisenhower. Of that memorable day, Larson later wrote:

> I was still working in Washington in the Foreign Economic Administration when General Eisenhower made his triumphal return from Europe. There was a big parade, and all government employees were turned loose for the occasion. I had managed to get myself a splendid vantage-point in the front row of the crowd at 14th and Constitution, where the cavalcade was to turn. As Eisenhower passed by me, in the back of an open car, I swear he looked

> right into my eyes and gave me a particularly dazzling version of the famous smile. I did not fully understand it at the time, but from then on I was a dedicated "Eisenhower man."[88]

Larson was so excited by this chance encounter that he rushed to his car after the parade ended and listened on the radio as Eisenhower addressed a joint session of Congress. This 20-minute speech, which recounted the Allied war effort since 1941, was noteworthy mostly for the evenhanded way Eisenhower acknowledged the contributions of all the key participants, including the late Franklin Roosevelt and the Soviet army and that country's people and their leaders. Like the face-to-face encounter earlier in the day, this speech had a great impact on Larson, cementing a lasting, highly favorable impression in his mind. As he later explained,

> It seemed to me that he [Eisenhower] made much better sense than anybody I had heard talk about public affairs for many, many years. Everything he said was right on the button, so far as I was concerned. So, there was a sort of a one-two punch: first the personal one and then the intellectual one. And I suddenly realized that deep in my heart somewhere I guess I made up my mind that if this man ever did run for President, I was going to be all for him.[89]

Larson's thinking on other important subjects had changed significantly by the end of World War II. As he grew into his middle thirties, Larson's views on religion increasingly moved away from the tenets of the Lutheran Church toward a nondenominational Protestantism. Contact with people and ideas outside the tightly knit Lutheran community of Sioux Falls seems to have been the key factor here. While he and Florence continued to attend church, they never found one that formed the center of their social world as First Lutheran in Sioux Falls had for his parents. The closest such experience appears to have been the small church he and Florence belonged to in Milwaukee. They had become very active there and were friends with the minister and his wife, John and Della Cyrus, but even this tended to move Larson away from his Lutheran roots, thanks to John Cyrus's unorthodox views on matters of theology. The other company Larson kept, which consisted mostly of young lawyers, artists, and theater people, also seems to have had a secularizing effect.[90]

The change in Larson's thinking about religion appeared clearly in a letter he wrote to Florence during September 1943 while visiting with the Cyruses at their new home in Arizona. Reading William James's *The Varieties of Religious Experience* and discussing theology with John Cyrus pushed Larson to decide what he actually had come to believe, which, he explained to Florence, "is about as far from Lutheranism or any other denominational creed as anything could be. . . . He [John] does not believe in the 'virgin birth' of Jesus, nor in the physical resurrection of the body. Well, when it comes to the showdown, it occurred to me that I had never believed any such ideas myself, and didn't see why anybody else should."[91] He continued to believe in God, as he would for the rest of his life, but in a steadily less formal and ever more individual way.[92]

That shift appears to have gone along with, and encouraged, a change in his values. In place of the morally traditional outlook he had acquired while growing up came a somewhat more relaxed attitude. Still very much what today one would call a square, Larson in the decade after returning from England became a less extreme, more tolerant version of that sort of person.

The clearest sign of that change could be seen in the way his views about alcohol evolved in the decade after he returned from England. Larson's earlier dismissive attitude, which had grown out of the drunkenness he saw at the University of South Dakota, at Oxford, and in the London pubs, had clearly eased by the mid-1940s. In part this had to do, one suspects, with the way in which the demise of Prohibition in 1933 altered the context in which Larson encountered drinking. Alcoholic beverages had once again become customary at many kinds of social events, and this was especially true for the elite Protestant social circles in which he and Florence mostly moved. This change, and contact with a peer group whose members tended to be less morally traditional than the Lutheran community Larson had known as a youth, moved him toward an appreciation for the pleasures of alcohol. Larson wrote Florence that "as soon as I arrived [at the Cyrus home], John and I had several beers, then I bought a bottle of rum, and John bought a bottle of bourbon. That afternoon we had long bacardis and Della was waltzing about as of old. A little later we switched to whiskey. We're off to quite a start."[93] This apparently sounded like too much of a good thing to Florence, who gently cautioned Larson in her next letter to "remember 'in the bottom of the whiskey glass lies the ruin of man.'"[94] All the indications are that he heeded her caution. Rather than moving from one extreme to the other, Larson settled instead for a middle position on drinking.[95]

The passage of time, changing social conditions, and a new peer group appear to have had a similarly loosening effect on Larson's thinking about partisan politics. Like so many Party of Lincoln Republicans, Larson had a difficult time identifying strongly with the national GOP during the 1930s and early 1940s, most of whose leaders, in Congress especially, took strongly anti–New Deal stands. His own response to Roosevelt's policies consisted of qualified support rather than sweeping condemnation. The most telling indication of Larson's distance from the dominant faction in the Republican Party was his voting record. Although Larson continued to think of himself of a Republican, he never bothered to register as one during FDR's presidency. In so doing, he became part of a larger national phenomenon, in which many moderate and liberal Republicans who had admired such former GOP presidents as Lincoln and Theodore Roosevelt dropped out of the party's primaries. Larson noted the uncertainty he felt in this area and others in a letter to Florence: "There are very few things about which I am sure. I am not sure what I believe about politics, or about religion, or about how to bring up children, or about what we are fighting for—or about any of the myriad other things on which many people seem to be completely satisfied with their opinions."[96]

Helping to steady him during this time of doubt was the love he felt for Florence, which had only grown stronger during their first eight years of married life. He made that clear in that same letter's next passage: "But I know I love you. And I know that nothing is more important than that. Not even religion."[97] His letters to her during the war years were filled with such sentiments, as were hers to him. The periods of separation produced by his business trips and her occasional visits home to South Dakota stimulated the expression of even more such thoughts. These letters leave no doubt that for both of them, their love and marriage constituted the foundation on which the rest of their lives was built.[98]

Their remarkably strong and successful marriage resulted in part from similar backgrounds, intellects, tastes, and interests, but there were other factors at work as well. One had to do with Florence's willingness to put his career above her own in making decisions about where they would live. When Larson began looking for a new job so that he could leave the OPA and explained in a letter that he would try for places where she, too, could pursue her career in theater, Florence made her views about this issue very plain:

> I just want to say one thing. You must consider your position first, and mine second. It would put too much responsibility on me if you did otherwise. I have the children, you know. I still think we can make some change which will give me a chance to work part time, and you a chance to do what you want most. I like the idea of living in L.A. for the babies. For myself, I like N.Y. best, but I am not sure that I want to be that selfish.[99]

Her response spoke volumes about the particular circumstances educated women of her generation faced and her own characteristically midwestern focus on marriage and family life. The economic conditions of the 1930s had greatly narrowed opportunities for secure, full-time jobs in the theater, which were hard to find even in more prosperous years. Such jobs ordinarily paid far less than the ones Arthur Larson held, which tended to tilt Florence's priorities in the direction she expressed above. The movement among employers toward job rationing during the worst years of the 1930s raised yet another obstacle for married women whose husbands still had work and made this kind of calculation all the more persuasive. This was especially true for younger women with professional aspirations such as Florence who first tried to enter the paid labor force in those same years. The only real job she managed to find was in Milwaukee with the WPA's Federal Theatre Project, which conservatives in Congress had voted out of existence two months before she and Larson left for Knoxville. And although a period of acute labor shortage soon arose after the United States formally entered World War II, by that point they had two small children of preschool age and no nearby relatives or quality day care program to help raise them. All of these considerations inclined Florence toward the conclusions she expressed in her letter. So, too, did her midwestern background, which had imbued her with a family-centered set of priorities, and a very healthy marriage, which suggested that she could rely on it to sustain her over the long term.[100]

Other factors, too, accounted for the success of that marriage, including Florence's traditionally feminine demeanor and social graces. Larson expressed his appreciation for them explicitly in another letter written in the summer of 1943 that praised what he called her "feminine graces and manners that make girls attractive as girls . . . the things which you have in such super-abundance. How to walk, to sit, to eat, to move your hands, to dress,—how to do all the little things in a graceful, delicate way."[101] Florence, for her part, seems to have been equally appreciative of his intelligent, sensitive nature, ease with words, commitment to children and home life, and genuine interest in art and music. And while his thinking here seems more old-fashioned and elitist than hers, there is no doubt that the bond between them was truly reciprocal.[102]

One other factor that strengthened that bond had to do with its physical side. They shared a deeply passionate love life, which the separations caused by his business trips seems only to have intensified. During one of Larson's business trips in June 1943, he wrote a twelve-page, handwritten letter to her about the joys of their lovemaking. Florence enjoyed the letter so much that she sometimes carried it about with her when he was away. This particular episode captures the dual nature of their attitudes toward sex as something that was central to their married life but was not publicly discussed.[103]

Florence's importance to his life emerged most clearly when she left Washington to visit relatives, leaving him on his own there. He found little to do during such periods except go to work and engage in light exercise such as cycling and swimming at the local YMCA. Larson went through these days "in a kind of trance," as he once described it in a letter to her.[104] His heavy dependence on her for companionship was intensified by the nature of life in wartime Washington, where most of the people he knew worked long hours in government offices and getting around the city often proved difficult due to its overcrowded buses.[105]

Larson had few fond memories of his four years in Washington during the first half of the 1940s, thanks to the city's wartime shortages, congested system of mass transit, and hot, humid, climate. Even more annoying were the area's housing shortage and high rents that, like the overcrowded system of mass transit, had resulted from Washington's rapid growth during the 1930s and early 1940s. D.C.'s metropolitan area grew from 601,000 in 1930 to over 1 million by 1941 and expanded by another 70,000 the following year. The huge influx of newcomers who filled New Deal and then wartime agencies transformed the nation's capital from an overgrown southern town into a real city for the first time, but one whose infrastructure failed to keep pace with that rapid growth.[106]

He and Florence felt that problem most directly with respect to the matter of housing. While looking for a place to rent in the fall of 1941 they could find nothing affordable in the district itself and settled instead for a less convenient house in northern Virginia. Far from desirable, given its location near railroad tracks, sooty air, unpleasant odors, and disagreeable owner, it nonetheless cost what was then the considerable sum of $80 a month. So unpleasant was their living arrangement that toward the end of 1943 they moved to another home in nearby Arlington. Living in Washington proved to be so expensive that they exhausted their savings during their first two years there and spent the next two living paycheck to paycheck on an income of about $5,500 a year.[107]

Larson's persistent back problems made life even more difficult for him. The pains came and went seemingly without rhyme or reason. The only certainty was that vigorous physical exercise could aggravate his condition, which dissuaded Larson from doing much swimming or anything that required him to bend over. So serious had the pain become in late 1941 that Larson underwent a third spinal operation at Johns Hopkins Hospital that December, but it did not end his troubles. The surgeon, who had also performed his previous operation, had nothing to suggest except still more surgery, but Larson balked at that advice. The failure of three back operations over the course of as many years to cure his problem had made him much more doubtful about the value of that approach. He experimented with various forms of exercise and a climate change by spending about four weeks in the southwest in the late summer of 1943, but none of these things improved his condition. Larson summarized it this way in a letter to his surgeon written the following April:

> I have reached the point where I can walk eight or ten blocks without developing sharp pains, although I still have my ups and downs from day to day. However, I am considerably encouraged by the fact that I have not had a severe recurrence—that is, one which keeps me in bed for a week or so—since last July. This is the first time in seven years that I have gone for over six months without such a recurrence.[108]

An army doctor confirmed the debilitating effects of Larson's back problems that same spring, when he had a pre-induction physical examination. Larson had tried to avoid what he later called this "humiliating experience," but the local draft board, eager for able-bodied men, had insisted.[109] The examining physician concluded that Larson was unfit for service, which clearly indicated that his back troubles remained serious even after five years of medical treatment.[110]

In addition to the discomfort he sometimes suffered, Larson's condition interfered with his search for a new job. Between his heavy duties at OPA and FEA and his back pains, Larson found that he simply did not have the strength to look hard for postwar work. By the time the Japanese government announced its intention to surrender on August 14, 1945, he had only one firm offer, which came from an eccentric lumberman named Julius Stulman. A highly successful businessman and devotee of nonmaterialist philosophy, Stulman had taken a liking to Larson when they met during one of his OPA business trips out west. Stulman explained that he planned to establish an export-import firm based in New York that would deal with European countries and Italy in particular as the expected postwar economic revival took hold there. He asked Larson to help manage this enterprise and Larson agreed. Leaving Florence and their two children behind in Washington at first, he moved to New York and began working out of an office in Trinity Square.[111]

But even as the orders began to come in, Larson's doubts about the wisdom of this course grew. He had never thought of himself as cut out for the business world, and this feeling grew inside him until he began to feel that he was making a serious mistake. His anxiety grew so great that it produced actual physical symptoms:

> I felt as though I were playing a part, as though none of this were real. Something deep inside me was certain that I was making the wrong decision, and it expressed itself in a disconcertingly tangible way. Although I had never had any eye trouble or even worn glasses, I was hit by a severe case of diplopia—double vision—which sometimes attends cases of *folie de doute* such as mine.[112]

At this critical juncture, fate intervened in the form of a query from Robert Stevens, the dean of the Cornell Law School, who had been impressed by Larson's application for a job there six years earlier and now had one to offer. One short visit to the university's campus early in the fall of 1945 proved enough to change Larson's mind and the direction of the rest of his professional life. He promptly submitted his resignation from the export-import job, which Stulman amicably accepted, and returned to the life of a law professor that so obviously suited him. With that decision, Larson's ten-year search for the right kind of career and place in which to pursue it finally and successfully came to an end.[113]

CHAPTER FOUR

Legal Scholar

LARSON'S ARRIVAL AT CORNELL in the fall of 1945 signaled the start of a distinctly different phase of his life, both personally and professionally. After a decade of moving about, he and his family settled into a much more stable existence. For the next eight years they would call the area around Ithaca, New York, where Cornell was located their home. One key reason for this new stability had to do with his and Florence's concern that their two young children be properly brought up. In the fall the Larsons moved to Ithaca, Lex turned six and began first grade and Anna turned five and started kindergarten. So concerned were Arthur and Florence that their children get off on the right foot in school that Lex and Anna and the family housekeeper, Mrs. Hamer, joined him in Ithaca even before Florence arrived there. Having accepted a teaching job in the Speech and Drama Department of George Washington University for the fall term of 1945 before Larson got the offer from Cornell, Florence felt obliged to remain in Washington until the following January. Larson took upon himself such tasks as finding a house to rent, enrolling the children in the local public school, and looking after them over the next few months when they came home each day.[1]

His willingness to do this stemmed both from his sense of responsibility to Florence and their children and from what appears to have been a genuine enthusiasm for domestic life. Unlike many highly educated professional men of that time, Larson seems clearly to have enjoyed domestic duties as well as his career. His letters to Florence during this period revealed his enthusiasm for fixing up and furnishing the old house he rented that first year and for spending time with Lex and Anna. The letters also made clear how very much he missed her. He soon began sending out inquiries to the Speech and Drama Departments at

Cornell and nearby Ithaca College about possible openings for Florence. When she arrived and eventually found a position teaching drama at the latter, their new situation seemed complete.[2]

Not everything about it was ideal, however. Cornell suffered in those days, like so many American universities, from too many students and not enough money. Returning veterans brought a big, albeit temporary, bulge in enrollment, causing overcrowded classes and a shortage of affordable student housing. At the same time, university budgets remained tight as Cornell dealt with expenses deferred during the difficult years of the Great Depression and World War II. By Larson's third year at Cornell, the university's $8 million budget was almost $1 million in the red. During the 1948–1949 academic year, acting president Cornelis W. de Kiewiet slashed spending by over $800,000, inaugurating a lean period in Cornell's history that lasted through the mid-1950s.[3]

For Larson, however, life was fairly sweet. His law school salary of approximately $7,000, when combined with income from various writing projects and Florence's annual pay from Ithaca College, netted them about $8,500 per year before taxes. Though not princely, this sum supported them and their two children quite comfortably. Robert Stevens helped out, too, by inviting Larson to co-author a casebook on corporations for students, which added to his income.[4]

Stevens had first been appointed dean of Cornell's law school in 1937, and his fondness for Larson helped smooth his way. Although Stevens had been born in 1888 and thus was old enough to be Larson's father, the two men had things in common. Stevens came from a family with deep roots in western New York State, an area that possessed much the same midwestern quality as Larson's native South Dakota. Like Larson, Stevens had spent part of his boyhood in Washington, D.C., where his family had acquired a house during his grandfather's service in Congress. While living there, Stevens had formed part of a lively circle of friends in Washington whose members included Theodore Roosevelt, Jr., and his younger brother Kermit, which exposed Stevens to the same kind of Republican outlook Larson had received from his parents. Stevens had also been part of the illustrious Harvard Class of 1910, which included such notables as T. S. Eliot, Walter Lippmann, and John Reed. Studying at Harvard then had given Stevens an educational experience similar in many ways to the one Larson acquired at Oxford. Stevens's published work, mostly on the subject of corporations, consistently advocated a "realistic" approach in dealing with the legal problems they created, much like Larson's intellectual approach to matters of law and public policy in general. Although Stevens, unlike Larson, had spent most of his adult life as a law professor and dean, he also served in the Lend-Lease and Foreign Economic Administrations during World War II. These similarities in experience and outlook helped establish a close working relationship and provided Larson with a valuable mentor.[5]

The Cornell Law School also helped Larson blossom as a scholar. With its imposing Gothic building, distinguished faculty, light teaching loads, and fine library, Cornell seemed an entirely different academic world from the one he had known at the University of Tennessee. Larson commented on the contrast in a letter to Florence shortly after he arrived in Ithaca: "There is a very tangible atmosphere of high-powered, high-standard activity. These guys are as different from the Tennessee faculty as night is from day."[6]

This happy and supportive environment helped make possible an extraordinarily productive period in Larson's professional life. Over the eight years after he arrived at Cornell Law School, he and Stevens co-authored a casebook on corporation law and Larson published five scholarly articles and a two-volume treatise on the law of workers' compensation. Of these, the last took by far the most time and effort and was the most significant as a work of scholarship. Writing the treatise on workers' compensation quite literally dominated Larson's professional life at Cornell. This work also had by far the greatest effect on the subsequent course of his career. For all of these reasons, the story of Larson's treatise stands at the center of this chapter in his life.[7]

Larson had not planned to write a book about workers' compensation law when he first joined the Cornell faculty. His decision to write it grew out of a more general belief that to make one's mark in academic life, or other fields for that matter, one needed to do something truly significant by age 40. Thirty-five years old when he arrived in Ithaca, Larson concluded that he needed to produce an authoritative book on some area of law over the next five years. At first he considered writing about business organizations, but when he discovered that the field of workers' compensation law lacked an authoritative treatise, he chose that subject instead. His experience with workers' compensation cases while at Quarles, Spence and Quarles and the article he wrote about that subject during his time at Tennessee Law School evidently persuaded Larson that he would have an edge in the workers' compensation area. He set to work on what he hoped would make his name in the world of legal scholarship.[8]

Arthur Larson chose a good time to write a treatise on the subject of workers' compensation. By the late 1940s, state legislatures had been experimenting with the administration of work-related injuries for a generation. A workers' compensation statute had gone into effect in every state, and courts and commissions across the country had worked over this area of the law extensively. A body of settled law, though still very much in the making, had begun to emerge. Serious problems still remained, however, in working out the basic rules of statutory interpretation. These problems stemmed mostly from uncertainty over the extent to which state workers' compensation statutes superseded preexisting tort law in this area. The result was a huge number of conflicting and confusing court decisions that poured out from every state each year by the late 1940s.[9]

This situation was exactly the sort that cried out for guidance by disinterested legal experts. And, in fact, there had been a few earlier efforts by legal academics during the 1930s and early 1940s to produce textual guides. The most notable of these was Samuel Horovitz's 1944 *Injury and Death Under Workmen's Compensation Laws.* The problems with Horovitz's book had to do with its intended audience (he wrote primarily for law students, not judges), its unabashed advocacy of the statutory approach, and, most important, its sharp and persistent criticism of the judiciary's tendency to take a backward-looking approach when interpreting workers' compensation acts. Horovitz wrote in the book's preface: "True neutrality in workmen's compensation is a myth. . . . The neutral is usually the vacillating individual who gives and takes, trying to satisfy both sides, and creating only enmity or confusion."[10] Not surprisingly, Horovitz's treatise received a cool reception from most judges. Thus, when Larson began working on a treatise of his own, the need for such a book—and the opportunity to make a name for himself by writing one—remained very real.[11]

Larson also had a model on which to draw, Robert Stevens's highly successful 1936 *Handbook on the Law of Private Corporations.* This text took a practical approach to its subject, rejecting the earlier tendency to accept uncritically the legal fiction that a corporation was equivalent to a person. "Stevens on Corporations," as it was popularly known, won praise not only for explaining the law as it was but also for expressing its author's cogent views of what the law ought to be.[12]

Despite these advantages, there was still the very big problem of coping with the ongoing river of reported appellate decisions, then running at a rate of about 2,000 per year, which had no doubt deterred other scholars from attempting to create a workers' compensation treatise, and the need to be very thorough, which made shortcuts impossible. In order for a legal treatise to succeed, lawyers and judges, who would be the basic market for such a work, needed to feel certain that it addressed the subject in a truly comprehensive fashion. Only then would they consider it reliable enough to be worth buying and using. Larson explained these pressures in a letter to Florence written shortly after he began teaching at Cornell:

> The standards of precision and thoroughness which legal writing requires are very demanding and consume a surprising amount of time. In many other fields, like speech, for example, you can sit down and write what you think, and if your ideas are good, your book is good. . . . But in law the task is double: you have to have the ideas, true; but you also have to build upon an unassailable foundation of decided case law and statutes. You may not agree with the cases and statutes, but you cannot ignore them. They must be accounted for somehow.[13]

The amount of work required to write a treatise on workers' compensation law must have seemed to many to be beyond the strength of any one person. Larson, however, decided to try. The regimen he imposed on himself while researching and writing the book was astonishingly severe. As he later recalled,

> I resigned from clubs, refused to serve on committees, declined almost all social invitations, gave no speeches, attended no conventions, conferences or symposia. . . . I worked day and night, weekends and holidays . . . for five years. To avoid burning out, I had a rigid cut-off point at night-just in time to hear Eric Sevareid's nightly news summary and commentary at eleven.
>
> No secretary. No research assistant. No Xerox. Only a battered Corona portable.[14]

A few serious setbacks along the way made that Herculean task even more daunting. Of these, lower back problems were the most significant. During Larson's third year at Cornell, the pain in his legs became so acute that he decided to undergo another round of surgery soon after spring semester classes ended. This time the doctor in question performed something called a "spinal fusion" in order to stabilize what he believed to be the source of the problem. After the procedure, which took place in New York City on June 1, 1948, Larson spent three and a half months in a body cast that stretched from his chin to his knees. Once it came off, Larson also had to contend with the bitter disappointment that this fourth operation had diminished his pain somewhat at first but had not cured him. Either too much exertion or too little could still bring back the shooting pains in his legs. For this he had spent so much money that he needed to sell the piece of property he had acquired in Maine for a summer home and accept a $4,000 loan from Florence's father in the fall of 1949 to help deal with the extra bills the surgery had brought. The untimely death of Larson's own father in 1950, before he had a chance to see the fruit of his son's labors, added still further to his woes.[15]

Refusing to give up, Larson pressed on with his work. While still in the body cast, he prepared an outline of his treatise based on the research already completed. Once out of the cast, Larson wrote steadily for the next few years and then hit another unexpected obstacle. He showed a draft of the manuscript to a representative of his publisher, Mathew Bender & Company, only to be told that it had to be longer than one volume, something the publisher had failed to mention when Larson first contracted with it. Even more maddening was the reason Bender's representative gave: lawyers did not trust one-volume works because they looked too much like law school texts. So Larson made it bigger and produced the requisite two-volume manuscript by the end of 1951. So jealously did he guard the manuscript, of which there was no duplicate, that when the time came to send it off to Mathew Bender in Albany, New York, Larson drove it there himself. He even slept with it at a motel during an overnight stop.[16]

After delivering his precious cargo, Larson faced one last challenge, which was to complete a table of all of the cases cited in his treatise. Although a customary feature in law books of all kinds, the very large number of precedents discussed in Larson's manuscript made his task unusually onerous. After filling and alphabetizing 5,000 index cards (with the help of Florence, Lex, and Anna), Larson realized that he would need approximately 10,000 more. Unable to buy them in London, where he had gone on sabbatical in January 1952, Larson hit upon the idea of using adhesive-backed paper divided like address labels instead.[17]

The published treatise arrived by mail at Larson's London apartment the following March. The memory remained vivid to him even when looking back many years later: "A heavy square package was delivered to our digs in Bayswater. I knew what it was, of course, but the suspense was still almost unbearable until I could get the wrappings off. There it was. My baby. A rich deep maroon, with gold lettering. Fine quality paper and elegant typography. This beautiful thing had arisen from my battered, scribbled-up mess of a manuscript. Life has few such moments."[18] Impressed by the treatise's weight, Larson put it on a bathroom scale and discovered that the two-volume set, some 1,593 pages in length, weighed just over twelve pounds. For this, the publisher had fixed a price of $40. All that remained by then was to see how the treatise fared in the marketplace of ideas.[19]

To Larson's pleasure, his great work met with immediate success, and judges began quoting it to support their rulings. Some judges explicitly followed interpretive suggestions Larson had made and even used his phraseology, which became part of the everyday legal vocabulary of workers' compensation rulings. In recognition of the treatise's importance, Harvard University bestowed on Larson its Henderson Prize for scholarship that contributed greatly to the administrative process. When viewed in retrospect, there is no question that Larson's creation was one of the most influential and successful legal treatises in American history.[20]

There are several reasons why Larson's treatise achieved those results. One is the fact that it met the need of lawyers, legislators, and judges for such a work. A second is that Larson's work, unlike Horovitz's, made no effort to vilify the earlier, and often very poor, judicial performance in interpreting the state statutes. Larson's treatise approached that situation as a consequence of a misunderstanding of the ultimate purpose those statutes were intended to serve rather than of malice or reactionary political commitments on the part of the judges involved.[21]

Larson first publicly explained his thinking on this key point in two special lectures on workers' compensation law that he delivered at the Cornell Law School on April 4 and 6, 1950. Having by then worked out the basic concepts on which his treatise would be based, Larson agreed to speak about them at the invitation of a former industrial commissioner in Massachusetts who wanted to encourage the study of workers' compensation in the nation's law schools. Larson's remarks reached a very wide audience because, as part of the arrangement, they were reprinted in the *Nacca Law Journal*, the periodical for experts in the workers' compensation field.[22]

Larson's first lecture, "The Welfare State and Workmen's Compensation," began by analyzing the character of the nation's existing array of social welfare laws. Larson started there in order to make clear that the various state workers' compensation statutes, rather than codifying older tort law in this area, formed instead a basic part of a truly new system of social security that had been emerging piecemeal in the United States since the second decade of the twentieth century. Although this might seem an obvious point to some, Larson contended that the incremental way in which the American welfare state had been created often led observers to miss the larger purpose served by the separate parts. He conceded that the United States had not yet adopted any form of public health insurance as the British had recently done but argued that such a scheme, whatever its merits, did not fit conceptually with America's existing social security laws. Such laws, Larson contended, were concerned fundamentally with the problem of lost income.[23]

Larson then explained what he saw as the underlying model of social organization on which the nation's social security laws had been based. In his view, that model was what today we would call the traditional or patriarchal family structure, in which a male acted as head of a household that included him, his wife, and his children and he alone earned the income needed to support them all. Larson made that point very explicitly: "The true social security system, based as it is on the theory of offsetting wage loss, centers entirely upon the wage-earner, the breadwinner. The underlying philosophy is not that the breadwinner's bills will be paid for him when they hit him too hard; it is that if he is protected against too severe inroads into his normal earnings he can take care of his own bills."[24]

In expressing these thoughts, which will no doubt strike many readers today as jarringly old-fashioned in their assumptions about gender roles and family structure, one can see the influence not only of Larson's research into the purposes social insurance laws had been intended to serve but also the changes in American life they had encouraged. Like the states' workers' compensation laws, the Social Security Act of 1935 and such other New Deal measures as the National Labor Relations Act of 1935 and the Fair Labor Standards Act of 1938, the much broader system of federal income taxation created during World War II, and the Servicemen's Readjustment Act of 1944 (popularly known as the G.I. Bill) had tended to encourage the formation of just the sort of families that Larson described. By 1950, when he gave his lecture, the ever-increasing number of families organized along those lines doubtless suggested to him, as it did to so many others then, that this model of social organization was both "normal" and destined to become something close to universal. Larson's receptivity to thinking in such terms probably also grew out of the household and community in which he grew up, which fit that description.[25]

These assumptions about gender roles and family structure could be seen most clearly in the name lawmakers had given to the state statutes dealing with workers' compensation and, consequently, the title Larson gave to his treatise. Even though these laws covered categories of employment rather than specific groups of people, legislators chose to call the laws "workmen's compensation acts." This nomenclature no doubt reflected, in part at least, the heavy preponderance of men in the job categories affected when legislatures first passed such laws during the second decade of the twentieth century. The persistence of such terminology over the next three decades even as women's participation in the paid labor force grew suggests, however, that the assumptions about gender roles and family structure Larson described also were involved. His decision to call his new treatise *The Law of Workmen's Compensation* showed just how deeply entrenched this terminology, and the assumptions that lay behind it, had become since the industrial revolution.[26]

Although later generations would find problems with the model of social organization Larson outlined to his audience, his matter-of-fact approach served at that time to bring order out of the confusion in workers' compensation law. Lawyers and judges alike had become confused, he argued, mostly because they thought of such statutes as having codified, with an important change, the preexisting tort law in this area rather than having made entirely new law. According to this view, the workmen's compensation laws had amended, not replaced, older tort law and made workplace accidents into a "strict-liability tort." The concept of strict liability, as used elsewhere in tort law, imposed responsibility on the manufacturers of defective products that harmed consumers even when the manufacturers acted carefully in producing the commodities in question. Judges had applied that idea in interpreting the workmen's compensation laws, and the result, Larson argued, was needless confusion.[27]

To prove his point, Larson explained that there were at least six basic differences between the nature of liability in workmen's compensation law and liability in tort. The most important of these had to do with the basic test of liability. Under the workmen's compensation laws, an employer was liable if the employee's injury was work related. Issues of fault on the part of either party, so central to tort law, in this area were entirely irrelevant. Aware that some of his listeners might be bothered by the notion of liability without a showing of fault, especially when it was the employee, rather than his or her boss, who had acted carelessly, Larson discussed the underlying social philosophy at work. In a passage that echoed his earlier workers' compensation article for the *Tennessee Law Review*, he explained that "to require the innocent employer to pay the 'guilty' employee might seem to flout the entire moral basis of law. In an entirely individualistic moral code, this might be so, but let us see what happens when considerations of social morality are introduced."[28]

Larson observed that society had three basic options with respect to the disabled. It could refuse aid and reduce them to the status of beggars, it could extend a government handout in the stigmatizing form of means-tested relief payments, or it could grant workmen's compensation, which avoided the humiliation of the means test and placed the cost of the injury on the consumers of the product whose manufacture caused the harm. He endorsed the third, arguing that it was the only morally satisfactory solution to the problem of the injured worker.[29]

And lest his listeners miss the point he was making about the most basic difference between strict liability in tort and workmens' compensation, Larson pointed out that the issue of fault mattered even in strict liability tort because in some instances one could escape liability by showing that another had been responsible for the harm done. The existence of these defenses demonstrated, Larson argued, that the doctrine of strict liability in tort had not eliminated considerations of fault entirely, as workmens' compensation had.[30]

Larson buttressed those key points by discussing four more reasons why workmen's compensation should not be viewed as a strict liability tort. First, he noted that in workmen's compensation, unlike tort, the only injuries compensated were those that produced disability and thus presumably diminished earning power. Second, he observed that workmen's compensation, unlike tort, did not try to compensate the injured worker for all of his lost income but only enough of it to allow him or her to live decently. Third, Larson pointed out that workmen's compensation payments stopped when a recipient died, unlike tort damages, to which the recipient's heirs might be able to lay a claim. Fourth, Larson noted that in workmen's compensation, the employer could pass the cost of such payments on to others in the form of higher prices for the product made by the enterprise in question. This stood in marked contrast to tort damages, which typically were borne solely by the party required to pay them. Larson summarized that last key difference in this way: "Tort litigation is an adversary contest to right a wrong between the contestants; Workmen's Compensation is a system, not a contest, to supply security to injured workers and distribute the cost among consumers of the product."[31]

Larson closed his first lecture by cautioning his listeners not to fall into the trap of assuming that the American system of workmen's compensation operated in exactly the same way as social insurance schemes did in the European countries that had pioneered them. In what would become a characteristic intellectual move, Larson argued that workmen's compensation in the United States had emerged as something that was neither entirely private (the old tort law approach) nor public (as in Western Europe and the British Commonwealth nations) but rather was something in between. In reaching that conclusion, Larson emphasized that the critical element had to do with how such systems were financed: "In the American [workmen's compensation system] it is typically premiums paid by the employer only and passed on to a particular consuming group; in the British it is 'premiums' paid equally by the employer and the employee, with a small addition by the government; in New Zealand it is general taxes."[32]

Larson also argued that in two key ways—the relationship of hazard to liability and the measure of benefits awarded—the American system of workmen's compensation occupied a middle position between tort and social insurance in the European sense. He noted that while the issue of fault had been eliminated under the American system, the system still placed responsibility for lost earnings on the industry in which the injured party worked and ultimately on those who consumed its products. In Western Europe and the Commonwealth countries, by contrast, employers in general or the tax-paying public assumed that responsibility.[33]

Larson argued in a similar vein that while the American system of workmen's compensation had clearly broken with older tort law with respect to how much compensation the worker should receive, the system fell far short of being a genuine relief system based purely on need: "In New Zealand, as well as in England, the size of benefits has nothing to do with previous earnings. It is fundamentally uniform for everyone, varying only according to the number of dependents. The typical American compensation act relates the award to the claimant's previous average weekly wage, within fixed minimum and maximum limits."[34] The American approach to determining compensation did, of course, rest upon a belief that an injured worker's need and previous average income were related, but that was not the same thing, Larson concluded, as using an actual means test to determine how much he or she should receive.[35]

Larson elaborated on how American lawyers and judges had become so confused about the nature of the nation's workmen's compensation system in his second lecture, which he entitled "The Future of Workmen's Compensation." Although most of his remarks dealt with ways to improve and expand the system, in the course of discussing needed changes he made one important point about how the drafting of the first workmen's compensation statutes had unwittingly encouraged judges to interpret them as codifications and amendments of preexisting tort law rather than as a wholly new departure from it. The early statutes, like the British act of 1897 on which they were based, all contained the phrase "arising out of and in the course of employment" to describe the injuries for which the new system would compensate. Lawmakers had drawn this key phrase from the area of tort law that dealt with an employer's liability for the wrongful acts of his or her employees. The problem with using this phrase in workmen's compensation statutes, Larson explained, was that it provided narrower grounds for compensation than the framers of the law had intended, because workers were sometimes injured as a consequence of work but not literally during it. Larson noted that some of the more recent workmen's compensation statutes had addressed this problem and praised in particular the wording of the 1945 Wyoming law that granted compensation for injuries "sustained as a result of employment." Even so, he added, the inclusion of the older, tort-derived language in the earliest compensation acts had led to great and continuing confusion, given the central role played by precedent in the American legal system.[36]

Even the way workmen's compensation was usually taught in the nation's law schools, Larson argued in an article published two years later, contributed to this mess. Following the confusing wording of the statutes and their erroneous interpretation by the courts, law schools typically dealt with workmen's compensation laws in the course on torts rather than recognizing the subject and other fields of social insurance law as different enough to deserve a separate course.[37]

Larson incorporated the material from his two Cornell lectures and this article into the first two chapters of his treatise and added a much more extensive discussion of the history of workers' compensation in the major industrial countries. So significant did Larson believe all of this material to be that he also published it separately as a law review article entitled "The Nature and Origins of Workmen's Compensation." The expanded historical discussion it contained shed still more light on how the United States had developed its unusual workers' compensation system and why courts had experienced so much difficulty in interpreting the laws that created it.[38]

Larson explained that Germany had invented the first modern workmen's compensation system during the mid-1880s and in so doing created an influential model for all subsequent forms of social insurance. The distinctive aspect of the German system had to do with its financing scheme, which included worker as well as employer contributions. Germany's long-standing and highly developed system of guilds helped make this possible by providing the mechanisms needed to collect worker and employer contributions and elect the representatives who managed the system. It quickly attracted favorable attention from other major industrial countries, including Britain and the United States. In 1897, the British Parliament enacted the first workmen's compensation law there, modeled to a large degree on the German one. When American state legislatures began working on this issue during the first decade of the twentieth century, they looked to those earlier examples, the German one especially, to guide them.[39]

Problems developed, however, when the state legislatures tried to replicate continental models, mostly because of the greater conservatism of the United States, especially its judiciary, when compared with Germany. At the same time that American state lawmakers were becoming interested in creating workmen's compensation systems, the federal and state courts were establishing sharp limits on what legislatures could do in this area. The courts struck down early and limited workmen's compensation laws in Maryland and Montana and the much broader New York workmen's compensation act of 1910 on the grounds that they violated state and federal constitutional provisions against taking property without due process of law. This judicial resistance led legislatures to craft workmen's compensation laws in the United States that were more awkward and fragmentary than their German and British predecessors on the theory that the weakness and incompleteness of such laws might ensure their constitutionality.[40]

Another important consequence of the more conservative American economic and political milieu and the related problem of judicial resistance to social insurance schemes, though not one that Larson stressed, had to do with how the state legislatures approached the issue of financing worker compensation systems. The United States had nothing like the German guilds, which would have facilitated employee contributions to those systems. There were, to be sure, some American labor unions that could have played such a role, but the courts were sufficiently hostile to the American labor movement as to make that kind of approach legally very questionable. And even if the practical problem of establishing a mechanism to collect employee contributions could have been surmounted, the judiciary would likely have found any such system unconstitutional on the grounds that it violated workers' "liberty of contract" as protected by the due process clause of the Fifth and Fourteenth Amendments. The U.S. Supreme Court's 1905 decision in *Lochner v. New York* had, in essence, given constitutional protection to the economic theory of laissez-faire, which posited that the employer and worker stood in equal relation to each other when establishing the terms of the employment contract between them, with which, therefore, the government ought not to interfere. This ruling, so at odds with the realities of the modern industrial economy, nonetheless stood for the next thirty-two years. It was during those years that most of the states enacted their workmen's compensation laws.[41]

Faced with this very serious legal obstacle, state legislatures chose to finance their compensation systems in a way that diverged significantly from the German practice. In the United States, workers' compensation emerged in principle and in practice as a unilateral system in which the employer assumed all of the costs and presumably passed them along to consumers in the form of higher prices. Lawmakers sought to make this approach palatable to the courts (and employers) by recognizing employers' equally unilateral right to control the workplace. If employers enjoyed that kind of undisputed authority, so the logic went, the responsibility for—and the cost of compensating for—workplace injuries rightly belonged on their shoulders alone.[42]

Although this approach proved successful in the sense that the courts upheld the constitutionality of workmen's compensation acts consistently beginning in 1917, funding the system through employer contributions alone made the American system much more problematic for employers and the courts than the German one. The reason for this was fairly simple, although Larson, interestingly, did not mention it. If workers contributed to the cost of the compensation system, they would acquire a strong disincentive to file excessive or fraudulent claims. A system financed by employer contributions only, on the other hand, lacked that sort of built-in brake on unreasonable worker demands for compensation. The specter of excessive and fraudulent worker claims that inflated product prices and possibly even drove employers out of business was most likely another important reason why judges resorted so often to irrelevant tort law doctrines to restrict workers' right to compensation and thereby made such a tangled mess of workers' compensation law. And lest this concern seem one-sided on the judges' part, one should keep in mind that if excessive and fraudulent claims were made, the resulting inflation and business failures would harm workers as well as employers.[43]

It is unclear whether Larson missed this issue or simply chose not to discuss it in his treatise. He tended to avoid controversial topics when the passage of time and the advent of new social conditions appeared to have rendered such controversies moot. The decision to avoid discussing the danger of excessive and fraudulent demands for compensation would have appeared much more sensible during the time when Larson researched and wrote his treatise, because the demise of the Lochner model and advent of the New Deal had substantially changed the context in which workers operated and, as a direct result, significantly reduced the likelihood of this problem. As American unions grew larger and more powerful during the 1940s and early 1950s, worker alienation and misconduct had declined, thanks to the improved wages and working conditions, a greater feeling of participation that unionization brought, and the help unions gave to management in policing worker misbehavior.[44]

Larson acknowledged that the elimination of fault had created a legitimate need to establish boundaries to compensation, but he did not do so by using irrelevant tort law doctrines. Instead, Larson addressed that concern by offering clearer and more realistic definitions of such key phrases in workmen's compensation law as "arise out of employment" and "during course of employment." Even more important, he came up with entirely original wording to encompass important aspects of workmen's compensation law. In this way, he dealt directly and effectively with judicial concern that ignoring older tort law concepts completely would open the way to compensation in almost every conceivable situation. Larson approached the new system the state laws had created as a middle position or compromise between the extremes of the older tort law (which had led courts to deny damages in the overwhelming majority of cases) and the possibility that under the new statutory schemes they would allow an award to almost every claimant.[45]

All of these reasons for the treatise's success followed from a more general one: Larson's ability to provide clear bases in policy for every interpretation of the law he advocated. This ability grew out of at least three different attributes. First, he approached the field from a broad legal-historical perspective. Here one can see clearly the mark of his legal training at Oxford. Having spent most of his time there studying legal history and jurisprudence, he was well prepared to provide an explanation of workers' compensation law grounded in basic principles of public policy. Second, he demonstrated genuinely heartfelt sympathy for the injured workers the state workmen's compensation laws had been enacted to protect. This is where Larson's Depression-era background, especially his brush with unemployment while suffering from a disabling back injury, seem to have made a real difference. Such experiences gave him a greater understanding of the insecurity and poverty that loomed perpetually over the heads of so many workers. Understanding workers' point of view went a long way toward thinking (and writing) clearly about the policies that lay behind the various statutory provisions. A third attribute that helped Larson provide clear policy reasons for his interpretations of the law in this area was his effectiveness as a writer. The style of his treatise is almost literary, for which Larson's Oxford education once again deserves much credit. The writing throughout *The Law of Workmen's Compensation* is clear, strong, and at times positively charming.[46]

At least four other reasons contributed to the treatise's success. One had to do simply with the passage of time and the changes in the judiciary that accompanied the New Deal. Over the two decades before the publication of Larson's treatise, many of the judges who had tried to apply tort law doctrines when interpreting workers' compensation law had retired. Their successors, on the federal bench especially, tended to understand better the break with the past made by welfare state legislation and to view such laws in a much more sympathetic way.[47]

Another reason Larson's treatise enjoyed such extraordinary influence over judicial rulings was its perceptive grasp of those directions the law was moving in. At times the lines of innovation were fairly clear in the new case law. In those situations, Larson's contribution was simply to summarize them in accessible words and phrases. In other instances, however, those directions could only be discovered by a painstaking observation of similarities that led to an understanding of larger patterns. Larson's great gift was an ability to come up with new and appealing expressions that conveyed clearly the patterns of innovation that were emerging. Among the leading examples of this phenomenon were the phrases "positional risk," "neutral risk," "personal risk," "so-close rule," and "quantum theory," all of which he coined. These terms were vehicles that drew together accident situations that seemed at first unrelated or directed attention to fine distinctions that thus far had eluded those working in the field of workers' compensation law. In this respect, as in others, Larson's treatise was at once thoroughly scholarly and highly useful.[48]

One more specific reason for that success was the treatise's encyclopedic coverage. *The Law of Workmen's Compensation* cited all of the significant reported decisions in the field and in most instances provided some explanatory comments about them. Such comprehensiveness led Larson over the years to expand the treatise's size to keep up with new rulings. It eventually grew to eleven volumes, the regular revision of which kept several lawyers employed full time.[49]

If these were the specific reasons why Larson's treatise proved so successful, a more general one had to do his overall perspective on the body of law it described and the larger social context in which *The Law of Workmen's Compensation* first appeared. Larson presented the newer statutory approach to work-related injuries as a moderate and sensible response to the modern industrial age at a time when moderation was in fashion. The political and intellectual milieu of the 1950s, with its faith in objectivity and expertise as the best way to address important social problems, both informed Larson's analysis and contributed to its successful reception. That milieu also tended to reward academics such as Larson who wrote comprehensive textbooks much more than it did scholars who produced narrowly focused works.[50]

The full extent of those rewards in Larson's case began to become clear shortly after he returned from England in the summer of 1952. Publication of his treatise, he later recalled, opened all the doors to his subsequent professional advancement: "That one book changed my life more than anything else. Everything changed after that book came out. The first thing was I started getting lots of job offers."[51] As the invitations to apply for positions at other law schools began arriving, Larson followed up the ones he saw as the most attractive. By January 1953, he had received a formal offer to become dean of the University of Pittsburgh Law School at the end of the spring semester, which he accepted. He and Florence put their house near Ithaca up for sale and packed and moved the entire family once school ended for the summer, thereby putting an end to the eight years of stability they had known there.[52]

Larson's decision to leave Cornell for this new job seems, at first, more than a little puzzling. He and Florence liked Ithaca and had bought a beautiful home in the nearby suburb of Cayuga Heights overlooking one of the area's many scenic gorges. Their two children had done well in the local schools, with Lex slated to begin high school in the fall of 1953 and Anna one grade behind him. Larson had attained the respect of his Cornell colleagues, who had promoted him to full professor even before his treatise was published. He also enjoyed a close relationship with the law school's longtime dean, Robert Stevens. Florence had found a measure of professional satisfaction in Ithaca, too, through her teaching at Ithaca College. Why then, did he and she decide to trade all of this for a move to Pittsburgh, which in the early 1950s, though cleaner than it used to be, still suffered from the sooty smoke belched by nearby steel mills?[53]

The reason for this seemingly inexplicable choice had to do, his son later explained, with Arthur Larson's sense that becoming a dean was a step forward professionally, even if the new environment seemed less attractive. This kind of reasoning showed just how fiercely ambitious Larson was for professional success. Although outwardly a warm and gentle man, he possessed an inner drive of extraordinary intensity. Over the next few years, it would carry him far higher than even he could have imagined.[54]

CHAPTER FIVE

To the Eisenhower Administration

LARSON ULTIMATELY SPENT only nine months at Pittsburgh Law School, a time notable chiefly for the part it played in advancing him to a high-ranking position in the U.S. Department of Labor. His brief tenure as dean, which began on July 1, 1953, gave him the modicum of administrative experience needed for such an appointment. Even more important, he finished writing a manuscript about the American social insurance system that established him as an expert on that subject.[1]

This writing project grew out of Larson's discovery while researching his treatise that workers' compensation constituted the first building block in the American social insurance system. Intrigued by that idea, he decided to write something about that system as a whole. What made Larson's approach original was its comparative dimension. The sweeping changes in British social insurance policy instituted by the Labour government during the second half of the 1940s appear to have inspired him to learn more about them and thus put the more limited American system in clearer perspective. Larson received a Fulbright fellowship to support nine months of research in London from February through October 1952, and he used this time to become familiar with the details of the greatly expanded British social insurance system. The result of his labors emerged one year later as a 97-page typewritten manuscript entitled "The American System: Structure, Coverage and Current Issues."[2]

The manuscript's most interesting features were its frank discussion of the shortcomings and needed reforms in the American system, its explanation of the ways it differed from the British system, its views on current social insurance policy debates, its thoughts on how the federal system of government and the partly public, partly private nature of the American social insurance system ought to shape its design, and its final conclusions.

Larson readily acknowledged that an income insurance approach did not protect against poverty in all instances. He observed that public assistance, or relief payments, as they had earlier been known, supposedly filled the gaps created by this kind of approach and addressed the needs of those who had not had a chance to qualify for protection under the more recently created income insurance programs such as Social Security. In time, he explained, the growth of such programs would steadily reduce public assistance for this latter reason, "until it is finally confined to the irreduceable [*sic*] residue of situations not capable of insurance treatment."[3] He noted that recently, for the first time, total old-age public assistance payments had begun to decrease and fall below total payments for old-age pensions under the Social Security Act.[4]

In keeping with his assumption that public assistance would continue to decline, Larson focused most of his attention on the income insurance programs. According to his statistical analysis, over one-tenth of the U.S. population was experiencing income loss against which the social insurance system was supposed to guard: "On any given day, there are perhaps 20 million people within these categories: 13 million aged, 3 million widows and children, 3 million of working age disabled, and 1 million unemployed."[5] He noted that providing income security to the aged constituted by far the biggest social problem. Although some of the elderly, Larson acknowledged, had sufficient means to support themselves in old age, all of the reputable studies showed that "the great majority of those now receiving social security checks really need them."[6] This was even more true, he observed, for recipients who were not elderly.[7]

What was most striking about Larson's analysis was the compassion it revealed for the casualties of the American economic and political system. That sympathy emerged most clearly when Larson related a story he picked out of his local newspaper on August 8, 1953, which described the untimely death of a middle-aged couple. After the husband had lost his job due to illness and exhausted their savings on medical bills, the couple decided to live apart, he in the county poorhouse and she, apparently, with her daughter. So miserable did this make the couple that they soon shot themselves in their car along the shoulder of the Pennsylvania Turnpike, leaving only a brief note behind to explain the despair that lay behind their decision. Larson summed up the lesson afforded by this sad story:

> [Here] are most of the arguments for social insurance as against old-fashioned relief, for neither public relief, nor the help of friends, nor the theoretical availability of help from a married daughter, could avert this tragedy. Insurance benefits for non-occupational permanent disability, if they had existed, would have averted it. If we want to sense the scope of the social insurance problem as it really is, we shall have to combine the social worker's personal

> insight into individual human suffering with the economist's and actuary's grasp of the impact of payments of many billions of dollars to many millions of families over a long period of years to come.[8]

Having issued this pointed reminder to keep in mind the human consequences of failing to provide social insurance, Larson assessed which kinds of situations leading to lost income the American system insured against and which it did not. Larson's most interesting comments on that topic had to do with the issue of non-occupational disability. He called the almost complete failure of the income insurance system to provide for this "the most astonishing feature of the American social security scene."[9] What made this omission so disturbing, Larson explained, was that the disabled man's plight was greater than that of the unemployed or the aged, given that the first still had his health and thus the possibility at least of future paid work and the second could conceivably work as well. A man disabled for reasons unrelated to employment, in contrast, lost both his income and his ability to work, ran up doctor and hospital bills, and likely had a wife and children to support. The American system not only provided such a man nothing but sometimes also made him forfeit his other benefits under it, such as unemployment and old-age insurance. This was because a man's eligibility for protection under the other income insurance programs that made up the American social insurance system depended on his holding a paying job for an extended period. Should he become disabled as a younger adult or have failed to come under the protection of those programs due to the gaps in their coverage, such a man could not become eligible for their protection once he could no longer work.[10]

As bad as this was, Larson pointed out that it appeared still worse when compared with the example set by the other major industrial countries, most of which adopted disability insurance (or sickness insurance, as it was called) first. Even in the United States, Larson related, sickness insurance was the first kind of social insurance to be seriously urged and studied, though it was not adopted there. All of this led Larson to consider why the American experience in this area had proven to be so different.[11]

Larson located the answer to this mystery in an accident of history. In the United States, most of the major social insurance programs emerged during the Great Depression, when policymakers were focused on the economic causes of unemployment rather than the physical ones. Larson argued that even the old-age pensions part of Social Security, which seemed to address a physical cause of unemployment, really had more to do with lawmakers' desire to move older workers out of paying jobs and thereby create more opportunities for younger unemployed people. Only later, he continued, did the rationale for old-age pensions shift to promoting the physical comfort and well-being of the elderly.[12]

Although there was surely something to Larson's explanation, it did not account for the emergence of workers' compensation laws twenty-five years earlier.

A more exact way of formulating the question would have been to ask why workers' compensation statutes appeared then but not sickness insurance ones. The most likely answer appears to be the same one that explained why the American workers' compensation system took the form that it did, which was the impossibility at the time it was created of requiring mandatory worker contributions, as the German system had. Without this mechanism for spreading the cost and discouraging excessive and fraudulent worker claims for compensation, the American business community most likely refused to accept a sickness insurance system in the early years of the twentieth century out of fear that a system financed by employers alone would prove so expensive as to be unworkable. And by the time the legal obstacle to mandatory employee contributions vanished during the mid-1930s, the focus of social insurance advocates had shifted to protecting against economic causes of unemployment, which had led to the serious gap in the American social insurance system's coverage that Larson pointed out.[13]

Larson argued that something needed be done to remedy this situation. He drew a clear distinction between short- and long-term disability. Although the cutoff between the two was, he readily admitted, somewhat arbitrary, the difference between them was greater than one of degree. When a man was permanently disabled, he explained, he was prematurely retired and deserved to be treated like other retirees. When he was temporarily disabled, the problem was tiding him over during a period of unemployment. The natural tendency of temporary disability legislation Larson concluded, was toward "either unemployment insurance or workmen's compensation, depending on whether you stress the 'unemployment' or the physical-injury aspect of the problem"[14] The care he gave to this question seems to have stemmed in part from his own experience with recurrent short-term disability. Larson's back problems had made him acutely aware of the serious trouble even temporary disability could create. Although in Larson's case it had not interfered seriously with his ability to earn money, he no doubt understood that the consequences of such an ailment for those holding most other kinds of paying jobs would likely have been much more severe. After weighing all of the various considerations, Larson endorsed the approach adopted by New York State in 1949, which financed temporary disability insurance through private insurance and, if necessary, through a state fund and administered the program through the already-existing state Workmen's Compensation Board. As for the problem of total permanent disability, Larson strongly endorsed dealing with this problem through public social insurance.[15]

He also endorsed extending the reach of the federal-state unemployment insurance system, where feasible, to those members of the nation's paid labor force who were as yet uncovered and extending the duration of unemployment insurance payments to a length of time consistent with the usual period of joblessness the temporarily unemployed experienced. At the same time, Larson opposed trying to address the problem of long-term unemployment through an income insurance approach on the ground that no actuarially sound calculations could ever be made to support such a program. Larson used an explicitly comparative argument, noting that even the much broader British social insurance scheme did not address this problem, despite the urgings of the British plan's primary architect, Sir William Beveridge, to do so.[16]

Apart from special situations like this, Larson consistently showed his openness to the extension and improvement of social insurance programs. The clearest sign of that intellectual flexibility appeared in his discussion of another major area of social insurance coverage that had to do with hospital and medical expenses. In keeping with the reasoning he had applied to workers' compensation programs in his treatise, Larson argued that including payment of unusual hospital and medical expenses that were caused by and coincided with the emergency that caused the lost income was consistent with the income insurance principle behind the American social insurance system. Larson noted that only workers' compensation systems had thus far provided for hospital and medical expenses but argued that providing for such expenses in disability and old-age income insurance systems would be consistent with the basic purpose they served.[17]

Lest he be misunderstood as having endorsed a comprehensive system of health insurance, Larson immediately added that what he was suggesting would be considerably more limited in its reach:

> The kind of plan in which payment of medical expenses occurs only after wage-loss would differ from complete health insurance both in that it would only be the insured income-earner himself whose medical expenses would be paid (not those of his wife and family) and in that there would be many expenses even of the income-earner which would not be associated with disability, such as dental care.[18]

In writing this very revealing passage, Larson signaled his openness in principle to a limited form of what eventually became known as Medicare. More than any other single suggestion in his manuscript, this one revealed the moderately conservative nature of Larson's views in the area of social insurance, for such an extension of that system had the most far-reaching potential of the various ones he had endorsed. And, as with his views on insuring against disability, Larson's intellectual flexibility here seemed to be a product in part of his own experience with expensive hospital bills.[19]

Larson observed that much of the thinking about extending social insurance to cover hospital and medical expenses was very confused because there were two very different rationales for doing so, which gave rise to different kinds of arguments. One could defend this kind of social insurance on the grounds of protecting economic security or public health, he explained. Although he conceded that there were some good arguments in favor of protecting public health in this way, he stated that they were not relevant to his analysis, based as it was on the view that American social insurance programs were intended simply to protect economic security.[20]

Good health and economic security were, of course, related to one another, and it was on that relationship that Larson focused. He noted that in sickness cases, the cost of hospital and medical care usually exceeded the amount of lost income. The problem with simply accepting the logical conclusion that such expenses should be covered through social insurance, Larson explained, had to do with the distinctly new area of coverage to which such an extension would lead and the inevitable effect it would have on how the nation's privately organized medical system worked. The second of these posed the biggest single obstacle. Simply establishing a public fund that the insured could draw on to pay unusual medical expenses would not in itself elicit strong opposition from private health care providers. What would prompt such resistance was the likelihood that a government official would exert control over which medical procedures would be covered and to what extent, thereby limiting the discretion of doctors and hospitals. Larson refrained from rehashing the debate surrounding this explosive issue because proposals for public health insurance introduced in Congress several years earlier had led nowhere and would likely not be revived "during at least the next few years."[21]

The only real answer he provided was the observation that currently the focus was on trying to do as much as possible via private medical insurance, which could be underwritten by a government subsidy for those unable to afford the premiums. Larson noted that slightly over half of the population was insured privately at the time he wrote and that there was no fundamental obstacle to allowing private insurance to do "the major part of this job."[22] The basic shortcoming of that approach for those who enjoyed such coverage, Larson acknowledged, was its limited nature. Private insurance plans did not pay for long periods of hospitalization or exceptionally expensive treatments because the premiums needed to insure against those contingencies would be prohibitively expensive for most people. The best way to minimize the likelihood of such expenses, Larson suggested, was good preventive medicine.[23]

Larson's discussion of how the British social insurance system differed from the American one was similarly balanced. He began by observing that while the British system's defenders tended to describe it as "comprehensive," that adjective was misleading. The British social insurance system did not address the problem of long-term unemployment, which could be considered a serious gap. Disability of whatever origin or duration was covered fully, but only if the claimant had made the requisite payroll contributions for at least three years, which constituted another gap. Occupational injuries were compensated for at a higher rate than non-occupational ones because the preexisting workers' compensation system had paid benefits more generous than the British government believed it could afford for non-occupational injuries. This kind of inconsistency would also likely occur in the United States, Larson noted perceptively, should it ever move toward a more comprehensive system, because the natural tendency would be to preserve existing programs and benefit levels rather than start anew. Additionally, the British system, like the American one, provided no survivor benefits to a widow if she had no children and was younger than a certain age (in the United Kingdom, fifty, in the United States, sixty-five).[24]

Larson also addressed the more fundamental differences between the British and American systems. He argued that the most basic difference was that Britain's system had gone beyond the income insurance principle into new categories of welfare state provision that had no analog in the United States. He gave as his first example the system of family allowances, which provided payments to mothers for each child beyond the first. Although the logic behind this measure was to alleviate one of the leading causes of poverty in Britain—large families—such benefits were paid to everyone, regardless of whether they participated in the national insurance system or had any real need. Larson wrote, "The Queen would be perfectly entitled to draw it for her second child."[25]

Larson cast serious doubt on the notion that Americans would ever adopt something like this program, even though it existed in every other country that had established a social insurance system. He argued that one key reason for adopting family allowances in Britain was to keep the wage level low in order to make British exports competitive in world markets. What this meant, in effect, he wrote, was that "the family allowance system is an admission that the average British wage will not support the average British family." Larson added, "The same could not be said in the United States."[26]

Implicit in Larson's analysis was his assumption that the United States could continue to prosper with an average wage level much greater than those of the other highly industrialized countries. In this he reflected the optimistic American outlook that had emerged since the early 1940s, a period when the nation had achieved unprecedented prosperity and high wage levels mostly through domestic production and consumption. Should that situation change and the need for American businesses to become more globally competitive increase as a result, Larson's confident conclusion would lose its persuasiveness.[27]

Larson also pointed out another motivation for family allowances in Britain, which was to encourage population growth through natural increase. He noted that the same basic motive lay behind the decision to provide various insurance grants for maternity, which not only replaced lost wages but also helped defray the cost of having children. While he did not say so explicitly, this consideration did not apply with equal force to the United States, where the birth rate since the early 1940s had risen to a twentieth-century high, producing the Baby Boom. Of course, this would change if the American birth rate should decline in the future to one more like that of postwar Britain. Larson seems not to have seriously considered that possibility at the time he wrote his manuscript, although he did note there that the Catholic Family Life Conference in Philadelphia had endorsed a proposal to establish family allowances in the United States.[28]

Larson also discussed another major difference from the American system—Britain's National Health Service. It provided medical, dental, and hospital services as well as drugs and appliances, all without charge and without reference to insurance contributions or status. Income (and income loss) was entirely irrelevant. Like the family allowance program, this one complemented and simplified the rest of the British social insurance system.[29]

Larson observed that those gains in comprehensiveness had come at a cost of unity of underlying purpose. In one of the clearest and most illuminating descriptions of how the two nations' social insurance systems had come to differ, he wrote:

> While the British system is more comprehensive than ours, then, it is not in every respect accurate to say that it is more unified. It is more unified in administration, of course, since it has nothing like our federal-state-private division of function. But in principle and objective, we retain a simplicity which the British no longer have. That is, we have the one all-pervading principle of restitution of wage-loss. We are not promoting the birth-rate. We are not using social insurance to keep down the wage level. We are not—to be perfectly blunt—even using it to promote public health.[30]

Larson also pointed out two other basic differences, which were closely related. Unlike the American Social Security system, the British equivalent, known as National Insurance, was financed through a flat-rate system of taxation and awarded benefits and pensions at the same rate. Thus, in Britain, every income earner made the same weekly contribution and received, when eligible, the same amount. This posed a significant contrast with the United States, where, as Larson noted, both the amount of the weekly contribution and the ultimate benefit were related to past earnings. The logic behind the British approach was that the benefit paid to everyone was pegged at the level needed to maintain bare subsistence according to a national average of prices for essential goods and services. In taking this approach, Britain had departed from the practice followed by most of the other countries that had adopted social insurance schemes, the United States included, which established a benefit level somewhere between bare subsistence and genuine comfort. The British practice in this area seemed even more striking, Larson continued, because all of the momentum in the American political system was toward raising benefit levels and the major disputes were over how much and how best to do this. While Larson observed that many viewed the British innovation as "a symptom of the 'leveling' process that has been going on in England," he did not spell out more explicitly the egalitarian objective that lay behind this decision to give the well-to-do no more than the poorest of the poor.[31]

Instead, Larson focused on the practical consequence for the British system of keeping the benefit level so low, which had placed a substantial and growing burden on the British equivalent of American public assistance. Reminding readers that in the United States public assistance payments had begun to fall, he pointed to a very different pattern in Britain. There, public assistance payments had continued to grow, despite the maturing of the national insurance system. The only possible explanation was the inadequate level of benefits for those living in unusually expensive areas, such as London. Thus, supplementing through public assistance had become "a permanent adjunct to the national insurance system."[32]

Larson's discussion of the current policy debates in the field of American social insurance revealed his moderately conservative views on that subject even more clearly. For him, the fundamental issue was the disagreement over whether American social insurance legislation should be considered comparable to social benefits provided by an enlightened society and government or to privately purchased annuities and insurance policies. Larson argued that the correct answer was "both." This explained the confused nature of the debate about the system and the existence of two distinctively different camps of critics:

> One group is impatient with the failure to attain a complete and efficient distribution of social benefits to everyone who needs them in proportion to their presumed needs, due to such insurance-based requirements as attaining covered status through the making of contributions; the other group is disturbed by the ways in which social insurance falls short of private insurance, by not giving all of the insureds the same dollar-for-dollar value on contributed premium, by not giving a man an absolute right to his pension at retirement age whether he goes on earning or not, and by ignoring in a grandiose fashion principles of financing accepted in private insurance circles.[33]

Larson discussed the various controversies that grew out of this difference of opinion, starting with one of the most explosive, the redistributive function of the American social insurance system. He pointed out that a person making $3,600 per year paid eighteen times as much into the Social Security system as a person making $200, but when the time came to collect benefits, the first person's benefit would be only three and a half times as great as the second person's. In a characteristically clear and memorable phrase, Larson wrote, "This disparity is one of the things that makes social insurance 'social.'"[34] And there were other redistributive features of that system, Larson pointed out, such as requiring employers to make contributions toward their employees' benefits and the policy of favoring latecomers over long-time contributors.[35]

Larson observed, by way of contrast, that the British system, with its flat-rate financing and equal benefits policy, did not include a redistributive function within the framework of its National Insurance program. Thus, the British depended on achieving redistribution mainly through progressive income taxation, aided by public assistance payments, free medical care, and subsidies for food and housing. Larson sharply criticized this road to redistribution on the grounds that it had conspicuously failed to eliminate what he called "the humiliation of direct relief" and its stigmatizing means test.[36] He also criticized the British approach for the very different reason that progressive taxes deterred initiative, which he called "unquestionably one of the primary reasons for Britain's economic plight."[37] The American system, on the other hand, created no such problem, Larson observed, because additional hours worked would be subject to the same Social Security tax rate.[38]

Larson's critique of the British approach to redistribution was an interesting mixture of compassion and conservatism. What he seems to have missed is the notion that creating disincentives to work more than usual could serve other socially worthwhile purposes, such as encouraging workers to spend more time with their families and engage in leisure, and inducing employers to spread employment around by hiring additional workers rather than requiring existing ones to work longer. The key question, of course, was whether those things benefited British society more than greater industriousness among the ranks of the already employed would have. Larson's comments here suggest that he believed Britain could ill afford such policies, given its postwar economic difficulties. His thinking on this issue also signaled one of the ways moderate conservatives like him distinguished themselves from moderate leftists of the sort found in labor union circles and the Democratic Party. While policy differences between those two camps had narrowed since the 1930s, they nonetheless remained meaningful.[39]

Larson also disposed of one final criticism, in this instance from the left, of existing American policy in this area. He noted that some had criticized the policy because it singled out covered employment as the only source of support that stopped benefits. Income from investments, rents, savings, or even noncovered employment did not disturb the right to the pension, Larson acknowledged, but he defended this discriminatory treatment as preferable to a policy that would, in effect, amount to a means test. If all forms of income were relevant to deciding whether one received pension payments through Social Security and payments were denied to those with substantial incomes based upon these other kinds of sources, the system would lose its insurance-based feature of broad reach and thus defeat one of the system's most fundamental goals. In Larson's words, "The means test is just what the insurance principle is supposed to be getting away from," and for that reason he opposed bringing all forms of income into consideration when deciding whether a pension should be paid.[40] The most he would favor in the way of reform was an extension of coverage to occupations presently excluded, which would reduce opportunities for this inequity though not eliminate them completely.[41]

Larson took a similarly cautious stand on proposals before Congress to change Social Security's financing system. They stemmed, he noted, from the ongoing debate over whether Social Security should be financed by a system of accumulated reserves or a pay-as-you-go approach. Larson noted that from its earliest days Social Security's financing had combined elements of both. In discussing the various controversies to which this mixed system of financing had given rise, he dismissed at the outset the most conservative criticism, which faulted the existing arrangement for not adhering to the strictest standard of actuarial soundness common in the private insurance industry. Larson called the application of such a standard to Social Security "pointless" for the simple reason that the government, unlike private companies, did not run the risk of going out of business and thus did not need to accumulate as much in the way of reserves as a private insurer would. He also rejected a pure pay-as-you-go scheme, which was backed by the U.S. Chamber of Commerce, on the grounds that waiting each year to see what Social Security's liabilities would be and then setting contribution rates to meet them would make planning for the future too difficult and leave nothing on hand for contingencies.[42]

Instead of those two extremes, Larson favored a more moderate solution to what he called the principal criticism of the present system. As it had steadily accumulated reserves during the 1940s and early 1950s, political pressure for ever higher benefits had also grown. Such pressure had been encouraged, Larson noted, by the illusion of a large surplus that the mounting reserves had created. Larson noted that not everything about such a misconception had been bad, because it had helped persuade Congress to increase benefits in line with the growing cost of living. He also argued that concerns about the tendency to increase benefits excessively were overblown because the payroll deduction feature served as an automatic check. All the government needed to do when faced with such demands, Larson explained, was tell constituents that any increase in benefits would require a corresponding rise in the payroll tax rate. Moreover, he argued, the existence of an actual fund of accumulated contributions had strengthened the sense among contributors and everyone else that those who had paid into it had a moral right to a benefit that was at least as large as their contributions would provide. Larson argued that while the system's financing diverged in some respects from that of a private insurance arrangement, the similarities were sufficiently strong to deter lawmakers in the future from reneging on Social Security's commitments to contributors. Although conceptually somewhat messy, the existing financing scheme made Social Security politically more secure, and Larson strongly supported it.[43]

As for the lively argument over whether the federal government should help fund Social Security through income tax revenues, thereby easing the burden imposed on employers and employees and facilitating improvements in benefits, Larson acknowledged the virtues of such an approach but cautioned that it could lead to income tax rates like those of Britain, with the resulting drawback that he had already mentioned. He observed that if the Social Security system were expanded to insure against non-occupational disability and health care costs, political pressure for subsidizing the system with income tax revenues would grow because the payroll tax rates otherwise would rise very high, perhaps to as much as 15 to 20 percent. The basic problem for Larson with using income tax revenue to help pay for social insurance seems to have been the practical one of finding some way to establish firm boundaries on how far the government could go in that direction, lest that practice culminate in what he saw as initiative-destroying income tax rates.[44]

Larson's discussion of the mixed federal-state and public-private aspects of the American social insurance system led him to make some of the most far-reaching and interesting observations in his manuscript. He acknowledged that the first impression created by the American system was of a complete hodgepodge. If one probed deeply enough, however, Larson argued, a very different conclusion would emerge:

> One can find a consistent pattern which is not only quite beautiful to observe, but which may well be the only kind of pattern which will work in this country. There are two simple principles on which the federal-state-private division of function has so far been worked out, consciously or unconsciously. One was enunciated by Abraham Lincoln, when he said that the role of government is "to do for the people what needs to be done, but which they cannot by individual effort do at all, or do so well." The second is implicit in our constitutional form of government: that if the thing must be done by the government, it should be done at as local a level as possible, and only if it cannot be done by the state should it done by the federal government.[45]

Larson observed that this was the opposite of the traditional socialist view but that it represented the prevailing one in America, especially under the present (Eisenhower) administration. If the validity of this formula is conceded, he concluded, the various parts of the American social security system would be found "right where they belong."[46]

Larson's formula reveals the extent to which his views on issues of federalism had evolved since the 1930s. Gone was his youthful enthusiasm for replacing state laws and courts with federal ones. In its place had come a more mature appreciation for the role the states played in a country so big and regionally diverse as to make uniform national rules hard to devise and administer. This did not mean, of course, that Larson had become averse to federal laws and programs. These he still endorsed if—and only if—the states could not handle the problems in question themselves as well as the federal government could. The key intellectual shift, then, was not a rejection of federal government solutions but rather a much greater awareness of the virtues of state lawmaking and administration in a country like the United States.

Larson tested his two-part formula by applying it to each of the various kinds of social insurance programs. Most noteworthy about this part of his analysis was Larson's firm conclusion that unemployment insurance and Social Security could never be handled by private means. The first of these, he argued, presented so many unpredictable contingencies as to make an actuarially sound private insurance approach prohibitively expensive. The second, if handled privately, would involve the accumulation of funds so large it would create an impossible investment problem. Larson's conclusions indicated the considerable distance that stood between him and the more conservative Republicans of that day, such as the recently elected U.S. senator from Arizona, Barry Goldwater. Although Goldwater and his like-minded supporters continued to believe that private insurance, savings, and charity could adequately meet the needs social insurance programs addressed, Larson's manuscript shows no such faith.[47]

Larson's views on whether the states or the federal government should operate such programs, and where to put the still-missing parts of the system, also set him apart from right-wing Republicans such as Goldwater. Larson's thinking in these areas also distinguished him from fervent New Deal liberals, who tended to favor federal administration of all social insurance programs. He thought the states had rightly been given the task of administering the unemployment insurance system because the required reserves were fairly small and the liabilities were not of such long duration that they would interfere seriously with interstate movement. The same considerations indicated to him that Social Security had been correctly assigned to the federal government because of that program's much larger reserves and longer periods of coverage.[48]

As for the gaps in the existing social insurance system, most notably insurance for temporary and permanent total disability, Larson argued that the success of New York State in handling the first of these via private insurance indicated that this was the appropriate course for the other states. Insuring against permanent total disability was a different matter, he argued, that was more suited to administration by the federal government because of the long periods when recipients might be eligible for payments and the problem of inhibiting movement of recipients across state lines.[49]

Larson also discussed at considerable length an important new development that seemed to violate his formula; the advent of employer-sponsored pension plans. American unions had begun pushing hard for these in the late 1940s as a way to supplement the inadequate retirement benefits Social Security paid. The key breakthrough had come in November 1949, when the Steelworkers Union succeeded in winning such a plan from United States Steel, the industry's leading firm. Over the next four years, such plans had spread rapidly in the heavily unionized sectors of the economy such as basic manufacturing, transportation, and construction.[50]

Larson perceived two serious dangers in the growth of this benefit. The first involved the problem of finance and investment. If everyone presently covered by Social Security succeeded in obtaining a supplementary private pension, the total reserves required to make them actuarially sound might reach $190 billion, he estimated, or double the value of all of the securities listed on the New York Stock Exchange at that time. Failing to fund such plans fully, as was routinely done, Larson continued, would avoid this first problem but only by creating a second one. Employees typically had to work for years in order to acquire vested pension rights, meaning rights that could never be rescinded even if the employees went to work at another company.[51]

Larson observed that this increased a covered employee's incentive to stay with his current employer until fully vested. Labor economists viewed this development with concern because it reduced the mobility of the labor force and consequently impaired future economic development. Larson shared that concern, although he focused more on the loss of freedom to the individual than harm to the health of the economy. He observed that some of this problem could be alleviated by developing multi-employer plans or plans based on region or the jurisdiction of a particular union but then pointed out that thus far such devices had played only a small part in the development of employer-sponsored pension plans. This situation drove Americans toward a kind of paradox in which a privately financed system protected individual freedom less effectively than a publicly financed one.[52]

The lesson Larson drew from this was very different from the one more-conservative Republicans surely would have:

> If we had to do it over again, it would probably have been better to do the whole old-age pension job under O.A.S.I. [Social Security], by bringing the entire level up to the point where it does not need a great deal of supplementation—leaving supplementation to take the form of savings and other voluntary efforts. This, in addition to avoiding the freedom and finance problems, would also prevent the discrimination now growing up between employees with strong bargaining power and those without.[53]

Although much of Larson's analysis made sense, he tended to assume that most workers greatly valued the freedom to move around the country. One could just as easily argue that most workers preferred the stability, security, and family and community ties that came from staying in one place. Larson also did not mention, and might not have understood, the underlying political problem that had led to the result he criticized. Labor leaders had also favored adequate Social Security payments and turned to the private pension device only after a coalition of the most conservative Republicans and Southern Democrats in

A judge's son poses for the camera. *Courtesy of Anna Larson and Lex Larson.*

Grandfather Peter Larson Sorlie and Grandmother Martha Goodman. *Courtesy of Anna Larson and Lex Larson.*

Father Lewis Larson and mother Anna Bertia Huseboe on their wedding day in 1903. *Courtesy of Anna Larson and Lex Larson.*

The Larson family, circa 1920: (*back row, left to right*) Marguerite, Anna, Palmer, Lewis; (*front row, left to right*) Richard, Donald, Arthur. *Courtesy of Anna Larson and Lex Larson.*

Courting in a canoe. *Courtesy of Anna Larson and Lex Larson.*

Larson (*center*) and his fellow rowers at Pembroke College, Oxford, circa 1933. *Courtesy of Anna Larson and Lex Larson.*

A PROFESSIONAL COMEDIAN AT THE OXFORD UNION: MR. GILLIE POTTER, WHO PROVED A MOST POPULAR DEBATER (FOURTH FROM LEFT), WITH MEMBERS OF THE UNION.

Mr. Gillie Potter, the comedian who is so popular with listeners to the wireless, made a hasty journey from Brighton to make his début at the Oxford Union on February 8. He appeared in order to support a motion (which was carried by 243 votes to 164) "that this generation must break with tradition in order to create a brave new world." Those seen here are (l. to r.) K. R. F. Steel-Maitland, Gordon Murray, I. G. Martin, Gillie Potter, L. A. Larson, D. F. Karaka (President), J. P. Hickerton, and C. S. M. Bereton.

Illustrated London News
Feb. 17, 1934

Larson (*center*) with other leaders of the Oxford Union, 1934.
Illustrated London News, *Feburary 17, 1934.*

Rhodes scholar, 1933. *Courtesy of Kay Vaughan.*

Actress (Florence Newcomb Larson), 1936. *Courtesy of Franklin Boruszak.*

Doting dad: Arthur and Anna, circa 1944.
Courtesy of Anna Larson and Lex Larson.

The Larsons, circa 1951: (*back*) Florence, Arthur; (*front*) Anna, Lex. *Courtesy of Anna Larson and Lex Larson.*

Above right: Labor Secretary James P. Mitchell announces his choice for under secretary, March 23, 1954. *Courtesy of Anna Larson and Lex Larson.*

Below right: Entertaining at home, January 1955. *Courtesy of Anna Larson and Lex Larson.*

The Larson family "orchestra," circa 1956.
Courtesy of Anna Larson and Lex Larson.

Eisenhower congratulates his new USIA director, December 18, 1956.
Courtesy of Anna Larson and Lex Larson.

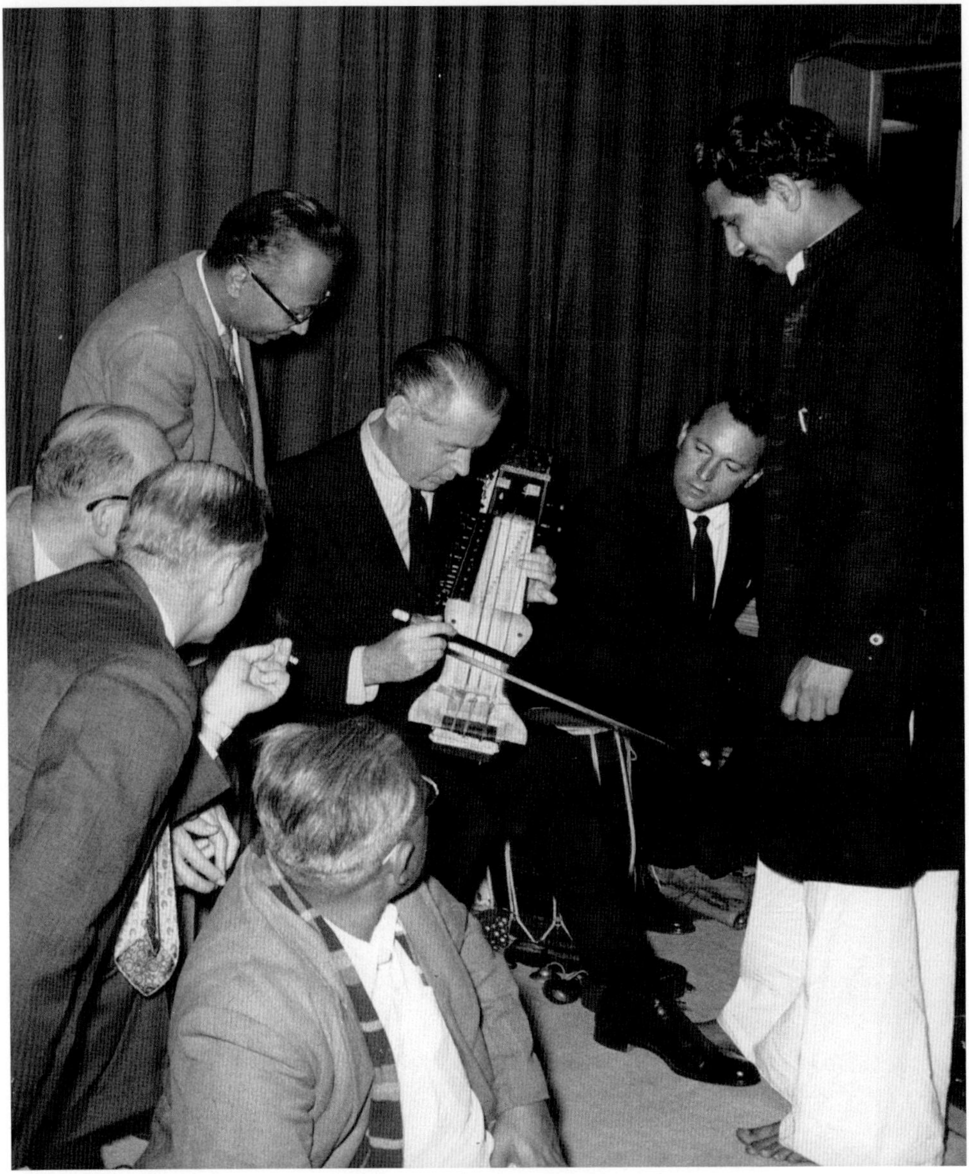

Demonstrating an instrument while in the Middle East, 1957.
Courtesy of Anna Larson and Lex Larson.

Larson and his staff at the World Rule of Law Center, Duke University.
Courtesy of Anna Larson and Lex Larson.

Campaigning against conservative extremists in the mid-1960s.
Courtesy of Anna Larson and Lex Larson.

Teaching law at Duke. *Courtesy of Anna Larson and Lex Larson.*

A sculptor and her biggest fan, at home in Durham, North Carolina, in 1984. *Jim Sparks, (Durham)* Herald-Sun.

Congress repeatedly blocked such a change. The private pensions approach promised to help millions of union members and their families—and many others too, as nonunion employers, wishing to compete with unionized employers for the best workers, increasingly decided to offer this fringe benefit. Larson was right, however, to point out that some of the long-term consequences of this outcome could prove highly undesirable. He correctly noted that the employer-sponsored health, hospitalization, and life insurance plans that unions had begun to win through collective bargaining presented the same kinds of reduced labor mobility problems and the same kinds of inequities between workers with varying degrees of bargaining power.[54]

Most striking about Larson's discussion of these and the larger issues raised by employer-sponsored plans was the firmness with which he dismissed private arrangements if they struck him as less beneficial than public governmental ones: "The conclusion as to our state-federal-private division is this: let the job be done as privately and locally as possible, but when the nature of the job calls for nation-wide government action, do not hesitate to take the federal action. It is just as bad for private business to try to do a federal job as it is for the federal government to invade areas which can better be handled privately."[55] This kind of strictly balanced observation, so characteristic of Larson's thinking and writing, helped make his analysis seem distinctly different from the more one-sided assessments so common during the preceding twenty years.[56]

That same quality was clear in Larson's treatment of the relationship between social insurance programs and private savings. He complained that Americans had become so insurance minded as to be in danger of forgetting its true purpose. Larson argued that social insurance should provide a fund to meet truly extraordinary emergencies—and no more. He decried the growing trend, in Britain especially, toward expanding coverage to smaller and smaller contingencies, which increased the administrative burden on and undermined the effectiveness of social insurance programs. Americans would do better, he suggested, to save for such small contingencies and deal with them that way than by overloading a system meant to address more important problems.[57]

Larson summed up his manuscript with a few very revealing comments. He argued that most of the defects of American social insurance could rightly be viewed as the "transitional growing pains of a young and immature system."[58] Some of those pains would cease with the passage of time as more Americans became eligible for coverage and for higher levels of benefits. The great danger he saw was that frustration with those growing pains and with the failure thus far to extend coverage to categories of employment and kinds of causes of lost income excluded by existing laws might lead to an abandonment of the underlying insurance principle in favor of something more socialistic. The logical conclusion, he suggested, was to extend coverage in these ways immediately:

> To the extent we delay this full coverage, we perpetuate discriminations and inequities, and thus invite increasing demands for scrapping the whole insurance idea. If we want to keep it, we had better perfect it now. Otherwise we shall end with a tax-supported hand-out system of some kind, a result far less consistent with the traditions of free enterprise and personal dignity which we have so far managed to maintain side by side with our social insurance legislation.[59]

Implicit in this prescription was Larson's sense, widely shared by moderate conservatives of his generation, that failure to reform social insurance in ways that strengthened the existing system would eventually lead to more radical policy outcomes from the left. This deeply rooted concern set him apart from more extreme conservatives such as Hoover and Goldwater, who tended to dismiss the possibility of such an alternative and objected to expanding welfare state programs out of fear that it might unwittingly bring socialist possibilities to life. But when Larson wrote his manuscript on social insurance in 1953, moderate conservatives like him had come to hold the upper hand in this debate for several reasons. The rise of the labor movement and left-wing political parties in the major market systems during the 1930s and 1940s, the emergence of more comprehensive social insurance schemes in Western Europe, and, above, all, the rise of nonmarket systems, most notably in the Soviet Union and the People's Republic of China, tended to convince moderate conservatives that the most likely alternative to an inadequate American welfare state would be something more radically leftist. At the same time, the tendency of social insurance to increase economic security among workers and weaken the appeal of radically leftist policies encouraged moderate conservatives to believe that the welfare state was a step away from the revolution, not toward it.[60]

Of course, these were not the only considerations. Larson's manuscript makes clear that he favored expanding coverage of social insurance programs on the ground of simple humanity. What gave his arguments extra force on the right was the combination of that concern with the fear that the most likely alternative to what he advocated would be even more collectivist and the belief that a welfare state kept within proper boundaries would tend to preserve the free enterprise system rather than undermine it. Just how much force his views had and how well they meshed with the political milieu of that time would become clear with surprising speed.[61]

Larson first circulated his manuscript in the form of a conference paper, which was discussed at a meeting organized by the American Assembly. Established by Dwight Eisenhower in 1950 while he was president of Columbia University, this group brought together representatives of business, labor, farm groups, professions such as law and medicine, the two major political parties, and government for an annual conference on an important public issue. The conferences usually lasted three or four days and were all held at Arden House, the onetime country estate of American railway tycoon Edward H. Harriman. Located on a high ridge amid an 8,000-acre tract of woods north of New York City, Arden House had been given to Columbia in 1950 by Harriman's son Averell, the former U.S. ambassador to the Soviet Union and secretary of commerce, for use as conference space. The American Assembly meetings embodied Eisenhower's faith that if leaders from various walks of life sat down together and approached public policy problems in a calm, nonpartisan fashion, away from the glare of the media spotlight, misunderstandings could be eliminated and constructive progress encouraged. After each conference, the assembly made the papers presented available to the media and provided discussion guides and pamphlets for use by "little American Assemblies" around the country and other interested civic groups. The first assembly conference, held in 1951, dealt with the relationship between the United States and Western Europe, and the second with inflation. In November 1953, one year after Eisenhower was elected president, the American Assembly held its third annual conference. This time the subject was "Economic Security for Americans: An Appraisal of the Past Half-Century, 1900–1953." Participants were given seven papers, including Larson's, on various aspects of that topic and then broke into smaller groups to discuss them.[62]

As the author of the paper on "The American System," Larson was asked to chair the roundtable discussion of his income insurance thesis and its public policy consequences, a responsibility he discharged so effectively as to set in motion a very consequential chain of events. At his right during this session, he later recalled, sat Under Secretary of Health, Education, and Welfare Nelson Rockefeller, and at Larson's left, Averell Harriman himself, who would be elected governor of New York one year later. At the other end of the table from Larson was Columbia economics professor Eli Ginzberg, who watched, listened, and came to the conclusion that Larson would make a good under secretary of labor. This had far-reaching consequences because, unbeknown to him, Ginzberg served the Eisenhower administration behind the scenes as a policy advisor and talent scout. Even more to the point, one of Ginzberg's close friends was Eisenhower's secretary of labor, James P. Mitchell. Formerly the chief labor negotiator for Bloomingdale's Department Store in New York, Mitchell was looking for someone in the winter of 1953–1954 to fill the Labor Department's number two post. It was Ginzberg's suggestion, based upon the positive impression Larson's paper and presentation made during the American Assembly meeting, that put him in Mitchell's mind as a candidate for under secretary of labor.[63]

The first sign of how this fortuitous chain of events would change Larson's life came early in March 1954, when he received a telephone call from a former law student named John J. Gilhooley, who was working as administrative assistant to Mitchell. Would Larson be willing to come to Washington right away to meet with Mitchell? Gilhooley asked, without explaining why his boss wanted to see him. Although Larson later recalled that "I had to think twice [about] who the Secretary of Labor was," he obligingly agreed and made the trip. He and Mitchell hit it off right away. After about twenty minutes of conversation on a topic Larson could not later remember, Mitchell asked him if he would like to be under secretary of labor. Larson replied impulsively, "I'd love it," and the two men shook hands on this understanding.[64]

As Larson walked toward the door leading out of Mitchell's office, however, one final consideration surfaced, seemingly as an afterthought. In his memoirs, Larson described the very revealing exchange that then ensued:

> We had said our goodbyes, and I was halfway out the door, when Mitchell said, "Oh, by the way, are you a Republican?"
>
> Much has been said and written about the low priority of partisan politics in the Eisenhower administration. But this little episode, for me, told it all. Here was the juiciest political plum in Washington. All the other top jobs had long since been filled. Almost every Republican senator had a candidate for the spot. But for Mitchell, considerations of political affiliation had barely managed to force themselves into his consciousness as an afterthought, too late in any event to affect his commitment.
>
> Fortunately, I was able to assure the Secretary that I was a Republican. I was born a Republican, but I did not rely on that rather intangible concept, particularly since my partisan political activity until 1952 had been zero. More to the point, in 1952 I had registered Republican at Cayuga Heights School in Ithaca, N.Y., for the express purpose of voting for Eisenhower.[65]

Larson's memory appears to have deceived him a little on that last point. He told one of his grandsons that he had first registered as a Republican when Eisenhower began to receive serious consideration as a presidential candidate. That had happened four years earlier, in the spring of 1948, when leaders in both of the two major parties had made overtures to the new president of Columbia. Eisenhower refused them, but the media's considerable attention to a possible Eisenhower candidacy that year appears to have motivated Larson to register as a member of the GOP. He listed himself one year later as a registered Republican in his official Cornell faculty biography, so he seems to have gotten the dates mixed up. The other factor at work here likely was Larson's lack of enthusiasm for the eventual GOP standard-bearer in 1948, New York governor Thomas Dewey, whose overly cautious presidential campaign had ended in an embarrassing defeat.[66]

Partisan political considerations did ultimately influence Larson's appointment as under secretary of labor, but only in a relatively minor sense. After a brief meeting with Eisenhower, in which he gave his consent to the appointment, Larson was turned over to the members of the White House staff charged with clearing his appointment with the appropriate elected officials. The key sticking point had to do with Larson's state of residence. Pennsylvania seemed the simple answer, despite Larson's newness to Pittsburgh, but the two Republican senators from that state so often disagreed on matters great and small that the White House staffers involved decided to investigate the other options. Larson innocently suggested that if voting registration was the determining factor, he could still be considered a New Yorker, given that he had not yet registered to vote in Pennsylvania. That brought the exclamation "Oh God, not that" from one staffer, who was tired of dealing with complaints that the administration had too many people from there already.[67]

According to Larson's memoirs, he then suggested South Dakota, which seemed like a good solution until Republican senator Karl Mundt, the same man who had coached Florence's college debate team and discouraged her romance with Larson, nixed it. Larson recalled hearing that Mundt responded to this query by saying that Larson had deserted South Dakota and was nothing but a "damned Easterner." Mundt's objection appears to have stemmed from hardheaded political calculation rather than any personal bias against Larson. Counting him as a South Dakotan would have diminished Mundt's ability to use his senatorial prerogative to obtain other presidential appointments for residents of his home state. This concern that he not "waste" some of his influence on someone who had left the state twenty years earlier seems to have led Mundt to take a firm stand against Larson's nomination as a South Dakotan, or so Larson heard at the time.[68]

Thus, the White House staffers concluded he would have to be nominated as a Pennsylvanian. They gave Larson the task of obtaining the consent of both of that state's U.S. senators, which he managed to get. What helped here was that one of these two, Edward Martin, had graduated from Pittsburgh Law School, and the other, James Duff, had helped organize the effort to draft Eisenhower for the GOP presidential nomination in 1952 and strongly supported his administration. Triumphantly announcing his achievement to the staff, Larson found himself faced with the need to perform one more feat of political diplomacy. The staffers told him that he needed to clear his appointment with the local Republican Party chairman in Pittsburgh first. This person, wanting to signal his annoyance with the failure of the White House to consult him beforehand, put Larson off for a week and then gave his assent.[69]

And so the matter finally was settled. On March 23, 1954, the White House announced Larson's nomination to the press. He owed his new job to his reputation as an expert on social insurance law, his administrative credentials as a law school dean, his very strong public speaking skills, and, above all, his public policy views, which closely corresponded with those of the Eisenhower administration. For all of these reasons, Arthur Larson, though just forty-three years old and without strong political connections, had arrived in the spring of 1954 as an important public official. Over the next two years, he would make the most of his unexpected opportunity.[70]

CHAPTER SIX

Of Theory and Practice

LARSON FORMALLY ASSUMED the office of under secretary of labor on April 12, 1954, following a brief and uneventful Senate confirmation process. Rather than resign as dean of Pittsburgh Law School, he opted to request an indefinite leave of absence, which was granted. Although not eager to return to Pittsburgh, Larson evidently wanted a sure way out in case his new situation proved unsatisfactory. Florence, Lex, and Anna stayed there until the school year ended and then went on vacation to Sioux Falls and Lake Bemidji for the summer. This four-month period of separation brought with it more than a little loneliness, but it gave Larson the chance to devote his undivided attention to learning his new job responsibilities.[1]

Larson's new boss, James Mitchell, helped with that process by clearly explaining early on how the senior administrative duties of the Labor Department would be divided between them. Mitchell's forte lay in the realm of mediating labor-management disputes. Under Presidents Roosevelt and Truman, a senior White House official had usually played this very important role, but once Eisenhower took office the pattern changed. In keeping with the new president's fondness for the orderly delegation of responsibility, Mitchell formally took charge of all labor mediation problems. Wanting to devote himself primarily to this time-consuming and high-profile work, Mitchell decided to delegate the rest of his responsibilities, which mostly had to do with welfare-state programs, to his new under secretary. Mitchell appears to have had just this kind of division of duties in mind when he asked Larson to serve as under secretary because it played to Larson's strengths as well as his own.[2]

Mitchell and Larson made an odd pair in many respects, with backgrounds and personalities that were a study in contrasts. Larson's new boss, ten years his senior, was the son of two Irish Catholic trade unionists from Elizabeth, New Jersey. After finishing high school, Mitchell had operated two small grocery stores there, and when they both failed in 1923, he took a series of jobs that included selling lumber and coal and driving trucks. Mitchell had then entered the field of personnel administration at Western Electric, and, in the 1930s, served as a relief administrator in New Jersey and New York City. During World War II, he headed the army's civilian personnel department and handled labor relations for all of its construction projects. After this, Mitchell served on the Hoover Commission on the Reorganization of the Executive Branch and returned to private industry as the head of labor relations at Bloomingdale's Department Store in New York. Although a Democrat, Mitchell had supported Eisenhower's presidential campaign in 1952. Soon after Eisenhower won, Mitchell re-registered as a Republican. His chance to become part of the Eisenhower Cabinet had materialized in the fall of 1953, when Eisenhower's first Labor Secretary, plumbers' union chief Martin Durkin, resigned in a huff because the president decided not back Durkin's proposed changes to federal labor laws. Mitchell then became, like Durkin before him, the one Catholic in the Eisenhower cabinet and the only member who had been, until very recently, a Democrat. The differences in personality were equally pronounced, for Mitchell was as intense and volatile as Larson was low-keyed and deliberate. Even their looks contrasted, with Mitchell stocky and dark-haired and Larson tall, angular, and blond.[3]

Despite their many differences, Mitchell and Larson developed a smooth and friendly working relationship, something made possible by their complementary skills and interests and common outlook on politics and public policy. Neither considered himself a strongly partisan Republican or a fervent opponent of the New Deal. Their genuine sympathy for American workers inclined them instead to take a less antagonistic, more practical approach to the domestic policy legacies of the Roosevelt and Truman administrations. Mitchell and Larson also shared a common moral and cultural sensibility. Both men were 1950s squares in their private lives and outward appearance. For all of these reasons, the top two officials in the Eisenhower Labor Department soon proved to be a harmonious and effective combination.[4]

When Larson arrived at his new job, he found Mitchell engaged in an administrative overhaul and housecleaning. Determined to reorganize the department's various bureaus and regional office staffs so that they interacted more efficiently, Mitchell had appointed a panel of five distinguished outside experts early in 1954 to make recommendations on restructuring. When their report came in, Mitchell implemented it so thoroughly that it gave the department the greatest reorganization in its 40-year history. In addition to tightening lines of authority, Mitchell called regular meetings of bureau heads, some of whom hardly knew each other. He brought regional office heads together, too, and established committees to deal with special problems of interest to more than one part of the department. Related to this overhaul was Mitchell's effort to weed out poorly performing employees at all levels. Martin Durkin had appointed a group of subordinates of very uneven quality, and Mitchell was gradually replacing the weakest of these when Larson assumed his new post. Mitchell put Larson to work on that task, too, and the related one of firing more junior holdovers from the Truman administration whose job performance was unsatisfactory or who had engaged in improper behavior, such as misuse of government funds. The 8.5 percent cut in the Labor Department's budget enacted by the Republican-controlled 83rd Congress also contributed to this Darwinian process. Some of the stickiest cases involved Labor Department employees whom the Defense Department and/or the FBI considered to be security risks. Mitchell took the position that hard evidence of wrongdoing would be required to dismiss someone for that reason and he backed up that stand by fighting for employees he believed to be unfairly accused of endangering national security.[5]

Larson shared that position on loyalty investigation issues. Both his training as a lawyer, with its emphasis on the importance of due process and presumption of innocence in criminal cases, and a run-in with the FBI during his OPA days seem to have shaped his views in this area. The incident involving the FBI had begun one day in the early 1940s when Larson received a summons to report to the Justice Department building. There three FBI agents had interrogated him about whether he had signed a pacifist petition in Tomah, Wisconsin, that was backed by the far left. Larson managed to persuade his unsmiling accusers, who questioned him "in precisely the same manner suitable to interrogation of a thrice-convicted safe cracker" that they had the wrong Arthur Larson, but he never forgot this disturbing experience.[6]

Larson's disgust with the irresponsible conduct of Wisconsin senator Joseph McCarthy and the climate in Washington it helped create seems also to have influenced his views on the issue of "security risks" in government. In Larson's second month as under secretary he witnessed first-hand the kind of confused thinking McCarthy's alarmist accusations had led to. The occasion was a dinner at Washington's Mayflower Hotel on May 29, 1954, sponsored by the National Federation of Lutheran Clubs. This group had invited Larson, as a Lutheran who had recently become a prominent member of the Eisenhower administration, to deliver the keynote address. Florence had come to town for the event, which took place in a ballroom that held over 700 guests.[7]

As Larson sat at the head table, however, listening to former senator Gerald Nye of North Dakota and a retired general named Fellows make some introductory remarks, he became disturbed by their anti-Eisenhower, pro-McCarthy tone. The catalyst for these themes was an executive order that Eisenhower had issued twelve days earlier that barred members of the executive branch from communicating with McCarthy unless they had the president's permission.

Eisenhower intended his order to put an end to McCarthy's reckless investigations of government agencies by cutting off his access to the kinds of people that fueled them, which it did. Larson listened with mounting incredulity as one speaker compared Eisenhower's order with the sort of Catholic Church doctrine against which Martin Luther had protested. Many years later Larson recalled his reaction to this twisted line of reasoning:

> One of the speakers had the bright idea of equating this [McCarthy's protest over the executive order] with Lutheranism . . . by saying that, well, it was like Luther you see. Luther had said that people cannot be denied the right to talk to God directly. And I thought, "Can I be hearing this right? God being equated with Joe McCarthy?" It finally sunk in, and I gave the high sign to my wife . . . and so the principal speaker . . . walked out the door of the Mayflower. . . . That was my first personal brush with McCarthyism.[8]

This episode, like his earlier encounter with the FBI, served only to strengthen Larson's concern that the entire issue of disloyal government employees had been greatly distorted. His perspective on these issues and Mitchell's strong stand against discharging people on security grounds without hard evidence helped make certain that the wave of Labor Department dismissals in 1954 was not used to carry out a witch hunt against leftists.[9]

Even the task of firing people for entirely legitimate reasons did not come easily to Larson. A gentle and essentially kindly man who had come to his new job from almost a decade in the much more secure world of academia, he appears to have found this responsibility the most difficult of the many he learned to handle during his first few months as under secretary. Larson managed to perform as expected but not without qualms, as a passage from a letter he wrote to Florence in July 1954 made clear: "It is reassuring to know that I am doing all right in this job. Believe me, Buddy, this is the most merciless environment I have ever been in. We are slaughtering old hands around here right and left. Nice guys. But not good enough. People we work with every day—but one day, poof, they're gone."[10]

Other things came much more easily for him, such as lobbying members of Congress, testifying at committee hearings, and giving speeches. He scored some notable early coups in the first of those three areas, impressing both Mitchell and the department's senior congressional liaison officer. Larson's first real triumph as a lobbyist came when an administration-backed bill to modernize the District of Columbia's unemployment insurance system and raise the maximum weekly benefit from $20 to $30 bogged down in Congress in late June. Larson attached great importance to this measure because Eisenhower himself had urged the states to raise their benefit levels, thereby creating a potentially embarrassing situation in which those in the District of Columbia, which the federal government alone controlled, were the lowest in the nation.

Upon hearing from the Labor Department's congressional liaison that no one could get the bill moving, Larson went up to Capitol Hill to see what he could accomplish. First came a visit to Senator Francis Case of South Dakota, who chaired the Senate Committee on the District of Columbia. Case listened and then summoned Senator James Glenn Beall of Maryland, who chaired the subcommittee with jurisdiction over the measure.[11]

Once these two men understood the broader considerations at work, they became enthusiastic about moving it along. Beall called Congressman Henry Talle, who chaired the equivalent subcommittee in the House. Talle had sponsored his own less generous measure on the same subject, so Larson went to see him next. After talking with this persuasive visitor for a while, Talle agreed to drop his own version of the bill and hold joint hearings with the Senate subcommittee on the administration's proposal during the following week. Larson proudly reported this accomplishment to Florence: "When I got back [to the Labor Department] an hour later and announced joint hearings for next Thursday morning, with Talle's bill withdrawn, the group at the office, including Mitchell, couldn't believe it."[12]

Larson pulled off a similar feat two weeks later when lobbying for an administration proposal to extend the federal-state unemployment insurance system to all firms with three or more employees, a significant change from the existing minimum of eight employees. Having read reports in the local newspapers that the bill would likely stall in the Senate Finance Committee, Larson went to see its chair, Eugene Millikin of Colorado, on Friday, July 12th. Larson informed Florence that he had given Millikin "the old deep massage on how important this bill was, but I couldn't quite tell whether he was 'sold' or not."[13] The result of this conversation became clear the following Monday, when Millikin's committee reported out the bill without hearings, thereby putting it on the fast track toward passage by the full Senate. The head of the Labor Department's office of congressional liaison, upon hearing this news, called Larson and told him in an awed voice that "everything you touch turns to gold."[14] So impressed was this person and Mitchell by Larson's achievements on Capitol Hill that they asked him to assume overall responsibility for the department's lobbying effort there. Larson declined, telling them he had plenty to do already, but he appreciated the implied compliment nonetheless.[15]

Larson's success in this area seems to have stemmed from a variety of factors, the most important of which was the rapport he could establish with the Republicans running Congress at that time. Most of the committee and subcommittee chairmen had never dealt with a senior Labor Department official who was a midwestern Republican, as so many of them were. After twenty years of being lobbied on labor issues by Democratic officials serving Roosevelt and Truman, Larson must have seemed like a breath of fresh air. That was certainly the case with the potentially troublesome Congressman Talle, as Larson explained in a letter to Florence: "I had looked [him] up and found [him] to be a Norwegian Lutheran from Luther College in Iowa. He knew all about me, and we got on beautifully."[16]

Larson's credibility with GOP congressional leaders was helped, too, by the fact that he had never belonged to a labor union, as so many senior Labor Department officials under previous administrations had. He even looked like a Republican, with his tall frame, blond hair, conservative suits, gleaming white shirts, and striped ties. Larson's obvious knowledge about the issues in question also surely helped, as did the way he characteristically made his case. Rather than resort to the kinds of emotional and populist appeals common during the Roosevelt and Truman eras, Larson argued in favor of his positions in a calm, academic fashion. This proved to be a winning combination during 1954, when the GOP had narrow majorities in both the House and the Senate.[17]

By July of that year, Larson had become conversant with all of his major duties as under secretary. In addition to managing the day-to-day operation of the Labor Department, lobbying and testifying before Congress on bills to improve social insurance programs, and giving an average of two speeches per week on aspects of social insurance to professional groups, he had several other major responsibilities. Although he had no one-on-one dealings with Eisenhower, Larson attended the weekly meetings of the president's Cabinet whenever Mitchell was away, which proved to be often. Larson also attended meetings of the subcabinet, which included all of the under secretaries from the cabinet-level departments. He oversaw the preparation of such Labor Department publications as its annual handbook and report to Congress and other public relations efforts such as helping to produce a television show on the department's work that aired on Labor Day that year. Larson also supervised the work of special departmental committees created to study the problems of older workers and newcomers to the paid labor force and ways to improve state workers' compensation laws. Learning all of these responsibilities required Larson to work long hours during his first four months on the job.[18]

As if that were not enough, he spent evenings and weekends working on a new book. Aimed at the educated general reader, it would explain the background of all of the various Social Security programs, including old-age pensions, aid to dependent children, and unemployment insurance; the income-insurance theory behind them; current controversies; and proposals for reform. In addition, Larson wanted to provide an easily understood account of Social Security's major provisions as they affected the employee, the beneficiary, and the employer. The catalysts for this new writing project were was the lack of any such book, which suggested to Larson that there might be a fairly big market for one, and Congress's consideration that same summer of an Eisenhower administration proposal to bring about the greatest single expansion in Social Security ever. This reform, which Congress approved in amended form, extended the system's coverage to most categories of paid employment not yet covered, such as agricultural laborers and domestics. Entitled *Know Your Social Security*, the 220-page volume was published one year later by Harper and Brothers and met with a favorable reception that included an unexpected public endorsement from Vice President Richard Nixon. As with Larson's earlier treatise on workers' compensation, his new book revealed a gift for expressing complicated rules and regulations in clear, concise prose.[19]

Although most of *Know Your Social Security* either restated ideas Larson had earlier expressed in his Arden House paper or dealt with such mundane matters as how to file a claim and estimate one's retirement benefits, the chapters dealing with the origins of social insurance, the government's proper role in this area, and current controversies expressed important ideas in ways that were different enough from Larson's earlier work to merit further discussion. In the chapter entitled "Where Did Social Security Come From?" Larson claimed that social insurance schemes had been invented by conservatives and thus could not be considered "socialistic" in nature. Although correct in attributing the specific proposals first put forward in Germany and in the other Western European countries to conservatives, Larson's discussion of the pattern of causation was nonetheless somewhat misleading. He acknowledged that German chancellor Otto von Bismarck first became interested in social insurance out of a concern about the growing political power of Marxian socialists and decided to deal with that problem by backing the creation of Prussia's influential social insurance system, but then he observed that "it is typical of the history of social security that it did not come in on a great wave of popular demand from the mass of people, as Marxians would now like for us to believe. It came largely because of the efforts of farsighted individuals, who were found as often as not among the ranks of those who would be called politically conservative."[20]

Larson's analysis tends to obscure the fact that but for pressure from below, from Marxists, socialists, and trade unionists, social insurance laws would never have come into being. While Larson was right to argue that the specific *form* of social insurance that emerged in Western Europe and the United States bore the imprint of conservatives there, he went too far in suggesting that they therefore deserved the sole or even primary credit for its creation. A more accurate reading would have given credit more clearly and evenly to pressure from below and a far-sighted response from above. Although Larson usually analyzed all kinds of issues in that balanced way, he seems to have been thrown off by an overriding concern with refuting the charge that social insurance was essentially a left-wing idea. Acutely aware of how many conservatives, in the United States especially, still held that view, Larson presented the historical record in the way most likely to reconcile these critics on the right.

Not all of them found his approach satisfactory, of course. When Larson first floated this interpretation in a speech to the Economic Club of Chicago the previous year, he received a dissenting response from the director of economic research for the U.S. Chamber of Commerce, Emerson Schmidt. Schmidt suggested that Larson might be overselling the virtues of social security while failing to point out the potentially dangerous growth of government power to which social security might lead: "You imply that you believe that the social security system in Germany launched by Bismarck stopped Communism. But it did not stop Hitler."[21]

Although aware of this kind of rebuttal, Larson persisted with his thesis, evidently believing it to be the best way to persuade those on the right of social security's value to a free society. In serving that worthwhile goal, so characteristic of the administration for which he worked, Larson sacrificed a certain amount of clarity and accuracy. His handling of this issue revealed how the shift from a purely academic role to a much more political one had begun to affect his thinking and writing.[22]

A similar pattern emerged in his discussion of the government's proper role in the area of social insurance. Larson suggested that Republicans had historically been more supportive of an expansive view of the government's role than Democrats. While certainly true in the nineteenth century, this had become steadily less so in the following one, something he did not mention. Here again, Larson wrote history with a well-intended purpose, but the result was less than fully accurate.[23]

The more politicized nature of his analysis also appeared in the chapter entitled "Some Current Controversies," where he addressed the issue of disability insurance. Larson's Arden House paper had strongly suggested that the United States should adopt a social insurance program for injuries and ailments that were not work related, but the relevant passages in his new book were much more vague. Larson no doubt understood that readers would naturally tend to think that the views expressed there were in line with those of the Eisenhower administration, given his high office within it. As there was no administration consensus on the issue of disability insurance, Larson evidently chose to express his view about the need for it only indirectly.[24]

The same concern about antagonizing more conservative elements lay behind Larson's decision around this time to substitute the term "income insurance" for "social insurance" when discussing the American system. From his perspective, "income insurance" not only had the virtue of greater accuracy, it also gave less offense to Old Guard Republicans and conservative Southern Democrats in Congress, who tended to associate the word "social" with socialism. So strongly did he feel about this change that he made it Labor Department policy for all official publications. The same kind of reasoning led him to describe income insurance programs and efforts to improve them as bulwarks against communism.[25]

In all of these various efforts to assuage the fears of conservatives still inclined to oppose the welfare state as "socialistic" and "un-American," one can discern a key feature of moderate conservatism: a determination not to provoke opposition from those farther to the right. That overriding concern tended to inhibit Larson and the Eisenhower administration from freely expressing their qualified support for the most durable and important of Roosevelt's and Truman's policies, both domestic and foreign. That same concern also encouraged Larson and like-minded conservatives, when arguing in favor of such New Deal policies as Social Security, farm subsidies, and federal funding for public works construction, to emphasize their value in preventing more radical change instead of their other constructive results. While this tactic no doubt helped reconcile conservatives to the continuation and even the expansion of those policies during the 1950s, it had the consequence of making Eisenhower and many of his aides sound more conservative than they actually were. The most astute observers understood this, but many others, then and afterward, did not.[26]

The desire not to provoke conservatives needlessly also led Larson to refrain from challenging existing policies he believed to be wrong unless the prospects for reform appeared real. One example of this tactic had to do with the practice of licensing Mexican citizens to work as farm laborers in the southwestern United States. These *braceros* tended to lower wage levels for agricultural workers, but the strong support of the farm lobby made this guest-worker program unstoppable, despite Larson's private objection to it. He complained about that in a letter to Florence written on July 17, 1954: "We import thousands of Mexican laborers for the big farmers of Texas, California and elsewhere. Why? So that these farmers can get masses of labor when they want it at low cost. If we didn't do this, these farmers would have to pay going rates to domestic laborers. I'd like to see the whole program cut out—but of course the agricultural lobby is the strongest in Congress by several times over."[27]

Although the need to mute his opposition to policies like this must have worn on Larson and other like-minded officials in the Eisenhower administration, their admiration for its head tended to make such self-restraint bearable. That was certainly the case for Larson, who had his first substantive conversation with the president during a stag dinner at the White House on August 4th. So excited was Larson by this experience that he wrote Florence about it that same night: "It is very late—but I must write you just a note to tell you that my dinner with Eisenhower was the most thrilling experience I have yet had. I sat opposite him at dinner, and next to him afterward and we talked for hours about everything and everybody—Eden, Mendes-France, India, Indonesia, Iran, Taft, Churchill, Israel, religion, principles,—everything."[28]

Soon after this memorable event, which made a nice capstone to Larson's four-month period of apprenticeship at the Labor Department, he rejoined his family and enjoyed a well-deserved vacation. During this time, he and Florence began organizing their new life together in Washington. At the end of the summer, they and their two children made the move to the nation's capital, where they had rented a house in the fashionable northwest section of the city. Lex and Anna—who turned fifteen and fourteen, respectively, in 1954—enrolled in private schools there that fall, he at St. Albans and she at the nearby National Cathedral School. The timing of this move proved fortuitous for them, in the sense that both children were able to spend most of their high school years in one place.[29]

The move had much more disruptive consequences for Florence, whose career in theater essentially came to a halt. No one, and certainly not Arthur Larson, had consciously intended that to happen. He had always been supportive of her work, which she had continued after leaving her teaching job at Ithaca College by acting in the Pittsburgh Playhouse under her maiden name. But there were limited opportunities for acting roles in Washington at that time, and parts for women over 40, as she was by then, tended to be few everywhere. Even more decisive was Florence's sense that she needed to assume entertaining duties as the wife of a high-ranking administration official. She also worked behind the scenes as the chief editor of her husband's speeches and other major writings. These factors and her family responsibilities essentially preempted Florence's career aspirations during the mid-1950s.[30]

Although Florence conceived of this change at first as only an interruption, it marked a more permanent turning point in her life. The root cause of this was the progress of Arthur's career and her strong support for it, which tended to undermine her own professional goals. This kind of growing imbalance, so common for middle-class couples of their generation, produced its share of regrets for Florence Larson. She gently expressed them to her own daughter in later years by encouraging Anna's career in music and repeatedly remarking to her that "it is by your works that ye shall be known."[31] What made this outcome bearable was the great pleasure Florence derived from her very stable and happy marriage to Arthur and the achievements of their talented and successful children. Her letters to him then and afterward glow with pride at his accomplishments and reflect as well the pleasure she took from raising Lex and Anna. In Florence's case, the 1950s social system both gave and took away, a trade-off she accepted graciously if not always happily.[32]

To facilitate the kind of home entertaining that ultimately consumed so much of Florence's time and energy, in the late spring of 1955 she and Arthur bought a three-story house with elaborate wrought-iron grillwork outside and a very large living room that took up all of the first floor. Located on Ordway Street in the fashionable neighborhood of Cleveland Park, this house was near the one they had been renting and the children's schools. For the next three years, the Larsons would call it home. They lived comfortably there on the $17,500 he earned as under secretary of labor and on the extra income from his writings, most notably the workers' compensation treatise. The highlights of their home life were the frequent parties they held in the salon-type first-floor room. These affairs usually featured guests associated with the Eisenhower administration who listened or joined in as Arthur and Florence made their own music, sometimes accompanied by Lex and/or Anna. The family photographs from this period convey an impression of both midwestern wholesomeness and East Coast formality. These somewhat contrasting images blended together to produce the outward appearance of a more urbane version of the *Leave It to Beaver* kind of family life. As with so many families during the 1950s, the underlying reality was more complicated and less carefree. Lex, in particular, experienced discomfort in playing the role his parents assigned to him but nonetheless dutifully did his part. In so doing, he and the other members of his family (and similar ones across America) projected a lasting, highly positive image of home life that later generations would look back on nostalgically.[33]

The decision to buy a house in Washington not only made entertaining easier; it also signaled Larson's deepening commitment to his new job there. Having learned the ropes during the spring and summer of 1954, he had begun moving ahead that fall with some pet projects of his own. The considerable success the Labor Department enjoyed that year in winning congressional approval for bills it had proposed encouraged such thoughts. Congress had passed Eisenhower administration bills to improve the nation's social insurance system, most notably the extension of Social Security to ten and a half million more workers and an increase in average monthly benefits of 13 percent. Congress had also enacted the improvements to the District of Columbia's unemployment insurance system Larson had lobbied for, raising the maximum weekly benefit from $20 to $30. A more limited version of the other measure he had pushed for, a proposal to extend unemployment insurance to small businesses, also passed. This new law extended coverage to 1.4 million more people, even though it did not go as far as the Eisenhower administration had proposed.[34]

Wanting to try again on that front and to move along the process of completing the nation's social insurance system more generally in accordance with the wage-loss theory behind it, Larson decided to focus the bulk of his efforts on the District of Columbia. Pushing for improvements in and additions to its various social insurance programs would, he hoped, benefit the city's 800,000 residents and set a good example that the states would choose to follow. At the same time, Larson also supported a new bill to extend federal unemployment insurance coverage to all businesses still outside the program. He also favored improving the workers' compensation system for longshoremen and harbor workers, who were covered in this area by federal law because they worked on both land and water. Larson also decided to push the Labor Department to provide assistance to any state interested in reviewing its existing social insurance laws or passing new ones. All of these ideas received James Mitchell's blessing, and all except the last one—which did not require presidential approval or new legislation—received that of the White House staff as well. They became official administration policy when Eisenhower's aides included them in the president's 1955 State of the Union message.[35]

This speech, which Eisenhower delivered to the new 84th Congress on January 6, 1955, briefly mentioned Larson's proposals for the District of Columbia in a single sentence. After the address, Larson filled in the details of his plans. They called for further improvements in the District's unemployment insurance program, this time by raising the maximum benefit level to 50 percent of average weekly wages for a maximum of twenty-six weeks. This proposal followed up on an earlier letter to state officials signed by Eisenhower and James Mitchell that urged them to adopt this approach. At the same time, the number of workers entitled to participate would be expanded and a new provision would be added to establish a retraining program for the chronically unemployed. All of this reflected Larson's view that the crucial criterion for deciding how much the district's unemployment insurance program should be improved and extended was not what the states had already done, which had shaped the previous year's legislation in this area, but what was needed to fulfill the program's basic purpose.[36]

Larson's proposals for reforming the workers' compensation program and adding a non-occupational disability insurance program in the District of Columbia reflected that underlying rationale. The key changes in the first area would increase benefits, extend coverage to on-the-job accidents and illnesses that were currently exempt from such benefits, and incorporate the best features of the various state systems. His proposal to create a disability insurance program for the district would close the widest gap in the income insurance system there. Larson called non-occupational disability insurance "today's frontier" in the area of income insurance.[37]

These proposals at first attracted little attention from the press—in part because Larson's ideas applied only to the District of Columbia. They were overshadowed, too, by the Eisenhower administration's other proposals in the field of labor, most notably a plan to raise the minimum wage from seventy-five to ninety cents an hour and amendments to the National Labor Relations Act, which regulated union organization and collective bargaining.[38]

One publication did perceive the far-reaching implications behind the Eisenhower administration's proposals for changing the District of Columbia's social insurance system: *Business Week*. In an article entitled "Pushing State Action for Labor" that appeared in the January 15, 1955, issue, the magazine's labor reporter explained the larger purpose behind these measures and named Larson as the key administration official advocating them. The article's author perceptively observed that Larson's campaign would be difficult because he faced opposition not only from management groups concerned about the cost to employers of these changes but also from labor unions, which shared Larson's ultimate objectives but wanted to accomplish them by federalizing state programs. Conceding at the outset that this would be a long-term effort, Larson nonetheless possessed the inner confidence of a man who believes himself to be on the right side of history. He conveyed this thought to his *Business Week* interviewer by saying, "I think there is a certain inner logic in systems of this kind that must eventually work itself out. Deficiencies in our administration of things will not go on forever."[39] With that characteristically optimistic view to sustain him, Larson set out in 1955 to see how much could be accomplished.

The makeup of the new Congress made his already difficult task much more so. In the off-year elections held the previous November, the GOP had lost its slim majority in the House and Senate. That result stemmed mostly from the political repercussions of the 1954 recession that followed the end of the Korean War, too many GOP candidates with Old Guard attitudes, Eisenhower's reluctance to involve himself directly in the congressional campaigns, and his absence from the ballot, which meant no coattail effect for Republicans contending with an opposition party that was still the dominant one nationally. The 84th Congress featured small Democratic majorities in both of its houses and new leadership in the form of Senate Majority Leader Lyndon Johnson and House Speaker Sam Rayburn. Both Texans, their elevation to the top jobs in their respective chambers reflected the dominant part southerners played in congressional Democratic circles at that time. That power was ultimately based on the congressional seniority system, which representatives and senators from the one-party South were better able to exploit than northern and western Democrats in Congress, who faced much more competitive general election races. This meant that Democratic majorities in the House and Senate would automatically bring southerners to the fore—not only to the top leadership offices but also to most of the committee chairmanships. Thus, as of the first week of January 1955, the Senate and House labor committees acquired heads who were Southern Democrats, Senator Lister Hill of Alabama and Representative Graham Barden of North Carolina. Barden in particular was more conservative than his GOP predecessor, which boded ill for any bill aimed at expanding social insurance programs.[40]

The return of the so-called Dixiecrats to leadership roles in Congress had other, even more troubling implications for Larson's plans, because they depended so heavily on using the District of Columbia as a model. Southern Democrats had long thought of Washington in that way, but primarily with respect to racial segregation. Dixiecrats had used Democratic majorities in Congress forty years earlier to spread Jim Crow practices in the nation's capital, thereby giving Washington a distinctively southern social structure. Related to this was an economic structure whose most notable features included low wages, few unions, and a system of social insurance among the poorest in the nation. Persuading the Southern Democrats running Congress in 1955 to go along with making the District of Columbia into a social insurance showcase must have seemed a very tall order, but Larson decided to push ahead.[41]

He did have some grounds for optimism. Although the Dixiecrats held most of the leadership posts, the new Congress as a whole had more liberal members than the previous one, given that most of the newcomers were northern Democrats, not southern ones. He also had the backing of his boss and the Eisenhower White House and could count on some support from GOP moderates in Congress. A kind of centrist coalition could be developed from these elements, as Larson had seen in the last Congress when it enacted improvements to the Social Security and unemployment insurance programs. Larson's ability to get his new proposals through depended ultimately on whether he could assemble a similar coalition behind them.[42]

During the early stages of this effort, Larson concentrated on drafting the needed bills with the help of Labor Department staff. Of the three measures under development, the one dealing with workers' compensation required the most preliminary research, for the simple reason that Larson intended to bring together the best provisions in all of the various state laws. This idea of drafting a model workers' compensation act had been in Larson's mind from the very start of his tenure at the Labor Department, even before he came up with the idea of using the District of Columbia as an example for the states to follow. He had established a special committee in May 1954 with himself as chairman to develop a model act and announced this initiative during a speech in Orlando, Florida, the following fall. In that address, Larson made clear that rather than displace state lawmaking in this area, he wanted to profit from what he saw as healthy experimentation among the states over the past forty years. In effect, Larson argued that the Labor Department was the logical clearinghouse for the states' best practices, a strategy that acknowledged the states' primacy in this area of law but still afforded the federal government room to take the initiative in drafting a model act. He also emphasized the value of such a project to state legislatures that were satisfied with the rules they already had in this area but wanted to be sure they had not missed situations that merited coverage. Larson explained that completeness was the most important goal of the model act.[43]

Devising a model act proved to be a time-consuming process not only because of the basic research involved but also because Larson decided to circulate a working draft to interested groups such as the national governors' conference, state program administrators, state legislators, the U.S. Chamber of Commerce, the National Association of Manufacturers (NAM), and various trade associations. More than the other proposals for the District of Columbia, and, indeed, more than anything else he ever did while under secretary of labor, this model workers' compensation act was his "baby." Thus, it offers an important indication of the nature of his experience in that post.[44]

At first, all seemed to go as planned. The various model provisions were gathered and discussed under Larson's expert supervision, and a legislative draftsman prepared a version for circulation and review outside the department. This "discussion draft" went out to interested parties in December 1955, and most of the responses that came in over the next four months were favorable. Larson's high hopes for his model workers' compensation act could be seen in his comments about it in a memo to James Mitchell that he wrote while the research and drafting process was under way:

> The more I work on this project, the more I am convinced that it is intensely valuable, and that this model act is going to contain a surprising amount of creative improvement of interest to every State in the Union, no matter how advanced its legislation may be. One of our plans is to have this Act submitted to the ILO [International Labour Organization] and have it become an ILO document, where it can serve as a model for the entire world.[45]

These high hopes soon came to naught, however, as spokesmen for the business community and some state administrators responded to the draft by voicing objections to the whole idea. Within business circles, reactions ranged from unenthusiastic to outright hostile. Representatives of the U.S. Chamber of Commerce met privately with Larson in mid-April 1956 to express their reservations about the model act. After several hours of discussion, Larson came away with the impression that he had made no real converts but had forestalled truly harmful opposition from that quarter. The NAM voiced its objections much more strongly. This group of mostly small- and medium-sized businesses expressed its opposition to Larson's brainchild in a May 1st letter signed by NAM president Cola G. Parker. Although many NAM members doubtless had reservations about how much the new provisions would cost them, this letter focused on the source of the model act. Parker argued that the federal government had no business telling the states what to do about workers' compensation or even making suggestions on that topic. Similar responses came from interested trade associations and some businesses, most notably insurance companies, that belonged to them.[46]

If this were not damaging enough, some of the state administrators, most notably Otto Kriese of Ohio, weighed in with the same basic objection. Opposition from this group seems to have taken Larson by surprise, precisely because his model act was, in essence, a compendium of the states' best practices. Neither the general concept nor the model act's specific provisions bothered Kriese and like-minded state officials. They did object strongly, however, to the U.S. Labor Department's role as compiler. Fiercely protective of the states' prerogatives in this area, Kriese and his colleagues argued in effect that a model act would have been acceptable had it come from some body created by the states instead of from the federal government. Kriese and company saw through Larson's subtle plan for getting around the concerns about federalism and wanted none of it.[47]

Not all of the responses were hostile, of course. In fact, the large majority of the ninety-nine letters commenting on the discussion draft that had come in by April 1, 1956, were positive, Larson reported to James Mitchell. And while many labor leaders and the most liberal Democrats in Congress would have preferred a federalized workers' compensation system, no strong protests emerged from those quarters.[48]

Even so, the formidable group of opponents the model act had aroused had no trouble blocking it. Larson tried to placate his plan's critics by conceding that he had erred in using the term "model act" because some had interpreted that phrase as implying that the federal government would pressure the states to adopt the act verbatim, when he had merely meant to create a guide states could use as they saw fit. Even this clarification failed to mollify his plan's critics. They used their influence in Congress to cut off funds for any more work on this project, in effect compelling Larson to give up.[49]

The disappointing outcome of his model act project did not mean that Larson's considerable efforts on its behalf had been entirely in vain. They drew attention to deficiencies in state workers' compensation systems and put pressure on state legislatures to make needed improvements. In the first seven months of 1955, for example, thirty states and the two territories of Alaska and Hawaii increased workers' compensation benefits. Larson's work on the model act also laid the groundwork for a similar, much more successful future venture.[50]

His other major legislative initiatives during 1955–1956 produced similarly mixed results. Opposition from conservative Southern Democrats completely blocked some of his proposals, most notably those having to do with the District of Columbia. The Dixiecrats objected to the cost of these initiatives and, one suspects, to providing the District of Columbia's large black population in particular with social insurance protections that would have been among the best in the country. Some of Larson's proposals also met with strong opposition from New Deal liberals in Congress, although the motive behind that opposition was very different from those of the Dixiecrats. The most ardent liberals there objected to Larson's plans to give the states, rather than the federal government, responsibility for dealing with such problems as chronic unemployment and non-occupational disability. The pressures from these extremes produced a variety of legislative outcomes with respect to the measures Larson championed. In the end, none of them emerged from the 84th Congress in the more moderate form he had favored.[51]

The fate of Larson's plan to improve the district's unemployment insurance system by establishing a program to retrain the chronically unemployed is instructive in this regard. Although the problem Larson sought to address was not new in the mid-1950s, it had become more serious beginning in 1954, when the post–Korean War recession led to lasting high unemployment in some of the nation's older manufacturing centers, mostly located in the Northeast and Midwest.

During that year, the migration of employers to other areas of the country where labor costs were lower, most notably the South, accelerated, and so did automation. Both of these strategies aimed at improving profitability, but they also led to higher levels of joblessness in older manufacturing areas even as the nation's economy recovered strongly in 1955. These developments helped Larson's retraining initiative attract immediate attention in the press when he first raised it publicly on December 29, 1954. Speaking to a conference of economists in Detroit, Larson proposed studying this idea, and when Mitchell and the White House staff gave their blessing, he pushed such a plan as an improvement to the District of Columbia's unemployment insurance system. Despite this interest, however, his bill to provide for such a program went nowhere in the 84th Congress.[52]

Dixiecrat objections to Larson's proposal went beyond the issue of whether the nation's capital should serve as a social insurance model for the other states. Southern Democrats also opposed Larson's bill and a similar proposal by Illinois senator Paul Douglas on the ground that a lack of jobs in areas of prolonged high unemployment, rather than a lack of skills, was the key problem and that the best solution was for the long-term unemployed to migrate to places where jobs were plentiful. In essence, southern conservatives and some like-minded northern and western ones argued that the proper solution to this problem was to let the market system work undisturbed by inducing people to move to places where they were needed most instead of establishing a government program that would interfere with that process. Implicit in this prescription, of course, was the idea that the most constructive course for northern workers displaced by deindustrialization was to move to the emerging Sunbelt, whose largely non-union environment and low wages and living costs were increasingly attracting employers from the North. This would tend, of course, to raise incomes in the South and narrow the substantial economic gap between that region, then the nation's poorest, and the rest of the country but in a way that would be very painful to many living in the industrial north.[53]

Dixiecrats in Congress made plain their lack of interest in any kind of "depressed areas" legislation, as it became known, during hearings held by the House Banking and Currency Committee in April 1956. The focus of these hearings was not Larson's proposal for the District of Columbia, which had died the year before, but rather a new Eisenhower administration bill that had been introduced in January 1956. This measure, a much more modestly funded alternative to Paul Douglas's bill, would have empowered the Commerce Department to administer a new $50 million loan program for communities suffering from chronic unemployment. Larson testified on behalf of this bill, an experience he described in a memo to James Mitchell: "The Committee's approach was so completely disorganized that it is impossible to predict what line it will take from this point on. Congressman [L. H.] Fountain [of North Carolina] flatly stated that the bill had no more chance of being reported out than a snowball had of surviving in hell. He did not enlarge upon this somewhat hackneyed simile."[54]

Interest among New Deal liberals in Congress, on the other hand, was quite genuine, and their perspective on this very difficult issue was in some ways closer to Larson's. Sensitive to the disruption in people's lives deindustrialization had begun to cause, in large part because the process was occurring in places liberals usually represented, they shared Larson's view that the government should do something to help the long-term unemployed. They, too, however, tended to oppose his bill and the subsequent administration measure.[55]

Liberals led by Democrat Paul Douglas favored a federal program instead, not separate state ones, and a much bigger federal commitment than the Eisenhower administration had proposed. Douglas's bill would have established an independent federal agency to administer retraining programs for rural as well as urban "depressed areas" and a $390 million federal loan program that would help such places attract new industries. By adding rural areas afflicted by chronic unemployment, Douglas hoped to address another serious social problem and in the process broaden support for depressed-areas legislation enough to make its enactment possible. At the same, however, the bulk of the funds and the focus of Douglas's proposal remained on the more urban communities experiencing economic decline.[56]

This kind of support among liberals for what in Europe was called "industrial policy" led them to view the Eisenhower administration's proposal for which Larson testified as too modest. In this area, as in others during the mid-1950s, the forces pushing for more extreme solutions on the right and left blocked the middle course. The resulting stalemate satisfied the Dixiecrats running Congress by allowing the ongoing process of economic change across regions to continue undisturbed.[57]

Larson's disability insurance proposal for the District of Columbia also went nowhere in Congress, albeit for a very different reason. The new Democratic majorities there, sensing that disability insurance could be a winning issue for them, instead backed the creation of a federal agency to oversee a disability program that the states would help administer. Even some of the leading Dixiecrats in Congress such as Lyndon Johnson and Sam Rayburn supported this measure, which passed the House in June 1955. Although the Eisenhower administration had taken no position on the proposal up to that point, as the Senate began its deliberations on the bill in early 1956, pressure mounted on Eisenhower and his aides to take a clear stand on the bill, which organized labor strongly supported and the American Medical Association just as strongly opposed.[58]

Larson did not figure prominently in this debate because the federal nature of the proposed program meant that the secretary of the recently created Department of Health, Education and Welfare (HEW), Marion Folsom, would serve as the administration spokesperson on this issue. A former executive at Eastman Kodak with a longtime interest in social insurance issues, Folsom delayed making a decision until March 1956 while he pondered what course to take. Although not close to Folsom, Larson did have connections at HEW, most notably to its under secretary, Nelson Rockefeller. Shortly after arriving in Washington to begin work at the Labor Department, Larson had become much better acquainted with Rockefeller and through him got to know Oveta Culp Hobby, the Federal Security Administrator, who oversaw the operation of Social Security and had a direct interest in the disability proposal. In fact, Rockefeller and Hobby were the two Eisenhower administration officials Larson knew best outside the Labor Department, thanks to their mutual interest in the Social Security extension bill that had passed in 1954. Through this informal network of administration officials concerned with social insurance issues, Larson was able to transmit his views on a variety of topics, including disability insurance.[59]

From Larson's perspective, the Democrats' plan went too far by creating a federal agency rather than leaving the matter entirely to the states and not far enough by excluding the partially disabled entirely and the completely disabled under the age of fifty from coverage. After much deliberation, Folsom and the Eisenhower administration came out against the Democrats' bill in March 1956. For Eisenhower and his top aides, the federal nature of the proposed program appears to have been the determining factor. Believing that this was properly something for the states to do by themselves, Folsom testified against the Senate bill, and Eisenhower threatened to veto the measure if it passed both houses of Congress. This disagreement culminated in a dramatic showdown vote on the Senate floor on July 17, 1956. By a margin of one vote, the proposal to create a federal program to provide insurance for the permanently disabled over the age of fifty passed, thereby opening the way to adoption of the bill's other provisions. Evidently feeling election-year pressures not to oppose the measure, Eisenhower reluctantly signed it into law, thereby signaling the death knell for the state-based approach to disability insurance that Larson had favored.[60]

Although clearly a defeat, this turn of events nonetheless had its positive aspects for Larson. The knowledge that under this new law the states would still play the primary administrative role and that gaps in coverage could be filled in later via legislative amendment (which eventually was done) must have taken away some of the sting. Above all, Larson could take satisfaction from seeing the nation begin at long last to fill in what he saw as the most serious hole in the nation's social insurance system. Still, the specific outcome in this area was another sobering reminder of the difficulties involved in completing that system along the lines he believed to be correct.[61]

This pattern of either getting nothing at all or more than he had asked for from the 84th Congress applied to most of the other bills pending in which Larson had taken a special interest. One example was the outcome of his proposal to improve the workers' compensation system for longshoremen and harbor workers. The relevant committees in both houses of Congress held hearings to consider the bill, at which Larson testified. Its specific proposals for minimum and maximum compensation levels soon encountered resistance, however, from a group of sixteen Senate liberals led by Warren Magnuson of Washington and Wayne Morse of Oregon. This group argued that Larson's proposed compensation levels were too low and sponsored their own, more expensive measure instead, which Larson opposed as so generous that it would discourage recipients from seeking rehabilitation and a return to gainful employment. Walter Mason, the union movement's lobbyist assigned to the bill, declared that both Larson's version and the Magnuson-Morse one were inadequate and proposed raising compensation levels even higher. In the end, Congress approved a compromise that was close to what Larson had wanted but with compensation levels he still considered to be too high.[62]

The one other measure he personally championed in the 84th Congress—a plan to give the federal government power to regulate the transportation of migrant farm workers—also passed, but in a limited form that did not reach all of the carriers involved. Although this measure did bring some improvements in health and safety, it could not put an end to the exploitation of migrant farm workers by large growers operating in the Southwest, as Larson wished. They used their formidable clout in Congress to keep the *bracero* program alive for the remainder of the Eisenhower presidency.[63]

Even the higher-profile items the Labor Department pushed in Congress tended to meet the same fate as Larson's pet proposals. The 33 ⅓ percent increase in the minimum wage (from 75 cents to $1 an hour) that Congress approved in 1955 was ten cents more than the Eisenhower administration had thought necessary to restore the purchasing power lost due to Korean War–related inflation. An increase that large also seemed potentially self-defeating, given the risk that it might bring another round of higher prices, but Eisenhower reluctantly concluded that this was the best he could do with a Democratic-controlled Congress and signed the measure into law. Eisenhower, Mitchell, and Larson favored extending coverage of the minimum wage to include workers in such low-wage sectors as textiles, sawmills, and sugar refining, but strong opposition from Southern Democrats in Congress blocked that part of the administration's minimum-wage proposal. Although pleased that the minimum wage had been raised, the net result, from the perspective of the Eisenhower administration, gave too much to too few.[64]

The other major bill the Labor Department backed in the 84th Congress, its proposed amendments to the National Labor Relations Act, fared even worse. Eisenhower had promised during his 1952 presidential campaign to win enactment of some improvements to the law and developed specific suggestions during his first year as president. Most of these proposed changes dealt with fairly technical issues. Although Eisenhower and his aides believed that these amendments would improve the existing statute, the 83rd Congress blocked any changes. Another attempt in 1955–1956 produced the same result, and for the same basic reason. Unwilling to disturb the existing détente between labor and management groups on issues of union organization and collective bargaining, the 84th Congress, like its predecessor, simply refused to make changes in this area.[65]

Larson did not fault James Mitchell for these less-than-stellar legislative results during 1955–1956. On the contrary, Larson formed an early positive impression of his boss's political and administrative skills and never changed his mind. The basis for that view lay in Mitchell's effectiveness in handling labor-management disputes and, more generally, in establishing himself as the most important figure within the Eisenhower administration on labor policy questions.[66]

Larson mentioned his early positive impressions of Mitchell in letters to Florence during the summer of 1954. Although Larson had begun with a favorable view of his new boss, the extent of Mitchell's political skills came as something of a surprise even to him. He confided in Florence in July that "Mitchell is shrewder politically than I realized. He wrote 250 letters last week to Republican congressmen and leaders, offering to appear with them in television programs, etc. to help in campaigns. He has already made one television film of this kind, and is spending all of Monday making some more. Incidentally, of course, the Labor Department gets a big boost."[67]

Mitchell's performance as labor secretary in the ensuing years only increased Larson's high opinion of him. When Larson looked backed during retirement on his career, which included collaborations with many impressive people, he said of Mitchell that "he was just a wonderful man. In fact, of all the people I've ever known in public life, he's the only one who is right up there with Eisenhower, so far as my own feelings and estimation are concerned."[68]

What explains the seeming contradiction between the Labor Department's mixed legislative record during the mid-1950s and the high opinion Larson, Eisenhower, and many others formed of Mitchell's abilities was the nature of the 1950s economic and political system. During this heyday of American corporatism, bargaining between organized interest groups such as labor, management, and agriculture and supervision of that process by executive branch agencies did far more to determine social conditions than legislation in Congress. Mitchell's great effectiveness as a mediator of the collective bargaining process and in getting the various federal agencies that regulated labor to act in concert helped give the United States during the mid-1950s the lowest peacetime unemployment rates ever recorded and the American working and lower middle classes some of the sunniest years they had ever known.[69]

This broader view of the Labor Department's record under Eisenhower helps put the legislative setbacks Larson experienced during 1955–1956 in clearer perspective. While they were significant, those defeats were of distinctly less importance than the Labor Department's other achievements during his tenure as under secretary. The fundamental reasons why Larson's experience in the secondary realm of congressional legislation during 1955–1956 did not match the Labor Department's overall performance had to do with the ambitious nature of his objectives, competition from groups pushing ideas about social insurance that were more extreme than his own, and the switch in January 1955 to a Dixiecrat-led Congress. The second and third of these mattered more than the first in determining the fate of Larson's social insurance proposals, which suggests that it was largely beyond his control.[70]

Rather than simply feeling disappointed by this turn of events, Larson appeared to be of two minds during 1956 about what was happening in the social insurance field. In an address to a business group on February 15th of that year, he sounded upbeat about the ongoing trend toward more emphasis on privately negotiated supplements to welfare state programs as an alternative to legislatively enacted ones. This speech, which Larson entitled "Outflanking the Welfare State," is interesting for Larson's comments on that subject and on the role of unions in American society. Clearly an exercise in trying to persuade a management group to view unions more sympathetically, Larson pointed out that they had helped keep the American social insurance system a partly private one by bargaining for fringe benefits that supplemented those provided by public programs. Although his earlier Arden House paper had argued that this trend was in some ways unfortunate, this time Larson mentioned only what he saw as its positive consequence.[71]

Larson used that point as the basis for making a much bigger one—that business should welcome more unionization because the stronger and more numerous unions became, the more they would be able to take care of workers themselves instead of relying on public welfare state programs to do so. Lest anyone in the audience think that this was simply the view of one official in the Eisenhower administration, Larson quoted Eisenhower's public statement the previous year that "strong, dedicated, democratic trade unionism is one of the bulwarks of our American way of life. Our democracy and our economy both make possible and draw strength from free trade unions."[72]

Larson's thesis is interesting for what it said about how his views had evolved over the preceding two and a half years. In his Arden House paper he had pointed to the problems that organized labor's quest for private supplements to welfare state programs would likely create, such as the difficulties associated with financing such supplemental benefit systems and their tendency to reduce labor force mobility by greatly increasing the incentive to stay permanently with one employer. These kinds of problems had led Larson then to conclude that it would have been better had this trend never developed. The most important reason for his change of opinion by 1956, one suspects, was simply a concession to reality. By that point, such fringe benefits had clearly become a durable feature of American life, which meant that dwelling on their drawbacks no longer made much sense.[73]

Larson also seems to have shifted his stance on the issue of private supplements out of an appreciation for their contribution to keeping the public welfare state within sharply defined boundaries. Eager to preserve the distinctive American variety of social insurance, Larson appears to have decided by 1956 that private supplements were not only inevitable but actually desirable for that reason. One corollary, of course, was support for more unionization of the economy in order to promote adequate levels of social insurance coverage for everyone.[74]

While there was a certain logic to Larson's views on this subject, one could also raise questions about them, as some of his listeners surely did. Larson tended to assume that as unions grew bigger and more powerful, their social insurance demands would mostly focus on private supplements rather than on expanded public programs, but whether unions would do so was not clear. Unions had been pushed into bargaining for private supplements only because of an earlier inability to win better public programs from Congress. That failure on the legislative front had stemmed from labor's weakness in certain parts of the country, most notably the South. One could argue, therefore, that more unionization might upset the balance of power that had encouraged the push for fringe benefits of this sort. Larson's remarks suggest that he believed that unions, having started down that road, would not turn back as they grew bigger and stronger, but he could not be sure of that. Another concern had to do with the possibility of excessive union demands in this area as organized labor grew in size and power. Larson tended to assume that American labor leaders could exercise the needed self-restraint, but that, too, remained an open question.[75]

Larson's thesis also rested on a somewhat controversial reading of history. He suggested that the historical record indicated that there are only two alternatives available to Americans: strong unions that bargain privately for many of the things governments provided in other countries or greater government intervention in American life. There had been a time, however, when the nation had possessed neither of these things, as the most conservative members of the business community were prone to point out. In effect, Larson was arguing that Americans had become accustomed to, and dependent on, certain kinds of institutions that cushioned the effects of a modern market economy and that they would not accept a return to the preexisting world of laissez-faire. Although his argument had a lot of force, there were still some in the American business community who had not accepted it.[76]

The uncertainty in Larson's mind about the future of social insurance programs can be seen in remarks he made toward the end of 1956. This address, which he delivered at Cornell's School of Industrial and Labor Relations, showed his sense of frustration with the slow pace of legislative action in this area. "The Future of Income Insurance" reviewed the recent record of Congress and state legislatures in light of Larson's goal of a complete, adequate, and coordinated system of income insurance. He sounded the two major themes: Congress and state legislatures continued to improve the system, but new kinds of problems were cropping up just as fast. He argued that in order to complete the system, a new wave of legislative reform was needed like that of the 1930s.[77]

Bringing about such a burst of reform was a great challenge, he observed, because the motivating forces behind earlier waves of activity in this area, such as what he called the "white-hot indignation against the cruelties of the common-law in its treatment of industrial injuries" and the Great Depression had passed into history. Larson told the audience that they could not count on political pressure from prospective beneficiaries to create the needed wave of reform because those most neglected by the current income insurance system were in the lower ranks of the working population and had little economic or political power.[78]

He also pointed out how the unforeseeable nature of the problems that income insurance addressed tended to suppress support for reform even among those who had more influence. The income insurance system protected against contingencies, Larson noted, that usually did not come to pass. Getting people together to fight for legislation that would protect them adequately against problems most of them would likely never encounter posed a basic structural obstacle to reform of the sort Larson called for.[79]

Even the rise of organized labor over the preceding quarter-century had not completely addressed this basic problem, Larson pointed out. In fact, he told his listeners, strong labor unions by then were contributing, however unintentionally, to the creation of a two-tiered system of social insurance by bargaining successfully for so-called fringe benefits that supplemented existing income insurance programs. Larson argued not that unions had abandoned their efforts to make those programs adequate for all but only that labor's "emphasis is apt to be on improving benefits available to those already covered."[80]

What seems to have disturbed Larson most about this state of affairs was the ongoing trend he perceived in the direction of greater inequality in the field of income insurance protections. Although fundamentally an optimist, he warned that if the current trend continued, the country would end up with a two-tiered system of labor in which the first-class worker received both Social Security and private supplementary benefits and the second-class worker received only basic Social Security. In his characteristically calm and tactful way, Larson hinted at the fundamental source of the unfortunate trend he described when explaining what he thought needed to be done to change it:

> I have thought and worried about this question a lot in recent years, and it seems to me there is only one answer. The only hope is that the American public in general, and the business community in particular, will become

> convinced before it is too late that a complete income insurance system is an indispensable adjunct both to a modern private-enterprise economy and to a modern individualistic free society.[81]

Larson saw this solution as a real possibility, he explained, because he believed that business executives who took the trouble to learn about the benefits a complete system of social insurance brought to the economy and society would be persuaded of its desirability.[82]

Larson made his already familiar arguments that he believed would bring business around, and he also made a new one. He pointed out the value of income insurance programs in maintaining consumer purchasing power during adverse situations such as disability or unemployment, which facilitated purchases made on credit of houses, cars, and appliances. The net result, he said, was to help deter severe economic downturns, thereby making the overall economy more stable and businessmen more prosperous.[83]

This speech nicely illustrates his greatest contribution to the Eisenhower administration: explaining and defending its policies through his writings and public addresses. Over the preceding thirty-two months in which he had served as under secretary of labor, Larson had given a great many speeches. Although they mostly reworked themes and issues already discussed, some expressed new ideas sufficiently important as to deserve discussion.

Larson gave the first such address on August 26, 1954, at the University of Pittsburgh's summer commencement exercises. "Liberty, Equality, Security" addressed the question of whether providing more economic security necessarily implied a loss of personal freedom. Larson explained to his audience he had chosen as his title an obvious parody of the rallying cry of the French Revolution in order to emphasize that in more recent times popular government faced a new demand—the demand for security. He called it "the word of the mid-twentieth century—the key word, the fighting word, in fact."[84]

The most original and interesting part of Larson's address dealt with the question of whether undergraduates then truly deserved the label "Silent Generation" that some intellectuals and social critics had given them. Larson rose to the defense of the 1950s college student, but not by arguing that the Silent Generation rubric was essentially untrue. Instead, he argued that the less strident quality of political debates among college students reflected a greater maturity and wisdom than the 1930s generation had possessed. Rather than being disturbed by the new trend, Larson welcomed it.[85]

Larson rejected the notion advanced by some of this generation's detractors that the real reason for its political quiescence stemmed from shrunken ambitions and an overriding concern with a comfortable suburban life. Such critics, he said, had reached such unflattering conclusions by comparing college life then with a nostalgic view of the more politicized campus climate of the 1930s.

The problem with such a comparison, Larson continued, was its essential unfairness. The stakes for all Americans and the country's role in the world had increased greatly since then, which meant that spouting simplistic and misguided political beliefs on American campuses during the 1950s would likely have had far more serious consequences than it had during the 1930s. This "sobering responsibility," Larson said, explained the emergence of a Silent Generation.[86]

His explanation of the quiet on many college campuses, although sound as far as it went, omitted two other factors at work. One was the antiradical hysteria that had been going on since the late 1940s, which had discouraged college students, and the population more generally, from openly expressing political ideas that fell outside the mainstream. Larson's omission of this factor seems very strange, given his own brush with McCarthyism earlier in the year. Perhaps his lack of vulnerability was the reason. Without any radical past of his own to put him at the mercy of the anticommunist witch-hunters, Larson may have missed the extent to which American students with extreme left-wing views had muted their voices out of fear. The other factor that Larson might have mentioned had to do with the way in which events during the 1920s, 1930s, and 1940s had diminished hopes, even among the young, for a brave new world. Efforts to create such a world during those years had led directly to the disasters of fascism and Stalinism. These hard lessons of the previous three decades had surely contributed as well to the shaping of the Silent Generation.[87]

Larson tackled a very different set of issues in another speech given later that year at Cornell Law School. "The Lawyer as Conservative" devoted a good deal of attention to the difference between what Larson called "good conservatism" and "bad conservatism." According to him, the first of these aimed to preserve time-honored ideals and values in ways that evolved in response to changing social conditions. "Bad conservatism," on the other hand, focused on preserving means, not ends, an error that usually led to counterproductive results.[88]

To illustrate his general point, Larson offered the modern income insurance system as an example of a good kind of conservatism. Although much of Larson's remarks covered familiar ground, his observations about how American economic life had changed and had prompted the adoption of new means to preserve cherished values deserve mention. Understanding that much of the sentiment against income insurance programs was concentrated among more prosperous Americans in rural parts of the country, Larson set out to explain why the kinds of self-help that had flourished there were not applicable to the large majority of Americans who lived in and around urban areas:

> The central fact now is that we live in a cash-wage economy, not an agrarian economy. This means that for the vast majority of Americans, when cash wages stop, stark disaster is not far away. They do not have hams and bacon stored in a smokehouse, nor a cellar full of turnips and apples; nor can they

> clothe themselves by spinning their own fleece; and, as for shelter, there is no great rambling family house which can accommodate a wide range of generations and relatives. Food requires cash; clothing may be had only for cash; shelter is only for those who can pay rent in cash.[89]

Larson moved on to address the most common response to this point raised by more extreme conservatives, which was to argue that private savings could meet this new social reality. Here Larson made very clear what he meant about updating the means to meet a traditional end by arguing forcefully that income insurance was a newer form of saving, as were home ownership, private insurance, and private contributory benefit plans through employers. All had emerged, he said, not for change's sake, but rather because the Great Depression had demonstrated "once and for all" that the old-fashioned private form of saving was inadequate protection against a modern business crash.[90]

A lawyer acted as a conservative in the best sense, Larson concluded, by finding for a client this new kind of means to preserve a long-standing and worthwhile end. This was true for the attorney who served a private party and the one who worked for a public entity. He elaborated on that last point by listing a series of contemporary problems such as highway accidents, juvenile delinquency, and racial discrimination that seemingly needed new means to preserve cherished American values. Larson emphasized the need to address these problems without endangering other traditional values, such as individual responsibility, sympathy for the young, and respect for local government. His analysis is interesting for what it says about how moderate conservatives of the 1950s variety tended to approach many of the decade's leading issues and how such conservatives differed from moderate New Deal liberals such as labor leader George Meany and Democratic presidential candidate Adlai Stevenson. Moderate conservatives such as Larson tended to be more aware of, and concerned with, the worthwhile things that could be lost by the steady progress of social reform. Such awareness did not usually lead to fundamental disagreements over public policy goals with moderate liberals. The main difference between these two groups was the attitude toward reform, especially the proper ways and means of achieving it. While moderate New Deal liberals pushed a reformist agenda enthusiastically, moderate conservatives such as Larson typically did so much more cautiously.[91]

Larson's list of social problems is noteworthy, too, for its allusion to school desegregation, one of the very few times he publicly mentioned the subject of race while serving as under secretary of labor. Larson's seeming inattention to racial issues did not signal any disagreement with the U.S. Supreme Court's ruling in *Brown v. The Board of Education of Topeka, Kansas* the previous May; on the contrary, he supported it. What explains Larson's behavior in this area is the way moderates on both the right and the left tended to think at the time about the problems blacks faced. To moderates of that era, those problems were essentially attributable to class, not color. In keeping with that perspective, Larson and the like-minded James Mitchell decided early in their tenure that the Labor Department would issue no more reports on blacks specifically. Mitchell made his thinking clear on this point when he received a May 10, 1954, memo from Larson announcing this decision at a recent policy meeting. To Larson's written statement there, which read "Oral agreement that we would issue no more publications on negroes," Mitchell appended by hand the qualification "as such."[92]

This did not mean that Mitchell and Larson had no interest in the issue of segregation. On the contrary, the two men wished to eradicate its vestiges in the Employment Service's regional offices and tried to find a way to accomplish that goal. On October 25, 1954, Larson sent a memo detailing his activities of the past two weeks to Mitchell: "We held a meeting on the question of desegregation of Employment Services offices in some of the Southern states. I have suggested it to [White House official] Max Rabb as an agenda item for the Sub-Cabinet, on the theory that all Federal Agencies must move together under a single Administration policy if anything is to be done."[93]

Despite this promising beginning, Mitchell and Larson soon dropped the idea. Although the record is unclear about the reason for this, it was most likely because of the return of the Dixiecrats to power in Congress in January 1955. Their control over the budgetary purse strings tended to inhibit all of the executive branch departments and agencies from tackling the issue of segregation within the public sector. The extent of Larson's interest in the issue can be seen, though, in his decision to raise it again fourteen months later. In a memo to Mitchell dated January 3, 1956, Larson reported that he had contacted Max Rabb with positive results but noted resistance from officials at HEW. In the end, neither Larson's nor James Mitchell's well-meaning efforts entirely achieved the desired goal. The Employment Service retained some segregated offices and other aspects of Jim Crow, most notably job listings with a racial qualification, throughout the life of the Eisenhower administration. A presidential committee to fight discrimination among employers doing business with the federal government headed by Mitchell and Vice President Nixon achieved similarly incomplete results.[94]

This did not mean, however, that all aspects of life for African Americans were disappointing during this period. Unemployment rates among blacks remained low by historical standards during Eisenhower's presidency, and various indicators such as years of formal education, life expectancy, and median income also showed substantial gains. This seemingly contrasting picture of black life in the 1950s reflected the class-oriented policies of the era, which contributed to important progress in living standards but did not eliminate entirely the federal government's participation in Jim Crow.[95]

That tendency to see all major social problems as ultimately rooted in class led Larson to approach the issue of gender in much the same way. In a meeting of the Labor Department's top policy committee on October 6, 1955, to discuss goals for the Women's Affairs Program, Mitchell led off by stating that he wanted the Labor Department to "advance the status of women who have to work."[96] Larson agreed and asked whether the department should try to state that explicitly so as to avoid confusion: He "questioned whether or not we should spell out the problem, that is, we are trying to assist women who need work, we are not encouraging women who have home responsibilities to abandon them."[97]

Implicit in both men's remarks were some crucial assumptions, the most notable of which were that only those women who sought paying jobs out of economic necessity required the Labor Department's help and that women's domestic obligations took precedence over working outside the home. These views, so jarring to many people today, reflected a view common among moderates in the 1950s that the most serious problems women faced grew out of poverty and class rather than gender-based discrimination. From that perspective, the Labor Department could aid women most effectively by concentrating its efforts on women with paying jobs who lacked other means of support or who belonged to a household in which the male breadwinner did not earn enough by himself to pay the bills. Even the concern that Larson expressed about not encouraging women to neglect their domestic responsibilities fit in with this view, by assuming a sexual division of labor in which women were expected to perform such duties and receive economic support from men in return. In this way of thinking, to encourage women, even unintentionally, to neglect their part of the bargain might have led the men who supported them to do so as well and thus make the economic status of women worse. There were, of course, many men (and some women) who favored the sexual division of labor for more simplistic reasons, such as the notion that it was "natural" and satisfactory to women as well as men. Although Larson was no doubt influenced by such thinking, his education and expertise gave him a much clearer understanding of the less obvious and more thoughtful rationales at work here.

Underlying all of this was the controlling assumption behind Larson's early writings on the American social insurance system that the steady growth in the number of this kind of household since the 1930s would continue until it became almost universal. Although he would doubtless have conceded that there would always be some women, such as his own spouse, who would seek a paying job either for the stimulation and/or economic independence it could bring, Larson would just as surely have viewed such women as exceptional and not in need of the Labor Department's special assistance.

The one other important assumption that deserves mention is the view that the overwhelming majority of women would choose to have children and devote themselves solely to the task of child raising for a period of several years. According to this view, while women might spend a substantial portion of their lives in paying jobs, they would not do so continuously, but rather would do so early and then later in life. Larson made that clear when giving a speech on June 28, 1955, about the Labor Department's efforts to aid the older worker, which was a special interest of his. Larson devoted a significant portion of that speech to "mature women" and discussed the employment concerns of older women in these terms:

> I think each one of us could probably find among our immediate relatives and friends at least several women who were trained as professional nurses, or teachers or secretaries, who got married, had a family, and lost touch with the labor market, and who now would like nothing more than to get back into the game again. I am not talking about tearing married women away from their children at a time when they are needed at home. I am thinking of women whose children have grown to the point where the mother's constant presence at home is no longer necessary.[98]

This kind of thinking and the class-oriented approach to the issue of women in the paid labor force more generally did not mean that women fared poorly in economic terms during the mid-1950s. On the contrary, they moved into paying jobs during this period in ever greater numbers. And while such women continued to earn less than men, the wages of full-time year-round women workers in the paid labor force reached 63.6 percent of those of men in 1957, the highest level recorded to that point. Married women also enjoyed more economic security than ever before, thanks mostly to the greater durability of marriage than in earlier (and later) periods.[99]

At the same time, women in the paid labor force remained largely confined to the lowest-paying jobs. When compared with men, women during that time actually lost ground in education and professional employment, and they continued to earn substantially less than men even when doing the same kind of work. Thus, women managed to gain ground economically during the mid-1950s, but not in ways that fostered greater independence. Women did not usually advance economically then as women but rather by belonging to households headed by men. To Arthur Larson and James Mitchell, this situation seemed both "normal" and likely to continue indefinitely, which explains their preoccupation with the concerns of women of limited means who lacked that form of support.[100]

Larson also appears to have had some qualms about the appropriateness of federal intervention to require equal pay for equal work, as some feminists and trade unionists were increasingly demanding. A sign of such doubt appeared during a meeting of the Labor Department's top policy committee on September 20, 1955, in which he; Mitchell; his special assistant for women's affairs, Alice Leopold; and senior civil servant Millard Cass discussed an equal pay bill. Larson observed "that he was not sure of the philosophy underlying this legislation since it interferes with the freedom to contract."[101] In the end, however, whatever misgivings Larson may have had about such legislation made no practical difference. Strong resistance to any equal pay law from congressional Dixiecrats in general and from House Labor Committee chairman Graham Barden in particular blocked its passage throughout the second half of the 1950s.[102]

Larson gave one other speech in 1956 that merits attention, precisely because it offers the clearest and most complete statement of what he thought the future would hold for the nation's workers. He gave this address, entitled "Working People in the Next Twenty Years," to a journalists' group that met in Los Angeles on June 20, 1956. Larson sounded a characteristically Republican theme at the beginning of his talk by criticizing former president Franklin Roosevelt's tendency during the 1930s to think that the American economy had reached a technological plateau. Quoting Roosevelt's remark in 1932 that "our industrial plant is built; the problem is now whether under existing conditions it is overbuilt," Larson observed that technological innovation over the following two decades had thoroughly discredited that notion.[103]

If the recent past was any guide, Larson pointed out, the rapid pace of technological change would likely continue indefinitely, producing far-reaching changes in the nature of work by the mid-1970s. Sustaining that process, he noted, were increasing demands for more services and more leisure, which might make jobs so plentiful over the next twenty years that teenagers would be discouraged from finishing high school. Ever more consumer demand and a rapidly growing population, he predicted, would likely combine to produce a 50 percent increase in the gross national product over those years. To this rosy (and accurate) forecast Larson added another, carefully qualified one: "If past trends continue, we may also assume that a relatively greater part of this increase will accrue to the benefit of lower income groups, so that the distribution of incomes will be narrowed."[104]

Turning to the issue of what kinds of jobs would likely be created in the next two decades, Larson noted a long-term trend toward openings that required higher-skilled workers and predicted it would continue indefinitely. Among the most important consequences, he argued, was the gradual disappearance of the working class in the traditional Marxian sense. Instead of a workforce composed primarily of those who labored in heavy industry, Larson predicted one in which most Americans performed tasks requiring less brawn and more education. Such a world was already emerging, he said, and from this he drew a truly revolutionary conclusion: "What all this adds up to is one single resounding new fact about working people: labor is not a class, and by 1976 there probably will have disappeared almost all vestiges of the concept of 'labor' as a sort of minority set apart from other people, having its own special interests and point of view."[105]

As for the future of income insurance and privately negotiated supplements, Larson sounded his familiar theme about the need for business to understand why improvements in that system were required. He also observed that labor unions everywhere would likely fight for a shorter working day and more supplemental fringe benefits, including benefits that cushioned manual laborers against the effects of automation-induced unemployment. This, Larson predicted, would have the effect of spreading work around and increasing the likelihood of regular employment.[106]

Larson was much more guarded about the issue of union growth. It ultimately depended, he argued, on "such matters as union policy, intensity and direction of organizing efforts, and economic conditions."[107] Beyond those specific factors, he continued, union growth would depend on the labor movement's ability to adapt to the changing nature of the workforce.[108]

Larson added one final prediction about the length of the working day in the future. Acknowledging that any such forecast from someone in an official capacity would likely cause controversy, he contented himself with noting the gradual decline in the length of the working day over the previous 125 years, and extrapolating from there, he suggested that average working hours for nonfarm employees would likely drop by 12 percent over the next two decades.[109]

Larson's predictions indicate an impressive degree of foresight, although one could argue with some of the conclusions he drew. His contention that "labor" in the sense of a discrete group would gradually fade over the next two decades was correct in the sense of the way people looked and thought rather than lived. Larson understood that fewer jobs in heavy industry would tend to diminish working-class visibility and consciousness, but he did not note the likelihood that a new kind of working class would emerge instead. Its members would do less heavy lifting, perhaps, but in other crucial respects, such as wages, benefits, and control over their working conditions, these workers would fit in the category encompassed by the term "labor."[110]

Larson's remarks obscured at least one other important development. His notion that keeping teenagers in school might prove difficult given the coming abundance of jobs ignored the differing appeal of jobs that paid well and had good benefits, which would presumably be very tempting to many 16- and 17-year-olds, and poorly paid jobs that offered few if any benefits, which would have considerably less allure. His conclusions about the future length of the working day similarly posited a uniform trend across job categories rather than diverging ones in which some people worked the same hours as before, or even longer ones, while others saw their participation in paid employment become increasingly casual. What Larson did not mention was the possibility that over the next two decades a hollowing out of the middle of the employment structure could occur, in which job opportunities available to those in the upper half of the income distribution became more lucrative and demanding while the opportunities for those living in the bottom half became less attractive and less regularly available.[111]

Related to this was the issue of the future of unions, about which Larson seemed genuinely uncertain. Should unions fail to organize the emerging sectors of the economy, services especially, this hollowing-out process would occur, because it was unionization more than anything else over the previous two decades that had fostered a large "middle class" of jobs in terms of wages, hours, and working conditions. Unable to discern what lay in store for organized labor, Larson evidently chose not to mention, or perhaps even contemplate, such a discouraging possibility. Like so many Americans in the mid-1950s, Larson tended to look ahead optimistically. The previous twenty years' record of impressive economic progress led him to hope, like the population in general, that the next two decades would bring more of the same.[112]

Larson ultimately spent about thirty-three months as under secretary of labor, which served as a kind of tutorial on the realties of contemporary politics. Like many an academic who took a high government post, before and since, Larson learned some hard lessons about the considerable gap that existed between theory and practice. His vision of a complete, adequate, and coordinated social insurance system remained intact—but his confidence in its imminence had clearly waned.[113]

Larson's experience at the Labor Department also revealed to his colleagues in the Eisenhower administration where his greatest gifts lay, which in the late spring of 1956 led to a major change in his duties. From that point onward, Larson would devote himself primarily to the tasks of writing and public speaking on the topic of what Eisenhower and his top aides sought, as a whole, to accomplish. In an administration heavy with experienced practitioners, Larson stood out for his ability to explain clearly and coherently the larger vision those practitioners were trying to realize. It was this talent that opened the door to a new, unexpected, and even more exciting chapter in Larson's life.[114]

CHAPTER SEVEN

A Republican Looks at His Party

LARSON'S ROAD TO GREATER prominence in Washington began at Cornell. His research on the law of workers' compensation and a course he sometimes taught called "Social Legislation" prompted him to try writing some essays that extrapolated a broader political philosophy from those subjects. When he became under secretary of labor and began making speeches on a wide range of topics, Larson decided to use some of these speaking obligations to work out the remaining chapters for an as-yet-incomplete book of essays. He sent the finished manuscript to Cornell University Press, only to receive a politely worded letter of rejection in return. Much later, he described this disappointing response: "It was a thoughtful letter saying that they liked the substantive content of the book, but that in the publishing business books of essays were poison—just a cut above books of sermons. However, if I would weave the same material into a unified book, I might have something."[1]

Choking back his chagrin over having wasted time and effort on the essay format, Larson proceeded to do as the letter had suggested. In recasting his manuscript, Larson received help from Florence and his brother Don, by then a professor of political science at Ohio Wesleyan University. The crucial period in terms of the actual writing came early in 1956, when Arthur Larson suddenly decided that the book would never get done unless he took a break from his duties at the Labor Department. Once again demonstrating the extraordinary drive that had carried him there, Larson opted to take what was officially billed as a vacation to Miami in late January and early February. While Don's family and Florence enjoyed the sights and sun by day, the two brothers toiled away on the manuscript. Don contributed suggestions intended to give it a broader outlook and remove any passages that might prove offensive. Arthur Larson responded to this constructive criticism by rewriting large sections of his earlier draft. On some of these days, he "sat at his typewriter . . . from eight in the morning until eleven at night," Florence reported to his mother.[2] The only breaks Arthur Larson took during this trip were a couple of fishing trips with Don and an occasional night on the town with Florence. She also worked on the manuscript, which after ten days of strenuous effort was complete, whereupon the "vacationers" returned from Florida.[3]

Before the venture could go forward, however, it needed to clear one other hurdle. Larson appears to have decided that in view of the manuscript's subject and his own post within the Eisenhower administration, he needed approval to publish from White House staff. The views of a relatively obscure Eisenhower administration official about its overall philosophy might not have interested publishers, but a book of that sort that the White House had officially endorsed had much greater prospects for success. Accordingly, Larson asked James Mitchell to raise the matter with the president's chief of staff, Sherman Adams, who expressed interest and circulated Larson's manuscript to White House special counsel Gerald D. Morgan, Special Assistant for Economic Affairs Gabriel Hauge, presidential speechwriter Kevin McCann, and Assistant Press Secretary Murray Snyder. Hauge and McCann enthusiastically favored publication, reported White House aide Arthur Minnich in a memo to Adams. The others had no serious objections to the book's contents, although some concern was expressed, Minnich noted, about the precedent that would be set by allowing an incumbent member of the administration to publish a book about it. All of those who had reviewed the manuscript, Minnich added, agreed that any profits from this venture ought to go to charity to head off criticism that Larson had used his public office for personal gain. With that understanding, Adams approved publication and Larson moved on to the next step.[4] Rather than send his revised manuscript back to Cornell University Press, Larson this time put out feelers to the major publishing houses in New York. To his surprise, Harper and Brother's editor Evan Thomas jumped at the idea of publishing it. The key factor was Harper's recent publication of a book by Truman's former secretary of state, Dean Acheson, *A Democrat Looks at His Party*. This work purported to explain what the Democratic Party stood for by the mid-1950s and prompted Thomas to cast about for an equivalent manifesto from the Republican perspective. Larson's manuscript appeared to fit the bill nicely, which led to an offer in March of a contract with Harper's and a fast-track schedule for publication. In return, Evan Thomas asked only that Larson accept the title *A Republican Looks at His Party*, which Larson liked.[5]

The degree of interest his new writing project aroused took even the optimistic Larson by surprise. During March 1956, *Reader's Digest*, *Life Magazine*, and the *New York Herald-Tribune* syndicate contacted him to express interest in publishing excerpts. Clearly excited by this attention, he allowed these publications to see the draft manuscript. The prospect of being published in *Life* interested Larson the most. It would bring nationwide attention to the book in a media outlet oriented toward moderate and liberal Republicans. *Life* editor Henry Luce, whose views on politics closely paralleled Larson's, ultimately decided not to publish extensive excerpts, on the advice of his aides Edward K. Thompson and C. D. Jackson that to do so would seem too self-serving and partisan. Instead, he decided to give the book substantial and favorable coverage as part of a cover story about Larson scheduled to appear after the Republican National Convention met in August.[6]

All of these signs of impending success helped persuade Larson to postpone a return to academia indefinitely. The chancellor's office at the University of Pittsburgh had indicated in February that Larson's leave would come to an end by the summer of 1956, forcing Larson to choose that year between returning to his deanship or staying in the less-secure job he held. Although neither he nor Florence looked forward to a return to Pittsburgh, Larson delayed making a final decision until Eisenhower had formally announced his intention to run again, which he did on February 29, 1956. With another term for the administration now likely and the media expressing strong interest in Larson's new book, he decided to cut his ties to his former employer. On March 13, 1956, Larson wrote the vice-chancellor at Pitt to convey the news that he would not be coming back and explained that the progress of his new book project had influenced this decision. A standing offer to join the faculty of the University of Chicago Law School, which Larson had received a short while earlier, helped dispel any concern he or Florence might have felt about what Larson would do when his work in government eventually came to an end.[7] Both his status within the administration and the already promising prospects for his new book substantially improved in late May that year, when Eisenhower decided to give Larson the task of drafting the presidential address to the upcoming GOP convention. Where Eisenhower got the idea of putting Larson to work as a speechwriter is something Larson did not mention in his memoirs, perhaps because he never knew or, if he did, out of a sense of embarrassment. The source, oddly enough, was South Dakota senator Karl Mundt, the same man who had tried to obstruct his romance with Florence back in college and refused to sponsor Larson's appointment as under secretary of labor.[8]

After Larson had joined the Eisenhower administration in 1954, he and Florence had made a concerted effort to get along with Mundt. Despite their previous problems with him, there must have seemed no real point in feuding with a U.S. senator from their own home state and party. And so, over the following two years, Arthur Larson had politely responded to Mundt's occasional requests for help with matters related to the Labor Department and Florence had held a luncheon in honor of Mundt's spouse. Although trying to treat Mundt civilly, neither Arthur nor Florence grew to like him. The biggest obstacles to such a friendship were Mundt's strident anticommunism and generally negative approach to anything that smacked of the New Deal. Florence Larson relayed reports about Mundt's behavior of this sort in her letters from South Dakota in the summer of 1954. She wrote Larson that her brother Parker also opposed Mundt for this reason: "You'll be interested to know that Parker is against Mundt. He says that all Mundt preaches out here is [anti]communism—'there is one behind every pillar' etc. Parker says . . . his speeches are all 'against'—never pro-anything. Always fear, fear, fear."[9]

Although the Larsons never warmed up to Mundt, he appears to have developed a liking for them. In part this seems to have stemmed from the pride Mundt took that a fellow South Dakotan had assumed a prominent place in the first Republican administration Washington had seen since 1933. More important, however, was Arthur Larson's assistance in getting a Mundt protégé a job at the Labor Department and help with a speech Mundt delivered to the Yale Political Union. The second of these actions had by far the greater impact. Larson sent copies of four of his addresses dealing with aspects of the Eisenhower program and the Republican Party to Mundt for use in preparing his Yale address. Mundt liked this material so much that he wrote back on May 19, 1956, to report he had read it from "cover to cover."[10] All of these speeches rehearsed favorite themes. The emphasis in "The Lawyer as Conservative" and "Outflanking the Welfare State" on the difference between good and bad conservatism and the way the American income insurance system had allowed the country to avoid a purely public system along Western European lines clearly appealed to Mundt. So, too, did the arguments presented in "Government for the People" and "Lincoln, Labor and Prosperity." "Government for the People" explained the "Lincoln formula" about the proper role of government ("to do for the people what needs to be done, but which they cannot by individual effort do at all, or do so well"), using social insurance as an example, as Larson had earlier done in his Arden House paper. Larson argued in this speech, which he wrote in the summer of 1954, that Eisenhower's presidency was guided by this same principle. Members of the White House staff, upon seeing the published version of Larson's address, had promptly endorsed that view and sent copies of the speech to public speakers employed throughout the executive branch. The accompanying memo described Larson's remarks about the Lincoln formula as "an eminently clear statement of a fundamental concept in the Eisenhower philosophy." Eisenhower himself used the Lincoln quote to explain what the Republican Party stood for in public remarks on August 2, 1955.[11] "Lincoln, Labor and Prosperity" made the argument that the Republican Party had its origins as a workingmen's movement and that Abraham Lincoln had believed that economic prosperity in general depended on the well-being of the common laborer. These arguments expanded on the suggestion Larson had made in *Know Your Social Security* that Republicans had historically been more supportive than Democrats of government intervention on behalf of workers and activist government more generally. Implicit in Larson's analysis was an argument that the GOP's rightward drift during the 1920s and 1930s had constituted an erroneous deviation from a longer-term pattern, which the party had corrected by the mid-1950s.[12] These four speeches so pleased Mundt, as he explained in his May 19th letter to Larson, that he wrote Eisenhower the same day to suggest that the president add Larson to the presidential speechwriting team for the upcoming campaign. Mundt also included copies of the four speeches, which Mundt described to the president in glowing terms. Unbeknown to Mundt, his suggestion had arrived at an opportune moment. Eisenhower, who had once served as a speechwriter for Army Chief of Staff Douglas MacArthur and took a strong personal interest in such matters, had lately become dissatisfied with his addresses out of a sense that they lacked freshness. Wanting his convention speech to present in an original and stimulating way his vision for his party's and country's future, Eisenhower was receptive to bringing a new mind to that assignment. Although he did not know Larson well, Eisenhower consulted with Sherman Adams, who evidently liked the idea and wrote Mundt on May 21st to inform him that "the President is deeply appreciative of your May nineteenth letter respecting Arthur Larson. I can assure you that this idea will be kept very much in mind as campaign plans and organizations develop."[13]

Eight days later, Larson paid a visit to the White House at Eisenhower's request to discuss the upcoming convention address. Larson took detailed notes of this important session, in which Eisenhower evidently did most of the talking. Eisenhower explained at the outset why he wanted Larson to try his hand at writing the presidential address to the upcoming GOP convention and what he wanted to accomplish with this speech. Larson recorded these remarks as follows:

> The President said that he had talked himself out over the past 10 years. He didn't want to give a speech just to hear his voice—he wanted to *say* something—have an *idea*—a *Q.E.D.*
>
> Only one theme—like Cato's—he wants to repeat: the appeal to youth.
>
> He is really not partisan at heart—doesn't want to paint Republicans all white and Democrats all black.[14]

After discussing for a while the limitations of his probable opponent that year, Adlai Stevenson, Eisenhower returned to the topic at hand. He observed that the GOP convention would seem much less exciting than the Democratic one "unless I get sick again," given that the Democrats had not yet settled on their national ticket.[15] The two men discussed how to make the Republican convention stimulating, to the young especially. Larson argued that Eisenhower's speech could convey the excitement of a middle-of-the-road approach to younger voters whose ideas were more shaped by contemporary conditions than the events of the 1930s. He added that the Republicans were more likely to be the party of the future because the Democrats were a "preposterous coalition of opposites" that would certainly blow up.[16] Larson's mention of the extremes in the American political system prompted an Eisenhower outburst against the most liberal Democrats such as Governors George Leader of Pennsylvania and Averell Harriman of New York, as well as the most conservative Republicans, such as Senators John Bricker of Ohio and Joseph McCarthy of Wisconsin.[17]

At that point, Larson spoke up to explain his thoughts about what the speech should contain and his other efforts to convey what the Republican Party stood for:

> I said middle-of-road was rough and he agreed. People shout from both ends at you. But this country should have assumed middle-of-road many years earlier.
>
> I commented: once we have a philosophy that fits our times, we can then go on to appeal to youth to solve the thousands of problems that are real—instead of bull-session arguments on issues out of the 1930's.
>
> I told him I had written a book and he was much interested. Also that I was to talk to Young Republican trainees next week on Philosophy of Administration.[18]

As this 30-minute conversation drew to a close, Eisenhower explained how annoyed he was by his opponents' charge that American prestige in the world had dropped to an all-time low. He showed real anger about this obviously false accusation and quoted a letter from the Indian ambassador saying that every foreign leader in the world wanted Eisenhower reelected that year. Larson listened politely and then told Eisenhower "there was nothing I'd rather do than write his convention speech."[19] They agreed it should run for about twenty-five minutes, with Eisenhower commenting that he did not mind public speaking as long as he had something worth saying.[20]

This first private discussion of substance with Eisenhower left a lasting impression in Larson's mind of the president's friendly, direct, and appreciative manner: "He was extremely cordial and warm—talked with great emphasis and spirit, and really beamed at me as we parted, indicating that he was genuinely grateful for some help."[21]

In closing, Eisenhower underscored the importance he placed on this assignment by saying that it was weighing on his mind more than anything else that summer and if he could stop worrying about it he would enjoy the season much more. To this Larson replied in his characteristically confident way: "Mr. President, you can stop worrying—I'll take care of it."[22] An obviously pleased Eisenhower told Larson to drop in again as soon as he had an outline of ideas, at which point they could talk some more, and on that note the first working meeting of Eisenhower and Larson came to end.[23]

Although Larson came up with an outline for the speech in just five days, he did not have a chance to discuss his ideas with Eisenhower until the third week of July. Eisenhower suddenly became ill on June 7th and was hospitalized for the next two weeks. Stricken with ileitis, a digestive disorder, Eisenhower had to undergo serious emergency surgery and recuperate in virtual seclusion. Although the president's doctors assured him and the press that the prospects for a rapid and full recovery were excellent, Eisenhower could not discharge most of his official duties during this time, including work on his convention address.[24]

This apparent setback had a silver lining, however, because it provided Eisenhower with an extended period of rest and reflection just as the advance copies of *A Republican Looks at His Party* arrived in Washington. On June 20th, Sherman Adams ferried one over to Eisenhower at Walter Reed, after marking several passages in it that sounded very much like the president's own previously expressed observations. Eisenhower dictated a brief letter of thanks to Larson the next day, to "assure you that I shall read it all, as soon as possible, with the greatest of interest."[25] Gabriel Hauge called the next day to pass along Sherman Adams's report that of all the books well-wishers had given Eisenhower to read, it was Larson's that was lying halfway open, face downward, on the president's bed.[26] The fruits of this involuntary period of study materialized later that summer, when a reporter asked Eisenhower at one of his televised press conferences what he thought of Larson's book. Eisenhower commented that while he could not recall every detail in *A Republican Looks at His Party*, "in general, I thought he expressed my philosophy of government as well as I have seen it in a book that size."[27] In the space of less than a minute, the fondest hopes of Larson and his publisher had been realized.

This presidential seal of approval helped *A Republican Looks at His Party* attract a great many readers and reviewers during the summer and fall of 1956. Most of the commentary was favorable, including James Reston's in the influential *New York Times*. Reston called the book "a serious contribution to the literature of the campaign" and "probably the most articulate argument for the Eisenhower Republicans since General Eisenhower entered politics." Reston also noted that Larson's book was important precisely because "it is being used already as a guidebook for the Republican campaigners."[28]

The object of all this attention was a slender 200-page volume bearing a red, white, and blue dust jacket that drew together the various ideas about moderate conservatism that Larson had been developing throughout his adult life into a single statement. The book's two basic premises were that in the United States of the mid-1950s there was more agreement than ever before—among people if not among politicians—on fundamental issues and that the Eisenhower administration's philosophy and actions reflected that consensus. The book's purpose,

Larson explained, was to show the truthfulness of these two ideas by deriving larger patterns from the specific actions and plans of the Eisenhower administration since it had taken office in January 1953.[29]

Aware that some of the president's critics believed that he and his supporters had no coherent political philosophy at all, Larson's book argued that the former general turned politician led a movement that was "deeply rooted in conscious principle" and aware of its future direction. This movement was rooted in the nation's oldest political traditions yet was different from any previous political philosophy.[30]

The reason many people had not understood these facts, Larson explained, was because this "New Republicanism" did not fit neatly within preexisting political categories such as "liberal," "New Deal," "prolabor," "probusiness," "left," or "right." Larson contended boldly that such categories, "drawn from earlier decades, are now largely obsolete."[31] He pointed to two older sets of ideas in particular as New Republicanism's chief competitors, which he called the "1896 ideology" and the "1936 ideology." The first of these, which had had its adherents in both the Democratic and Republican Parties, Larson described as having emphasized states' rights, deference to private enterprise, hostility and even contempt for labor, and indifference to the needs of the individual citizen. The 1936 ideology, on the other hand, had emphasized the centralization of authority in Washington, D.C., hostility to business and a view of it as incapable of operating without government supervision and stimulation, concern for labor out of a belief that unions needed the government's help to overcome employers' bargaining advantage, and sensitivity to the needs of individuals but also an inclination to view them from a distance and en masse. With characteristic tactfulness, Larson declined to discuss the appropriateness of these views during the times in which they had emerged full blown. Instead, he argued simply that whatever the merits of these public philosophies in their respective heydays, neither "fit the facts" facing the United States by the mid-1950s.[32]

Larson listed what he saw as the key changes in conditions facing the country since those earlier eras. Of these, the first and most important, he contended, "is that we have neither a nation-wide depression, nor a nation-wide war emergency." He explained that such crises by their very nature tended to call legitimately for greater action by the federal government. Larson conceded that the nation was committed to heavy spending on national defense and surrounded by world tensions but argued that this state of affairs differed from a true wartime footing, which required centralization of governmental authority. In a similar vein, Larson contended that the nature of unemployment in America had changed, from the central social problem to much a more modest one that stemmed mostly from special or local causes.[33] Other important changes had made the older political ideologies irrelevant, Larson continued. The nature of capital and labor had evolved from distinct and antagonistic interests to more intertwined and cooperative ones. The problem of inflation, once viewed as inevitable in a prosperous economy, had all but vanished in recent years. Business attitudes toward government had become more positive as business leaders had come to understand how government intervention into economic affairs could contribute to a stable and prosperous market system. Government influence over the economy and society had grown as the volume of public spending had increased. The basis of the American economy itself had changed, from agriculture to heavy industry, which had greatly increased the potential for future economic growth. Activities such as school and road construction, once viewed as essentially local in character, had become issues of national concern, which was changing relationships between federal, state, and local governments. And finally, America's international responsibilities had become so great as to demand a more mature approach to the conduct of the nation's foreign policy.[34]

Keeping his focus on matters domestic, Larson argued that the older ideologies and the New Republicanism could be evaluated by testing their domestic policy stands against what he called the federal government's "four main internal relations." These he listed as its relations to state governments, to private enterprise, to labor, and to individual persons. The New Republicanism, he argued, mistrusted neither the states nor the federal government. Instead, Eisenhower Republicans favored giving the states as much authority as they could properly exercise, which, Larson contended, was significantly more than New Deal liberals had believed appropriate but was still not the old states' rights position so popular in the nineteenth century. Larson used the same basic argument with relations to private enterprise and labor, arguing that "this Administration is against neither but is for both."[35] By the same token, Eisenhower and his supporters sought to restore as much responsibility as was practicable to individuals. Larson summed up the general tenor of his remarks with a characteristically clear formulation: "In all this, the key word is *balance*."[36] In taking this middle way between what Larson depicted as the older, misguided extremes, Eisenhower and his aides, he argued, had "discovered and established the Authentic American Center in politics." Larson distinguished this from the center in more polarized European societies, which he characterized as "an uneasy and precarious mid-point between large and powerful left-wing and right-wing elements of varying degrees of radicalism." The American version of the center, he argued, consisted of "a common meeting ground of the great majority of our people on our own issues, against a backdrop of our own history, our own current setting and our own responsibilities for the future."[37]

Larson saw the proof of this assertion in the fact that many self-described independents and Democrats had supported Eisenhower from the time he had first announced his intention to seek the presidency in 1952. And lest anyone argue that such voters had been attracted that year solely by the former general's distinguished war record and magnetic personality, Larson observed that as

Eisenhower's political philosophy had become clearer through his words and actions as president, his popularity with independents and the most moderate Democrats had actually increased. While the most extreme elements on the left and right still remained, which Larson lumped together under the rubric "The Opposition," they had become, he suggested, a fairly small minority.[38] This broad agreement on matters of politics and public policy, Larson argued, had recently emerged for five reasons, three of them gradual and two more short term. The first of these essentially restated the thesis of historian Louis Hartz that America's lack of a feudal past had precluded the emergence of clearly defined and highly self-conscious classes of aristocrats and proletarians.[39]

Larson also echoed Hartz's argument that this "common social origin" had been reinforced by a second factor, which Larson called "a studied ideological position" that grew out of the American Revolution.[40] He argued that the ideas expressed in the Federalist Papers, the Constitution, and the Declaration of Independence, which were influenced by the writings of Locke, Hume, Montesquieu, Rousseau, and others, had "laid down a solid ideological platform upon which all subsequent American thought could be built."[41]

A third reason for the appearance of the American consensus, Larson argued, was "the gradual maturing and moving-together of the interests which have provided our principal conflicts."[42] He gave as examples the business and labor leaders who had come to see themselves as having fundamental interests in common, the business community's acceptance of the modern regulatory state, and decline in tension between farmers in the South and West and bankers in the East, thanks in part to the advent of government price support policies that enabled many farmers to stay out of debt.[43]

Larson argued that two more proximate factors had contributed to the appearance of the American consensus. The first was the advent of a serious challenge to American values from communist nations. This challenge had forced Americans to take stock of their own values and increased awareness of how much most Americans had in common politically when compared with the tenets of Soviet socialism. This turn of events had also strengthened the center in America, Larson continued, by "putting an end to the luxury of toying with extremism."[44] The familiar phenomenon in intellectual circles during the 1930s of the parlor communist, he added, had disappeared forever and extremism was "being reduced to the hard core of those who really mean business."[45] The other proximate cause for the emergence of the American consensus was that the Eisenhower administration had given it definition and voice and put its principles into practice. Larson felt this point was crucial and explained that neither of the two major political parties was a center party as such. Historical factors had led both Democrats and Republicans to incorporate conservatives, moderates, and liberals in their ranks. In such a situation, the ascendancy of centrists was far from automatic. Thus, Eisenhower's success in marshalling the moderate forces behind him was a feat of great political importance because it had contributed greatly to the emergence of the American consensus in the 1950s.[46] In making this point, Larson explicitly rejected the notion voiced by many liberal Democrats—and conservative Republicans—that Eisenhower had simply accepted and perpetuated New Deal domestic policies. Larson acknowledged that some domestic policies of the New Republicanism had been adapted from the New Deal but asserted that "a very large part" of the New Republicanism's domestic program involved a sharp change in direction from that of the Roosevelt and Truman administrations. Larson emphasized this key point: "In fact, most of this book is devoted to a delineation of this marked change, for it frequently involved a reversal of a trend that had been going on not only in this country but all over the world for perhaps twenty years."[47]

Larson characterized the Democratic Party of the 1950s as one whose two largest factions—the "ultra Fair Dealers" and the Southern Democrats—were the most liberal and conservative forces, respectively, in American politics. He conceded that the GOP also had its conservative and more liberal wings but argued that the degree of difference in the Republican Party was less extreme, which allowed for constructive compromises of a moderate nature. Larson contended that the Democratic Party could not speak for the American consensus because too many Democratic politicians had come to rely upon antibusiness themes in order to get elected. This habit posed an insuperable obstacle for more thoughtful Democrats who were trying to move their party to the center.[48]

Larson closed this discussion by contending that the future success of both major parties depended on their ability to promote moderate policies that fell within the American consensus. He predicted that Republicans would stay on this path in the years ahead and nominate moderate presidential candidates in the Eisenhower mold who would give the party a strong chance of staying in power. In the same paragraph, however, he also warned that should the GOP chose a more rightward course instead and the Democrats move to embrace "the middle way," then the fortunes of the two major parties would almost surely reverse. "In politics—as in chess," Larson contended, "the man who holds the center holds a position of almost unbeatable strength."[49]

Having laid out his main arguments in the book's first chapter, Larson devoted the next four to elaborating on those themes. Here he presented in detail the various arguments that had appeared in his earlier writings, such as the need to avoid concentrating any more authority in the federal government than was absolutely necessary, to take a realistic approach to the existence of both large corporations and labor unions and seek to make them do as much public good as possible, and to accept the American social insurance system as a necessary part of the country's economy and society.[50]

Most of this now-familiar material needs no further explication, but a few new issues in Larson's analysis deserve mention. In the chapter on federalism, he described New Dealers in favor of a strong presidency as "centralizers" following a European political theory. Larson's suggestion that New Dealers had followed a foreign model while Republicans favored an authentically American one seems unfair. A more balanced discussion would have pointed out that both the moderate leftism associated with the New Deal and the moderate conservatism backed by the Eisenhower Republicans had their roots in European political ideas and could best be thought of as distinctive American variations of them. Larson had explicitly acknowledged in his earlier writings the European roots of the American system of social insurance that Eisenhower Republicans favored and so should have known better than to discuss the differences between New Dealers and New Republicans on issues of federalism in such a different and one-sided way. At most Larson should have argued merely that Eisenhower-era conservatism was more deeply rooted in American political traditions, whereas New Deal–style leftism reflected a newer way of thinking. As in other places in *A Republican Looks at His Party*, Larson's essentially partisan purpose appears to have clouded his thinking and writing on this important subject. The result was an assertion—and a way of thinking about the New Deal in general—that would eventually get Larson into a good deal of trouble.[51]

The enthusiasm he expressed in this chapter for giving state governments more responsibility, while not without merit, also deserves criticism for not acknowledging the problems this might cause disadvantaged minorities, especially those trying to dismantle the Jim Crow system of legalized racial segregation. Segregationists' enthusiasm for states' rights stemmed from their fear that more federal authority over local matters would likely spell the end of the existing system of racial subordination. Larson's omission here seems strange, given the ongoing controversy over the recent U.S. Supreme Court ruling in the *Brown* decision. While his reasons for avoiding this sensitive subject are not entirely clear, doing so undercut the force of Larson's plea "that we bend every effort to make state governments, state agencies and state legislation more effective."[52] Until segregation had been removed, Larson's prescription was very problematic. What one could say on behalf of Larson's argument here, as in some other areas, was that it was ahead of its time. That visionary quality influenced Larson's approach to the entire federalism issue, which was reflected in his tendency to assume that all state governments were basically alike. For example, he defended the Eisenhower administration's decision to transfer control over offshore oil lands from the federal government to the states adjoining coastal areas. In response to liberal critics who charged that this amounted to a giveaway that corrupt state governments would mismanage, Larson argued that this initiative had returned control to the people of those states. A more even-handed response would have acknowledged that some states had much more developed governmental structures and procedural safeguards than others and that the possibility of mismanagement or outright corruption would vary depending on the character of the state government involved. Apparently carried away by the larger point he was trying to make about the value of the role of states in America's federal system, Larson simply ignored that kind of distinction. Once the states with weak systems of governmental administration improved them sufficiently, however, this sort of objection would lose its validity.[53]

The next three chapters showed the same pattern of mostly sound arguments to support the premise that New Republicanism took a distinctive and coherent middle position between the older political ideologies. Nowhere did that pattern emerge more clearly and convincingly than in the chapter devoted to the proper relationship between business and government. Larson explained that New Republicanism's basic perspective on that key question favored policies that encouraged the inherent energies of a free enterprise system, accompanied by just enough government activity (and no more) to avoid extreme economic booms and busts, to protect the public against harmful business practices, and to provide adequate protections against the human hazards associated with this kind of economy. He described the basic difference between this and the New Deal liberal perspective as one between "having faith in private enterprise, and not quite having faith in it."[54] In his explanation of this basic point, Larson's moderately conservative perspective prevailed throughout. He criticized New Deal policies during the 1930s for having failed to achieve a lasting prosperity and noted in particular that Franklin Roosevelt's antibusiness attitude from 1935 onward had so weakened confidence among business executives that it discouraged the kind of investment needed to help the economy recover. At the same, time, however, Larson rejected the older Republican economic orthodoxy of the 1920s. To Calvin Coolidge's oft-quoted remark that "the business of America is business," Larson offered the rejoinder, "The business of government is government, not business."[55] He rejected, too, the notion so popular among more extreme conservatives that the federal government bureaucracy was large and wasteful with words that showed how far the New Republicanism stood from the perspective of the GOP's Old Guard:

> Cutting government expenditures is not so easy as some might have you believe. The old notion that the federal government is a sort of gigantic rabbit warren filled with paper-pushing bureaucrats most of whom have been hired in order to make their boss a bigger man is absolutely false. Where it is possible to compare the number of people for a given operation in a private business as against government, you will often find the private business using many times the personnel for the same work.[56]

Larson took a similarly moderate approach to the issue of inflation, which he called "our most underestimated issue."[57] He noted that real wages had actually declined from 1944 to 1952, albeit only slightly, because the almost 50 percent increase in paychecks had been eroded by heavy inflation. In contrast, real wages during Eisenhower's first three years as president had risen by about 8 percent, while prices had remained fairly stable. Thus, Larson argued that economic policies aimed at slowing the economy when it seemed to be overheating had the potential to help the many, rather than just the privileged few. He suggested that many New Dealers had not fully understood this point but that the Eisenhower Republicans surely did.[58]

Larson sketched out a cautious middle position regarding the touchy subject of the Tennessee Valley Authority (TVA), which he rightly observed had been a lightning rod for philosophical debates about the government-business relationship. To those who argued that the massive hydroelectric power project should have been left to private initiative—or not done at all—Larson suggested that only the federal government could have built the series of dams and power plants that together constituted the heart of TVA. He argued that it was right for the government to bring electricity and prosperity to an impoverished region but that ongoing operation of these facilities might be privatized to some degree.[59]

Larson also devoted substantial portions of this chapter to debunking what he called "the big business fable" and the myths surrounding the politics of tax cuts. The first of these had grown out of persistent attacks from New Deal liberals on "big business" since the mid-1930s, which Larson argued made no sense in the world of the 1950s. The reason was simple: by then the nation's largest corporations tended to be the most unionized and provide the best wages, benefits, and job security. In contrast, the small employer, so often lionized by populist-minded liberals, typically had no union, paid lower wages, and offered no fringe benefits. As for federal tax policy, Larson pointed out that Eisenhower's tax cut proposals, denounced by liberals as a "sellout to big business," had aimed at encouraging investment and new business startups, which promised over time to generate many good new jobs and not just more income for wealthy investors.[60]

Two other themes that Larson introduced in this chapter had to do with the composition of the Eisenhower Cabinet and the administration's farm policy. Clearly annoyed with the charge of liberal Democrats that Eisenhower's top advisors were mostly rich businessmen, Larson listed the twenty-one senior officials who usually attended Cabinet meetings and pointed out that of these, only five had backgrounds as business executives. Most of the others had risen to prominence in the professions of law, education, and the military, and three had come from careers in elective politics.[61]

By far the most interesting comments Larson made in this chapter concerned farm policy. He strongly endorsed the array of subsidies and special services for farmers that had emerged over the past century. This marked a major shift from the comments Larson had made in earlier letters to his parents and Florence, which tended to credit the existence of such programs to the political strength of the agriculture lobby in Congress. He now stoutly defended farmers' special benefits as necessary given the unusually competitive and unpredictable nature of the farming business. Perhaps the influence of his political scientist brother Don had brought about this change in outlook, although there is no evidence of that. The amount of attention he gave to agricultural issues was not very great, but what little Larson did have to say strongly endorsed the existing institutional arrangements and what he saw as Eisenhower's moderate approach of trying to target federal agricultural subsidies to the larger, more economically viable farm enterprises that were still family owned and operated, rather than more marginal ones or corporate-run agribusinesses.[62]

Larson's analysis in this chapter suffered from some exaggerations and omissions. For example, he portrayed the Eisenhower administration's approach to dealing with the 1954 recession as very different from the way Truman had handled a similar downturn five years earlier. In fact, however, the recession-fighting policies pursued in both instances were very similar, which signaled the degree to which Eisenhower Republicans had assimilated Keynesian economic ideas that New Dealers had endorsed first.[63]

Larson also overstated the degree of difference between New Deal and New Republican economic policies when he said that the first required war to bring prosperity while the second did not. Although this assertion was literally true, it left out the important additional truth that very high levels of military spending had continued even after the Korean War ended and provided crucial stimulus to the mid-1950s economic boom. The roughly 10 percent of gross national product spent on armies and armaments in the 1950s was an extraordinarily high level for a major industrial society ostensibly at peace and put Larson's boast that New Republicans had brought "Peace and Prosperity" in a rather different light. Here, as elsewhere, Larson did not acknowledge adequately that prosecuting the Cold War had placed the United States on something like a wartime footing indefinitely.[64]

Larson's chapters on the federal government's relations to labor and the individual made similarly centrist arguments. Much of the discussion covered already familiar ground, such as the view that labor unions were needed to make a market system more humane and stable and that a complete system of social insurance had become a necessity in the modern wage-based economy. There were a few new themes, such as what Larson argued was the key difference between Eisenhower Republicans and New Deal liberals with respect to labor. This, he explained, had to do with the nature of the federal government's role in the collective bargaining process. Unlike New Dealers, who tended to favor a good deal of government intervention in that process, New Republicans favored a more limited, though still significant, role for government: "The role of the government is to insure . . . fairness, to settle disputes about the rules governing the fair-bargaining process, to tender its good offices in the form of mediation and conciliation services to aid in arriving at agreement on the substance of a dispute, and only in rare cases of genuine national emergency to intervene more directly in a labor dispute."[65]

The most specific difference between New Dealers and Eisenhower Republicans Larson mentioned had to do with who should determine workers' proper share of the fruits of postwar prosperity. Larson strongly disagreed with the argument of many New Deal liberals that the federal government should try to determine how much worker productivity had increased and thus what fraction of growing corporate profits workers deserved. In his view, both management and labor representatives had matured sufficiently in their approach to collective bargaining to make them, and that process, reliable and safe determinants of the right result. Of crucial importance here, he explained, was that leaders on both sides had come to accept a belief (which New Republicans strongly endorsed) in the mutuality of interest between both parties and a rejection of what Larson called "the class struggle lie."[66] Continuing economic growth promised to reward both owner and worker, he observed confidently, thereby discrediting the Marxian notion that more industrialism would breed more poverty. He noted, too, that Eisenhower Republicans gave a higher priority to increasing overall output than they did to equalizing shares, which was the opposite of the New Deal position.[67]

Larson also mentioned, but gave much less attention to, the issue of employment discrimination based on age, race, or gender. He indicated that New Republicans opposed such discrimination and called for much more emphasis "by government and everyone else" on providing training, apprenticeship, and educational opportunities to all who sought them.[68]

Much of Larson's handling of this controversial set of issues deserves praise, but his analysis also had its weaknesses. For example, his discussion of the nature of collective bargaining tended to ignore parts of the country, such as the South and Southwest, and sectors of the economy, such as agriculture and services, where many employers still fiercely opposed unions and organized labor remained weak or nonexistent. He also tended to leave out references to irresponsible union behavior in places such as Chicago and New York City and sectors of the economy such as construction and transportation in which organized labor possessed extraordinary strength. Larson discussed the issue of labor-management relations in the mid-1950s as though one uniform pattern had emerged across the economy and society, but in fact the United States was an unusually diverse place with respect to employer attitudes toward unions, labor union strength, and patterns of collective bargaining. Implicit in much of Larson's analysis was an unstated assumption that the trend of the previous two decades toward bigger and more responsible employers and unions in the major industrial states of the Northeast, the Midwest, and the West Coast would expand so as to approach universality.[69] Larson's comments about unfair discrimination in employment also deserve criticism for suggesting that providing more and better job training alone would be enough to open job opportunities to aged, non-white, and female workers. Although Larson was clearly right to point out the fundamental importance of access to education and job training for members of these groups, he did not acknowledge that many workplaces and kinds of jobs remained closed to them regardless of their qualifications. His remarks instead implied a considerable degree of optimism that education would in time dissolve the attitudes that had led to barriers of this sort.[70]

In the last three chapters of *A Republican Looks at His Party*, Larson returned to the issue of how best to define what he called the New Republicanism. This part of his book restated many ideas he had developed earlier. Some of Larson's comments about where American-style conservatism had come from warrants attention, for he had not expressed such thoughts in his earlier writings. Larson argued that the American version of conservatism differed from British and Continental varieties and could best be understood as a revolt against those bodies of right-wing thought. He characterized these schools of European conservative thought as endorsing the views that people live in a permanent, stratified class structure and that a large central government and the sacrifice of a good deal of personal freedom were needed to maintain social order.[71]

Here, as in elsewhere in his book, Larson revealed a tendency toward overstatement. While he was right in pointing out that American conservatism was somewhat less elitist, class-conscious, and statist than its Western European counterparts, he neglected to make clear that those differences had narrowed considerably since 1776. Larson persisted in seeing the kind of moderate American conservatism associated with President Eisenhower as something fundamentally different from the sort represented by British prime minister Anthony Eden, French general Charles de Gaulle, Italian premier Alcide De Gasperi, and West German chancellor Konrad Adenauer, but the political programs of all five were in many respects essentially the same. Rather than arguing that Eisenhower Republicanism was uniquely American (and that the New Deal was "Europe-based"), Larson would have done much better to point out those aspects of it that derived from abroad and those that had emerged from the nation's own experiences. Determined to demonstrate that moderate conservatism had deep roots in the nation's past and make the differences between the New Republicanism and the New Deal appear as sharp as possible, Larson evidently got carried away by the direction of his own arguments. Although much of his thesis made sense, this type of exaggeration weakened its overall force.[72]

A similar problem affected the one brief reference to foreign affairs Larson made in these concluding chapters. He contended that unlike communist leaders, the United States did not seek to impose its values on the world at large: "We are not setting out to convert the world to our own ideas and to remake others in our image, as has been tried sometimes by others in the past, and as is being tried by the Communists now. Rather, we are trying in every possible way to help other countries realize their own potentials, within the framework of their own cultures."[73] The problem with this formulation is that some administration spokesmen, most notably Secretary of State John Foster Dulles, at times sounded more like missionaries for what they proudly called "the American way of life" than defenders of self-determination for foreign lands.[74]

The one other new and important point Larson made came in the chapter entitled "Principles of the New Republicanism." Most of these were already familiar and summed up the book's main arguments. The first such principle that Larson listed, however, dealt with an issue about which he had said almost nothing earlier in the book: "We begin by acknowledging reverently the existence of a God of order, justice and love."[75] He elaborated on this point by explaining that New Republicans' demands for the highest standards of behavior in government and efforts to help the less fortunate were not based on purely practical considerations or sentiment but rather stemmed ultimately from their religious beliefs. In writing this, Larson made clear that while New Republicans endorsed no one creed in particular, they did view religion itself as the driving force behind their political principles and efforts to translate them into concrete results.[76]

Considered as a whole, *A Republican Looks at His Party* carried a political message that resembled Larson himself: highly intelligent, moderately conservative, sensible, and often highly persuasive, though at times overly optimistic, simplistic, and self-serving. That message in effect updated earlier conservative ideas associated with such figures as Alexander Hamilton, Abraham Lincoln, William McKinley, and Theodore Roosevelt. It was closest to the views of the last two, but new conditions had led to significant departures from Progressive-era Republicanism. The Great Depression, World War II, and the advent of the Cold War had reshaped moderate conservatives' priorities in significant ways. These seismic events had increased their concern with promoting economic growth, the welfare state, labor unions, a large military establishment, and collective security arrangements and had diminished somewhat their concern about environmental conservation, legal equality for blacks and women, entrepreneurship, low levels of taxation, and limits on overseas involvement. At the most basic level, the Eisenhower-Larson kind of Republicanism contemplated more of a role for the state than most moderately conservative Progressives had favored. The implicit message of *A Republican Looks at His Party* was that social conditions had changed so much since the early years of the twentieth century that government was required to do more (though not as much as New Dealers thought it should).[77] The book ought to have conveyed that message under a different title, however, for Larson's theme was not the views of the Republican Party as such but rather those of Eisenhower and his supporters. Four years earlier they had prevailed over the presidential candidate of the GOP's Old Guard, Ohio senator Robert Taft, but only narrowly. The bulk of Taft's delegates to the

1952 Republican National Convention were committed party activists and prominent GOP members of Congress, who looked with suspicion on more moderate newcomers to the fold such as Eisenhower. Had Larson called the book *A Republican Looks at the Eisenhower Administration* or *A Republican Looks at His Party's Dominant Faction*, the prospective reader would have received a more accurate clue as to its contents.[78] Larson's choice to go along with his publisher's suggestion for a title meant that *A Republican Looks at His Party* would prove annoying to both the GOP's right wing, which disagreed with many of Eisenhower's and Larson's views, and liberal Democrats, who knew from bitter experience just how different Old Guard Republicans were from the Eisenhower Republican variety.[79]

Those problems lay down the road, however, for when the book first appeared in July 1956, it met with a degree of success that even Larson could not have expected. Propelled by its own merits and Eisenhower's personal endorsement, *A Republican Looks at His Party* soon made the bestseller lists and remained there for months. It made much more of an impression on educated general readers than Dean Acheson's book had. The closest analogue in liberal circles was not Acheson's book but rather the much more widely read book by historian Arthur Schlesinger, Jr., entitled *The Vital Center*, which had appeared seven years earlier. All of this attention, most of it favorable, established Arthur Larson as the best-known expert on Eisenhower-era Republicanism, just as that point of view reached its zenith.[80]

Larson's work that summer on the presidential address to the 1956 GOP convention increased his visibility even more within Washington's political community. Although Eisenhower rejected the heavily historical approach of Larson's seven-page outline, with its emphasis on the GOP's early origins and support for legislative innovations faithful to the spirit of the Homestead Act that would enable Americans to succeed on their "new frontiers," the president clearly liked much of what Larson had written.[81] At their first meeting after Eisenhower returned from the hospital, he told Larson "You're off to a hell of a good start on this speech" and suggested various revisions, setting in motion a genuinely collaborative effort.[82] Eisenhower's great interest in the speech led him to meet with Larson seven more times in July and August to discuss the organization and wording of the various drafts. Reporters noted Larson's frequent appearance on the president's daily appointment list, and one journalist asked Eisenhower at a press conference on August 8th what the two men talked about during these meetings. The president's playfully mysterious reply—"Well, I could [tell you], but I don't think I will"—generated even more interest in the under secretary of labor's new status, which was unprecedented for someone in that post.[83] Articles in the media about Larson's book began referring to him as the president's political "guru" and the administration's "philosopher."[84]

Eisenhower formally delivered the fruits of this collaboration on the evening of August 23, 1956, at the Cow Palace convention center in San Francisco. To the assembled GOP Convention delegates and guests, including an eagerly attentive Arthur Larson, Eisenhower presented in a more complete and coherent form than ever before his view of what the Republican Party should stand for in the years to come. As his renomination had been uncontested, and his chief rival from four years ago, Senator Taft, had died in July 1953, Eisenhower's listeners in the hall that night consisted mostly of his kind of Republican rather than Old Guard ones. Thereby blessed with a live audience to encourage him that was highly receptive if not truly representative of the party as a whole, Eisenhower moved quickly to his main theme. He began with one of Arthur Larson's favorite quotations from Ibsen: "I hold that man is in the right who is most clearly in league with the future."[85] Calling the GOP "the Party of the Future," Eisenhower devoted his speech to explaining five reasons why he believed this to be true.[86]

First, Eisenhower argued that the GOP deserved this rubric because "it is the Party of long-range principle, not short-term expediency."[87] He gave three examples to prove his point from the areas of farm policy, labor policy, and federal-state relations. His administration had refused to yield to pleas for more money for farm price supports, he explained, because they had led in recent years to mounting crop surpluses that further depressed prices. Instead, Eisenhower and his aides had taken a principled position in favor of policies that kept agricultural commodity prices stable over the long term, even if that meant smaller government subsidies for farmers than they had known in the recent past.[88] Eisenhower similarly criticized what he believed had been the overly activist policies of his predecessor in the field of labor-management relations. Eisenhower said that his administration had chosen to adhere to the principle of "free collective bargaining without government interference," which he called "the cornerstone of the American philosophy of labor-management relations."[89] The more activist alternative, he argued forcefully, would only prove self-defeating over the long run: "If the government charges impatiently into every major dispute, the negotiations between parties will become a pointless preliminary farce, while everyone waits around to see what the government will do."[90]

He approached the issue of federal-state relations in much the same way, arguing that making all public policies through the federal government might yield faster results but at an unacceptable longer-term cost, which he defined as "the growth of a swollen, bureaucratic, monster government in Washington, in whose shadow our state and local governments will ultimately wither and die." Instead, Eisenhower argued, the Republican Party had committed itself to the principle that "geographical balance of power is essential to our form of free society."[91] Eisenhower argued in effect that while the federal government could do too little, it could also do too much, which would produce highly undesirable long-term consequences.[92]

Eisenhower moved to the Republican Party's concentration on contemporary problems rather than past ones as a second reason it was the party of the future. He emphasized that "our opponents" continued to dwell on the danger of renewed depression, which had blinded them to the demands of a different and much more prosperous era. Eisenhower's list of the new issues that had supplanted such older ones focused on those facing the roughly two-thirds of the country's population living in major metropolitan areas, for whom better roads, schools, water, and power were high priorities. The Republican Party believed, Eisenhower said, that Americans should turn their attention to finding solutions to these problems rather than fighting irrelevant battles from the nation's past over again.[93]

The third reason why the GOP deserved to be regarded as the party of the future, Eisenhower said, was because "it is the party that draws people together, not drives them apart."[94] He decried the technique of pitting group against group for what he called "cheap political advantage" and argued that from its beginnings, the GOP had established a record of bringing together workers, farmers, small businessmen, writers, and reformers of all kinds.[95] Eisenhower tacitly acknowledged that the party had not remained true to its origins but argued that by 1956 it had reclaimed that heritage. He rejected the charge sometimes leveled by its opponents that the GOP had become a single-interest party in a negative sense. Instead, Eisenhower retorted, the Republicans were "a one-interest" party only in the sense of favoring what was best for all Americans. Implicit throughout this part of his speech was a notion of mutuality of interest among all citizens and rejection of the Marxian idea of class struggle.[96]

Next Eisenhower turned to the fourth reason in support of his main thesis: "The Republican Party is the Party of the Future because it is the party through which the many things that still need doing will soonest be done—and will be done by enlisting the fullest energies of free, creative, individual people."[97] Eisenhower elaborated on this point, which Larson had not made explicitly in his original speech outline, by arguing that the GOP placed a heavy emphasis on policies that stimulated private activity for public purposes rather than relying primarily on the government itself to solve social problems.[98]

In one of the more striking passages of his speech, Eisenhower warned against the dangers of complacency and made clear that he wanted more than just Republicans to participate in addressing social problems:

> In our time of prosperity and progress, one thing we must always be on guard against is smugness. True, things are going well; but there are thousands of things still to be done. There are still enough needless sufferings to be cured, enough injustices to be erased, to provide careers for all the crusaders we can produce or find.
>
> We want them all! Republicans, independents, discerning Democrats—come on in and help![99]

Eisenhower pointed to the problem of unfair discrimination in general terms as an example of the kind of social ill that required citizen participation to solve and explained what his administration had done to help. He strongly implied that while the Truman administration had offered bolder words in this area, Eisenhower's administration had helped bring more concrete results.

> A wide range of quietly effective actions has brought about more genuine—and often voluntary—progress toward equal justice and opportunity in the last three years than was accomplished in all of the previous twenty put together. Elimination of various kinds of discrimination in the Armed Services, the District of Columbia, and among the employees of government contractors provides specific examples of this progress.[100]

Eisenhower's fifth and final reason why the Republican Party deserved to be considered a forward-looking party was its commitment to peace, without which, he added pointedly, "there is no future."[101] He noted that his administration had proposed a plan for sharing nuclear technology with friendly nations that would use it solely for peaceful purposes. Under the auspices of this program, which became known as "Atoms for Peace," over thirty nations had signed agreements with the United States to develop nuclear research reactors, seven had done so to build nuclear power plants, and many other such agreements were under consideration. Eisenhower observed that the administration continued to work for disarmament, "so that the labor of men could with confidence be devoted to their own improvement rather than wasted in the building of engines of destruction."[102]

The president made an unusually personal and firm statement about the need to establish lasting peace between nations. Alluding to his almost-40-year career in the U.S. Army prior to entering politics, Eisenhower said, "No one is more aware than I that it is the young who fight the wars, and it is the young who give up years of their lives to military training and service. It is not enough that their elders promise 'Peace in our time'; it must be peace in their time too, and in their children's time; indeed my friends, there is only one real peace now, and that is peace for all time."[103]

Eisenhower outlined what he saw as the three essential requirements for achieving such a peace. The first he called "the elementary necessity of maintaining our own national strength" to deter aggression.[104] By this he meant not just military preparedness but also economic and moral strength, all three of which, he suggested, were closely related. Eisenhower pointed with pride to his administration's record in this area and observed that building this kind of strength depended not just on governmental action but also the work of each and every citizen.[105]

The second of what Eisenhower called "the three imperatives of peace" was collective security, through which many friendly nations had banded together to protect themselves against common hazards. He reiterated his belief that such alliances must not simply promote military strength or a mindless conformity about all aspects of life. Mindful that there were more than a few diehard isolationists in America, Eisenhower argued eloquently against the notion that the United States could pursue such an outdated policy successfully:

> There can be no enduring peace for any nation while other nations suffer privation, oppression, and a sense of injustice and despair. In our modern world, it is madness to suppose that there could be an island of tranquility and prosperity in a sea of wretchedness and frustration. For America's sake, as well as the world's, we must measure up to the challenge of the second imperative; the urgent need for mutual economic and military cooperation among the free nations, sufficient to deter or repel aggression wherever it threatens.[106]

Even this, and the commitment to building national strength, were not enough in an age of nuclear weapons that could obliterate cities and travel across continents. With these advances in weaponry, "war has become not just tragic, but preposterous." The need to avoid war had become so great that it gave rise to a third requirement for peace, an active effort to bridge the gap that separated free peoples from those living under communist rule. Acknowledging that there had to be a willingness on both sides to reach out in order for that to happen, Eisenhower argued that signs of interest had appeared in the communist world in fostering what he called "some small degree of friendly intercourse among peoples." Indirectly acknowledging the potential risk that such exchanges might make communist espionage and propaganda campaigns more effective, Eisenhower emphasized the cautious way his administration was approaching this effort at mutual understanding and gave concrete examples of the forms it might take, such as educational and cultural exchanges.[107]

Adherence to these three requirements for peace, Eisenhower argued, promised to bring a future far better for later generations. Advances in science and technology, labor-saving methods, management, labor organization, education, medicine, and "not least, politics and government" all were bringing such a future within reach. Eisenhower described his vision for that future in a paragraph imbued with Larsonian foresight and optimism:

> Travel all over the world, to learn to know our brothers abroad, will be fast and cheap. The fear and pain of crippling disease will be greatly reduced. The material things that make life interesting and pleasant will be available to everyone. Leisure, together with educational and recreational facilities, will be abundant, so that all can develop the life of the spirit, of reflection, of the arts, of the full realization of the good things of the world. And political wisdom will ensure justice and harmony.[108]

Having expressed his faith in the possibility of such a bright future for humanity, Eisenhower closed on a more cautionary note. He argued that such an era would not be attained by revolution or what he called "the sordid politics of pitting group against group."[109] Only free peoples working together could bring such a future about. The continuing deep division between the free world and the communist one constituted a serious obstacle to the realization of these hopes. Eisenhower underscored that point by recalling a passage from the Bible that Abraham Lincoln had quoted from memorably on the eve of the American Civil War:

> Lincoln, speaking to the Republican State Convention [of Illinois] in 1858, began with the biblical quotation, "A house divided against itself cannot stand."
>
> Today the world is a house divided.
>
> But—as is sometimes forgotten—Lincoln followed this quotation with a note of hope for his troubled country: "I do not expect the house to fall," he said, "but I do expect it will cease to be divided."[110]

Eisenhower argued that Americans a century later needed that same kind of conviction about what the future would bring. In making this point, Eisenhower struck another theological note, suggesting that religious faith and God's help would bring a better world to pass.[111]

Larson listened proudly throughout the address, so much of which had emerged from his (and Don's and Florence's) efforts. This occasion, and the 1956 GOP convention more generally, made such a lasting impression on Larson's memory that thirty years later he could vividly recall the events of that week:

> I had written not only the President's Acceptance Speech, but also part of [Washington] Governor [Arthur] Langlie's Keynote Address, as well as the seconding speech on behalf of Labor. I sat there in my box, listening to my words, and reveling in the applause. . . . I was on the "Today Show" and "Meet the Press." I did a two-part interview with the *New Republic,* and suggested to the editors that it might be appropriate for the *New Republic* to become the organ of the New Republicanism—which they didn't find amusing. *Time Magazine* went through the entire process of doing a cover story on me, shooting hundreds of pictures all over San Francisco. (The story was preempted by the British invasion of Suez, for which I could never forgive Anthony Eden).[112]

The good times did not end there. Eisenhower soon asked Larson for help with some campaign addresses, which elaborated on the themes in his convention acceptance address. Larson recalled later that he wrote about half of Eisenhower's principal campaign speeches that fall, cementing a close and continuing relationship with him. The end result of their joint efforts could not have been more satisfying for Arthur Larson. Eisenhower not only won reelection, as most experts had expected, he achieved an even bigger landslide over Adlai

Stevenson than in 1952. The GOP national ticket carried forty-one of the forty-eight states in 1956, even though registered Democrats outnumbered registered Republicans by a margin of approximately 5 to 4. The clearest sign of just how broad Eisenhower's victory was on November 6th and how popular his message was came from staunchly Democratic Chicago, which went Republican in a presidential contest for the first time since 1928.[113]

The crowning moment for Arthur Larson, however, came later that night, when Eisenhower appeared at the Sheraton-Park Hotel in Washington to thank a tired but jubilant crowd of his supporters. Disappointed that he had not been able to bring Republican congressional majorities in with him, as he had four years earlier, and certain that too many GOP candidates for Congress with Old Guard attitudes was the reason, Eisenhower decided to talk about the need for Republicans to follow his moderate path if they wished to do better in the future. To Larson's delight, wild cheers erupted when Eisenhower made clear that the victory they celebrated that night was one not just of a person or a party but a distinct philosophy, to which the president gave a new label: "And now let me say something that looks to the future: I think Modern Republicanism has now proved itself. And America has approved of Modern Republicanism."[114]

The events of 1956 must have seemed to Larson like a dream come true. At the year's outset, he had been toiling away in relative obscurity as an under secretary in one of the smallest Cabinet-level departments. By Election Day, in contrast, he had written a best-selling book, become a personal aide to the president, acquired a national reputation as a result, and seen Eisenhower's—and his own—political ideas win an overwhelming victory. The president had come to have so much confidence in his new speechwriter that Eisenhower suggested to a group of GOP politicos in Seattle during a campaign stop that Larson should be considered a serious contender for the Republican presidential nomination next time. Although that idea struck even the highly self-confident Larson as preposterous, his future, like the ideas with which he was so closely identified, had never seemed so bright.[115]

CHAPTER EIGHT

Caught in the Crosscurrents

LARSON'S WRITING AND public speaking skills so impressed Dwight Eisenhower in the summer and fall of 1956 that the president decided immediately after the election to groom him for higher things. Eisenhower's plans for Larson's future grew out of a larger interest in developing a corps of talented younger officials who could advance the cause of Modern Republicanism in the years ahead. Acutely aware that Old Guard Republicans would like nothing better than to recapture control of the party once the president completed his second term, Eisenhower intended, as he told Larson at a meeting on November 9, 1956, "to start getting some of you young fellows ready for 1960."[1] Eisenhower by this point saw the forty-six-year-old Larson as one of the most promising members of a group that included the president's younger brother Milton, an academic economist who had worked in government and then as a university president; former Texas oil man, secretary of the navy, and secretary of the treasury Robert Anderson; former supreme allied commander in Europe and Red Cross president Alfred Gruenther; and former Health, Education and Welfare under secretary and Special Assistant to the President for Cold War Strategy Nelson Rockefeller. That none of these men had ever run for public office before did not bother Eisenhower much. His rapport with Larson and the others stemmed in part from the fact that they, like him, had not entered high government office from a career in partisan politics, a background that did not impress him. Eisenhower tended to look for successors who had achieved distinction outside politics and to give less serious consideration to the two professional politicians in his Cabinet, Vice President Richard Nixon and U.S. Ambassador to the United Nations Henry Cabot Lodge.[2]

With these thoughts in mind, Eisenhower informed Larson at their meeting on November 9th, which Secretary of State John Foster Dulles also attended, that two high-level posts had become vacant: secretary of the Department of Health, Education and Welfare and director of the United States Information Agency (USIA), which carried America's official message to the outside world. Although Larson's expertise in the area of social insurance made the first of these seem the more appropriate choice, Eisenhower urged him to take the second. In this way, the president explained, Larson could acquire experience in foreign policy and thus round out his credentials for higher office.[3]

Even though Larson did not take the idea of a political future seriously, he did nothing to dissuade Eisenhower or Dulles about that possibility. In part this appears to have stemmed from Larson's unwillingness to admit to them that his back problems could seriously disable him without warning. They had eased somewhat in recent years, thanks in part to the skilled treatment he received from the White House masseur, whose services Eisenhower and Sherman Adams had thoughtfully made available to him. Even so, Larson understood from many years of experience that he could not bend over safely and thus could never have withstood the rigors of a national political campaign. In his memoirs, Larson acknowledged that hard fact in the circumspect fashion he used whenever referring to his back trouble: "All of this was very flattering, although I myself knew that the idea of me as President was preposterous. By now I had had a chance to observe at close range what it takes not only to arrive at that eminence, but to survive there. I could never understand why anyone in his right mind would really want to let himself in for that kind of punishment."[4] Had Larson made these thoughts clear to all concerned, however, his chances for the new and interesting job assignments put before him might well have disappeared. So Larson accepted the USIA directorship, which would allow him to pursue a long-standing interest in foreign policy, and voiced no objection to the president's rationale behind this appointment.[5]

Taking this course had the effect of increasing Larson's already considerable visibility within the Eisenhower administration. In part this was simply a result of moving from an under secretary's position to that of agency head. The shift in his formal duties from domestic to foreign policy signaled even more clearly to Washington insiders that Larson's star was on the rise. Favorable attention in the press and, even more, his speeches during the winter of 1957 to such influential groups as the Washington press corps, the Business Advisory Council, and the Advertising Council only strengthened that impression. Although none of this portended a future race for the White House in Larson's mind, many of those in Washington's political community, not knowing of his disability, understandably thought otherwise. This misleading impression posed no obstacle to his confirmation as USIA director by the Senate but would soon create serious problems for Larson's tenure in that office.[6]

At first, however, everything about Larson's new job seemed highly satisfactory to him. His immediate predecessor, Theodore Streibert, had left the sometimes-controversial agency in good order and with a bigger budget and staff than ever before. The USIA had achieved formal independence from the State Department only three and a half years earlier, through legislation passed by the Republican-controlled 83rd Congress and signed by Eisenhower. Like so many other parts of the country's national security apparatus, what ultimately became the USIA had first emerged during World War II, in this particular instance to combat Axis propaganda efforts. Although some members of Congress clearly would have liked to see what was known first as the Foreign Information Service and later as the Office of War Information abolished after V-J Day, the advent of the Cold War had provided the organization with a new lease on life as part of the State Department. The grumbling in Congress about this during Truman's presidency continued, however, because conservatives tended to view any kind of government propaganda agency with suspicion and had feared since the early 1940s that it would be used to promote New Deal policies at home and abroad. Eisenhower's election to the presidency had help quiet those concerns and persuade Congress to go along with the plan of new secretary of state John Foster Dulles to make what was then called the International Information Administration into an independent agency. Firmly believing that the State Department should focus on its core missions of formulating and executing foreign policy, Dulles sought to divorce ancillary activities that distracted U.S. diplomats from that task. Streibert had managed the newly named USIA so well during its first three and a half years of existence that it gained prestige within the federal government and a badly needed sense of stability.[7]

This new equilibrium had been reached in part by defining the agency's basic principles and purposes during the Cold War more clearly. Early in Streibert's tenure as USIA director, the agency's staff had developed a memo entitled "U.S. Information Agency Strategic Principles" to guide future operations. This eighteen-page document spelled out clearly that the USIA's basic function was to influence foreign governments to support U.S. foreign policy objectives by using communication techniques that affected public opinion in those nations. This formulation explicitly ruled out any USIA role in trying to influence American public opinion, one of the activities that had made the Office of War Information so controversial with congressional conservatives during World War II. The statement also made clear that while the USIA contributed to the formation of American foreign policy with respect to information considerations, the agency did not have the authority to anticipate policy developments or promulgate U.S. policy and objectives on its own. These restrictions tended to keep the USIA out of the kind of controversy the Office of War Information had sometimes encountered by carefully limiting the agency's role in the realm of foreign policy.[8]

The statement's discussion of how best to describe American values and achievements seemed calculated to avoid offending conservatives and contributed to keeping the USIA out of trouble during its early years of independent existence. In addition to emphasizing the need to present facts rather than opinion, this document listed the following examples of basic American values and achievements that were appropriate for USIA communication and explained how to communicate them:

> Belief in a deity, individual and national freedom, in ownership of property and in human rights, in a peaceful world and the common humanity of men and nations compromising their differences and cooperating in the United Nations. The military strength of the U.S., its economic system, its standard of living, its technical development and productive capacity make fruitful and effective subjects of propaganda if presented without self-praise in ways which show the U.S. capacity to resist aggression and to give powerful assistance in the creation of a peaceful world order.[9]

The statement made clear that the purpose to be served by all such references to American values and achievements was the provision of evidence to other peoples that U.S. goals and policies were in harmony with their own aspirations for freedom, progress, and peace.[10]

As important, if not more so, in reassuring congressional conservatives that the USIA deserved their support was the agency's focus during the mid-1950s on reaching nations outside the Soviet bloc where the population appeared undecided about whether the Americans or the Soviets offered the more promising model for future development. This did not mean that the USIA had given up its efforts to reach the peoples of Eastern Europe living under communist rule. Such efforts continued steadily throughout this period. The crucial point is that in addition to that task, the USIA had committed itself to working hard to resist the spread of communism beyond places where it had already achieved dominance. In keeping with that view, the statement of strategic principles committed the agency to a single overarching theme: "Unite the free world in order to reduce the Communist threat without war."[11]

The approach spelled out in the statement of strategic principles evidently pleased the still-cautious congressional committees that oversaw the USIA's work. During Streibert's tenure, the USIA's budget and staff had grown steadily, from $84.2 million and 10,727 employees in fiscal year 1954 to $113 million and 12,589 three years later. Members of Congress continued, however, to signal their reservations about the whole idea of a public information agency by refusing to make the USIA's overseas foreign service officers career civil servants with job tenure. Attracting high-quality people to work in such an insecure situation proved a continuing challenge for USIA officials and gave the agency a reputation for employing people of widely varying ability overseas. Such was the nature of the agency for which Larson assumed formal responsibility on December 18, 1956, following a swearing-in ceremony over which Eisenhower personally presided.[12]

Upon assuming his new office, Larson began pushing an initiative that grew out of his discussions with foreign policy experts. During this early period of preparation, he spoke at length about the USIA's mission and operations with Eisenhower himself as well as USIA staff members in Washington, senior State Department officials such as John Foster Dulles and Under Secretary of State Herbert Hoover, Jr., and former presidential special assistant Nelson Rockefeller, who by then had returned to New York to help run the Rockefeller Brothers Fund. Taking careful notes of these talks in the small memo books that he had begun carrying about with him regularly, Larson came to one major conclusion about the USIA's future. He decided that for all of the agency's progress over the previous three and a half years, the USIA had spent too much time communicating what the United States opposed and not enough explaining what it favored. Determined to present "a constructive message for the world," Larson began planning for more USIA programs that would communicate that message clearly and completely.[13]

Larson also drew upon the advice of the foreign policy experts in developing such programs and other specific proposals to further his goal. He decided to push for more USIA activity in critical countries, especially those in the Middle and Far East and in Africa. He favored new programs for Eastern Europe as well, most notably an expansion of the USIA magazine, *America Illustrated*. Larson also endorsed more use of radio and the rapidly emerging medium of television, the construction of a high-powered radio transmitter in the Eastern Mediterranean to increase the reach of Voice of America broadcasts in the Middle East, and more low-cost books and other forms of media. Most of these ideas were not new. Larson's predecessor, Theodore Streibert, had specifically asked Congress one year earlier for more money to do everything mentioned above except the expansion of *America Illustrated* and the construction of the new transmitter, but the House and Senate appropriations committees had refused to provide sufficient funds to pay for his proposals. Larson's prospects for making these projects and his two new ones happen would depend on administration support and his own skillful advocacy before these committees. In keeping with his generally optimistic outlook, Larson decided to seek a 24 percent increase in the USIA's annual budget, from the $113 million Congress had appropriated in 1956 to $140 million, and new legislation establishing a career service for USIA personnel stationed overseas. With these, Larson believed, he could carry out his plans for the USIA effectively.[14]

Strong support from the White House encouraged Larson to pursue this ambitious course of action. Sharing his view that the nation needed to do a better job of presenting a positive message to foreign nations, Eisenhower decided to insert Larson's requests into the president's 1957 State of the Union Address, the only agency or department budget specifically mentioned there. To underscore his backing for this item, Eisenhower also invited Larson to attend a special New

Year's Day meeting at which the president, his top aides, and congressional leaders discussed Middle East policy and the budget and gave the new USIA director time there to make his case personally. Larson received an assist at this session from Vice President Richard Nixon, who echoed Larson's pleas for more USIA funding, in the area of radio broadcasting especially. Although the response at this meeting from House Majority Leader John W. McCormack was less than enthusiastic, all of this support from the high reaches of the Eisenhower administration led Larson to believe that more money could be obtained from Congress. So, too, did the president's decision to give Larson time at the Cabinet meeting held on January 17, 1957, to make an extensive presentation on the USIA's work and future plans and solicit assistance from all of the Cabinet-level departments.[15]

Five days after that session, Larson set off on a three-week trip abroad to inspect USIA missions in the Middle East and India and educate himself about the workings of his agency, in preparation for his testimony before the congressional appropriations committees scheduled to begin in late February. Before reaching his first official stop, Larson took a brief detour to England to accept a doctor of civil laws degree from Oxford on January 24, 1957. Although plagued by poor weather, Larson enjoyed this honor and the pageantry that went with it.[16]

Larson did find disturbing the anti-American sentiment he encountered in Britain during his stopover there. Many Britons still resented the Eisenhower administration's decision to resist the British and French effort to retake the Suez Canal by force after the Egyptian government headed by Gamal Abdel Nasser nationalized the waterway on July 26, 1956. The fallout from the resulting Suez Crisis, which compelled the British and French governments to make an embarrassing retreat and British prime minister Anthony Eden to resign, had made British public opinion unusually sensitive to apparent American slights. Larson learned the reasons for this unusual state of affairs from talking with the American ambassador in London, Winthrop Aldrich, British foreign secretary Selwyn Lloyd, and other officials. Larson reported his findings to Florence in a letter written on January 26th: "Anti-Americanism—at least as to policies—is very noticeable in Britain—and it all converges on [John Foster] Dulles. Today's papers all headline his statement about 'American boys might not want to have British or French soldiers at their side if they fought in the Mid-East.' It is being taken as a great insult—which of course it wasn't."[17]

Larson proceeded on his whirlwind tour of USIA missions in Turkey, Lebanon, Pakistan, India, Iraq, and Egypt. The close relationship he enjoyed with the president and rumors reported in the *New York Times* that Larson was launching an administration-backed propaganda offensive in the Middle East helped him go far beyond the usual inspection trips to USIA facilities. Prime ministers in no less than five of the six countries he visited met with him privately, including Jawaharlal Nehru of India, M. T. F. Suhrawaddy of Pakistan, Nuri-as-Said of Iraq, Sami Soulh of Lebanon, and Egypt's Nasser.[18]

Larson's conversations with these men and other experts in the region proved to be of very mixed value. He learned a good deal in India from a 45-minute interview with Nehru at his home and an unexpected encounter with former American ambassador to India Chester Bowles, who remembered Larson from their days together at the Office of Price Administration and happened to be in Delhi when Larson visited there. At his meeting with Nehru, the charge d'affaires broke the ice by mentioning Larson's earlier stop in England to accept his D.C.L. degree from Oxford. Nehru looked impressed, and the two men began talking about the degree ceremony, with Nehru explaining that he had studied at Cambridge University's Trinity College. Clearly warming up to his visitor, Nehru turned to talking about Indian history and noted that 1957 marked the tenth anniversary of the Indian republic's founding, the centennial of what he called, with a grin, "the so-called Indian mutiny" against British colonial rule, and the bicentennial of the beginnings of British imperialism in India.[19] Nehru then proceeded to give Larson a history lesson on the origins of British rule there, evidently intended to counteract whatever Anglophilic tendencies the new USIA director had developed from his association with Oxford. Larson took notes of this mini-lecture, which he summarized as follows: "He [Nehru] recounted how the British had taken advantage of the decaying Indian empire—bribed right and left—so that there were still rajahs who were traitors who had sold out—and the people & other rajahs have never forgot."[20] The conversation then turned to other matters, with Nehru recommending that Larson visit a particular tomb, the name of which the Indian prime minister helpfully wrote down in Larson's notebook. The two men also discussed ideas about improving India's economy, with Nehru observing that efforts to improve life at the village level were "the most revolutionary of all."[21] After a few final pleasantries, Larson took his leave, having seen firsthand Nehru's pride in India's progress since independence from Britain and his hostility to western imperialism.[22]

Larson's discussion with Chester Bowles, which took place at the American ambassador's residence where Larson was staying, focused on more immediate concerns. Bowles, drawing upon his experience as ambassador to India during the Truman administration, offered several recommendations to improve U.S.-Indian relations. He suggested that the United States reschedule India's payments on American loans to ease the financial pressures the country faced and refrain from providing Pakistan more military aid. The Eisenhower administration had considered increasing such military assistance as part of the recently announced "Eisenhower doctrine," which committed the United States to helping Middle Eastern countries that sought to resist the spread of communism. Bowles warned, however, that giving Pakistan more arms would likely prove counterproductive by alienating Nehru and encouraging Indian neutralism in the conflict between East and West. Bowles explained that Nehru was afraid that such a move would embolden Pakistan's army to keep fighting with

India over the disputed province of Kashmir. Bowles also argued that the United States could provide much-needed assistance to India and improve America's standing there by getting more American businessmen involved with economic development programs at the village level. He also pointed out that the United States had hurt its relations with India by not sending high-level U.S. government diplomats to visit the country regularly. Clearly sympathetic to Bowles's views and impressed by his knowledge, Larson later characterized this briefing as "superb" and "better than anything I'd had up until then."[23]

Much less helpful were meetings with Suhrawaddy of Pakistan and Nuri-as-Said of Iraq. Larson jotted down his impressions of Suhrawaddy as "a small, fat, conceited, sensual fellow—with a penchant for heavy banter."[24] Suhrawaddy told Larson that Russia was making headway in Asia through Syria and Afghanistan and that China was also "pressing in" through such nations as Japan, Burma, Indonesia, and Vietnam.[25] The Pakistani prime minister observed that neutralism of the sort Nehru represented was possible only when one's country was not in danger and that India would eventually find itself forced by communist advances to side with the West. Although Suhrawaddy no doubt intended this alarmist picture of communist gains to encourage the United States government to provide more military assistance, he clearly failed to impress Larson in the way Nehru and Chester Bowles had.[26]

Nur-as-Said displeased Larson in a different way. He found the Iraqi prime minister positively jarring with his repeated demands for radio-jamming equipment to use in blocking inflammatory Arab nationalist messages coming from Syria and Radio Cairo. Larson told him that the U.S. government did not do this on principle and that jamming was counterproductive. Larson came away from this meeting and others with various official groups in Baghdad with the impression, as he noted in his memo book, that the "principal concern here is Israel."[27] The Jewish state's successful military campaign to occupy the Gaza Strip during the Suez crisis and reluctance to leave thereafter had made anti-Israel attitudes very visible during Larson's visit to Baghdad.[28]

Larson's meeting with Egypt's charismatic leader was the last major one of the trip and lasted for an hour and a quarter at Nasser's home. After fifteen minutes or so of pleasantries, Larson noted, Nasser "took the ball" and began talking about information policy. Nasser explained that it had been a specialty of his before coming to power and that he had found the psychological aspects of the subject useful in understanding his own people. Nasser told Larson that Egyptians' strong sense of history made them wary and even suspicious by nature. They also tended to be sentimental and emotional, he continued, and would not stand for foreign domination. Nasser added that "any [Egyptian] leader who is suspected of being a foreign agent is thru."[29]

After elaborating a bit more on that last theme, Nasser lit into the American press. "This," Larson noted, "is his No[.] 1 obsession. He plainly believes it is a gigantic conspiracy to discredit him."[30] So passionate did Nasser sound on this subject that Larson could recall this part of the discussion vividly many years later in his memoirs:

> Nasser's decisions seemed to have been made primarily with an eye on the reaction of the press. For example, he suddenly asked me, "Do you want to know why I made that deal for Soviet weapons?" I did indeed. "I'll tell you why. The *New York Times* has been saying over and over that Israel can lick me with one hand tied behind their back—and I decided to show them." Again and again, he would cite the editorial positions of major newspapers, and one got the impression of an actor on the world stage who lives for nothing but his reviews in the morning papers.[31]

Eventually Nasser turned to another point, which was how his studies at the War College and elsewhere had taught him a basic lesson of Middle Eastern history. He told Larson it showed clearly that Arabs could achieve nothing politically without unity.[32]

As Larson listened patiently to all of this, he formed several strong impressions and conclusions. First, he was convinced that Nasser sincerely believed that neither he nor any other Egyptian leader could afford to become identified in his people's eyes as the tool of a foreign power. "This means," Larson concluded, "he will never willingly become a Russian stooge."[33] Larson also detected an undercurrent of nervousness on Nasser's part throughout the substantive part of their discussion and observed that "he is evidently worried."[34] Toward the end of the conversation, Nasser complained about the new Eisenhower Doctrine, which he felt had created a breach in Arab unity. The way in which Nasser discussed this issue, however, gave Larson the impression that the Egyptian leader also objected to the Eisenhower Doctrine because he saw the policy as aimed at him. Larson came away from this talk with the sense that Nasser "is getting ready to turn toward us" and that he needed more evenhanded coverage in the American press in order to bring that about.[35] The overall impression that Nasser conveyed was one of insecurity, of a leader who believes he is losing support among his own people and in other Arab nations. Larson summed up his impression of Nasser from this meeting as "a man given to oversimplification and emotion."[36]

Larson did not confine his research to high-level meetings of this sort. He also spoke at length with USIA staff in each of the countries he visited as well as journalists, diplomats, and other foreign government officials. Understanding that even these sources of information might not provide a complete picture of Middle Eastern problems, Larson also met with some younger American-educated intellectuals and professionals, most notably in Iraq, whose complaints about the government's resistance to them and their ideas made a lasting impression. Larson later wrote of his meeting with Iraqi intellectuals:

> The essence of their grievance was mostly this: they had spent years getting the finest education that America offered, as lawyers, engineers, scientists, doctors, and the like, and had returned to Iraq with high hopes for putting their talents and training into the development of a new country. But what they found was that they were relegated to the very bottom of the totem pole, with the dead weight of thousands of hack politicians and bureaucrats above them, barring them from the really interesting and significant jobs for which they felt qualified.[37]

Although aware from his talks that the places he had seen faced serious problems and that many people there tended to blame the United States for them, Larson continued to view the future of those nations optimistically. That came through clearly in the list of observations and conclusions about the Middle East he jotted down at the end of his visit there. Among the most important of Larson's observations was that there was still "a vast amount" of needless misunderstanding among Middle Easterners about the United States; that although they were basically friendly to Americans, they believed that Eisenhower's emphasis on containing communism in the region did not deal with what they saw as the real threat to the region's stability, which was Israel; that Middle Easterners viewed the conflict between France and Algeria as a key battleground in the struggle against colonialism; and that Soviet influence was growing in the Middle East.[38]

From these impressions and the many others Larson gleaned during his trip, he drew several conclusions. First, the solution in terms of U.S. information policy was to emphasize American interest in helping promote freedom and economic progress for each Middle Eastern country and to explain efforts to contain communism as only a necessary prerequisite to these greater goals. Second, more resources ought to be devoted to communicating that message, via radio, television, personal contacts, presidential speeches, and other official material concerning the Middle East. Third, the United States needed to refrain from increasing aid to Israel and mount "a vigorous attack" on the Palestinian refugee problem in order to improve American standing in the region. Fourth, the United States should seek to avoid siding with France in the Algerian conflict. Fifth, the Soviet invasion of Hungary had caused many second thoughts among Arab leaders and the United States ought to use that opportunity to its advantage, especially in Jordan, Lebanon, and Egypt. Sixth, and in some ways most important, Larson noted, "All of this *confims* that there is much more to our job than anti-communism."[39]

Larson's thoughts about the Middle Eastern political situation showed an impressive grasp of its complexities. Rather than a single-minded fixation with the communist "threat" there, his notes from this trip reveal an awareness of the other considerations at work and the need to address them with a positive message from the United States about the region's future. Larson's conclusion about the need for the United States to refrain from allying with France in Algeria in particular revealed his ability to think outside simplistic Cold War categories. Radical Algerian nationalists had begun an armed struggle in 1954 to free their country from French rule. Unlike many of the more hawkish American experts on foreign policy, who tended to see this rebellion in purely East-West terms, Larson appears to have perceived the serious threat to the interests of the United States in the Middle East that could arise should the United States behave in ways that suggested that it backed a continuation of colonialism. Larson's overall analysis of the Middle Eastern situation could be faulted, perhaps, for its overly optimistic view that better American information policy could make a big difference to the region's future, but even that somewhat doubtful notion reflected an understandable excitement about the possibilities of his new job.[40]

Larson's basically hopeful outlook at the end of this trip no doubt also reflected his own background and situation at that particular moment. He had a sunny view of humanity's destiny, which his comfortable upbringing, religious beliefs, happy home life, and considerable personal success all tended to reinforce. The astonishingly rapid progress of his career over the previous twelve months no doubt also contributed to this rosy outlook. On the heels of all the good news Larson had received and the heady experience of speaking directly with a series of foreign leaders came word of another important accomplishment. Near the end of his trip, he learned via cable from the USIA in Washington that Harvard had awarded him its Henderson Prize for his treatise on worker's compensation. News of this honor and the $1,000 that came with it "really knocked me flat," he wrote Florence.[41] By the time Larson reached home on February 11, 1957, he must truly have felt on top of the world.[42]

Over the next two weeks, Larson carefully prepared his remarks for the first of the congressional hearings at which he would be testifying on the USIA's behalf. That initial appearance took place on February 26th before the House Appropriations Subcommittee. In the previous two years, this body had given USIA budget requests rougher treatment than its counterpart in the Senate, thanks mostly to the unfriendly attitude of the House subcommittee's chairman, Congressman John J. Rooney of Brooklyn. Having been warned that Rooney doubted the value of the USIA in general, Larson developed a comprehensive defense of the agency's role and specific budgetary needs and presented it with his characteristic effectiveness. Larson's remarks so impressed subcommittee member Frank Bow of Ohio, an administration loyalist, that he sent a message to Eisenhower later that same day, reporting that Larson had "made the best presentation of the needs and place of USIA in government I have ever heard."[43] The response from Rooney signaled even more clearly how well Larson had done. Instead of putting him on the defensive by asking hard and even unfair questions he could not easily answer, as Rooney had done to other USIA directors in the past, the chairman found himself unable to rattle Larson or make any headway in the face of his clear, calm, and persuasive replies.[44]

This debater's triumph was followed by another, even more noteworthy, one later that same week, when Larson spoke at the Washington press corps' annual Gridiron Dinner. The organizers of the 1957 event had asked Larson to speak on behalf of the Republicans and Adlai Stevenson to speak for the Democrats. In keeping with the custom, Larson gave a funny yet pointed defense of the Eisenhower administration. When Stevenson spoke a bit later, he ruefully acknowledged in his usual witty way that his rival had succeeded in upstaging him. Stevenson joked that he "had heard of a Larson pitching a no-hitter, but didn't think a Larson would pitch one against him."[45] Humorously alluding to Larson's role as Eisenhower's speechwriter, Stevenson quoted a Roman aphorism about "fearing Caesar's ghost more than Caesar."[46] Stevenson complimented his opponent that night in yet another way, Larson noted in his memo book, by offering to welcome him into the Democratic Party "any time I am tired of being a missionary to the heathen."[47] The twice-defeated presidential candidate then lashed out at the assembled reporters for what he believed had been their unfair coverage of his most recent presidential campaign. By the end of this attack, which fell flat with the audience, Larson had clearly made the better impression on its members.[48]

This particular oratorical victory came at a high price. Among those listening that night was Senate Majority Leader Lyndon Johnson, who had begun to think seriously about running for the presidency in 1960. As insecure as he was ambitious, Johnson responded to Larson's success by turning to a dinner companion and remarking—within earshot of an Eisenhower aide—"We're going to have to get that guy Larson; he'll be up for the Presidency some day."[49] When exactly Larson learned of this remark is unclear, but even if he had found out about it immediately, Larson was not the sort of person who would have taken such a statement seriously. An essentially gentle, kind, and trusting man, he did not think in such terms or expect others to do so. Larson's lack of experience with the rougher side of partisan politics contributed to a kind of innocence about rivals in that world and the ways in which they might respond to his new prominence. Although these qualities apparently endeared him to Eisenhower, they left Larson unprepared for what Johnson might do.[50]

This same naiveté made Larson unready for attacks from Old Guard Republicans in Congress, angry about his advocacy of "the new Republicanism" and what they saw as the excessive size of Eisenhower's proposed budget for fiscal year 1958. At $73.3 billion dollars, it was Eisenhower's biggest budget request yet and a record for peacetime. The dollar amount was, however, more than a little misleading. The most meaningful figure was the fraction of the nation's gross national product taken up by federal spending, and Eisenhower's proposal amounted to less than 18 percent of the gross national product, the lowest since 1939. The trend indicated by these figures nonetheless angered many right-wing Republicans by suggesting that the president's program did not portend a sharp break with the taxing and spending policies of the Roosevelt and Truman administrations, as such conservatives had hoped, but only a more modest reduction in the federal government's share of a rapidly expanding GNP. Even the specific areas targeted for substantial increases offended members of the GOP's Old Guard. Most of the additional money Eisenhower asked for was earmarked for such things as foreign aid, resource development, social insurance programs, and school construction.[51]

Also animating Old Guard opposition to Eisenhower's proposed budget was the emergence of inflation during early 1957 as a serious economic problem. The product of a complex set of causes, most notably wage-price spirals in the heavily unionized sectors of the economy, balance-of-payment difficulties with the nation's major trading partners, and heavy government spending on armaments, inflation seemed likely to grow steadily unless something was done to rein it in. Treasury secretary George Humphrey reflected his concern over that alarming prospect when he commented at a press conference held the same day the White House staff sent Eisenhower's budget proposal to Congress that "if we don't [reduce government spending and taxing] over a long period of time, I will predict that you will have a depression that will curl your hair."[52] Eisenhower's remarks at his own press conference one week later, which seemed to suggest that he and Humphrey did not disagree about the need for fiscal restraint, and budget director Percival F. Brundage's efforts to make such reductions only emboldened the would-be budget cutters in Congress and demoralized Modern Republicans there.[53]

For all of these reasons, the substantial increase in appropriations Eisenhower and Larson had proposed for the USIA acquired symbolic importance in the minds of more fiscally conservative Republicans in Congress. Determined to send Eisenhower and his aides a message, these members of the GOP's Old Guard decided to vent their opposition to Modern Republicanism, and the level and kinds of public spending it implied at the USIA's expense. Right-wing Republicans were joined in this quest by some of the more partisan Democrats, eager to pose opportunistically as defenders of fiscal restraint and hostile to Larson for his success in promoting a moderate Republican alternative to New Deal liberal ideas.[54]

The first sign of how much opposition he and his ideas had stirred up came in early April, when the House Appropriations Committee signaled its intention to reduce rather than increase the USIA's budget from the $113 million level appropriated the previous year. Despite a personal plea from Eisenhower to committee chairman Clarence Cannon, he and a majority of his colleagues backed a cut, which the House of Representatives approved. Instead of the $140 million Eisenhower and Larson had asked for in January, the House voted an appropriation of $106.1 million for the USIA that spring. Although Larson tried to increase that amount by winning the Senate's support for a larger appropriation, the same basic constellation of forces and an aroused Lyndon Johnson awaited him there, boding ill for his prospects.[55]

Larson managed to make matters even worse by giving a partisan political speech to a Republican group in Hawaii on April 16th, only three weeks before his Senate testimony. Officially billed as a "Lincoln Birthday Address," it had been postponed due to Larson's foreign tour and his many other speaking obligations in March and early April. Florence came along on this trip, their first to what was still the territory of Hawaii. With statehood fast approaching, the leaders of the islands' nascent Republican Party had invited him there to "help pep them up," as Larson explained in a letter to his mother.[56] Drawing heavily on the themes of *A Republican Looks at His Party*, Larson gave a speech at the Kaiser Dome in Honolulu entitled "As Our Case Is New," urging Hawaii Republicans to follow the Modern Republican path. Although there was nothing original in Larson's remarks that day, his decision to repeat aloud some of the more controversial aspects of his thesis was a major mistake. Larson's statement that during the Roosevelt and Truman administrations "the country was in the grip of a somewhat alien philosophy, imported from Europe" and his contrasting view of Modern Republicanism as "a truly American ideology and program" evidently did not bother his partisan Republican audience, but the response from Senate Democrats would soon prove to be very different.[57]

When Larson first appeared before the Senate Appropriations Subcommittee on the afternoon of May 2, 1957, he seems to have felt confident that he could repeat his successful showing before the equivalent House panel the previous February. To his great surprise, subcommittee chair Lyndon Johnson and allies Allen Ellender of Louisiana, William Fulbright of Arkansas, and Mike Mansfield of Montana never gave Larson a chance. They barraged him with one sarcastic and hostile question after another, and when he answered as he had before Rooney's subcommittee, Johnson simply ignored the response and directed Larson to answer again. The proximate cause of this torrent of verbal harassment emerged when Ellender and Johnson confronted Larson with his remark about "alien influence" and demanded to know if he had said it.[58] Larson's explanation that the offending comment had been taken out of context satisfied none of the Democrats present.[59]

Over the course of what became four days of questioning, even the uncommonly decent Mansfield announced that he was "very much disturbed" by Larson's recent speech: "I happened to be in office during the latter days of the New Deal, all the period of the Fair Deal, and during the period of the present Republican Administration. I was never aware of the fact that I was in the grip of an alien philosophy during any of those years."[60]

The failure of Republicans on the subcommittee to defend Larson effectively made his ordeal even worse. The leader of the Senate Republicans, California senator William Knowland and his colleague, Everett Dirksen of Illinois, signaled the Old Guard's hostility to Modern Republicanism and its advocates by refusing to come to Larson's aid. The more moderate Leverett Saltonstall of Massachusetts and Edward Thye of Minnesota tried to protect him, but to no avail.[61]

Even if the Republicans had been united behind him, rescuing Larson would have been beyond their power. With Johnson firmly in control as both subcommittee chair and Senate majority leader, and determined to put an abrupt end to Larson's rise, neither he nor his defenders could stop this abuse of the hearings process. Larson later described Johnson's pivotal and thoroughly cynical role in this tawdry episode:

> Lyndon Johnson personally presided at all the sessions, backed by a crew of the most hostile Democrats on the [sub]committee. Johnson grilled me for hours every day . . . , and no matter what I said, he would come back with something like, "You haven't answered my question. Why don't you go home and do your homework?" . . . At one point he even leaned over with the Johnson leer and said, "You know, this hurts me more than it does you."[62]

In this time of trouble, Larson drew support and comfort from Florence. The way in which his career preempted hers in the mid-1950s had intensified the bond between them by giving Florence the time to act as his chief editor and thus involving her much more closely in his work. The end of her career in theater also made Florence into a truly constant companion to her husband. One sign of that second change was the sudden decrease in the number of letters between Arthur and Florence that began in the mid-1950s and continued for the rest of their lives. They no longer needed to write to each other much because from that point forward he and she were seldom apart.[63]

Larson also consoled himself during this traumatic time by taking a trip to the Guitar Shop on M Street and treating himself to a new classical guitar. Deciding to channel all of the negative emotional energy stirred up by the hearings into something positive, he began to take lessons from Sophocles Pappas, who had studied with Andres Segovia. Larson continued to play his new instrument for many years, thereby succeeding in his quest to make something good out of what had obviously been a very unpleasant experience.[64]

Larson could perhaps have avoided this ambush. If he had characterized both New Deal and Modern Republican ideas more tactfully—and accurately—as distinctive American variations on European ideas, he would have eliminated the key pretext for the Democrats' attack. He could also have made himself less vulnerable by refraining from making speeches to Republican groups after being named USIA director. Although he informed a friend soon after his appointment that he would be taking "a slight holiday from politics," Larson evidently could not resist the temptation to continue in his role as chief public advocate for Modern Republicanism.[65] The USIA's mission of presenting

America's official message to the outside world made partisan speechmaking on the director's part especially perilous, something Larson seems not to have fully understood. A sympathetic Eisenhower took that view, telling Larson that his Hawaii speech in particular "was the one mistake [he] had made."[66] Larson also damaged his cause by vigorously defending the USIA news service at a time when the head of one of the nation's leading wire services had come to see it as a rival. This quarrel led to a lot of unfavorable press coverage of the USIA at the very moment it came under attack in Congress. Even if Larson had managed to avoid these missteps, however, he seems likely to have run into trouble. The most basic reason for this was his strong public identification with the Modern Republican cause at a time when opposition to it had begun to grow.[67]

There were, of course, other prominent spokesmen for that point of view who did not meet with the same fate as Larson did. Three others in particular enjoyed something like the importance he did to the explication of Modern Republican ideas. Of this trio, the earliest was *Fortune* writer and editor Russell Davenport, who had worked as a senior aide to Wendell Willkie during his unsuccessful campaign for the presidency in 1940. Davenport's Manhattan think tank, the Institute for Creative Research, served as a source of Modern Republican ideas during the 1940s and early 1950s. Eisenhower thought so highly of him and his ideas that he kept a copy of Davenport's book, *My Country*, on his desk in the Oval Office during the early months of his presidency. Columbia economist Eli Ginzberg also developed similar ideas through his Conservation of Human Resources Project, which Eisenhower had helped him start while serving as the university's president in the late 1940s. And there was also Gabriel Hauge's work as research director for Eisenhower's 1952 presidential campaign and then as Eisenhower's special assistant for economic affairs. None of these three enjoyed, however, anything like Larson's public prominence at the point when the tide began shifting against their mutually shared set of beliefs. Davenport was dead by then, and Ginzberg had never left Columbia, where he made his contributions to the Eisenhower administration outside the media spotlight. Hauge held an important job within the Eisenhower administration but worked in the White House, a venue that sheltered him from the kind of encounter with Congress that proved so damaging to Larson. Only Larson presented the combination of public visibility, high office, and apparent electoral prospects that had made him such an inviting target.[68]

The full extent of the opposition to him and his ideas from both Old Guard Republicans and opportunistic Democrats became clear when Congress finished its work on the USIA budget for fiscal year 1958. The Senate, under Lyndon Johnson's direction and with minority leader William Knowland's approval, passed an appropriation of $90.2 million for the agency, approximately 20 percent less than the USIA had received the year before. The House-Senate Conference Committee, despite some strong nudging by Eisenhower, agreed to provide only $95.1 million, which compelled Larson to make substantial reductions in the USIA's radio and television broadcasting, motion picture production, and information service. The cuts hit USIA operations hard in Western Europe, the Far East, Latin America, and the Middle East. The smaller budget also forced Larson to make 650 layoffs. These deep cuts, and the embarrassing public attack on the USIA director himself, damaged the agency's morale and effectiveness for years to come.[69]

Despite these setbacks, Larson tried hard to frame a more positive message for the USIA to carry. He had laid out the main themes of that message in a speech at Philadelphia on March 31st entitled "What Hopes for Peace?" In this address, Larson argued that the key to such hopes was improving understanding of the United States elsewhere in the world. He stated that foreigners needed to learn that what America stood for and sought for people around the globe was in line with what he called "basic human motivations."[70] He discussed five of these, the first of which was freedom. Larson's discussion of this crucial point focused on freedom in the political sense, rather than the economic one, and he suggested that no government could completely squelch a people's desire for it.[71]

Next came property, which he said was something so innate that even a small child felt a sense of ownership in his crib. So powerful was this motivation, Larson continued, that if there was a challenge here it was to persuade people to accept the idea that ownership had limits and that property must be used "with due regard for the property rights of others."[72] From this innate sense of ownership, Larson added, followed an instinctive belief that a man was entitled to the fruits of his own toil and an innate willingness to fight against violations of that right.[73]

The third of these fundamental human traits Larson called justice. Like the belief in property, Larson argued, a sense of justice was essentially innate in all human beings. Although the vicissitudes of life might cause one to doubt whether justice always prevailed, "that sense of justice and injustice never leaves us. No fancy theory about justice being whatever serves the ends of the State can ever blot it out."[74]

Fourth was "national pride, or pride in whatever group claims a person's principal allegiance." Observing that at that point in history loyalty to the nation was most common, Larson acknowledged that this could interfere with efforts to work together across national boundaries, but then went on to say that no one could ignore the power of this belief: "The sophisticated may lament this, and urge us all to be world citizens. But in this imperfect world of today, we might as well face the fact that it is through the vehicle of the particular nation that most people are striving to achieve their economic and political objectives and assert their ultimate traditions."[75]

Larson's fifth and final universal human trait was that of religion. He argued that while it took many forms the world over, the religious impulse existed everywhere and in every person and would continue to seek some kind of expression.[76]

Larson then compared how the United States and the communist countries dealt with these motivations. Not surprisingly, he found that the American system tended to promote all of them while the communist system tried to resist them. To Larson, this basic difference conclusively proved communism's illegitimacy.[77]

Understanding that listeners might wonder how such an "unnatural" system could ever have come into being, Larson explained that it had done so not by the consent of the people living under communist rule but rather by concentrating economic and political power in the hands of what he called "a small group of fanatical agitators and leaders." Even they, he added, had found themselves forced to make compromises with what Larson called "that same old human nature" in order to remain in power.[78]

Rather than give in to despair over the prospects for peace in these circumstances, Larson argued that peace could be promoted by encouraging people living under communism to assert what he saw as their basic human motivations. He pointed to "a new class" of people who had grown up under that system and increasingly questioned communist orthodoxy. Larson gave as his example the nation of Hungary, where the uprising against communist rule in late 1956 had "demonstrated once and for all that you cannot brainwash an entire population into accepting the Communist mythology as a substitute for their own deepest beliefs and desires."[79] Larson defined the American role as communicating through every possible medium that the United States favored those beliefs and desires. This would lead, he said, to mutual understanding between peoples and increase the likelihood of a lasting peace.[80]

Larson's speech managed to be both profound and parochial. Much of what he had to say about fundamental human motivations rang true, but his heavy emphasis on "human nature" ignored the extent to which socialization could affect popular beliefs and desires. He also did not acknowledge the possibility that different historical experiences elsewhere and the modern industrial order itself might have given rise to newer, competing human aspirations, such as equality and cooperation, that communists had sought to advance. Like so many conservatives of his generation, Larson took seriously the economic and military challenge posed by the leading communist nations but not the notion that some of the basic values they promoted might actually enjoy popular support there.

Larson followed this speech with another talk one week later, devoted to the ways and means the USIA could send this new message. Formally entitled "The United States Information Service: How Effective Is It?" Larson's remarks addressed the issues of whether the USIA's informational arm was reaching its intended audience, whether its message was increasing understanding of the United States abroad, and what the best ways were to improve that effort's effectiveness. Larson informed his listeners, members of New York's Union League Club, that the latest intelligence indicated that Voice of America radio broadcasts were reaching large audiences in the Soviet Union and Eastern Europe, despite jamming operations there. The 326,000 "fan letters" that the USIA received from around the world in 1956, he added, also provided clear and convincing evidence that its broadcasts and print publications were reaching a great many people. Larson noted that the two magazines with the largest circulation in Southeast Asia were both USIA publications: *Free World* and *The World Today*, the second of which appeared in Chinese. Also highly successful was the USIA traveling exhibit entitled "Atoms for Peace," which explained the nonmilitary uses of nuclear technology. Fourteen million people had seen this exhibit thus far, Larson reported, and the clearest sign of its great effectiveness had come in Japan. He described this unexpected development:

> A dramatic illustration [of the exhibit's success] is what happened when we brought our Atoms-for-Peace exhibit to—of all places—Hiroshima. Over wild leftist protests, the civic leaders put it in the Peace Museum, actually displacing most of the relics of the atomic bombing in the process. In three weeks, 120,000 people, one third of the population[,] had seen the exhibit, and six civic and educational organizations were conducting special programs on peaceful uses of atomic energy.[81]

Other forms of media and efforts to communicate also showed clear signs of success, Larson explained, such as the Information Agency's 143 lending libraries and its English classes, in which 90,000 students were enrolled. One of the most effective recent USIA ventures, he continued, was the extensive reporting on Soviet premier Nikita Khrushchev's secret 1956 speech to the Twentieth Soviet Communist Party Congress acknowledging Stalin's cruelties and incompetence. This had led to outright defections from overseas Communist parties, Larson noted, and had also led one major socialist leader in Western Europe, Italy's Pietro Nenni, to break formally with Moscow.[82]

One of the clearest signs that Voice of America broadcasts were having an effect, Larson continued, was the large amount of money Soviet and Eastern European governments spent on radio jamming efforts. Larson informed his listeners that the Soviet government had devoted more money to jamming than the entire USIA budget. The Polish government had also spent more on their jamming operation than the agency's broadcasting budget until, he added, "they got tired of the expense and quit."[83] Popular hostility in Poland to the jamming effort had led students there to attack and seriously damage Polish jamming stations in Bydgoszcz and Poznan, Larson said. All of these signs and many others indicated that U.S. Information Service messages and materials were making a difference in what foreigners thought of the United States and its kind of economic and political system.[84]

Larson then discussed how the USIA could increase its effectiveness. He listed several ideas, the most important of which, Larson said, were to improve the content of the USIA's message and expand exchanges between private groups in the United States and counterparts abroad.[85]

He told his listeners that "the age of tricky propaganda is about over" and that persuasiveness increasingly required highly factual and accurate messages.[86] Larson added that the USIA could do better if it focused more of its efforts on presenting a constructive message about the United States to the outside world with evidence of specific American actions consistent with that message. Even more promising, he continued, was the president's "People to People" program, which encouraged reputable private organizations to arrange educational and cultural exchanges with similar foreign groups to promote mutual understanding. Hitting a very Modern Republican theme, Larson pointed out that the great promise of this program lay in tapping the energy and initiative of private citizens' organizations rather than trying to set up a government-funded and -controlled exchange program. If private groups responded as he hoped, Larson said, "the People-to-People approach could soar far beyond the governmental approach in importance and effectiveness."[87]

Like Larson's tenure in the Labor Department, his stint at the USIA revealed a gap between Modern Republican theory and practice. The congressional budget cuts did much to undermine his plans for enhancing the effectiveness of the U.S. Information Service. So, too, did resistance from within its own ranks, especially the émigré broadcasters at Voice of America. Hired primarily for their knowledge of the languages spoken in the Eastern European countries that communists had forced them to flee, these broadcasters typically wanted to fill their radio programs with a litany of communism's failings rather than a more positive message about what America offered. Understandably traumatized by the onset of communist rule in their native lands, such USIA employees often actively resisted Larson's efforts to accentuate the positive in programming. His inability to ascertain personally whether these broadcasters actually followed the scripts they were given seriously undermined Larson's efforts to reshape the content of Voice of America broadcasts.[88]

A similar kind of resistance, albeit from a different source, hampered Larson's efforts to promote cultural and educational exchanges during his tenure as the USIA's director. The excessively fearful view of Soviet intentions and capabilities promoted by the U.S. government over the previous decade had the consequence of encouraging public resistance to People-to-People exchanges with the Soviet Union and its Eastern European neighbors, apparently out of concerns that communist governments would use such contacts to promote their propaganda and espionage efforts. Although Eisenhower and Larson both personally endorsed People-to-People exchanges with all parts of the world, such interactions with Communist countries advanced slowly during the late 1950s.[89]

These setbacks, like those experienced by some of the more-forward-looking aspects of the Modern Republican program, showed that Larson's agenda for the USIA in 1957 was not so much impractical as simply ahead of its time. The budget cuts passed by partisan Democrats and Old Guard Republicans in Congress that year would not last once the special circumstances that motivated that action had passed. One could also reasonably expect, even during the late 1950s, that as the years went by and foreign-language training in the United States expanded, the USIA would become less dependent on its Eastern European émigré broadcasters. Even those who remained would presumably become less emotional about fighting communism as memories of the traumas associated with the beginnings of communist rule in Eastern Europe faded. Such changes would over time make possible the more constructive, accurate, and calm kind of USIA message for which Larson had pushed. As experience with educational and cultural exchanges diminished American hostility and fear of Soviet and Eastern European peoples, one could also reasonably expect that Eisenhower and Larson's People-to-People initiative would go as far as they hoped. Larson's achievement at the USIA, like his championing of Modern Republicanism more generally during the 1950s, did not so much change U.S. government policies greatly as begin to move them in different directions.[90]

Larson himself lost whatever opportunity he might have had to witness firsthand the early fruits of his efforts at the USIA when Eisenhower and Sherman Adams decided to remove him from the agency's directorship in October 1957. This action did not stem from any disagreement with Larson about the policies he had pursued there. On the contrary, all the indications are that Eisenhower and Adams genuinely liked Larson and his ideas for the USIA and also appreciated his hard work on its behalf. The reason for this sudden move had to do instead with the sense among senior White House officials that they could not put Larson (and the USIA) through another round of congressional budget hearings in the spring of 1958 like the one he had already experienced. With no reason to expect that Johnson or the Old Guard Republicans would behave any differently the next time, Eisenhower and Adams decided that Larson would have to leave, and early enough for a new director to prepare himself for the upcoming budget battle with Congress.[91]

Accordingly, Eisenhower and Adams met separately with Larson at the White House on the morning of October 1, 1957, to discuss his future. During the first of these two sessions, a private one with Eisenhower that lasted thirty minutes, Larson began by telling the president that the task he had given him to handle at the USIA was "nearly done."[92] By this Larson meant, he said, that the guidelines for the content of the agency's message had been changed as Eisenhower had wished. Larson also frankly explained his problems with the Senate Appropriations Subcommittee that Lyndon Johnson headed and his sense that Johnson and his allies there were "dedicated to discrediting me."[93] Eisenhower then related what he had learned about this matter, including Johnson's "tall tale" to the president that Larson had given the subcommittee no real facts, just speeches, and the news that Minority Leader William Knowland had echoed the same line. Neither man had fooled Eisenhower, he told Larson, but the completely imaginary quality of these charges made refuting them difficult.[94]

Eisenhower also reviewed his own well-intentioned motives in putting Larson in such an exposed position, telling him, as Larson noted in his ever-present memo book, "that he had wanted me to take this job to get prominence in the *public mind* in international affairs. He said that he wanted to build up a stable of promising bright young men, so that when the [Republican] National Convention came round, we wouldn't have to go back to the Spanish-American war for leaders."[95]

With that, Eisenhower turned to the topic of what Larson should do next. The president asked Larson if he would be interested in coming to the White House to work officially as a presidential speechwriter. The variety of challenges facing the administration, which included the budget battle with Congress; the school desegregation showdown in Little Rock, Arkansas; and continuing Cold War tensions, had placed heavy demands on Eisenhower and his staff. The president suggested that Larson could greatly ease this burden by writing speeches for him on these kinds of subjects.[96] The only drawback in Eisenhower's mind to this assignment, Larson noted, was the president's concern that such a job "was not one that brought you into the public eye—it rather involved anonymity—and that's not what he wants for me." On the other hand, Eisenhower observed, such a role would "permit me to make speeches myself much more freely—as Hauge did, for example."[97]

Larson voiced his interest in the assignment Eisenhower had proposed. He added that his ideal would be to plan ahead by developing a set of speeches on major topics likely to require presidential comment over the next twelve months. Having such an inventory of speeches available to Eisenhower, Larson explained, would prevent the kind of backlog that had recently developed. Eisenhower "decidedly agreed," and the two of them discussed the kinds of settings in which the proposed speeches could be used. Pleased that Larson appeared receptive to leaving the USIA and coming to the White House to help him, Eisenhower appears to have tried to take some of the sting out of this change by offering some words of encouragement. Eisenhower commented that "he didn't think my 'little setbacks' had hurt me in [the] public mind—and [that] he is still looking for ways to build me up." Larson responded by agreeing to think over the proposed change in duties and told Eisenhower that an upcoming inspection tour of USIA operations in the Far East meant that "it would be weeks before I could do anything."[98] After a brief discussion about possible successors as USIA director, the session came to a close.[99]

Next came a conversation with Sherman Adams, during which Larson recounted the details of his meeting with the president and asked about such matters as a title and salary to go with the proposed position. Adams replied that

Larson could take the slot of special assistant to the president that Nelson Rockefeller had recently vacated, which carried with it a salary "in [the] 20's," Larson noted, that was not very different from the $21,000 he currently earned as the USIA's director.[100] Evidently still a bit doubtful, Larson asked Adams whether this move would be a step back. Adams replied by asking rhetorically, "Now how could [becoming a] special assistant to the President be [a] step back?"[101] Reassured by Adams's enthusiasm, Larson replied, "I knew this was so, and that it was a great honor."[102] Still wanting to go on the two-month overseas inspection trip he had been planning for some time, Larson then said he could not make the change until after Christmas, to which Adams crisply replied, "Let's figure on that then."[103] The two men discussed possible successors for the USIA director's post, and then parted, with the job change and its particulars seemingly quite settled.[104]

This very civilized arrangement came apart in the course of finding a new USIA director. Eisenhower and Adams decided, with Larson's support, that veteran diplomat George V. Allen, then serving as U.S. ambassador to Greece, should be offered the job. Choosing a career foreign service officer would satisfy Congress, reasoned Eisenhower, Adams, and Larson, and thus put a stop to the kind of harassment there that Larson had endured. But Allen, understanding the rather thankless nature of the job at that particular time, raised various objections to the idea during a meeting at the White House on October 16, 1957. In an effort to change Adams's mind, Allen pointed out that Larson was scheduled to leave very soon on an extended tour of USIA facilities, and thus a change immediately after he returned could hardly be considered appropriate. Grasping Allen's point that such a move would make Larson's tour look like a needless waste of the taxpayers' money, the presidential chief of staff picked up his telephone and called Larson at the USIA. To his dismay, Adams informed him that the change they had discussed needed to take place at once and asked him to submit his letter of resignation as USIA director that same day. When Larson protested that "all the arrangements and appointments have been made" for the foreign tour, Adams replied with characteristic firmness, "So sorry Arthur; I'm afraid you'll have to give that up."[105] Disappointed but still dutiful, Larson reluctantly agreed, and with that obstacle now removed, Adams told George Allen that the news of his and Larson's new appointments would be announced immediately. Thus did Larson's ten-month stint as USIA director come to an untimely end.[106]

The most perceptive journalists noted not only this change but also its larger significance. The article about Larson's resignation as USIA director in the highly respected political periodical *The Reporter* commented on the link between his reputation as Modern Republicanism's "philosopher" and the fate of the USIA budget in Congress. Although clearly sympathetic to Larson and his ideas, this same article concluded that his sudden departure from the

USIA essentially constituted "a dismissal."[107] Pieces about Larson's move to the White House staff in the *New York Times, Time, Newsweek, U.S. News & World Report,* and the *Christian Century* all drew the same conclusion. Though still high in Washington's political sky, Larson's star had clearly begun to wane.[108]

CHAPTER NINE

The President's "Ghost"

LARSON JOINED THE White House staff just as it was struggling to develop an effective response to the public hysteria created by the news on October 4, 1957, of the Soviets' successful launch of their Sputnik satellite. Although Eisenhower reacted calmly to this turn of events, it clearly rattled some of his own senior advisors, such as Sherman Adams and defense secretary Charles Wilson. Larson appears to have been influenced by their view that the United States needed to do something dramatic to demonstrate that the American space program had not fallen behind the Soviet one. At a meeting of the National Security Council one week before Larson formally resigned as USIA director, he proposed giving serious thought to such a step.[1]

Eisenhower immediately responded with words that signaled both his respect for his speechwriter's advice and his view of the need to keep the Soviets' recent achievement in proper perspective:

> The President replied to Mr. Larson by stating that while he could hardly quarrel with Mr. Larson's conclusions if the Soviets were to win every time, the fact remained that the United States couldn't possibly set up a whole vast scientific program of basic research in areas about which we don't know anything, and then attempt to outdo the Russians in each aspect of such a program. We must, above all, still seek a military posture that the Russians will respect.[2]

After Richard Nixon pointed out that Congress would surely respond to the public concern about Sputnik by investigating the ongoing U.S. missile program, Larson reiterated his suggestion for "planning for a U.S. win in the next great break-through."[3] Over the next several weeks, Eisenhower resisted this kind of pressure. Firmly believing that more spending on missiles was unnecessary and inflationary, Eisenhower brushed off advice to make a dramatic move in this area to reassure jittery members of Congress, the American people, and the nation's friends and allies abroad.[4]

Despite this unfavorable response from the president, Larson continued to push for such a step. Even if the Soviets had not really moved significantly ahead of the United States' own missile and satellite development programs, he reasoned, the need for such a triumph to reassure Congress, the public, and America's overseas allies loomed large. Larson soon decided that the most feasible step was to do something that dramatized the peaceful uses of atomic energy. Five days after the National Security Council meeting where responses to Sputnik had been discussed, Larson wrote Eisenhower and Lewis Strauss, the chairman of the Atomic Energy Commission, to convey another suggestion. In his letter to the president, Larson acknowledged that his earlier ideas such as manned satellites, sending a missile to the moon, or a space platform appeared upon further reflection to be too uncertain and expensive. He made a new proposal to create a harbor where none had previously existed by using a large nuclear bomb. Larson elaborated on this idea in his letter to Lewis Strauss. Aware that the public might find such a feat frightening, given the horrific Japanese experience with fallout from the Hiroshima and Nagasaki bombings, Larson explained that he favored the development and use of a "clean" bomb that did not pose that kind of danger. Public fears about radioactive fallout, he continued, would likely dissipate following a successful test of such a device. Clearly confident that the technological and public relations obstacles could be easily surmounted, Larson urged Strauss to move on this idea right away: "Why not get right to the point, and demonstrate it just as soon as possible? . . . We could do something both constructive and 'clean' like creating a harbor with one blast, for example—perhaps in Alaska, or actually on the coast of the continental United States, if possible."[5]

Larson's remarks speak volumes about the Modern Republican attitude toward nuclear power. Like so many of his contemporaries in the Eisenhower administration, Larson tended to favor increasing use of nuclear technology on the optimistic assumption that its most serious side effects, such as radioactive fallout and waste, could be addressed safely. Nowhere in Larson's writings during this time can one find any attention to the environmental problems that nuclear weapons testing (or very rapid economic growth) was creating. Although nothing ever came of his specific proposal, those problems did not go away.[6]

Eisenhower did decide, however, that something must be done in the fall of 1957 to calm the public about the progress of the Soviet satellite program. Rather than push hard for a comparable American feat, he decided to give a series of speeches on the state of American science and national security. In a meeting with Larson on October 22nd, Eisenhower explained this assignment, which would be Larson's first in his new role as the president's chief speechwriter. The two men agreed that the first speech in the series should explain the administration's view of Sputnik's significance and American efforts to develop similar technology. Eisenhower emphasized that the purpose of this speech, and the series as a whole, was to reduce public anxiety about Soviet satellites by making clear that they did not constitute a major threat to the United States.[7]

Eisenhower's determination to convey the message that there was no reason for alarm came through clearly when Larson suggested next that the speech should call upon Americans to put aside their own private needs in the wake of the Soviet breakthrough. Instead of responding enthusiastically to this suggestion, Eisenhower expressed concern that it might be misinterpreted. Larson recorded this revealing exchange in his notebook: "I expressed my idea that after 5 years of prosperity maybe what the country needs is a call to sacrifice. He [Eisenhower] wasn't sure. This might imply a greater threat than existed."[8]

Eisenhower elaborated on that point in a memo to Larson two weeks later. It came in response to an early draft of the first speech in the series, which Larson had prepared after reading through several briefing papers on the state of the nation's armed forces. Eisenhower criticized Larson's draft because it failed to mention how much effort the United States was already making to develop ballistic missiles, the scientific survey conducted as part of the administration's "New Look" at national defense, or the huge sums being spent by the Defense Department on research and development. Eisenhower also criticized the draft for failing to emphasize enough that the president had been in "informal but close contact with scientists" throughout his presidency and that his decision to create an official scientific advisor would simply "regularize these connections and make them broader, permanent" and coordinate relations between the scientific community and the White House.[9] Eisenhower pointedly criticized those who argued that spending more on defense would ensure the nation's future safety. Rather than endorse that view, so popular with the most hawkish politicians and like-minded members of the foreign policy establishment, Eisenhower informed Larson that "finally, it should be pointed out that money alone will not solve this problem."[10] Above and beyond this critique of the fine points in Larson's draft, Eisenhower observed that the speech needed to do a better job of conveying his determination not to sacrifice the very kind of freedom the country was fighting for just to match the Soviets' accomplishment and his confidence that Americans could successfully compete with them in the scientific realm without compromising the nation's most cherished values.[11]

With the speech scheduled for delivery only two days after Larson received this memo, he had to work very swiftly to incorporate the president's changes. Larson's efforts were also informed by input from Eisenhower's scientific advisors and from Sherman Adams, Gabriel Hauge and Richard Nixon. Eisenhower's decision to split the speech into two to give the various issues under discussion the degree of attention he saw fit made Larson's workload bearable. To his gratification, the first half of this very important address, which Eisenhower delivered via live television broadcast from the Oval Office on the evening of November 7, 1957, met with positive reviews from both the press and the public.[12]

In this first talk on the subject of "Science in National Security," Eisenhower explained that he intended to focus on its most immediate aspects. He discussed in detail the great strengths of the nation's armed forces, including their extensive programs of missile development. Eisenhower conceded that the Soviets "are likely ahead" in some missile and special areas and were "obviously ahead" in satellite development. In the next sentence, however, he argued that the overall military strength of the United States and its allies was "distinctly greater" than that of the communist countries. Eisenhower confidently predicted that Americans would "close ranks and get on with the job to be done."[13] The key to future progress, he argued, was more sharing of scientific discoveries among the free societies, "greater concentration of effort and improved arrangements within the government in the fields of science, technology and missiles."[14]

The president then explained the specific actions he was taking to improve national security by advancing science. The first of these was the creation of the office of special assistant to the president for science and technology, a post that would be filled by Massachusetts Institute of Technology president James R. Killian. This important change was accompanied by four others. The first two were intended to address the problems that arose from interservice rivalries among the army, navy, and air force, all of which had developed missile technology. Eisenhower announced that he had directed the secretary of defense to give the head of the nation's overall missile development program the authority needed to make the various military service branches work together in developing their ongoing missile programs. He also stated that all new missile programs would come under the direction of a single manager without regard to the separate armed services. The two other actions Eisenhower announced that night had to do with encouraging the sharing of scientific information among the United States and its friends abroad and his support for a plan to organize a scientific committee at NATO. A similar committee would be considered for the Southeast Asian Treaty Organization (SEATO), he added, and for other comparable organizations. To facilitate these moves, the secretary of state would appoint a science advisor and see that science attachés were appointed in appropriate places abroad.[15]

Having laid out the principal steps he had taken to meet the challenge Sputnik represented, Eisenhower moved on to deliver a characteristic warning about the dangers of doing too much. He cautioned that the nation could not afford to waste its resources and explicitly rejected calls for an across-the-board increase in military spending:

> In this whole effort it is important to see that nothing is wasted on non-essentials. Defense today is expensive, and growing more so. We cannot afford waste.
>
> It misses the whole point to say that we must now increase our expenditures of all kinds on military hardware and defense—as, for example, to heed demands recently made that we restore all personnel cuts made in the armed forces.[16]

Very mindful of the dangers to the nation's economic well-being posed by rising inflation, Eisenhower added that the country could have both a sound national defense and a sound economy if Americans established sound priorities and stuck to them and if everyone carried a share of the overall burden.[17]

Clearly wanting to close on a more optimistic note, Eisenhower proceeded to acknowledge that science offered far more than the prospect of military strength and that such strength was intended to promote peace rather than endanger it. He expressed his hope that in the near future the United States and the Soviet Union could make a disarmament breakthrough and thereby reduce the need for such heavy spending on armaments.[18]

Eisenhower followed this first installment with a second one six days later, which addressed the topic of national security in a broader context. Larson submitted a draft of this separate address to Eisenhower, National Science Foundation director Alan Waterman, and Secretary of State John Foster Dulles for their comments, which arrived only a few days before Eisenhower was scheduled to deliver it. Luckily for Larson, his readers liked the draft and suggested mostly minor or technical changes. As usual, Eisenhower proved to be the most exacting critic. Very much in charge, he told Larson in a meeting on November 11th that he was rearranging the sequence of remarks at the beginning of the speech. Eisenhower also emphasized that it needed to convey "the idea that there are some places where money can speed up security and others where it can't."[19] Eisenhower followed up these remarks with a memo in which he observed pointedly that "the present draft gives too much of an impression that we must spend a *lot* more money on our military defenses. I think we should put in a disclaimer on this in the very first part."[20]

Larson continued to revise in accordance with Eisenhower's wishes, an intensive process that went on constantly in the last few days before the speech was to be delivered in Oklahoma City. Eisenhower's determination to call for action but not wasteful military spending appears to have kept him fussing with the speech. So, too, did his concern that it lacked an overall point, or what he liked to call a QED. As a result, Larson spent most of his waking hours on November 11th through the 13th in Eisenhower's presence and accompanied him to Oklahoma City on Air Force One. The two men kept working on the details of the speech until the plane landed.[21]

Eisenhower addressed a live audience at the Municipal Auditorium in Oklahoma City that evening and the nation as a whole via radio and television. The main theme of "Our Future Security" was the communist challenge in science and technology and the way in which the free world must meet it. In response to Nikita Khrushchev's boastful prediction that the Soviet Union would preside over the demise of the capitalist societies, Eisenhower drew an analogy to Hitler's plan for world domination in *Mein Kampf.* Not enough people had taken the Nazi leader seriously, Eisenhower said, and observed, "We shall not make that mistake again."[22]

Eisenhower described briefly some of the newest and most powerful American weapons and their extraordinary cost and restated his belief that the Soviet satellite program, while impressive, did not signal a breach in America's defenses. The correct conclusion to draw from the launch of Sputnik, Eisenhower argued, was that American efforts in the related fields of science and security should be reexamined with an eye to making improvements. He believed it was necessary to expand the number of U.S. bases for bombers and missiles, increase the speed with which they could respond to an enemy attack, improve the system for tracking incoming planes and missiles, and "develop an active missile defense against missiles."[23] The last of these, Eisenhower noted, was "undergoing intensive research and development within the Defense Department."[24]

In addition to these steps, the United States needed to add long-range ballistic missiles to its arsenal. Eisenhower warned, however, that ongoing American efforts to develop this kind of missile, which had lifted the Sputnik satellite into orbit, could not be speeded up by more spending. He also warned that long-range missiles, once available for manufacture, deployment, and installation, would be very costly. Having issued what was in effect a gently worded rebuke to the more hawkish critics of the administration's missile programs and overall defense policy, Eisenhower rounded out his list of new military needs by arguing for improvements in compensation for those in the armed forces and for moving ahead with the American satellite program.[25]

Eisenhower candidly acknowledged the heavy price of these new initiatives and the consequent need to cut spending elsewhere. The right place to start, he said, was with the rest of the defense budget. At the same time, he insisted, there should be no attempt to eliminate conventional armed forces and rely solely on nuclear retaliation. "Such a course," he argued forcefully, "would be completely self-defeating." Nor, he added, should military and economic aid to the nation's friends and allies abroad be reduced, lest that weaken the collective security arrangements into which the United States had entered with forty-two other countries.[26]

Eisenhower turned next to the politically very difficult issue of making reductions in civilian expenditures to accommodate increased military expenses. Here, he said, the country would be forced to make "some tough choices." He elaborated on this point: "Some [domestic] programs, while desirable, are not absolutely essential. In this I have reached a clear conclusion. Some savings may still be squeezed out through the wringer method. This will be one of the hardest and most distasteful tasks that the coming session of Congress must face. And pressure groups will wail in anguish."[27]

At the same time, Eisenhower made clear that he believed overall spending by the federal government would continue to increase and that needed spending on national security would not be deferred to maintain a balanced budget. Over the long run however, he quickly added, a balanced budget was "one indispensable aid in keeping our economy and therefore our total security, strong and sound."[28]

Next, Eisenhower discussed other, nonmilitary ways to improve national security, most notably by longer-term steps to strengthen scientific education and the nation's basic research effort. He noted that the Soviet Union had more people employed in science and engineering than the United States did and that improvements in Soviet schools and universities meant that America's qualitative edge no longer offset the Soviets' quantitative one. Eisenhower called this trend "disturbing" and reported that his scientific advisors believed that it was "the most critical problem of all." Sounding a very Modern Republican theme, he argued that the federal government could not address this problem alone and that the task was "a cooperative one" that needed to involve federal, state, and local governments and "our entire citizenry." Eisenhower said he believed this cooperative effort should be directed toward several educational reforms: "a system of nation-wide testing of high school students; a system of incentives for high-aptitude students to pursue scientific or professional studies; a program to stimulate good-quality teaching of mathematics and science; provision of more laboratory facilities; and measures, including fellowships, to increase the output of qualified teachers."[29]

Eisenhower called on American citizens to help bring these ideas to fruition. Lest his listeners mistakenly conclude that he believed scientists and engineers alone were required, Eisenhower affirmed his belief that the nation needed leaders in every field who "can meet intricate human problems with wisdom and courage."[30]

Eisenhower also elaborated on the need to encourage basic research. He reminded his listeners that in this area, too, the federal government could not do all that was needed. He pointed out that industry and private organizations undertook approximately 70 percent of all such research and that "the biggest share of the job" was in their hands.[31]

Eisenhower closed by reminding his listeners that the country's overall goal was still "peace with justice" and reiterated the hope expressed in his earlier speech that the Soviets would cooperate in achieving that objective. Clearly wanting to signal to Americans and the world at large that more U.S. spending on armaments did not signal an aggressive intent, Eisenhower said firmly:

> Our defense effort, large as it is, goes only far enough to deter and defeat attack.
>
> We will never be an aggressor. We want adequate security.
>
> We want no more than adequacy. But we will accept nothing less.[32]

This second address also met with positive responses from the public and the press, which added to the already considerable satisfaction Larson felt with his new job. In these first few weeks, he found himself greatly enjoying it, despite the often-hectic pace. Helping make the workload bearable were Florence's help as an editor and Sherman Adams's decisions to place all presidential speechwriting under Larson's control and allow him to have a small staff of his own to help with the research and writing. In a letter to his mother, Larson reported on these last two factors, which went far beyond anything Eisenhower's earlier speechwriters had been allowed:

> Only a few people know what the new job is. There has never been one like it before. I am systematically planning everything the President is going to say publicly for a long period of time ahead. . . .
>
> I have asked for three assistants, and will get them. This is something entirely new around the White House; but I intend to do this job right. I want to read everything of importance that comes out, and have plenty of time to think, and I told the President this.[33]

Larson liked the sense of being in the center of things so much that he confided in a late November letter to a friend the news that "incredible as it may sound, the [speechwriting] work is even more exciting than the USIA was."[34]

Working so closely with Eisenhower appears to have been the most stimulating aspect of the work for Larson, although he clearly relished the writing side of it as well. The president and his new chief speechwriter enjoyed an unusually close relationship, which Larson likened to that of father and son. They spent long afternoons together, working on speeches and talking about whatever else was on Eisenhower's mind. This kind of closeness was reflected by Larson's physical proximity to the president and the White House chief of staff. Sherman Adams assigned Larson two separate offices to facilitate interaction among this trio. The first of these spaces was located in the West Wing directly above where Eisenhower and Adams worked and the second in the East Wing, off of the executive mansion's main living quarters. Another indication of the intimate nature of the Eisenhower-Larson relationship was Eisenhower's decision to allow Larson to attend meetings of the National Security Council and the Cabinet. In this way, Eisenhower explained to Larson, he could stay current on matters facing the president and keep background research on speeches to a minimum.[35]

Even Eisenhower's heavy editing, for which he was notorious, did not cast a shadow over these highly satisfactory terms of employment. On the contrary,

Larson, the former debate champion, clearly enjoyed the give-and-take with him over how best to convey his thoughts. So competitive did Larson become about such matters that at times, he later confessed, he would almost forget that the other person on the couch with whom he was so vigorously disagreeing was the president of the United States. Eisenhower occasionally became exasperated enough to remind him whose speech it was they were working on. In one memorable instance, Eisenhower did so by saying, "Damnit Arthur, if you don't let me write this in, I'll extemporize it in anyway!"[36] Eisenhower also complained about Larson's argumentativeness through Sherman Adams, who told Larson on November 8th "the President liked my writing very much—liked my ideas, etc. etc. But then—rather reluctantly—he [Adams] told me the President wished I wouldn't argue so much with him. After all, it's *his* speech. I should try to get his ideas and incorporate them."[37] Larson promised to respect the president's wishes but did not abandon entirely this kind of advocacy.[38]

In the wake of the Oklahoma City speech, Larson moved ahead with drafting the third in the series, scheduled for delivery in Cleveland on November 26th. This installment focused on the role American foreign aid and trade could play in meeting the Soviet challenge. In keeping with Eisenhower's preferences, Larson used the term "mutual aid" throughout when referring to foreign aid, to convey the president's belief that American military and economic assistance to other nations benefited the giver as well as the various recipients. Larson also began planning for one more address in this series, which had "a security theme running through all four."[39] It was a characteristic one for both Modern Republicans and New Deal liberals. The twin traumas of economic depression in the 1930s and world war in the 1940s had led both the moderate right and the moderate left during the 1950s to focus on promoting security, especially in the economic and military senses. Larson continued during the fall of 1957 to develop plans for a wide range of presidential addresses on other timely topics to build an inventory of speeches that would help prevent future bottlenecks.[40]

All of these plans went up in smoke when Eisenhower suffered a mild stroke the day before he was to deliver the Cleveland speech. Although this "brain spasm," as the doctors later described it, affected only Eisenhower's ability to speak and not his other motor functions or his reasoning, this was still a potentially career-ending setback for an American president. Eisenhower's secretary, Ann Whitman, understanding the gravity of the situation after listening to Eisenhower speak gibberish to her, telephoned Larson during the night of November 25th–26th with the alarming news that "the President can't talk," something Sherman Adams confirmed the following morning.[41] Eisenhower's inability to speak properly for the next three weeks put an end to both the address on foreign aid and the science and security series as well. This shocking development clearly upset Larson, who described himself the day after the stroke as "close to tears."[42]

Things went from bad to worse when a highly publicized rocket launch ended in a fiery failure ten days later. This piece of bad luck, Larson later recalled, greatly undermined the effect of the two earlier speeches in reassuring the American people, the press, and allies that recent advances in Soviet rocketry and satellites posed no serious danger.[43]

Uncertainty over the president's prospects for recovery only added to the confusion Larson felt then. At first, he assumed the worst. In his words,

> I rushed down to the White House [after Ann Whitman's call], and there were several other people who had got there. The atmosphere of gloom and despair and grief around that place was beyond description. We all really thought the President this time was finished. I mean, he had had a heart attack [in September 1955], ileitis [in June 1956], and now, of all things, a stroke.[44]

Meetings with Eisenhower and Sherman Adams two weeks later about the upcoming State of the Union address only strengthened Larson's belief that the president would never fully regain his health. Even though Eisenhower had canceled his public appearances during his illness, this customary speech would have to be delivered in early January, and it became the focus of Larson's work in December 1957. During the first week of that month, Larson drafted a brief State of the Union address on the theory that Eisenhower would not be able to deliver any more. The president had recovered somewhat by that point, but not completely, and Larson decided that an unusually concise version of the customary review of administration policies and accomplishments seemed the most sensible course. To his chagrin, Larson learned from Eisenhower at a meeting on December 12th that he "had not liked my short draft too much."[45] Even more troubling was Eisenhower's failure to make constructive suggestions. In a private discussion afterward with Sherman Adams, Larson asked him if Eisenhower had communicated any ideas about what the State of the Union address should contain in his other meetings with his chief of staff. Adams's reply disheartened Larson, as his record of this exchange makes clear: "Adams, with great tenderness, said 'This man is not what he was. We'll have to work it out. You couldn't have learned any more from him than I did.' At almost this point I began to accept the idea of a sort of protectorate, an idea I have resisted until now."[46]

Larson's frustration with the almost complete lack of guidance on what was bound to be one of the most carefully watched addresses of the Eisenhower presidency prompted the following, highly revealing, outburst on the next page of his ever-present memo book:

> The process of preparing the President's speeches so as to reflect his ideas is rather like trying to construct a dinosaur skeleton out of a fragment of ankle bone.

> If I get even a word as a clue—I can take it from there, but without that clue, I never know if I'm on the right track or not. . . .
>
> For the State of the Union message, all I have is the general idea that we as Americans do indeed have great resources to bring to bear.[47]

This passage did not signal, of course, that Eisenhower had no firm ideas that he wanted expressed in his major addresses. On the contrary, Larson's memo books and other records from his speechwriting for Eisenhower indicate very clearly that the president edited heavily with respect to matters of intellectual content as well as writing style. What Eisenhower apparently expected, however, was that his speechwriter should develop a draft on the basis of a few general suggestions and then he could revise it to conform with his own views. The problem with the upcoming State of Union address, however, was that Eisenhower had been even less forthcoming with basic themes than usual, and his medical condition in early December seemed to rule out the heavy editing and frequent exchanges in which he and Larson had engaged in the past.[48]

Larson later described the specific problems with Eisenhower's articulation as mostly having to do with occasional, but still very noticeable transpositions. Larson explained this symptom of the president's stroke as follows: "For a time he couldn't talk straight at all. Then he started getting better, so he could talk, but what was so embarrassing and even scary about it was that as his power of speech began to return, it would trip him up every little while. He would seem to be going along all right, and without his even knowing what was happening, words would come out backwards."[49]

To Larson's relief, the president's remarkable recovery in the second half of December enabled him to help prepare and deliver the 1958 State of the Union address properly. Eisenhower attended a NATO summit conference on December 13–19 and managed to speak correctly, albeit briefly and rather simply, at all of the events connected with it. A more confident Eisenhower then turned his attention to the upcoming State of the Union address. In view of his diminished facility with words, Eisenhower and his staff decided that this speech should focus on a few of the most pressing problems facing the nation rather than the more comprehensive review of public policy that he had delivered on these occasions in years past. In keeping with Eisenhower's wishes, Larson wrote a speech that dealt only with the nation's strength and the pursuit of peace.[50]

Preparing this address proved a maddening experience for Larson, as other members of the White House staff began interfering with his handiwork. When he returned from a brief trip out of town around Christmastime, Larson discovered that this latest draft had been circulated without his permission to the senior staff, who had come up with a very different version instead. Among the worst offenders, from Larson's perspective, was Bryce Harlow, who worked in the office of congressional liaison. Acting on instructions from Sherman Adams, who evidently believed that Eisenhower's speaking problems required a simpler text than Larson had prepared, Harlow had redrafted the entire address to make it easier to read. Larson grumbled about the result in his memo book, observing there that Harlow "tries to sound like Hemingway, and ends by sounding like McGuffie's [*sic*] first reader."[51] Rather than simply accept what Harlow and other White House staffers had done to "his" speech, Larson proceeded to revise many of the revisions out of existence in a gradual process that required eight more drafts to complete.[52]

The reason for this uncharacteristically erratic behavior on the part of Eisenhower's White House staff had to do with Sherman Adams's change in outlook after the president's stroke. With Eisenhower clearly able to contribute less to the speechwriting process, Adams had evidently decided that others needed to do more, lest Larson's penchant for writing his own ideas in his own way go unchecked. On December 12th, Adams had told him to solicit more input from other members of the staff in preparing subsequent drafts of the upcoming State of the Union message. By January 1, 1958, this change in Adams's attitude had produced a palpable shift in the way other members of the White House staff behaved toward Larson and his work, which he described in his memo book in this way:

> There is a curious atmosphere around the White House these days.
> At times, I have the distinct feeling that some of the staff are trying to insulate me from the President and cut down my influence on speeches. I have sat through repeated staff conferences where everyone has a crack at changing not only words but whole pages [of the State of the Union address].[53]

Eisenhower delivered the final result of this somewhat confused drafting process on the evening of January 9th. In essence, the speech combined and restated the ideas expressed in his earlier science and security addresses. Only the sections dealing with foreign aid and trade covered ground he had not publicly discussed before, and even this material reprised the themes of the never-delivered Cleveland address. In speaking of what he liked to call "mutual aid," Eisenhower focused on its benefits to the United States. Very aware that some members of Congress and the public thought of economic aid to other countries as wasteful, Eisenhower listed three main ways in which it redounded to the benefit of the giver. He noted that recipients of American economic assistance tended to become what he called "bulwarks against communism" because this kind of aid helped bolster the military defenses and overall economy of countries that received it.[54] Second, Eisenhower pointed out that such aid helped recipients develop economically to the point that mutually beneficial trade with the United States could expand beyond its present levels. Third, Eisenhower pointed to the benefits such aid brought the United States in the way of closer ties and greater understanding with foreign nations. He then proposed strengthening the existing program of economic aid through greater use of repayable loans.[55]

Lest his listeners in Congress that night miss the larger point he was making about the value of economic assistance to foreign lands, Eisenhower directly attacked the most common argument used against it, that foreign aid amounted to a "give-away program." He stoutly rejected that idea, arguing forcefully that helping friendly foreign lands in this way paid great dividends to the United States.[56]

Eisenhower called for extending and improving the nation's existing laws governing foreign trade and eloquently explained the Modern Republican stance in favor of lower trade barriers. He pointed out that although most of what Americans produced in the 1950s never left the country, by 1958 that situation was beginning to change. In addition to the argument that world trade created jobs and profits for American industry and agriculture, he noted the importance of international trade for assuring the raw materials U.S. industry needed, allowing American free enterprise to develop on a worldwide scale, creating and strengthening friendships with foreign nations, and laying the groundwork for peace by making free societies stronger.[57]

Eisenhower also pointed to the potential economic benefits for Americans that could come from lowering trade barriers even more and dismissed protectionism as a policy that Americans had long since outgrown. He reminded his audience that in terms of overall value of goods imported and exported, the United States had become the world's leader in international trade and urged Americans to draw the right conclusion from that fact:

> If we use this great asset wisely to meet the expanding demands of the world, we shall not only provide future opportunities for our own business, agriculture and labor, but in the process strengthen our security posture and other prospects for a prosperous, harmonious world.
>
> As President McKinley said, as long ago as 1901, "Isolation is no longer possible or desirable. . . . The period of exclusiveness is past."[58]

The only other ideas in this speech that the public had not heard before concerned Eisenhower's proposals to try working with the Soviets in some scientific areas, such as efforts to eradicate malaria from the earth, and to find cures for what he called "the diseases that are the common enemy of all mortals—such as cancer and heart disease."[59]

Eisenhower's conclusion to the speech appeared to signal his understanding that the public concern created by Sputnik's launch and the failure of the U.S. Vanguard rocket launch required a somewhat stronger response from the administration. Having opposed Larson's suggestion for the first science and security address of an emphatic call to sacrifice on the ground that such a statement might imply more of an emergency than actually existed, Eisenhower this time underscored that idea. He told his listeners that his proposed actions in response to the Soviet challenge "demand and expect two things of the American people: sacrifice, and a high degree of understanding."[60] In the next sentence, however, Eisenhower cautioned his listeners not to overreact to his words. The president warned that "for sacrifice to be effective, it must be intelligent. Sacrifice must be made for the right purpose and in the right place—even if that place happens to come close to home!"[61]

Although Eisenhower did not say much in this address that was truly new, he managed to deliver it clearly and correctly. The only obvious sign of the change wrought by the stroke had to do with the rate at which he spoke that night. Projected to run between thirty-five and forty minutes, the address took Eisenhower forty-four to deliver. Evidently wanting to show their appreciation for the president's courageous performance and for his apparent recovery from his latest illness, members of Congress interrupted him over and over again with loud and enthusiastic applause. The press also raved about the speech, although seemingly for much the same reasons.[62]

Many of Eisenhower's remarks that night merited praise, but his decision to say nothing about segregation in general or the recent confrontation at Central High School in Little Rock, Arkansas, in an address that purported to deal with the most serious problems facing the United States at that time, seems strange. The entire Little Rock episode weighed heavily on Eisenhower's mind in the fall of 1957, and the stress it caused him may well have contributed to his stroke. Such was the view of his secretary, Ann Whitman, who had told Larson the day after Eisenhower fell ill that

> the President had not really been himself since the pressure began building up at the time of Little Rock. She said that the idea he was thick-skinned and never read the papers was a pure fiction. He read lots of them. One morning before 8:00 he asked her, "Did you see that letter to the editor in the [*New York*] *Times*?"
>
> He suffered a great deal under criticism, and this [stroke] was the result[, she said].[63]

Eisenhower's views on the subject of segregation were more complex and thoughtful than many observers, including Arthur Larson, realized at that time. Larson's first impression of the president's thinking in this area was formed in July 1956, during their work on the nomination acceptance address. At a meeting with Larson on July 20th, in the course of discussing how best to word the passage dealing with the problem of unfair treatment of racial minorities, Eisenhower elaborated on his views by saying that "he wanted to be sure to make clear that social equality of political and economic opportunity does not mean necessarily that everyone has to mingle socially—or that a Negro should court my daughter."[64]

Even though Eisenhower was obviously being metaphorical here—he had no daughter—his comment startled Larson, who apparently interpreted it to mean that Eisenhower harbored a prejudice against blacks. Eisenhower's comments about the Supreme Court's decision in the *Brown* case, which he made privately to Larson one year later, only strengthened that perception. The catalyst for this discussion appears to have been a suggestion from Larson that Eisenhower send an open letter to the schoolchildren at Central High School in Little Rock encouraging them to behave in a "democratic manner that does justice to our proud heritage."[65] Eisenhower decided against that idea and told Larson on October 1, 1957, while discussing the administration's response to the confrontation in Little Rock that the Supreme Court had erred in finding the principle of separate but equal in public education to be unconstitutional. Larson noted down the president's remarks, which Eisenhower never uttered publicly or in his memoirs, as follows:

> He stressed his desire to stay within his constitutional bounds [in dealing with the Little Rock crisis]. He did not want to take sides on the merits of the S. Ct. decision. In fact, he told me he thought it was wrong.
>
> He believes Ct. should have gone no further than to require equal opportunities—and that to require integration was not necessary. He recognized the Ct.'s argument, which I reminded him of, that segregation in itself damaged the pride and spirit—but did not find it compelling.[66]

In all of this, Eisenhower appears to have reflected both the perspective of the lower-middle-class world in which he had grown up and the southern white one in which he had lived during much of his time in the military. From the first of these had come an acute sense of the difficulties faced by those who engaged in interracial socializing, especially intermarriage. While affluent Americans and urban bohemians who lived this way might be able to insulate themselves against the social ostracism and even more dire consequences that would likely follow, so this reasoning went, the large majority from more typical class and social backgrounds could not. This thinking, so common among lower-middle-class whites (and blacks) of Eisenhower's generation, did not so much embrace prejudice as recognize its reality and the unhappiness that would likely befall ordinary Americans who tried to challenge it in this way. Of course, some whites who harbored feelings of antipathy toward members of racial minority groups doubtless used this rationale as a face-saving excuse. There is no convincing evidence, however, that Eisenhower was one of them.[67]

His many years of living in and around racially segregated military installations in the South did affect Eisenhower's views on Jim Crow. From these experiences Eisenhower had acquired a very clear sense of the difficulties involved in trying to dismantle the southern system of segregation and a pessimistic view of the likely consequences of trying to use the federal government's power to do so. Until attitudes among prejudiced whites there changed, he argued privately, efforts to compel racially integrated schools in the South would lead only to efforts on the part of such whites to avoid them, one way or another.[68]

Eisenhower had other objections to the *Brown* ruling. He rejected out of hand the notion that separating whites from blacks during schooling was necessarily injurious to the latter, as the Supreme Court had concluded. His experience with the segregated world he had known for much of his adult life had taught him that all-black schools run by black administrators and teachers could benefit their pupils by eliminating the kind of tension and prejudice from whites that would have interfered with learning and by providing role models with whom black students could identify strongly. Eisenhower also feared that efforts to dismantle Jim Crow by federal court order would divide the country in ways that would be injurious to everyone, including blacks.[69]

Eisenhower's strong sense of the depth of southern white hostility to ending segregated schools also lay behind his refusal, prior to the confrontation at Little Rock, to make clear that he would use the powers of his office to enforce the Supreme Court's school desegregation ruling. Had he done so, Eisenhower's liberal critics argued, this confrontation might never have occurred. Eisenhower believed, however, that presidential statements in support of the *Brown* decision prior to the Little Rock confrontation would have had a polarizing and even inflammatory effect, on many white southerners especially, and might have produced exactly the result they were intended to forestall. The disappointing experience in 1957 of trying to win passage of a new federal civil rights law, which Southern Democrats in Congress amended to the point of almost complete ineffectuality, also discouraged Eisenhower from using the bully pulpit of the presidency to try to fight segregation.[70]

Above and beyond these specific objections in explaining Eisenhower's refusal to do more about the segregation issue were Eisenhower's firmly held views about the president's proper role in the American constitutional system. He saw the power of that office as so great, even when kept within its proper boundaries, that no president ought to expand that power through the various means at his disposal, even if the end was a noble one. This, Larson later said, went a long way toward explaining Eisenhower's approach to the civil rights issue:

> He did not believe it was the job of the President to go out and lead a crusade about civil rights.
>
> When it came to his job, what was his job as President to do about civil rights, he did all kinds of things that people may have forgotten. He abolished [by executive order] segregation in absolutely every institution that was under the direct control of the federal government, including the District of Columbia, the veterans' hospitals, and everything that the federal government had anything direct to say about.[71]

These considerations about the president's proper role, about respecting the roles of state and local governments in the federal system, and the other considerations more specific to the segregation issue itself undoubtedly lay behind Eisenhower's decision not to mention it in his 1958 State of the Union address.

Although Larson, like many other northern moderates and liberals of his day, tended to dismiss Eisenhower's views on segregation, especially the notion that an all-black educational environment was not necessarily harmful to black children, the passage of time increased Larson's respect for Eisenhower's perspective. Larson never came to share it, but he did come to believe by the early 1990s that Eisenhower's critique of the Supreme Court's reasoning in the *Brown* case had more substance than he had earlier thought:

> The basis of Brown against Board of Education at the time was a somewhat debatable psychological assumption that segregation was psychologically damaging to the young children. That was the absolute foundation on which the case was based. He [Eisenhower] didn't agree with that, necessarily. And as the years have gone by, I would say, if anything, there are more people today, probably, that are questioning whether this original psychological assumption was good psychology or not.[72]

Despite Eisenhower's disappointing omission of Little Rock and the segregation issue more generally from his 1958 State of the Union address, Larson basked briefly in the glow of its favorable reviews. He had fought to keep the speech in line with Eisenhower's basic philosophy, and his own, and his patience and tenacity had paid off. The speech turned out to be something of a last hurrah for Larson, however, as Eisenhower and his aides began moving away from some of the Modern Republican stands they had earlier taken. Eisenhower's annual budget message, which was prepared by his economic advisors and delivered to Congress just four days after the State of the Union address, signaled the change. Markedly more conservative in tone and substance than his earlier budget messages, it sounded the call for restraints on spending, especially on domestic programs. As Eisenhower and his aides traveled down this road and seemingly embraced the Old Guard stance on the growth of the welfare state, Larson gradually disappeared from public view. By April 1958, an article in *Time* had labeled him the Eisenhower administration's "forgotten man."[73]

The underlying cause of this shift to a more conservative position did not signal a change in heart but rather a hardheaded response to changing economic conditions. By the second half of 1957, those new conditions had emerged as unexpected by-products of earlier public policy successes. Marshall Plan assistance to the nations of Western Europe and U.S. foreign aid to Japan had contributed to those countries' economic comeback but had also helped revive significant foreign competition in basic manufacturing. Strong labor unions in the United States had raised workers' wages significantly beyond what their

Western European and Japanese counterparts received, which tended to increase American manufacturers' vulnerability to foreign competition. Increasing imports also undermined the stability of the Bretton Woods system of fixed currency exchange rates developed toward the end of World War II. Higher wages, increasing imports, rapid economic growth, and heavy government spending, on armaments especially, had also combined to create a rising wave of general price inflation that menaced the long-term prosperity of all Americans.[74]

Faced with these growing challenges, the Eisenhower presidency moved to meet them in 1957–1958. Deeply concerned about the related problems of growing foreign competition and rising inflation, Eisenhower and his senior economic advisors decided to make significant changes in the administration's economic policies. The leading figures in this process, besides Eisenhower, all joined the administration around this time: Council of Economic Advisors chairman Raymond "Steve" Saulnier, who replaced Arthur Burns early in 1957; treasury secretary Robert Anderson, who succeeded George Humphrey in July 1957; budget director Maurice Stans, who replaced Percival Brundage in March 1958; and Special Assistant to the President for Economic Affairs Don Paarlberg, who succeeded Gabriel Hauge in that post in September 1958. Together they pushed successfully for higher interest rates and cuts in federal domestic spending. These unpopular changes in monetary and fiscal policy did bring inflation down, but they also caused the economy to stall in August 1957 and unemployment to rise steadily for nine months. By April 1958, the recession's trough, the nation's official unemployment rate had reached 7 percent, which was the highest since 1950.[75]

The continuing public concern over Sputnik and pressure in Congress for more military spending as a result only made matters worse from the perspective of Modern Republicans such as Larson. Eisenhower's stroke and the Vanguard setback diminished somewhat the administration's ability to resist that kind of pressure, but the more Eisenhower and his aides yielded to it, the more Stans demanded cuts in domestic programs, lest inflationary pressures increase. Even more disturbing, in some respects, was the way this kind of reasoning led Eisenhower and his economic advisors to oppose the creation of major new domestic programs, most notably a health care plan for the elderly, regardless of need. By the spring of 1958, this more rigid stance against further improvements in the still-unfinished social insurance system had become clear, to the dismay of Larson and like-minded Republicans.[76]

How fully Larson understood the nation's underlying economic problems and thus the reason for the administration's shift toward a more fiscally conservative position remains unclear. He had neither a background in business nor any formal training in economics and seems not to have grasped immediately that the inflationary surge of the later 1950s differed both in cause and consequence from earlier ones. Had Larson dealt with collective bargaining matters while in the Labor Department, he might have acquired a better sense of what had gone wrong, but James Mitchell, in keeping with his own expertise and preferences, had handled all of the high-level negotiations between labor and management. Larson's focus on social insurance programs had, in contrast, made him more aware of what needed to be done in order to complete and perfect the system instead of the economic problems that more government spending on such programs or more employer-sponsored programs could intensify.[77]

Perhaps the clearest sign of this shift in the administration's policies, from Larson's perspective, came when Eisenhower began to downplay the term Modern Republicanism. In part this change stemmed from his growing awareness of how much this rubric tended to provoke opposition from more conservative Republicans and thus to divide the GOP's ranks. Eisenhower's efforts to address that problem by explaining what he meant more clearly gradually petered out in 1957–1958, just as his more conservative economic policies were implemented. This conjunction suggests that Eisenhower eventually decided to drop the Modern Republican terminology not only because it had proved divisive but also because his administration's shift toward more conservative monetary and fiscal policies had narrowed the differences between his brand of Republicanism and that of the Old Guard and thus made the Modern Republican label even more problematic.[78]

Whatever the exact reasons for this noteworthy change in semantics on Eisenhower's part, it, like the shift in economic policy, appears to have been a strong signal to Larson and like-minded members of the administration that it was retreating from its earlier, more moderate position. Rather than stay and fight a seemingly hopeless battle with Stans and his allies, Larson and many of the other Modern Republicans chose to leave when an appealing job offer came along.[79]

In his case, the catalyst materialized in the late spring and early summer of 1958 in the form of an offer from Duke University Law School to become director of a center to promote the rule of law in resolving international disputes. The key figure behind this invitation was Charles Rhyne, a prominent attorney and Duke trustee who had sparked the center's creation. While serving as president of the American Bar Association during 1957, Rhyne had made a speech in favor of strengthening the use of law to resolve international disputes.[80]

The most basic cause of the growing interest in that idea was the intensifying arms race between East and West. Like the economic problems facing the United States in the late 1950s, that frightening competition was an unintended result of earlier public policy successes. The creation after World War II of a very large permanent American military establishment and collective security arrangements such as NATO and SEATO had increased national security but also helped spark an arms race that threatened both sides with nuclear Armageddon should war come. When Charles Rhyne gave his speech, leaders on both sides had come to feel increasing pressure to find other, safer ways to promote peace than ever greater military strength.[81]

Rhyne's interest in the issue had led to the creation one year later of an Special Committee on World Peace Through Law in the American Bar Association that Rhyne agreed to chair. On May 3, 1958, he had delivered a forceful address at Duke elaborating on that basic idea and calling for the creation of a rule of law center. Rhyne had followed up on his earlier statements in this vein by persuading Eisenhower to proclaim May 1, 1958, as the first National Law Day and to make it an annual observance. Eisenhower's need to issue a message in connection with the first Law Day was what initially involved Arthur Larson with this issue. In the course of doing research on the Law Day message, Larson had become intrigued by the effort to promote the development of international rules of dispute resolution. Larson's interest in the project and success in drafting the presidential Law Day remarks evidently led Rhyne to think of him as the right person to head the World Rule of Law Center after Rhyne persuaded the Duke trustees to establish it there.[82]

The idea appealed to Larson for several reasons. It intersected with both his long-standing interest in foreign affairs and his orientation toward law as the best way to resolve conflict. This proposal also was in tune with Larson's essentially gentle nature and religious beliefs, which tended to resist the use of force unless absolutely necessary. Promoting the world rule of law also resonated with Larson's youthful enthusiasm for peaceful solutions to international conflict, a feeling the "peace through military strength" emphasis of the early Cold War years had never entirely displaced. The Progressive-era origins of the idea of the world rule of law also attracted him to it. Its champions then had been Elihu Root, who had served in Theodore Roosevelt's administration as secretary of state, and Root's law partner, Grenville Clark. Root had advanced two proposals at the international disarmament conferences held in the Hague during 1899 and 1904 that helped inspire the creation of the permanent International Court of Justice at The Hague in 1946. Clark, in collaboration with law professor Louis Sohn, had developed a blueprint for a judicial body with much greater reach than the International Court of Justice had thus far achieved. This plan appeared in the book *World Peace through World Law* in 1958.[83]

For all of these reasons, Larson decided to meet with Duke's president, Hollis Edens, and law school dean, E. R. Latty, in June 1958 to discuss the proposal. Pleased and excited by what they told him, Arthur Larson sounded out Florence, who was amenable to the idea, given how much more it appealed to him than a return to more conventional law teaching. Enthusiastic support for this venture from Eisenhower, Nixon, John Foster Dulles, and Henry Luce also helped persuade Larson to accept. So, too, in a different way, did Sherman Adams's travails that summer. After Adams gave a partisan political speech in January 1958 that blamed the Pearl Harbor attack and the Soviet advantage in satellites on the Democrats, congressional leaders used their investigating authority to harass him. By July, Adams was facing mounting pressure to resign, a turn of events that Larson found so unfair as to be disgusting. All of these factors and his more basic unhappiness with the administration's increasingly rigid opposition to new domestic spending led Larson to write a letter of resignation on August 8, 1958, effective September 1st. With that step, his ten and a half months as chief presidential speechwriter and four and a half years with the Eisenhower administration came to a bittersweet end.[84]

CHAPTER TEN

Dueling with the New Right

When Arthur and Florence Larson arrived in Durham, North Carolina, in mid-September 1958, they took up residence in an area unlike any they had lived in before. The closest earlier experience for them had been their two-year stay in Knoxville, Tennessee. Knoxville, however, had been urban, with a diversified economy; rates of income, home ownership, and literacy that were high for the South; and a strong two-party political system at the local level. Durham, while not entirely different, contrasted sharply with Knoxville in some important ways. Although census takers in 1960 counted 78,302 residents, it still had the feel of a small southern town. The area's economy also differed sharply from Knoxville's. Durham and North Carolina recovered quickly from the 1957–1958 recession, but both remained highly dependent on the traditional sources of Tar Heel prosperity: tobacco, textiles, and forest products. The first two of these were sectors of the economy notorious for very low wages, and they helped give North Carolina some of the lowest wage levels in the country. Durham's tobacco-processing plants reflected the statewide pattern, as did Durham's very low rate of unionization. And while the area Arthur and Florence began to call home boasted three major institutions of higher learning (Duke, North Carolina State University, and the University of North Carolina), it lagged significantly behind national norms for literacy and years of schooling. Even the local political situation posed a contrast with Knoxville. In North Carolina, Dixiecrats dominated the important elective offices and the local Republican Party organization in Durham was weak.[1]

The Duke Law School faculty, which Larson joined that fall, also differed from the ones of which he had earlier been part. Although Duke's law school was stronger than the Tennessee Law School, it had not yet achieved national distinction. In that sense, Larson's decision to teach at Duke constituted something of a step down from Cornell and Pittsburgh. The nature and terms of his appointment at Duke were, however, far more prestigious and lucrative than those enjoyed by other members of its law faculty. He had been hired primarily to create a major research center and teach courses related to its work rather than the standard offerings he had been obliged to teach earlier in his academic career. At Eisenhower's suggestion, Larson had insisted on a salary equal to what he had earned as the president's speechwriter, even if the center venture did not work out and he remained at Duke solely as a law professor. This arrangement guaranteed him an income, he noted in a letter to his mother, "much higher than any non-administrative university salary I have seen."[2]

These unusually favorable terms of employment and the substantial amount Larson earned annually from his workers' compensation treatise and various other writings gave him and Florence the means to buy a large and very attractive Tudor-like house in the affluent Hope Valley section of Durham. There they established a home for themselves and their college-age children and set out to make new colleagues and friends. This latest transition proved much easier for Arthur Larson than for Florence. For him, this new setting provided another exciting job and the various personal connections that came with it. He also continued to commute up to Washington one to two days a week to work part-time on Eisenhower's speeches, in collaboration with political scientist Malcolm Moos of Johns Hopkins. At Larson's suggestion, Eisenhower had appointed Moos, who had earlier worked as a speechwriting aide to Larson, as his successor. The two men enjoyed a close and friendly working relationship. His frequent trips to Washington also enabled him to keep up with the other friends he had made there. This combination of jobs clearly provided Arthur Larson with a very happy, if at times rather hectic, existence in the late 1950s. His deeply satisfying relationship with Florence and the success of Lex and Anna at Haverford and Sarah Lawrence increased his contentment even more.[3]

For Florence, the move to Durham proved much more problematic, especially at first. Durham did not have much of a theater scene in those days, and she found herself unable to restart her career there. The area's very traditional social structure only increased her sense of isolation. Most of the women she met during her first few years in Durham, although educated and socially graceful, did not have serious professional aspirations or experiences. Socializing with them could only have made Florence feel like the odd person out. The newly empty nest at home increased her feelings of loneliness. Helping to sustain Florence then were the very happy marriage she enjoyed with Arthur, the stimulation and new experiences that grew out of his professional success, and the progress of their two children. In time, Florence would create a more satisfying outside life for herself in Durham, although it never equaled her husband's. Like so many other highly intelligent educated women of her generation, she learned to make the best of this kind of situation, but not without regrets.[4]

The process of transformation then just beginning in North Carolina, especially in what became known as the Research Triangle, helped them put down roots in Durham. This collaborative venture between the three major universities in the area helped attract many talented newcomers who strengthened those schools' faculties and student bodies and propelled the area's economy and cultural life forward steadily. And while North Carolina was a much more polarized place politically than he and Florence were used to, the election in 1960 of moderately liberal gubernatorial candidate Terry Sanford signaled that the state would eventually comply peacefully with the U.S. Supreme Court's school desegregation rulings. All of this gradually made Durham and the nearby communities of Raleigh and Chapel Hill much more diverse, stimulating, and pleasant places for people like the Larsons to live and work.[5]

All of that lay in the future, however, when, on September 15, 1958, the World Rule of Law Center at Duke formally began its existence with Arthur Larson as its director. During his first two years in this job, Larson established the center's basic operating procedures, hired other academic experts in the field and support staff to help carry out the center's mission, and obtained grants to help fund this new venture. Although not the only cause to which he devoted his energies then, the center consumed by far the largest of them.[6]

In coming up with a plan for this new venture, Larson drew upon the ideas not only of Elihu Root, Grenville Clark, Louis Sohn, and Charles Rhyne but also the speeches and writings on the idea of world peace through law of distinguished legal scholar Roscoe Pound and Judge John J. Parker. Also influential was an American Bar Association report on this subject that Rhyne had commissioned in 1957. A committee headed by former New York governor and presidential candidate Thomas E. Dewey had prepared this report, which appeared in 1958. An address by media company head Henry Luce on the same topic also had a significant impact. Larson spoke at length with Dewey and Luce, among others, in the course of developing the center's organizational plan.[7]

Larson first explained it publicly in "World Rule of Law: The Time Has Come," a speech he delivered on May 1, 1959, at Harvard Law School's second annual Law Day observance. This important speech laid out the basic premises under which the center would operate and the specific objectives it and the other scholars working in this area should seek to realize.[8]

Larson acknowledged that the early pioneers in this field such as Root and Clark had not succeeded in bringing about an international legal system but pointed out the signs of renewed interest in their ideas. The reason for this, Larson suggested, was the inability to eliminate international conflict without offering a positive alternative. He pointed to action taking place on three fronts: the American Bar Association (which was studying the idea seriously), universities and foundations (which were devoting more resources to it), and government (with Larson leading the way as Eisenhower's special consultant on the world rule of law). All of these efforts, he noted, sought to create a more orderly, less violent approach to solving international disputes.[9]

The first governmental move, Larson explained, was a push in the U.S. Senate for changes in a treaty provision known as the Connally amendment. Enacted in 1946, it excluded any essentially domestic matter from the jurisdiction of the International Court of Justice and stipulated that the U.S. government would be the sole judge of what was domestic and what was international for this purpose. This sort of "self-judging" clause, which the United States and several other countries had adopted, had greatly limited the usefulness of the international court. In fact, at the time Larson spoke, the court had heard less than one truly contentious case per year since its creation. Larson noted that the president, vice president, secretary of state, and U.S. attorney general had all recently called for revisiting the Connally amendment and that Minnesota senator Hubert Humphrey had introduced a Senate resolution calling for American acceptance of an enlarged degree of jurisdiction for the international court.[10]

Larson's discussion of the Connally amendment was bound to become controversial because strongly conservative Americans tended to fear that the international court might try to meddle in matters that were essentially domestic by taking an unduly expansive view of what constituted an international issue. He seems to have underestimated the depth of the opposition on the right to changes in the Connally amendment specifically and toward moves in the direction of a system of international law in general.[11]

The intensity of such opposition had surfaced in the early 1950s during the Bricker amendment controversy. This proposed constitutional amendment would have prohibited the negotiation of any treaty that abridged any right or freedom under the U.S. Constitution or affected any other matters essentially within the domestic jurisdiction of the United States. Although partly motivated by a desire to restrain the growth of presidential power in the realm of foreign policy, the Bricker amendment was also inspired by the same sorts of concerns that had led to the Connally amendment's enactment. That the Eisenhower administration had been obliged to fight a grueling battle in the Senate to defeat the Bricker amendment, which ultimately failed by only one vote, should have alerted Larson to the long odds against repealing or modifying the Connally amendment. So, too, should the wording of the Dewey Committee's report on behalf of the American Bar Association, which had avoided making a direct recommendation on that issue. Thomas Dewey had also cautioned Larson against becoming heavily involved in a battle to repeal the Connally amendment, but the more optimistic Larson viewed substantial changes to it as a real possibility.[12]

As Larson was launching this crusade, he finished a new book that plunged him into a second, related contest. This was the struggle to determine what the country ought to stand for in the years ahead. The catalyst behind his new book, which Larson entitled *What We Are For,* was his effort while USIA director to spell out more clearly what the United States stood for, not just what it stood against. He had begun writing a manuscript devoted to this theme while serving as Eisenhower's chief speechwriter and, with help from Florence and his brother Don, finished it around the time he arrived at Duke.[13]

What We Are For, which appeared in January 1959, mostly restated ideas Larson had expressed in earlier writings and speeches while USIA director, but it also contained a few new concepts and ways of expressing older ideas that deserve mention. Larson added a new item to his list of "basic human motivations" (freedom, property, justice, group allegiance, and religion) the American system promoted, which he called individuality. By this Larson meant the idea that most people wanted to be recognized as "separate, identifiable, and somewhat special persons."[14]

Another new theme in *What We Are For* was an increased concern with the way more extreme conservatives were defining the American system's basic principles. As the New Right, led by journalist and editor William F. Buckley, Jr., and Arizona senator Barry Goldwater, began to gain ground in the late 1950s, the number of New Right books and pamphlets about the American system steadily multiplied. Rather than personalize his disagreements with such people, Larson tactfully refrained from mentioning them by name in *What We Are For.* Instead, he emphasized that the problem with their writings was that they could offend newly developing countries in the Third World if people there accepted at face value such extremely conservative descriptions of what the United States stood for in the 1950s.[15]

That last qualifying remark constituted a crucial distinction for a moderate conservative such as Arthur Larson. He did not quarrel with much that New Rightists had written about the early days of the American republic and the beliefs of its founders. His concern, Larson explained, was that these kinds of tracts about the small-government, laissez-faire American system of that time ignored the important ways the country had changed in the past century. If Third World peoples came to believe that the United States still possessed its original economic and political system, they would surely view it as irrelevant to their own situation. The likely result of such a misunderstanding, Larson argued forcefully, would be communist gains in the Third World.[16] Rather than allow that to happen, he urged Americans to describe their system accurately and suggested the term "enterprise democracy" to convey its essentials in brief.[17]

Another change in terminology in *What We Are For* had to do with American welfare state programs. Unlike *Know Your Social Security* and *A Republican Looks at His Party,* in which Larson had called that array of programs an "income insurance system," in *What We Are For* Larson mostly used the more common term "social insurance." Although in Larson's mind the two were essentially synonymous, his decision to return to using the second term (like his call for describing the American system as it had become, rather than what it had earlier been) would irritate those farther to the right, who tended to equate the word "social" with "socialism."[18]

What We Are For also offered a new formula that Larson developed to summarize his case for a pluralistic economic and political system. He argued that when economic and political forces were dispersed and balanced as they were in the United States, the result was freedom. Conversely, when those forces were combined and concentrated as they were in the Soviet Union, the result was tyranny. He expressed that thought in an equation: T = E + P, which stood for "Tyranny equals Economic plus Political Power." Although this was a useful insight, he did not adequately recognize the wide range of agreement within the American business community on many fundamental issues and the great collective power it exerted on the workings of the nation's economic and political system. While more dispersed than in the Soviet Union, economic and political power in the United States were still more narrowly concentrated than Larson suggested, as leftist critics increasingly pointed out.[19]

Even though *What We Are For* did not depart greatly from the basic themes of Larson's earlier writings, it met with less success and more controversy than they had. Timing was critical here. The broad agreement of the mid-1950s had begun to erode by 1959, and the clearest sign of that had come the previous fall, when the off-year elections had gone very badly for the Republicans. The Eisenhower administration's recent shift toward more conservative economic policies and the growing strength of the GOP's most right-wing elements persuaded many moderate voters to swing back to the Democrats and inaugurated a more contentious and uncertain political environment. These and other developments portended a period of greater public disagreement about what the United States stood for, which greatly complicated the task of explaining that subject. Larson's new book also had less appeal on the right than his earlier writings had because it devoted so little attention to the growing problems with the 1950s economic system, which were beginning to push many highly knowledgeable conservatives toward more extreme positions.[20]

Mixed reactions emerged fairly quickly after *What We Are For* appeared. John F. Kennedy gave the book a basically positive evaluation in a review that appeared on the front page of the Sunday Book Review section of the *New York Times*. Eisenhower and Nixon, however, greeted *What We Are For* with a conspicuous silence. And leaders of the emerging New Right, most notably William F. Buckley, Jr., and Barry Goldwater, explicitly rejected Larson's views in books of their own.[21]

The reactions from Buckley and Goldwater were the most noteworthy, because they signaled the widening rift within the Republican Party over its future direction. Buckley's book, entitled *Up from Liberalism*, appeared the same year as *What We Are For* and disputed Larson's ideas about politics in the wittily sarcastic style for which the *National Review* editor had become well known. The book attacked Modern Republicanism as an unprincipled position aimed at winning the maximum possible favor with the electorate. Buckley criticized in particular what he saw as the Modern Republican proclivity to make so many concessions to liberalism as to make conservatism almost invisible and singled out *A Republican Looks at His Party* as a leading example of this phenomenon. Buckley did praise Larson's effort to state the Modern Republican position for its "verve and spirit." Buckley also acknowledged the book's considerable impact, albeit snidely, by commenting that it "had the singular distinction of being read by President Eisenhower."[22] With this faint praise out of the way, Buckley belittled Larson's reliance on the so-called Lincoln formula by suggesting that its strictures were so vague as to offer no meaningful guide to the basic differences between American liberals and conservatives and dismissed Larson's new political formula in *What We Are For* as pseudo-scientific.[23]

Barry Goldwater's response, which came one year later, was much rougher. His manifesto, entitled *The Conscience of a Conservative*, announced its thesis on the very first page: "I have been in a position to observe first hand how Conservatism is faring in Washington. And it is all too clear that in spite of a Conservative revival among the people the radical ideas that were promoted by the New and Fair Deals under the guise of Liberalism still dominate the councils of our national government."[24] Like *Up from Liberalism*, to which Goldwater had contributed a brief introduction, *The Conscience of a Conservative* mentioned Larson by name when discussing moderate conservatism's supposed failure in the 1950s. Goldwater blasted the Lincoln formula as a rationalization for abandoning the principle of limited government, especially because, he claimed, Larson believed the government should decide what needed to be done, not the people themselves.[25]

Not content to stop there, Goldwater linked this view of government's proper function with fascism and Stalinism. He warned readers to take very seriously Dean Acheson's statements in support of an activist government in *A Democrat Looks at His Party* and Larson's arguments in his Republican rebuttal to it, for both, Goldwater claimed, posed the same basic threat to liberty. Goldwater went to attack "the Achesons and Larsons" for having imperiled the republican form of government itself by allowing older restraints on the growth of government to wither. Resorting to the apocalyptic terminology so popular with the far right, Goldwater wrote that the overall result had been "a Leviathan, a vast national authority out of touch with the people and out of control."[26] A key reason for this, he argued, was the emphasis in recent times on public policies that promoted security at the expense of freedom.[27]

On and on the argument went for 123 pages, almost every one of which featured statements at odds with Larson's writings. In addition to the points already mentioned, two others deserve mention here. Goldwater devoted a chapter of his book to an argument against the inevitability of the welfare state in the modern industrial society. Instead, he said, the size and cost of welfare programs should be reduced and private charity should be encouraged. The disagreement with Larson's support for an expanded and completed system of social insurance could hardly have been starker.[28]

As troubling, if not more so, was Goldwater's call to wage the Cold War more aggressively. Goldwater emphasized military means to achieve that end, including what he called "small, clean nuclear weapons" and argued that the United States should act more independently of foreign countries to protect its interests.[29] Both themes conflicted directly with Larson's emphasis on resolving international conflicts with law, not force, especially his call in *What We Are For* to take steps that encouraged foreign nations to identify with the United States. The difference in tone and outlook could hardly have been more pronounced. Urging the United States to deal with foreign countries "like a great power," Goldwater argued for an end to foreign aid except in the form of loans or technical assistance. Even these should be extended, he said, only to anticommunist nations willing to help the United States wage the Cold War. Goldwater also stated that the United States should declare that communist countries were international outlaws, terminate diplomatic relations with them, and actively encourage and support internal rebellions against communist rule. All in all, this was a world apart from Larson's views.[30]

Happily for Larson, the GOP's choice to succeed Eisenhower the year Goldwater's book appeared was the much more moderate Richard Nixon. Larson had established a reasonably good rapport with Nixon, thanks to similarities in age, background, and outlook. Nixon, who turned forty-seven in 1960, was just three years younger than Larson and, like him, came from a family with midwestern Republican roots. Both were highly intelligent and ambitious and had risen from comfortable but not affluent households through hard work and good luck. Their career paths shared other important features. Nixon, too, had excelled at debate and the study of law (at Duke) but then found himself bored and unhappy in private practice. Like Larson, Nixon had gone on to work at the Office of Price Administration during World War II. Both men had been unfairly victimized by partisan political attacks, although in Nixon's case it was his nasty and sometimes deceitful style of campaigning for the House and Senate that had provoked reprisals. Larson's decision to accept a position at Duke Law School gave them that in common as well. Much more important in explaining the rapport between two men with such different temperaments, however, was the evolution in Nixon's views during the 1950s in a more moderate direction. By the time Larson left the Eisenhower White House, Nixon's stands on the issues had come to correspond fairly closely with Larson's, especially in the area of foreign policy.[31]

Even so, Larson, like so many others, appears to have harbored inner reservations about Nixon, thanks mostly to Eisenhower's complaint that "Dick is too political."[32] By this Eisenhower meant that Nixon paid too much attention to the electoral consequences of choosing one policy over another rather than simply doing what seemed best and dealing with the political fallout as effectively as possible. The first way of thinking, so common among career politicians like Nixon who hoped to rise high in the system, differed greatly from Eisenhower's philosophical bent, which emphasized doing what was best for the country. Larson later explained Eisenhower's disdain for the more politicized approach Nixon favored in this way: "If you wanted to get into trouble with Eisenhower fast, all you had to do was say 'This . . . is going to cost us votes in North Dakota or . . . with this particular group or that particular group.' He would throw you out."[33]

Of course, either perspective, if taken to an extreme, presented serious problems. A politician who refused to take unpopular stands would likely do a disservice to his constituents. So, too, would a politician whose indifference to public opinion helped bring about the election of those who favored shortsighted or wrongheaded policies. Most politicians could be found somewhere in between. Eisenhower and Nixon tended to occupy opposite ends of this continuum, hence the friction between them on this fundamental way of approaching public affairs. And in this respect Larson the academic stood much closer to Eisenhower the career military man turned president than to Nixon the professional politician. For Eisenhower, Larson, and others, the chief concern about Nixon becoming president was not his views but whether he would act on them when some other course seemed more likely to advance his career.[34]

In addition to this basic reservation, Eisenhower had also privately voiced to Larson a concern about whether Nixon possessed the requisite gravitas for the presidency. Eisenhower had communicated this only indirectly by noting toward the end of Larson's time as chief speechwriter that "Dick has matured."[35] Eisenhower here seems to have been thinking not just of Nixon's persona but also of his age. Nixon was young enough to be Eisenhower's son, and that large gap in years appears to have contributed to his concern that Nixon was not yet ready to become president.[36]

Florence's unenthusiastic response to Nixon added to Larson's doubts. This likely stemmed, at least in part, from Nixon's lack of interest in women and visible discomfort around them even when, as in Florence's case, they knew a lot about politics. This quality, so different from her own husband, very likely put off Florence Larson when she encountered Nixon at official functions. His close association with Joseph McCarthy during the height of the anticommunist hysteria may well have been another reason. Whatever the exact motivation, Florence's lack of enthusiasm for Nixon had an impact on Arthur Larson, who greatly respected her judgment.[37]

Despite these concerns, Larson decided during the summer of 1958 to support Nixon's presidential aspirations. In keeping with Larson's role as chief theoretician of Modern Republicanism, he wanted very much to elect as a successor to Eisenhower someone who shared those views, and in that vital respect Nixon evidently appeared acceptable and electable to him. Larson had been impressed, too, by Eisenhower's observation that Nixon "isn't the sort of person you turn to when you want a new idea, but he has an uncanny ability to draw upon others' ideas and bring out their essence in a cool-headed way."[38] Another motive, perhaps, was to increase Larson's own chances for an appointment in a future Nixon administration. When the two of them met on July 9, 1958, to discuss the job offer from Duke, Larson used the occasion to tell Nixon "he could count me among his supporters" in 1960.[39] Larson noted Nixon's reaction to this news:

> He was visibly pleased and said that I had been a real "leaven" that was much needed. If you weren't "controversial" you were nothing.
>
> I observed that everyone at a comparable level had been worked over sooner or later—he more than most. He said I would have to keep myself available, because government couldn't do without this kind of talent.[40]

Once at Duke, Larson asked for and received an autographed picture of Nixon that helped symbolize this new connection.[41]

Although the two men were friendly during the late 1950s, they could hardly have been considered close. One indication of this was Nixon's refusal to endorse *What We Are For* or even to write a foreword for a proposed paperback edition of *A Republican Looks at His Party* that Larson wanted printed during the year of Nixon's presidential campaign. Unwilling to antagonize New Rightists such as Buckley and Goldwater, Nixon studiously avoided any action that might identify him as a firmly committed member of the GOP's Modern Republican wing.[42]

Another telling sign was Nixon's unwillingness to visit Duke at Larson's invitation to speak at the law school. Anti-Nixon faculty at Duke had blocked the awarding of an honorary degree to him in 1954, which had prompted him to cancel a planned commencement address and avoid the campus thereafter. Never one to forgive or forget a slight of that sort, Nixon gently rebuffed Larson's overtures to visit Duke, even during the 1960 presidential campaign.[43]

Still more revealing of the distance that separated the two men was Nixon's reaction to Larson's input during the campaign. Larson suggested two themes, one domestic and one foreign, that he believed Nixon should sound during his race against Kennedy. Larson urged Nixon to endorse a public health insurance program for the elderly and the disabled—a version of what later became known as Medicare—and the idea of world peace through law. Nixon politely declined both suggestions.[44]

His decision about the first of these did not surprise Larson greatly, given

Nixon's earlier statements criticizing the Medicare concept. Larson's letter to Nixon on this issue explained that this new proposal differed from the plan backed by some liberal Democrats to pay the hospital and medical bills of all Social Security recipients. Under Larson's plan, only the aged and the disabled who lost income through illness would receive payments for such bills. He conceded that making such fine distinctions clear was not always easy but argued that it could be done. He also recognized that taking such a stand during the campaign might be awkward for Nixon, given some of his earlier statements in this area. Larson's understanding of these obstacles appears to have led him to accept without rancor Nixon's refusal to embrace this suggestion. His letter of response also gave Larson cause for hope, because in it Nixon said "Your application of the principle of 'restoration of wage loss' [to hospital and medical expenses] would seem to be both sound and feasible" and did not rule out support for Larson's proposal in the future.[45]

Larson was greatly dismayed, though, by Nixon's opportunistic retreat from the earlier stance he had taken in favor of reconsidering the Connally amendment. Nixon wrote Larson a letter reciting the arguments against the "peace through law" theme, culminating in a conclusion that it had "no political sex appeal."[46] And then, under pressure from the GOP's increasingly militant right wing, Nixon issued a statement that characteristically attempted to placate both sides on the issue. Unfortunately for him, ultraconservative opponents of any change in the Connally amendment saw through the statement immediately, while those who favored repeal or amendment interpreted Nixon's gambit as an abandonment of his previous position. This way of campaigning, so indicative of why Eisenhower had never really liked Nixon, discouraged Larson. He later criticized Nixon's efforts by observing that "he ended by having no theme at all."[47]

Nixon's opponent had more appeal in some ways, but Larson never seriously considered supporting him. Larson had first become acquainted with Kennedy during the mid-1950s. Both were considered rising stars within their respective parties and so agreed to make some joint appearances to discuss the issues of the day. USIA deputy director Abbott Washburn, who attended these events, recalled later that Larson and Kennedy "made an attractive pair." Both, he said, exuded charisma and intelligence. Larson, the former debate champion, enjoyed the encounters and admired Kennedy's articulate, witty rejoinders. The friendly tenor of the discussions and the closeness on the issues between the two men became obvious when Larson asserted at one point that Kennedy was "really A Modern Republican and didn't know it" and Kennedy countered that Larson was "really a Democrat and didn't know it."[48] Kennedy had also won favor with Larson by coming to the defense of the USIA's budget and mission when Lyndon Johnson launched his partisan political attack on them in the spring of 1957. Larson later characterized Kennedy as "my chief defender in some ways" during that painful time.[49] Kennedy's keen interest in new ways of thinking about foreign policy and his decision in 1957 to champion the cause of Algerian independence also likely appealed to Larson. The two men met again to debate the issues shortly after Kennedy's review of *What We Are For* had appeared in the *New York Times,* this time at a symposium sponsored by CBS at the Rockefeller Institute in New York. Kennedy's "New Frontiers" campaign theme, the same one Larson had proposed that Eisenhower use four years earlier, must have struck a responsive chord. Kennedy's support for Medicare undoubtedly did so as well.[50]

Despite all of these considerations, other, more basic ones kept Larson firmly within the Nixon camp. Larson's strong sense of identification with the GOP and previous commitment to Nixon's candidacy ruled out an endorsement of Kennedy. The much greater likelihood of being offered a high-level post by Nixon also probably mattered. Kennedy's decision to select Lyndon Johnson as the Democrats' vice presidential candidate must have influenced Larson as well. The presence of his chief tormentor during his USIA days on the Democratic ticket furnished yet another powerful reason to stay with Richard Nixon, despite Larson's misgivings about him. The contrast with Nixon's choice as his running mate, U.S. Ambassador to the United Nations Henry Cabot Lodge, with whom Larson had worked in the past, only underscored that factor. Nixon's support, however muddled, for a stronger world court also surely had an impact, given that Kennedy had not taken such a stand. Finally, there was Larson's tendency to view the election as a kind of referendum on the eight-year record of the Eisenhower presidency. The unfairness of some of Kennedy's attacks on the administration's performance clearly put Larson off, as they did Eisenhower himself and many other like-minded Republicans. This last factor motivated Florence to offer to make some speeches on Nixon's behalf, although her desire for a GOP victory in order to make a quick return to Washington and thus escape her own isolated situation in Durham may well have contributed to that offer. For all of these reasons, Nixon's very narrow loss on November 8, 1960, appears to have disappointed and frustrated both Larsons. While hardly a decisive repudiation, the election's outcome had clearly dealt a blow to the Modern Republican cause and their own personal fortunes.[51]

With the advent of a Democratic administration in Washington came some important changes in Arthur Larson's professional life. He would likely remain at Duke for several years at least rather than just the initial two-year period to which he had committed himself. And while there was still plenty of work for him to do at Duke, the election outcome placed the future of Larson's center in some doubt, given that neither Kennedy nor Johnson had expressed much interest in the cause it championed. Nixon's defeat tended to make Larson's mission to establish a world rule of law more difficult in another way, because the end of GOP control of the White House greatly diminished pressure on the party's most conservative elements to accept more moderate policies. Despite these discouraging developments, Larson persevered in his twin quests for peace through law and Modern Republicanism.[52]

The clearest sign that the world rule of law effort faced formidable obstacles was the lack of progress in the U.S. Senate on changes to the Connally amendment. Even before Nixon's loss to Kennedy, this important part of Larson's world rule of law crusade had stalled. This was partly attributable to the changing composition of the Senate after the off-year elections of 1958. The deep recession that year and division in Republican ranks nationwide over what the party's future direction should be had produced a major shift in the Senate's makeup. What had been a fairly narrow Democratic majority became a majority of 64 to 34 after the 1958 elections. In view of this unhappy turn of events, Eisenhower and his legislative aides had decided to let moderately liberal Democratic senators who had expressed strong interest in changes to the Connally amendment, such as Hubert Humphrey of Minnesota and Stuart Symington of Missouri, take the lead on that issue.[53]

This seemingly sensible concession to a new political reality had failed to yield the desired result, however, due to Senate majority leader Lyndon Johnson's opposition. Searching opportunistically by that point for ways to differentiate himself from such rivals for the presidency as Humphrey, Nixon, and Symington, Johnson evidently decided to oppose enlarging the jurisdiction of the International Court of Justice to curry favor with conservatives opposed to such a move. He may also have opposed the idea on its own merits, although one cannot be sure of that. Whatever Johnson's exact motivations were here, the consequences for the effort to repeal or amend the Connally amendment during 1959–1960 were very clear. Using his powerful Senate post and the wheeler-dealer methods for which he became famous, Johnson blocked any changes in the existing law through the end of Eisenhower's presidency.[54]

Larson's sense of frustration at this turn of events was compounded by the reaction to it from some of Eisenhower's senior aides. Once the inability to make any headway in the Senate became clear, some of them began pushing Eisenhower to let the idea drop. Resistance from the most conservative Republicans may well have been a factor in that kind of thinking. One clear sign of this change was the administration's decision to back off from creating a special advisory commission on the Connally amendment issue. Another was the Justice Department's evident lack of enthusiasm. Larson strongly disagreed with those counseling retreat, however, and kept pressing Eisenhower to restate his support for the Connally amendment's repeal. Only a very personal and forceful effort on Larson's part succeeded in keeping Eisenhower on record in support of that reform. The net result of this kind of infighting within the executive branch, however, was an impression in Congress and the media that administration support for repealing the Connally amendment was only lukewarm.[55]

Not all of the signs were discouraging, of course. After a full-court press from

Eisenhower and Larson, delegates to the American Bar Association convention that met in August 1960 adopted a resolution in favor of the amendment's repeal. The vote had been very close, however, and only reaffirmed a stand the organization had first taken in 1947. More substantial signs of progress came from abroad, as Britain, France, India, and Pakistan opted to abolish their own "self-judging" clauses in the late 1950s. By 1961, the United States was the only major power that retained a self-judging clause in its treaty concerning the World Court. More than anything else, these actions by foreign governments suggested to Larson that his quest for a change in the U.S. position was far from hopeless. He kept pushing in the early 1960s for such a change, despite the lack of any real progress in Congress and increasingly intense opposition from the New Right.[56]

At the same time, he entered a different kind of battle with the new Kennedy administration, which greeted Larson's crusade against the Connally amendment with marked indifference. This disheartening response reflected, at least partly, a different set of priorities. Kennedy and his top aides were preoccupied at first with other issues, such as increasing economic growth and employment, improving and expanding public education, creating a health insurance program for the elderly, and containing the spread of communism in the Third World. The lack of a reliable majority in Congress for Kennedy's domestic program during the early 1960s only intensified those preoccupations by requiring him and his aides to wage an intensive effort on Capitol Hill each time a major administration bill underwent congressional consideration. The resulting indifference to Larson's crusade, though hardly an outright rejection, signaled even more strongly that the effort to repeal the Connally amendment had ground to a halt.[57]

The Kennedy administration's decision to sponsor the so-called Bay of Pigs invasion of Cuba on April 17, 1961, hurt Larson's world rule of law crusade even more. This disastrous venture, which involved 1,400 anti-Castro Cuban exiles who had been organized, trained, armed, and transported by the CIA, ended in defeat at the hands of the Cuban army less than three days later. While most American critics of the operation attacked it as ill considered, Larson also believed it to be downright illegal. In a guest editorial in the *Saturday Review* that appeared one month later, he denounced the incident as "a flagrant violation of law."[58] Larson explained that both a federal criminal statute and an international agreement to which the United States was a party—the 1928 Treaty of Havana—prohibited any government from allowing, let alone helping, exiles organize themselves for a raid on their native land. Lest anyone think he was making too much out of legal technicalities, Larson pointed out firmly that "we are not dealing here with the fringes of international law and conduct. This is the very heart of the matter: the integrity of national states; the right of freedom from interference in domestic affairs; the illegality of force in international relations."[59]

Larson kept trying to bring about a more orderly and peaceful international system during the early 1960s, despite the setbacks of the rejection of the Connally amendment and the illegal action of the Bay of Pigs. Among the most illuminating ventures he participated in were private discussions with influential Soviets about ways to promote international law. These conversations took place at two important conferences financed by the Ford Foundation that were intended to improve understanding between the United States and the Soviet Union.[60]

The prime movers behind these meetings were Eisenhower, *Saturday Review* editor Norman Cousins, and Larson. Eisenhower had met with Cousins in the late 1950s, shortly before the editor visited the Soviet Union as part of the People to People exchange program. While discussing the possibility of further exchanges with the Soviets, Eisenhower suggested to Cousins that he sound them out about the possibility of holding conferences of private citizens to explore issues of common concern, given that official diplomacy seemed stuck.[61]

Cousins did what he could to advance this idea. While in Moscow he addressed the leading body of the Soviet Union's Peace Committee and proposed a conference of private citizens who enjoyed the confidence of their respective governments to address outstanding issues informally. Although no positive response materialized then, when Cousins reported his invitation to Eisenhower, the president urged Cousins to keep asking the Soviets, even if they declined such overtures at first. Eisenhower also suggested that Cousins speak with Larson about this matter and keep him informed of any progress.[62]

Acting on this advice, Cousins paid a visit to Larson's White House office and thus began a collaboration that eventually yielded the desired result. He and Larson decided to consult with leading foreign policy experts within the government about the idea. The two men contacted Special Assistant to the Secretary of State for Soviet Affairs Charles E. Bohlen; USIA's deputy director for policy and plans, Saxton Bradford; Assistant Secretary of State for Educational and Cultural Affairs Robert H. Thayer; and the State Department's East-West Group. These officials raised no objections but refrained from giving a formal endorsement in view of the private nature of the proposed event. With this kind of unofficial blessing from his government, Cousins issued more invitations to the Soviets to attend such a conference. After declining at least four times, the Soviet government finally sent a telegram to Cousins agreeing to send twenty prominent Soviet intellectuals to a conference in the United States. After a telephone call from an excited Cousins with this news, Larson wrote invitations to a group of prominent Americans, and the meeting was on.[63]

The conference took place on the campus of Dartmouth College in early November 1960, its president, John Dickey, having offered the facilities of his school for that purpose. Economist Walt Rostow of the Massachusetts Institute of Technology, a foreign policy advisor to John F. Kennedy, headed the fifteen-member American delegation at this meeting, which included former Connecticut senator William Benton, who was also close to Kennedy; international lawyer Grenville Clark; former U.S. ambassador to the USSR George Kennan; Philip Mosely of the Council on Foreign Relations; Waldemar Neilsen and Shepard Stone of the Ford Foundation; and several other prominent writers and intellectuals, including Larson. The nine-member Soviet group featured legal expert Victor Chkhikvadze; playwright Alexander Korneichuk, a member of the Communist Party's Central Committee who knew Khrushchev well; and several others prominent in Soviet arts and sciences.[64]

The mostly pleasant tone of what became known as the Dartmouth meetings surprised Larson and the other Americans present, given the poor state of U.S.-Soviet relations at the time. The meetings took place only six months after the downing of an American U-2 spy plane inside Russia, which had provoked Nikita Khrushchev to stalk out of an important disarmament conference in Paris. Khrushchev's belligerent remarks thereafter and the strongly anti-Soviet themes sounded by both Kennedy and Nixon during their respective presidential campaigns had heightened those tensions and led Larson to expect some difficult exchanges with the Soviet delegates. They did refer repeatedly to American military intervention in Siberia during 1918, which had been part of an effort by Western powers to halt the Bolshevik Revolution, but to his surprise did not spend most of the time reciting this kind of party line view of which side had started the trouble between them. Instead, Larson found the Soviet delegates to be cordial, concerned about making progress toward disarmament, and receptive to his ideas about promoting the world rule of law. The mood of good fellowship proved so strong that Larson and a Soviet composer named Vano Muradeli obtained a guitar and sang together. Larson's effectiveness at the conference so impressed Cousins, Florence Larson reported to her friend Ruth Tidmarsh, that the editor "wants to make him President."[65] The clearest sign that the meeting had gone well came when the Soviet delegation proposed a follow-up round to be held six months later in the Soviet Union and the Americans agreed.[66]

Larson's trip to the Soviet Union to attend the second conference, which Florence made as well, proved very educational in more ways than one. The meeting took place in the Crimean town of Nizhnyaya Oreanda during the week of May 22–29, 1961, and was followed by a week of sightseeing in Kiev, Leningrad, and Moscow. This time the American delegation included seventeen members, including luminaries such as the singer Marian Anderson, Harvard Law School dean Erwin Griswold, former Eisenhower advisor on economic matters Gabriel Hauge, anthropologist Margaret Mead, Yale's Department of Economics chairman Lloyd Reynolds, and Harvard law professor and world rule of law advocate Louis Sohn. The eighteen-person Soviet group included three members of the Communist Party's Central Committee and one candidate member as well as two of the Soviet judges on the International Court of Justice, Vladimir Koretsky and F. I. Kozhevnikov, whose presence signaled clear Soviet interest in Larson's ideas. Having broken the ice at their previous session, the conference delegates felt free to engage in more spirited and at times heated exchanges on such topics as disarmament; secrecy; the Soviet roles in the Congo, Hungary, and Vietnam; and the different meanings the two nations tended to assign to the terms "peaceful coexistence" and "international law."[67]

In the course of these discussions, Larson became more aware of the difficulties involved in trying to build a world rule of law system that included communist countries. He discovered that two of the Soviet delegates objected to the term "world law" because it seemed to negate national sovereignty. They endorsed the idea of international law in general, but in this area, as in others, the Soviets were unwilling to debate crucial specific issues, most notably the kind of forum that would resolve disagreements arising under an expanded body of international law. Soviet delegates repeatedly stated their preference for "settlement of disputes by negotiation and mutual concessions" instead of with a judicial approach.[68] The Soviets' strong emphasis on the need to protect national sovereignty convinced Larson that Grenville Clark and Louis Sohn's conception of revising the UN's charter to create a genuine world government was unworkable. He noted in his conference diary that one Soviet lawyer had even characterized the Clark-Sohn plan "as another kind of world imperialism."[69] Larson remained optimistic, however, that his more limited concept of greater use of treaties between sovereign nations to establish legal rules to regulate their behavior could succeed.[70]

The biggest single problem in understanding the Soviets, Larson concluded from these talks, was how to reconcile what called he "their wildly inconsistent words and actions" in the international arena. In marked contrast with more conservative Americans, who tended to see Soviet statements in favor of peace and friendship with the United States as a mere ruse, Larson suspected that more than one factor lay behind such inconsistency. A key reason for rejecting the more simplistic explanation of outright dishonesty, Larson noted in his diary, was the Soviet delegates' obviously sincere desire for peace and fear of war.[71]

These impressions led him to consider and note down in his conference diary other possible explanations, such as the tendency of the large Soviet bureaucracy to thwart those in the USSR who favored friendlier relations with the United States. He saw a parallel here to the problems he had encountered at the USIA from some of the émigré language experts, who had undermined his policy of communicating what was positive about America in favor of talking about what was negative about the Soviet Union. Larson also surmised that the Soviet government and newspapers were still filled with Stalinists who disliked the more recent emphasis on peace and friendship. The sophisticated way in which he approached the entire issue of Soviet inconsistency is clear in the summary notes Larson jotted down in his conference diary:

> As a group, they [the Stalinists] are sufficiently numerous, strong and strategically placed to get away with it [obstructing the new party line]. In addition, perhaps it suits the government to let them get away with it.
>
> Thus, it is quite possible that the anti-Americanism and the peace-friendship elements are both valid and, in a way, sincere.[72]

The distance between Larson's views on this issue and those of more conservative Americans can also be seen in his rejection of the totalitarian model that political scientist Hannah Arendt had used to explain the Soviet political system. According to Arendt, the Soviet state's efforts to mobilize the Soviet people into a mass movement aimed at transforming the world, the concentration of power in the hands of state bureaucrats, the glorification of the nation's leader, the official propaganda campaigns, the practice of spying on ordinary citizens by the secret police, and the repression of dissidents had all combined to create a system of government similar to that of Nazi Germany. Larson believed, however, that the very different conditions facing Germany in the mid-1930s and the USSR twenty-five years later belied such a comparison, despite its superficial appeal. He observed in his conference diary that

> one should note that the USSR in 1961 does *not* resemble Hitler's Germany in many ways. The mood is entirely different. Germany was depressed, bitter, unpleasant. True, Germany displayed show-pieces—and had strength-thru-joy circuses, etc. But among the people the atmosphere was unhealthy—hate was in the air. The propaganda stressed, not peace and friendship, but Lebensraum, master race, hatred of Jews, glory of war, etc. There is none of that in the USSR of today. The mood on the streets appears to be friendly . . . cheerful and hopeful.[73]

Larson's impressions of the Soviet people gained from touring Kiev, Leningrad, and Moscow clearly pushed him away from Orwellian notions of Soviet life. Besides the common American reactions to the seemingly endless rows of suburban apartment buildings and the sight of muscular Soviet women doing manual labor, Larson's diary from the trip noted the friendliness toward Americans expressed by casual acquaintances and people he encountered at random. Instead of a belligerent attitude among the Soviet people, Larson's strongest general impression was of "a driving urge to improve." His visit to a collective farm outside Kiev conveyed that sense especially strongly. The high quality of the country's traditional performing and folk arts also impressed him, although he found the contemporary arts there "miserable." Nowhere did he get the feeling that ordinary Russians or Ukrainians viewed their country as one enormous prison, as the most anti-Soviet writers sometimes suggested they did. The overall impressions of dynamism and hope indicated to Larson that the Soviet system would likely endure indefinitely. He observed in his diary that "obviously it is too late—and it would be pointless—to quarrel with Russia's internal system. It may or may not be the best for the given problem—but as of today it is working and it is here to stay." From this Larson concluded that Americans and Soviets would have to learn to live with each other in peace and control the arms race in which they had joined.[74]

He hit upon the law of outer space as a good place in which to start U.S.-Soviet discussions about building an expanded international legal system. The lack of existing law governing extraterrestrial bodies and the U.S.-Soviet monopoly over space exploration apparently suggested to Larson that space law would be easier to develop than rules governing other kinds of international disputes. The receptivity of the Soviet delegates at the Oreanda conference encouraged Larson to push for another follow-up session to discuss space law specifically.[75]

However, the Dartmouth and Oreanda conferences failed to generate any real momentum in 1961 for such negotiations because of the chilly relations between the Soviet and American governments at that time. In the week after the Oreanda conference, Kennedy and Khrushchev met in Vienna for a superpower summit that only worsened relations between their two countries. Serious disagreements over such sensitive subjects as the future of Berlin, Cuba, a nuclear test ban treaty, avoiding accidental war between the two nations, and revolutions in the Third World produced a hardening of attitudes on both sides and inaugurated a new round of intense East-West conflict for the next two years. Although both Kennedy and Khrushchev favored steps toward a more peaceful U.S.-Soviet relationship, the two leaders also felt compelled to satisfy their most hawkish critics. The result was an incoherent and sometimes reckless foreign policy on both sides during the rest of 1961 and 1962 that undermined Larson's efforts to promote peace through international law.[76]

He kept trying, mostly by writing and speaking in favor of that cause. Larson emphasized the importance of referring international disputes to the United Nations instead of pursuing unilateral or bilateral approaches. He perceived a dangerous trend away from the Truman and Eisenhower administrations' policy of using the United Nations whenever possible. The Kennedy administration seemed, he thought, to have embraced a "pick and choose" policy of using the UN only when the short-term disadvantages did not appear to outweigh the long-term interest in adhering to its charter. "Do it through the UN" became something of a personal mantra for Larson, then and afterward, whether the issue was the Arab-Israeli conflict in the Middle East, civil war in the Congo, or a combination of communist infiltration and civil war in Vietnam. He used the phrase as the title of an article that appeared in the August 25, 1962, issue of the *Saturday Review* that advocated that the U.S. government refer both the Vietnam issue and plans to test a nuclear weapon in outer space to the United Nations for its decision.[77]

The approach to the Vietnam issue Larson spelled out in this article is worthy of some attention, given the far-reaching implications of American policy there during the 1960s. Larson began his discussion of Vietnam by noting that President Kennedy had explicitly called the situation in Southeast Asia a "threat to peace" in a speech to the UN General Assembly on September 25, 1961. Despite this official characterization, the formal procedure for bringing that threat to peace before the Security Council had not been invoked. Since that time, the conflict in Vietnam had continued and the U.S. military had become seriously involved.[78]

Larson conceded that the UN charter did not require member nations to bring their disputes to the Security Council at the very beginning and that members were free to pursue other avenues to resolve such conflicts. He pointed out, however, that Article 37 of the Charter required member nations to refer such disputes to the Security Council when other avenues to peace had failed. Larson stated that that time had come:

> When matters have reached the point where American troops are being sent to South Vietnam and Thailand and Americans are being killed and wounded on "technical," "training," and "support" assignments, it seems clear that the parties have failed to settle a dispute which is "likely to endanger the maintenance of international peace" through use of "peaceful means of their own choice." It is then time to bring the problem under the aegis of the U.N.[79]

In the conclusion to this influential article, which the American Association for the United Nations reprinted and distributed across the country, Larson set forth his view of the UN's basic purpose. The UN was not simply a mechanism for facilitating negotiations between countries in conflict, he argued. Instead, it marked a new departure in international relations and sought to resolve issues based on right, not might. Larson's commitment to using the United Nations whenever possible and his expansive view of its proper function grew partly out of his long-standing enthusiasm for the ideals that lay behind the UN's founding. The clearest sign of that enthusiasm was Larson's decision in 1950 to join the United World Federalists, which sought to build support for a world federal government as a way to achieve peace. His world rule of law crusade only strengthened that basic orientation, thereby making him one of leading advocates for the United Nations in the United States at a time when the organization's popularity had begun to decline there.[80]

There were four basic reasons for the change in American public opinion toward the United Nations during the early 1960s. The first stemmed from the increase in membership of the UN General Assembly, which had grown from 76 countries in 1955 to 104 seven years later, mostly because of the decline of colonialism in the Third World. By 1962, a majority of that expanded membership, some 54 nations in all, lay in Africa and Asia. This change in the General Assembly's balance of power tended to diminish respect for American perspectives and consequently weakened public support for the United Nations in the United States. These changes in membership and outlook were what had encouraged the Kennedy administration to resort to the UN more selectively than previous administrations had done, and that shift also contributed to a decline in the organization's prestige in the United States. At the same time, American and British efforts to expand the UN's peacekeeping function over French and Soviet objections, most notably in the Congo and Middle East, helped bring on a funding crisis, as those two leading dissenters against UN peacekeeping policy increasingly withheld funds needed to support it. This development also bred resentment of the United Nations in the United States because of the pressure it came under to increase its already large share of the UN's budget.[81]

Larson argued that, if resolved properly, these challenges could lead to an even more activist phase in the UN's history, but in the early 1960s no such trend became evident. A sense of quiet crisis developed at the United Nations instead, as members argued over what its proper mission ought to be and how to ensure that agreements about funding be kept. The disputes over peacekeeping and finances also began to hurt the International Court of Justice, especially after it issued an advisory opinion in 1962 that the costs of the Congo and Middle East operations were "expenses of the Organization" and thus binding on members. For the next four years, member nations would refrain from bringing any new cases before the World Court, thereby signaling even more clearly just how troubled the UN and its affiliated bodies had become. Larson continued to argue for his expansive vision of the United Nations and the International Court of Justice during the early 1960s, but without success. In this, as with his world rule of law crusade more generally, Larson's efforts attracted mostly favorable attention from the media but did not produce other concrete results.

In the late spring and summer of 1963 a ray of real hope finally appeared. Its origins lay in the frightening confrontation of the previous fall over the installation of Soviet missiles in Cuba. This episode, which might have sparked a U.S.-Soviet war, persuaded the governments of both nations to work harder for better relations. A major turning point came on June 10, 1963, when President Kennedy delivered a commencement address at American University that called on the Soviet Union and the United States to help "make the world safe for diversity." The speech, which Kennedy made after Norman Cousins had urged him to do so, renounced any intention by the U.S. government to seek a world peace on terms that would essentially require a Soviet surrender. The government of the USSR responded to this overture in several unusual ways, such as allowing the Soviet press to publish the full text of the speech, dropping its jamming of Voice of America's Russian-language broadcast of it to the Soviet Union and Eastern Europe, and stopping all other jamming of Western broadcasts. Just as suddenly, the Soviet government's representatives in Vienna agreed to the principle of inspection by the International Atomic Energy Agency to make certain that its reactors were used for peaceful purposes only. And then, on July 2, Nikita Khrushchev made a speech in East Berlin praising Kennedy's recent address and endorsing an atmospheric nuclear test ban treaty of the sort that had been under serious discussion for the previous four years. On July 25, 1963, just six weeks after Kennedy's speech at American University, American, British, and Soviet diplomats signed this arms control agreement, the first they had ever negotiated.[82]

Larson greeted this development with real excitement. After almost five years of trying hard to promote world peace, a concrete step in that direction had finally materialized. Understanding that Eisenhower's support for the treaty could be crucial in securing its ratification by the U.S. Senate, Larson wrote to him four days after the agreement had been signed, urging the former president to endorse it publicly. Larson explained that two reasons why Eisenhower should do so were the tepid response to the treaty thus far from most Senate Republicans and Barry Goldwater's outright opposition.[83]

Eisenhower eventually endorsed the test-ban agreement, but in a letter to Larson he showed much less enthusiasm for it than Larson had communicated: "I am astonished that you seem to think that such a Treaty as this is practically an automatic guarantor of constantly improving relationships between the East and West, with almost assured progress in satisfactory disarmament measures and marked decrease in cold war activity."[84]

With the help of Eisenhower's influential backing, the Senate voted to approve the treaty on September 24, 1963, by a vote of 80 to 19—fourteen more than the required two-thirds. The bipartisan nature of the bloc that voted in favor must have pleased Larson. Support for the measure among Senate Republicans, who endorsed it by a margin of 25 to 8, amounted to just over three-quarters of their caucus and included, crucially, Senate GOP leader Everett Dirksen of Illinois. Although the margin among Senate Democrats was slightly higher at 55 to 11, no one could argue that the Republican Party had failed to back this historic early step toward meaningful arms control and détente.[85]

The test ban treaty hardly portended a new millennium, of course, as Larson well knew. The agreement banned nuclear tests in the atmosphere, in outer space, and under water only. Underground tests could and would continue. Another limit to the agreement's reach appeared when China and France, heavily engaged in nuclear weapons development programs of their own, refused to sign even this partial test ban treaty. Still more troubling, the arms race between the Soviet Union and the United States showed no signs of slowing in the summer of 1963. On the contrary, spending on nuclear missiles and bombers was growing, as both sides tried to strengthen their arsenals following the previous fall's showdown over Cuba. Superpower conflict over that nation also continued, as the Soviets' decision to leave most of their 42,000 soldiers and technicians stationed on the island became clear and the U.S. government continued to search for ways to oust Castro, including assassination. Despite all of these discouraging considerations, however, the test ban treaty signaled a welcome move away from the acrimony between the superpowers of the previous three years, and Larson viewed it as a very significant and satisfying achievement.[86]

Kennedy's successful negotiation of the treaty also marked a turning point in Larson's estimation of him and his administration. Although Larson had liked Kennedy's campaign promise to "get the country moving again," his appealing style, and the way he inspired the young, the Bay of Pigs fiasco and militantly anticommunist rhetoric Kennedy so often used during his first two years as president had briefly disillusioned Larson. Kennedy's fondness for informal meetings, direct contacts, and small task forces to deal with individual issues also put Larson off. Kennedy had made these changes to encourage the flow of new ideas, which bureaucratic structures sometimes stifled, at a time when he believed new ways of thinking were badly needed. Larson, however, perceived the risks created by such changes in the administrative process as too great. Larson firmly believed that Eisenhower's policy of going through proper channels had tended to prevent mistakes such as the Bay of Pigs invasion.[87]

The Kennedy administration's tendency to try to resolve international crises without resorting to the United Nations had also troubled Larson. Despite this, Larson approved of the administration's negotiations with Laos, China, the Soviet Union, North Vietnam, and nine other nations during the first year and a half of Kennedy's presidency, which avoided a superpower confrontation in Laos. Diplomacy even of this more limited sort, Larson believed, was vastly preferable to a unilateral and illegal military action of the kind Kennedy had approved against Cuba.[88]

The first signs of Larson's increasing enthusiasm for Kennedy's policies came in the fall of 1962. In September he accepted the administration's request to become a consultant to the State Department on the problems facing the United Nations. When the Cuban missile crisis erupted only a few weeks later, Larson mobilized his World Rule of Law Center staff to study the legality of the U.S. blockade, or "quarantine," as Kennedy and his aides like to call it, of Cuba. Larson and his colleagues concluded that this action was lawful because of the essentially defensive nature of the operation and Kennedy's decision to obtain the approval of the Organization of American States first.[89]

The administration's actions regarding some domestic issues of special concern to Larson also gradually improved his opinion of it. Larson supported Kennedy's push to enact a Medicare plan in 1962. Even though Congress rejected the proposal, Larson liked the administration's advocacy of an idea he strongly favored. Even more pleasing was the Kennedy Labor Department's unexpected help in reviving the model state workers' compensation statute Larson had developed while under secretary of labor. Kennedy Labor Department official Daniel Patrick Moynihan's request in 1961 that Larson head up this effort surprised and pleased him. He later recalled the episode:

> The Council of State Governments had decided to sponsor the drafting of a new Model Act, for inclusion in its regular ongoing program of suggested state legislation. My first question was naturally whether a Model Act would fare any better today than it had in 1954. The answer was that as long as the whole effort was under *state* auspices, no one would complain, since the bugaboo of federalization could not possibly be found in a state-organization-sponsored program of legislation.[90]

Working with this group of workers' compensation experts from around the country proved both pleasurable and productive for Larson. It met all day once a month for the next four years, drafting a revised model act that ultimately won the group's unanimous support on all but one or two relatively minor points. He wrote a section-by-section commentary explaining the specific choices the group had made, and the Council of State Governments distributed this material widely. State legislatures used it extensively to revise workers' compensation laws, vindicating Larson's original idea. Larson's opinion of the other members of the drafting committee was so high that he later observed, "I have never worked with a more conscientious and capable group."[91]

Kennedy's eloquent and emotional televised address on June 11, 1963, in favor of new federal legislation to protect the civil rights of black Americans also pleased Larson. Eisenhower's unwillingness to embrace the civil rights cause had deeply disappointed Larson, who firmly believed in an end to legalized segregation. Kennedy's civil rights speech must have been especially liberating for Larson, who had earlier pushed Eisenhower for such a statement on that issue.[92]

While these actions by the Kennedy administration pulled Larson toward it, Barry Goldwater's growing popularity within the GOP pushed Larson away from the Republican Party. Goldwater's hostile reaction to the nuclear test ban treaty, so different from Kennedy's articulate advocacy in favor of it, crystallized that shift in Larson's attitude. He made that plain in the draft of an extraordinary letter to Eisenhower written on August 9, 1963. Larson began this very revealing missive by explaining that "I am going to risk the friendship between us—which is one of the most precious things in my life—by writing a letter with a degree of candor which is not customary in letters to Presidents."[93]

From there Larson went on to recount what he saw as the key political developments of the past several years. He reminded Eisenhower that during his presidency he had given a very high priority toward taking practical steps to avoid nuclear war and observed that President Kennedy had recently begun to do the same. Larson expressed disappointment that Eisenhower's initial response to the test ban treaty was not more enthusiastic, given that it had been his administration that had first proposed an agreement of this kind. Next, Larson stated that he was well along on a sequel to *A Republican Looks at His Party* that addressed the question of how a political party with 16 million fewer registrants than the Democrats could become the country's majority party. Larson said that his first point in this new manuscript was that the Republican Party had a golden opportunity to achieve such status during Eisenhower's presidency but that implacable opposition to Eisenhower's more moderate form of conservatism from "the Mundts, and Bridges and Goldwaters" had left the party in about the same place it had been before Eisenhower's first election.[94]

Larson explained that his new book's main purpose would be to propose two or three big ideas that could lift the Republican Party to an entirely new level of public acceptance and that the first of these ideas needed to be a fresh program to build world peace. He noted that he had tried very hard to sell Nixon on that last point and suggested that Nixon's refusal to campaign on that theme had been the decisive factor in his very narrow defeat. Larson argued firmly that unless Republicans took hold of the peace issue, made it their own, and convinced the public that they had the most constructive answer to it, the party "will not see the inside of the White House for another generation—barring some catastrophe that none of us wants to see."[95]

Larson's reasons for writing all this emerged clearly as he pointed out that the conspicuous silence on the test ban treaty from most GOP congressmen, senators, and governors had lent even greater prominence to Goldwater's attacks on it. The net result was that the identification of the Republican Party with the peace issue was being lost. The other main reason Larson had written, he explained, was that he had just read a newspaper column stating that Eisenhower had been invited to attend a dinner in Hershey, Pennsylvania, at which Goldwater would be the principal speaker. Larson observed that he supposed Eisenhower would be under increasing pressure to take a stand on Goldwater and tried hard to make certain Eisenhower publicly denounced Goldwater's views. The depth of Larson's feelings surfaced in the following passage: "I have made a methodical examination of Goldwater's position on every major domestic and international issue. If Goldwater had his way, it is no exaggeration to say that practically everything that I have spent my life to try to achieve on the domestic and international scene would be destroyed—and I think that the same can be said of you."[96]

Larson stated that he could not understand the reluctance among leading Republicans to oppose Goldwater's view publicly, and complained that he, Larson, had recently experienced just this sort of equivocation during an appearance on a national television show with former Republican National Committee chairman Meade Alcorn and his successor, Thruston Morton. When moderator Harry Reasoner had asked if they would support all of the men most often mentioned as possible GOP presidential candidates in 1964, Larson had forthrightly replied that he could not support Goldwater under any circumstances "because he was either utterly wrong or utterly unrealistic on every foreign and domestic issue."[97] To Larson's dismay, not only Morton but also Alcorn had refused to go along with Larson's stand. He could understand

Morton's statement that he would support any good Republican, given Morton's role as party chairman, Larson wrote, but not Alcorn's refusal to answer the question directly, given that he no longer held any official position within the GOP and was free to say what he liked. That Alcorn had proceeded to tell Larson privately after the cameras were turned off that he of course did not favor Goldwater only added to Larson's sense of frustration. The consequence of all this reticence, Larson continued, created a false impression in the mind of many Republicans that Goldwater enjoyed acceptance from mainstream officials in the party.[98]

Finally, and most explosively, Larson stated that he could not stomach the idea of Republicanism at any price:

> I have put a great deal of research and thought into this matter, and I have determined in advance where, as a matter of principle, the breaking point lies at which loyalty to my beliefs will take precedence over loyalty to the Republican Party. I think it is only fair to say, therefore, that if Goldwater were nominated, there would be organized on the following day a Republicans for Kennedy movement, with me at the head of it, if somebody else did not beat me to it, and I have no doubt that the bulk of the Republican Party would go along.[99]

Larson concluded this remarkable letter by adding that although he did not think matters would ever reach this point, taking the current political contest within the GOP more seriously might help prevent it.[100]

Larson never sent this letter, which he seems to have drafted in the heat of the moment. He must have had second thoughts about how Eisenhower would likely react to this outburst, especially to Larson's intention to support Kennedy's reelection should the Republicans decide to nominate Goldwater for the presidency in 1964. Larson knew that Kennedy's criticism during the 1960 presidential campaign of the Eisenhower administration's record had deeply offended Eisenhower and that he had never warmed up to his successor thereafter. Rather than risk alienating Eisenhower completely, Larson evidently decided to keep his own counsel for the time being on the upcoming presidential race.[101]

The politically suicidal actions of Goldwater's strongest potential rival, New York governor Nelson Rockefeller, also likely contributed to Larson's decision to stay out of partisan politics during 1963. Rockefeller had divorced his wife of thirty-two years, Mary Todhunter Clark, in March 1962, and then stunned the political world by marrying a woman nineteen years his junior named Margaretta Fitler ("Happy") Murphy fourteen months later. Rockefeller's decision to marry a woman who had recently left her husband—and surrendered her right to see their four children (aged three to twelve) as a condition of her divorce from him—deeply offended many morally traditional Americans. It also effectively ended Rockefeller's chances for the GOP presidential nomination in

1964, even though he stubbornly refused to accept that hard political fact. This turn of events must have shocked Larson, given that his first impression of Rockefeller, formed when they became acquainted in the spring of 1954, was that he was a devoted family man. Although Larson respected Rockefeller's views on public affairs, his divorce and remarriage put considerable distance between the two men. Rockefeller's hawkish foreign policy views, on Cuba especially, also likely put Larson off his candidacy. Whatever the exact amount of weight accorded to these factors, Larson avoided Rockefeller's emerging presidential campaign in 1963, a decision that left Larson without an active candidate of his own to back. By September of that year he had lost interest in partisan politics and had no plans to involve himself much in it during 1964 unless Goldwater won the GOP presidential nomination.[102]

Lyndon Johnson's accidental accession to the presidency on November 22, 1963, following Kennedy's assassination in Dallas changed Larson's outlook almost immediately. In December he gave some serious thought to writing a book critical of Johnson. Although Richard Nixon urged him to do it, Larson soon decided against such a project, apparently because he felt uncomfortable with the role of attacker. Larson chose instead to accentuate the positive by writing about what the GOP ought to do to win the upcoming presidential election. He abandoned his book-length sequel to *A Republican Looks at His Party* in favor of articles, which could reach influential readers much more quickly. These pieces, which appeared that winter in such publications as the *Saturday Evening Post*, the *Saturday Review*, and *The Nation*, mostly restated Larson's by-then familiar views on the GOP's need to nominate a moderate conservative who favored activist government but only within proper boundaries.[103]

A few aspects of Larson's thesis were new. In an article for the *Saturday Evening Post* entitled "How the Republicans Can Win," Larson argued that in order to prevail in 1964, the GOP's presidential candidate should hit two major campaign themes, one domestic and the other foreign. These should be, he suggested, a solution to the problem of growing blue-collar unemployment and an emphasis on using the United Nations to resolve such knotty international disputes as Berlin and Vietnam.[104]

Larson's discussion of the first of these two ideas is especially interesting, because he had never before written extensively on that topic. It so engaged him that he produced a 67-page manuscript that greatly expanded on his discussion in the *Saturday Evening Post* piece. Although "A National Progress-Sharing Program" was rejected by the editors of *Fortune* magazine and never appeared in print anywhere, it deserves attention here for what it says about Larson's understanding of the nation's domestic problems in the mid-1960s and his moderately conservative prescription for dealing with them.[105]

Larson observed in this piece that the distinctive American problem was the presence of a growing body of unemployed workers as an apparently permanent feature of the economy. Until recently, he continued, economists and policymakers had tended to assume that a higher rate of economic growth could shrink this group substantially. Instead, he noted, the American economy had gone through a series of recessions and recoveries in recent years, producing an overall result at odds with that earlier optimistic assumption. Even though most major economic indicators had recovered after each recession ended and had moved upward once more to all-time highs, the added unemployment produced by these slowdowns was never fully taken up by the ensuing recoveries. Economists had begun to face up to what Larson called, with his characteristic clarity, "the new dilemma of the American economy: increasing production accompanied by increasing unemployment."[106]

Larson noted in passing that Kennedy's campaign theme of "getting the country moving again" had been related to the approach of increasing economic growth to address this problem but that this solution and the labor movement's prescription of a shorter work week were both inadequate. The reason for this, Larson argued, had to do with automation, the ultimate cause of growing structural unemployment. The process of replacing workers with machines was far from new, he continued, but the very rapid pace of automation in the United States in the early 1960s was. He argued that more economic growth of the sort Kennedy and Johnson had called for would not stop technological unemployment, as it was sometimes called. The labor movement's call for a shorter work week without any reduction in weekly pay would actually make matters worse, Larson suggested, by increasing both blue-collar workers' real hourly wages and management's interest in replacing such workers with machinery wherever possible.[107]

In his solution to this problem, Larson drew an analogy to an earlier period in American history, when the Republican Party had pushed for the Homestead Act of 1862 in order to reduce unemployment. That measure had permitted any citizen or prospective citizen to buy 160 acres of land for a small fee after living on it for five years. Larson's updated version of this idea was to provide workers with what he called "capital estates." He suggested that American businesses greatly expand programs that paid workers partly in company stock. This, he argued, would allow workers' income to grow in a way business could afford, which would tend to push employment up and inflation down. It would also encourage greater worker productivity and discourage strikes by aligning the interests of the worker and the company more closely. All of this would help keep business competitive with foreign imports and diminish the pressure on American firms to automate jobs out of existence. He noted that the best-known example of using stock as a form of employee compensation to help keep a company competitive in recent years had been at American Motors Corporation, whose management had concluded an agreement of that sort with its unionized workforce. Larson came up with the term "progress-sharing program" to describe his proposal. He contended that government policies could encourage the spread of such plans enough to reverse the trend toward more blue-collar unemployment and that this kind of approach to the problem would be acceptable to managers and workers and would fit within established American traditions.[108]

In the first clear sign of how Larson meant for this plan to affect the race for the 1964 Republican presidential nomination, he praised former American Motors chief executive officer George Romney by name for having pioneered progress-sharing at that company. Larson had first met Romney in June 1958, when they shared a commencement platform at a private school in Michigan. The two men had liked each other immediately, thanks to strong similarities in background, philosophy, and temperament. When Romney had moved on from American Motors to win the Michigan governorship in November 1962, Larson, like many others, began to think of this handsome, moderate, competent, forthright, and morally traditional midwesterner as a promising presidential candidate.[109]

The profit-sharing approach Romney inaugurated at American Motors and Larson wanted to expand had its merits, but it also had some serious limitations. The plan can be thought of as a kind of middle way of dealing with the problem of rising unemployment among blue-collar workers. The scheme avoided the expansion of what Larson saw as a demeaning public-assistance model, which was the course of action Lyndon Johnson and his top advisors had begun to take, and what Larson saw as the unrealistic and even callous policy of leaving the unemployment problem to market forces, private charity, and state and local governments for resolution, as Goldwater and his followers wanted to do. The basic problem with Larson's plan was the considerable length of time that would likely be needed to implement it fully. "Progress sharing" in that sense was a visionary solution that promised no quick fix to the new unemployment problem.[110]

The large number of attractive moderate contenders for the 1964 GOP presidential nomination encouraged Larson, however, in believing that his "progress-sharing" and "do it through the UN" themes might be used successfully by one of them in a race against Lyndon Johnson. The rather muddy state of the GOP field by late winter led Larson to visit Eisenhower, to discuss how best to proceed with the plan of nominating a centrist alternative to Goldwater. Eisenhower and Larson met on March 9th at the former president's vacation home in Palm Desert, California. Eisenhower, clearly energized by the battle going on within the GOP between moderate and more extreme conservatives, took the lead in talking about the various candidates. The appeal of extreme conservative positions to young people troubled him, Eisenhower told Larson. He recorded the former president's thoughts on that point:

> He was disturbed by the number of students who adopt dogmatic ideas and particularly by those who become Goldwater fanatics unreasoningly. The

> trouble with Goldwater [Eisenhower said] is that he has a positive opinion on every subject anyone brings up. No one can be that sure of everything. It reminded him of the definition of the Indian River—an inch deep and a mile wide—too deep to plow and too shallow to drink. That's how Goldwater's opinions are on the issues. "The guy is nuts," says D.D.E.[111]

Eisenhower indicated that his choice among the leading moderate contenders was Pennsylvania governor William Scranton, whom Eisenhower described as "a suave polished man who didn't seem to take himself too seriously."[112] Eisenhower also told Larson that two of the three other moderates most often mentioned that year, George Romney and Henry Cabot Lodge, would make good candidates and that the third, Nelson Rockefeller, was certainly qualified by virtue of experience. Of Nixon, Eisenhower said only that his defeat in the 1962 California gubernatorial election and disastrous press conference the next day had seriously injured his chances in 1964. Eisenhower also confided that he was constantly working on the problem of the right GOP ticket and for that reason had taken the trouble to meet most of the Republican governors.[113]

Larson clearly found this session encouraging, precisely because Eisenhower appeared open to supporting any of the likely candidates except Goldwater, which was Larson's position as well. He was also pleased that Eisenhower gave the impression of being willing to back Romney strongly should he jump into the race; the Michigan governor was Larson's first choice. The tenor of this conversation conveyed both men's confidence that a moderate candidate would emerge from this crowded field to prevail over Goldwater and his very zealous supporters.[114]

The self-assurance of late winter vanished the following spring as the GOP moderates fell into disorder and then defeat. There were several reasons for this unexpected turn of events. First, the strength of the leading moderate contenders that year had always been more illusory than real. Romney and Scranton had been elected to their respective governorships less than two years earlier and lacked the requisite experience, in foreign policy especially, for national office in 1964. Nelson Rockefeller had the necessary background by then, but his divorce and remarriage had fatally harmed his candidacy that year. Neither Nixon nor Lodge, having flubbed the previous presidential election that many experts had expected them to win, appealed greatly to party regulars. The sheer number of moderate contenders also worked against their wing of the party by fragmenting it in the face of a stiff challenge from more extreme conservatives who had united behind Goldwater's candidacy.[115]

The zeal of the Goldwaterites also made a big difference. In the states that used the party convention method to select delegates to the 1964 Republican National Convention, intensely committed minorities could sometimes prevail over less-energetic majorities. The intensity of Goldwater's support among the most conservative Republicans also weakened the moderates' cause in another way, by discouraging Republican officeholders who disagreed with the Arizona senator's views from publicly condemning his candidacy. Fearful that such opposition might provoke retribution in the form of a primary challenge from the right when these officeholders sought reelection, they mostly muffled their protests during the 1964 primary season.[116]

The Goldwater campaign's pioneering efforts in the area of direct-mail fundraising also contributed significantly to the moderates' defeat. This revolutionary means of raising campaign contributions directly from voters gave the GOP right wing's candidate much more money than in previous years at a time when expensive television advertising was becoming more important in determining election outcomes. This greater ability of the right to raise money when compared with the party's moderate wing also reflected the increasing wealth of the emerging Sunbelt, where support for Goldwater was strongest, and the economic decline of Modern Republican strongholds in the industrial northeast and midwest. The success of the Goldwater campaign in raising money also helped intimidate even more those Republican officeholders who feared retaliation if they openly opposed Goldwater's candidacy.[117]

Changing conditions, both foreign and domestic, also tipped the balance against the GOP moderates in 1964. The success of the Cuban revolution, the shift in power in the UN General Assembly toward emerging Third World countries, the spread of communism there, Soviet advances in rocket and satellite technology, and a growing fear on the right that arms control agreements such as the Nuclear Test Ban Treaty could turn out to be a trap if the Soviets cheated increased conservatives' sense that America was endangered. So, too, in a different way, did growing inflation and foreign competition, in manufacturing especially. These related trends, which business executives recognized sooner and understood better than most other Americans, posed a serious long-term threat to the health of the nation's economy by the mid-1960s. As a direct result, many businessmen began responding much more positively and energetically to the far right's calls to get rid of unions and reduce federal government regulating, spending, and taxing. Many conservative people became even more so at that time in response to greater Supreme Court activism, rising crime, and the more general decline in traditional morality. Kennedy and Johnson's push to expand the federal government's role in society, especially their efforts to dismantle Jim Crow, also increased conservatives' concerns about centralized government power. What they saw as the news media's irresponsible and unfair reporting of these new developments also provoked them. These various changes in social conditions helped New Right Republicans seize the intellectual initiative within the GOP in 1964 as the policy prescriptions offered by moderates such as Larson appeared to be steadily less relevant and effective.[118]

All of these factors combined to put the New Right's candidate over the top at the 1964 Republican National Convention, to Larson's great dismay. With

Goldwater's nomination on July 15th, whatever future Larson's "progress-sharing" and "do it through the UN" policies might have had in the mid-1960s disappeared. Goldwater made that very clear in his nomination acceptance address the next day, which directly contradicted not only those policy proposals but Larson's more basic political commitments as well. In the same San Francisco convention hall in which Dwight Eisenhower had accepted his party's renomination for president eight years earlier, Goldwater pointedly told GOP convention delegates and Republicans watching via television across the country that "our people have followed false prophets" and pledged to return to "proven ways." Perhaps most galling, Goldwater used the occasion to attack moderation itself. In a thinly veiled slap at the Modern Republicans, Goldwater told his listeners to "let our Republicanism, so focused and so dedicated, not be made fuzzy and futile by unthinking and stupid labels. Those who do not care for our cause we do not expect to enter our ranks in any case. *I would remind you that extremism in the defense of liberty is no vice! And let me remind you also that moderation in the pursuit of justice is no virtue!*"[119]

Modern Republicans responded with understandable outrage. Larson, at home in North Carolina, watched as much of the speech as he could stand before stalking out of the room. Goldwater's remarks made Larson so angry that he spent most of the next few days in his woodshop, working off the negative emotional energy by making a baby-changing table for his daughter's new child. Dwight Eisenhower, for his part, publicly labeled the speech an offense to "the whole American system."[120] Richard Nixon, who had made the introductory remarks prior to the address, described his reaction more simply. He said the speech made him feel "almost physically sick."[121]

Goldwater's explicit rejection of Modern Republicanism prompted Larson to do something that six months earlier would have seemed inconceivable, which was to endorse Lyndon Johnson's bid for a four-year term as president in his own right. Less than three weeks after the GOP convention ended, Larson expressed that decision to his former OPA colleague John Kenneth Galbraith, who passed this news along to Johnson. Still upset with Johnson over the USIA hearings ambush, however, and doubtful of his competence to be president, in the area of foreign policy especially, Larson avoided an active role in the fall campaign. He did agree to serve on a panel of foreign policy experts that Johnson organized in September 1964 to give him advice on major international problems, a commitment that had the intended effect of identifying Larson with the administration. He also wrote a short letter to the president endorsing his re-election that was released to the press on September 19th.[122]

The most Larson would do on behalf of Johnson's presidential campaign, though, was to give a single speech in Raleigh, North Carolina, endorsing the Democratic national ticket. Even that came relatively late—on October 21st—and consisted mostly of attacks on Goldwater's stands on the issues rather than support for Johnson's candidacy. Larson's lack of enthusiasm for the presidential candidate he found himself compelled to endorse that year manifested itself in another way as well. His speech at Raleigh praised Johnson's running mate, Minnesota senator Hubert Humphrey (for his efforts to promote arms control, disarmament and the United Nations) more than it did the president. For this act of principle, Larson received a telegram from the local Republican organization urging him to change his party registration to Democrat.[123]

Rather than spend his time campaigning for a Democratic presidential candidate he did not really trust, Larson instead concentrated his energies that fall on a crusade against extreme right-wing propaganda groups, most notably the John Birch Society. On September 22nd, he announced the formation of a new group with that goal called the National Council for Civic Responsibility. The council's eighty members included former cabinet members, governors, union heads, educators, and scientists who lent their names to this effort to expose the errors in the material then being circulated by far-right groups. At a press conference in New York City, Larson explained that the Public Affairs Institute in Washington, a nonprofit educational organization, would provide funds to the council. It would use those resources to issue books and other printed material that documented the false statements coming from far-right groups. Larson noted that radio and television programs from the far right numbered 7,000 per week by then at an estimated cost of $10 million a year. One of the first efforts of the council to combat this wave of propaganda was the publication of three books that documented in detail the nature of far-right groups and their alarmist, false, and often bigoted assertions.[124]

Although the Council on Civic Responsibility was an avowedly nonpartisan organization that took no stand on the 1964 presidential campaign, the two were nonetheless related because of Barry Goldwater's unwillingness to disavow support from extreme right-wing groups, even if he disagreed with some of their stands and methods. As a result, such groups strongly supported Goldwater's candidacy, which tended to merge it with them in the minds of many Americans. For these reasons and others, Larson felt personally vindicated by Goldwater's crushing defeat on November 3rd. In the face of a very vigorous challenge, moderation had prevailed, or so Larson thought at the time.[125]

In hindsight, however, the outcome of the 1964 election appears to have been much more ambiguous. Although Goldwater did lose badly, in the process dealing a blow to the far-right groups that backed him, the magnitude of his defeat stemmed in no small part from the Arizona senator's angry speech to the GOP convention and poorly organized fall campaign. New Right spokesman Ronald Reagan made Goldwaterite conservatism's appeal clear to the most perceptive observers during 1964 by giving effective speeches on the GOP candidate's behalf in a calmer, friendlier manner. Even more important, Goldwater's nomination had brought about a decisive shift in power within the GOP that year from the party's moderate wing to its more conservative one. Although their candidate was soundly beaten in 1964, New Right Republicans achieved a much more lasting increase in influence within the party's high councils. More than anything else, the outcome of the 1964 presidential election signaled an increasing polarization of American politics and society. That trend would soon push Arthur Larson and people like him toward the margins of public life. By the end of 1964, moderate conservatism of the sort he favored had clearly gone into decline.[126]

CHAPTER ELEVEN

Victories and Defeats

As 1965 OPENED, Larson busied himself with his new venture to expose the falsehoods and misconduct of far-right groups. Although he was working on other causes, his role as head of the National Council on Civic Responsibility made its efforts a very high priority that year. The council had grown quickly during the last few months of 1964, from an initial roster of eighty prominent Americans to about 300. This kind of backing, which included people from many fields and professions, lent substance to the council's attacks on extreme conservative groups, especially the John Birch Society. Larson also aided this cause by prodding the more respectable members of the New Right to break with the Birchers. In a debate with William F. Buckley, Jr., on April 30th, Larson reminded him that the GOP's recent embrace of extreme conservatism had ended in electoral disaster. Although the extent to which Larson's efforts moved Buckley and other like-minded conservatives to act against the John Birch Society remains unclear, act they certainly did. In the October 19, 1965, issue of Buckley's *National Review*, columnists James Burnham and Frank Meyer denounced the Birchers, dealing their organization a devastating blow. Buckley also chose to publish in that issue many of the angry letters he had received from Birchers in the past, the tone and substance of which reinforced the view of that group as extreme to the point of irrationality. From that point onward, the John Birch Society and other similar groups declined steadily in visibility and influ-ence, to Larson's great relief.[1]

The quest to create a public health insurance program for the elderly, something Larson had long supported, also achieved a real breakthrough in 1965. Goldwater's disastrous defeat the previous November had led to the election of so many liberal Democrats to Congress that the enactment of Medicare was finally possible. Larson served on two advisory panels during the mid-1960s that helped shape Medicare legislation. The first, the National Committee on Health Care of the Aging, was explicitly nonpartisan and private. Organized by two influential senators, Republican Jacob Javits of New York and Democrat Clinton Anderson of New Mexico, the Javits Committee, as it became known, carefully prepared a revised version of the Medicare plans Congress had earlier voted down. Larson felt at home with the group, in part because its members included Marion Folsom and Arthur Flemming (its chair), both of whom had served in the Eisenhower administration as secretary of health, education and welfare. Larson also liked the Javits Committee because it included members drawn from the medical profession, hospitals, the insurance industry, and other interested groups, who approached the Medicare issue in a calm, thoughtful way.[2]

Under Arthur Flemming's capable leadership, the Javits Committee held several daylong meetings to develop a report on the entire Medicare issue. Larson described the outcome of this effort as "a rather detailed, quite sophisticated report which went down the line for medicare, but with a lot of the troublesome, controversial sub-issues dealt with I think with more painstaking and professional care than they were apt to get in the typical public discussion."[3] The report met with a very favorable response from the media when it appeared in November 1963, Larson later remembered, and helped reorient the Medicare debate away from whether there should be such a program to what form it should take.[4]

Larson drew upon his experience with the Javits Committee in serving on a second Medicare-related group, the 1965 Advisory Council on Social Security. Congress created this body to study the Social Security system and develop specific legislative proposals in the event reforms appeared necessary. Headed by Social Security commissioner Robert M. Ball, the council's thirteen members included experts drawn from all the relevant fields and groups save for the still-recalcitrant American Medical Association. The council turned to the thorny Medicare issue last, but out of many meetings came a concrete Medicare proposal that won almost unanimous support on all of its key features. The council promptly submitted its Medicare plan to Congress, which passed it that summer in a somewhat modified form.[5]

Larson disagreed strongly with only two aspects of the council's final Medicare proposal and the Medicare Act itself. The first had to do with the failure to insure those with total permanent disabilities. In keeping with his overall theory of income insurance, Larson believed that someone who had become completely and permanently disabled would likely not be able to afford the cost of unusual medical expenses and would likely incur them. For those reasons, Larson firmly believed, the completely and permanently disabled deserved the same kind of public health insurance that the elderly would receive under Medicare. Larson's second dispute with Medicare as it emerged in 1965 concerned the extent of its insurance. He would have gone farther than the council and Congress ultimately did by providing Medicare recipients with insurance not only for the cost of hospitalization but for surgical and medical costs as well.[6]

Despite these disagreements, Larson took great satisfaction from the creation of Medicare in 1965. It marked the most significant step in many years toward a more comprehensive system of social insurance. That Modern Republicans had played a noteworthy part in bringing about Medicare's enactment also pleased him greatly. Both the Medicare Act and the way it came into being afforded clear evidence that the ideas to which he had devoted so much of his professional life continued to exert a very real influence.[7]

Larson also took pride in the advances the nation made during the middle and late 1960s in dismantling the legal basis of racial segregation. In a speech in Louisville, Kentucky, on December 1, 1964, Larson focused on the foreign policy implications of the civil rights issue. "International Implications of Civil Rights in America" is notable chiefly for its emphasis on persuading conservatives to comply with the Supreme Court's school desegregation decisions and the Civil Rights Act of 1964, which Congress had passed the previous summer.[8]

He argued that further resistance to the ongoing changes in American law and life regarding race would aid the international communist movement in the largely nonwhite Third World. This situation required the United States to pursue two specific courses of action, Larson said. First, the nation needed to avoid even the appearance of support for colonial governments in the Third World. In order to escape that taint, he said, the U.S. government should work within the framework of the United Nations in dealing with such ongoing disputes as the civil war in the Congo and the conflict in Vietnam. And second, Larson contended, the United States needed "to assume vigorous and conspicuous leadership of the world movement for human and civil rights."[9] The most obvious way to do that was "to set the best possible example in the way we handle our own racial and human rights problems."[10]

Four years later, Larson returned to the theme of American progress in the area of civil rights when he gave a series of lectures on that topic at the University of Wisconsin Law School's centennial observance. In "The New Law of Race Relations," he argued that the time had come to consider race relations law as a distinctive area within the law school curriculum and the realm of legal scholarship. He pointed to the advent of workers' compensation as a distinct legal field in response to changing social conditions and argued that since 1954 something similar had happened in the area of race relations. The change there had been so far-reaching as to make the issue of race relations "the most important domestic issue on the American scene."[11] Thus, it was fitting that race relations should henceforth become a field of law unto itself rather than just an adjunct of constitutional law.[12]

Although the bulk of Larson's Wisconsin lectures consisted of a very detailed discussion of the various components of race relations law, toward the end he made some more general and very revealing comments about what he believed law could do to improve race relations in America. He characteristically rejected the views of the most extreme on the left and right that law could not bring about constructive change in this area. In a thinly veiled criticism of Eisenhower's views on that subject, Larson explained why he thought the more right-wing view of the law's limitations in this area made no more sense than that of the black militants who had dismissed legal changes in race relations law as worthless: "As so often happens in respect to extremist views, the same low opinion of the rule of law has often, and indeed much earlier, been voiced by traditionalists. In their case it takes the form of the cliché that changes in race relations cannot be brought about by laws but only by changes in the 'hearts and minds of men.'"[13]

Larson explained that this idea had done a great deal of damage because it had influenced the Supreme Court's interpretation of the equal protection clause of the Fourteenth Amendment. In the landmark *Plessy v. Ferguson* decision, he said, which had established the separate-but-equal rule in American life for sixty years, this very limited sense of what the law could accomplish had overcome ample legal authority in support of a ruling against such segregation. In Larson's words, "the majority . . . suggested that it was the problem of control of conduct by law that was decisive" in upholding the separate-but-equal policy in public transportation.[14] The fundamental problem with the Court's ruling in *Plessy,* he argued, was that it gave the force of law to a race relations system that prevented the needed changes in hearts and minds.[15]

Having dismissed the notion that law could not overcome prejudice, Larson proceeded to attack another extreme view, the idea that once antidiscrimination statutes and judicial decisions had been placed on the books, the struggle for equality was essentially won. The ability of such statutes and decisions to bring about meaningful changes in behavior depended, he said, on a variety of factors: "How strong and ingrained and widespread the opposition is to the ordained line of conduct, and to what extent the opposition to the legal norm is the result of emotion, ingrained bias, economic considerations, fear of loss of political power, and other factors. It will also depend on the character of the sanctions or incentives adopted to secure compliance with the law."[16]

Larson stoutly rejected the notion that there were areas of race relations law where popular attitudes in favor of discrimination were so strong as to render legislation pointless. He suggested instead that failure to make more headway in desegregating schools, housing, and employment stemmed from the fact that only weak sanctions had thus far been used to combat those very serious problems. Using stronger sanctions would, he concluded, bring about the changes in law that new civil rights laws and court rulings had promised.[17]

During the second half of the 1960s, Larson's expansive sense of the possible also led him to continue championing the cause of arms control and to witness another significant victory in an area of special concern to him. The specific issue was the effort to negotiate an international agreement that would limit the spread of nuclear weapons technology. After the U.S. Senate adopted a resolution in favor of negotiating such an agreement by a vote of 84 to 0 on May 17, 1966, Larson became actively involved in trying to bring it about. He helped organize and agreed to chair a new lobbying organization called the Educational Committee to Halt Atomic Weapons Spread. Like the National Council for Civic Responsibility, from which Larson evidently drew most of this new group's members, it was essentially a "name" committee. Approximately 300 distinguished Americans signed a statement urging President Johnson to move forward with the negotiation of a nuclear nonproliferation treaty through the United Nations. Larson, in his capacity as chairman of the committee, transmitted this document to the White House in September 1966, thus beginning a two-year campaign to build support for such an agreement.[18]

Larson's specific efforts in that regard fell into two main areas. First, he used the access to Johnson that came with membership on his panel of outside foreign policy consultants to press for postponing further underground nuclear weapons testing, lest it interfere with progress toward such an agreement. Believing that a planned underground test might disrupt the increasing momentum overseas in favor of a nonproliferation treaty, Larson firmly expressed his opposition to the test, which was code-named Cabriolet, in early 1967. Concerned about the possibility Larson had raised and about how such a test might affect other ongoing efforts at diplomacy, Johnson decided to postpone Cabriolet for a year, during which nonproliferation treaty negotiations moved forward steadily. By the time the test finally took place on January 26, 1968, the momentum in favor of the treaty had grown so strong that no disruption occurred as a result.[19]

Larson's other contribution to this cause was to push for it in his published writings. He made a strong case for quick action on a nonproliferation agreement in a *Saturday Review* article that appeared the week of October 7, 1967. Larson also wrote a booklet entitled *Questions and Answers on the Spread of Nuclear Weapons,* which his center at Duke published in the spring of 1968. Widely distributed prior to the UN General Assembly debate on the proposed nuclear nonproliferation treaty, the booklet helped educate the American public about the reasons to support that pact.[20]

To Larson's gratification, the General Assembly approved the agreement on June 12th of that year and the U.S. Senate formally ratified it by a vote of 83 to 15 on March 13, 1969. One year later, the agreement, having gained the requisite amount of support by other nations, took effect, thereby rewarding his efforts and those of many others to achieve that goal. Although a less than fully effective means of preventing the spread of nuclear weapons technology, the treaty did greatly slow that process, thus giving the nations of the world valuable time to cope with the consequences of proliferation.[21]

In addition to these specific achievements were others that he aided to a lesser degree. The quintessential organization man, he lent his name and sometimes his energies to many other worthwhile causes and in so doing demonstrated his openness to the kinds of changes at work in American society. One notable example of Larson's flexibility came in January 1964, when he agreed to serve on the sixteen-person Commission on the Status Of Women appointed by North Carolina governor Terry Sanford. This body, headed by Duke history professor Anne Firor, followed up on the work of the President's Commission on the Status of Women that John F. Kennedy had established by executive order in December 1961. The North Carolina commission, like those established around the same time in forty-eight other states, aided in documenting women's unequal status. In addition, the North Carolina commission, at Governor Sanford's request, developed a plan of action for reforming state laws in the areas of employment, legal and property rights, family relations, education, vocational training, welfare, and day care. This kind of activity by the states contributed significantly both to a revival of feminism and changes in women's status during the latter half of the 1960s.[22]

All of Larson's accomplishments then were overshadowed, however, by other, more fundamental defeats. His campaign for world peace through law had stalled by 1964, something so clear even to him that Larson decided to drop the word "World" from the name of his center at Duke that year. Henceforth his think tank would be known simply as the Rule of Law Center and would expand its activities to include domestic as well as foreign policy issues.[23]

Larson hoped to keep pushing for his world rule of law program, but the Johnson administration's actions with regard to the Dominican Republic and Vietnam during 1965 killed whatever chance remained for the success of that cause. When a coup took place in the Dominican Republic on April 24, 1965, the new leader, Juan Bosch, failed to establish control. Fearful that the disorder there might pave the way for a Communist takeover, Johnson sent in 14,000 Marines on April 28th to overthrow Bosch and stabilize the situation. Although a popular move with Americans and successful in the narrow sense that it replaced Bosch with a more moderate ruler named Joaquin Balaguer, Johnson's action deeply offended Larson. To him, the Dominican intervention was even more illegal than the Bay of Pigs invasion. The Kennedy administration had at least tried to preserve the outward appearance that the Bay of Pigs intervention was a military action conducted by exiled Cuban nationals. The Dominican action, on the other hand, featured uniformed members of the U.S. military overthrowing another nation's government. Larson also strongly objected, as did many other experts, to Johnson's utter disregard for the feelings and legal rights of the other nations in the Western hemisphere. In marked contrast with the Kennedy administration's conduct during the Cuban missile crisis, Johnson refused to consult with the Organization of American States before taking military action against the Dominican government.[24]

Larson blasted the U.S. military intervention in the Dominican Republic in an article published nineteen months later in *The Progressive*. There he called Johnson's action and the earlier Bay of Pigs invasion "stark examples of flouting of law."[25] Larson argued that the Dominican intervention was not only illegal but counterproductive because it had increased the credibility and popularity of communist movements in Latin America. He stoutly rejected the U.S. State Department's view that for the United States to have refrained from acting would have produced an even less desirable outcome—that is, a communist takeover of the Dominican Republic.[26]

In a crucial part of his critique, Larson rejected the analogy, so often made in official Johnson administration circles, between the Dominican Republic and Cuba. He pointed out that the Cuban revolution had come about as the result of a long-term, well-organized buildup of revolutionary military force that proceeded to seize power in a methodical fashion. In the Dominican Republic, the situation was very different. The maxim most applicable to this disgraceful episode, Larson argued forcefully, was that "the road to ruin is paved with false analogies."[27]

As discouraging as all of this was to Larson, the Johnson administration's handling of the Vietnam issue bothered him much more. Deeply disappointed by what he perceived as a lack of direction in foreign affairs generally and with regard to Vietnam in particular during Johnson's first year as president, Larson decided to write something substantial that argued for a new approach. As he had when working on *A Republican Looks at His Party*, Larson sought the assistance of his brother Don, a political scientist who had recently returned from Pakistan, where he had been teaching courses in public administration at the University of the Panjab in Lahore. The fruits of their joint effort appeared early in May 1965 as a booklet entitled *Vietnam and Beyond: A New American Foreign Policy and Program*.[28]

This forty-two page paperback made the case for cutting back the policy of attempting to contain the spread of communism everywhere in the world. The Larson brothers argued that the most basic flaw in that policy was the way it prevented a judicious weighing of the costs and benefits associated with American military intervention in specific situations. The Larsons also criticized the current approach to containment for making American conduct too predictably reactive, which tended to yield the initiative to the nation's communist rivals. Finally, the Larsons faulted the existing version of the containment policy on purely practical grounds. In their words, "The most serious defect in the policy is that it is not working."[29]

The Larson brothers argued instead for what they called a policy of "selective containment," by which they meant guaranteeing full aid and protection to every foreign land "whose protection would serve the basic self-interest of the United States and would promote the type of world we seek to foster." The key difference between this formulation of containment and the existing one, the Larsons explained, had to do with the degree of weight accorded to the danger of the "physical spread of communist influence." Under the existing version of containment, that consideration outweighed all others, but under a policy of selective containment, that danger would be only one major factor to be considered among other relevant ones.[30]

The Larsons proposed the application of five specific tests in deciding whether to commit American military force to the defense of a foreign land: one, the present and future importance of the area to the U.S. defense of the noncommunist world; two, the economic viability of the area in question; three, the extent to which the area involved was committed not just to anticommunism but also to freedom in the American sense; four, the extent to which the area involved had been associated with the United States historically, traditionally, and legally in the pursuit of common goals; and five, the extent to which the area in question would constitute an actual burden to the communist world if communists came to power there.[31]

Aware that some might challenge such an approach for, in effect, abandoning large parts of the world to communist domination, risking the nation's prestige overseas, or retreating into isolationism, the Larsons offered some interesting responses to those kinds of objections. They stoutly rejected the notion the fates of all foreign lands were inextricably linked, as the so-called domino theory suggested. Calling that theory "a wholly unproved hypothesis," the Larsons argued instead that the United States could write off Vietnam as a hopeless cause without bringing about the loss of all of Southeast Asia to the communists.[32] The key here, the Larsons contended, was to make very clear what criteria the United States had used in reaching its decision about Vietnam and to apply those criteria consistently elsewhere. One of the most important factors was the attitude of the population in the country at stake. They approvingly quoted George Kennan's testimony before a House foreign affairs subcommittee on March 11, 1956, that the only foreign peoples for whom American economic and military assistance would truly make a difference were those already strongly committed to trying to defend themselves against communist subversion.[33]

To the charge that a more selective approach to containment might diminish American standing in the world, the Larsons replied that the current approach also carried that risk, especially with respect to Vietnam. The way to make such a change in policy without losing prestige and support abroad was to explain and execute the new approach in a clear, effective, and consistent fashion.[34]

Finally, the Larsons argued that selective containment would not constitute a kind of neo-isolationism because such a policy would make American efforts overseas more productive and free up wasted resources for new, more promising initiatives. In an interesting twist, the Larsons argued that the policy of trying to contain communism everywhere had led the United States in an isolationist direction because the country's foreign policymakers increasingly ignored the United Nations when it did not support American military intervention in the Third World. Italicizing this passage so as to give it the greatest possible emphasis, the Larsons tartly observed that "*if there is any real 'neo-isolationism,' it is that of 'go-it-alone' unilateral involvement, isolating ourselves from the world community body expressly created to handle these peacekeeping problems by joint action.*"[35]

The Larson brothers moved on to a discussion of the nature of the American commitment in Vietnam. The need for clearer understanding of that key issue appeared very urgent in the spring of 1965, they explained, because the "point of no return" in terms of a major American military intervention in Vietnam seemed to be approaching rapidly. Noting that President Johnson had repeatedly argued that the need to honor the commitments the U.S. government had made to the government of South Vietnam since 1954 was leading him to increase American military involvement there greatly, the Larsons reviewed the diplomatic and historical record to make clear what those commitments were.[36]

They began by reminding readers that Johnson had based his statements about American commitments to South Vietnam on an October 1, 1954, letter from Eisenhower to Ngo Dinh Diem, then president of South Vietnam, and on the terms of the Southeast Asia Collective Defense (SEATO) Treaty and Protocol ratified in February 1955. They quoted extensively from the Eisenhower letter, whose highly tentative terms stressed hopes for South Vietnam's future, in order to demonstrate that one could not fairly characterize anything in it as an American commitment to guarantee South Vietnam's security. The letter did commit the United States to a modest amount of economic and military assistance, but even that pledge was expressed in conditional terms that required the South Vietnamese government to maintain a strong state capable of resisting communist aggression and to make "needed reforms."[37]

The nature and amount of the aid given during Eisenhower's administration confirmed this characterization of the relationship between the United States and South Vietnam then, the Larsons argued. They noted that less than one-fourth of the assistance given South Vietnam during Eisenhower's presidency had been classified as military; the rest was economic. The small size of the military component could be seen in the announcement during Eisenhower's last year as president that the group of American military advisors in Vietnam would increase from 327 to 685. Thus, the Larsons concluded, "The nearest thing to a commitment at this stage was an indicated willingness, subject to some stiff (and as yet unsatisfied) conditions and understandings, to provide economic and technical assistance, including military advisers, material and training."[38]

The Larsons argued forcefully that the United States had no obligation to South Vietnam (or anyone else) under the SEATO treaty to use American forces in the defense of that country. They offered three specific reasons in support of this view. First, they argued that the events calling for direct action set forth in the treaty had not occurred. They quoted as support for that interpretation the statements of treaty author John Foster Dulles, who had observed that American military intervention in Indochina pursuant to the SEATO treaty would depend upon, among other things, evidence of concern by the United Nations and a collective effort by the SEATO powers, neither of which had materialized thus far. Second, the Larsons argued that the SEATO powers had not even agreed on what measures to take with respect to the Vietnam situation, let alone act jointly in support of such steps. Third, the Larsons continued, any SEATO obligation to defend South Vietnam was inoperative as long as the other treaty signers failed to recognize such a duty.[39]

The Larsons buttressed this view of what the United States had promised South Vietnam by highlighting President Kennedy's comment on the subject in the course of a televised interview on September 2, 1963. They quoted Kennedy's response to a question from CBS newsman Walter Cronkite: "In the final analysis, it is their [the South Vietnamese people's] war. They are the ones who have to win it or lose it. We can help them, we can give them equipment, we can send our men out there as advisers, but they have to win it—the people of Vietnam—against the Communists."[40] This statement, the Larsons argued, confirmed the limited nature of Kennedy's conception of the American obligation to South Vietnam.

The Larsons also contended that none of the major documents, speeches, press conferences, or communiqués dealing with the relationship of the United States with South Vietnam used the word "commitment" until Johnson became president. The Larsons conceded that Special Assistant to the President for National Security Affairs McGeorge Bundy had used the word in a statement issued on September 30, 1963, but dismissed this as having "no significance" because "a Special Assistant to the President has no authority to commit anybody in his own right." Only with the advent of the Johnson administration had words such as "commitment," "obligation," and "pledge" begun to appear in official statements made by the president and the secretary of defense.[41]

Johnson and his aides had compounded this error, the Larsons argued, by claiming that such "pledges" had been given by the two previous administrations and that the nation would dishonor itself if it reneged on those commitments. They argued that "what President Johnson has done is to convert imperceptibly a diplomatic statement on policy based ultimately on considerations of American security, into an unconditional moral obligation to another country, suffused with overtones of national integrity and honor."[42]

The trouble with this approach, the Larsons added, was that repeated

Johnson administration statements that changing course in Vietnam would bring dishonor to the United States had the effect of robbing the nation of flexibility with respect to future policy changes on that issue. Calling such flexibility "the prime essential of international relations," the Larsons contended that the more sophisticated members of the world community would not interpret a change in American policy toward Vietnam as dishonorable or cowardly, assuming such a change was based on hardheaded considerations of national interest. Johnson's strategy, however, had made certain that the United States would look very foolish to outside observers if it made such a change in policy at some future time.[43]

The Larsons argued that the one clear obligation was to refer the entire matter to the UN Security Council, in accordance with Article 37 of the UN Charter. The situation in South Vietnam clearly constituted a threat to peace, which the parties involved had been unable to resolve by themselves. In such a situation, Article 37 required member nations to refer such a dispute to the Security Council. If there was a danger of dishonor to America, it lay in failing to abide by this obligation, which the Larsons characterized as "unconditional, overriding, peremptory—and real."[44]

Toward the end of *Vietnam and Beyond*, the Larsons discussed how best to withdraw from the Vietnam War honorably. First, they argued that the need for an alternative to the pattern of ever-increasing military involvement was "urgent in the extreme" in the spring of 1965. In an especially farsighted passage, they observed that "the people of the United States do not want to become bogged down in what Secretary [of State Dean] Rusk has called a 'mean, dirty war' on the Asiatic mainland—a war that is becoming meaner and dirtier than any we have ever become embroiled in, what with news of napalm, nauseous gas, defoliation of forests, burning of villages, and mistaken killing of one's own troops increasingly filling our [news]papers."[45] The two most disturbing consequences of this situation were the downgrading of the legal systems established earlier to handle peacekeeping and the danger the conflict posed to détente between the United States and the Soviet Union.[46]

The saddest aspect of American military involvement in Vietnam, the Larsons added, lay in the lack of considered judgment behind it. Rather than the result of conscious planning, escalation in Vietnam had come about in a haphazard fashion that gradually transformed the original U.S. policy into something very different. And while U.S. policymakers had "nibbled our way into this dangerous mess," those same decision makers "cannot nibble our way out."[47]

The only way to accomplish that goal was by a series of bold actions. First, the United States should convene a meeting of the SEATO powers and ask them to develop a joint policy for action with respect to Vietnam. If the other SEATO powers refused to assume some of the responsibility for military action there, as seemed likely, that treaty would not obligate the United States to shoulder such responsibility itself. Instead, the United States should next refer the matter to the UN Security Council. The Larsons conceded that the Soviet Union might veto any UN peacekeeping operation in Vietnam, and they argued that the United States should then call for a special session of the UN General Assembly to address the Vietnam situation. Acknowledging that the General Assembly at that time was in a state of virtual paralysis due to disputes over previous peacekeeping operations, most notably in the Congo, the Larsons urged the Johnson administration to strike a deal with the countries that had balked at paying their peacekeeping assessments. The basic terms of such a bargain would be American support for a UN agreement to forgive the failure of those nations to pay their share of previous peacekeeping operations in return for these nations' support of American efforts to resolve the Vietnam situation through the General Assembly.[48]

The analysis presented in *Vietnam and Beyond* defies easy evaluation. The Larsons' critique of the trend toward mounting military involvement and its consequences and the Johnson administration's dishonesty in suggesting that the United States had no other choice deserves high praise. The Larsons deserve criticism, however, for at times overstating their case, especially with respect to the idea that the two previous administrations would have disagreed with Johnson's reasoning. The changing nature of the situation in South Vietnam from 1954 through 1965 made such comparisons suspect. This was especially true of the Larsons' suggestion that President Kennedy would, had he lived, have taken a different course in Vietnam. They accurately quoted his reply to Walter Cronkite's question about Vietnam but failed to note that at other times during Kennedy's presidency he had made more interventionist-sounding remarks, including in the speech he was to give in Dallas on the day he died. The stance of Johnson's immediate predecessor on the Vietnam issue was not the clear and firm one the Larsons had implied but rather a study in ambiguity. A more careful and complete use of the historical record in this regard would have led the Larsons to argue merely that Kennedy's Vietnam policy had sought, above all else, to retain flexibility regarding future steps there, an objective Johnson had essentially abandoned.[49]

Vietnam and Beyond can also be faulted for its specific prescription with respect to the Vietnam issue. The likelihood that the United Nations would have assumed a peacekeeping role there in 1965 seems low. Indeed, unhappiness among some leading UN members, most notably France and the Soviet Union, about earlier peacekeeping operations was what had precipitated the very serious funding dispute that had almost paralyzed the General Assembly by the spring of that year. Negotiations between the United States and other major powers did manage to resolve the controversy by the end of 1965, but only by conceding, in effect, that the earlier policy of trying to expand the UN's function considerably beyond the facilitation of discussion and negotiation should be abandoned. Thus, the Larsons' specific suggestion about how best to handle the Vietnam issue in 1965 appears to have been unworkable.[50]

Rather than address in detail the possibility that the appeal to the UN might not work, *Vietnam and Beyond* took no clear stance on what the United States ought to do in that case and ignored the issue of what having tried and failed at the UN would mean for American policy toward Vietnam thereafter. The reason for those omissions was simple, Larson explained in his memoirs twenty-five years later. At the time *Vietnam and Beyond* was written, he did not believe that the United Nations would refuse to take on the Vietnam issue, because it had until then shouldered similarly difficult peacekeeping missions in Korea, the Suez, and the Congo.[51]

A sense of how difficult the choices would then become for the United States in Vietnam may also have inhibited the Larsons from addressing that possibility. Arthur Larson suggested in his memoirs that if the United Nations had refused to take jurisdiction over the Vietnam conflict in 1965, the United States ought to have withdrawn its forces on the theory that the UN's refusal to act would have absolved Americans of any obligation to contribute further to the defense of the government of South Vietnam. Such a conclusion would have been highly controversial and even explosive in 1965, and it did not appear anywhere in *Vietnam and Beyond*.[52]

That gap in the Larsons' analysis left it open to the following objection: if the United States went to the United Nations with the Vietnam issue and was rebuffed, the legality and acceptability of any subsequent unilateral moves by the United States government would thereby become much more suspect. The Larsons' decision to say nothing about that possibility and their argument that the UN might well assume jurisdiction over the Vietnam issue allowed hawkish critics to attack the Larsons' Vietnam policy prescription as ill considered and unrealistic.

Such was the response from Secretary of State Dean Rusk, who dismissed Larson's "do-it-through-the-UN" approach to the Vietnam conflict as utterly impractical. Rusk and Arthur Larson had first clashed over that idea back in the spring of 1962, when a delegation from the national board of the American Association for the United Nations had met with Rusk and other State Department officials to express concern about the Vietnam situation. The goal of this five-man delegation, which included Larson, was to urge that the facilities of the UN be used to deal with the Vietnam problem. Completely unsuccessful in persuading Rusk then, Larson decided to try again three years later. This time the discussion took place during a meeting of the foreign policy experts Johnson had appointed in the fall of 1964 to advise the administration. Johnson and his aides did not intend initially to meet with this group; instead, they wanted to solicit advice and receive suggestions from individual members with expertise on a particular issue. The administration's decision in the late winter and early spring of

1965 to escalate drastically American military involvement in Vietnam appears, however, to have persuaded Johnson, Rusk, and Defense Secretary Robert McNamara to call a meeting of the outside experts in the hope of enlisting their support for that planned action. The session took place in Rusk's office at the State Department on July 8th of that year, just as the massive scope of the military buildup Johnson and his aides intended in Vietnam had begun to be clear to interested observers.[53]

The intensity of Larson's belief in the need to use the United Nations to address the Vietnam conflict and his opposition to Johnson's decision to pursue a course of unilateral military action there instead appears vividly in Larson's memoirs. He described the July 8th encounter with Rusk and his aides as follows:

> I sensed this would probably be my last chance to say directly to the decision makers what I had been saying and writing since 1962, and perhaps I monopolized the conversation a bit too much. At lunch I was seated next to Rusk, and was keeping up my barrage for his benefit. At last the unflappable Rusk turned purple and shouted "Art, I'm not going to take Vietnam to the U.N. *just to please you*!" I observed that "pleasing me" had been for some time very low on the hierarchy of State Department motivations—and the tension relaxed somewhat. Needless to say, I was never called back as a consultant.[54]

The arguments made in *Vietnam and Beyond* failed to win the support of other prominent figures such as Eisenhower and Nixon, whom Larson tried to influence by sending them copies of the booklet. Eisenhower did, however, take the time and trouble to write two and a half single-spaced typed pages in response. This very revealing letter, dated May 18, 1965, and marked "personal and confidential," set forth in detail Eisenhower's views on the Larsons' analysis of the Vietnam issue. Eisenhower began by praising *Vietnam and Beyond* for "setting the record straight" about how the United States reached the point that it had with respect to Vietnam.[55] He then qualified that endorsement by observing that he disagreed with criticizing Johnson publicly for the steps he was taking to deal with the Vietnam issue. The reason for this, Eisenhower explained, was his view that in any international crisis the president must speak for all Americans because the Constitution placed upon him sole responsibility for conducting foreign relations. Accordingly, Eisenhower urged that any such criticism should be expressed directly and privately.[56]

Eisenhower also took issue with some of the most crucial parts of the Larsons' analysis. He pointed out that in discussing the domino theory, *Vietnam and Beyond* had not considered what the fall of South Vietnam would likely mean to its neighbors to the west, Cambodia and Laos, and to other nearby countries. Eisenhower revealed his belief in the domino theory: "In my opinion, their [Cambodia's and Laos's] fall would be the next thing to a certainty; after that Indonesia, already verging on Communism, would scarcely make a pretense of neutrality. What then would be the fate of Malaysia and Burma—even assuming that Thailand could hold out for a time?" The longer-term result, he added, would be to undermine the American position in the Philippines and Taiwan and even, eventually, Japan.[57]

For that reason, and "in the circumstances as of the spring of 1965," Eisenhower explained, "I must confess that I see no alternative to what the President is now doing." Eisenhower conceded the value of George Kennan's emphasis on giving economic and military aid to foreign peoples who actively sought to resist communism themselves but argued that the more pressing issue had to do with whether America's vital interests were at stake. Eisenhower observed that "in many ways I admire and respect George Kennan. But the advice (as to policy) that you quote from him is itself a generality. The big point is *where are our vital interests involved*? One such spot, in my opinion, is Vietnam."[58]

Eisenhower softened his criticism of *Vietnam and Beyond* toward the end of his letter by explaining that these observations were just random ones, written rapidly after what he confessed was "a hasty reading of your book."[59] Obviously wanting to spare Larson's feelings as much as possible, Eisenhower commented in a final paragraph that he agreed with some of the Larsons' recommendations regarding the fullest possible uses of SEATO and the UN, adding that he had "just wanted to say that problems of this kind are so complicated as to admit of no simple formula."[60]

The impact of the Larsons' analysis on other readers proved no more helpful. Richard Nixon wrote a brief, noncommittal thank-you note to Arthur Larson upon receiving a copy of *Vietnam and Beyond* but apparently never followed up with the more detailed comments Larson had invited. The *Saturday Review* gave the Larsons' arguments greater visibility by publishing the part of the booklet dealing with strategies for an honorable withdrawal as an article in the April 24, 1965, issue, but all to no avail. In the year *Vietnam and Beyond* appeared, the Johnson administration essentially Americanized the war in Vietnam by dispatching almost 200,000 U.S. soldiers there. The Larson brothers' commendable effort to head off that misguided act had failed.[61]

As the number of American soldiers in Vietnam climbed toward 400,000 over the course of 1966, Arthur Larson's alienation from Johnson's foreign policies grew commensurately. Disgusted by Johnson's aversion to multilateral approaches to resolving the Vietnam conflict, Larson decided to write a general condemnation of that aspect of the administration's record. This dissent appeared in two parts in the November and December 1966 issues of *The Progressive* magazine. These articles blasted Johnson's actions in Vietnam and argued that a resort to military force was characteristic of Johnson's entire approach to foreign policy.[62]

Not content to fight Johnson's policies by writing articles, Arthur Larson eagerly signed on to Michigan governor George Romney's emerging presidential campaign in the winter of 1967. The election results of the previous fall had revealed a strongly Republican trend across the country, which encouraged Larson in believing Romney could beat Johnson in the next presidential election. So, too, did the backing Romney received from GOP governors. Convinced that the large number of moderate GOP presidential contenders in 1964 had fragmented their wing of the party and opened the door to Goldwater's nomination, the GOP governors agreed that Romney should be the sole candidate from their ranks in 1968. New York's Nelson Rockefeller in particular played the leading role in brokering this December 1966 agreement to "let George do it." Determined to see a candidate from the party's moderate-to-liberal wing win the GOP presidential nomination the next time, Rockefeller also helped out by pledging financial support and lending some members of his own staff to advise Romney's fledgling campaign.[63]

Those encouraging developments and the basic congruence between Romney and Larson in background, temperament, and philosophy soon brought the two men together. Larson had first written Romney on November 11, 1966, to congratulate him for winning reelection as governor by a margin of over 500,000 votes. Larson also took the opportunity to inform Romney that "you have always been my first choice for the man to lead the Republican Party nationally."[64] Romney's friendly reply and news reports that he was looking for foreign policy advice inspired Larson to write again two months later, this time to offer his services to Romney's emerging presidential campaign. When Romney promptly accepted and invited Larson to come to East Lansing to participate in upcoming speechwriting sessions, he enthusiastically agreed to make the trip. On February 14, 1967, Larson flew in from Durham for two days of discussion and speechwriting with Romney and members of his campaign staff. The opportunity Larson had long awaited both for the country and himself had finally arrived.[65]

At that time, Romney was on the eve of his first major speaking tour to promote his presidential prospects. Officially billed as an exploratory trip rather than a campaign one, it would take him to Alaska and several of the Rocky Mountain states. Romney decided not to discuss Vietnam during this maiden effort, apparently because he had not yet worked out his own views on that tangled subject. Larson strongly supported that decision for many reasons. Among the most important of these, he explained in a letter to Romney, was the very fluid nature of the Vietnam situation at that time. What seemed to be a constructive stance on that issue in the winter of 1967 might appear positively misguided by general election day in 1968, should events in Vietnam change significantly in the interim. Thus the focus of this first major round of speechwriting was on other topics, most notably Romney's critique of Johnson's Great Society policies and his approach to foreign policy more generally.[66]

Larson had already made a contribution to clarifying Romney's stands in those areas by sending him copies of relevant speeches and articles he had written earlier. Romney had used Larson's term "the Great Façade" in a Lincoln Day speech in Louisville, Kentucky, that attacked Johnson's domestic policies. Larson had come up with this rubric to illustrate what he saw as the hollowness of Johnson's Great Society programs. In a January 20th memo to Romney that commented on a first draft of the Louisville speech, Larson explained what he meant by such terminology. The Great Society, he wrote, "reminds one of the façade of a typical western movie set, with showy store and shop fronts advertising groceries, hardware, beer and free lunch—but if you walk through the door you see only the empty desert sands stretching away in the distance."[67] Larson used the rest of this revealing memo to lay out the other main points he thought Romney should hit when criticizing Johnson's domestic policies. Larson emphasized at the outset that no one could dispute the good intentions behind the Great Society programs. The main objection to them, he wrote, was how poorly they had been administered. The other reason for calling the Great Society a "Great Façade," Larson explained, stemmed from what he believed to be Johnson's essentially opportunistic support for those programs. The proof of this could be seen, Larson added, in the way Johnson had begun to back away from them at the first signs of growing political opposition.[68]

Above and beyond these weaknesses in Johnson's Great Society programs, Larson continued, loomed a broader problem of administrative incompetence. He urged Romney to sound the theme that Lyndon Johnson and his aides "simply do not know how to run a government." Larson likened the Democratic Party in this regard to the Labour Party in England. Labour's program, he observed, was at times "closer to the hearts of the people" than that of the rival Conservatives, but even in those circumstances Labour did not always prevail because of the public's sense that the party could not govern effectively.[69]

The main reason for this problem of administrative incompetence in Washington had to do, Larson contended, with Johnson's refusal to delegate authority and allow the system of government to work through proper channels. A related theme that Romney should hit, Larson continued, was the country's trend toward "one-man government that violates our deepest democratic and constitutional traditions."[70] Larson argued that Johnson's policies and administrative approach were drawing power from state and local governments and concentrating it more and more in Washington, especially in the executive branch. As a result, the benefits of the system of separated powers and checks and balances were being lost. Even the decision to go to war in Vietnam, Larson noted, had essentially been Johnson's alone.[71]

In concluding this memo to Romney, Larson made two final points. First, he argued that Romney should point to his own record of effective administration and that of similar GOP governors in contrast to Johnson's poor one as president. Second, Larson urged Romney to contrast the Eisenhower administration's success in making and keeping the peace with the very different foreign policy record of most recent Democratic administrations. Aware that Republicans had shied away in the past from making that point directly, Larson advised Romney that it was "extremely delicate to handle" but nonetheless should be kept in mind.[72]

All the indications are that Romney and his staff found this memo's advice to be highly persuasive, and so it was. Despite a tendency at times toward overstatement, Larson's memo summed up with characteristic insight and clarity many of the biggest flaws in Johnson's presidency and policies. Romney showed he agreed by using the memo and related materials Larson had sent as the basis for three different speeches planned for delivery during the upcoming tour of western states. Romney also underscored his approval of what Larson had written by repeatedly telling him during the February 1967 visit that, as Larson noted in his memo book, "I was the most accomplished idea man and writer he knew of."[73]

Larson left East Lansing on February 16th in an upbeat mood, but the optimism inspired by two days of productive discussions and speechwriting soon diminished. That change stemmed not from any friction with Romney or his staff, with whom Larson had established a real rapport, but rather from the disappointing response to Romney's speaking tour in the West. Everywhere he went reporters hounded him with questions about Vietnam, which journalists understandably saw as the most pressing issue of the day. Romney had intended to postpone any discussion of that issue until later but lacked the self-discipline required to refrain from making off-the-cuff remarks about it. That tendency to shoot from the hip had not hurt Romney as governor due to the much narrower range of issues before him in that office, but campaigning for the presidency soon exposed that very serious flaw in his candidacy. Romney's confusing comments to reporters about Vietnam and, even more, his candid admission that he simply did not know yet what he would do about it took attention away from his attack on Johnson's other policies. By the time Romney returned to Michigan, the media covering his speaking tour had termed it a failure.[74]

Romney and his aides made a valiant effort to revive his candidacy by deciding he should give a major speech on Vietnam in the spring. They turned to Larson to write this address in the hope that it could lay to rest Romney's problems with the press and the public on that topic. Larson agreed to take on this critical task and returned to East Lansing at the end of March 1967 to compose the speech in consultation with Romney and his aides. Larson later recalled the instructions he received at the outset as follows:

> Romney briskly sketched out the problem: he must have a speech that unmistakably disavowed Johnson's Vietnam war policy, yet it could not be too "soft," and must take into account not only the hawkish views of many Republicans but indeed some earlier statements of Romney himself that were not exactly dovish. Over and over he hammered one point: the most disas-

trous outcome that could befall him would be for the speech to be called a "me-too" endorsement of Johnson's position.[75]

Larson also received guidance in the form of a first draft of the speech prepared by Romney speechwriter Jonathan Moore. That initial effort made the following three main points: Lyndon Johnson's original decision to escalate drastically American military involvement in Vietnam during 1965 had been a mistake, but once American forces had been committed to that degree, the United States needed to see the matter through to a satisfactory conclusion. The way to do this was to implement more effectively Johnson's middle course between all-out war and simply giving up.[76]

With all of those ideas whirling through his brain, Larson set to work on a new, more serviceable speech than Moore had produced. By writing more or less around the clock for two days Larson managed to produce a draft Romney and his aides liked. It began by listing the major arguments against further escalating American involvement, as the most hawkish critics of Johnson's Vietnam policy had begun demanding. Larson's draft pointed out the danger such a course of action could pose to American standing in the world, especially in the Third World. To use the full military power of the United States against a relatively weak Asian nation such as North Vietnam would allow the communists to paint Americans as "ruthless oppressors and colonialists—the very opposite of our traditional role in the world."[77] Larson also pointed out that the application of more American force against North Vietnam would likely be met with increased Chinese and Soviet involvement in the conflict. Thus, greater escalation would likely prove futile and even dangerous by increasing the risk of war between the United States and China, the Soviet Union, or both.[78]

The speech recounted the various errors that had led to the Vietnam mess in the first place and moved to the crucial issue of what to do next. The list of errors mostly restated ideas Larson had expressed earlier, but the passages dealing with what to do next showed how his thinking had evolved in response to changing circumstances. Agreeing with the premise that Johnson's decision to intervene militarily in a big way ruled out a simple withdrawal thereafter, Larson's draft called instead, as Moore's had, for a more effective prosecution of the war effort. The key passage on that point and, indeed, in the entire speech, read as follows:

> From what I have said up until now, I trust no one will conclude that my views on the past handling of Vietnam can be described as reflecting unqualified admiration. And so I think I can speak from a background like that of a very large number of Americans when I say that, however we may feel about how we became involved in Vietnam, *we must stay the course and see it through!* . . .
>
> Having put our hand to this job and carried it this far, we have an overwhelming obligation to complete it. Otherwise the security and safety of

> millions of people we set out to help will be far worse off than if we had never taken on the task in the first place.[79]

Larson's speech draft then discussed what might be done to wage the Vietnam War more effectively and argued that "a major increase in emphasis on the pacification program" aimed at Communist guerillas in the South, rather than more force against North Vietnam, would achieve the desired military result.[80]

This formulation of the Vietnam problem and its solution revealed how completely Johnson's policy had entrapped its moderate critics. Their sense of responsibility led them to support the heavy commitment of American military force in Vietnam once that step had been taken. Johnson's policy of escalation had turned would-be doves into hawks, just as he had intended. The basic problem with taking the stand enunciated in Larson's draft was that the same arguments he marshaled against using even more force also applied to the ongoing American military effort. That campaign, especially the bombing operation code-named Operation Rolling Thunder, was damaging U.S. standing abroad. And as American military involvement had increased, so, too, had support from China and the Soviet Union for North Vietnam, which suggested that U.S. military intervention in Vietnam was essentially an exercise in futility. More than anything else, Larson's draft signaled how difficult the task of staking out a sensible middle position on Vietnam had become by the spring of 1967.[81]

The subsequent fate of Larson's formulation also underscored the dilemma of moderate conservatives with respect to Vietnam policy. Romney decided that copies of Larson's draft should be sent to Eisenhower, Nelson Rockefeller, and former Federal Reserve Board chairman Marriner Eccles for their comments before Romney delivered the speech in Hartford, Connecticut, on April 7th. Larson agreed to carry a copy of the speech to Eisenhower and hurried out to his vacation home in Palm Desert, California, to meet with the former president on April 3rd. Eisenhower made a few minor but useful suggestions, which Larson dutifully jotted down, and then said of the draft "I think this is very good."[82] For a brief moment all seemed well, until Romney actually delivered the speech. To Larson's great surprise, it departed heavily from the version he had written and shown to Eisenhower. Gone was the list of mistakes that had led to American involvement in the first place. Also excised was the call for shifting from a focus on conventional warfare against North Vietnam to an emphasis on defeating the guerrillas in the South. Instead, Romney endorsed the existing policy of seeking conventional military victories against the North Vietnamese and the Communist guerrillas. The only really new idea in the speech was Romney's call for an amnesty in South Vietnam once the war had ended so that all factions could participate in governing the country thereafter. So closely did this statement parallel the Johnson administration's policy that the president and his aides actually hailed Romney's speech as an endorsement.[83]

The reason for this disastrous outcome stemmed from Nelson Rockefeller's vehement objections to the views contained in Larson's draft. A closet hawk, Rockefeller opposed the passages in the speech draft that argued against escalation. He also rejected the proposed shift in emphasis from conventional warfare against North Vietnam to efforts to "pacify" guerrillas in the South, apparently out of a belief that focusing on North Vietnam held the promise of a satisfactory military result. Rockefeller's strong objections to Larson's draft caused Romney to backtrack, in deference to Rockefeller's greater experience with foreign policy and, even more, one suspects, out of a sense that he could not afford to alienate so important a backer of his presidential candidacy. Whatever the precise weight accorded to those considerations, Larson felt their impact immediately and directly. After giving the newly revised Vietnam speech in Hartford, Romney never spoke to Larson again.[84]

His foray into GOP presidential politics having ended in frustration, Larson decided to avoid any further participation until the Republican National Convention chose a candidate in August 1968. The outcome there appeared uncertain until the first ballot ended, thanks to the lack of broad enthusiasm for any of the contenders. Romney's mishandling of the Vietnam issue and his inability to refrain from making ill-considered remarks to reporters soon took the bloom off his presidential prospects. The primary beneficiary of that development, Richard Nixon, saw his hopes for a comeback revive in the latter half of 1967. Even Nixon's success in the 1968 presidential primaries, however, stemmed more from a lack of strong opposition than from enthusiastic support among Republicans for his candidacy. Larson's attitude toward Nixon's campaign was instructive in this regard. Although an early backer of Nixon's candidacy in 1960, eight years later Larson politely declined the Nixon campaign's requests for an endorsement prior to the GOP convention. Doubts about Nixon's electability in 1968 and his vague statements about Vietnam left Larson unenthusiastic about the prospect of a second Nixon run for the White House.[85]

With Nixon's nomination on August 8th, Larson came around, as did so many other loyal, if doubting, Republicans. He had begun talking in early July to Nixon campaign officials about policies and potential Nixon administration appointees, and for a brief time that summer, the possibility of Larson's return to high office seemed bright. Nixon had established a big lead in the polls over his likely opponent that year, Vice President Hubert Humphrey, who had entered the race after Johnson withdrew on March 31st. Johnson's decision not to run again due to the intense opposition among many liberals and leftists to his Vietnam policy had greatly improved Nixon's chances of winning. Instead of running against an incumbent, Nixon found himself facing a Democratic Party in disarray. The disorderly and divisive Democratic convention that met in Chicago during the last week of August 1968 served only to confirm the impression in the minds of many voters that the party could not govern effectively. By the time the Democrats adjourned on August 30th, Nixon's return to high office, and Larson's as well, appeared highly likely.[86]

The publication of Larson's latest book two days later, however, ended his chance of a return to government service. A biography of the president Larson had served entitled *Eisenhower: The President Nobody Knew*, it drew upon Larson's notes of his experiences with its subject over the previous twelve years. In keeping with those experiences, the book depicted Eisenhower as a principled moderate who strongly disagreed with most of the views of the Republican Right. The book's disclosure that Eisenhower had privately opposed the U.S. Supreme Court's decision in the landmark school desegregation case made news by contradicting Eisenhower's own memoirs on that point. Larson's revelations of Eisenhower's doubts about Nixon's leadership abilities attracted much less attention in the media, because an earlier memoir by Eisenhower speechwriter Emmet Hughes had contained similar information. However, the timing of Larson's disclosures could not have been worse from the perspective of Nixon's staff. Just as their candidate entered the fall campaign, a new book had surfaced that revived older doubts about Nixon's fitness to serve as president. Although Larson's book did not play a major role in the 1968 presidential election, Nixon's aides never forgave or forgot what Larson had done. Thus, despite Nixon's narrow victory over Humphrey on November 5th, Larson's prospects of a return to high office were extinguished.[87]

He still had his center at Duke to run, of course, but even that increasingly became a casualty of the Vietnam War. The center's mission of world peace through law had already lost momentum before Johnson escalated American military involvement in Vietnam, but with that development even many foreigners sympathetic to the cause of international law lost interest in what Americans such as Larson had to say about it. The disrespect Johnson and his aides showed for multilateral means of resolving international disputes in general and the Vietnam conflict in particular made American-backed initiatives to promote the United Nations and the rule of international law seem naive and even hypocritical. As a result, the grant money that had sustained the Rule of Law Center's personnel and programs gradually dried up during the second half of the 1960s. By the end of 1969, the center's full-time staff had shrunk from the nine international lawyers it had employed in 1965–1966 to only four. Although Duke did not formally abolish Larson's center, by early 1970 it had ceased to be a major academic enterprise there.[88]

This special grievance with what Johnson and his aides had done in Vietnam, like Larson's other objections to that policy, pushed him increasingly in new directions by 1970. He gave two speeches in the spring that year that illustrated vividly how the war had changed his stands on politics and public policy to an extent that was unusual for someone about to turn sixty years old. The first of these two addresses dealt with the issue of radicalism and student protest. Larson gave this speech, which he entitled simply "Extremism in America," at Eisenhower College in Seneca Falls, New York, on April 9, 1970. In this talk Larson frankly admitted that changing conditions in the country and the Vietnam War in particular had encouraged protest on college campuses, and he welcomed that change. Larson made those points as broadly and forcefully as possible:

> If the main thrust of the protest movement has been opposition to the Vietnam war, it follows that the protest movement was and is right and legitimate. Those who have protested the war were and are right. Those who got us in, secretly pushed us further in, and refused every chance to get out were wrong. They were wrong morally, legally, diplomatically, militarily, politically, historically, and, above all, in terms of human suffering.[89]

To those who argued that the student protesters should have avoided marches, demonstrations, sit-ins, and the like in favor of "democratic means," Larson replied passionately, "What chance have the young people of this country had to do anything whatever by democratic means about the Vietnam war? For that matter, what chance has anybody had to do anything about the Vietnam war by democratic means?"[90]

Larson defended those very controversial statements in three ways. First, he noted that Lyndon Johnson had campaigned in 1964 on a platform of "no wider war," only to take precisely the opposite course after winning reelection. Second, Larson observed that even though public disapproval of Johnson's handling of the Vietnam War had driven him from office in 1968, "the war still goes on, and now even is in serious danger of spreading beyond Vietnam into all of old Indochina."[91] Third, Larson pointed out that despite the Constitution's provision giving Congress alone the power to declare war, that body had been "largely bypassed" during the process of launching and expanding American military involvement in Vietnam.[92]

For all of those reasons, Larson endorsed further student protests aimed at halting American participation in the Vietnam War. Stoutly rejecting what he suggested was the grim complacency of "the silent majority," Larson told his college-age audience that he hoped there would be no letup on the part of the antiwar protestors. To them, Larson said, "stay with it, and more power to you."[93]

The way in which the Vietnam War had influenced his thinking on politics and public policy could also be seen in an address he delivered just two days after the one at Eisenhower College. Larson gave this second speech, "The Military-Industrial Complex Ten Years Later," to the faculty and students of Virginia Military Institute (VMI), one of the oldest and most prestigious military colleges in the country. Larson's theme was the warning Eisenhower had issued in his farewell address on January 17, 1961, against "the acquisition of unwarranted influence, whether sought or unsought, by the military-industrial complex."[94]

Although Larson's successor as presidential speechwriter, Malcolm Moos, had written the farewell address, Larson had some inside knowledge of Eisenhower's views on that particular theme, which formed the basis for Larson's speech. First, he assured his listeners that Eisenhower had truly believed in the existence of a military-industrial complex and the problems it could create. Larson illustrated that point by confiding that Eisenhower had complained privately about the "glacier-like movement of the military budget" in the face of his earnest efforts to reduce it substantially.[95] Larson also pointed to the scandals in military procurement in which millions of taxpayer dollars had been wasted due to a lack of both adequate competition in bidding and government oversight. Larson argued that Eisenhower's concern with the procurement system in particular had been one of the motives behind the warning in his farewell speech.[96]

As serious as this problem had been under Eisenhower, Larson continued, it had grown far worse during the nine years since Eisenhower left office. In making this assertion, Larson drew upon what he had learned one year earlier from serving as chairman of a conference on the military budget and national priorities. That meeting had been organized by several members of Congress, most of them liberal Democrats such as Senators George McGovern of South Dakota and Gaylord Nelson of Wisconsin, and featured presentations by nationally known academic experts such as George Kistiakowsky of Harvard and Hans Morgenthau of the University of Chicago. That conference and Larson's own reading and research had convinced him that Eisenhower had been "the last American president to retain control of the military budget."[97] Since then, Larson said, "the Pentagon has largely been writing its own ticket" and offered as proof the enormous increase in spending on military equipment during the 1960s.[98]

Beyond wasting public funds, Larson went on, this problem had contributed to what he called "the militarization of American foreign policy."[99] What he meant by that provocative phrase was that Eisenhower had believed deeply that the government of the United States should determine foreign policy and then tailor its military programs to fit that policy. Instead, Larson argued, under the three presidents who had served since Eisenhower, "military policy has dictated foreign policy."[100] Larson gave as "the most stark illustration of this change" the growing American military involvement in Vietnam since 1960 and the extent to which that involvement had reshaped American foreign policy.[101] Lest his listeners think that an isolated case, Larson added such other examples as CIA covert operations that had snowballed into major military involvements from which turning back became almost impossible, American arms sales to foreign powers that altered the balance of power in regional conflicts, and the way in which the U.S. military's plans to build an anti–ballistic missile system had interfered with efforts to negotiate arms control and disarmament agreements with the Soviet Union.[102]

Larson concluded that those examples pointed to a general conclusion that "when foreign policy is militarized it is almost invariably wrong."[103] The reason for that was the presence of some unforeseen contingency or factor that military leaders failed to consider, such as the attitude and political inclinations of a local population. He pointed to Cambodia as a prime example of this tendency of a military-driven foreign policy to reach the wrong conclusion. In an especially far-sighted passage, Larson observed:

> One can easily imagine the tremendous pressure being applied by those in the Pentagon who dream of sweeping Cambodia clean of Communists, thus destroying the Communist sanctuary that has complicated the operations in the southern part of South Vietnam, and paving the way for total victory, at least in the southern sector. Tempting as this sounds, this once more leaves out of account the fact that . . . any such attempt would merely produce on Cambodian soil a carbon copy of the hopeless situation in South Vietnam, where Communists have not been cleaned out of various areas even when they are completely surrounded.[104]

American military efforts to escalate the war against North Vietnam were similarly flawed, Larson argued, because they failed to take into account the great likelihood that the Soviet Union would simply offset such escalation by increasing Soviet military assistance to the North Vietnamese. In a characteristically clear statement, Larson pointed out that "our military always seem to jump to the conclusion that the option for escalation is all on our side."[105]

From that hard fact of life Larson drew a sweeping conclusion. He argued that military force had lost its effectiveness as a means of settling international disputes. For that reason, Congress should regain control over runaway military spending, place a freeze on all advanced weapons development and use while the United States and the Soviet Union tried to negotiate an arms-control agreement, and abolish the draft immediately. Such steps could be taken, he added, because public opinion, among younger Americans especially, had begun to change in favor of them.[106]

Larson contended that the stakes at issue were even higher than he had thus far suggested. The militarization of foreign policy had interfered not only with the development of effective foreign relations but with democracy itself in America. The "survival of the United States as a free, democratic society" depended on putting a stop to a military-driven foreign policy, Larson argued, thereby concluding an address that likely stunned many of the VMI faculty and students who heard it.[107]

Larson's VMI address spoke volumes about how far his thinking on military matters had come since the mid-1950s. In the intervening decade and a half he had moved away from the view, so prominent during Eisenhower's presidency, of American military strength as a deterrent to aggression and thus a force for peace. Although much of what Larson said in his VMI address made sense, it could be faulted, like some of his other speeches and writings, for overstating his case. His contention that military force had proven ineffective as a means to resolve the Vietnam conflict was highly persuasive, but his conclusion that the use of such force would always produce such unsatisfactory results appears much more doubtful. The most that can be said for Larson's view on that broader point is that over the long run he might well have been right.[108]

Instead of qualifying his views in that way, Larson in the spring of 1970 moved even farther from the Vietnam policy stance of the Nixon administration and the mainstream of the Republican Party. After Nixon's televised announcement on April 30th of a U.S. military invasion of Cambodia sparked demonstrations at college campuses across the nation and the shooting at Kent State, Larson finally broke completely with Nixon's Vietnam policy. During a teach-in at the Duke Law School on the evening of May 12, 1970, Larson called for an unconditional withdrawal of American military forces from Vietnam. With that step, his role as an influential spokesman in GOP circles finally came to an end.[109]

Epilogue

After his break with the Nixon administration over Vietnam, Arthur Larson entered the final stage of his life and career. Although he gradually lost the public prominence he had enjoyed in the 1950s and 1960s, Larson found ways to continue making important contributions. In the early 1970s, he returned to the subject of workers' compensation law and produced several major articles on that topic. Not content simply to expand horizons in a field he already knew well, Larson broke new ground in 1974 by producing a treatise on employment discrimination law. The subject interested him so much during the 1970s that he developed new courses on race and sex discrimination. During that final decade of teaching at Duke, Larson's new courses and his evenhanded approach to the material they covered drew many enthusiastic students. When he reached the mandatory retirement age of seventy in 1980, the editors of the *Duke Law Journal* recognized his many achievements as a scholar and teacher by publishing a special tribute, to which several of his colleagues contributed.[1]

Larson's extracurricular activities during the 1970s and 1980s reflected that same unusual capacity for continuing growth. At age sixty-four, he began taking weekly singing lessons and sang the roles of Hans Sachs in *Die Meistersinger* and King Melchior in *Amahl and the Night Visitors*, among others. Larson played an active role in Duke's Collegium Musicum, where he sang and played the viola da gamba. During the late 1970s, he also began a scholarly study of the songs of Edvard Grieg, taking lessons in Norwegian to do justice to that topic. Larson's musical activities were so numerous and varied that a colleague observed that "his participation in the musical affairs of the university would justify a place of honor even if his contributions to the law were ignored."[2] In order to conduct concerts in their own home more easily, Arthur and Florence moved in 1984 to a new house in Durham. This strikingly attractive low-slung dwelling featured a very large living and concert area, where many memorable performances and parties took place.[3]

Florence renewed herself in a different way during the late 1960s and 1970s by becoming an artist. She made a serious commitment to working as a sculptor, something Arthur Larson lovingly supported. Their new house provided studio and gallery space for Florence's work, which gave her a much more purposeful life in Durham. Although hardly the kind of career she had earlier hoped for, Florence made the best of her situation, and all the indications are that she enjoyed herself greatly in these later years of her life. In part this stemmed from her warm, optimistic nature, which her professional setback had not altered. Florence's deeply satisfying family life was another major factor. She delighted in the companionship of her erudite, gentle, and wise husband and their two accomplished children. Lex followed in his father's footsteps by earning a law degree (at Harvard) and then became a successful attorney in Washington. Toward the end of his father's career, Lex succeeded him as the head of the legal team at Durham that kept the workers' compensation treatise up to date. Anna earned a Ph.D. in music composition from the University of Maryland and pursued the kind of career as a composer, playwright, and music director Florence had wanted for herself. Arthur and Florence's six grandchildren, sons of Lex and Anna, who often came to visit, also added to Arthur and Florence's feelings of contentment in their later years.[4]

All of this helped ease the sting of disappointment the Larsons felt during the 1970s and 1980s as the Republican Party moved steadily to the right. That shift made Arthur Larson in particular an increasingly isolated figure politically, whose public policy stands in important areas positioned him nearer to the Democrats then than the mainstream of his own party. In part Larson's return to relative obscurity stemmed from the death or retirement of the most prominent Modern Republicans, most notably Eisenhower himself, who died on March 28, 1969. Larson's disgust with Richard Nixon for his hawkish Vietnam War policy and disgraceful conduct during the Watergate scandal also contributed to Larson's increasing sense of distance from the GOP during the 1970s. Ronald Reagan's presidency over the next eight years only deepened that sense of alienation. In 1986, thirty years after the publication of *A Republican Looks at His Party*, Larson lamented to one of his grandsons that only a few Republicans with that kind of philosophy still remained in high elective office. By that point, Larson had returned more or less to where he had started as a young man in thinking of himself as a Republican but taking no part in GOP affairs.[5]

Above and beyond those specific reasons for Larson's gradual return to obscurity loomed more fundamental ones. Changing social conditions during the 1960s, 1970s, and 1980s made the views he had explained in *A Republican Looks at His Party* steadily less workable then. The shifts in Larson's views during the 1960s and early 1970s reflected his understanding of the need for change. What set him apart from many conservatives then and afterward, however, were his positions in the key areas of economic policy and national security. As the problems of increasing foreign economic competition and inflation mounted during the 1960s and 1970s, conservatives moved in the direction of more market-oriented solutions to social problems. At the same time, rightists tended to resist efforts to shrink drastically the size and power of the nation's military and national security establishment. Larson, however, tended to think that in the economic realm conservatives had gone too far and in the national security realm not far enough. Those two major deviations from the new conservative orthodoxy increasingly left Larson on the margins of the American Right.[6]

Such a turn of events would likely have discouraged a less optimistic person, but even during the heyday of the New Right, Larson remained hopeful about the future of the political philosophy for which he was best known. Near the end of his life in the early 1990s, Larson thought he detected signs of Modern Republicanism's revival. In a memoir written then, he quoted approvingly from a column by syndicated columnist David Broder of the *Washington Post* that argued George Bush, Sr., had "recreated the Eisenhower presidency."[7] Larson also quoted at length from another of Broder's columns, which surveyed the results of the gubernatorial elections held in 1990 and concluded that "forceful new Republicans, many of them with urban voting bases, are taking over in California and the northern tier states where Lincoln-Teddy Roosevelt-Eisenhower Republicanism had its roots."[8]

Although not entirely sure Broder was right, Larson felt cautiously optimistic by then that Modern Republicanism had finally begun to make a comeback. Such a development made sense to Larson because he firmly believed that moderate conservatism remained the dominant American political tradition. The more polarized politics of the 1970s and 1980s had disrupted that pattern, he thought, but only temporarily. Any society's dominant political tradition ultimately must reflect what works best in light of that society's history, customs, and specific conditions, and to Larson, moderate conservatism of the sort he had described in his writings clearly met that test for the United States. Thus, by the early 1990s he saw good reason for believing that the Modern Republican cause would not only endure but would ultimately prevail.[9]

It was an outcome, however, that Arthur Larson himself did not live to see. His health began to decline in the 1980s, and not even Larson's extraordinary energy and zest for life could counteract that unwelcome development entirely. He had trouble getting around by himself but stubbornly refused to use either a walker or a wheelchair, apparently because he disliked the way they would have publicly labeled him as disabled. Florence's death in 1991 also hit him hard by taking away not only a companion but a source of great physical and emotional support as well. As is so often the case in such circumstances, his own death on March 27, 1993, followed fairly soon after hers. The moderate conservative cause to which both of them had given so much had finally passed from their hands to those of the next generation.[10]

NOTES

Abbreviations

ABL	Anna Barbara Larson interview, September 18, 2000
AH	Arthur Huseboe
AHTI	Telephone interview with Arthur Huseboe, August 3, 2000
AHL	Anna Huseboe Larson
AHL-HR	Typed transcript of correspondence between Anna Huseboe Larson and Helen Rothie
AL	Arthur Larson
ALICY	Arthur Larson interview for *Contentious Years* television show, June 5, 1992, Larson Family Papers
AL-KL I	Recording of Ken Larson's first oral interview with Arthur Larson, March 14, 1986, Larson Family Papers
AL-KL II	Recording of Ken Larson's second oral interview with Arthur Larson, March 14, 1986, Larson Family Papers
AL-KL III	Recording of Ken Larson's third oral interview with Arthur Larson, March 16, 1986, Larson Family Papers
ALP	Arthur Larson Papers
ALS	Arthur Larson Scrapbooks
AL-YM	Transcript of Yanek Mieczkowski's interview with Arthur Larson, April 11, 1989
AS	Administrative Series
ASCUP	Archives Services Center, University of Pittsburgh, Pittsburgh, Pennsylvania
ATCL	Arthur Larson, *A Twentieth-Century Life* (Sioux Falls, S.D.: Center for Western Studies, 1997)
AWF	Ann Whitman File
AWTI	Telephone interview with Abbott Washburn May, 31, 2002
BAC	Business Advisory Council
BG	Barry Goldwater
CF	Chronological File
CFS	Central File Series
CIS	Congressional Information Service
CU	Columbia University, New York, New York
DDE	Dwight D. Eisenhower

DDEDS	Dwight D. Eisenhower Diary Series
DDEL	Dwight D. Eisenhower Presidential Library, Abilene, Kansas
DDEP	Dwight D. Eisenhower Papers
DDEPPP	Dwight D. Eisenhower Post-Presidential Paper
DDRS	Declassified Documents Reference System
DL	Don Larson
DLP	U.S. Department of Labor Papers
FN	Florence Newcomb
FNL	Florence Newcomb Larson
GC	General Correspondence
GR	George Romney
HB	Helmer Blegen
HSTL	Harry S. Truman Presidential Library, Independence, Missouri
JFK	John F. Kennedy
JPM	James P. Mitchell
JPMP	James P. Mitchell Papers
LBJ	Lyndon Baines Johnson
LBJL	Lyndon Baines Johnson Presidential Library, Austin, Texas
LBJP	Lyndon Baines Johnson Papers
LFP	Larson Family Papers, Chapel Hill, North Carolina
LFRR	Larson Family Reunion Recording
LKL	Lex K. Larson Interview, March 23, 2000
LL	Lewis Larson
LMC	Larson-Moos Collection
LMS	Legislative Meetings Series
LOD	Arthur Larson's Office Diary
MB	Arthur Larson's Memo Book
MCTI	Telephone interview with Millard Cass, November 22, 1995
MFP	Memorandum for the President
NARA II	National Archives and Records Administration II, College Park, Maryland
NF	Name File
NSC	National Security Council
OF	Official File
OHC	Oral History Collection
PL	Palmer Larson
PPF	President's Personal File
PUL	Princeton University Library, Princeton, New Jersey
RG	Record Group
RMCKLCU	Rare and Manuscript Collections, Kroch Library, Cornell University, Ithaca, New York
RMN	Richard M. Nixon
RMNP	Richard M. Nixon Papers
RMNL	Richard Nixon Library and Birthplace, Yorba Linda, California
RMNPPP	Richard M. Nixon Pre-Presidential Papers (Pacific Southwest Region, National Archives)
SFS	Subject File Series
SGMML	Seeley G. Mudd Manuscript Library
SSP	Social Security Project
WHCF	White House Central Files

WHO	White House Office
WHOF	White House Office Files
WHOSSP	White House Office of the Staff Secretary's Papers

1. *Native Son of the Upper Midwest*

1. *ATCL*, 1–20; AL-KL I.

2. Theodore C. Blegen, *Norwegian Migration to America: The American Transition* (Northfield, Minn.: Norwegian-American Historical Association, 1940), 3–36; Briant Lindsay Lowell, *Scandinavian Exodus: Demographic and Social Development of 19th-Century Rural Communities* (Boulder, Colo.: Westview Press, 1987), 1–61, 159–241; Donald Sneen, *Through Trials and Triumphs: A History of Augustana College* (Sioux Falls, S.D.: Center for Western Studies, 1985), 2–3; Roger Daniels, *Coming to America: A History of Immigration and Ethnicity in American Life*, (New York: HarperCollins, 1990), 172–176; *ATCL*, 11; AL-KL I.

3. *ATCL*, 11. See also AL-KL I.

4. *ATCL*, 11–15; AL-KL I; AH to the author, December 29, 2000, 1; Daniels, *Coming to America*, 172–176; Herbert S. Schell, *History of South Dakota* (Lincoln, Neb.: University of Nebraska Press, 1961), 110–113.

5. *ATCL*, 11–15; AL-KL I; Schell, *History of South Dakota*, 175–202; O. E. Rolvaag, *Giants in the Earth: A Saga of the Prairie* (New York: HarperPerennial, 1991).

6. Guy V. Aldrich, "Judge Lewis Larson," unpublished ms., LFP; *ATCL*, 11; AL-KL I.

7. *ATCL*, 11; AL-KL I.

8. *ATCL*, 11 (see also 8); AL-KL I; Aldrich, "Judge Lewis Larson"; typed transcripts of letters from AH to Helen Rothie, 1–3, all in LFP; AHTI.

9. Blegen, *Norwegian Migration to America*, 100–174; Daniels, *Coming to America*, 174–175; AH to Helen Rothie, 3, LFP.

10. AHTI. The wedding photo is reprinted in *ATCL*, 5.

11. *ATCL*, 5. I am indebted to Kathy Larson for her perceptive observations about the Larson family photographs.

12. R. E. Bragstad, *Sioux Falls in Retrospect* (Sioux Falls, S.D.: n.p., 1967), 1–10; Schell, *History of South Dakota*, 336–337, 352; John R. Borchert, *America's Northern Heartland: An Economic and Historical Geography of the Upper Midwest* (Minneapolis: University of Minnesota Press, 1987), 22–23, 69.

13. Schell, *History of South Dakota*, 363, 365–367.

14. Bragstad, *Sioux Falls*, 49–51, 123–125.

15. T. D. Griffith, *South Dakota* (New York: Fodor's, 1994), 76; Bragstad, *Sioux Falls*, 123–125; AHTI; Schell, *History of South Dakota*, 337–340; Fred Shannon, *The Farmer's Last Frontier: Agriculture, 1860–1897* (White Plains, N.Y.: M. E. Sharpe, 1945), 291–295.

16. Schell, *History of South Dakota*, 261–262; Bragstad, *Sioux Falls*, 168–170; Griffith, *South Dakota*, 76–78.

17. AL-KL I.

18. Ibid.; *ATCL*, 4; Schell, *History of South Dakota*, 186; Aldrich, "Judge Lewis Larson", and AHL-HR, 3–4, both in LFP; AHTI; Bragstad, *Sioux Falls*, 25; *ATCL*, 1.

19. AHL-HR, January 18, 1912, LFP. See also *ATCL*, 1; Federal Writers' Project, *Washington: City and Capital* (Washington, D.C.: U.S. Government Printing Office, 1937), 81–84.

20. AL-KL I; *ATCL*, 1.

21. AHL-HR, January 18, 1912, LFP. For the beautification projects in Washington, see Charles Moore, *Washington Past and Present* (New York: The Century Company,

1929), 257–293; Federal Writers' Project, *Washington: City and Capital*, 95–99.

22. AHL-HR, March 22, 1912, LFP.

23. Ibid. See also *ATCL*, 6.

24. Schell, *History of South Dakota*, 259–262; Julie Bolding, "The Patriarch of Progressive Reform," in The Argus Leader, *South Dakota 99* (Sioux Falls, S.D.: Ex Machina, 1989), 61–62; Herbert T. Hoover and Larry J. Zimmerman, *South Dakota Leaders: From Pierre Chouteau, Jr. to Oscar Howe* (Vermillion, S.D.: University of South Dakota Press, 1989), 199–202.

25. Schell, *History of South Dakota*, 262; Bolding, "The Patriarch," 61–62; Hoover and Zimmerman, *South Dakota Leaders*, 203; *ATCL*, 1.

26. Schell, *History of South Dakota*, 223–241, 260–264, 380; Howard R. Lamar, *Dakota Territory, 1861–1889, A Study of Frontier Politics* (New Haven, Conn.: Yale University Press, 1956), 280; Hoover and Zimmerman, *South Dakota Leaders*, 202–203; Edmund Morris, *The Rise of Theodore Roosevelt* (New York: Ballantine Books, 1979), 270–341.

27. Schell, *History of South Dakota*, especially 158–188, 265–269; Lamar, *Dakota Territory*, especially 283–284; AHTI; D. W. Meinig, *The Shaping of America*, vol. 3, *Transcontinental America, 1950–1915* (New Haven, Conn.: Yale University Press, 1998), 275–276, 286; Blegen, *Norwegian Immigration to America*, especially 100–130; Jon Gjerde, *The Minds of the West: Ethnocultural Evolution in the Rural Middle West, 1830–1917* (Chapel Hill: University of North Carolina Press, 1997), 9–22, 135–185.

28. Schell, *History of South Dakota*, 262–264; Hoover and Zimmerman, *South Dakota Leaders*, 203–204; AL-KL I; *ATCL*, 1.

29. William Leuchtenburg, *The Perils of Prosperity, 1914–32* (Chicago: University of Chicago Press, 1958), 100–103; David M. Kennedy, *Over Here: The First World War and American Society* (New York: Oxford University Press, 1980), 242–244; Bragstad, *Sioux Falls*, 1, 132–133; Borchert, *America's Northern Heartland*, 51–78; Schell, *History of South Dakota*, 277–281, 343–346, 363, 365, 368, 370–371, 377; Robert S. Lynd and Helen Merrell Lynd, *Middletown: A Study in Modern American Culture* (New York: Harcourt, Brace, Jovanovich, 1929).

30. AHTI; Aldrich, "Judge Lewis Larson," LFP; AL-KL I; *ATCL*, 65.

31. AH to the author, December 29, 2000, 1; *ATCL*, 1–20; AHL-HR, 1, LFP; AHTI; AL to AHL, June 1919 and June 22, 1922, LFP; AL-KL I and II.

32. *ATCL*, 189 (see also 17, 190–204); AHTI; AL-KL I; LFRR.

33. *ATCL*, 191 (see also 190, 192–204); LKL; ABL; LFRR.

34. *ATCL*, 191; AHTI; Daniel J. Czitrom, *Media and the American Mind: From Morse to McLuhan* (Chapel Hill: University of North Carolina Press, 1982), 60–79; Lynd and Lynd, *Middletown*, 225–312.

35. *ATCL*, 2–4.

36. Ibid., 4–6, 21–23; Borchert, *America's Northern Heartland*, 143; AHTI.

37. *ATCL*, 4–6; *Lowell School Facing Prairie Avenue: 1891* (Sioux Falls, S.D.: n.p., 1967) (pamphlet at Sioux Falls Public Library); AL-KL II.

38. *ATCL*, 8 (see also 6).

39. AL-KL I. See also *ATCL*, 205.

40. Stanley Olsen, *One Hundred Years of Ministry: First Lutheran Church* (Sioux Falls, S.D.: n.p., 1977), 1–7; Borchert, *America's Northern Heartland*, 143; Blegen, *Norwegian Migration*, 100–174; Sydney E. Ahlstrom, *A Religious History of the American People* (New Haven, Conn.: Yale University Press, 1972), 760–761.

41. Olsen, *One Hundred Years of Ministry*, 2–3, 5–7; Blegen, *Norwegian Migration*, 100–174; Ahlstrom, *A Religious History*, 760–762.

42. Olsen, *One Hundred Years of Ministry*, 8; AHTI.

43. H. J. Glenn to LL, September 26, 1918, quoted in Olsen, *One Hundred Years*, 8–9 (see also 7, 10). See also Daniels, *Coming to America*, 174–176; Gjerde, *Minds of the West*, 271–272, 319–325; Kennedy, *Over Here*, 66–69; Schell, *History of South Dakota*, 270–273. In 1910, the year of AL's birth, just over 40 percent of the 1 million Norwegian Lutherans living in the United States were foreign born, and they were assimilating more slowly than Swedish Lutherans. On that point, see Martin Marty, *Modern American Religion: The Irony of It All, 1893–1919* (Chicago: University of Chicago Press, 1986), 170–171.

44. AL-KL I. See also Olsen, *One Hundred Years of Ministry*, 8–13.

45. *ATCL*, 205.

46. Ibid.

47. Ibid.

48. Ibid., 39.

49. Ibid., 21–23, 41; *The Monogram: Yearbook of the Senior Class of the Washington High School, Sioux Falls, South Dakota* (Sioux Falls, S.D.: Washington High School, 1927); Ken Kessinger, *Sioux Falls Washington High School Sports Heritage, 1899–1989* (Freeman, S.D.: Pine Hill Press, 1990); AL-KL I; AHTI.

50. *ATCL*, 22. See also *The Monogram*; AHTI.

51. *The Monogram*; *ATCL*, 22; AHTI.

52. *ATCL*, 23. See also "[Newcomb Family] Genealogy," 2, LFP; "The Debate Season of '26–'27," in *The Monogram*; AL-KL I; "L. Arthur Larson is Dead at 82," *New York Times*, April 1, 1993.

53. *ATCL*, 23.

54. "The Debate Season of '26–'27"; *ATCL*, 23.

55. *ATCL*, 23.

56. Ibid., 23–24.

57. Ibid., 24.

58. Ibid., 25 (see also 24).

59. Ibid., 25.

60. Ibid.

61. Ibid., 25–26 (see also 27–30).

62. Ibid., 27 (see also 28); LL to AL, August 13, 1923, LFP; AL-KL I.

63. *ATCL*, 28.

64. Ibid., 28–30.

65. See "[Newcomb Family] Genealogy," 2, LFP. On the tendency of religious differences between Catholics and Protestants to separate young people in this fashion, particularly in midwestern communities of that time, see Lynd and Merrell Lynd, *Middletown*, 110–117.

66. FN to AL, "Wed. At College 1:00," LFP. See also *ATCL*, 28.

67. FN to AL, October 11, 1929, LFP. See also her other letters to him from 1928 to 1929; "Family History of the Robert Kingsbury Newcomb Family"; "[Newcomb Family] Genealogy"; and AL to his parents postmarked July 18, 1929, all in LFP; *ATCL*, 31–37.

68. See letters from FN to AL from 1928 to 1930, all in LFP; *The Edda* (Sioux Falls, S.D.: Student Association of Augustana College, 1931); AHTI; *ATCL*, 29, 39–41.

69. FN to AL, March 11 and 25, 1930, LFP; *ATCL*, 23, 117; *The Edda*, 161–162; Jim Protexter, "Committee Power Felt at Home and Abroad," in The Argus Leader, *South Dakota* 99, 136–141.

70. FN to AL, December 20, 1930, LFP; Schell, *History of South Dakota*, 281–284.

71. *ATCL*, 121; Schell, *History of South Dakota*, 281–283; FN to AL, 1929–1932, LFP.

72. FN to AL with the heading "Y.W.C.A. Rooms, School. E. Wing 3:15 Wednesday," probably written in the fall of 1929, LFP. See also her other letters to him from 1929 to

1930 in that same collection, especially March 11, 1930, March 25, 1930, April 22, 1930, and the first one from 1931, which is headed "Madison[,] Sunday."

73. FN to AL, not dated and probably written early in 1932, LFP. See also her other letters to him from 1931 to 1932 in LFP.

74. See FN to AL, "Sat.," LFP. See also September 11, 1930 and others from later that year and 1931–1932, all in LFP; ABL; *ATCL*, 37.

75. See FN to AL marked "Monday," and the others from 1931 to 1932, all in LFP.

76. *ATCL*, 28–29; Sneen, *Through Trials and Triumphs*, 1–76.

77. Sneen, *Through Trials and Triumphs*, 74–85.

78. *The Edda*, 158–162; AHTI; AL to HB, 1932–1935, LFP; *ATCL*, 44; Sneen, *Through Trials and Triumphs*, 80, 82–84.

79. Sneen, *Through Trials and Triumphs*, 83–84; *The Edda*, 149, 152, 158–162.

80. *ATCL*, 39. See also Sneen, *Through Trials and Triumphs*, 85–86.

81. *ATCL*, 39–41; H. J. Glenn to AL, October 6, 1931, 4, and AL to LL, October 6, 1931, both in LFP.

82. H. J. Glenn to AL, October 6, 1931, 4, LFP. See also *ATCL*, 39, 41.

83. *ATCL*, 39.

84. ABL; AHTI; *ATCL*, 41.

85. *ATCL*, 42.

86. Ibid., 44 (see also 43). See Theodore C. Hume to AL, n.d., LFP. Hume, who was one of Larson's examiners in Des Moines, wrote: "Our committee was impressed quite as much by your genuine spirit of public service as by your splendid record, and ability."

87. *ATCL*, 44 (see also 42); and the four letters from AL to his parents from the fall of 1931, all in LFP.

88. *ATCL*, 44.

89. Ibid., 44–45.

90. See FN's letters to AL from late 1931 and 1932, LFP.

91. *ATCL*, 45.

2. *Oxford's Imprint*

1. *ATCL*, 47.

2. AL to HB, November 1, 1932, 2, LFP.

3. See, for example, AL to LL, March 9, 1933, 9, AHL; AL to LL, December 3, 1933, 4, LFP.

4. AL to his parents, January 16, 1933, 1, LFP. See also his letters to his parents, October 9, 1932, 2, and LL, January 1, 1933, 1, all in LFP; Laurence A. Crosby, Frank Aydelotte, and Alan C. Valentine, eds., *Oxford of Today: A Manual for Prospective Rhodes Scholars* (New York: Oxford University Press, 1927), 29–39, 117–150; Douglas MacLeane, *A History of Pembroke College Oxford* (Oxford: Clarendon Press, 1897).

5. AL to his parents, January 16, 1933, 2–6, LFP. The bill, which came to a total of $416, is in LFP. This was for the first of the three eight-week terms per academic year, while AL's scholarship provided him with 400 British pounds (then approximately $1,400) per annum on which to live. See, on that last point, AL to LL, November 12, 1933, 8, LFP; Carlton Kemp Allen, *Forty Years of the Rhodes Scholarships* (Oxford: Oxford University Press, 1944), 9.

6. AL to HB, November 1, 1932, 5, LFP (see also 3–4); AL to PL, January 16, 1933, 2, LFP; *ATCL*, 72–73. For Rhodes scholars and the Oxford tutorial method of instruction, see Frank Aydelotte, *The American Rhodes Scholarships: A Review of the First Forty Years* (Princeton, N.J.: Princeton University Press, 1946), 64–70.

7. See Christopher Hobhouse, *Oxford: As It Was and As It Is Today* (New York: Oxford University Press, 1946), 83–108; Joseph A. Soares, *The Decline of Privilege: The Modernization of Oxford University* (Stanford, Calif.: Stanford University Press, 1999), 1–37.

8. AL to PL, January 21, 1933, 2, LFP. See also AL to HB, November 1, 1932, 3, LFP.

9. AL to his parents, October 9, 1932, 2, LFP.

10. AL to PL, January 21, 1933, 2, LFP. See also AL to his parents, October 17, 1932, 4, and AL to HB, November 1, 1932, 2–3, both in LFP; *ATCL*, 71, where he discussed the limitations of Oxford's lecture system.

11. AL to LL, March 9, 1933, 2, LFP.

12. Ibid., 2–4.

13. See AL to LL, March 9, 1933, 5–8, AL to AHL, June 26, 1933, 3–4, AL to LL, September 21, 1933, 3, and AL to AHL, October 11, 1933, 3–5, and October 20, 1933, 1–3, all in LFP.

14. AL to LL, March 9, 1933, 9, LFP. See also AL to AHL, May 2, 1933, 2, LFP.

15. *ATCL*, 47. For the popularity of the left at Oxford during the 1930s, see David Walter, *The Oxford Union: Playground of Power* (London: Macdonald, 1984), 72–117.

16. *ATCL*, 47.

17. See AL to his parents, October 17, 1932, 1–2, LFP; *ATCL*, 47–49.

18. *ATCL*, 49.

19. See AL to LL, May 15, 1933, 2–3, AL to AHL, March 22, 1933, 6, both in LFP.

20. AL to LL, May 15, 1933, 2–3, LFP.

21. AL to HB, June 3, 1933, 5, LFP (see also 3–4, 6); AL to his parents, October 24, 1932, 4–5, and AL to AHL, November 19, 1932, 9–12, both in LFP.

22. AL to DL, November 12, 1932, 5–6, LFP.

23. See AL to his parents, October 9, 1932, 3–4, October 17, 1932, 1, 3–4, October 24, 1932, 3–4, 6, and November 19, 1932, 1–2, all in LFP; *ATCL*, 58–59.

24. AL to PL, January 21, 1933, 2, LFP (see also 3–5), AL to his parents, October 24, 1932, 3–4, AL to Don Larson, November 12, 1932, 1, AL to AHL, January 16, 1933, 8–9, all in LFP; *ATCL*, 53–55.

25. See AL to PL, January 21, 1933, 2–3, AL to LL, February 11, 1933, 3–4, AL to DL, February 17, 1933, 1–8, AL to AHL February 23, 1933, 1–5, and AL to LL, November 12, 1933, 8, and the Pembroke College program for the Togger Races, known formally as "The Torpids," all in LFP; *ATCL*, 55–57.

26. *ATCL*, 58. See also AL to AHL, February 12, 1933, 8, LFP.

27. *ATCL*, 57–58.

28. Ibid., 58. See also AL to AHL, February 12, 1933, 7–8, and February 23, 1933, 5–8, both in LFP.

29. Christopher Hollis, *The Oxford Union* (London: Evans Brothers, 1965), especially 153–183; Walter, *The Oxford Union*, especially 47–74; AL to his parents, October 9, 1932, 7, AL to AHL, February 12, 1933, 7–8, and AL to DL, February 17, 1933, 8–9, all in LFP.

30. AL to LL, March 9, 1933, 14, LFP (see also 13); AL to AHL, February 12, 1933, 7, AL to DL, February 17, 1933, 9–10, all in LFP; Hollis, *The Oxford Union*, 185–190; Walter, *The Oxford Union*, 79–91.

31. For the popularity of pacifism in the United States during the 1920s and early 1930s, see William Leuchtenburg, *The Perils of Prosperity, 1914–32* (Chicago: University of Chicago Press, 1958), 104–119; Joan Hoff Wilson, *Herbert Hoover: Forgotten Progressive* (Prospect Heights, Ill.: Waveland Press, 1992), 8–9, 168–208; Alan Dawley, *Struggles for Justice: Social Responsibility and the Liberal State* (Cambridge, Mass.: Belknap Press of Harvard University, 1991), 322–324.

32. See AL to LL, March 30, 1933, 1–2, AL to AHL, June 26, 1933, 4–7, AL to LL, July 1, 1933, 1–3, and AL to AHL, July 12, 1933, 2, all in LFP.

33. See AL to AHL, April 17, 1933, 5–9, LFP; John Stevenson, *British Society, 1914–45* (Middlesex: Penguin Books, 1984), 108, 114, 269–274.

34. AL to AHL, April 17, 1933, 5, LFP. For the attitudes of middle-class Americans toward political radicals during the mid-1930s, see William E. Leuchtenburg, *Franklin D. Roosevelt and the New Deal* (New York: Harper & Row, 1963), 242–243; Dawley, *Struggles for Justice*, 384–385.

35. AL to AHL, August 4, 1933, 9, LFP (see also 4–8, 10).

36. Ibid., 5.

37. AL to AHL, September 12, 1933, 1, LFP. For AL's impressions from his travels in Europe during 1932–1935, see his letters to his parents and his brothers Palmer and Don for those years in LFP; and *ATCL*, 50–52, 65–68.

38. AL to AHL, September 12, 1933, 7–8, LFP (see also 2–6); *ATCL*, 50–51.

39. See also on this point, AL to LL, September 21, 1933, 4–5, LFP.

40. Ibid., 5 (see also 4).

41. Ibid., 4.

42. AL to his parents, December 11, 1932, 3–4, LFP. For the social life he and Florence enjoyed during their time in England, see the rest of their correspondence from this period in LFP. During the mid-1930s, the top 1 percent of the British population owned approximately 55 percent of the country's wealth and the top 5 percent owned approximately 80 percent. On that point, see Stevenson, *British Society*, 330. On the world of elite Britons at that time, see 331–355.

43. FN to DL, March 2, 1933, 2–3, LFP. See also AL to LL, October 6, 1932, 3–4, AL to AHL, November 19, 1932, 2–3, 5–12, AL to his parents, December 11, 1932, 1–3, and AL to AHL, February 12, 1933, 3–5, and March 22, 1933, 2–4, all in LFP; *ATCL*, 59.

44. AL to his parents, December 11, 1932, 4, LFP.

45. AL to AHL, March 22, 1933, 3, LFP. See also his letters more generally from 1932 to 1935 in LFP for evidence of AL's preference for music and drama over other forms of entertainment.

46. AL to HB, June 3, 1933, 3, LFP.

47. AL to AHL, April 17, 1933, 4, LFP.

48. AL to AHL, October 20, 1933, 2, LFP (see also 1).

49. AL to DL, November 25, 1933, 5, LFP (see also 1–4).

50. "The Union," *Isis*, November 1, 1933, 12, clipping in ALP. See also AL to AHL, November 4, 1933, 1, LFP.

51. AL to AHL, November 4, 1933, 1, LFP.

52. AL to AHL, February 11, 1934, 4–5, LFP (see also 1–3); AL to DL, November 25, 1933, 7–10, AL to AHL, January 13, 1934, 3, AL to LL, February 22, 1934, 1–3, and the various clippings from Oxford magazines reporting his Oxford Union speeches, all in LFP.

53. AL to AHL, December 3, 1933, 7, LFP (see also 8–10); AL to DL, November 25, 1933, 5–7 and AL's correspondence more generally during 1933–1935, where he discussed his activities in the Oxford Union, LFP; Hollis, *The Oxford Union*, 193–197; Walter, *The Oxford Union*, 72–80, 91–98.

54. AL to AHL, December 3, 1933, 8, LFP (see also 7).

55. Ibid., 9.

56. See David Burner, *The Politics of Provincialism: The Democratic Party in Transition, 1918–1932* (New York: Norton, 1975), 158–197; Leuchtenburg, *Franklin D. Roosevelt and the New Deal*, especially 31–61.

57. AL to LL, November 12, 1933, 11, LFP.

58. AL to HB, November 1, 1932, 8, AL to LL, May 15, 1933, 1, both in LFP; *ATCL*, 115–116; Alan Brinkley, "The Missions of Henry Luce," paper presented to the Diplomatic History Workshop, Ohio State University, May 7, 1998.

59. Wilson, *Herbert Hoover*, 209–231; Arthur M. Schlesinger, Jr., *The Crisis of the Old Order, 1919–1933* (Boston: Houghton Mifflin, 1957), 324, 328, 330, 339, 344, 349, 355–356, 482–483; Leuchtenburg, *Franklin D. Roosevelt and the New Deal*, especially 41–69; "Oxford Union's 'New Deal,'" (London) *Daily Telegraph*, November 16, 1934; "Union Just Prefers New Deal," *Isis*, February 13, 1935, 13.

60. See AL to AHL, November 17, 1934, 1–3, LFP; *ATCL*, 75–76.

61. *ATCL*, 8, 21–30, 35–38, 76; AL to his parents, December 11, 1932, 3–4, AL to AHL, February 12, 1933, 7, and AL to DL, February 17, 1933, 8–9, all in LFP.

62. AL to AHL, November 17, 1934, 3, LFP (see also 4).

63. Quoted in "Oxford Union Society's Greatest Experiment," unidentified press clipping, LFP. See also "Oxford Union's 'New Deal'"; "Victory for Women at Oxford," unidentified clipping in LFP; AL to AHL, November 17, 1934, 3–4, LFP; *ATCL*, 76.

64. "Oxford Union Society's Greatest Experiment," and AL to AHL, November 17, 1934, 4, both in LFP; *ATCL*, 76.

65. See AL to AHL, November 17, 1934, 4–5, LFP; *ATCL*, 76.

66. "Union Just Prefers New Deal"; Robert Skidelsky, *John Maynard Keynes: The Economist as Savior, 1920–1937* (New York: Penguin Books, 1992), 338–571; Wilson, *Herbert Hoover*, 122–167; Leuchtenburg, *Franklin D. Roosevelt and the New Deal*, especially 30–60.

67. "Union Just Prefers New Deal." See also AL to LL, January 30, 1935, 4, LFP; Bentley Brinkerhoff Gilbert, *David Lloyd George: A Political Life* (Columbus: Ohio State University Press, 1992), II:23, 419.

68. "Union Just Prefers New Deal"; AL to AHL, February 13, 1935, 1–2, LFP. Megan Lloyd George clearly impressed AL, who escorted her back to her guestroom. He wrote his mother that "she's a funny, tiny woman, but quite a politician, for all that." See page 2 of the letter cited above.

69. See Harold Macmillan, *Winds of Change* (New York: Harper & Row, 1966), 326–340; Alistair Horne, *Harold Macmillan*, vol. I (New York: Viking, 1988), 97–105; Skidelsky, *John Maynard Keynes*, 231–232; Walter, *The Oxford Union*, 96–97; AL to LL, January 30, 1935, 4, and AL's correspondence during 1933–1935, in LFP.

70. Horne, *Harold Macmillan*, I:105; Skidelsky, *John Maynard Keynes*, 231–232; Robert O. Paxton, *Europe in the Twentieth Century*, 2nd ed. (New York: Harcourt, Brace, Jovanovich, 1985), 329–333; AL to AHL, December 3, 1933, 9, and AL to LL, February 22, 1934, 4, both in LFP.

71. AL to LL, March 6, 1935, 1–3, LFP; *ATCL*, 76–77.

72. AL to AHL, November 17, 1934, 5, LFP. See also AL to AHL, October 19, 1934, 2, LFP, where he related the news of his nomination for membership and described the Carlton as "the ritziest club in Oxford"; Hollis, *The Oxford Union*, 193, 196–197.

73. AL to his parents, December 22, 1932, 1, LFP (see also 4–10); AL to AHL, November 19, 1932, 3; AL to his parents, December 11, 1932, 6, and December 22, 1932, 1, 3; AL to PL, January 21, 1933, 8, and AL to AHL, September 5, 1934, 1, all in LFP; *ATCL*, 66–68; Paxton, *Europe in the Twentieth Century*, 400–402.

74. AL to LL, March 9, 1933, 10, LFP (see also 11); AL to LL, January 3, 1933, 2–4; AL to PL, January 21, 1933, 5–8, all in LFP.

75. AL to LL, November 12, 1933, 11, LFP.

76. Ibid., 8 (see also 9); Leuchtenburg, *Franklin D. Roosevelt and the New Deal*, 202–203, 210–230.

77. AL to DL, March 16, 1934, 12, LFP (see also 10–11).

78. AL to AHL, April 7, 1934, 6, LFP.

79. AL to DL, January 5, 1935, 5, LFP (see also 4).

80. AL to LL, November 12, 1933, 11–12, LFP (see also 10); AL to AHL, February 23,

1933, 8, AL to LL, March 9, 1933, 11, AL to AHL, June 26, 1933, 7, August 4, 1933, 1, 4–10, August 18, 1933, 1–8, and AL to LL, August 25, 1933, 1–8, all in LFP.

81. AL to LL, November 12, 1933, 13, LFP.

82. AL to DL, March 16, 1934, 7, LFP (see also 6, 8); Paxton, *Europe in the Twentieth Century*, 275–277, 342–344.

83. AL to DL, March 16, 1934, 8–9, LFP.

84. For corporatism in Italy and Italian military expansion after 1934, see Paxton, *Europe in the Twentieth Century*, 342–344, 419–421. On the admiration for Italian fascism in the United States during the 1920s and early 1930s, see Alan Brinkley, *The End of Reform: New Deal Liberalism in Recession and War* (New York: Alfred A. Knopf, 1995), 39, 154–155.

85. For corporatism more generally, see Charles S. Maier, *Recasting Bourgeois Europe: Stabilization in France, Germany and Italy in the Decade after World War I* (Princeton, N.J.: Princeton University Press, 1975) and *In Search of Stability: Explorations in Historical Political Economy* (Cambridge: Cambridge University Press, 1987); Philippe C. Schmitter and Gerhard Lehmbruch, eds., *Trends Toward Corporatist Intermediation* (Beverly Hills, Calif.: Sage, 1979) and *Patterns of Corporatist Policymaking* (Beverly Hills, Calif.: Sage, 1982); and Suzanne Berger, ed., *Organizing Interest Groups in Western Europe* (Cambridge: Cambridge University Press, 1981). For corporatist structures in immigrant communities of the upper Midwest, see Jon Gjerde, *Minds of the West: Ethnocultural Evolution in the Rural Middle West, 1830–1917* (Chapel Hill: University of North Carolina Press, 1997), 9–22, 135–185. Gjerde argues that immigrant leaders in the upper Midwest were "influenced by corporatist ideas [that] stressed the significance of institutions that mediated between the individual and the state, such as the family and the church community, which were deemed essential to the proper operation of society" (21).

86. AL to DL, March 16, 1934, 9, LFP.

87. Ibid., 10.

88. Unidentified newspaper clipping quoting Larson, in LFP. See also the debate program and AL to DL, March 16, 1934, 10, LFP.

89. AL to DL, January 15, 1935, 2–3, LFP. See also the unidentified newspaper clipping summarizing Larson's speech, LFP.

90. AL to DL, January 15, 1935, 2, LFP. See also Hollis, *The Oxford Union*, 174–201; Walter, *The Oxford Union*, 72–117.

91. AL to DL, March 16, 1934, 10, LFP.

92. See AL to AHL, November 19, 1932, 2–3, June 26, 1933, 7, 2; AL to LL, July 14, 1933, 2–4, September 26, 1933, 1–6, April 18, 1934, 1–10; AL to AHL, May 3, 1934, 1–18; AL to his parents, May 20, 1934, 1–4; and AL to HB, June 3, 1933, 1–3. All in LFP.

93. AL to PL, January 21, 1933, 5, LFP. See also AL to AHL, September 12, 1933, 13, LFP, where he wrote that in France "everyone [is] fundamentally mad."

94. AL to AHL, September 12, 1933, 13, LFP.

95. AL to AHL, September 5, 1934, 2, LFP. See also AL to AHL, September 22, 1934, 2, LFP, where he reported that a general strike was expected soon and observed "I can't imagine what difference it will make, for I've never seen anyone working here yet."

96. AL to AHL, September 5, 1934, 2, LFP. See also AL to PL, January 21, 1935, 5–6, where he expressed his determination to visit France again and develop an appreciation for its people, in LFP.

97. See, generally, AL to family and friends from September 1932 through June 1935, LFP.

98. AL to DL, January 15, 1935, 2, LFP. See also on this point AL to his mother, April 7, 1934, 5–6, LFP, where he wrote that "London . . . has recently elected a Socialist gov-

ernment. They're a pretty good lot, as a whole, however, and won't do much but improve social services, especially slum clearance."

99. AL to DL, January 15, 1935, 6, LFP.

100. Ibid., 2. With respect to the 1934 elections, see Leuchtenburg, *Franklin D. Roosevelt and the New Deal*, 116–117. Leuchtenburg observed that the 1934 elections "almost erased the Republican party as a national force. They left the GOP with only seven governorships, less than a third of Congress, no program of any substance, no leader with a popular appeal and none on the horizon" (117).

101. AL to DL, January 15, 1935, 2, LFP. For Lippmann and his views, see Ronald Steel, *Walter Lippmann and the American Century* (Boston: Little, Brown, 1980), especially 269–312.

102. See AL to DL, January 15, 1935, 6–7, LFP; Walter Lippmann, *The Method of Freedom* (New York: Macmillan, 1934); Steel, *Walter Lippmann*, 304–309.

103. AL to DL, January 15, 1935, 4, LFP (see also 3); Lippmann, *The Method of Freedom*, especially 45–71; Steel, *Walter Lippmann*, 307–309.

104. AL to DL, January 15, 1935, 5, LFP.

105. Ibid., 6.

106. Ibid., 6.

107. See *ATCL*, 96; AL to DL, January 15, 1935, 5–6, LFP.

108. AL to LL, September 21, 1933, 1–2, LFP. For his diligence in doing his work, see FN to AL's parents, October 18, 1933, 1, LFP.

109. AL to LL, September 21, 1933, 2–3, LFP.

110. *ATCL*, 73.

111. AL to AHL, June 26, 1933, 4, LFP.

112. See Felix Frankfurter's essay on Cardozo in Robert Livingston Schuyler, ed., *Dictionary of American Biography*, Supplement Two (New York: Scribner's, 1958) 93–96; Richard Polenberg's essay on Cardozo in John C. Garraty and Mark C. Carnes, eds., *American National Biography* (New York: Oxford University Press, 1999), 4:373–375; Liva Baker, *The Justice from Beacon Hill: The Life and Times of Oliver Wendell Holmes* (New York: HarperCollins, 1991).

113. AL to AHL, October 20, 1933, 1, LFP. See also AL to LL, May 15, 1933, 4, and AHL, June 26, 1933, 2, both in LFP.

114. See AL to AHL, October 20, 1933, 3, and December 3, 1933, 10, and AL to LL, March 6, 1935, 3–4, all in LFP; Thomas J. Schaeper and Kathleen Schaeper, *Cowboys into Gentlemen: Rhodes Scholars, Oxford, and the Creation of an American Elite* (New York: Berghahn Books, 1998), 81; Gifford Prosser, *Oxford and the Rhodes Scholarships* (n.p.: n.p., 1958), 14; *ATCL*, 73, 80.

115. See FN's letters to AHL, November 2, 1932, 9–10, January 21, 1933, 1–2, October 18, 1933, 2, AL to his parents, December 22, 1932, 2–3, AL to AHL, January 27, 1932, 3, March 22, 1933, 2, July 12, 1933, 5–6, August 4, 1933, 1–2, and AL to LL, March 30, 1933, 2, all in LFP; *ATCL*, 64–65.

116. See AL to LL, December 27, 1933, 8, AL to AHL, January 13, 1933, 4, March 17, 1934, 4, April 7, 1934, 2–3, and AL to DL, April 13, 1934, 1, all in LFP; *ATCL*, 64–65.

117. See AL to DL, April 13, 1934, 22–24, May 1, 1934, 1–2, July 26, 1934, 1–2, AL to AHL, November 20, 1934, 3–4, December 21, 1934, 1–2, January 1, 1935, 1–2, AL to LL, December 6, 1934, 1–4, December 25, 1934, 1–2, AL to FN, June 27, 1935, 1–2, and FN to DL, June 9, 1933, 1–3, all in LFP; *ATCL*, 77–80.

118. AL to LL, January 7, 1935, 13, LFP (see also 1–12, 14–16); AL to LL, December 6, 1934, 3–4, and December 25, 1934, 2, and AL to AHL, November 20, 1934, 3, December 21, 1934, 1–2, and January 1, 1935, 2, all in LFP; *ATCL*, 80.

119. See AL to LL, October 1, 1934, 1, and the photographs of Larson taken during his final year at Oxford, all in LFP; Lex K. Larson, e-mail to author, February 10, 2001; Henry S. Reuss, "A Tribute to Arthur Larson," *Duke Law Journal* 1980 (June 1980): 405.

120. See AL to LL, January 7, 11–12, January 20, 1935, 1–4, January 30, 1935, 2–3, March 6, 1935, 1–2, April 28, 1935, 1–4, and AL to AHL, March 10, 1935, 1–6, March 27, 1935, 1–4, all in LFP; Laura Kalman, *Legal Realism at Yale, 1927–1960* (Chapel Hill: University of North Carolina Press, 1986), 115–138.

121. AL to LL, January 20, 1935, 4, LFP. See also AL to LL, January 7, 1935, 12, and May 25, 1935, 1–4, LFP.

122. See Leroy J. Burlingame to AL, May 15, 1935, and the related material with it, and AL to LL, May 25, 1935, 2–3, all in LFP.

123. AL to LL, May 25, 1935, 2–3, LFP.

124. See AL to AHL, May 24, 1935, 1–2, AL to LL, May 25, 1935, 1–4, and AL to FN, June 27, 1935, 1, all in LFP.

125. AL letters to AHL, September 12, 1933, 14, and AL to LL, September 26, 1933, 6, January 30, 1935, 8, all in LFP; William L. Prosser, John W. Wade, and Victor E. Schwartz, *Torts: Cases and Materials*, 7th ed. (Mineola: Foundation Press, 1982), 1–3; *ATCL*, 82; Crosby, Aydelotte, and Valentine, *Oxford of Today*, 83–86.

126. *ATCL*, 82.

127. Prosser, Wade, and Schwartz, *Torts*, 1–3; *ATCL*, 82.

128. AL to LL, June 23, 1935, 2–3, AL's Oxford diploma, and the letter from the Pembroke College bursar explaining that AL's First entitled him to a book prize, all in LFP; *ATCL*, 81–83. AL's final grades placed him in the top fifth of the Rhodes scholars who earned Oxford degrees during the 1930s. On that point, see Schaeper and Schaeper, *Cowboys into Gentlemen*, 98–99.

129. See AL to FN, June 27, 1935, 1–2, and the formal announcement of their wedding, both in LFP; *ATCL*, 83–85.

3. *A Few False Starts*

1. *ATCL*, 85–86; AL to LL, January 7, 1935, 1–6, January 20, 1935, 4, and May 25, 1935, 1–4, AL to AHL, May 24, 1935, 1, AL to FN, June 27, 1935, 1, and Leroy J. Burlingame to AL, May 15, 1935, and the related material, all in LFP.

2. John R. Borchert, *America's Northern Heartland: An Economic and Historical Geography of the Upper Midwest* (Minneapolis: University of Minnesota Press, 1987), 76, 79–84, 93–97.

3. See AL to LL, January 7, 1935, 8, 12, January 20, 1935, 4, and May 25, 1935, 2, and Theodore C. Hume to AL, all in LFP; Blegen, *Norwegian Migration*, 485–489; *ATCL*, 100–101; Writers' Program (U.S.) Wisconsin, *Wisconsin: A Guide to the Badger State* (New York: Duell, Sloan and Pearce, 1941), 54–65; Robert C. Nesbit, *Wisconsin: A History* (Madison: University of Wisconsin Press, 1973), 399–495.

4. John D. Hicks, "A Political Whirlpool," in John J. Murray, ed., *The Heritage of the Middle West* (Norman: University of Oklahoma Press, 1958), 80–81; Writers' Program (U.S.) Wisconsin, *Wisconsin*, 240–242; H. Russell Austin, *The Milwaukee Story: The Making of an American City* (Milwaukee, Wisc.: Journal Company, 1946), 175–176, 193–195; Bayrd Still, *Milwaukee: The History of a City* (Madison: State Historical Society of Wisconsin, 1948), 476–501; John Gurda, *The Making of Milwaukee* (Milwaukee, Wisc.: Milwaukee County Historical Society, 1999), 284–294.

5. Still, *Milwaukee*, 433–475; Writers' Program (U.S.) Wisconsin, *Wisconsin*, 241–247. Of the twenty-five most populous American cities during the late 1930s, only two had a smaller proportion of black residents; see Still, *Milwaukee*, 471.

6. Writers' Program (U.S.) Wisconsin, *Wisconsin*, 240–242; Austin, *The Milwaukee Story*, 175–176; Still, *Milwaukee*, 446–453, 515–568; Gurda, *The Making of Milwaukee*, 295–297; *ATCL*, 87.

7. AL-KL II. See also AL to AHL, September 11, 1936, 1, LFP; *ATCL*, 87.

8. J. V. Quarles to AL, May 16, 1935, 1–2, Frank Aydelotte to AL, May 17, 1935, both in LFP; AL-KL II; Still, *Milwaukee*, 476–514; *ATCL*, 87–89; Henry S. Reuss, "A Tribute to Arthur Larson," *Duke Law Journal* 1980 (June 1980): 405; Henry S. Reuss, *When Government Was Good: Memories of a Life in Politics* (Madison: University of Wisconsin Press, 1999), 11.

9. *ATCL*, 89.

10. Ibid.; Leroy J. Burlingame to AL, May 15, 1935, 1–2, LFP.

11. See AL to AHL, October 3, 1935, 2, November 4, 1935, 2, and AL to LL, October 21, 1935, 1–3, and November 14, 1935, 1–2, all in LFP.

12. See AL to AHL, November 13, 1935, 1–2, January 24, 1936, 1–2, March 18, 1936, 2, all in LFP; Reuss, *When Government Was Good*, 11; Reuss, "Tribute," 405; *ATCL*, 88–89.

13. Ibid., 206.

14. Ibid., 208 (see also 206).

15. See AL to AHL, October 3, 1935, 2, November 4, 1935, 2, and January 24, 1936, 1, and AL to LL, October 21, 1935, 1–3, and November 14, 1935, 2, all in LFP; William E. Leuchtenburg, *Franklin D. Roosevelt and the New Deal* (New York: Harper & Row, 1963), 143–163; Arthur M. Schlesinger, Jr., *The Politics of Upheaval* (Boston: Houghton Mifflin, 1960), especially 385–423; Dawley, *Struggles for Justice: Social Responsibility and the Liberal State* (Cambridge, Mass.: Belknap Press of Harvard University, 1991), 371–417; Reuss, "Tribute," 405.

16. AL to AHL, November 26, 1935, 2, (see also 1), AL to AHL, October 3, 1935, 1, November 4, 1935, 1–2, January 24, 1936, 1, March 18, 1936, 1–2, and AL to LL, October 21, 1935, 2–4, all in LFP; *ATCL*, 92–94.

17. AL to AHL, March 18, 1936, 2, LFP.

18. AL-KL II. See also *ATCL*, 3–4, 91–95.

19. AL letters to AHL, December 2, 1937, 2, January 18, 1938, 1–2, February 17, 1938, 2–3, and June 5, 1939, 2, all in LFP; *ATCL*, 87, 91–95.

20. Quoted in *ATCL*, 96 (see also 95); AL-KL I; Leuchtenburg, *Franklin D. Roosevelt and the New Deal*, 244–249; Still, *Milwaukee*, 480–481.

21. AL-KL I. See also AL to AHL, May 2, 1933, 3, April 29, 1939, 1–2, and June 5, 1939, 1, in LFP; ABL; *ATCL*, 96.

22. AL-KL I.

23. *ATCL*, 96. See also AL-KL I. Although enacted into law in the summer of 1935, the Social Security system did not begin paying benefits to anyone except the indigent elderly and dependent children until January 1940 in order to give the trust fund time to accumulate sufficient reserves; see David M. Kennedy, *Freedom from Fear: The American People in Depression and War, 1929–1945* (New York: Oxford University Press), 271–272.

24. AL to LL, January 7, 1935, 8, LFP. See also Larson's other correspondence from 1935 to 1939, LFP; *ATCL*, 87–95.

25. *ATCL*, 108–109.

26. Writers' Program (U.S.) Wisconsin, *Wisconsin*, 247; Austin, *The Milwaukee Story*, 174–175, 199; John Gunther, *Inside U.S.A.* (New York: Harper & Brothers, 1946), 321–323; Reuss, *When Government Was Good*, 10, 14. Reuss, the product of a staunchly Republican household who shared AL's basic outlook, characterized the Wisconsin political scene in the late 1930s as "desolate."

27. See AL to AHL, March 27, 1935, 4, and April 14, 1935, 1–2, both in LFP; *ATCL*, 96; Reuss, *When Government Was Good*, 12–13.

28. AL-KL II; AL to AHL, January 18, 1938, 1, LFP; *ATCL*, 96, 106.

29. *ATCL,* 96.

30. Betsey Beeler Creekmore, *Knoxville* (Knoxville: University of Tennessee Press, 1958), 170–171; Michael J. McDonald and William Bruce Wheeler, *Knoxville, Tennessee: Continuity and Change in an Appalachian City* (Knoxville: University of Tennessee Press, 1983), 4–5, 50–69; *ATCL,* 96–97.

31. Creekmore, *Knoxville,* 92–112; McDonald and Wheeler, *Knoxville,* 11–14; Michael Barone and Grant Ujifusa, *The Almanac of American Politics 1988* (Washington, D.C.: National Journal, 1987), 110.

32. Creekmore, *Knoxville,* especially 171–174, 224–244; McDonald and Wheeler, *Knoxville,* 10–66; Gunther, *Inside USA,* 653–675.

33. Creekmore, *Knoxville,* 226–235; McDonald and Wheeler, *Knoxville,* 61–69.

34. Quoted in *ATCL,* 96–97.

35. Quoted in ibid., 97.

36. For the black boy at camp, see AL to LL, June 2, 1935, 2–3, LFP. For details of the University of Tennessee's policy of racial segregation, see Creekmore, *Knoxville,* 170–174; James Riley Montgomery, Stanley J. Folmsbee, and Lee Seifert Greene, *To Foster Knowledge: A History of the University of Tennessee, 1794–1970* (Knoxville: University of Tennessee Press, 1984), 101–105, 199.

37. *ATCL,* 97.

38. Ibid., 97–98.

39. Ibid., 98.

40. Quoted in ibid., 99 (see also 98).

41. Ibid., 99. See also Jack B. Weinstein, et al., *Cases and Materials on Evidence,* 7th ed. (Mineola, N.Y.: Foundation Press, 1983), 834–842.

42. Lex Larson, e-mail to the author, March 9, 2001; FNL to AHL, December 30, 1939, 2, AL to AHL, September [n.d.], 1940, 1–2, September 20, 1940, 2–4, November 12, 1940, 1–4, May 25, 1941, 1, and FNL to LL, "Monday," 1, all in LFP; *ATCL,* 99.

43. American Bar Association Survey Committee, *The Law Schools of Tennessee: Report of the Survey Committee* (Knoxville, Tenn.: University of Tennessee, 1938), 45 (see also 43–44); Clyde Conley Street, "A History of Legal Education in Tennessee" (M.A. thesis, University of Tennessee, 1941), 65–68; AL to AHL, February 8, 1940, 1, and February 28, 1940, 2, LFP; James Riley Montgomery, "Threshold of a New Day? The University of Tennessee, 1919–1946," *University of Tennessee Record* 74 (1971): 116–135, 146–149; Montgomery, Folmsbee and Greene, *To Foster Knowledge,* 181–194, 201.

44. American Bar Association Survey Committee, *The Law Schools of Tennessee,* 42, 44; Street, "A History of Legal Education in Tennessee," 65–68; Montgomery, "Threshold of a New Day?" 146–149; AL to AHL, March 11, 1940, 1–2, LFP.

45. University of Tennessee, *University of Tennessee Record* (Knoxville: University of Tennessee, 1940 and 1941), 43:269–271 and 44:89; AL to AHL, December 30, 1939, 1, February 8, 1940, 1, February 28, 1940, 1–2, March 11, 1940, 1–2, September [n.d.], 1940, 1–2, September 20, 1940, 3–4, AL to LL, November 18, 1940, 1–2, and FNL to LL, "Monday," all in LFP.

46. FNL to LL, "Monday," 1, LFP.

47. Ibid., 1; *ATCL,* 100.

48. AL to AHL, February 28, 1940, 2, LFP. See also AL's other letters to her and to LL from this period in LFP.

49. AL to AHL, March 11, 1940, 1, LFP.

50. See Montgomery, Folmsbee, and Greene, *To Foster Knowledge,* 181–182, 194; undated handwritten curriculum vitae and AL to AHL, November 12, 1940, 4, LFP; *ATCL,* 96–97, 99.

51. Arthur Larson, "Has the President an Inherent Power of Removal of His Non-Executive Appointees?" *Tennessee Law Review* 16 (April 1940): 259–260; David E. Lilienthal, *The Journals of David Lilienthal*, vol. I, *The TVA Years, 1939–1945* (New York: Harper & Row, 1964), 69–74; William E. Leuchtenburg, *The Supreme Court Reborn: The Constitutional Revolution in the Age of Roosevelt* (New York: Oxford University Press, 1995), 52–81.

52. AL to AHL, February 28, 1940, 1–2, LFP; Larson, "Has the President an Inherent Power of Removal?" 259–290.

53. Larson, "Has the President an Inherent Power of Removal?" 275. See also *A. E. Morgan v. Tennessee Valley Authority, et al.*, 28 F. Supp. 732 (E. D. Tenn. 1939); *Morgan v. Tennessee Valley Authority*, 115 F.2d 990 (6th Cir. 1940); *Morgan v. Tennessee Valley Authority*, 312 U.S. 701 (1941).

54. Leuchtenburg, *Franklin D. Roosevelt and the New Deal*, 91–92, 171; Arthur M. Schlesinger, Jr., *The Coming of the New Deal* (Boston: Houghton Mifflin, 1958), 486–489 and *The Politics of Upheaval*, 518–523; Larson, "Has the President an Inherent Power of Removal?" 264; Walter Lippmann, *The Good Society* (Boston: Little, Brown, 1937); Ronald Steel, *Walter Lippmann and the American Century* (Boston: Little, Brown, 1980), 322–326.

55. Arthur Larson, "The American Presidency," *Tennessee Law Review* 16 (December 1939–June 1941): 758–759; see also Harold Laski, *The American Presidency: An Interpretation* (New York: Harper and Brothers, 1940); Schlesinger, *The Politics of Upheaval*, 170–174.

56. See Arthur Larson, "The Doctrine of 'Constitutional Fact,'" *Temple University Law Quarterly* 15 (February 1941): 185–221; Wex S. Malone, "A Tribute to Arthur Larson," *Duke Law Journal* 1980 (June 1980): 392–393; Roy Lubove, *The Struggle for Social Security, 1900–1935*, 2nd ed. (Pittsburgh, Pa.: University of Pittsburgh Press, 1986), 45–65.

57. Larson, "The Doctrine of 'Constitutional Fact,'" 189–190. For the relationship between workers' compensation laws and the creation of the modern American welfare state, see Lubove, *The Struggle for Social Security*, especially 45–65.

58. Thurman Arnold, *Bottlenecks of Business* (New York: Reynal and Hitchcock, 1940); Alan Brinkley, *The End of Reform: New Deal Liberalism in Recession and War* (New York: Alfred A. Knopf, 1995), 106–122.

59. Arthur Larson, "Bottlenecks of Business," *Tennessee Law Review* 16 (December 1939–June 1941): 759–760.

60. Arthur Larson, "A Century of Social Thought," *Tennessee Law Review* 16 (December 1939–June 1941): 1014; see also *A Century of Social Thought; A Series of Lectures Delivered at Duke University during the Academic Year 1938–1939 as a Part of the Centennial Celebration of That Institution* (Durham, N.C.: Duke University Press, 1939).

61. Larson, "A Century of Social Thought," 1014.

62. Ibid., 1015. For Hoover and Taft, see Herbert Clark Hoover, *Addresses Upon the American Road, 1933–1938* (New York: Scribner's, 1938), 300–324, and *Addresses Upon the American Road, 1940–1941* (New York: Scribner's, 1941), 3–114; Joan Hoff Wilson, *Herbert Hoover: Forgotten Progressive* (Prospect Heights, Ill.: Waveland Press, 1992), 232–248; Clarence E. Wunderlin, ed., *The Papers of Robert A. Taft*, vol. I, *1889–1938* (Kent, Ohio: Kent State University Press, 1997), 393–200; James Patterson, *Mr. Republican: A Biography of Robert A. Taft* (Boston: Houghton Mifflin, 1972), 195–202, 237–250; John Morton Blum, *V Was for Victory: Politics and American Culture during World War II* (New York: Harcourt Brace Jovanovich, 1976), 271–273.

63. AL-KL I; Reuss, *When Government Was Good*, 14–15; Reuss, "A Tribute," 405–406; *ATCL*, 99–100.0.On the nature of the New Deal's third phase, see Richard Polenberg,

War and Society (Philadelphia: Lippincott, 1972); Blum, *V Was For Victory;* Brinkley, *The End of Reform,* 175–271; and Kennedy, *Freedom from Fear,* 615–668, 746–797.

64. Gunther, *Inside USA,* 761. See also AL-KL I; *ATCL,* 99–100; McDonald and Wheeler, *Knoxville,* 67–69; Montgomery, "Threshold of a New Day?" 133–134.

65. McDonald and Wheeler, *Knoxville,* 69; Montgomery, "Threshold of a New Day? 133–134; *ATCL,* 99–100.

66. See AL to FNL, "Friday Night," and his letters to AHL, September 10, 1941, 1–2, and September 25, 1941, 1–4, all in LFP; Laurence E. Tilley, *Chronology of the Office of Price Administration* (Washington, D.C.: U.S. Government Printing Office, 1946); Andrew H. Bartels, "The Office of Price Administration and the Legacy of the New Deal, 1939–1946," *Public Historian* 5 (Summer 1983): 5–29; John Kenneth Galbraith, *A Life in Our Times* (Boston: Houghton Mifflin, 1981), 106–165.

67. Galbraith, *A Life in Our Times,* 134–136; AL-KL I; *ATCL,* 100; Tilley, *Chronology of the Office of Price Administration.*

68. Bartels, "Office of Price Administration," 12–18; Galbraith, *A Life in Our Times,* 163–170; Tilley, *Chronology of the Office of Price Administration* ; Sterling MacMillan, *Individual Firm Adjustments under OPA: A Study in the Dynamics of Flexible Pricing* (Bloomington, Ind.: Principia Press, 1949), especially 89–117.

69. AL-KL I. See also AL to FNL, May 19, 1943, 1, "Sunday," 1–4, May 25, 1943, 2–3, and May 30, 1943, 2–3, all in LFP; Harvey C. Mansfield and Associates, *A Short History of the OPA* (Washington, D.C.: Office of Price Administration, 1947), 209–210; *ATCL,* 100.

70. See AL to FNL, May 1, 1942, 1–3, May 2, 1942, 1–6, September 5, 1942, 1–5, March 16, 1943, 1–2, May 19, 1943, 1–3, "Sunday," 1–4, June 23, 1944, 1–4, June 24, 1944, 1–4, and June 29, 1944, 1–5, and AL to AHL, September 10, 1941, 1–2, September 25, 1941, 1–4, all in LFP; *ATCL,* 100; Galbraith, *A Life in Our Times,* 179–189; Meg Jacobs, "'How About Some Meat?': The Office of Price Administration, Consumption Politics, and State Building from the Bottom Up, 1941–1946," *Journal of American History* 84 (December 1997): 910–941; and Brinkley, *The End of Reform,* 46–48.

71. Galbraith, *A Life in Our Times,* 124–189; Brinkley, *The End of Reform,* 146–148; Bartels, "Office of Price Administration," 5–29; Jacobs, "'How About Some Meat?'" 910–913; David Brinkley, *Washington Goes to War* (New York: Alfred A. Knopf, 1988), 133–134. On the OPA's extraordinary nature, see especially Alan Brinkley's observation in *The End of Reform* that "the OPA may have been the most intrusive federal bureaucracy ever created in America" (147). Andrew Bartels suggests in his article cited above that a more comprehensive price control regime could have been implemented immediately after the attack on Pearl Harbor (12), but that seems doubtful. For the issue of state capacity, see Peter B. Evans, Dietrich Rueschemeyer, and Theda Skocpol, eds., *Bringing the State Back In* (Cambridge: Cambridge University Press, 1985).

72. AL to FNL, May 2, 1942, 1 (see also 2–6), AL to FNL, April 29, 1942, 2, September 5, 1942, 3–4, and March 16, 1943, 1–2, all in LFP.

73. AL to FNL, June 24, 1944, 4, LFP.

74. Brinkley, *End of Reform,* 147; Brinkley, *Washington Goes to War,* 133; Blum, *V Was for Victory,* 117–140; Jacobs, "'How About Some Meat?'" 917; Howell Harris, *The Right to Manage: Industrial Relations Policies of American Business in the 1940's* (Madison: University of Wisconsin Press, 1982), especially 20–47.

75. AL to his parents, January 11, 1942, 2, LFP.

76. See ibid., 1. See also with respect to this controversy, Bartels, "Office of Price Administration," 10–16; Galbraith, *A Life in Our Times,* 140–141, 151–152. On the origins of the "parity" concept, see William Leuchtenburg, *The Perils of Prosperity, 1914-32* (Chicago: University of Chicago Press, 1958), 102–103.

77. AL to his parents, January 11, 1942, 2, LFP. See also Brinkley, *Washington Goes to War*, 133–134; Brinkley, *End of Reform*, 145–148; Galbraith, *A Life in Our Times*, 177–189.

78. AL to FNL, June 1, 1943, 1, LFP.

79. See AL to FNL, September 5, 1942, 3–4, June 23, 1944, 1–4, and June 24, 1941–1942, all in LFP.

80. See FNL's letters to AL postmarked August 31, 1943, 1–2, August 20, 1943, 3, FNL to AL, September 2, 1943, 2–3, AL to FNL, postmarked September 4, 1943, 3–4, September 17, 1943, 3, AL to FNL, September 8, 1943, 2, September 16, 1943, 2–4, September 17, 1943, 2, June 21, 1944, 2, June 23, 1944, 1–4, June 24, 1944, 4, June 29, 1944, 5–6, his handwritten résumé, his letter to Claude Watkins, August 1, 1944 and Watkins's reply, August 4, 1944, all in LFP; *ATCL*, 102.

81. *ATCL*, 102; Blum, *V Was for Victory*, 283–284.

82. *ATCL*, 102.

83. Ibid.

84. See AL to FNL, March 19, 1945, 1–8, March 20, 1945, March 22, 1945, 1, March 26, 1945, 1, March 27, 1945, 1, March 28, 1945, 1, his two letters to her dated March 30, 1945, and AL to FNL, April 4, 1945, 1–4, April 6, 1945, 1–2, April 9, 1945, 1, LFP; AL-KL I; *ATCL*, 102–104.

85. *ATCL*, 102–104; Arthur Larson, "The Northern Countries," in Mordecai Ezekiel, ed., *Towards World Prosperity: Through Industrial and Agricultural Development and Expansion* (New York: Harper and Brothers, 1947), 107–127; Marquis Childs, *Sweden: The Middle Way* (New York: Penguin, 1948); Robert O. Paxton, *Europe in the Twentieth Century*, 2nd ed. (New York: Harcourt, Brace, Jovanovich, 1985), 328–329.

86. Larson, "The Northern Countries," 119 (see also 117–118, 120–127). For Ezekiel's emphasis on economic growth as the remedy for depression and authoritarianism, see the various references to him in Brinkley, *End of Reform*.

87. See Larson, "The Northern Countries," 117–127.

88. *ATCL*, 116.

89. AL-KL II. See also the transcript of DDE's speech to the joint session of Congress, which is reprinted in full in U.S. Congress, *Congressional Record*, vol. 91, Part 5, 79th Congress, 1st Session (Washington, D.C.: U.S. Government Printing Office 1945), 6243–6245.

90. See AL to FNL, "Saturday," 2, "Friday," 3–4, "Thursday," (postmarked September 7, 1943), 1–4, September 9, 1943, 1–8, September 11, 1943, 1–3, FNL to AL postmarked September 8, 1943, 1–3, and Della Cyrus to FNL, May 22, 1943, 1–2, all in LFP; LKL; AHTI.

91. AL to FNL, "Thursday" (postmarked September 7, 1943), 2–3 (see also 1, 4), and "Saturday," 2, "Friday," 3–4, September 9, 1943, 1–8, September 11, 1943, 1–3, all in LFP.

92. *ATCL*, 208.

93. AL to FNL, "Friday," 2–3, LFP.

94. FNL to AL, August 30, 1943, 1, LFP.

95. See AL to FNL, "Saturday,"1–2, written shortly after the letter cited in note 94. See also on this point their correspondence more generally, all of which is in LFP.

96. AL to FNL, "Tuesday," 3, LFP. See also Leuchtenburg, *Franklin D. Roosevelt and the New Deal*, 271–274; Blum, *V Was for Victory*, 221–222, 234–235; George H. Mayer, *The Republican Party, 1854–1964* (New York: Oxford University Press, 1964), 428–474; James T. Patterson, *Congressional Conservatism and the New Deal: The Growth of the Conservative Coalition in Congress, 1933–1939* (Lexington: University of Kentucky Press, 1967).

97. AL to FNL, "Tuesday," 3, LFP.

98. See the correspondence between AL and FNL from 1941 to 1945, LFP.

99. FNL to AL, postmarked September 20, 1943, 2–3, LFP.

100. These conclusions emerge from FNL's many letters to AL from the 1930s and early 1940s, all of which are in LFP. For the trend toward rationing one paying job per household during the Depression, see Susan Ware, *Holding Their Own: American Women in the 1930s* (Boston: Twayne, 1982), 27–30. The demise of the Federal Theatre Project on June 30, 1939, is noted in Leuchtenburg, *Franklin D. Roosevelt and the New Deal*, 272–273.

101. AL to FNL, September 14, 1943, 2, LFP (see also 1, 3–4).

102. See FNL to AL, April 28, 1942, 5, "Monday" (postmarked May 24, 1943), 2, August 29, 1943, 13, "Tuesday," 3, "Later," 1, September 20, 1943, 1–2, and AL to FNL, April 29, 1942, 2–3, March 16, 1943, 2, May 19, 1943, 2, May 30, 1943, 3, "Friday" (postmarked September 4, 1943), 4, September 18, 1943, 2, and September 15, 1943, 4, all in LFP.

103. See AL to FNL, June 6, 1943, his June 11, 1943, covering note, and FNL to AL, September 2, 1943, 3, all in LFP.

104. AL to FNL, June 1, 1943, 1, "Sunday" (postmarked May 23, 1943), 3–5, May 25, 1943, 1, and May 30, 1943, 2–3, all in LFP.

105. See FNL to AL, postmarked September 13, 1943, 1–2, LFP; *ATCL*, 102.

106. *ATCL*, 101–102; see Brinkley, *Washington Goes to War*, 103–137 for an insightful portrait of life in the nation's capital during World War II.

107. See AL to AHL, September 10, 1941, 2, FNL to AHL, September 23, 1941, 1–2, AL to FNL, "Friday," 6, June 21, 1944, 1, FNL to AL, August 28, 1943, 1–2, "Thurs. A.M." (postmarked August 28, 1943), 2–3, 6, August 29, 1943, 4, "Sunday" (postmarked September 8, 1943), 5, September 9, 1943, 1–3, "Sat." (postmarked September 20, 1943), 1, and the copy of AL's 1942 income tax return, March 13, 1943, which listed his net income for that year as $5,347.64, and his handwritten resume, all in LFP.

108. AL to Dr. Walter Dandy, April 5, 1944, 1, LFP. See also AL's other letters to Dandy, February 17, 1942, March 18, 1942, and March 25, 1942, AL to his parents, January 11, 1942, 1, AL to the OPA office manager, Harold Vincent, requesting sick leave in December 1941, AL to Local Draft Board No. 4 in Knoxville, Tennessee, August 12, 1942, AL to FNL, April 29, 1943, 1–2, May 1, 1942, 1, "Sunday" (postmarked May 23, 1943), 5–6, "Friday" (postmarked August 27, 1943), 5–6, "Wednesday" (September postmarked, 1943), 1–3, and FNL to AL, September 9, 1943, 1–2, all in LFP.

109. AL-KL I. See also the Selective Service System's order to AL to report for a preinduction physical on April 12, 1944, LFP.

110. AL-KL I.

111. See FNL to AL, September 9, 1943, 1–2, AL to Claude Watkins, August 1, 1944, and Watkins to AL, August 4, 1944, all in LFP; *ATCL*, 104–105.

112. See AL to Julius Stulman, November 9, 1945, 1–2, LFP; *ATCL*, 105.

113. AL-KL I; *ATCL*, 105–106. See also AL to FNL, October 31, 1945, 2, LFP, where he wrote "so far as law schools are concerned, if it hadn't been for Cornell, what would my prospects have been? I shudder to think of it."

4. Legal Scholar

1. See the correspondence between AL and FNL from October 1945 through January 1946, and AL to Julius Stulman, November 9, 1945, all in LFP; AL-KL I; *ATCL*, 106–107.

2. See *ATCL*, 107.

3. Morris Bishop, *A History of Cornell* (Ithaca, N.Y.: Cornell University Press, 1962), 477–483, 554–609; Robert S. Stevens, "The Cornell Law School from 1919 to 1954," *Cornell Law Review* 54 (February 1969): 332–357.

4. The details of the Larson family's income during this time are contained in AL to

FNL, January 16, 1946, 3–4, LFP. The casebook appeared in 1947 under the title *Cases and Materials on the Law of Corporations* (St. Paul, Minn.: West Publishing Company, 1947).

5. See the material dealing with Stevens in the Cornell Faculty Biographical Files, Box 13, RMCKLCU; AL to FNL, January 10, 1946, 2, and January 16, 1946, 2–3, LFP; John W. MacDonald, "Robert Sproule Stevens: His Impact on the Cornell Law School," *Cornell Law Quarterly* 50 (Summer 1965): 579–586; Harry G. Henn, "Robert Sproule Stevens: His Influence on Corporation Law," *Cornell Law Quarterly* 50 (Summer 1965): 587–598; Gray Thoron, "Robert Sproule Stevens," *Cornell Law Review* 54 (February 1969): 327–357; Ronald Steel, *Walter Lippmann and the American Century* (Boston: Little, Brown, 1980), 12–22; and *ATCL*, 106.

6. AL to FNL, October 29, 1945, 5, LFP. See also Bishop, *A History of Cornell*, 477; Kermit Carlyle Parsons, *The Cornell Campus: A History of Its Planning and Development* (Ithaca, N.Y.: Cornell University Press, 1968), 239; and Stevens, "The Cornell Law School," 332–352.

7. See "Writings [of] Arthur Larson," *Duke Law Journal* 1980 (June 1980): 407–415; AL to FNL, January 16, 1946, 1–3, LFP; AL-KL I; *ATCL*, 107–113.

8. AL to FNL, November 3, 1945, 1–2, LFP; *ATCL*, 107–109.

9. Wex S. Malone, "A Tribute to Arthur Larson," *Duke Law Journal* 1980 (June 1980): 392–394; *ATCL*, 109–110.

10. Samuel Horovitz, *Injury and Death under Workmen's Compensation Laws* (Boston: Wright & Potter, 1944), vii. See also Malone, "A Tribute to Arthur Larson," 393; *ATCL*, 175.

11. Malone, "A Tribute to Arthur Larson," 393; *ATCL*, 108–110.

12. Henn, "Robert Sproule Stevens," 593–594.

13. AL to FNL, December 4, 1945, 1, LFP. See also *ATCL*, 109–110.

14. *ATCL*, 110. For AL's work habits, see his letters to FNL, November 3, 1945, 1, November 29, 1945, 1, January 10, 1946, 2, January 13, 1946, 4, and AL to AHL, March 30, 1951, 2, all in LFP.

15. Three years after this operation, AL wrote the surgeon who performed it to report that "between the acute attacks and the chronic pains, the fusion episode represents a loss and not a gain"; AL to Dr. L. A. Lantzounis, September 17, 1951, LFP. See also AL's other letters to Lantzounis, May 17, 1948, May 21, 1948, January 16, 1950, and September 17, 1951, Lantzounis to AL, May 19, 1948, AL to the Magistrate's Court, City of New York, April 2, 1949, AL to FNL, January 16, 1946, 3, and "Saturday" [June 5, 1948], AL to Ralph B. Cheney, April 29, 1949, AL to Robert Newcomb, September 29, 1949, and AL to Mrs. [?] Craumann, February 12, 1951, all in LFP; *ATCL*, 107–108. For LL's final illness and death, see AL to LL, October 11, 1949, November 28, 1949, December 31, 1949, January 11, 1950, January 17, 1950, January 26, 1950, February 6, 1950, LL to AL, October 8, 1950, and "Judge Lewis Larson," all in LFP; AL-KL I.

16. See AL to LL, November 28, 1949, 2, and January 11, 1950, 2–3, AL to AHL, March 30, 1951, 2, AL to "Cousin [Orvin?] Larson, September 17, 1951, 1, all in LFP; *ATCL*, 108–111.

17. See AL to Clara, May 23, 1951, 2, LFP; Lex Larson, e-mail to author, January 21, 1999; *ATCL*, 111–112.

18. *ATCL*, 112.

19. The details about the book's size, weight, and price are noted in "New Man," *Time Magazine*, April 5, 1954, 20.

20. See Malone, "A Tribute to Arthur Larson," 393–395; A. Kenneth Pye, "A Tribute to Arthur Larson," *Duke Law Journal* 1980 (June 1980): 400–404; and Harvard

University's press release, January 31, 1957, announcing the award of the Henderson Prize, in LFP.

21. Malone, "A Tribute to Arthur Larson," 394; Pye, "A Tribute to Arthur Larson," 400; Arthur Larson, "The Welfare State and Workmen's Compensation," *Nacca Law Journal* 5 (May 1950): 18–36; Arthur Larson, "The Nature and Origins of Workmen's Compensation," 37 *Cornell Law Quarterly* (Winter 1952): 206–234.

22. See AL to LL, January 11, 1950, 3, LFP; the April 3, 1950, press release from Cornell's Office of Public Relations and Information explaining the lecture series, in the file on AL in Faculty Biographical Material, Box 13, RMCKLCU; Larson, "The Welfare State and Workmen's Compensation," 18–36.

23. Larson, "The Welfare State and Workmen's Compensation," 19–25. For the relationship between state workers' compensation laws and the creation of the modern American welfare state, see Roy Lubove, *The Struggle for Social Security, 1900–1935,* 2nd ed. (Pittsburgh: University of Pittsburgh Press, 1986), 45–65; David A. Moss, *Socializing Security: Progressive-Era Economists and the Origins of American Social Policy* (Cambridge, Mass.: Harvard University Press, 1996), 33, 68–71.

24. Larson, "The Welfare State and Workmen's Compensation," 23.

25. For the way in which American welfare state measures, especially those associated with the New Deal, tended to encourage a patriarchal social system, see Barbara J. Nelson, "The Origins of the Two-Channel Welfare State: Workmen's Compensation and Mother's Aid," in Linda Gordon, ed., *Women, the State and Welfare* (Madison: University of Wisconsin Press, 1990), 123–151; Linda Gordon, *Pitied But Not Entitled: Single Mothers and the History of Welfare* (New York: Free Press, 1994); Michael Willrich, "Home Slackers: Men, the State and Welfare in Modern America," *Journal of American History* 87 (September 2000): 460–489; Alice Kessler-Harris, *In Pursuit of Equity: Women, Men, and the Quest for Economic Citizenship in 20th-Century America* (New York: Oxford University Press, 2001).

26. Arthur Larson, *The Law of Workmen's Compensation* (Albany, N.Y.: Mathew Bender, 1952); LKL.

27. Larson, "The Welfare State and Workmen's Compensation," 25.

28. Ibid., 28 (see also 27).

29. Ibid., 28.

30. Ibid., 29.

31. Ibid., 31 (see also 30).

32. Ibid., 33 (see also 32).

33. Ibid., 34–35.

34. Ibid., 35.

35. Ibid.

36. Arthur Larson, "The Future of Workmen's Compensation," *Nacca Law Journal* 6 (November 1950): 38–39.

37. See AL to Henry S. Manley, March 17, 1948, 1, LFP; Arthur Larson, "Social Legislation and the Law Schools," *American Bar Association Journal* 39 (1952): 237–239.

38. See Larson, "Nature and Origins of Workmen's Compensation," 221–234.

39. Ibid., 228–231. On the importance of the German workers' compensation system to other industrial countries, see Daniel Rodgers, *Atlantic Crossings: Social Politics in a Progressive Age* (Cambridge, Mass.: Belknap Press of Harvard University, 1998), 245–266.

40. Larson, "Nature and Origins of Workmen's Compensation," 231–233. For U.S. judiciary rulings that constricted the emergence of the American welfare state, see Rodgers, *Atlantic Crossings*, 206, 238, 379, 427, 443, 445; Arnold N. Paul, *Conservative Crisis and the Rule of Law: Attitudes of Bar and Bench, 1887–1896* (Ithaca, N.Y.: Cornell University

Press, 1960); Paul Kens, *Lochner v. New York: Economic Regulation on Trial* (Lawrence: University Press of Kansas, 1998), 154–176.

41. See Larson, "Nature and Origins of Workmen's Compensation," 206–207, 231–234; Benjamin R. Twiss, *Lawyers and the Constitution: How Laissez Faire Came to the Supreme Court* (Princeton, N.J.: Princeton University Press, 1942); *Lochner v. New York*, 198 U.S. 45 (1905); Kens, *Lochner v. New York*; John Fabian Witt, "The Transformation of Work and the Law of Workplace Accidents, 1842–1910," *Yale Law Journal* 107 (1998): 1467–1502. Daniel Rodgers points out that the German system did not require employee contributions in principle but did so in practice by requiring that German workers exhaust their sickness benefits before receiving payments from the workers' compensation system; Rodgers, *Atlantic Crossings*, 248–249.

42. See Larson, "Nature and Origins of Workmen's Compensation," 206–207, 231–234; Witt, "The Transformation of Work and the Law of Workplace Accidents," 1467–1502.

43. Mandatory worker contributions could also have provided the means to pay higher levels of compensation. See the report of the New York Commission, whose recommendations became the basis for the landmark New York workmen's compensation statute of 1910, at 25 N. Y. Sen. Doc. No. 38 (1910). The report's authors noted that "could we see a practical way to put a [such a] scheme of compensation in force . . . we would recommend it. The German system on some such lines seems admirable. But practically we see no way to accomplish this by force of compulsory law" (67). On the differences in financing between the European and American workers' compensation systems, see Larson, "Nature and Origins of Workmen's Compensation," 206–207, 232–234; and Rodgers, *Atlantic Crossings*, 248–266.

44. For an example of Larson's tendency to avoid controversial subjects that seemed moot, see "Nature and Origins of Workmen's Compensation," where he wrote, "At the present time, with the constitutionality of all types of compensation acts firmly established, there is no practical purpose to be served by tracing out the elaborate and violent constitutional law arguments provoked by the early acts" (232). On the demise of Lochner and the emergence of the New Deal industrial relations system, see Alpheus T. Mason, *The Supreme Court from Taft to Burger*, 3rd ed. (Baton Rouge: Louisiana State University Press, 1979), 40–128; Leuchtenburg, *The Supreme Court Reborn*, 213–236; and David L. Stebenne, *Arthur J. Goldberg: New Deal Liberal* (New York: Oxford University Press, 1996), 9–153.

45. Larson, "Nature and Origins of Workmen's Compensation," 206–234; Malone, "A Tribute to Arthur Larson," 394.

46. See Malone, "A Tribute to Arthur Larson," 394–395; Reuss, "A Tribute," 405 and the discussion on pages 85–88, 93–94, and 105–110.

47. Leuchtenburg, *The Supreme Court Reborn*, 220; conversation with James Brudney, November 18, 1999.

48. Malone, "A Tribute to Arthur Larson," 394–395; Pye, "A Tribute to Arthur Larson," 400.

49. Malone, "A Tribute to Arthur Larson," 395; LKL.

50. For the intellectual milieu of the 1950s, see John Patrick Diggins, *The Proud Decades: America in War and Peace, 1941–1960* (New York: Norton, 1988), 247–257; Richard H. Pells, *The Liberal Mind in a Conservative Age: American Intellectuals in the 1940s and 1950s* (Middletown, Conn.: Wesleyan University Press, 1985), especially 96–147.

51. AL-KL I; *ATCL*, 113.

52. See AL to Carl [?], January 18, 1953, AL to General Electric, January 22, 1953, Arthur E. Sutherland to AL, January 28, 1953, the clipping from the *Pittsburgh Post Gazette* entitled "Cornell Professor Named Pitt Law Dean," all in LFP; AL-KL I; *ATCL*, 113–114.

53. See AL to FNL, January 16, 1946, 4, AL's petition for admission to the New York Bar, 2, AL's letter of resignation from the Cornell faculty to Robert Stevens, February 17, 1953, AL to Carl, April 27, 1953, the letters from AL and FNL to his parents from 1945 to 1953, all in LFP; AL-KL I; ABL; LKL; and *ATCL*, 106–107, 113–114.

54. LKL.

5. *To the Eisenhower Administration*

1. AL's starting date as dean of Pittsburgh Law School is noted in W. Edward Sell, *The Law Down A Century Remembered:* A *100 Year History of the University of Pittsburgh Law School* (Pittsburgh, Pa.: W. Edward Sell, 1995), 95.

2. See AL to Clara [?], May 23, 1951, 2, LFP; AL-KL I; AL Memoir, Social Security Project, OHC, CU, 2, 9–12; Arthur Marwick, *British Society since 1945* (Harmondsworth: Penguin Books, 1982), 49–63; AL, "The American System: Structure, Coverage and Current Issues," in the file on AL at the ASCUP; *ATCL*, 111, 115, 127.

3. Larson, "The American System," 4.

4. Ibid. The turning point came in February 1951, when the value of welfare payments to the aged dropped below the value of insurance payments for the first time. See Edward D. Berkowitz, "The Historical Development of Social Security in the United States," in Eric R. Kingson and James H. Schulz, eds., *Social Security in the 21st Century* (New York: Oxford University Press, 1997), 28. See also Brian Gratton, "The New Welfare State: Social Security and Retirement in 1950," *Social Science History* 12 (Summer 1988): 172–174.

5. Larson, "The American System," 7.

6. Larson, "The American System," 8 (see also 7).

7. Ibid., 8–9.

8. Ibid., 10 (see also 7–9).

9. Ibid., 27.

10. Ibid., 27–28.

11. Ibid., 28. For the early creation of sickness insurance systems in other major industrial countries, see Deltev Zöllner, "Germany," 24–27; Yves Saint-Jours, "France," 111; A. I. Ogus, "Great Britain," 182–187; Herbert Hofmeister, "Austria," 285–287 and 302–306, all in Peter A. Kohler and Hans F. Zacher with Martin Partington, eds., *The Evolution of Social Insurance, 1881–1981: Studies of Germany, France, Great Britain, Austria and Switzerland* (London: Frances Pinter, 1982); and International Labour Office, *An Introduction to Social Security* (Geneva: Kundig, 1970), 10–12.

12. Larson, "The American System," 28–29. Social security's objective of creating job openings by promoting retirement is discussed in William Graebner, *A History of Retirement: The Meaning and Function of an American Institution, 1885–1978* (New Haven, Conn.: Yale University Press, 1980), 120–214. On the emergence of Social Security in the late 1930s, see Stefan A. Riesenfeld with Richard C. Maxwell, *Modern Social Legislation* (Brooklyn, N.Y.: Foundation Press, 1950), 15–16; J. Douglas Brown, *An American Philosophy of Social Security: Evolution and Issues* (Princeton, N.J.: Princeton University Press, 1972), 131–150; W. Andrew Achenbaum, *Social Security: Visions and Revisions* (Cambridge: Cambridge University Press, 1986), 32–37; Edward D. Berkowitz, "The First Advisory Council and the 1939 Amendments," in Edward D. Berkowitz, ed., *Social Security after Fifty: Successes and Failures* (New York: Greenwood Press, 1987), 55–78; Bruno Stein, "Pay-as-You-Go, Partial Prefunding, and Full Funding in American Social Security," *History of Political Economy* 23 (1991): 79–83; and William R. Brock, "From New Deal to New Liberalism," *Reviews in American History* 23 (December 1995): 713.

13. For resistance to disability insurance legislation, see Brown, *An American Philosophy of Social Security*, 151–156; Edward D. Berkowitz, "Disability Insurance and the Social Security Tradition," in Gerald D. Nash, Noel H. Pugach, and Richard F. Tomasson, eds., *Social Security: The First Half Century* (Albuquerque: University of New Mexico Press, 1988), 279–285; and Edward D. Berkowitz, "The Historical Development of Social Security in the United States" and Jerry L. Mashaw, "Disability Why Does the Search for Good Programs Continue?" both in Kingson and Schulz, *Social Security in the 21st Century*, 31 and 105–108, respectively.

14. Larson, "The American System," 29.

15. Ibid, 30–37.

16. Ibid., 38–44.

17. Ibid., 45.

18. Ibid., 45.

19. On the origins of Medicare, see Charles McKinney, "The Role of Organized Labor in the Quest for Compulsory Health Insurance, 1912–1965" (Ph.D. diss., University of Wisconsin, 1969); Brown, *An American Philosophy of Social Security*, 194–196; Monte M. Poen, *Harry S. Truman Versus the Medical Lobby: The Genesis of Medicare* (Columbia: University of Missouri Press, 1979).

20. Larson, "The American System," 46.

21. Ibid., 47; on the stalemate in Congress at that time, see Poen, *Harry S. Truman Versus the Medical Lobby*, 174–210.

22. Larson, "The American System," 48 (see also 47).

23. Ibid., 48–49.

24. Ibid., 48–56, especially 50–51.

25. Ibid., 51. Arthur Marwick explained the decision to make such payments to the mother alone as "a very rudimentary sign of feminist influence on social legislation, which recognized women's role as child-rearers, and was designed to prevent husbands from spending the money on drink or horses." See *British Society since 1945*, 51. Of course, one could also see this as an antifeminist policy for its tendency to imply that women alone were responsible for childrearing and for offering an inducement to women to have more children than they otherwise might choose to.

26. Larson, "The American System," 52.

27. On the optimism among policymakers and academics bred by the spectacular growth of the U.S. economy during the 1940s and early 1950s, see Alan Brinkley, *The End of Reform: New Deal Liberalism in Recession and War* (New York: Alfred A. Knopf, 1995), 227–271; Robert Lekachman, *The Age of Keynes* (New York: McGraw-Hill, 1966), 144–202; and John Kenneth Galbraith, *Economics in Perspective* (Boston: Houghton Mifflin, 1987), 237–265.

28. Larson, "The American System," 52. For the American Baby Boom, see John Patrick Diggins, *The Proud Decades: America in War and Peace, 1941–1960* (New York: Norton, 1988), 181, which notes that the U.S. population "leaped from 130 million in 1940 to 165 million by the mid-1950's, the biggest increase in the history of the Republic." See also Elaine Tyler May, "Cold War—Warm Hearth: Politics and the Family in Postwar America," in Steve Fraser and Gary Gerstle, eds., *Rise and Fall of the New Deal Order, 1930–1980* (Princeton, N.J.: Princeton University Press, 1989), 153–155; Andrew Cherlin, *Marriage, Divorce, Remarriage* (Cambridge, Mass.: Harvard University Press, 1981), 6–32; For comparisons with European demographic patterns, see Hugh Carter and Paul C. Glick, *Marriage and Divorce: A Social and Economic Study* (Cambridge, Mass.: Harvard University Press, 1976), 22–41.

29. Larson, "The American System," 52–53. On the creation of Britain's National

Health Service, see Marwick, *British Society since 1945*, 53–58. Marwick noted that its creation was "widely seen, both at the time and since, as the most significant and successful social innovation of the period" (56).

30. Larson, "The American System," 53.

31. Ibid., 54; Marwick, *British Society since 1945*, 51–53.

32. Larson, "The American System," 55; Marwick, *British Society since 1945*, 52–53. Marwick noted that the level of British public assistance payments during the 1950s cloaked the degree to which national insurance benefits were inadequate because "save in emergencies, National Assistance would only be paid out after a personal needs test; it later transpired that many in need were in fact deterred by this from applying for it" (53).

33. Larson, "The American System," 57.

34. Ibid., 58.

35. Ibid., 58–59.

36. Ibid., 59. On the intense hostility of the British working class to the means test, see Marwick, *British Society since 1945*, 50–51, where the author wrote that "the 'means test' . . . sounded in Labour ears as once the phrase 'Spanish inquisition' had sounded in the ears of Protestant zealots."

37. Larson, "The American System," 60.

38. Ibid., 60–61.

39. On Britain's postwar economic problems, see Robert O. Paxton, *Europe in the Twentieth Century*, 2nd ed. (New York: Harcourt, Brace, Jovanovich, 1985), 531–533; Pauline Gregg, *A Social and Economic History of Britain, 1760–1970*, 6th ed. (London: George G. Harrap & Co., 1971), 549–576. For the views of a representative and influential moderate leftist in this same period, see David L. Stebenne, *Arthur J. Goldberg: New Deal Liberal* (New York: Oxford University Press, 1996).

40. Larson, "The American System," 64.

41. Ibid.

42. Ibid., 65.

43. Ibid., 65–67.

44. Ibid., 68–69.

45. Ibid., 81.

46. Ibid.

47. Ibid., 81–82. BG had won election to the U.S. Senate in November 1952 with the help of what he called DDE's "good, stiff coattail." For that observation and more about BG's libertarian outlook, see his memoir in OHC, DDEL, 1–12. See also BG's manifesto *The Conscience of a Conservative* (Shepherdsville, Ky.: Victor Publishing Company, 1960), 68–75; Robert Alan Goldberg, *Barry Goldwater* (New Haven, Conn.: Yale University Press), 3–109; Rick Perlstein, *Before the Storm: Barry Goldwater and the Unmaking of the American Consensus* (New York: Hill and Wang, 2001), especially 3–68.

48. Larson, "The American System," 82. For New Deal liberals' unhappiness with the shortcomings of locally based relief efforts during the Depression and enthusiasm for a nationalized social insurance system, see William R. Brock, *Welfare, Democracy and the New Deal* (Cambridge: Cambridge University Press, 1988), 171–201, and Brock, "From New Deal to New Liberalism," 713.

49. Larson, "The American System," 83.

50. Ibid., 83–87. For the emergence of employer-sponsored pension plans, see Nelson Lichtenstein, "From Corporatism to Collective Bargaining: Organized Labor and the Eclipse of Social Democracy in the Postwar Era," in Steve Fraser and Gary Gerstle, eds., *The Rise and Fall of the New Deal Order, 1930–1980* (Princeton, N.J.: Princeton University Press, 1989), 142–144; and Stebenne, *Arthur J. Goldberg*, 66–67, 74–75, 142–143.

51. Larson, "The American System," 83–84.
52. Ibid., 84–85.
53. Ibid., 85–86.
54. Ibid., 86. For the way in which the most conservative members of Congress blocked labor's quest for an expanded welfare state in the mid-1940s and labor's consequent push for privatized solutions, see Stebenne, *Arthur J. Goldberg*, 62–63, 66–67, 74–76, 142–143.
55. Larson, "The American System," 86–87.
56. On the way in which the earth-shaking events of the 1930s and 1940s tended to polarize debates about domestic policy, see Arthur M. Schlesinger, Jr., *The Politics of Upheaval* (Boston: Houghton Mifflin, 1960), especially 515–547; and Brinkley, *The End of Reform*, especially 137–174.
57. Larson, "The American System," 88–89.
58. Ibid., 96.
59. Ibid.
60. On the issue of how these events influenced the thinking of moderate conservatives, see Ronald Steel, *Walter Lippmann and the American Century* (Boston: Little, Brown, 1980), 297–344; Robert Griffith, "Dwight D. Eisenhower and the Corporate Commonwealth," *American Historical Review* 87 (February 1982): 90–103; E. J. Dionne, Jr., *Why Americans Hate Politics* (New York: Touchstone, 1991), 147–172.
61. Larson, "The American System," 7–11, 27–28.
62. The American Assembly, *Economic Security for Americans*; "A Brief History of the Arden House," available online at http://www.ardenhouse.com/ardenhouse.htm (accessed May 29, 2001); Stephen E. Ambrose, *Eisenhower* (New York: Simon & Schuster, 1983), 1:482; Griffith, "Eisenhower and the Corporate Commonwealth," 93–100, 109–112.
63. While president of Columbia, DDE had worked with Ginzberg to develop an important research project on human resources. Upon hearing from JPM of Ginzberg's help to him, DDE wrote Ginzberg a personal note of thanks for "the significant contribution you have made as a consultant in helping him [Mitchell] improve the programs, policies and organization of the Department of Labor." See DDE to Ginzberg, February 5, 1955, folder Eisenhower, Dwight D. (2), Box 1, Eli Ginzberg Papers, DDEL. See also "Origins of the Conservation of Human Resources Project," in the same folder, and the Eli Ginzberg Memoir, OHC, 6–35, 108, both in DDEL; AL-KL I; ALICY; Ambrose, *Eisenhower*, 1:484; Stephen E. Ambrose, *Eisenhower* (New York: Simon & Schuster, 1984), 2:118; "Educator Named High Labor Aide," *New York Times*, March 24, 1954.
64. AL-KL I; ALICY; *ATCL*, 115.
65. *ATCL*, 115–116. Republican National Committee Chairman Leonard Hall recalled a conversation he had with DDE prior to his inauguration that illustrated DDE's lack of concern with partisanship in staffing decisions. Asked by Hall what role the Republican Party would play in this process, DDE had replied, "You're . . . too late on that because . . . I was told that the cabinet members should pick their own people, and I told everyone of them to do it." See Leonard Hall Memoir in OHC, DDEL, 56.
66. See AL-KL II; AL's Biographical Information Form, Office of Public Relations and Information, Cornell University, September 14, 1949, where, under the heading of "political party preference," AL had typed "registered as a Republican"; in folder 1210, Box 13, Cornell University Archives, RMCKLCU; Ambrose, *Eisenhower*, 1:476–478.
67. *ATCL*, 117 (see also 116).
68. *ATCL*, 117.
69. Ambrose, *Eisenhower*, 1:516–517, 519; *ATCL*, 117–119. The official record of AL's appointment is more ambiguous. JPM's official memorandum of nomination sent to

White House Chief of Staff Sherman Adams dated March 18, 1954, listed the nominee as "Arthur Larson of South Dakota" and reported that JPM had been "informed, through the Republican National Committee, that the appointment of Mr. Larson has the approval of Senators Mundt and Case of South Dakota." This report appears to have been premature, however, because the one reference to Larson's appointment in the Congressional Record referred to him as "Arthur Larson, of Pennsylvania." See JPM's memo and the attached material in folder 1954 Administration—Arthur Larson [Recommendation for Under Secretary; employment-unemployment insurance], Box 79, JPMP, DDEL; U.S. Congress, *Proceedings and Debates of the 83rd Congress, 2nd Session,* vol. 100, part 4 (Washington, D.C.: U.S. Government Printing Office, 1954), 4315.

70. AL-KL I; ALICY; "Educator Named High Labor Aide," *New York Times,* March 24, 1954.

6. *Of Theory and Practice*

1. See U.S. Congress, *Proceedings and Debates of the 83rd Congress, 2nd Session,* vol. 100, part 4 (Washington, D.C.: U.S. Government Printing Office, 1954), 4315; "Schedule for Swearing-In Ceremony," April 12, 1954, and the accompanying press release, folder Labor Dept.—Swearing In Ceremonies 1954, Box 21, ALP, DDEL; AL to Vice Chancellor Charles Nutting, April 2, 1954, Nutting's reply, April 5, 1954, and University Secretary John Weber to AL, May 17, 1954, AL to FNL, April 6, 1954, and the correspondence between them from June through August 1954, especially AL to FNL, July 18, 1954, 1–3, all in LFP.

2. AL-KL II; "Secretary or Chief of Staff?" *Fortune,* December 1953, 61–64; "Inside Man," *Fortune,* May 1954, 62; "Mitchell—A Man in the Middle," *Fortune,* February 1955, 61–62, 64; Stephen E. Ambrose, *Eisenhower* (New York: Simon & Schuster, 1984), 2:45, 344–345.

3. See "Pushing State Action for Labor," *Business Week,* January 15, 1955, 144–146; Henry P. Guzda, "James P. Mitchell," in John A. Garraty, ed., *Dictionary of American Biography,* Supplement 7 (New York: Charles Scribner's Sons, 1981), 542–544; and Ambrose, *Eisenhower,* 2:24, 116–118.

4. See AL to FNL, July 9, 1954, 3, LFP; AL-KL I; ALICY.

5. *Fortune* magazine's labor columnist, Daniel Bell, reported in February 1955 that "privately, many labor people like Mitchell (and [the] C.I.O. in particular has reason to admire his courage in facing up to the Defense Department on a security-issue case)." See "Mitchell—A Man in the Middle," 61 (see also 62). On the situation at the Labor Department during Larson's first few months there, see also AL to FNL, July 7, 1954, 2–3, July 12, 1954, 4, and July 17, 1954, 3–4, LFP; "Ike's Labor Team," and "Durkin's Troubles," *Fortune,* September 1953, 66–67, "Secretary or Chief of Staff?" 62; and "Inside Man," 62.

6. *ATCL,* 100–101; AL to FNL, July 17, 1954, 3–4, LFP; ALICY.

7. ALICY.

8. Ibid. See also AL's memo of a telephone conversation the next day to White House aide Gabriel Hauge, which recounted the details of this episode, in LFP. For DDE's executive order and its consequences, see Sherman Adams, *Firsthand Report: The Story of the Eisenhower Administration* (New York: Harper & Brothers, 1961), 149–152; William Bragg Ewald, Jr., *Eisenhower the President: Crucial Days, 1951–1960* (Englewood Cliffs, N.J.: Prentice Hall, 1981), 135–143; Ambrose, *Eisenhower,* 2:186–189.

9. See AL to FNL, July 17, 1954, 3–4, LFP, where he wrote that "I have three cases now, involving three top people, two of whom are under some kind of attack for security reasons (actually with almost no substance—but involving the risk of public discussion,

which in their cases must be avoided at all costs)." See also ALICY; and "Mitchell—A Man in the Middle," 61.

10. AL to FNL, July 12, 1954, 4, LFP. See also AL to FNL, July 7, 1954, 2–3, and July 17, 1954, 3–4, LFP.

11. AL to FNL, July 1, 1954, 2–4, LFP; "Down the Middle," *Fortune*, February 1954, 75.

12. AL to FNL, July 1, 1954, 4, LFP (see also 2–3); "Down the Middle," 75. AL represented the department at the hearings. See "Hearings on a Bill to Amend the D.C. Unemployment Compensation Act and for Other Purposes," House Committee on the District of Columbia and Senate Committee on the District of Columbia, July 8, 1954, CIS No. 83 SD-T.75, Seattle Unpublished Hearings Collection.

13. AL to FNL, July 12, 1954, 1, LFP. For more details of this measure, see "Down the Middle," 75; and AL's testimony in "Unemployment Insurance," House Committee on Ways and Means, June 8–11, 1954, CIS No. 83 H1450-1, SUDOC:Y4.W36:Un 2/3/1954.

14. AL to FNL, July 12, 1954, 2, LFP (see also 1).

15. See AL to FNL, July 9, 1954, 3–4, LFP.

16. AL to FNL, July 1, 1954, 3, LFP.

17. Before DDE's administrations, Republican administrations typically staffed the upper echelons of the Labor Department with career trade union politicians, but once Harrison Hobart, who had held a high-ranking office in the Brotherhood of Locomotive Engineers, left, the Eisenhower administration had none in such positions. See "Ike's Labor Team," *Fortune*, September 1953, 66; "Secretary or Chief of Staff?" 61; "Inside Man," 62.

18. See AL to FNL, June 29, 1954, 1, July 7, 1954, 2–3, letter postmarked July 11, 1954, 4, July 12, 1954, 2–3, July 17, 1954, 1–4, 8, letter postmarked July 21, 1954, 2–3, August 2, 1954, 1–3, and AL to AHL, June 12, 1955, 1, all in LFP; AL's memos to JPM, May 10, 1954, 1–3, May 11, 1954, 1–2, May 13, 1954, 1–2, May 14, 1954, 1–2, May 29, 1954, 1–9, all in folder 1954—Administrative—Arthur Larson (Under Secretary of Labor) [Daily Activities, May], the "Summary of Action," memo of the Secretary's Program and Operations Committee, August 5, 1954, in folder 1954—Secretary's Policy Committee—Material from the Secretary's Notebook (5), all in Box 71, and AL's memo to JPM, October 25, 1954, 1–7, in folder 1955—Administrative—Arthur Larson—Reports, Box 79, JPMP, DDEL; AL to Sig Mickelson, September 10, 1954, folder General Correspondence J-M, Box 1, General Correspondence of [James T.] O'Connell and Larson 1954–56 A-Z, DLP, RG 174, NARA II; "Labor '54," *Variety*, September 8, 1954, 40; "Pushing State Action for Labor," 144–146.

19. Social Security expert Wilbur Cohen's review of *Know Your Social Security* described it as "an outstanding piece of work" and observed that "nobody has produced a better short account . . . in the twenty years since social security was established." See Wilbur Cohen, "Know Your Social Security," *Social Casework* 37 (March 1956): 140. On the writing of this book, see AL to FNL, July 1, 1954, 1–2, July 4, 1954, 1–4, July 7, 1954, 3–4, July 9, 1954, 4, July 12, 1954, 3–4, July 17, 1954, 3, and his letters to her postmarked July 21, 1954, 3–4, and July 25, 1954, 3, and AL to AHL, October 30, 1955, 1, all in LFP; AL thanking RMN for his endorsement, October 21, 1955, folder "Larson, Mr. Arthur," Box 438, Series 320, GC, RMNPPP.

20. Arthur Larson, *Know Your Social Security* (New York: Harper and Brothers, 1955), 10–11.

21. Emerson P. Schmidt to AL, May 28, 1954, 2, folder General Correspondence, A-C, Box 1, General Correspondence of O'Connell and Larson, 1954–56 A-Z, RG 174, NARA II. See also "Income Insurance and Labor Relations," *Employment Security Review* (August 1954): 27; and "Social Security Extension Advanced as Bulwark of Free Economy," *Toledo Blade*, May 30, 1954.

22. On the emphasis placed by DDE himself and his administration more generally

on trying to reconcile conservatives and businessmen to the modern welfare state, see the memoir of DDE's first chief of staff, Sherman Adams, *Firsthand Report,* 27–28, 459–460; Alan Brinkley, "A President for Certain Seasons," *Wilson Quarterly* (Spring 1990): 110–119, especially 115–116; and E. J. Dionne, Jr., *Why Americans Hate Politics* (New York: Touchstone, 1991), 170–173.

23. See Larson, *Know Your Social Security,* 12–14. On the two major parties' shifting attitudes toward governmental activism, see Mayer, *The Republican Party,* especially 300–335; and David Burner, *The Politics of Provincialism: The Democratic Party in Transition, 1918–1932* (New York: Norton, 1967).

24. Larson, *Know Your Social Security,* v, xvi; Wilbur Cohen, "Know Your Social Security," *Social Casework* 37 (March 1956): 140.

25. AL first used the term "income insurance" in his speech to the Economic Club of Chicago on May 18, 1954, observing at the outset that "I am using the term Income Insurance rather than the more familiar term 'social insurance,' because I have learned from experience that there are quite a few people who feel a trace of suspicion about anything with the word 'social' in it." The address is reprinted under the title "Income Insurance and Labor Relations," *Employment Security Review* 21 (August 1954): 26–28. See also on this issue, "GOP Watches Speeches of Democrats Who 'Like Ike,'" *Jacksonville* (Florida) *Times-Union,* June 7, 1954.

26. For discerning views of this aspect of DDE and his presidency, see Fred I. Greenstein, *The Hidden-Hand Presidency: Eisenhower as Leader* (New York: Basic Books, 1982), 66–73, 233, 239; and Ambrose, *Eisenhower,* 2:219–222, 294. For examples of analyses that tend to take the more conservative-sounding public utterances of DDE and his aides at face value, see Gary W. Reichard, *The Reaffirmation of Republicanism: Eisenhower and the Eighty-Third Congress* (Knoxville: University of Tennessee Press, 1975); and Griffith, "Eisenhower and the Corporate Commonwealth."

27. AL to FNL, July 17, 1954, 5, LFP. *Bracero* is the Spanish word for "field hand."

28. AL to FNL, August 4, 1954, 1, LFP. See also AL to FNL, August 2, 1954, LFP.

29. FNL to AHL, July 21, 1954, 1–2, and AL to FNL, August 4, 1954, both in LFP; LKL; ABL.

30. The observations expressed above are based on ABL; LKL; and the correspondence between AL and FNL, especially the years from 1945 to 1953, in LFP; "Pitt's Larson a Lawyer, Professor and Author," undated press clipping in Larson's biographical file, ASCUP; "Labor Undersecretary's Wife Interrupts Her Acting Career," March [?], 1955, press clipping in ALS, LFP; "Mrs. Larson Fills Bill for USIA Wives," *Washington Star,* November 18, 1956; *ATCL,* 151.

31. ABL.

32. See FNL to AL, July 1, 1954, July 4, 1954, July 5, 1954, July 7, 1954, July 9, 1954, July 11, 1954, July 12, 1954, and July 18, 1954, and the letters postmarked July 14, 17, and 21, 1954, all in LFP.

33. AL to AHL, May 22, 1955, 1, and June 12, 1955, 1–2, and the Larson family photographs from 1954 to 1958, all in LFP; "Larson Happy, Surprised to Get Labor Post," press clipping in AL's biographical file, ASCUP; LKL; ABL. On the nature of middle-class family life in America during the 1950s, see Elaine Tyler May, "Cold War—Warm Hearth: Politics and the Family in Postwar America," in Steve Fraser and Gary Gerstle, eds., *Rise and Fall of the New Deal Order, 1930–1980* (Princeton, N.J.: Princeton University Press, 1989), 153–181; Alan Ehrenhalt, *The Lost City: Discovering the Forgotten Virtues of Community in the Chicago of the 1950s* (New York: Basic Books, 1995), 193–249; and John Patrick Diggins, *The Proud Decades: America in War and Peace, 1941–1960* (New York: Norton, 1988), 211–219.

34. The measure passed by Congress extended coverage from firms with eight or more employees to those with four or more, but the Eisenhower administration favored coverage for firms with three or more employees. See "Down the Middle," 75; "Labor and the Eighty-Fourth Congress," *Fortune,* December 1954, 64. On the home purchase and Larson's work there, see AL to AHL, May 22, 1955, 1, June 12, 1955, 1–2, and July 1, 1954, 2–3, LFP. See also Chester J. Pach, Jr., and Elmo Richardson, *The Presidency of Dwight D. Eisenhower,* rev. ed. (Lawrence: University Press of Kansas, 1991), 56; Edward D. Berkowitz, "The Historical Development of Social Security in the United States," in Eric R. Kingson and James H. Schulz, eds., *Social Security in the 21st Century* (New York: Oxford University Press, 1997), 30–31; and AL, "Outflanking the Welfare State," 2, speech to the Midwinter Personnel Conference, American Management Association, Chicago, Illinois, February 15, 1956, folder 1956—Administrative—Arthur Larson, Box 79, JPMP, DDEL.

35. Extending unemployment insurance coverage to all businesses not yet covered would have added another 2 million workers to the system. See "Labor and the Eighty-Fourth Congress," 64; "Income Insurance and Labor Relations," 27; "Outflanking the Welfare State," 2–14; "Pushing State Action for Labor," 144–146; and *Public Papers of the Presidents of the United States: Dwight D. Eisenhower 1955* (Washington, D.C.: National Archives and Records Service, 1959), 7–30, especially 26.

36. *Public Papers of the Presidents of the United States: Dwight D. Eisenhower 1955,* 26; "Income Insurance and Labor Relations," 27; "Economist Backs Annual-Pay Move," *New York Times,* December 30, 1954; AL memo to JPM, May 14, 1954, 1–2, folder 1954—Administrative—Arthur Larson (Under Secretary of Labor) [Daily Activities, May], Box 79, JPMP, DDEL.

37. "Pushing State Action for Labor," 144–146.

38. Ibid., 144; *Public Papers of the Presidents of the United States: Dwight D. Eisenhower 1955,* 26; "The Effects of a Varying Rise in the Minimum Wage," *Fortune,* May 1955, 59.

39. "Pushing State Action for Labor," 146 (see also 144–145); "Income Insurance and Labor Relations," 26–28.

40. Ambrose, *Eisenhower,* 2:217–219, Adams, *Firsthand Report,* 161–168; Dewey Grantham, *The Life & Death of the Solid South: A Political History* (Lexington: University of Kentucky Press, 1988), especially 58–77, 102–124; "Labor and the Eighty-Fourth Congress," 64; Paul H. Douglas, *In the Fullness of Time: The Memoirs of Paul H. Douglas* (New York: Harcourt, Brace, Jovanovich, 1971), 196–221.

41. Grantham, *The Life & Death of the Solid South,* 66–68; C. Vann Woodward, *Origins of the New South, 1877–1913* (Baton Rouge: Louisiana State University Press, 1951), 456–481; Kathleen L. Wolgemuth, "Woodrow Wilson and Federal Segregation," *Journal of Negro History* 44 (April 1959): 158–173; Nancy J. Weiss, "The Negro and the New Freedom: Fighting Wilsonian Segregation," *Political Science Quarterly* 84 (March 1969): 61–79; AL to FNL, July 1, 1954, 2–3, LFP.

42. "Labor and the Eighty-Fourth Congress," 64; "Pushing State Action for Labor," 144; "Ambrose, *Eisenhower,* 2:48, 115, 158, 160; "Outflanking the Welfare State," 1–3.

43. AL address to the Sixth Annual Conference of the Southern Association of Workmen's Compensation Administrators, Orlando, Florida, on October 28, 1954, was published as "The Model Workmen's Compensation Act," *Tennessee Law Review* 23 (April 1955): 838–845; AL memos to JPM, May 13, 1954, 2, and May 29, 1954, 2, folder 1954—Administrative—Arthur Larson (Under Secretary of Labor) [Daily Activities, May], Box 79, JPMP, DDEL.

44. See AL's memos to JPM, October 25, 1954, 7, and January 18, 1955, 3, folder

1955—Administrative—Arthur Larson—Reports, and AL's memo to JPM, July 18, 1955, 2, folder Weekly Activity Reports: Under Secretary and Deputy Under Secretary (Apr. 1–Nov. 18, 1955) (1), all in Box 79, JPMP, DDEL; "The Model Workmen's Compensation Act."

45. AL memo to JPM, July 18, 1955, 2, folder Weekly Activity Reports: Under Secretary and Deputy Under Secretary (Apr. 1–Nov. 18, 1955) (1), 2, Box 79, JPMP, DDEL. See also AL's memo to JPM, August 2, 1955, 1, in that same folder; "Summary of Action," September 20, 1955, 2, folder 1955 Secretary's Policy Comm. Chronological—Meeting #166 (Sept. 7)—#174 (Sept. 28), Box 73, and AL's memo to JPM, January 23, 1956, 3–4, folder Weekly Activity Reports: Under Secretary and Deputy Under Secretary (Nov. 25, 1955–June 25, 1956) (1), Box 81, both in JPMP, DDEL; "Proposed Model of Compensation Laws Distributed," *Trades Union News* (Philadelphia), December 9, 1955.

46. See AL's memos to JPMP, January 23, 1956, 3–4, April 2, 1956, 5, April 16, 1956, 2–3, April 26, 1956, 1, and May 11, 1956, 1, folder Weekly Activity Reports: Under Secretary and Deputy Under Secretary (Nov. 25, 1955–June 25, 1956), Box 81, JPMP, DDEL; AL to Edwin E. Witte, December 27, 1955, L. K. Pollard to JPM, February 13, 1956, AL to L. K. Pollard, February 29, 1956, AL to Cola Parker, May 17, 1956, Leavitt R. Barker to Howard Pyle, June 1, 1956, and AL to Pyle, June 25, 1956, all in folder Workmen's Compensation: Correspondence re Model Act and re Orlando Speech M-Z, Box 15, General Subject Files of Under Secretary James T. O'Connell, 1954–1960, RG 174, NARA II; "Model State Law Gets Sidetracked," *Business Week*, September 1, 1956, 122–123.

47. See LOD, February 13, 1956, folder Memorandum Book Labor Dept., Box 21, ALP, DDEL; *ATCL*, 177–178.

48. Memos from AL to JPM, April 2, 1956, 5, and April 26, 1956, 1, folder Weekly Activity Reports: Under Secretary and Deputy Under Secretary (Nov. 25, 1955–June 25, 1956) (1), Box 81, JPMP and LOD, January 21 and May 22, 1956, ALP, all in DDEL; "Proposed Model of Compensation Laws Distributed"; "Model State Law Gets Sidetracked," 122–123; "Labor and the Eighty-Fourth Congress," 64.

49. The House and Senate Appropriations Committees formally approved the budget cut in August 1956; see "Model State Law Gets Sidetracked," 122–123. On the opposition to Larson's proposal and his attempts to disarm it, see AL to Howard Pyle, June 25, 1956, 1–3, folder Workmen's Compensation: Correspondence re Model Act and re Orlando Speech M-Z, Box 15, General Subject Files of Under Secretary James T. O'Connell, 1954–1960, RG 174, NARA II; "Model State Law Gets Sidetracked," 122–123.

50. AL memo to JPM, May 14, 1956, 1, folder Weekly Activity Reports: Under Secretary and Deputy Under Secretary (Nov. 25, 1955–June 25, 1956) (1), Box 81, JPMP, DDEL; "State Labor Scores," *Fortune*, August 1955, 60; *ATCL*, 177–178.

51. See U.S. Department of Labor, *Annual Report 1956* (Washington, D.C.: U.S. Department of Labor, 1956), 5.

52. AL memo to JPM, May 29, 1954, 4, folder 1954—Administrative—Arthur Larson (Under Secretary of Labor) [Daily Activities, May], AL's memo to JPM, September 20, 1955, 1, folder Weekly Activity Reports Under Secretary and Deputy Under Secretary (April 1–Nov. 18, 1955) (1), both in Box 79, JPMP, DDEL. See also the collection of press clippings from late December 1954 and throughout 1955 reporting on AL's proposal, especially "Economist Backs Annual-Pay Move," *New York Times*, December 30, 1954, all of which are in ALS for 1954–1957, ALP, DDEL; "Factories on the Move," *Fortune*, July 1954, 36–40; "Push-Button Labor," *Fortune*, August 1954, 50–52; "The First 'Automation' Strike," *Fortune*, December 1955, 57–58; Roger H. Davidson, *Coalition-Building for Depressed Areas Bills: 1955–1965* (Indianapolis, Ind.: Bobbs-Merrill, 1966), 1–3; DDE's 1956 State of the Union Message, which endorsed legislation in this area, in *Public Papers of the*

Presidents of the United States: Dwight D. Eisenhower 1956 (Washington, D.C.: National Archives and Record Service, 1958), 17–18.

53. Davidson, *Coalition-Building for Depressed Areas Bills,* 2, 6–7; Douglas, *In the Fullness of Time,* 512–516; Bruce J. Shulman, *From Cotton Belt to Sunbelt: Federal Policy, Economic Development, and the Transformation of the South, 1938–1980* (New York: Oxford University Press, 1991), 112–134; Dewey W. Grantham, *The South in Modern America: A Region at Odds* (New York: HarperCollins, 1994), 259–280; and John P. Worsham, Jr., *The Sunbelt Issue: The 'Decline' of the North and the Rise of the 'South'* (Monticello, Ill.: Vance Bibliographies, 1978), 1–9.

54. AL memo to JPM, April 13, 1956, 1, folder Weekly Activity Reports: Under Secretary and Deputy Under Secretary (Nov. 25, 1955–June 25, 1956) (1), Box 81, JPMP, DDEL. See also AL's memo to JPM, September 20, 1955, 1, folder Weekly Activity Reports: Under Secretary and Deputy Under Secretary (Apr. 1–Nov. 18, 1955) (1), Box 79, JPMP, DDEL; Davidson, *Coalition-Building for Depressed Areas Bills,* 3–7; "Area Assistance Act of 1956," House Committee on Banking and Currency, 12–13, 18–19, 23–26, April 1956, CIS No. 84 H1552-6, SUDOC:Y4.B22/1:Ar3.

55. See "President's Proposal for Domestic 'Point IV' Program," *St. Louis Post-Dispatch,* October 3, 1955; Davidson, *Coalition-Building for Depressed Areas Bills,* 3–8; "Hearings on Area Redevelopment, Part 2," Senate Committee on Labor and Public Welfare, February 24, 25 and 27, March 20, 22–23, 26, 28, 29, and April 26, 1956, CIS No. 84 S1172-4-B, SUDOC:Y4.L11/2:Ar3/pt. 2; Douglas, *In the Fullness of Time,* 512–517.

56. See Davidson, *Coalition-Building for Depressed Areas Bills,* 3–5; Douglas, *In the Fullness of Time,* 512–517.

57. See "President's Proposal for Domestic 'Point IV' Program," *St. Louis Post-Dispatch,* October 3, 1955; Davidson, *Coalition-Building for Depressed Areas Bills,* 5–8; Douglas, *In the Fullness of Time,* 516–517.

58. AL's memos to JPM, July 18, 1955, 1, and August 2, 1955, 1, folder Weekly Activity Reports: Under Secretary and Deputy Under Secretary (Apr. 1–Nov. 18, 1955) (1), Box 79, JPMP, DDEL; Edward Berkowitz and Daniel M. Fox, "The Politics of Social Security Expansion: Social Security Disability Insurance, 1935–1986," *Journal of Policy History* 1 (1989): 233–234, 244–248; Edward Berkowitz and Kim McQuaid, *Creating the Welfare State: The Political Economy of Twentieth-Century Reform* (New York: Praeger Publishers, 1980), 153–154.

59. Berkowitz and Fox, "The Politics of Social Security Expansion," 236–237, 247; Berkowitz and McQuaid, *Creating the Welfare State,* 153–154; Sanford M. Jacoby, "Employers and the Welfare State: The Role of Marion B. Folsom," *Journal of American History* 80 (September 1993): 525–556; AL to FNL, April 6, 1954, 1–2; June 29, 1954, 1, July 1, 1954, 4, and July 17, 1954, 2–3, LFP; ALICY.

60. For AL's views on this issue, see his Arden House paper, "The American System: Structure, Coverage and Current Issues," 27–37, in the file on AL at the ASCUP. On the Eisenhower administration's actions and the bill's passage in Congress, see AL's memos to JPM, July 18, 1955, 1, August 2, 1955, 1, and September 20, 1955, 1, folder Weekly Activity Reports: Under Secretary and Deputy Under Secretary (Apr. 1–Nov. 18, 1955) (1), Box 79, JPMP, DDEL; Berkowitz and McQuaid, *Creating the Welfare State,* 154–155; Berkowitz and Fox, "The Politics of Social Security Expansion," 235–236, 247–248. A good short explanation of the law's major provisions is in "A Chronology of Significant Events in Social Security, 1935–1985," in Gerald D. Nash, Noel H. Pugach, and Richard F. Tomasson, eds., *Social Security: The First Half Century* (Albuquerque: University of New Mexico Press, 1988), 317.

61. Larson, "The American System," 27–37; Berkowitz and Fox, "The Politics of Social Security Expansion," 248–249.

62. See "Longshoremen's and Harbor Workers' Compensation Act," Senate Committee on Labor and Public Welfare, June 23–24, 1955, CIS No. 84 S1134-1, SUDOC:Y4.L11/2:L86/2; "Longshoremen's and Harbor Workers' Compensation Act," House Committee on Education and Labor, 12–14, March 26, 1956, CIS No. 84 H1533-2, SUDOC:Y4.Ed8/1:L86/2; "Longshoremen's and Harbor Workers' Compensation Act (Third Party Liability)," House Committee on Education and Labor, May 23–24 and June 11, 1956, CIS No. 84 H1567-5, SUDOC:Y4.Ed8/1:L86/3; "Higher Injury Payments Sought for Port Workers," *Corpus Christi Caller*, June 24, 1955; "Labor Dep't Urges Longshoremen Be Given $15 Compensation Hike," *Portland* (Maine) *Press-Herald Telegram*, June 24, 1955; *Public Papers of the Presidents of the United States: Dwight D. Eisenhower* 1956, 23, 116–117; *U.S. Statutes at Large* 1956 (Washington, D.C.: Federal Register Division, National Archives), 70:654–656; U.S. Department of Labor, *Annual Report* 1956, 5.

63. See "Transportation of Migrant Farm Workers," House Committee on Interstate and Foreign Commerce, May 18, 1956, CIS No. 84 H1575-5, Y4.IN8/4:T687/21; "Solution of Migratory Labor Problem Indicated," *Bakersfield Californian*, February 21, 1955; *U.S. Statutes at Large* 1956, 958.

64. "Pushing State Action for Labor," 144–146; "Down the Middle," 75; "Labor and the Eight-Fourth Congress," 64; "Mitchell—A Man in the Middle," 61–62, 64; "The Effects of a Varying Rise in the Minimum Wage," *Fortune*, May 1955, 50; "Amendment to Increase the Minimum Wage," House Committee on Education and Labor, June 1–3, 7–10, 14–15, 17, 21–24, and 28–30, 1955, CIS No. 84 H1501-4, SUDOC:Y4.Ed8/1:W12/4; *Public Papers of the Presidents of the United States: Dwight D. Eisenhower* 1955, 435–436, 551–553, and *Public Papers of the Presidents of the United States: Dwight D. Eisenhower* 1956, 22–23, 116–117, 855–856, 906–907; Dwight D. Eisenhower, *Mandate for Change* (Garden City, N.Y.: Doubleday, 1963), 498.

65. On the nature of the postwar labor-management détente, see the articles published under the heading "The Postwar Social Contract: Perspectives from France, Germany, Japan and the United States," *International Labor and Working Class History* 50 (Fall 1996): 114–156. On the effort to revise Taft-Hartley, see Gerald Pomper, "Labor Legislation: The Revision of Taft-Hartley in 1953–1954," *Labor History* 6 (1965): 143–149; Ambrose, *Eisenhower*, 2:24, 116–117; "Mr. Taft Proposes," *Fortune*, January 1953, 63–66; "Eisenhower's Labor Liaison," *Fortune*, March 1953, 77–80; "Down the Middle," 75; "Labor and the Eighty-Fourth Congress," 64; "Mitchell—A Man in the Middle," 61–62, 64; "Pushing State Action for Labor," 144–146; *Public Papers of the Presidents of the United States: Dwight D. Eisenhower* 1956, 26, 906.

66. See AL to FNL, July 9, 1954, 3, July 12, 1954, 2, and July 17, 1954, 6–7, LFP; AL-KL I; "Secretary or Chief of Staff?" 61–62, 64; "Mitchell—A Man in the Middle," 61–62, 64.

67. AL to FNL, 7, (see also 6), July 9, 1954, 3, and July 12, 1954, 2, LFP.

68. AL-KL I. Other knowledgeable observers shared that high opinion of JPM. See, for example, *Fortune* labor correspondent Daniel Bell's articles on Mitchell: "Eisenhower's Labor Liaison," March 1953, 77–80; "Down the Middle," February 1954, 64; and "Mitchell—A Man in the Middle," February 1955, 61–62, 64. Longtime Labor Department civil servant Millard Cass, who worked for every secretary of labor from 1933 to 1963, said simply that "Mitchell was the best Labor Secretary the country ever had—and I'm a Democrat!" AFL-CIO president George Meany agreed. JPM's successor, Arthur J. Goldberg, said of him that "his contribution to the nation was an enduring one, both in what he accomplished and the way he accomplished it." Those observations are drawn from MCTI; and Guzda, "James P. Mitchell," 544.

69. On the corporatist nature of the postwar economic and political system, see David

L. Stebenne, *Arthur J. Goldberg: New Deal Liberal* (New York: Oxford University Press, 1996), 42–43, 184–187, 207–221; on the positive social consequences for working-class Americans, see 142–148; Diggins, *The Proud Decades*, 128–139, 177–119; James Patterson, *Grand Expectations: The United States, 1945–1974* (New York: Oxford University Press, 1996), 311–342; Ehrenhalt, *The Lost City*, 90–189.

70. These conclusions are based on AL, "The Future of Income Insurance," speech delivered at Cornell University, November 15, 1956, in folder 1956—Administrative—Arthur Larson, Box 79, JPMP, DDEL; and *ATCL*, 174–187.

71. Larson, "Outflanking the Welfare State," 5–6.

72. Quoted in ibid., 12. For the full text of DDE's telegraph message on the occasion of the opening of the Teamsters' Building in Washington, see *Public Papers of the Presidents of the United States: Dwight E. Eisenhower 1955*, 838.

73. See Larson, "The American System," 83–87.

74. Larson discussed his concern with keeping the welfare state within what he called "proper boundaries" in ALICY.

75. On the way in which organized labor's economic and political weakness, in the South especially, pushed it toward the pursuit of private supplements to the provisions of the welfare state, see Lichtenstein, "From Corporatism to Collective Bargaining," 122–145; Stebenne, *Arthur J. Goldberg*, 53–77; and Robert H. Zieger, *The CIO: 1935–1955* (Chapel Hill: University of North Carolina Press, 1995), 312–328. The difficulties labor leaders experienced during the mid-1950s in restraining union members' excessive collective-bargaining demands are discussed in Stebenne, *Arthur J. Goldberg*, 131–153.

76. On the persistence of such managerial attitudes, especially at firms located in the Sunbelt, see Howell Harris, *The Right to Manage: Industrial Relations Policies of American Business in the 1940s* (Madison: University of Wisconsin Press, 1982), 179–204; Robert Collins, *The Business Response to Keynes, 1929–1964* (New York: Columbia University Press, 1981), 158–172; and Barry Goldwater Memoir, 9–12, OHC, DDEL.

77. Larson, "The Future of Income Insurance," 1–2; "Larson Urges New Social Legislation," *Ithaca Journal*, November 16, 1963; ALICY.

78. Larson, "The Future of Income Insurance," 5 (see also 2–4).

79. Ibid., 5–6.

80. Ibid., 6.

81. Ibid., 8 (see also 6–7).

82. Ibid., 8.

83. Ibid., 8–12.

84. AL, "Liberty, Equality, Security," address delivered to the University of Pittsburgh's summer commencement, August 25, 1954, 1, in collection 0/10/5/1 FF16, UA Collection; and Larson to University of Pittsburgh chancellor R. H. Fitzgerald, August 4, 1954, in AL's biographical file, all in ASCUP.

85. Larson, "Liberty, Equality, Security," 7; see also "502 Pitt Graduates Hear Larson," *Pittsburgh Sun-Telegraph*, August 26, 1954.

86. Larson, "Liberty, Equality, Security," 9 (see also 7–8).

87. See David Caute, *The Great Fear: The Anti-Communist Purge under Truman and Eisenhower* (New York: Simon & Schuster, 1978), especially 403–430; Ellen W. Schrecker, *No Ivory Tower: McCarthyism and the Universities* (New York: Oxford University Press, 1986), 84–125. See also Joan Didion's observation in *The White Album* (New York: Simon & Schuster, 1979) about the mood at Berkeley in the mid-1950s: "We were that generation called 'silent,' but we were silent neither, as some thought, because we shared the period's official optimism nor, as others thought, because we feared its official repression. We were silent because the exhilaration of social action seemed to many of us

just one more way of escaping the personal, of masking for a while that dread of the meaningless which was man's fate" (206–207).

88. AL's Frank Irvine Lecture at the Cornell Law School on December 15, 1954 was published as "The Lawyer as Conservative," *Cornell Law Quarterly* 40 (Winter 1955): 183–194 (see especially 183). See also the press release issued by Cornell's Office of Public Relations and Information, December 9, 1954, and the one issued by the U.S. Labor Department entitled "Larson Explains the True Conservative," December 16, 1954, both of which are in file 1210, Box 13, Cornell Faculty Biographical Files, RMCKLCU.

89. Larson, "The Lawyer as Conservative," 184–185.

90. Ibid., 185–187.

91. For the views of Meany and Stevenson, see Joseph C. Goulden, *Meany* (New York: Atheneum, 1972), 207–232; Robert H. Zieger, "George Meany: Labor's Organization Man," in Melvyn Dubofsky and Warren Van Tine, eds., *Labor Leaders in America* (Urbana: University of Illinois Press, 1987), 324–349; John Bartlow Martin, *Adlai Stevenson of Illinois* (Garden City, N.Y.: Anchor/Doubleday, 1977); and *Adlai Stevenson and the World* (Garden City, N.Y.: Anchor/Doubleday, 1977); and Jean H. Baker, *The Stevensons: A Biography of an American Family* (New York: Norton, 1996).

92. AL memo to JPM, May 10, 1954, folder 1954—Administrative—Arthur Larson (Under Secretary of Labor) [Daily Activities, May], Box 79, JPMP, DDEL. See also AL to FNL, letter postmarked August 2, 1954, 1–2, LFP; and ALICY.

93. AL memo to JPM, October 25, 1954, 6, folder 1955—Administrative—Arthur Larson-Reports, Box 79, JPMP, DDEL.

94. AL memo to JPM, January 3, 1956, 4, folder Weekly Activity Reports: Under Secretary & Deputy Under Secretary (Nov. 25, 1955–June 25, 1956) (1), Box 81, JPMP, DDEL. On the persistence of segregation in the U.S. Employment Service into the early 1960s, see Stebenne, *Arthur J. Goldberg*, 245–247; the work of the presidential Committee on Government Contracts is described on page 243. See also "How Big a Stick?" *Fortune*, November 1955, 70–72.

95. William H. Harris observed that "black workers fared better in the labor market during the 1950s than at any other time, including World War II." See *The Harder We Run: Black Workers since the Civil War* (New York: Oxford University Press, 1982), 128. On the positive and negative aspects of the black experience during these years, see also Harvard Sitkoff, *The Struggle for Black Equality, 1954–1980* (New York: Hill & Wang, 1981), 3–96; Eric F. Goldman, *The Crucial Decade and After* (New York: Vintage, 1960), 12–66, 182–187, 264, 293–294; Diggins, *The Proud Decades*, 275–296; Marty Jezer, *The Dark Ages: Life in the United States, 1945–1960* (Boston: South End Press, 1982), 155–159, 296–303.

96. See "Summary of Action," Meeting 178 of the Secretary's Policy Committee, October 6, 1955, 1, folder 1955—Secretary's Policy Committee—Chronological—Meeting #176 (Oct. 4)–#178 (Oct. 10), Box 73, JPMP, DDEL.

97. "Summary of Action," 2.

98. AL, "A Six-Point Plan to Aid the Older Worker," address given to the Eighth Annual Conference on Aging, University of Michigan, June 28, 1955, 13 (see also 12, 14–15), folder Speech, June 28, 1955, Box 17, ALP, DDEL; "Summary of Action, Regional Directors' Conference, December 16–17, 1954," 6, folder 1954—Secretary's Policy Comm.—Material from the Secretary's Notebook (5), Box 71, and AL memos to JPM, July 18, 1955, 3, and September 20, 1955, 6, folder Weekly Activity Reports: Under Secretary and Deputy Under Secretary (Apr. 1–Nov. 18, 1955) (1), all in Box 79, JPMP, DDEL.

99. See Daniel Bell, "The Great Back-to-Work Movement," *Fortune*, November

1956, 90–93, 168, 170, 172; Diggins, *The Proud Decades*, 211–219; Patterson, *Grand Expectations*, 31–38, 361–369; Cynthia Harrison, *On Account of Sex: The Politics of Women's Issues, 1945–1968* (Berkeley: University of California Press, 1988), 25, 90–91; May, "Cold War—Warm Hearth," 153–181; William Chafe, *The American Woman: Her Changing Social, Political and Economic Roles* (New York: Oxford University Press, 1972), 174–225; Eugenia Kaledin, *Mothers and More: American Women in the 1950s* (Boston: Twayne, 1984), 43–80.

100. See "Summary of Action," Secretary's Policy Committee Meeting No. 178, October 6, 1955, 1–2, folder 1955—Secretary's Policy Committee—Chronological—Meeting #176 (Oct. 4)–#178 (Oct. 10), Box 73, JPMP, DDEL; Jezer, *The Dark Ages*, 220–234.

101. "Summary of Action," Secretary's Policy Committee Meeting No. 170, September 20, 1955, 4, folder 1955—Secretary's Policy Committee Chronological—Meeting #166 (Sept. 7)–#174 (Sept. 28), Box 73, JPMP, DDEL. For the details of the push for equal-pay legislation in the mid-1950s, see Harrison, *On Account of Sex*, 34, 39–51, 83.

102. U.S. Department of Labor, *Annual Report* 1956, 5; Harrison, *On Account of Sex*, 49–51.

103. AL, "Working People in the Next Twenty Years," address delivered to the International Association of Industrial Editors, June 20, 1956, Los Angeles, California, 3, folder 1956—Administrative—Arthur Larson, Box 79, JPMP, DDEL (see also 1–2). New Deal critic and 1944 and 1948 GOP presidential candidate Thomas Dewey emphasized this point in his speeches and other writings. See, in particular, the passage from his most important manifesto, *The Case against the New Deal* (New York: Harper and Brothers, 1940), 5–11.

104. Larson, "Working People in the Next Twenty Years," 6 (see also 3–5).

105. Ibid., 8 (see also 7, 9). The shift away from jobs in heavy industry of which Larson spoke began in Northern and Western Europe even earlier. The proportion of factory workers there leveled off at around one-third of the total population in the 1890s and declined gradually thereafter. See Paxton, *Europe in the Twentieth Century*, 217–218.

106. Larson, "Working People in the Next Twenty Years," 9–11.

107. Ibid., 11.

108. Ibid., 12.

109. Ibid., 12–13.

110. On the rise of this new kind of American working class, see Daniel Bell, "Beyond the Annual Wage," *Fortune*, May 1955, 92–95, 205–210, "No Boom for Unions," *Fortune*, June 1956, 136–137, 174–186, "Where Does Labor Go from Here?" *Fortune*, December 1957, 153–155, 256–262; and Bell, *The Coming of the Post-Industrial Society* (New York: Basic Books, 1973), 129–164.

111. On the hollowing out of middle-range jobs during the 1960s and 1970s, see Bell, *The Coming of the Post-Industrial Society*, 129–164; and Juliet B. Schor, *The Overworked American: The Unexpected Decline of Leisure* (New York: Basic Books, 1991), especially 43–82.

112. On the tendency of unions to create a broad "middle class" of employment opportunities, see Richard B. Freeman and James L. Medoff, *What Do Unions Do?* (New York: Basic Books, 1984), 43–93, 150–161. The pervasive optimism of the mid-1950s is noted in Diggins, *The Proud Decades*, 177–219; and Patterson, *Grand Expectations*, 311–342.

113. See especially AL's Cornell speech in November 1956, which he described to the audience as "my last utterance while I am in the Labor Department" and "an occasion for summing up." See Larson, "The Future of Income Insurance," 1.

114. AL-KL II; ALICY; *ATCL*, 127–128.

7. *A Republican Looks at His Party*

1. *ATCL*, 127.

2. FNL to AHL, February 9, 1956, 1, (see also 2), FNL to AHL, March 9, 1956, 1–2, and AL to AHL, October 30, 1955, 1, all in LFP; *ATCL*, 127.

3. See FNL's letters to AHL, February 9, 1956, 1, and March 9, 1956, 1–2, both in LFP.

4. See FNL to AHL, March 9, 1956, 2, LFP; LOD, February 12, 1956, MB Labor Dept., Box 21, ALP; and Arthur Minnich's memo to Sherman Adams, February 20, 1956, 1, folder 103-W Book Publishing by Government Officials, Box 475, Office Files, DDEP, both in DDEL.

5. See LOD, February 12 and 28, 1956; FNL to AHL, March 9, 1956, 2, LFP; Dean Acheson, *A Democrat Looks at His Party* (New York: Harper and Brothers, 1955); *ATCL*, 127–128.

6. See FNL to AHL, March 9, 1956, 2–3, AL to AHL, March 15, 1956, 1, LFP; LOD, March 9 and May 3, 1956; memo from Edward K. Thompson to C. D. Jackson, March 13, 1956, 1–3, and the attached cable from Jackson to Henry Luce, April 18, 1956, folder La-Misc. (2), Box 64, C. D. Jackson Papers, both in DDEL; remarks about Henry Luce's political philosophy by Alan Brinkley at the Diplomatic History Workshop, Ohio State University, May 7, 1998; *ATCL*, 130.

7. AL to Charles B. Nutting, March 13, 1956, 1 (see also Nutting's response, March 19, 1956), Edward H. Litchfield to AL, February 14, 1956, AL's reply, February 17, 1956, and AL to AHL, March 15, 1956, 1, all in LFP; Dwight E. Eisenhower, *Waging Peace, 1956–1961* (Garden City, N.Y.: Doubleday and Company), 3–5.

8. See AL to AHL, April 6, 1956, 1, LFP; *ATCL*, 130.

9. FNL to AL, July 5, 1954, 4 (see also FNL to AL, July 9, 1954, 4, and the letter postmarked July 17, 1954, 2–3), and FNL to AHL, not dated, on letterhead of the Brown Palace Hotel, Denver, 1, all in LFP; AL to Mundt, August 6 and 23, 1954, and May 23, 1956 and Mundt's letters to him, August 10, 1954, and May 19, 1956, folder General Correspondence J-M, Box 1, General Correspondence of O'Connell and Larson, 1954–56, RG 174, NARA II.

10. Karl E. Mundt to AL, May 19, 1956, 1, folder General Correspondence J-M, Box 1, General Correspondence of O'Connell and Larson, 1954–56 A-Z, RG 174, NARA II.

11. See the memo from the Executive Branch Liaison Office, both in August 27, 1954, and the attached remarks, "Speech by Arthur Larson, August 1954," Box 14, Stephen Benedict Collection, and "Quotes from the President on What the Republican Party Stands For—8/2/55," folder DDE Book Materials and Clippings, Box 16, ALP, both in DDEL. AL had planned to deliver this speech on July 31st of that year, but inclement weather forced him to postpone his remarks. On that point, see "13 Hurt as Wind Rips Grandstand at Granite City," *St. Louis Post-Dispatch*, August 1, 1954; Karl Mundt to AL, May 19, 1956, folder General Correspondence J-M, Box 1, General Correspondence of O'Connell and Larson, 1954–56 A-Z, RG 174, NARA II; *ATCL*, 125–126.

12. AL delivered this address on February 9, 1956. No copy of it has survived, although there are drafts on this topic entitled "The Forgotten Origins of the Republican Party" and "On a Republican Philosophy of Labor," folder Articles on Various Subjects (1955–1958), Box 15, ALP, DDEL. See also Arthur Larson, *A Republican Looks at His Party* (New York: Harper & Brothers, 1956), 142–144; Arthur Larson, *Know Your Social Security* (New York: Harper and Brothers, 1955), 12–14.

13. Sherman Adams to Karl E. Mundt, May 21, 1956, 1, folder 101–JJ Presidential Speeches and Speech Suggestions 1956, Box 426, WHOF, DDEP, DDEL. See also Mundt to DDE, May 19, 1956, folder General Correspondence J-M, Box 1, General Cor-

respondence of O'Connell and Larson, 1954–56 A-Z, RG 174, NARA II; Mundt to AL, May 19, 1956, in that same file; LOD, May 28, 1956; AL's notes entitled "Interview with the President 5/29/56," MB #1 May 1956, Box 22, ALP, DDEL; AL to AHL, June 3, 1956, 1, LFP. On DDE's work as a speechwriter for MacArthur and his strong interest in writing, see Dwight D. Eisenhower, *At Ease: Stories I Tell to Friends* (New York: Eastern Acorn Press, 1981), 212–215, 323–324; ALICY.

14. "Interview with the President 5/29/56," 1.

15. Quoted in AL to AHL, June 3, 1956, 1, LFP. DDE alluded here to the serious heart attack he had suffered on September 23, 1955. For the details of that episode, see Dwight D. Eisenhower, *Mandate for Change* (Garden City, N.Y.: Doubleday, 1963), 535–546.

16. "Interview with the President, 5/29/56," 2.

17. The typewritten version of these notes prepared by the Eisenhower Library staff reads "Bircher" instead of "Bricker," but AL's handwritten record makes clear that this is a misspelling. See "Interview with the President, 5/29/56," 2; and the handwritten notes in MB #1, May 1956, Box 22, ALP, DDEL.

18. "Interview with the President, 5/29/56," 2.

19. Ibid., 3. See also AL to AHL, June 3, 1956, 1, LFP.

20. "Interview with the President, 5/29/56," 3.

21. Ibid.

22. Quoted in AL to AHL, June 3, 1956, 1, LFP; see also "Interview with the President, 5/29/56," 3.

23. See AL to AHL, June 3, 1956, 1, LFP.

24. See ibid.; AL's notes entitled "Sequel to the July 20 Visit with the President," MB #2 July 1956, Box 22, and the speech outline in folder Material Relating to DDE Speeches, 1956–58, Box 28, both in ALP, DDEL; Eisenhower, *Waging Peace*, 9–10; *ATCL*, 128.

25. DDE to AL, June 21, 1956, folder I-L June 1956, Box 206, PPF, DDEL. See also Sherman Adams, *Firsthand Report: The Story of the Eisenhower Administration* (New York: Harper & Brothers, 1961), 298.

26. See LOD, June 22, 1956; Adams, *Firsthand Report*, 298.

27. Transcript of the President's News Conference of August 31, 1956, reprinted in *Public Papers of the Presidents of the United States: Dwight D. Eisenhower 1956* (Washington, D.C.: National Archives and Record Service, 1958), 722.

28. James Reston, "New G.O.P. Philosophy," *New York Times*, July 12, 1956. See also "Combating the New Deal," *Chicago Tribune*, July 15, 1956; Samuel Lubell, "With an Eye on November," unidentified press clipping, July 15, 1956, folder Larson, Mr. Arthur, Box 438, Series 320, General Correspondence, RMNPPP; "Ike's Draftsman," *Newsweek*, August 20, 1956, 28–29; "G.O.P. Philosopher," *Wall Street Journal*, September 13, 1956; "The Authentic American Center," *Time*, August 20, 1956, 14; "A Talk with Arthur Larson," *New Republic*, September 3, 1956, 5–6; "Ike's New 'Idea Man,'" *U.S. News & World Report*, September 7, 1956, 85–86; AL to AHL, June 3, 1956, 1, and July 15, 1956, 1–2, LFP.

29. Larson, *A Republican Looks at His Party*, vii–viii.

30. Ibid., 1.

31. Ibid., 2.

32. Ibid., 2–3, 8–9.

33. Ibid., 4.

34. Ibid., 4–8.

35. Ibid., 9 (see also 8).

36. Ibid., 9 (see also 10).

37. Ibid., 10.

38. Ibid., 11–12.

39. Ibid., 12–13. For the Hartz thesis, see Louis Hartz, *The Liberal Tradition in America* (New York: Harcourt, Brace & World, 1955) and the discussion of it in Richard Pells, *The Liberal Mind in a Conservative Age: American Intellectuals in the 1940s and 1950s* (Middletown, Conn.: Wesleyan University Press, 1989), 155–162; and James T. Kloppenberg, "In Retrospect: Louis Hartz's *The Liberal Tradition in America*," *Reviews in American History* 29 (September 2001): 460–478.

40. Larson, *A Republican Looks at His Party*, 13; see also Hartz, *The Liberal Tradition in America*, 35–66.

41. Ibid., 13.

42. Ibid.

43. Ibid., 13–14.

44. Ibid., 15 (see also 14).

45. Ibid., 15 (see also 16).

46. Ibid., 16–17.

47. Ibid., 17.

48. Ibid., 18.

49. Ibid., 19.

50. Ibid., 20–166.

51. Ibid., 23. The links between centrist political ideas in the United States and Europe are discussed in Philippe C. Schmitter and Gerhard Lehmbruch, eds., *Trends Toward Corporatist Intermediation* (Beverly Hills, Calif.: Sage, 1979); Margaret Weir and Theda Skocpol, "State Structures and Possibilities for 'Keynesian' Responses to the Great Depression in Sweden, Britain and the United States," in Peter B. Evans, Dietrich Rueschemeyer, and Theda Skocpol, eds., *Bringing the State Back In* (Cambridge: Cambridge University Press, 1985); Charles S. Maier, *In Search of Stability: Explorations in Historical Political Economy* (Cambridge: Cambridge University Press, 1987); Nelson Lichtenstein, "From Corporatism to Collective Bargaining: Organized Labor and the Eclipse of Social Democracy in the Postwar Era," in Steve Fraser and Gary Gerstle, eds., *The Rise and Fall of the New Deal Order, 1930–1980* (Princeton, N.J.: Princeton University Press, 1989), 122–125; and the articles published under the heading "The Postwar Social Contract," *International Labor and Working-Class History* 50 (Fall 1996): 114–156.

52. Larson, *A Republican Looks at His Party*, 27–28 (see also 29–31).

53. Ibid., 32–33. On the Tidelands oil controversy, see Eisenhower, *Mandate for Change*, 203–208; Adams, *Firsthand Report*, 305–306; James Patterson, *Grand Expectations: The United States, 1945–1974* (New York: Oxford University Press, 1996), 271.

54. Larson, *A Republican Looks at His Party*, 39.

55. Ibid., 67 (see also 40–66, 68–74).

56. Ibid., 62.

57. Ibid., 49.

58. Ibid., 49–59.

59. Ibid., 70–73. On the symbolic aspect of TVA in public policy debates, see William E. Leuchtenburg, *Franklin D. Roosevelt and the New Deal* (New York: Harper & Row, 1963), 12, 54–55, 86–87, 164–165, 341–342; and Alan Brinkley, *The End of Reform: New Deal Liberalism in Recession and War* (New York: Alfred A. Knopf, 1995), 6, 72, 242–243, 265–271.

60. Larson, *A Republican Looks at His Party*, 76–88.

61. Ibid., 90–92.

62. Ibid., 92–106.

63. See ibid., 40–42; A. E. Holmans, "The Eisenhower Administration and the Recession, 1953–5," *Oxford Economic Papers* (1958): 34–54; Robert Collins, *The Business*

Response to Keynes, 1929–1964 (New York: Columbia University Press, 1981), 152–158. Holmans concluded from his detailed study of this issue that "the differences between their [Truman's and Eisenhower's antirecession] policies were slight indeed" (50).

64. See Larson, *A Republican Looks at His Party*, 43–47; Jezer, *The Dark Ages*, 119–123; Robert O. Paxton, *Europe in the Twentieth Century*, 2nd ed. (New York: Harcourt, Brace, Jovanovich, 1985). Paxton observed that American (and Soviet) military spending during the 1950s was comparable to the share of Germany's GNP devoted to such purposes during the late 1930s (459n11).

65. Larson, *A Republican Looks at His Party*, 111.

66. Ibid., 142 (see also 111).

67. Ibid., 129–132, 142.

68. Ibid., 119–120.

69. On the unusually mixed nature of America's political economy during the mid-1950s, see Lichtenstein, "From Corporatism to Collective Bargaining," 122–152; and David L. Stebenne, *Arthur J. Goldberg: New Deal Liberal* (New York: Oxford University Press, 1996), 120–187.

70. Larson, *A Republican Looks at His Party*, 119–120. On the obstacles to good jobs in the professions and heavy industry for highly educated women, blacks, and blue-collar workers, respectively, during the 1950s, see William H. Chafe, *The Paradox of Change: American Women in the 20th Century* (New York: Oxford University Press, 1991), 175–193; William H. Harris, *The Harder We Run: Black Workers since the Civil War* (New York: Oxford University Press, 1982), 123–146; and Patterson, *Grand Expectations*, 15–38, 375–406.

71. See Larson, *A Republican Looks at His Party*, 172–175.

72. Ibid., 174–197. On the commonalities between moderate American conservatism in the 1950s and the Western European varieties, see Paxton, *Europe in the Twentieth Century*, 533–542, 555–577; and the articles published under the heading "The Postwar Social Contract," *International Labor and Working-Class History* 50 (Fall 1996): 114–156.

73. Larson, *A Republican Looks at His Party*, 177.

74. On the missionary impulse in American foreign policy during the late 1940s and 1950s, see Thomas G. Paterson, *On Every Front: The Making and Unmaking of the Cold War* (New York: Norton, 1979), 69–137; and Patterson, *Grand Expectations*, 105–136, 276–310.

75. Larson, *A Republican Looks at His Party*, 198 (see also 199–204).

76. Ibid., 198–199.

77. On the views of Hamilton, Lincoln, McKinley, and Theodore Roosevelt and their supporters, see Stanley Elkins and Eric McKitrick, *The Age of Federalism* (New York: Oxford University Press, 1993), especially 92–131, 258–263; Eric Foner, *Free Soil, Free Labor, Free Men: The Ideology of the Republican Party before the Civil War* (New York: Oxford University Press, 1970); David Herbert Donald, *Lincoln* (Simon & Schuster, 1995); and James Kloppenberg, *Uncertain Victory: Social Democracy and Progressivism in European and American Thought, 1870–1920* (New York: Oxford University Press, 1986), especially 145–160.

78. On the key roll call at the 1952 GOP Convention, the Eisenhower forces prevailed over those of Taft by a margin of 607 to 531; see Stephen E. Ambrose, *Eisenhower* (New York: Simon & Schuster, 1983), 1:540. On the split within the party that year, see Barton J. Bernstein, "Election of 1952," in Arthur M. Schlesinger, Jr., and Fred Israel, eds., *History of American Presidential Elections* (New York: McGraw-Hill, 1974), 4:3224–3232.

79. E. J. Dionne, Jr., *Why Americans Hate Politics* (New York: Touchstone, 1991), 170–176; *ATCL*, 127–128.

80. See AL to AHL, July 15, 1956, 1–2, LFP; Arthur M. Schlesinger, Jr., *The Vital Center, The Politics of Freedom* (Boston: Houghton Mifflin, 1949); Dionne, *Why Americans Hate Politics*, 172–176; *ATCL*, 128–130.

81. See AL's speech outline, which is headed "Convention Address," 5, 7, for this phrase, folder Materials Relating to DDE Speeches, 1956–58, Box 28, ALP, DDEL.

82. See AL's notes of his meeting with DDE, July 17, 1956, MB 1, Box 22, Larson Papers, DDEL.

83. DDE's reply to the question posed by Fred W. Perkins of Scripps-Howard is in the transcript of his weekly press conference, August 8, 1956, which is reprinted in *Public Papers of the Presidents of the United States: Dwight D. Eisenhower 1956*, 665. The notes of AL's meetings with DDE on July 17, 20, 26 and August 6, 7, 9, 14, and 15 are in MB 1–5, Box 22, Larson Papers, DDEL. The two men also discussed the speech at length over the telephone. On that point, see "Phone Calls—8/15/56 (2)," folder Aug. '56 Phone Calls, Box 16, DDEDS, AWF, DDEP, DDEL. AL noted the unprecedented nature of his role in a letter to his mother: "This is the sort of thing I can't advertise around here, but Secretary Mitchell knows it, of course, and is extremely happy about it, because it means that the Labor Department, for the first time, is getting somewhat on the inside track at the White House"; June 3, 1956, LFP.

84. "Ike's New 'Idea Man,'" *U.S. News & World Report*, September 7, 1956, 85–86; "G.O.P. Philosopher," *Wall Street Journal*, September 13, 1956; ALICY; *ATCL*, 130. Some journalists also used such terms as "chief ideologist" and "administration egghead" to characterize AL's role. See "Ike's Draftsman," *Newsweek*, August 20, 1956, 28–29; "A Talk with Arthur Larson," *New Republic*, September 3, 1956, 5–6; "Candled Egghead," *Newsweek*, October 28, 1957, 29–30.

85. Dwight D. Eisenhower, "Address at the Cow Palace on Accepting the Nomination of the Republican National Convention," August 23, 1956, reprinted in *Public Papers of the Presidents of the United States: Dwight D. Eisenhower 1956*, 704 (see also 702–703); Eisenhower, *Waging Peace*, 13. AL's notes on the speech indicate that he was the source of this quotation. See MB 1, Box 22, ALP, DDEL.

86. Eisenhower, "Address at the Cow Palace," 704–705.

87. Ibid. This line appeared in AL's original speech outline on page 6.

88. Eisenhower, "Address at the Cow Palace," 705–706. AL had made the exact same argument in *A Republican Looks at His Party*, 97–102, and in his speech outline on pages 5–6.

89. Eisenhower, "Address at the Cow Palace," 706 (see also on this point AL's speech outline on page 5).

90. Eisenhower, "Address at the Cow Palace," 706.

91. Ibid., 707.

92. Edward K. Thompson of Time-Life, in evaluating AL's book manuscript for Henry Luce, described this aspect of AL's thesis as reminiscent of "Goldilocks and the Three Bears." See Thompson's memo to Luce aide C. D. Jackson, March 13, 1956, 1–2, folder La-Misc. (2), Box 64, C. D. Jackson Papers, DDEL.

93. Eisenhower, "Address at the Cow Palace," 708 (see also 707); Larson, *A Republican Looks at His Party*, 7. AL made the point about focusing on today's problems in his speech outline on page 6.

94. Eisenhower, "Address at the Cow Palace," 708 (see also on this point AL's speech outline on pages 3, 6).

95. Eisenhower, "Address at the Cow Palace," 708. AL made this point in his speech outline on page 7.

96. Eisenhower, "Address at the Cow Palace," 708–709 (see also Larson, *A Republican Looks at His Party*, 135–142; AL's speech outline, page 4).

97. Eisenhower, "Address at the Cow Palace," 709 (see AL's expression of this idea in a more limited way in *A Republican Looks at His Party*, 39, 201).

98. Eisenhower, "Address at the Cow Palace," 709 (see AL's original speech outline, page 7, where he had alluded to Eisenhower's main point much less directly).

99. Eisenhower, "Address at the Cow Palace," 709. This passage, like the previous one quoted, did not appear in AL's original speech outline.

100. Eisenhower, "Address at the Cow Palace," 710. There was no mention of these things in AL's original speech outline, although he had discussed the lever of government contracts in *A Republican Looks at His Party*, 6. On DDE's support for framing the problem of unfair discrimination broadly so as to appeal to as many Americans as possible, see AL's notes of his discussion with DDE, July 26, 1956, MB 2, Box 22, ALP, DDEL.

101. Eisenhower, "Address at the Cow Palace," 711. AL had called the GOP the "party of peace" in his original speech outline but did not elaborate except to say that the young had the greatest interest in peace. See page 6 of the outline.

102. Eisenhower, "Address at the Cow Palace," 711.

103. Ibid.

104. Ibid.

105. Ibid., 712.

106. Ibid., 712–713. For AL's very similar formulation of the argument for collective security, see *A Republican Looks at His Party*, 177.

107. Eisenhower, "Address at the Cow Palace," 713.

108. Ibid., 714. AL's original speech outline contained these thoughts about the future expressed in words almost identical to the ones in the final draft. See AL's outline, 6–7.

109. Eisenhower, "Address at the Cow Palace," 714. This remark followed closely one in AL's original speech outline on page 7.

110. Eisenhower, "Address at the Cow Palace," 714–715. For details of Lincoln's "House Divided" speech on June 16, 1858, see David Herbert Donald, *Lincoln* (New York: Simon & Schuster, 1995), 206–209.

111. Eisenhower, "Address at the Cow Palace," 715; see also Larson, *A Republican Looks at His Party*, 198–199.

112. *ATCL*, 130. The British attack at the Suez Canal took place on November 5, 1956, on the eve of the American presidential election. For details of this event and the larger crisis of which it was part, see Eisenhower, *Waging Peace*, 69–99; Stephen E. Ambrose, *Eisenhower* (New York: Simon & Schuster, 1984), 2:367–374; Peter L. Hahn, *The United States, Great Britain, and Egypt, 1945–1956: Strategy and Diplomacy in the Early Cold War* (Chapel Hill: University of North Carolina Press, 1991), 211–239.

113. See the notes of AL's meetings to discuss speeches with DDE, 24, 25, 27, 28, and September 29, 1956, MB 5, Box 22, AL's memo to Sherman Adams, September 20, 1956, and the speech drafts in folder Material Relating to DDE Speeches, 1956–58, Box 28, all in ALP, DDEL; *ATCL*, 130; ALICY; AL-KL II; Samuel Lubell, *Revolt of the Moderates* (New York: Harper & Brothers, 1956), 103–125; Eisenhower, *Waging Peace*, 19; Ambrose, *Eisenhower*, 2:370.

114. Dwight D. Eisenhower, "Radio and Television Remarks Following the Election Victory," November 7, 1956, reprinted in *Public Papers of the Presidents of the United States: Dwight D. Eisenhower 1956*, 1090. DDE was the first victorious presidential candidate since 1848 whose party did not win control of at least one house of Congress. On that point, DDE's election night remarks, his reasons for making them, and the response they evoked, see Stephen E. Ambrose, *Nixon* (New York: Simon & Schuster, 1987), 1:421–422; *ATCL*, 130; Adams, *Firsthand Report*, 299; Stewart Alsop, "Just What is Modern Republicanism?" *Saturday Evening Post*, July 27, 1957, 18–19.

115. See Eisenhower speechwriter Emmet Hughes's recollection that "I had heard him [DDE] tell a group of local political leaders in Seattle, in the middle of the 1956 campaign, to look to Arthur Larson as a promising Presidential possibility for 1960," in Emmet John Hughes, "The Eisenhower I Knew," *Look*, December 4, 1962, 44. See also *ATCL*, 131–132.

8. *Caught in the Crosscurrents*

1. Quoted in *ATCL*, 131. See also AL's notes of this meeting in MB 6 USIA, Box 22, ALP, DDEL; Stephen E. Ambrose, *Eisenhower* (New York: Simon & Schuster, 1984), 2:152–153, 276–177; Stephen E. Ambrose, *Nixon* (New York: Simon & Schuster, 1987), 1:369–371; Emmet John Hughes, "The Eisenhower I Knew," *Look*, December 4, 1962, 44–46. DDE was the first president of the United States barred by the Constitution's Twenty-Second Amendment from seeking a third term.

2. See AL's notes of his conversation with DDE, MB October 1957 #1, Box 22, ALP, DDEL; "Warning from Gruenther," *U.S. News & World Report*, November 23, 1956, 22; Hughes, "The Eisenhower I Knew," 44–46; AL-KL II; ALICY; *ATCL*, 130–131.

3. See the notes of this conversation, MB 6 USIA, Box 22, ALP, DDEL; AL's Interview, September 22, 1965, 5–6, John Foster Dulles OHC, SGMML, PUL; *ATCL*, 131–132.

4. *ATCL*, 132. See also the notes of the November 9, 1956, meeting, MB 6 USIA, Box 22, ALP, DDEL; FNL to AHL, March 1, 1955, 2, and AL to AHL, September 28, 1957, 1, LFP.

5. See the notes of the November 9, 1956, meeting; AL's interview, 5–6, John Foster Dulles OHC; LKL; *ATCL*, 131–132.

6. See "Larson Rated GOP's 'Find of the Year,'" *Washington Post*, undated clipping, LFP; "Acquainting the World with the U.S.A.," *New York Herald Tribune*, November 12, 1956; "America's New 'Voice,'" *U.S. News & World Report*, November 23, 1956, 22; "Spokesman of America to the World," *Life*, January 21, 1957, 45–46; "USIA Boss Larson Paces 'New GOP,'" *New York Times*, January 21, 1957; AL to Bertha S. Adkins, February 21, 1957, folder Republican National Committee, 1956–58, Box 26, and AL's notes of the Gridiron dinner, MB USIA 4, Box 22, both in ALP, DDEL; "Nominations Sent to the Senate on January 14, 1957" and the attached material, and Gabriel Hauge's MFP, March 4, 1957, all in folder 247 1957 (1), Box 910, OF, DDEP, DDEL; BAC Meeting Minutes, March 14, 1957, 5, folder BAC-1, Box 69, Charles Sawyer Papers, HSTL; AL to AHL, March 17, 1957, 1, LFP; *ATCL*, 132–134.

7. On the history of the USIA, see "USIA: Summary of Positions since Becoming an Independent Agency" and "Summary of Appropriations since Becoming an Independent Agency," both dated November 13, 1956, Roll 12, USIA Director's CF, 1953–1964, RG 306, and the administrative history of the USIA in the finding aid to that collection, all in NARA II; John W. Henderson, *The United States Information Agency* (New York: Praeger, 1969), 29–55; John Morton Blum, *V Was for Victory: Politics and American Culture during World War II* (New York: Harcourt Brace Jovanovich, 1976), 21–45; AL's interview, 6–9, John Foster Dulles OHC, SGMML, PUL; Andrew H. Berding Memoir, 17, OHC, DDEL; *ATCL*, 139–140.

8. "U.S. Information Agency Strategic Principles," 1–2, 7, folder OCB 040, USIA (1) [Nov. 1953–May 1957], Box 20, OCB CFS, NSC Staff Papers, WHO, DDEL; Blum, *V Was for Victory*, 31–45. Although the strategic principles memo was not dated, its contents and location in the files pertaining to the USIA indicates that it was produced some time in 1954.

9. "U.S. Information Agency Strategic Principles," 3 (see also page 4).

10. Ibid., 3.

11. Ibid., 16 (see also 10–15, 17–18); "Report of the U.S. Information Agency to the National Security Council—Period January 1, 1954 through June 30, 1954," September 21, 1954, 2–3, 8–9, folder OCB 040 USIA (5) [Nov. 1953–May 1957], Box 20, OCB CFS, and "The USIA Program," 7–9, folder 35 NSC 5611, Box 7, Executive Secretary's SFS, both in NSC Staff Papers, WHO, DDEL.

12. See "USIA: Summary of Positions since Becoming an Independent Agency" and "Summary of Appropriations since Becoming an Independent Agency," both dated November 13, 1956, Roll 12, and AL's draft passage about the USIA for DDE's 1957 State of the Union message, 2, Roll 9, all in USIA Director's CF, 1953–1964, RG 306, in NARA II; the historical material about the USIA's directorship on the Department of State historian's website, www.state.gov/www/about_state/history/officers/usia.html; "Report of the U.S. Information Agency to the National Security Council—Period January 1, 1954 through June 30, 1954," September 21, 1954, 1–14, folder OCB 040 USIA (5) [Nov. 1953–May 1957], Box 20, OCB CFS, and "The USIA Program," 1–18, folder 35 NSC 5611, Box 7, Executive Secretary's SFS, both of which are in NSC Staff Papers, WHO, DDEL; "Nixon Hits 'Corn Ball' U.S. Envoys," *New York Herald Tribune*, March 17, 1957; Roy W. Howard to Sherman Adams, March 20, 1957, and attached material, and "Nominations Sent to the Senate on January, 14, 1957" and the attached material, all in folder 247 1957 (1), Box 910, OF, DDEP, DDEL; "Larson Becomes Chief of Information Agency," *New York Times*, December 19, 1956.

13. The "constructive message" remark is in MB 6 USIA, Box 22, ALP, DDEL. See also AL's notes there of his meeting with DDE, January 8, 1957, where they discussed the USIA at length. This memo book has notes of his other conversations regarding USIA programs. See also Theodore Streibert to AL, November 14, 1956, Roll 12, USIA Director's CF, 1953–1964, NARA II; "Itinerary for Under Secretary Larson," November 28, 1956, folder 1956 Administrative—Arthur Larson, Box 79, JPMP, DDEL; "USIA Boss Larson Paces 'New GOP,'" *New York Times*, January 21, 1957; *ATCL*, 137–146.

14. See AL's MB 6 USIA, Box 22, ALP, DDEL; "United States Information Agency Summary of Increases Requested in Fiscal Year 1957 Budget," 1–3, folder Legislative Leaders Meetings 1956 (2) [March-April], Box 2, LMS, AWF, and "Memorandum Regarding Current Legislative Needs of the U.S. Information Agency," 1–2, and the attached material, folder 247 1957 (2), Box 911, OF, all in DDEP, DDEL; Andrew H. Berding Memoir, 17, OHC, DDEL; "U.S. Information Agency Summary of Appropriations since Becoming an Independent Agency Fiscal Years 1954 thru 1957," Roll 12, USIA Director's CF, 1953–1964, RG 306, NARA II.

15. McCormack asked AL whether USIA broadcasts had encouraged pro-Western Hungarians to revolt against the communist government there in the belief that the United States would come to the rebels' aid. AL stoutly denied that the USIA had played such a role in sparking the Hungarian revolt, which Soviet military forces had easily crushed in November 1956. See "Notes on Presidential–Bipartisan Congressional Leadership Meeting," January 1, 1957, 9, folder Legislative Leaders Meetings 1957 (1) [January–February], Box 2, LMS, AWF, DDEP, DDEL; Robert O. Paxton, *Europe in the Twentieth Century*, 2nd ed. (New York: Harcourt, Brace, Jovanovich, 1985), 584–586. For Larson's effort to improve the USIA's message, see his draft passage about the USIA for DDE's 1957 State of the Union message and USIA deputy director Abbott Washburn's covering memos to A. J. Goodpaster and Kevin McCann, both dated December 28, 1956, and Washburn's memo to I. Jack Martin, December 31, 1956, all on Roll 9, and Washburn to New York senator Jacob Javits, April 18, 1957, Roll 14, USIA Director's CF, 1953–1964, RG 306, NARA II; "Annual Message to the Congress on the State of the Union,

January 10, 1957," in *Public Papers of the Presidents of the United States: Dwight D. Eisenhower 1957* (Washington, D.C.: National Archives and Records Service, 1958), 27; Dwight D. Eisenhower, *Waging Peace, 1956–1961* (Garden City: Doubleday and Company), 178–179; AL's prepared remarks to the January 17th Cabinet meeting, folder Cabinet Presentation on Communist Propaganda, 1–8, Box 28, ALP, DDEL.

16. AL to FNL, January 26, 1957, 1, LFP. The diploma is in Scrapbooks, 1954–57, Box 27, ALP, DDEL. On the purpose of AL's foreign trip, see AL to Peggy Burdick, December 6, 1956, and AL to Robert H. Steele, December 28, 1956, both on Roll 9, USIA Director's CF, 1953–1964, RG 306, NARA II; *ATCL*, 140.

17. AL to FNL, January 26, 1957, 1, LFP. See also AL's notes of his conversations with American and British government officials in England in USIA MB 2, Box 22, ALP, DDEL; Peter L. Hahn, *The United States, Great Britain, and Egypt, 1945–1956: Strategy and Diplomacy in the Early Cold War* (Chapel Hill: University of North Carolina Press, 1991), 194–239.

18. *ATCL*, 140–145; AL to FNL, January 26 and 28, 1957, and February 5 and 8, 1957, in LFP; AL's notes of his conversations during this trip in USIA MB 2 and 3, Box 22, ALP, DDEL.

19. AL's notes of meeting with Nehru, January 29, 1957, USIA MB 2, Box 22, ALP, DDEL.

20. Ibid.

21. Ibid.

22. Ibid.

23. *ATCL*, 142 (see also 141); AL's notes of conversation with Bowles, USIA MB 2, Box 22, ALP, DDEL. On the Eisenhower doctrine and Nehru's response, see Eisenhower, *Waging Peace*, 177–183; J. A. S. Grenville, *A History of the World in the 20th Century* (Cambridge, Mass.: Belknap Press of Harvard University, 2000), 472–475; on Bowles's views about India, see Chester Bowles, *Promises to Keep: My Years in Public Life, 1941–1969* (New York: Harper & Row, 1971), 248, 631–637.

24. AL's notes of meeting with Suhrawaddy, February 1, 1957, USIA MB 2, Box 22, ALP, DDEL.

25. Ibid.

26. Ibid.; *ATCL*, 142.

27. AL's notes of his meeting with Nuri-as-Said and other Iraqi officials in USIA MB 3, Box 22, ALP, DDEL. See also *ATCL*, 142–143.

28. See AL's notes of meetings in Iraq, USIA MB 3, Box 22, ALP, DDEL. On the issue of Israel's occupation of the Gaza Strip in 1956–1957, see Eisenhower, *Waging Peace*, 183–189.

29. AL's notes of meeting with Nasser, February 7, 1957, USIA MB 3, Box 22, ALP, DDEL; see also AL to FNL, February 8, 1957, 1, LFP.

30. AL's notes of meeting with Nasser, February 7, 1957.

31. *ATCL*, 140; see also AL's notes of meeting with Nasser, February 7, 1957.

32. See AL's notes of meeting with Nasser, February 7, 1957; *ATCL*, 140.

33. AL's notes of meeting with Nasser, February 7, 1957.

34. Ibid.

35. Ibid. On the weakness of Nasser's position after Suez, see Grenville, *A History of the World in the 20th Century*, 474–475.

36. AL's notes of meeting with Nasser, February 7, 1957.

37. *ATCL*, 143. See also AL's notes of this meeting in USIA MB 3, and notes of his other meetings with USIA staff members, journalists, and government officials in that memo book and USIA MB 2, both in Box 22, ALP, DDEL.

38. USIA MB 3, Box 22, ALP, DDEL.

39. Ibid. On the turn in Middle East public opinion against the West, including the United States, following the Suez crisis and the way it destabilized the region, see Hahn, *The United States, Great Britain, and Egypt*, 240–247; Grenville, *A History of the World in the 20th Century*, 472–475.

40. On the Algerian struggle for independence from France of 1954 to 1961 and its far-reaching repercussions, see Paxton, *Europe in the Twentieth Century*, 566, 627; Grenville, *A History of the World in the 20th Century*, 548–549; Albert Hourani, *A History of the Arab Peoples* (Cambridge, Mass.: Belknap Press of Harvard University Press, 1991), 369–372.

41. AL to FNL, February 8, 1957, 1, LFP; see also FNL to AHL, January 30, 1957, 1, LFP.

42. AL to FNL, February 8, 1957, 2, LFP.

43. One of the members of DDE's congressional liaison staff, Bryce Harlow, quoted Bow's remark in a MFP, February 26, 1957, folder 247 1957 (1), Box 910, OF, DDEP, DDEL. See also "Hearings on the Departments of State and Justice, the Judiciary, and Related Agencies Appropriations for 1958," Subcommittee of the Committee on Appropriations of the House of Representatives, February 26–27, 1957, CIS No. 85 H1597-1; on Rooney's attitude, see George V. Allen Memoir, OHC, DDEL, 66–67; *ATCL*, 134.

44. See "Hearings on the Departments of State and Justice, the Judiciary, and Related Agencies Appropriations for 1958"; *ATCL*, 134.

45. See AL's notes of Stevenson's remarks, USIA MB 4, Box 22, ALP, DDEL. Stevenson referred here to New York Yankees pitching star Don Larson. For details of the Gridiron Dinner held on March 2, 1957, see AL to AHL, March 17, 1957, 1, LFP; John Bartlow Martin, *Adlai Stevenson and the World* (Garden City, N.Y.: Anchor/Doubleday, 1977), 403–405; *ATCL*, 132.

46. See AL's notes of Stevenson's remarks.

47. Ibid.

48. Ibid.; see Gabriel Hauge's MFP, March 4, 1957, which reported that AL "had much the better of the day over Adlai," and the attached letter to from Hauge to AL congratulating him for "representing us all brilliantly"; in folder 247 1957 (1), Box 910, OF, DDEP, DDEL; Martin, *Adlai Stevenson and the World*, 403–405; *ATCL*, 132–133.

49. Quoted in *ATCL*, 134 (see also 133); on LBJ's ambitions and insecurities and the petty behavior they often inspired, see Robert A. Caro, *The Years of Lyndon Johnson: Means of Ascent* (New York: Alfred A. Knopf, 1990), 194–412; Robert Dallek, *Lone Star Rising: Lyndon Johnson and His Times* (New York: Oxford University Press, 1991), especially 468–508.

50. See, on this point, ABL; LKL; the comment of Booth Mooney, who had worked as a journalist in Texas and as LBJ's executive assistant, that AL "was utterly unfitted by temperament and training to deal with a hostile Lyndon Johnson" is in Mooney's memoir *The Politicians: 1945–1960* (Philadelphia: J. B. Lippincott, 1970), 262.

51. See the remarks of Republican congressman Noah M. Mason of Illinois in the *Congressional Record*, March 11, 1957, folder Larson, Mr. Arthur, Box 438, Series 320, General Correspondence, RMNPPP; Sherman Adams, *Firsthand Report: The Story of the Eisenhower Administration* (New York: Harper & Brothers, 1961), 298–300; Emmet John Hughes, *The Ordeal of Power: A Political Memoir of the Eisenhower Years* (New York: Atheneum, 1963), 235–236; Chester J. Pach, Jr., and Elmo Richardson, *The Presidency of Dwight D. Eisenhower*, rev. ed. (Lawrence: University Press of Kansas, 1991), 167–169; Mooney, *The Politicians*, 255–262; Ambrose, *Eisenhower*, 2:388–391.

52. Humphrey's remark at his press conference, January 16, 1957, is quoted in Ambrose, *Eisenhower*, 2:389 (see also 390–391). See also Hughes, *The Ordeal of Power*, 236–

237; Iwan W. Morgan, *Eisenhower Versus "The Spenders": The Eisenhower Administration, The Democrats and the Budget, 1953–60* (London: Pinter Publishers, 1990), 74–83; on the roots of rising prices in the later 1950s, see David L. Stebenne, *Arthur J. Goldberg: New Deal Liberal* (New York: Oxford University Press, 1996), 154–157, 175–187, 197–215.

53. Hughes, *The Ordeal of Power*, 236–237; Morgan, *Eisenhower Versus "The Spenders,"* 83–84.

54. See AL to AHL, May 5, 1957, 1, LFP; Adams, *Firsthand Report*, 298–300; Morgan, *Eisenhower Versus "The Spenders,"* 84–85; Hughes, *The Ordeal of Power*, 237; Pach and Richardson, *The Presidency of Dwight D. Eisenhower*, 167–169; Mooney, *The Politicians*, 255–262; Ambrose, *Eisenhower*, 2:388–391.

55. On the House's handling of the USIA's budget in 1957, see DDE to Cannon, April 9, 1957, and the attached material, DDE's correspondence with Frederic R. Coudert, Jr., and Abbott Washburn to Alfred M. Gruenther, May 20, 1957, all in folder 247 1957(1), Box 910, OF, DDE to Budget Director Percival Brundage, April 16, 1957, marked "Personal and Confidential," and the "Supplementary Notes of Legislative Leadership Meeting," April 16, 1957, folder Legislative Leaders Meetings 1957 (2) [March-April], Box 2, LMS, AWF, all in DDEP, DDEL; "'Philosopher' under Fire," *U.S. News & World Report*, April 26, 1957, 16.

56. AL to AHL, March 17, 1957, 1, LFP. See also AL to Bertha S. Adkins, March 6, 1957, and AL to Mrs. Anne Wheaton, March 25, 1957, folder Republican National Committee, 1956–58, Box 26, ALP, DDEL; AL's speech "As Our Case Is New," 1–3, folder Larson, Mr. Arthur, Box 438, Series 320, General Correspondence, RMNPPP; AL's Interview, 23, John Foster Dulles OHC, SGMML, PUL.

57. For the quoted passages from AL's speech, see "As Our Case is New," 8 and 12, respectively.

58. "Subcommittee of the Senate Committee on Appropriations," in "Hearings on the Departments of State, Justice, the Judiciary and Related Agencies Appropriations for 1958," May 2, 1957, CIS No. 85 S1204-2, Y.4.Ap6/2:St2/958, 488 (see also 449–487, 489–530); AL's notes of the hearings, MB March 1957, Box 22, ALP, DDEL; "Democrats Attack USIA Chief on Speech," *Washington Post*, May 3, 1957; "Arthur Larson Testifies," *New Republic*, May 27, 1957, 5–6; Dallek, *Lone Star Rising*, 515–516; *ATCL*, 134.

59. "Subcommittee of the Senate Committee on Appropriations, May 2, 1957," 488–530.

60. "Subcommittee of the Senate Committee on Appropriations, May 10, 1957," 1129–1130 (see also 1119–1128, 1131–1249, and the hearings on May 8–9, 1957, 797–975); AL's notes of the hearings, MB March 1957, Box 22, ALP, DDEL; "Democrats Attack USIA Chief on Speech," *Washington Post*, May 3, 1957; "Arthur Larson Testifies," *New Republic*, May 27, 1957, 5–6; Dallek, *Lone Star Rising*, 515–516; *ATCL*, 134.

61. See "Senate Committee on Appropriations, May 2, 1957," 488–530, and May 8–10, 1957, 797–975, 1119–1249; AL's notes from the hearings, MB March 1957, Box 22, ALP, DDEL; *ATCL*, 134.

62. *ATCL*, 134.

63. Ibid., 151; ABL; LKL.

64. *ATCL*, 134, 191–192.

65. AL to W. Raymond Blackard, December 6, 1956, Roll 9, USIA Director's CF, 1953–1964, RG 306, NARA II. AL also addressed a GOP women's group in the same month he gave his Hawaii speech. See AL to Bertha S. Adkins, March 6, 1957, and her letter of thanks to him, April 16, 1957, folder Republican National Committee, 1956–58, Box 26, ALP, DDEL.

66. See AL's notes of this conversation, MB October 1957 #1, Box 22, ALP, DDEL.

67. On the wire service imbroglio, see the correspondence between Roy W. Howard and Sherman Adams in folder 247 1957(1), Box 910, OF, DDEP, DDEL; AL to AHL, May 5, 1957, 1, LFP. On the most basic reason for the attacks on AL, see Adams, *Firsthand Report*, 298–301.

68. For Davenport, see Marcia Davenport, *Too Strong for Fantasy* (New York: Charles Scribner's Sons, 1967), 259–284; the material in the folders 1–3 of Davenport, Russell—Institute for Creative Research, and the folder Davenport, Russell—Political Matters, all in Box 5, Edwin N. Clarke Papers, DDEL. For Ginzberg's role, see his oral history and "Origins of the Conservation of Human Resources Project," folder Eisenhower, Dwight D. (1), Box 1, Eli Ginzberg Papers, both in DDEL; Ambrose, *Eisenhower*, 1:484; Ewald, *Eisenhower*, 170–171. On Hauge's role, see Stewart Alsop, "Just What Is Modern Republicanism?" *Saturday Evening Post*, July 27, 1957, 90; AL's notes of his meeting with DDE, October 1, 1957, MB October 1957 #1, Box 22, ALP, DDEL; Dwight D. Eisenhower, *Mandate for Change* (Garden City, N.Y.: Doubleday, 1963), 118, 487–489, 566.

69. See Abbott Washburn's Memo to Sherman Adams, May 11, 1957, Abbott Washburn to Alfred M. Gruenther, May 20, 1957, and the attached memo "Gruenther Appearance," May 3, 1957, and AL to John J. Rooney, July 15, 1957, all in folder 247 1957 (2), Box 9111, OF, DDEP, DDEL; AL's notes of his conversation with DDE about the USIA Budget, MB October 1957#1, Box 22, ALP, DDEL; Dallek, *Lone Star Rising*, 516; Mooney, *The Politicians*, 263.

70. AL, "What Hopes for Peace?" address to the Philadelphia Bulletin Forum, March 31, 1957, 4, folder 247 1957(1), Box 910, OF, DDEP, DDEL (see also 1–3).

71. Larson, "What Hopes for Peace?" 5 (see also 4).

72. Ibid., 5.

73. Ibid., 5.

74. Ibid., 6 (see also 5).

75. Ibid., 6.

76. Ibid., 6.

77. Ibid., 6–7.

78. Ibid., 8 (see also 7).

79. Ibid., 9 (see also 8).

80. Ibid., 9–10.

81. AL, "The United States Information Service: How Effective Is It?" address delivered at the Public Affairs Luncheon, Union League Club of New York, N.Y., April 4, 1957, in *Vital Speeches* 23, June 1, 1957, 494 (see also 492–93).

82. Larson, "The United States Information Service," 493–494. On the Khrushchev speech and its consequences, see Paxton, *Europe in the Twentieth Century*, 580.

83. Larson, "The United States Information Service," 494.

84. Ibid.

85. Ibid.

86. Ibid.

87. Ibid., 495. AL later elaborated on the need for a fact-based approach in a guidance paper he developed for all USIA personnel. See "U.S.I.A. Basic Guidance Paper," 1–6, and the covering letter from USIA Deputy Director for Policy and Plans Saxton Bradford, October 22, 1957, folder Articles 1955–58 (1), Box 15, ALP, DDEL; *ATCL*, 145.

88. *ATCL*, 146.

89. On the People-to-People program and the roots of resistance to it, see DDE's "Memorandum for Governor Adams," August 12, 1957, AWF, DDEDS, and AL's notes of his meetings with DDE on October 1 and 10, 1957, MB October 1957 #1, Box 22, ALP, all in DDEL; *ATCL*, 137–138; Thomas G. Paterson, *On Every Front: The Making and*

Unmaking of the Cold War (New York: Norton, 1979), 113–137; Michael J. Hogan, *A Cross of Iron: Harry S. Truman and the Origins of the National Security State* (Cambridge: Cambridge University Press, 1998), especially 1–22.

90. On this general tendency of Eisenhower's presidency, see the introduction to Louis Galambos and Daun Van Ee, eds., *The Papers of Dwight D. Eisenhower: The Presidency: The Middle Way* (Baltimore, Md.: Johns Hopkins University Press, 1996), XIV:xv–xx.

91. See AL's notes of meetings with DDE and Sherman Adams on October 1, 1957, MB October 1957, Box 22, ALP, and George V. Allen Memoir, 58–63, OHC, both in DDEL.

92. AL's notes of meeting with DDE, October 1, 1957.

93. Ibid. AL codified the new directions in form and content in "U.S.I.A. Basic Guidance Paper."

94. AL's notes of meeting with DDE, October 1, 1957.

95. Ibid.

96. Ibid.

97. Ibid.

98. Ibid. On the inspection tour, see AL to AHL, September 28, 1957, 2, and October 6, 1957, 1, LFP.

99. AL's notes of meeting with DDE, October 1, 1957.

100. AL's notes of meeting with Sherman Adams, October 1, 1957, MB October 1957, Box 22, ALP, DDEL. On the USIA director's salary, see "America's New 'Voice,'" 22.

101. AL's notes of meeting with Sherman Adams, October 1, 1957.

102. Ibid.

103. Ibid.

104. Ibid.

105. Quoted in George V. Allen Memoir, 63, OHC, DDEL (see also 58–62); "The Newsmaker: George V. Allen of USIA," *Newsweek*, October 28, 1957, 30.

106. See AL's letter of resignation as USIA director to DDE, October 16, 1957, and DDE's reply the following day, both of which are in folder 247 1957 (2), Box 911, OF, DDEP, DDEL; George V. Allen Memoir, 63–64, OHC, DDEL; "Larson Named White House Assistant," *New York Times*, October 17, 1957.

107. "A Republican Looks At His President," *The Reporter*, October 31, 1957, 2 (see also 3).

108. "Larson Named White House Assistant"; "In Propaganda War—A New Team," *U.S. News & World Report*, October 25, 1957, 20; "Candled Egghead," *Newsweek*, October 28, 1957, 29–30; "Young Man with a Book," *Time*, October 28, 1957, 21; "Modern Republican Is Kicked Upstairs," *Christian Century*, November 6, 1957, 1308–1309.

9. *The President's "Ghost"*

1. "Discussion at the 339th Meeting of the NSC, Thursday, October 10, 1957," October 11, 1957, 7, DDRS. On the uproar at the White House about Sputnik (and DDE's calm response), see AL's Interview, 28–29, John Foster Dulles OHC, SGMML, PUL; AL to Yanek Mieczkowski, November 22, 1988, 1–2, and AL-YM, both in folder Interviews 1988–92, Box 21, ALP, DDEL; Stephen E. Ambrose, *Eisenhower* (New York: Simon & Schuster, 1984), 2:423–435. The public hysteria over Sputnik is conveyed very effectively in the film *The Satellite Sky* (1990).

2. "Discussion at the 339th Meeting of the NSC, Thursday, October 10, 1957," 8.

3. Ibid. On the overreaction to Sputnik in Congress, especially on the part of Lyndon

Johnson, see William E. Burrows, *Deep Black: Space Espionage and National Security* (New York: Berkley Books, 1988), 88–90.

4. See AL-YM, folder Interviews 1988–92, Box 21, ALP, DDEL; Ambrose, *Eisenhower,* 2:423–435.

5. AL to Lewis Strauss, October 15, 1957, 1–2, DDRS. See also AL's accompanying memo, 2, where he confidently predicted that "the relatively small amount of fallout from a 90% 'clean bomb' could be handled with little trouble"; AL's MFP, October 15, 1957, 1, DDRS; AL's notes of his remarks at the October 10th NSC meeting, MB Oct. 1957 #1, Box 22, ALP, DDEL.

6. AL discussed the demise of the nuclear dynamite proposal in *ATCL,* 152. On this subject, see also Dan O'Neill, *The Firecracker Boys* (New York: St. Martin's Press, 1994). On the attitudes of DDE and his top aides toward nuclear power, see Ambrose, *Eisenhower,* 2:131–135, 147–151. On the administration's inadequate response to the environmental problems created by nuclear weapons testing and rapid economic growth, see James Patterson, *Grand Expectations: The United States, 1945–1974* (New York: Oxford University Press, 1996), 276–278; John Patrick Diggins, *The Proud Decades: America in War and Peace, 1941–1960* (New York: Norton, 1988), 325–331; Marty Jezer, *The Dark Ages: Life in the United States, 1945–1960* (Boston: South End Press, 1982), 146–151.

7. AL's notes of meeting with DDE, October 22, 1957, MB Oct. 1957 #2, Box 22, ALP, DDEL. For the advent of this series of speeches, see also AL to Yanek Mieczkowski, November 22, 1988, 1, and AL-YM, 2, both in folder Interviews 1988–92, Box 21, ALP, DDEL.

8. AL's notes of meeting with DDE, October 22, 1957, MB Oct. 1957 #2, Box 22, ALP, DDEL.

9. DDE, "Memorandum for the Honorable Arthur Larson," November 5, 1957, 1, in folder November '57 D.D.E. Diary, Box 28, DDEDS, AWF, DDEP, DDEL. See also AL's notes of meetings with DDE on November 4 and 5, 1957, MB Nov. 1957 #1, Box 22, ALP, DDEL. The briefing papers that AL consulted are in folder Science and Security: Background Material: Defense and John Hamlin, Box 3, LMC, DDEL.

10. DDE, "Memorandum for the Honorable Arthur Larson." On the enthusiasm for more military spending in the wake of the Sputnik launch, see Patterson, *Grand Expectations,* 418–420.

11. DDE, "Memorandum for the Honorable Arthur Larson," 1–2.

12. See AL's notes of meeting with Sherman Adams, October 28, 1957, MB Oct. 1957 #2, AL's notes of his meeting with the President's Science Advisory Committee, n.d., MB Nov. 1957 #1, Box 22, ALP, DDEL; the memo from RMN to AL, November 6, 1957, folder Larson, Mr. Arthur, Box 438, Series 320, General Correspondence, RMNPPP; "Radio and Television Address to the American People on Science in National Security," November 7, 1957, in *Public Papers of the Presidents of the United States: Dwight D. Eisenhower 1957* (Washington, D.C.: National Archives and Records Service, 1968), 789; AL to AHL, November 17, 1957, LFP.

13. Eisenhower, "Science in National Security," 794 (see also 789–793).

14. Ibid., 796 (see also 795).

15. Ibid., 796–797.

16. Ibid., 798.

17. Ibid.

18. Ibid., 799 (see also 798). The Soviet government soon rejected the new disarmament proposals the United Nations had approved because they, like most earlier proposals, would have required on-site inspection within the Soviet Union, which Soviet leaders refused to permit throughout the 1950s. See Ambrose, *Eisenhower,* 2:149–151.

19. See AL's notes of meeting with DDE, November 11, 1957, MB Nov. 1957 #2, Box 22,

ALP, DDEL. See also the memo from Alan T. Waterman to AL, November 12, 1957, folder President's Speeches: Science and Security Background Material Used for Nov. 7 and Nov. 13, 1957, Box 3, LMC, DDEL; DDE's memo to AL, November 12, 1957, in Louis Galambos and Daun Van Ee, eds., *The Papers of Dwight David Eisenhower, The Presidency: Keeping the Peace,* vol. XVIII (Baltimore, Md.: Johns Hopkins University Press, 2001), 561.

20. DDE's memo to AL, November 12, 1957, in Galambos and Van Ee, *The Papers of Dwight David Eisenhower,* XVIII:561.

21. See AL's notes of discussions with DDE, November 11–13, 1957, MB Nov. 1957 # 2, Box 22, ALP, DDEL. On Eisenhower's fondness for what he called a QED, see AL to Saxton Bradford, November 14, 1957, folder Chronological: Oct., Nov., Dec., Box 1, LMC, DDEL.

22. "Radio and Television Address to the American People on 'Our Future Security,'" November 13, 1957, in *Public Papers of the Presidents of the United States: Dwight D. Eisenhower* 1957, 809 (see also 807–808).

23. Eisenhower, "Our Future Security," 811 (see also 809–810).

24. Ibid., 811.

25. Ibid., 811–812.

26. Ibid., 813 (see also 812).

27. Ibid.

28. Ibid.

29. Ibid., 814 (see also 813).

30. Ibid., 815 (see also 814).

31. Ibid., 816 (see also 815).

32. Ibid., 816.

33. AL to AHL, October 20, 1957, 1 (see also his letters to her, November 17 and 24, 1957, LFP; AL-KL II; and ALICY; MB Nov. 1957 #2, Box 22, ALP, DDEL; *ATCL,* 151.

34. AL to Robert C. Hill, November 29, 1957, folder Chronological: Oct., Nov., Dec., Box 1, LMC, DDEL. See also AL to AHL, November 17, 1957, LFP.

35. AL-KL II; ALICY; AL to AHL, October 20, 1957, and November 17, 1957, LFP.

36. AL recorded this remark in his notes of a November 5, 1957, meeting with DDE, MB Nov. 1957 #1, Box 22, ALP, DDEL; see also AL-KL II; ALICY. For DDE's penchant for heavily editing his speechwriters' work, see his memo to AL, January 13, 1958, where he observed: "At heart you must understand that I am an editor; no written text appeals to me until I have inserted my own particular mannerisms of style." This memo is reprinted in Galambos and Van Ee, *The Papers of Dwight David Eisenhower,* XVIII:663–664. On this point, see also Emmet John Hughes, *The Ordeal of Power: A Political Memoir of the Eisenhower Years* (New York: Atheneum, 1963), 24–25, 61–62, 150, 192–193; Sherman Adams, *Firsthand Report: The Story of the Eisenhower Administration* (New York: Harper & Brothers, 1961), 81–83.

37. See AL's notes of meeting with Adams, November 8, 1957, MB Nov. 1957 #1, Box 22, ALP, DDEL.

38. See, on that point, AL's notes of meeting with Adams, December 12, 1957, MB Dec. 1957, Box 23, ALP, DDEL.

39. AL's MFP, November 12, 1957, folder Chronological: Oct., Nov., Dec., Box 1, LMC, DDEL. See also on this third speech, AL's notes on "Comments Concerning Mutual Aid Speech," MB Nov. 1957 #2, Box 22, ALP, and DDE's memo to AL, November 23, 1957, and the attached pages, folder President's Speeches: Peace 2/25/58 (Drafts including Cleveland Drafts for 11/26/57), Box 4, LMC, all in DDEL. On DDE's use of the term mutual aid, see AL's memo to Fred Fox, February 3, 1958, folder Chronological: January, February 1958, Box 1, LMC, DDEL.

40. On the preoccupation with security for those who came of age in the 1930s and 1940s, see David M. Kennedy, *Freedom from Fear: The American People in Depression and War, 1929–1945* (New York: Oxford University Press). For details of AL's plans to create an inventory of speeches, see AL to Saxton Bradford, Milton Eisenhower, and JPM, all November 14, 1957, and Larson's MFP, November 19, 1957, in folder Chronological: Oct., Nov., Dec., Box 1, LMC, DDEL.

41. AL-KL II. On the nature of DDE's stroke, see Dwight D. Eisenhower, *Waging Peace, 1956–1961* (Garden City, N.Y.: Doubleday and Company), 227–230; Ambrose, *Eisenhower*, 2:436–440.

42. See AL's notes for November 26, 1957, which are headlined "A Black Day at the White House," MB Nov. 1957 #2, Box 22, ALP, DDEL. On the consequences for the science and security series, see AL-KL II; AL to Yanek Mieczkowski, November 22, 1988, and AL-YM, 2, folder Interviews 1988–92, Box 21, ALP, DDEL; *ATCL*, 148.

43. AL-YM, 1–2, folder Interviews 1988–92, Box 21, ALP, DDEL. On the results of this sequence of events, see AL-KL II; Eric F. Goldman, *The Crucial Decade and After: America, 1945–1960* (New York: Vintage, 1960), 308–311; Ambrose, *Eisenhower*, 2:423–435.

44. AL-KL II.

45. See AL's notes headed "Meeting with the President . . . 12/12/57," MB Dec. 1957, Box 23, ALP, DDEL. See also the copy of AL's first draft of the 1958 State of the Union address, December 4, 1957, folder Material Relating to D.D.E. Speeches, 1956–58, Box 28, ALP, DDEL.

46. See AL's notes headed "Meeting with the President . . . 12/12/57."

47. Ibid.

48. On DDE's medical condition in the first few weeks after his stroke, see AL-KL II; Eisenhower, *Waging Peace*, 227–230; Ambrose, *Eisenhower*, 2:436–440.

49. AL-KL II.

50. See AL's Draft #3 of the 1958 State of the Union address, December 21, 1957, folder Material Relating to D.D.E. Speeches, 1956–58, Box 28, ALP, DDEL; Eisenhower, *Waging Peace*, 229–232, 240; *Public Papers of the Presidents of the United States: Dwight D. Eisenhower 1957*, 830–832, 835–844; Ambrose, *Eisenhower*, 2:439–440; AL-KL II; ALICY. DDE admitted in his memoirs, which were published seven years later, that the stroke permanently reduced his effectiveness as a speaker. He reported that "from that time [of the stroke] onward I have frequently experienced difficulty in prompt utterance of the word I seek. Even today, occasionally, I reverse syllables in a long word and at times am compelled to speak slowly and cautiously if I am to communicate correctly"; Eisenhower, *Waging Peace*, 229.

51. See MB January 1958, Box 23, ALP, DDEL. On the White House staff's meddling with the 1958 State of the Union address, see MB Dec. 1957 in that same collection; Raymond J. Saulnier to AL, December 29, 1957 and the three attached pages, Material Relating to D. D. E. Speeches, 1956–58, Box 28, ALP, DDEL; *ATCL*, 148.

52. Larson, *Twentieth Century Life*, 148. The speech eventually required seventeen complete drafts. See, on that point, DDE's memo to AL, January 13, 1958, in Galambos and Van Ee, *The Papers of Dwight David Eisenhower*, XVIII:664.

53. See MB Dec. 1957, Box 23, ALP, DDEL.

54. Dwight D. Eisenhower, "Annual Message to the Congress on the State of the Union," January 9, 1958, in *Public Papers of the Presidents of the United States: Dwight D. Eisenhower 1958* (Washington, D.C.: National Archives and Records Administration, 1959), 10 (see also 2–9, 11–15).

55. Eisenhower, "Annual Message to the Congress on the State of the Union," January 9, 1958, 10.

56. Ibid.

57. Ibid., 11 (see also 10).

58. Ibid., 11. On DDE's fondness for the free trade and internationalist ideas expressed in McKinley's speech to the Pan-American Exposition in Buffalo, New York, on the day before his assassination, see AL's notes of meeting with DDE, August 6, 1956, MB #4 July 1956, Box 22, ALP, DDEL.

59. Eisenhower, "Annual Message to the Congress on the State of the Union," January 9, 1958, 14 (see also 11–13).

60. Ibid., 15. On DDE's continued determination not to overreact to Sputnik, see AL's notes of meeting with DDE, January 6, 1958, MB Dec. 1957, Box 23, ALP, DDEL, where DDE objected to even stronger wording in the speech, and AL's observation there that "this is about the fourth time he has opened up on me for viewing this period as one of special/new danger."

61. Eisenhower, "Annual Message to the Congress on the State of the Union," January 9, 1958, 15.

62. On DDE's delivery of the 1958 State of the Union address and the enthusiastic response to it, see AL's notes headed "Telephone Conversation with the President 1/1/58," and AL's notes headed "Cabinet Meeting 1/10/58," MB Dec. 1957, Box 23, ALP, and "Congratulations Received by President on the State of the Union Message," folder State of the Union Message, Box 3, LMC, all in DDEL; DDE's memo of thanks to AL, January 13, 1958, in Galambos and Van Ee, *The Papers of Dwight David Eisenhower,* 18:663–664; AL-KL II; Eisenhower, *Waging Peace,* 240–241; *ATCL,* 148–149.

63. See AL's notes of this conversation under the heading "11/26/57 A Black Day at the White House," MB [Nov.] 1957 #2, Box 22, ALP, DDEL. On the confrontation at Little Rock in 1957 and DDE's response, see his "Radio and Television Address to the American People on the Situation in Little Rock," September 24, 1957, in *Public Papers of the Presidents of the United States: Dwight D. Eisenhower 1957,* 689–694; Harvard Sitkoff, *The Struggle for Black Equality, 1954–1980* (New York: Hill & Wang, 1981), 30–33; Ambrose, *Eisenhower,* 2:414–423, and Patterson, *Grand Expectations,* 413–416.

64. See AL, "Interview with the President 7/20/56," MB #3 July 1956, Box 22, ALP, DDEL.

65. AL to DDE, September 30, 1957, folder USIA (1), AWF, AS, DDEP, DDEL. See also Arthur Larson, *Eisenhower: The President Nobody Knew* (New York: Charles Scribner's Sons, 1968), 127; AL, "Meeting with the President 10/1/57," MB Oct. 1957 #1, Box 22, ALP, DDEL.

66. See AL, "Meeting with the President 10/1/57." See also Larson, *Eisenhower: The President Nobody Knew,* 124–126; Mary L. Dudziak, *Cold War Civil Rights: Race and the Image of American Democracy* (Princeton, N.J.: Princeton University Press, 2000), 137–138. In his memoirs, DDE endorsed the *Brown* decision, but he evidently wrote this (during the early 1960s) in order to avoid adding to the already great tensions within the southern and border states about the ongoing efforts to end Jim Crow schools. See Dwight D. Eisenhower, *Mandate for Change* (Garden City, N.Y.: Doubleday, 1963), 229–230.

67. On the lower-middle-class environment in which DDE grew up, see Dwight D. Eisenhower, *At Ease: Stories I Tell My Friends* (New York: Eastern Acorn Press, 1981), especially 64–92; and Stephen E. Ambrose, *Eisenhower* (New York: Simon & Schuster, 1983), 1:28–42. On lower-middle-class blacks' views on interracial dating and marriage in the 1950s, see Renee C. Romano, *Race Mixing: Black-White Marriage in Postwar America* (Cambridge, Mass.: Harvard University Press, 2003), especially 82–144.

68. On the southern and border-state world in which DDE mostly lived during the period 1916 to 1935, see Eisenhower, *At Ease,* 111–154; Ambrose, *Eisenhower,* 1:55–103; and

Patterson, *Grand Expectations*, 392–393. On DDE's belief that federal efforts to force the end of segregated southern schools would backfire, see ALICY; Adams, *Firsthand Report*, 331–332, 341–342; Hughes, *The Ordeal of Power*, 201–202; Ambrose, *Eisenhower*, 2:190; and Patterson, *Grand Expectations*, 393–394.

69. On DDE's disagreement with the assumption that segregated schools necessarily harmed blacks, see ALICY; and Larson, *Eisenhower: The President Nobody Knew*, 126–128. On DDE's concern that federal efforts to compel school desegregation would divide the country in ways harmful to everyone, see Ambrose, *Eisenhower*, 2:304–309, 408–410.

70. On DDE's refusal to make clear that he would use the powers of his office to enforce the *Brown* decision prior to the Little Rock confrontation and his reasons for this refusal, see Adams, *Firsthand Report*, 331–343; Hughes, *The Ordeal of Power*, 201–202; Ambrose, *Eisenhower*, 2:190–192, 304–309, 406–410; and Patterson, *Grand Expectations*, 394. On the 1957 Civil Rights Act, see Ambrose, *Eisenhower*, 2:406–410; and Patterson, *Grand Expectations*, 412–413.

71. ALICY. On DDE's use of his presidential powers to fight segregation, see Eisenhower, *Mandate for Change*, 234–236; Adams, *Firsthand Report*, 333–335.

72. ALICY. On the doubtful nature of this core assumption behind the Supreme Court's decision in *Brown*, see Patterson, *Grand Expectations*, including Patterson's observation that "in 1954 [when the Court decided the *Brown* case] there simply did not exist sufficient research that could 'prove' whether any particular racial mix in schools was superior—or in what ways—to any other" (391).

73. See "Behind the Story," *Time*, April 14, 1958, 33. On AL's delight with the response to the 1958 State of the Union address, see his notes headed "Cabinet Meeting 1/10/58," MB Dec. 1957, Box 23, ALP, and "Congratulations Received by President on the State of the Union Message," folder State of the Union Message, Box 3, LMC, both in DDEL; AL-KL II; *ATCL*, 148–149. The jarring shift from the State of the Union address to the 1958 budget message is described in Hughes, *The Ordeal of Power*, 258–259. The address is reprinted in *Public Papers of the Presidents of the United States: Dwight D. Eisenhower 1958*, 17–74.

74. On the changes pushing the Eisenhower administration to the right in the later 1950s, see David L. Stebenne, *Arthur J. Goldberg: New Deal Liberal* (New York: Oxford University Press, 1996), 154–157; Ambrose, *Eisenhower*, 2:411–486; William Bragg Ewald, Jr., *Eisenhower the President: Crucial Days, 1951–1960* (Englewood Cliffs, N.J.: Prentice Hall, 1981), 290–291; and Patterson, *Grand Expectations*, 407–441.

75. Eisenhower, *Waging Peace*, 212–213, 379–380; Ewald, *Eisenhower the President*, 290–291; *ATCL*, 130; Stebenne, *Arthur J. Goldberg*, 81, 154–157, 183; Ambrose, *Eisenhower*, 2:388–391, 433, 441, 460–461, 518; Iwan W. Morgan, *Eisenhower Versus "The Spenders": The Eisenhower Administration, The Democrats and the Budget, 1953–60* (London: Pinter Publishers, 1990), 9–13, 93–126. Morgan noted that this economic decline, though ultimately brief, "was one of the sharpest since the Civil War" (93).

76. See Hughes, *The Ordeal of Power*, 259.

77. The sense that AL's understanding of the economic problems the country faced was limited grows out of his letter to JPM, December 5, 1957, and JPM's reply, December 17, 1957, both in folder State of the Union Message (Working Papers), Box 3, LMC, DDEL; AL-KL II; and the contents of his memo books from 1957 to 1962, Boxes 22–24, ALP, DDEL.

78. On DDE's concern about the divisions within the GOP caused by his use of the term Modern Republicanism, his efforts to deal with that problem by defining this term in ways less objectionable to the Old Guard, and his decision in 1958 to stop using the term, see his letter to Republican National Committee chairman Meade Alcorn, August

30, 1957, marked "Personal and Confidential," 1–6, folder DDE Diary—7/1/57–8/31/57, Box 25, DDEDS, AWF, DDEP, DDEL; DDE's letters to Bion Rose East, September 12, 1957, and Clifford Roberts, March 27, 1958, in Galambos and Van Ee, *The Papers of Dwight David Eisenhower*, XVIII:434–437 and XIX:801–802; AL's notes entitled "Trip to Kansas City and Back with President 1/29/58," MB January 1958, Box 23, ALP, and AL's second and third drafts of "Eisenhower's Remarks at R.N.C.," January 29, 1958, and January 30, 1958, respectively, folder President's Speeches: Jan. 31, 1958 Remarks to Republican National Committee, Box 4, LMC, all in DDEL; excerpts from DDE's remarks at the Republican National Committee breakfast, January 31, 1958, and the transcript of the president's news conference of November 5, 1958, in *Public Papers of the Presidents of the United States: Dwight D. Eisenhower 1958*, 135–140 and 836–837, respectively; Eisenhower, *Waging Peace*, 375.

79. *ATCL*, 130; Ewald, *Eisenhower the President*, 290.

80. Charles S. Rhyne, "A World-Wide Challenge to Lawyers," *Vital Speeches*, 24 (June 1, 1958): 483; John Leonard Meyer, "Arthur Larson: Campaigner for World Peace through Rule of Law—Research as Rhetoric" (Ph.D. diss., University of Minnesota, 1970), 21, 30–34; *ATCL*, 155–156.

81. On the origins of the arms race of the 1950s and its destabilizing consequences, see Patterson, *Grand Expectations*, 82–136, 276–310, 418–424.

82. DDE's Law Day message is reprinted in *Public Papers of the Presidents of the United States: Dwight D. Eisenhower 1958*, 89–90. On the creation of the center at Duke, see the Duke University press release "Presidential Assistant Arthur Larson Resigns Post to Become Head of New 'Rule of Law' Center at Duke," August 11, 1958, and "Law for World Peace Goal of Arthur Larson," *Duke Chronicle*, September 19, 1958, both in folder Scrapbooks, 1958–65, Box 27, and AL's "Memo to the Files," October 23, 1958, folder Clippings, Memos, Letters, 1958–60 & Connally Amendment, Box 25, both in ALP, AL to DDE, August 8, 1958, 1, folder Larson, Arthur [August 1958], in Alpha Subseries, Subject Series, WHOSSP, Box 16, and AL to James Hagerty, February 5, 1959, folder Larson, Arthur (Only) (3), Alpha File, both in DDEP, all in DDEL.

83. See, generally, AL's notes of his meetings with DDE and Dulles on July 2, 1958, in MB May 1958, AL's notes of his meetings with Dewey and Luce, July 16, 1958, in MB July 1958, and AL's MBs for September–December 1958, all in Box 23, ALP, DDEL; AL's interview for the John Foster Dulles OHC, September 22, 1965, 31–33, John Foster Dulles OHC, SGMML, PUL; Grenville Clark and Louis B. Sohn, *World Peace through World Law* (Cambridge, Mass.: Harvard University Press, 1958); Meyer, "Arthur Larson," 30–32; *ATCL*, 55–56.

84. See AL to FNL, June 17, 1958, 2, FNL to AHL, June 25, 1958, 3, and "Thursday," 1, AL to AHL, July 8, 1958, 1–2, all in LFP; ALICY; AL's notes of meetings with Eisenhower, Nixon, Luce, Thomas Dewey, and William Rogers, MB July 1958, Box 23, ALP, AL to Henry Luce, August 1, 1958, folder Chronological: June, July, August 1958, Box 1, LMC, AL letter of resignation to DDE, August 8, 1958, and DDE's reply, n.d., both in folder Larson, Arthur [August 1958], Box 16, Alpha Subseries, SFS, WHOSSP, and "Presidential Assistant Arthur Larson Resigns Post to Become Head of New 'Rule of Law' Center at Duke," all in DDEL; "Larson to Head Duke Law Center," *Durham* (North Carolina) *Morning Herald*, August 12, 1958; "Solicitor of Justice," *Time*, August 18, 1958; "Arthur Larson Resigns as Ike's Aide," *U.S. News & World Report*, August 22, 1958. On the Sherman Adams controversy, see "Washington's Rival Regents," *Economist*, December 21, 1957, 1049–1050; AL's notes of "Talk with Adams 1/21/58," MB January 1958, Box 23, ALP, DDEL; Adams, *Firsthand Report*, 435–451; Mooney, *The Politicians*, 288–297; Ambrose, *Eisenhower*, 2:467–469, 480–482.

10. *Dueling with the New Right*

1. *ATCL*, 155–157; John Leonard Meyer, "Arthur Larson: Campaigner for World Peace Though Rule of Law—Research as Rhetoric" (Ph.D. diss., University of Minnesota, 1970), 101–102; Hugh Talmadge Lefler and Albert Ray Newsome, *North Carolina, The History of a Southern State*, 3rd ed. (Chapel Hill: University of North Carolina Press, 1973), 630–693; William S. Powell, *North Carolina: A Bicentennial History* (New York: Norton, 1977), 194–195; Thomas C. Parramore, "Sit-Ins and Civil Rights," in Lindley S. Butler and Alan D. Dawson, eds., *The North Carolina Experience: An Interpretive and Documentary History* (Chapel Hill: University of North Carolina Press, 1984), 408–409; Earl Black and Merle Black, *The Vital South: How Presidents Are Elected* (Cambridge, Mass.: Harvard University Press, 1992), 66–67.

2. AL to AHL, July 8, 1958, 1, LFP. On the other points raised in this paragraph, see AL's notes of his meeting with Charles Rhyne, June 24, 1958, and with DDE, July 3, 1958, in MB July 1958, Box 23, ALP, DDEL; Lefler and Newsome, *North Carolina*, 659; Meyer, "Arthur Larson," 21–23, 101–108.

3. See AL to John K. Lundberg, May 13, 1958, folder March, April, May 1958, Box 1, LMC, and AL's notes of "Meeting with the President," July 3, 1958, MB July 1958, Box 23, ALP, both in DDEL; AL to Lt. G. H. Weyrauch, November 17, 1958, and AL to AHL, July 8, 1958, 1, both in LFP; Malcolm Moos Memoir, 6–9, OHC, CU; ABL; LKL; *ATCL*, 157.

4. AL to FNL, June 14, 1958, 3, and October 19, 1960, 1–3, and FNL's letters to AHL, June 25, 1958, 3, and "Thursday," FNL's letters to Ruth Tidmarsh, January 5, 1960, 1–4, and "Sunday" (postmarked November 7, 1960), 1–4, and the flier marked "Mrs. Arthur Larson—Lecture Topics," all in LFP; LKL; ABL.

5. Lefler and Newsome, *North Carolina*, 659, 685–693; Powell, *North Carolina*, 192–207; Parramore, "Sit-ins and Civil Rights," 408–414; Douglas M. Knight, *Street of Dreams: The Nature and Legacy of the 1960s* (Durham, N.C.: Duke University Press, 1989), especially 95–160; LKL.

6. Meyer, "Arthur Larson," 101–109; "Meeting with the President," July 3, 1958, 2.

7. See, generally, Larson's notes of his meetings with DDE and Dulles on July 2, 1958, in MB May 1958, and AL's notes of his meetings with Dewey and Luce, July 16, 1958, in MB July 1958, and AL's MBs for September–December 1958, all in Box 23, ALP, DDEL; AL's interview for the John Foster Dulles OHC, September 22, 1965, 31–33, SGMML, PUL; Grenville Clark and Lewis P. Sohn, *World Peace through World Law* (Cambridge, Mass.: Harvard University Press, 1958); Rhyne, "A World-Wide Challenge to Lawyers," 483; Henry R. Luce, "Our Great Hope: Peace Is the Work of Justice," *American Bar Association Journal* 43 (May 1957), 407–411, and Luce to DDE, December 15, 1958, folder Rule of Law—World Peace Through Law, Box 644, OF, DDEP, DDEL; Meyer, "Arthur Larson," 30–32; *ATCL*, 55–56.

8. A copy of the speech is in the folder Miscellaneous Articles and Speeches, Box 17, ALP, DDEL.

9. Larson, "World Rule of Law," 1–4.

10. Ibid., 4–5. On the issue of the "self-judging" clauses and the way they limited use of the International Court of Justice, see Louis Henkin, Richard Pugh, Oscar Schachter, and Hans Smit, *International Law: Cases and Materials* (St. Paul, Minn.: West Publishing Company, 1980), 858–869.

11. Larson, "World Rule of Law," 18. On the history of the Connally amendment, see Leo Gross, "The International Court of Justice: Consideration of Requirements for Enhancing Its Role in the International Legal Order," *American Journal of International Law* 65 (1971): 253–326, especially 262–263; Louis Henkin, "The Connally Amendment

Revisited and, Hopefully, Contained," *American Journal of International Law* 65 (1971): 374–377.

12. On the Bricker amendment controversy and the concerns that lay behind it, see Dwight D. Eisenhower, *Mandate for Change* (Garden City, N.Y.: Doubleday, 1963), 278–285, 432; and Chester J. Pach, Jr., and Elmo Richardson, *The Presidency of Dwight D. Eisenhower*, rev. ed. (Lawrence: University Press of Kansas, 1991), 59–62. For Dewey's advice to AL regarding the Connally amendment, see his notes of his meeting with Dewey, July 16, 1958, MB July 1958, Box 23, ALP, DDEL.

13. On the genesis of *What We Are For*, see AL's MBs from 1957 to 1958, especially #6 USIA and USIA #2–#4, Boxes 22–23, and the speech "What We Are For," that Larson gave at Washington and Lee University, American University, and the University of Michigan during 1958, in folder Papers What We Are For, Box 17, all in ALP. See also AL to Harvey Wheeler, January 14, 1958, and February 3, 1958, AL to Carl G. Brandt, February 6, 1958, folder Chronological: January, February 1958, AL to John K. Lundberg, May 13, 1958, folder Chronological: March, April, May 1958, and AL to Frederick Davis, August 9, 1958, folder June, July, August 1958, all in Box 1, LMC, all in DDEL; AL to AHL, March 2 and 8, 1958, and April 7, 1958, FNL to AHL, June 25, 1958, 2, and the transcript for the television show *The Open Mind*, on which AL appeared on October 26, 1958, 1–18, all in LFP; *ATCL*, 145–146.

14. Larson, *What We Are For*, 112. Although Larson had not mentioned individuality in his earlier speech, which he had delivered on March 31, 1957 under the title "What Hopes for Peace?" he included the word on page 12 of the "U.S.I.A. Basic Guidance Paper" that was finished just as he left that agency six months later. In folder Articles 1955–58 (1), Box 15, ALP, DDEL.

15. On the emergence of the New Right in the mid- to late 1950s, see Sidney Blumenthal, *The Rise of the Counter-Establishment: From Conservative Ideology to Political Power* (New York: Perennial Library, 1988), 3–54; E. J. Dionne, Jr., *Why Americans Hate Politics* (New York: Touchstone, 1991), 147–175; and Rick Perlstein, *Before the Storm: Barry Goldwater and the Unmaking of the American Consensus* (New York: Hill and Wang, 2001), 3–76. On page 6 of his "What We Are For," on which his new book was based, Larson singled out right-wing ideologue Russell Kirk's book, *The American Cause* (Chicago: H. Regnery, 1957), as a "recent and typical example" of this kind of writing. For Kirk's importance to the New Right, see Dionne, *Why Americans Hate Politics*, 156–157.

16. Larson, *What We Are For*, 6–8.

17. Ibid., 6–8, 15. The inspiration for this label may well have been Eisenhower's view, which he expressed during a National Security Council meeting on May 22, 1958, that to people in the Third World, "capitalism means imperialism. . . . Need to coin a new phrase." See, on this point, AL's notes of this session in his MB May 1958, Box 23, ALP, DDEL, and his notes of the Cabinet meeting on May 16, 1958, where the term "Enterprise Democracy" was first used in this way.

18. Larson, *What We Are For*, 23–28.

19. Ibid., 38–45. For a leading statement of the pluralist position, see David B. Truman, *The Government Process*, 2nd ed. (New York: Alfred Knopf, 1971). On the weaknesses of pluralist political theory in explaining the workings of highly industrialized market systems, see Nicos Poulantzas, *Political Power and Social Classes* (London: Verso, 1978), 266–270, 327–328; Theda Skocpol, "Political Response to Capitalist Crisis: Neo-Marxist Theories of the State and the Case of the New Deal," *Politics and Society* 10 (1980): 155–201; and Theda Skocpol and Kenneth Finegold, "State Capacity and Economic Intervention in the Early New Deal," *Political Science Quarterly* 97 (1982): 255–278.

20. On the mounting problems the 1950s system faced, see David L. Stebenne, *Arthur*

J. Goldberg: New Deal Liberal (New York: Oxford University Press, 1996), 154–187; and James Patterson, *Grand Expectations: The United States, 1945–1974* (New York: Oxford University Press, 1996), 375–430. The shift in conservative circles toward a more right-wing position in the late 1950s is discussed in Blumenthal, *The Rise of the Counter-Establishment*, 28–39; Dionne, *Why Americans Hate Politics*, 172–176; and Perlstein, *Before the Storm*, 3–75.

21. John F. Kennedy, "If the World's to Know Us Better," *New York Times Book Review*, February 8, 1959, 1, 22; *Public Papers of the President: Dwight D. Eisenhower 1959* (Washington, D.C.: National Archives and Records Service, 1960); RMN to AL, April 25, 1960, in folder Larson, Mr. Arthur, Box 438, Series 320, General Correspondence, RMNPPP; William F. Buckley, Jr., *Up from Liberalism* (New Rochelle, N.Y.: 1959), 189–192; Barry Goldwater, *The Conscience of a Conservative* (Shepherdsville, Ky.: Victor, 1960), 15–30.

22. Buckley, *Up from Liberalism*, 189 (see also 117, 125–128); Blumenthal, *The Rise of the Counter-Establishment*, 28–29.

23. Buckley, *Up from Liberalism*, 190.

24. Goldwater, *The Conscience of a Conservative*, 1.

25. Ibid., 15–16. See also Buckley, *Up from Liberalism* for BG's two-page introduction endorsing Buckley's thesis.

26. Goldwater, *The Conscience of a Conservative*, 20 (see also 19).

27. Ibid.

28. See ibid., 68–75.

29. Ibid., 119 (see also 86–118).

30. Ibid., 119–123.

31. AL's notes of his meeting with RMN, July 9, 1958, MB July 1958, Box 23, ALP, DDEL; RMN to Charles F. Van Cleve, November 30, 1961, folder Larson, Mr. Arthur, Box 438, Series 320, GC, RMNPPP; Roger Morris, *Richard Milhous Nixon: The Rise of an American Politician* (New York: Henry Holt, 1990); Stephen E. Ambrose, *Nixon*, vol. 1 (New York: Simon & Schuster, 1987). On the similarities between AL's and RMN's views then, see especially RMN's letter to Van Cleve, where he wrote that "he and I share substantially the same views on most major world problems" (1).

32. See AL's notes of his meeting with DDE, October 1, 1957, MB October 1957 #1, Box 22, ALP, DDEL; ALICY; AL, *Eisenhower: The President Nobody Knew* (New York: Charles Scribner's Sons, 1968), 10.

33. ALICY. On Nixon's careerism and Eisenhower's dislike for it, see Stewart Alsop, *Nixon & Rockefeller: A Double Portrait* (Garden Citym, N.Y.: Doubleday, 1960), 176–179; Stephen E. Ambrose, *Eisenhower* (New York: Simon & Schuster, 1984), 2:297–299, 319–320, 512–513.

34. See AL's notes of his meeting with DDE, October 1, 1957, MB October 1957 #1, Box 22, ALP, DDEL; ALICY; Larson, *Eisenhower: The President Nobody Knew*, 10; Alsop, *Nixon & Rockefeller*, 176–179; Ambrose, *Eisenhower*, 2:297–299, 319–320, 512–513. Among the other prominent critics of RMN on this score were his leading rivals in the GOP, BG and Nelson Rockefeller, both of whom privately disdained RMN's willingness to compromise his principles for votes. See Goldberg, *Barry Goldwater*, 142, 144; author's interview with former Rockefeller aide Everette E. Dennis.

35. Larson, *Eisenhower: The President Nobody Knew*, 10.

36. Emmet John Hughes, "The Eisenhower I Knew," *Look*, December 4, 1962, 44; Ambrose, *Eisenhower*, 2:512–513, 545–546.

37. ABL; Ambrose, *Nixon*, 1:313–314, 340–341, 585–586.

38. Larson, *Eisenhower: The President Nobody Knew*, 10. See also AL's notes of his conversation with RMN, July 9, 1958, MB July 1958, Box 23, ALP, DDEL; *ATCL*, 127–136.

39. See AL's notes of his conversation with RMN, July 9, 1958, MB July 1958, Box 23, ALP, DDEL.

40. Ibid.

41. Nixon autographed the photo "To Arthur Larson with appreciation for his dedicated service to nation and with every good wish for success in his exciting new work at Duke University from his friend Dick Nixon." The photo is in LFP; see also AL to RMN, August 27, 1958, folder Larson, Mr. Arthur, Box 438, Series 320, GC, RMNPPP.

42. See AL to RMN, February 16, 1960, and RMN's reply, April 25, 1960, in folder Larson, Mr. Arthur, Box 438, Series 320, GC, RMNPPP; Ambrose, *Nixon*, 1:483–510, 535–538.

43. See Stephen R. Braswell to AL, August 2, 1960, folder Richard Nixon, 1960–62, Box 25, ALP, DDEL; AL to RMN, August 18, 1960, 2, and RMN's reply, August 29, 1960, in folder Larson, Mr. Arthur, Box 438, Series 320, GC, RMNPPP; Ambrose, *Nixon*, 1:347.

44. See AL to RMN, June 23, 1960, folder Larson, Mr. Arthur, Box 438, Series 320, GC, RMNPPP; AL Memoir, SSP, OHC, CU, 1–25; RMN to AL, June 27, 1960, folder Richard Nixon, 1960–62, Box 25, ALP, DDEL; Larson, *Eisenhower: The President Nobody Knew*, 116.

45. RMN to AL, June 27, 1960, folder Richard Nixon, 1960–62, Box 25, ALP, DDEL. See also AL to RMN, June 23, 1960, folder Larson, Mr. Arthur, Box 438, Series 320, GC, RMNPPP; AL Memoir, 25, SSP, OHC, CU; Larson, *Eisenhower: The President Nobody Knew*, 116.

46. Quoted in Larson, *Eisenhower: The President Nobody Knew*, 117 (see also 116).

47. Ibid., 117. See also Goldberg, *Barry Goldwater*, 142, regarding BG's concern with RMN's "recent avowal for the World Court." DDE's unhappiness with the way RMN conducted his 1960 presidential campaign is discussed in Theodore H. White, *The Making of the President 1960* (New York: Atheneum Publisher, 1961), 14, 337–340; and Ambrose, *Eisenhower*, 2:593–594, 599–604.

48. Quoted in *ATCL*, 130. See also AWTI.

49. AL Memoir, 24, SSP, OHC, CU. See also on this point, John W. Henderson, *The United States Information Agency* (New York: Praeger, 1969), 21–22.

50. For JFK's openness to new ideas in foreign policy, see his book, which Columbia University historian Allan Nevins edited, entitled *The Strategies of Peace* (New York: Harper & Brothers, 1960); and Hugh Brogan, *Kennedy: Profle in Power* (London: Longman, 1996), 57–61. On JFK's call for Algerian independence, see *The Strategies of Peace*, 65–81. An audiotape of AL's and JFK's appearance at the "Great Challenge" symposium, which aired on March 22, 1959, is in the Audiovisual Division, DDEL. On JFK's use of the New Frontiers concept as the basic theme of his nomination acceptance address to the 1960 Democratic National Convention, see Theodore C. Sorensen, *Kennedy* (New York: Harper and Row, 1965), 167. On the Medicare issue in the campaign, see AL Memoir, 24–25, SSP, OHC, CU.

51. Larson, *Eisenhower: The President Nobody Knew*, 116–118; *ATCL*, 127–135; FNL to Charles McWhorter, August 20, 1960, McWhorter's reply, August 29, 1960, and RMN to AL, August 29, 1960, all in folder Larson, Mr. Arthur, Box 438, Series 320, GC, RMNPPP; Ambrose, *Eisenhower*, 2:593–594, 597–604; Theodore H. White, *The Making of the President 1960* (New York: Atheneum Publisher, 1961), 14.

52. See AL's notes of "Meeting with the President," July 3, 1958, MB July 1958, Box 23, ALP, DDEL; Larson, *Eisenhower: The President Nobody Knew*, 112–116; Perlstein, *Before the Storm*, 99–157.

53. On the shift in DDE's tactics on the Connally amendment issue after the 1958 elections, see AL to Malcolm Moos, December 2, 1958, Malcolm Moos to AL, December 4, 1958, and AL's "Memorandum for Mr. Moos," January 5, 1959, all in folder Con-

nally Amendment, Rule of Law Center, 1959, 1963, Box 28, ALP, DDEL; the memo for the files of a White House meeting held on August 10, 1959 regarding "Presidential 'Rule of Law' Statement," folder Larson, Mr. Arthur, Box 438, Series 320, GC, RMNPPP; AL to White House Counsel David Kendall, August 13, 1959, LFP.

54. RMN had told AL in November 1959 that "all Northern Democrats and Presidential candidates would be for it [revisiting the Connally Amendment]—except Lyndon Johnson." See AL's notes of his meeting with RN, in MB November 1959, Box 23, ALP, DDEL. On LBJ's opportunistic quest for issues to use in winning the presidency, see ALICY; Dallek, *Lone Star Rising*, 544–570; Robert A. Caro, *The Years of Lyndon Johnson: Master of the Senate* (New York: Alfred A. Knopf, 2002), especially 1004–1034.

55. See AL's notes of his meetings with DDE, with *Time* reporter John Steele, November 25, 1959, and with RMN, MB November 1959, Box 23, AL's notes of his meetings with DDE on August 15 and 29, 1960, MB August 1960, Box 24, James Reston to AL, December 14, 1959, his reply, December 17, 1959, and AL to David Kendall, December 31, 1959, all in folder Clippings and Memos, Letters, 1958–60—Connally Amendment, Box 25, all in ALP, DDEL; Larson, *Eisenhower: The President Nobody Knew*, 114–115.

56. Larson, *Eisenhower: The President Nobody Knew*, 114–116; AL to RMN, August 18, 1960, folder Larson, Mr. Arthur, Box 438, Series 320, GC, RMNPPP; AL to James Reston, December 17, 1959, folder Clippings and Memos, Letters, 1958–60—Connally Amendment, Box 25, ALP, DDEL; AL to FNL, October 19, 20, and 22, 1960, LFP; Arthur Larson, "Peace through Law: The Role and Limits of Adjudication—Some Contemporary Applications," *American Society for International Law Proceedings* 54 (January 1960): 8–15; Arthur Larson, "The Self-Judging Clause and Self-Interest," *American Bar Association Journal* 46 (July 1960): 729–731; Arthur Larson, "The Facts, the Law, and the Connally Amendment," *Duke Law Journal* 74 (Winter 1961): 74–119; Meyer, "Arthur Larson," 21–24, 73–99, 229–257. On the far right's long-standing fear of American participation in multinational organizations and the World Court in particular, see Alan Brinkley, *Voices of Protest: Huey Long, Father Coughlin and the Great Depression* (New York: Vintage, 1983), 134–137, 150–153; Perlstein, *Before the Storm*, 8–10.

57. Larson, *Eisenhower: The President Nobody Knew*, 116; Irving Bernstein, *Promises Kept: John F. Kennedy's New Frontier* (New York: Oxford University Press, 1991); and Stebenne, *Arthur J. Goldberg*, 233–315.

58. Arthur Larson, "The Cuba Incident and the Rule of Law," *Saturday Review*, May 13, 1961, 28. For details of the Bay of Pigs invasion, see Sorensen, *Kennedy*, 294–309; and Patterson, *Grand Expectations*, 492–496.

59. Larson, "The Cuba Incident," 28.

60. See Norman Cousins, "A Tribute to Arthur Larson," *Duke Law Journal* 1980 (June 1980): 389–391; folder Trip to Russia—1961—Impressions and Reflections (hereafter AL's conference notes), Box 28, ALP, DDEL; "U.S.-Soviet Group Ends Closed Talk," *New York Times*, November 13, 1960; "U.S.-Soviet Talks to Open in Crimea," *New York Times*, May 13, 1961; "Private U.S.-Soviet Talks End; Gain in Understanding Reported," *New York Times*, June 1, 1961; "Benton Describes Parley in Soviet," *New York Times*, June 18, 1961; "That Quiet Talk in Crimea," *Kansas City Times*, June 21, 1961.

61. Cousins, "A Tribute to Arthur Larson," 389.

62. Ibid. DDE described AL to Cousins as "a person of extraordinary intelligence and historical knowledge who brought special qualities of vision and good will to any enterprise in which he was engaged."

63. See ibid., 389–390; AL's conference notes; "U.S.-Soviet Group Ends Closed Talk."

64. See Cousins, "A Tribute to Arthur Larson," 390; AL's conference notes; "U.S.-Soviet Group Ends Closed Talk."

65. FNL to Ruth Tidmarsh, "Sunday" (postmarked November 7, 1960), 3 (see also 2), LFP. Cousins, "A Tribute to Arthur Larson," 390; AL's conference notes; "U.S.-Soviet Group Ends Closed Talk"; "Benton Describes Parley in Soviet"; "That Quiet Talk in Crimea."

66. "U.S.-Soviet Group Ends Closed Talk."

67. See AL's conference notes ; "Private U.S.-Soviet Talks End; Gain in Understanding Reported"; "U.S.-Soviet Talks to Open in Crimea"; "Benton Describes Parley in Soviet"; "That Quiet Talk in Crimea."

68. See AL's conference notes.

69. See ibid. See also Clark and Sohn, *World Peace through World Law,* especially xi–xxxiii.

70. See AL's conference notes.

71. Ibid.

72. Ibid.

73. Ibid. For the details of Hannah Arendt's influential thesis, see her book *The Origins of Totalitarianism* (New York: Harcourt, Brace, 1951); and Richard H. Pells, *The Liberal Mind in a Conservative Age: American Intellectuals in the 1940s and 1950s* (Middletown: Wesleyan University Press, 1985), 83–96.

74. See AL's conference notes.

75. Ibid., and "Dr. Larson to USSR Meeting," May 20, 1961, unidentified press clipping, folder Scrapbooks, 1958–65, Box 27, in ALP, DDEL.

76. For the June 3–4, 1961, superpower summit and its consequences, see Sorensen, *Kennedy,* 543–550; Arthur M. Schlesinger, Jr., *A Thousand Days: John F. Kennedy in the White House* (Greenwich, Conn.: Fawcett, 1965), 320–325, 333–348; Strobe Talbot, ed., *Khrushchev Remembers* (Boston: Little, Brown, 1970), 458–460; Patterson, *Grand Expectations,* 497–509; and Michael Beschloss, *The Crisis Years: Kennedy and Khrushchev, 1960–1963* (New York: Edward Burlingame Books, 1991), especially 191–236.

77. See AL, *When Nations Disagree: A Handbook on Peace Through Law* (Baton Rouge: Louisiana State University Press, 1961) and *A Warless World* (New York: McGraw-Hill, 1963); his articles "Common Sense and the United Nations," *Saturday Review,* February 24, 1962, 17–20, 62; "Road Map for the U.N.," *Saturday Review,* April 28, 1962, 11–13, 39–40; "What Every U.N. Critic Should Know," *Saturday Review,* June 15, 1962, 13–15, 84–85; and "Do It Through the U.N.," *Saturday Review,* August 25, 1962, 10–12, 47. See also Meyer, "Arthur Larson," 72–99; and *ATCL,* 160–161.

78. Larson, "Do It Through the U.N.," 10.

79. Ibid.

80. See "Larson Appointed Consultant to U.S. State Department," *Durham Morning Herald,* October 4, 1962; John C. Holt II to AL, February 26, 1950, LFP.

81. Seymour Maxwell Finger, *American Ambassadors at the UN: People, Politics and Bureaucracy in Making Foreign Policy* (New York: Holmes & Meier, 1988), 132–141, 170; John G. Stoessinger, *The United Nations and the Superpowers: China, Russia and America* (New York: Random House, 1973), 103–120; Sorensen, *Kennedy,* 519–523.

82. Khrushchev told American negotiator Averell Harriman that JFK's American University address was "the best speech by any President since Roosevelt." See Sorensen, *Kennedy,* 733. On the emergence of the treaty, see 79–32, 734–736; Ambrose, *Eisenhower,* 2:267, 399, 401–404, 477–480, 489–494, 521–523, 538; Patterson, *Grand Expectations,* 498–509; Schlesinger, *A Thousand Days,* 811–830; Beschloss, *The Crisis Years,* 576–627.

83. AL to DDE, July 29, 1963, 1–2, folder Eisenhower, Dwight D. (4), Box 21, ALP, DDEL; AL's letter of support for the treaty is in *New York Times,* August 13, 1963; Sorensen, *Kennedy,* 736–737.

84. DDE to AL, August 31, 1963, 2, folder Eisenhower, Dwight D. (3), Box 21, ALP, DDEL. DDE's earlier letter to AL also showed a marked lack of enthusiasm for the test ban treaty. See the text of DDE to AL, August 12th, 1963, folder Eisenhower, Dwight D. (4), Box 21, ALP, DDEL.

85. Sorensen, *Kennedy*, 738–740; Schlesinger, *A Thousand Days*, 830–834; Beschloss, *The Crisis Years*, 633–637.

86. See AL to DDE, July 29, August 27, and September 6, 1963, and AL's draft of letter to DDE, August 9, 1963, in folders Eisenhower, Dwight D. (3) and Eisenhower, Dwight D. (4), Box 21, ALP, DDEL; Patterson, *Grand Expectations*, 508–509; Sorensen, *Kennedy*, 740. AL's observation that the "test ban was greatest achievement of J.F.K." is in MB Undated (1), Box 24, and AL's notes entitled "In Relation to Kennedy" folder DDE Book Materials and Clippings, Box 16, both in ALP, DDEL.

87. See AL's conference notes and AL's notes entitled "In Relation to Kennedy" folder DDE Book Materials and Clippings, Box 16, both in ALP, DDEL; Larson, *Eisenhower: The President Nobody Knew*, 118–119; ALICY; AL, "The Cuba Incident and the Rule of Law"; AL, "Do It Through the U.N."; Sorensen, *Kennedy*, 639–648; Schlesinger, *A Thousand Days*, 156, 158, 160, 202, 302–317; Patterson, *Grand Expectations*, 497; and *ATCL*, 160–161. The strengths and weaknesses of Kennedy's organizational approach are discussed in Sorensen, *Kennedy*, 281–285; and James N. Giglio, *The Presidency of John F. Kennedy* (Lawrence: University Press of Kansas, 1991), 30–37.

88. See AL, "The Cuba Incident and the Rule of Law"; AL, "Do It Through the U.N."

89. "Larson Appointed Consultant to U.S. State Department," *Durham Morning Herald*, October 4, 1962; "Quarantine of Cuba Legal, Larson Says," *Durham Sun*, December 6, 1962; "World Rule of Law Center Called on for Solutions to Many Issues," *Durham Morning Herald*, April 26, 1963; Meyer, "Arthur Larson," 167; Larson, *Eisenhower: The President Nobody Knew*, 120–121.

90. *ATCL*, 177–178. For AL's support for Medicare and the Kennedy administration's efforts to secure the measure's enactment in 1962, see Arthur Larson Memoir, 33–50, SSP, OHC, CU; "Health Benefits Get Larson's Endorsement," *Durham Morning News*, May 27, 1962; Bernstein, *Promises Kept*, 246–258.

91. *ATCL*, 178.

92. JFK's June 11th speech on civil rights legislation and its origins are discussed in Sorensen, *Kennedy*, 488–496; Schlesinger, *Robert Kennedy*, 352–374; Taylor Branch, *Parting the Waters: America in the King Years, 1954–1963* (New York: Simon and Schuster, 1988), 803–825; Patterson, *Grand Expectations*, 478–481.

93. Draft of AL to DDE, August 9, 1963, 1, folder Eisenhower, Dwight D. (4), Box 21, ALP, DDEL.

94. Ibid., 2 (see also 1, 3).

95. Ibid., 3.

96. Ibid., 4 (see also 3). On the details of the dinner at Hershey, see Lewis Strauss's letter of invitation to AL, August 15, 1963, folder Eisenhower, Dwight D. (3), in that same collection. AL's forty-three-page analysis of the views BG expressed in *The Conscience of a Conservative* is in folder 1963–64 Articles, Press Releases, Memos, Letters, Box 8, ALP, DDEL.

97. Draft of AL to DDE, August 9, 1963, 5, folder Eisenhower, Dwight D. (4), Box 21, ALP, DDEL.

98. Ibid.

99. Ibid., 7 (see also 6).

100. Ibid., 7.

101. On DDE's oft-expressed criticism of JFK's leadership qualities during the 1960

campaign and record as president thereafter, see Ambrose, *Eisenhower*, 2:597–599, 603–608, 637–641; and Schlesinger, *A Thousand Days*, 914–916.

102. See Perlstein, *Before the Storm*, 194–197, 200; AL to FNL, April 6, 1954, 1–2, LFP; AL to Nelson Rockefeller, November 5, 1958, folder Nelson Rockefeller 1958–65, Box 26, ALP, DDEL; FNL to Ruth Tidmarsh, September 3, 1963, 1–2, LFP; AL to Ruth Tidmarsh, January 28, 1964, 2, folder Ruth Tidmarsh, and AL's notes of his meeting with DDE, March 9, 1964, 4–5, MB 1963–64, Boxes 28 and 24, respectively, ALP, DDEL.

103. See FNL to Ruth Tidmarsh, January 27, 1964, 1, AL to Ruth Tidmarsh, January 28, 1964, folder Ruth Tidmarsh, Box 28, ALP, DDEL; RMN to AL, December 23, 1963, and AL's reply, December 31, 1963, in RMNL; DDE to AL, January 23, 1964 and AL's reply, January 28, 1964, both in folder Dwight D. Eisenhower (3), Box 21 ALP, DDEL; AL, "How the Republicans Can Win," *Saturday Evening Post*, January 25, 1964, 21–23; AL, "What Is Liberal Republicanism?" *Saturday Review*, February 29, 1964, 14–17; AL, "The GOP: Liberal Origins and the Future," *The Nation*, March 9, 1964, 236–239.

104. "How the Republicans Can Win."

105. A copy of this manuscript, which Larson sent to *Fortune* on January 29, 1964, is the folder (1964) (Articles), Box 9, ALP, DDEL.

106. Larson, "A National Progress-Sharing Program," 1. On the problems of automation and rising unemployment in the late 1950s and early 1960s, see Hobart Rowen, *The Free Enterprisers: Kennedy, Johnson and the Business Establishment* (New York: G. P. Putnam's Sons, 1964), 253–297.

107. Larson, "A National Progress-Sharing Program," 1–4.

108. Ibid., 3–31.

109. Ibid., 33–36; AL to FNL, June 14, 1958, 1, LFP; AL to GR, November 11, 1966, folder George Romney, 1966–67, Box 26, and AL's notes of his meeting with DDE, March 9, 1964, 3–4, MB 1963–64, Box 24, both in ALP, DDEL; Perlstein, *Before the Storm*, 170, 183, 199, 238, 274.

110. For the origins of LBJ's War on Poverty and its limitations, see Patterson, *Grand Expectations*, 447, 532–542. For BG's more privatized approach and AL's critique of it, see Goldwater, *The Conscience of a Conservative*, 58–75; and AL's notes criticizing that work in folder 1963–64 Articles, Press Releases, Memos, Letters, Box 8, ALP, DDEL, 35–36.

111. See AL's notes of this meeting, MB 1963–64, Box 24, ALP, DDEL.

112. Ibid.

113. Ibid.

114. Ibid.

115. Theodore White, *The Making of the President 1964* (New York: Signet, 1965), 123–196; Perlstein, *Before the Storm*, 313–370.

116. White, *The Making of the President 1964*, 123–169; Perlstein, *Before the Storm*, 313–332.

117. Perlstein, *Before the Storm*, 187–188, 198, 254, 267, 340–341.

118. White, *The Making of the President 1964*, 111–196; Perlstein, *Before the Storm*, 313–370; Lisa McGirr, *Suburban Warriors: The Origins of the New American Right* (Princeton, N.J.: Princeton University Press, 2001).

119. Quoted in Perlstein, *Before the Storm*, 391. The italics represent underlining in BG's speech text; see White, *The Making of the President 1964*, 261.

120. Quoted in Perlstein, *Before the Storm*, 392. AL's reaction to the speech is from ABL.

121. Richard M. Nixon, *RN: The Memoirs of Richard Milhous Nixon* (New York: Grosset & Dunlap, 1978), 260.

122. For AL's decision to serve on the advisory panel and endorse LBJ in 1964, see John Kenneth Galbraith to LBJ, August 3, 1964, folder Lar, Box 147, WHCF, LBJP, LBJL;

"President Names His 16 Advisers," *New York Times*, September 10, 1964; McGeorge Bundy to AL, September 15, 1964, folder Misc. Corresp. 1960–64, Box 25, ALP, DDEL; AL letter of explanation to DDE, September 16, 1964, folder La (4), Box 42, Principal File 1964, DDEPPP, DDEL; "Ex-Aide to Eisenhower Is Supporting Johnson," *New York Times*, September 20, 1964.

123. See the copy of AL's endorsement speech entitled "Why Republicans (and Everyone Else) Should Vote for Johnson and Humphrey," folder Articles 1964, Box 10, ALP, DDEL; "GOP Here Ask Dr. Larson to Terminate Party Ties," *Durham Morning Herald*, October 24, 1964; Larson, *Eisenhower: The President Nobody Knew*, 48–49. For AL's doubts about LBJ's qualifications to be president, see Larson, "How the Republicans Can Win"; and "GOP Author Hits Policies of LBJ," *Pittsburgh Post-Gazette*, April 16, 1964.

124. See "New Group's Aim: Expose Ultra Rightists," *New York Herald Tribune*, September 23, 1964; "'Errors' of Reactionary Fronts to be Exposed," *Denver Post*, September 23, 1964; the other clippings on the National Council for Civic Responsibility in folder Extreme Groups, Box 2, ALP, DDEL; "A Republican Looks at Extremism," *Look*, January 26, 1965, 24–26.

125. See Perlstein, *Before the Storm*, 471–516; "Larson Scoffs at Rightist 'Victory,'" *Seattle Times*, November 26, 1964.

126. On the reasons why BG lost so badly, see Perlstein, *Before the Storm*, 488–516; and Nixon, *RN*, 260–263. On Reagan's effectiveness as a campaigner for the New Right cause in 1964, see Perlstein, *Before the Storm*, 297, 336, 350, 352, 372, 422, 499–504; Nixon, *RN*, 263. The shift in power within the GOP in 1964 from the moderates to more extreme conservatives is discussed in Dionne, *Why Americans Hate Politics*, 180–186. For an overview of the growing polarization of American politics and society during the 1960s, see Patterson, *Grand Expectations*, 442–457.

11. *Victories and Defeats*

1. Arthur Larson, "International Implications of Civil Rights in America," 6, speech delivered at Louisville, Kentucky on December 1, 1964, folder Articles, Box 10, ALP, DDEL; "A Republican Looks at Extremism," *Look*, January 26, 1965, 24–26; "Menace on the Right," and "Monitoring of Right-Wing Programs Is Begun by Newly Formed Council," press clippings in folder Extreme Groups, Box 2, and "Conservative and Liberal Debate GOP's Future, Among Other Things," press clipping May 1, 1965, in folder Scrapbooks, 1965–1970, Box 28, all in ALP, DDEL; Craig Allen Swarts, "The John Birch Society: A New Perspective on Far-Right Conservatism" (M.A. thesis, Ohio State University, 1997), 62, 81–85; "Right Wing Losing Its Voice?" *Kalamazoo Gazette*, October 25, 1965; Arthur Larson, "Extremism in America," speech at Eisenhower College, April 9, 1970, 3–4, folder Articles, Box 14, ALP, DDEL.

2. AL Memoir, 40–42, SSP, OHC, CU; Jacob K. Javits with Rafael Steinberg, *Javits: The Autobiography of a Public Man* (Boston: Houghton, Mifflin, 1981), 293–300.

3. AL Memoir, 41, SSP, OHC, CU.

4. AL Memoir, 42–43, SSP, OHC, CU; see also Javits with Steinberg, *Javits*, 300.

5. AL Memoir, 44–47, SSP, OHC, CU; James Patterson, *Grand Expectations: The United States, 1945–1974* (New York: Oxford University Press, 1996), 572–574; Berkowitz, "The Historical Development of Social Security in the United States," in Edward R. Kingson and James H. Schulz, eds., *Social Security in the 21st Century* (New York: Oxford University Press, 1997), 32–35.

6. AL Memoir, 48 (see also 447, 49), SSP, OHC, CU. Part B of the Medicare Act provided voluntary coverage for doctors' services instead of the mandatory insurance Larson

favored. On the creation of Part B, see J. Douglas Brown, *An American Philosophy of Social Security: Evolution and Issues* (Princeton, N.J.: Princeton University Press, 1972), 197–198; and W. Andrew Achenbaum, *Social Security: Visions and Revisions* (Cambridge: Cambridge University Press, 1986), 52.

7. See, generally, AL Memoir, SSP, OHC, CU. On the Republican contribution to Medicare's enactment, see Javits with Steinberg, *Javits*, 293–301.

8. Arthur Larson, "International Implications of Civil Rights in America," 2, speech delivered at Louisville, Kentucky on December 1, 1964, folder Articles, Box 10, ALP, DDEL. For the passage of the Civil Rights Act of 1964, see Patterson, *Grand Expectations*, 542–547.

9. Larson, "International Implications of Civil Rights in America," 15 (see also 2–14).

10. Ibid, 16 (see also 15).

11. Arthur Larson, "The New Law of Race Relations," *Wisconsin Law Review* (1969): 472 (see also 470–471).

12. Ibid., 472.

13. Ibid., 511.

14. Ibid., 512.

15. Ibid.

16. Ibid.

17. Ibid., 513–514.

18. For the origins of the nuclear nonproliferation treaty and the Senate resolution sponsored by John Pastore of Rhode Island, see Glenn T. Seaborg with Benjamin S. Loeb, *Stemming the Tide: Arms Control in the Johnson Years* (Lexington, Mass.: D. C. Heath, 1987), 59–182. For AL's new committee, see Bill Moyers to Stanley Marcus, August 31, 1966, AL to Walt Rostow, September 14, 1966, and LBJ to AL, September 21, 1966, all in folder Arthur Larson, Box 63, NF, WHCF, LBJP, LBJL; AL to Arthur Flemming, August 9, 1966, and Flemming's reply, August 23, 1966, folder Lar-Lea, Box 15, Flemming Papers, DDEL; "Rule of Law Research Center Annual Report 1968," 5–6, folder Articles, Box 14, ALP, DDEL.

19. See AL's telegram to LBJ, January 31, 1967, AL to LBJ, February 1 and November 1, 1967, all in folder Arthur Larson, Box 63, NF, WHCF, and Dean Rusk to AL, November 6, 1967, folder Gen Co/5/ 6/1/67–7/31/68, Box 50, WHCF CO 151, all in LBJP, LBJL; Walt Rostow's memo to LBJ, March 3, 1967, DDRS; and Seaborg with Loeb, *Stemming the Tide*, 183–198, 249–306, 327–339, 344–347.

20. Arthur Larson, "Last Chance on Nuclear Nonproliferation?" *Saturday Review*, October 7, 1967, 21–24; "Rule of Law Research Center Annual Report 1968," 4–6, folder Articles, Box 14, ALP, DDEL.

21. See AL's telegram to LBJ, January 25, 1968, folder Arthur Larson, Box 63, NF, WHCF; AL and Jo Pomerance to LBJ, January 6, 1969, and LBJ's reply, January 8, 1969, folder EX ND 21 7/10/68–, Box 424, WHCF ND 21, LBJP, LBJL; Seaborg with Loeb, *Stemming the Tide*, 355–387.

22. John Leonard Meyer, "Arthur Larson: Campaigner for World Peace through Rule of Law—Research as Rhetoric" (Ph.D. diss., University of Minnesota, 1970), 23–26; "Governor Names 16 to Women's Status Group," *Durham Morning Herald*, January 5, 1964; "Four Here Will Help Study Women's Status," *Durham Sun*, January 7, 1964; Susan M. Hartmann, *From Margin to Mainstream: American Women and Politics since 1960* (New York: Alfred A. Knopf, 1989), 50–53.

23. Meyer, "Arthur Larson," 151–154.

24. For details of the Johnson administration's actions in the Dominican Republic in 1965, see John Morton Blum, *Years of Discord: American Politics and Society, 1961–1974*

(New York: Norton, 1991), 222–225; and Patterson, *Grand Expectations*, 611–612. For AL's views of this event, see AL, "Power and Law in World Affairs, *The Progressive*, November 1966, 12–15; *ATCL*, 161.

25. Larson, "Power and Law in World Affairs," 13.

26. Ibid.

27. Ibid., 14.

28. *ATCL*, 160–163; AL to Ruth Tidmarsh, April 13, 1965, 1–2; Don R. Larson and Arthur Larson, *Vietnam and Beyond: A New American Foreign Policy and Program* (Durham, N.C.: Rule of Law Research Center, Duke University, 1965).

29. Larson and Larson, *Vietnam and Beyond*, 6 (see also 4–5).

30. Ibid., 6.

31. Ibid., 6–15.

32. Ibid., 7 (see also 6, 15).

33. Ibid., 7–12.

34. Ibid., 15.

35. Ibid., 16 (see also 15).

36. Ibid., 17.

37. DDE to President Ngo Dinh Diem, October 1, 1954, quoted in Larson and Larson, *Vietnam and Beyond*, 18. The full text of the letter is in *Public Papers of the Presidents of the United States: Dwight D. Eisenhower 1954* (Washington, D.C.: National Archives and Records Service, 1960), 948–949.

38. Larson and Larson, *Vietnam and Beyond*, 20.

39. Ibid., 20–26.

40. Ibid., 26.

41. Ibid., 27.

42. Ibid.

43. Ibid., 28–29.

44. Ibid., 29.

45. Ibid., 30.

46. Ibid., 30–31.

47. Ibid., 31.

48. Ibid., 30–42.

49. On the changing nature of the circumstances in Vietnam from 1954 to 1965, see Leonard C. Meeker to AL, April 3, 1965, folder Misc. Corresp. 1965, Box 25, ALP, DDEL; George C. Herring, *America's Longest War: The United States and Vietnam, 1950–1975*, 2nd ed. (New York: Alfred A. Knopf, 1986), 43–132. On the ambiguous nature of JFK's record with respect to Vietnam and his emphasis on keeping his options open, see Frederik Logevall, *Choosing War: The Lost Chance for Peace and the Escalation of War in Vietnam* (Berkeley: University of California Press, 1999), 1–42, 395–400.

50. On the UN funding crisis and the way it was resolved, see John G. Stoessinger, *The United Nations and the Superpowers: China, Russia and America* (New York: Random House, 1973), 120–121; Seymour Maxwell Finger, *American Ambassadors at the UN: People, Politics and Bureaucracy in Making Foreign Policy* (New York: Holmes & Meier, 1988), 132–141, 170–172. Seymour Finger observed that the funding controversy "was really a conflict between those who wanted to maintain the United Nations as 'static conference machinery' (the USSR and Gaullist France) and those who wished to endow it with increasing strength and executive authority" (141).

51. *ATCL*, 162.

52. Ibid.

53. On Johnson's effort to build support for escalation, and this meeting, see Logevall,

Choosing War, 333–374; McGeorge Bundy to AL, June 26, 1965, and LBJ to AL, July 10, 1965, both in folder WHCF Name File, Box 63, LBJP, LBJL; *ATCL*, 161–162.

54. *ATCL*, 162–163.

55. DDE to AL, May 18, 1965, 1, folder LAR, Box 31, Principal File 1965 Alpha, DDEPPP, DDEL. See also AL to DDE, May 11, 1965, folder Eisenhower, Dwight D. (2), Box 21, ALP, DDEL.

56. DDE to AL, May 18, 1965, 1, folder LAR, Box 31, Principal File 1965 Alpha, DDEPPP, DDEL.

57. Ibid., 2.

58. Ibid.

59. Ibid., 3.

60. Ibid.

61. AL to RMN, May 7, 1965, and his reply, May 10, 1965, both in folder L, RMNP, RMNL; Don R. Larson and Arthur Larson, "A Plan for Peace in Vietnam," *Saturday Review*, April 24, 1965, 21–24; Stanley Karnow, *Vietnam: A History* (New York: Penguin Books, 1984), 435–481.

62. Herring, *America's Longest War*, 150; "Larson-Headed Parley Asks Halt to North Viet Bombing," *Durham Morning Herald*, February 16, 1966; "Dr. Larson Hits U.S. War Stand," *Durham Sun*, April 13, 1966; "Action by U.S. in Vietnam Violates Charter of U.N., Former USIS Head Asserts," *Sioux City Journal*, November 8, 1966; AL, "Power and Law in World Affairs," *The Progressive*, November 1966, 12–15, and December 1966, 35–37.

63. See AL to GR, November 11, 1966, and January 11, 1967, GR to AL, November 29, 1966, and January 23, 1967, all in folder Romney, George (2), Box 26, ALP, DDEL; Theodore White, *The Making of the President 1968* (New York: Atheneum, 1969), 36–41, 49–52.

64. AL to GR, November 11, 1966, folder Romney, George (2), Box 26, ALP, DDEL.

65. See GR to AL, November 29, 1966, and January 23, 1967, AL to GR, January 11, 1967, and February 1, 1967, "Romney Steps Up National Drive; Aide Plans a Big Research Office," *New York Times*, January 5, 1967, and William S. White, "Pressure on Romney," *Durham Morning Herald*, n.d., all in folders Romney, George (1) and Romney, George (2), and MB Romney—Planning His Speeches, folder George Romney, Vietnam Speech and Others, all in Box 26, ALP, DDEL.

66. AL to GR, January 11, 1967, 3, folder Romney, George (2), MB Romney—Planning His Speeches, folder George Romney, Vietnam Speech and Others, all in Box 26, ALP, DDEL; White, *Making of the President 1968*, 56.

67. AL memo "Comments on Lincoln Day Speech Notes," January 20, 1967, 1, folder George Romney, 1966–67, Box 26, ALP, DDEL. See also the speeches and other materials AL sent GR in that file and MB Romney—Planning His Speeches, folder George Romney, Vietnam Speech and Others, all in Box 26, ALP, DDEL.

68. Larson, "Comments on Lincoln Day Speech Notes," 1–3.

69. Ibid., 3.

70. Ibid., 4.

71. Ibid., 4–6.

72. Ibid., 7 (see also 6); on GR's record as a leader with "a knack for getting things done," see White, *The Making of the President 1968*, 37.

73. See MB "Romney—planning his speeches."

74. Ibid.; *ATCL*, 166–167; White, *The Making of the President 1968*, 56.

75. *ATCL*, 167. See also Lucretia Duke to E. L. Haywood regarding the details of AL's second trip to East Lansing, April 24, 1967, folder Romney, George (1), Box 26, ALP, DDEL.

76. See "Romney Hartford Speech—First Draft—Jonathan Moore—Mar. 28, 1967," folder Romney—Vietnam Speech 1967 (2) and MB Romney—Planning His Speeches, folder George Romney, Vietnam Speech and Others, both in Box 26, ALP, DDEL.

77. See the speech marked "Vietnam A.L. 2nd Draft," 1–3, folder Romney Vietnam Speech 1967 (3), Box 26, ALP, DDEL. See also *ATCL*, 167.

78. "Vietnam A.L. 2nd Draft," 3–4.

79. Ibid., 11–12 (see also 5–10).

80. Ibid., 12–16.

81. For the way LBJ manipulated would-be opponents of his Vietnam policy into reluctant supporters, see Logevall, *Choosing War*, 375–413; and Herring, *America's Longest War*, 108–143. On AL in particular, see "Realistic in His Vietnam Views," *Kansas City Times*, April 11, 1966. On the decline in American prestige resulting from the escalation policy and its futility, see Herring, *America's Longest War*, 144–185; Karnow, *Vietnam*, 474–514; and Gabriel Kolko, *Anatomy of a War: Vietnam, the United States, and the Modern Historical Experience* (New York: Pantheon, 1985), 293–340.

82. See AL's notes of his conversation with DDE, April 3, 1967, folder Eisenhower, Dwight D. (1), Box 21, ALP, DDEL. See also *ATCL*, 167–168.

83. See the copy of the GR speech in folder Romney—Vietnam Speech 1967 (1), Box 26 ALP, DDEL; "Romney Calls for Victory; War Policy Like Johnson's," *New York Times*, April 8, 1968; "President 'Grateful' for Romney's Speech," *Washington Post*, April 8, 1967; *ATCL*, 168.

84. "Late Changes in Text," *New York Times*, April 8, 1967; White, *The Making of the President 1968*, 56–57; *ATCL*, 168.

85. White, *The Making of the President 1968*, 41–61, 126–149, 224–229; Maurice Stans and Fred Seaton to AL, June 1, 1967, Stans to AL, February 13, 1968, W. Walter Williams to AL, June 17, 1968, Glenn A. Olds to AL, July 3 and 15, 1968, in folders 1–3 of Nixon, Richard, 1966–69, Box 25, ALP, DDEL; LKL; ABL; "Larson Lauds U.S., Soviet Pact," *Durham Morning Herald*, March 9, 1968.

86. See Glenn A. Olds to AL, July 3 and 15, 1968, folder Nixon, Richard, 1966–69 (1), Box 25, ALP, DDEL; ABL; A. Kenneth Pye, "A Tribute to Arthur Larson," *Duke Law Journal* (1980): 403; White, *The Making of the President 1968*, 277–324.

87. Arthur Larson, *Eisenhower: The President Nobody Knew* (New York: Charles Scribner's Sons, 1968); "Rule of Law Research Center Annual Report 1968," 5, folder Articles 1964–70, Box 14, ALP, DDEL; "Portrait of Eisenhower," *Wall Street Journal*, September 20, 1968; "The Private Man Behind the Public Figure," *Providence Journal*, September 22, 1968; "Highly Subjective," *New York Times*, October 13, 1968; Emmet John Hughes, *The Ordeal of Power: A Political Memoir of the Eisenhower Years* (New York: Atheneum, 1963), 173, 183, 200, 250, 270, 319; "Writer Says Eisenhower Had Doubts on Nixon," *Durham Sun*, November 20, 1962; Pye, "A Tribute to Arthur Larson," 403.

88. Meyer, "Arthur Larson," 126–135, 169–171, 174–181; LKL; *ATCL*, 160–161, 168–169. John Meyer concluded that Larson's world rule of law center "seems to have succeeded in carrying out its specific aims and programs but failed in its overall goal of advancing the use of law." See Meyer, "Arthur Larson," 180.

89. AL, "Extremism in America," 7, address delivered at Eisenhower College, April 9, 1970, folder Articles 1970, Box 14, ALP, DDEL.

90. Ibid., 8.

91. Ibid., 9 (see also 8).

92. Ibid., 9.

93. Ibid., 26 (see also 10–25).

94. Quoted in Dwight D. Eisenhower, *Waging Peace, 1956–1961* (Garden City, N.Y.:

Doubleday and Company), 616 (see also 614–615); Arthur Larson, "The Military-Industrial Complex Ten Years Later," 1, address delivered at Virginia Military Institute, April 11, 1970, folder Articles, Box 14, ALP, DDEL.

95. Larson, "The Military-Industrial Complex," 3 (see also 2).

96. Ibid., 3–8.

97. Ibid., 8. See also "Larson to Head Congressional Conference on Military Budget," *Durham Morning Herald,* March 28, 1969.

98. Larson, "The Military-Industrial Complex," 8 (see also 9–14).

99. Ibid., 15.

100. Ibid., 16 (see also 15).

101. Ibid., 16 (see also 17–18).

102. Ibid., 18–22.

103. Ibid., 23.

104. Ibid., 23–24.

105. Ibid., 24 (see also 25–27).

106. Ibid., 27–33.

107. Ibid., 33.

108. On the emphasis among Modern Republicans in the 1950s on achieving peace through military strength, see Chester J. Pach, Jr., and Elmo Richardson, *The Presidency of Dwight D. Eisenhower,* rev. ed. (Lawrence: University Press of Kansas, 1991), 75–104, 187–210.

109. See "Larson Says U.S. Should Withdraw Unconditionally," *Duke Chronicle,* May 13, 1970; on Nixon's Vietnam policy, see Herring, *America's Longest War,* 221–256; and Patterson, *Grand Expectations,* 743–770.

Epilogue

1. See "A Tribute to Arthur Larson," *Duke Law Journal* 1980 (June 1980): 387–415. On AL's shift to a focus on workers' compensation and employment discrimination law, see *ATCL,* 169–172, 175–176.

2. A. Kenneth Pye, "A Tribute to Arthur Larson," *Duke Law Journal* 1980 (June 1980): 403; see also *ATCL,* 196, 201–202.

3. LKL; ABL; *ATCL,* 202–204.

4. ALB; LKL; *ATCL,* 207.

5. AL-KL III; see also LKL.

6. On the conservative shift toward free market ideas in the 1960s, 1970s, and 1980s and the disagreement of more moderate conservatives such as AL with the extent of that trend, see, E. J. Dionne, Jr., *Why Americans Hate Politics* (New York: Touchstone, 1991), 147–208, 242–299. For AL's views on how much the national security establishment should be curbed, see "'Drastic Cutback' of CIA Advocated," *Santa Barbara News-Press,* December 16, 1973.

7. Quoted in *ATCL,* 135; see also "Arthur Larson Still an Optimist," *Raleigh News and Observer,* January 15, 1984.

8. *ATCL,* 136 (see also 135).

9. See ALICY; *ATCL,* 135–136, 166; "L. Arthur Larson Is Dead at 82; Top Eisenhower Aide and Writer," *New York Times,* April 1, 1993.

10. LKL; "L. Arthur Larson Is Dead at 82."

Index

ABOUT THE AUTHOR

David L. Stebenne earned a B.A. from Yale and a J.D. and Ph.D. in history from Columbia. He is author of *Arthur J. Goldberg: New Deal Liberal* and has written articles about various aspects of modern U.S. history. He has taught at Yale and Ohio State University, where he is currently an associate professor of history and adjunct professor of law.